BizTalk™ Server:
The Complete Reference

For Mam and Dad—
I miss you
but I know you're always with me
in everything I do.

And for Naomi—
my best friend, my love, my lobster.

BizTalk™ Server:
The Complete Reference

David Lowe
With Xin Chen, Todd Mondor,
Tomislav Rus, Ned Rynearson,
Ben Smith, Steve Wright, and
Tom Xu

Osborne/**McGraw-Hill**
New York Chicago San Francisco
Lisbon London Madrid Mexico City
Milan New Delhi San Juan
Seoul Singapore Sydney Toronto

Osborne/**McGraw-Hill**
2600 Tenth Street
Berkeley, California 94710
U.S.A.

To arrange bulk purchase discounts for sales promotions, premiums, or fund-raisers, please contact Osborne/**McGraw-Hill** at the above address. For information on translations or book distributors outside the U.S.A., please see the International Contact Information page immediately following the index of this book.

BizTalk Server: The Complete Reference

1234567890 DOC DOC 01987654321

Book p/n 0-07-222271-9 and CD p/n 0-07-222268-9, 0-07-222269-7, 0-07-222270-0 parts of
ISBN 0-07-213498-4

Publisher
  Brandon A. Nordin

Vice President & Associate Publisher
  Scott Rogers

Editorial Director
  Tracy Dunkelberger

Acquisitions Coordinator
  Emma Acker

Technical Editors
  Jeff Dalton, Ben Smith

Proofreader
  Linda Medoff

Indexer
  Irv Hershman

Computer Designers
  Tabitha M. Cagan, Elizabeth Jang,
  George Toma Charbak, Roberta Steele

Illustrators
  Michael Mueller, Lyssa Wald

This book was composed with Corel VENTURA™ Publisher.

About the Authors

David Lowe, MCSE, MCT, is a Subject Matter Expert/Instructional Software Design Engineer with Microsoft Corporation. Prior to this, he was an e-Business Consultant and Senior Lecturer in Internet Technologies with the Center for Advanced Technology Training (CATT) in Dublin, Ireland, a division of Siemens Business Services. During his time at CATT, David was frequently involved in the development and delivery of Microsoft Official Curriculum on XML, BizTalk Server 2000, and Commerce Server 2000, and was often invited to deliver beta and trainer preparation courses for Microsoft in Redmond, Washington. David regularly speaks on XML and BizTalk Server technologies at international conferences and has given presentations at Microsoft TechEd in Amsterdam and Barcelona, and at Microsoft Technology Week in San Diego. In whatever spare time he can find, he also runs www.xmltrainer.com.

Xin Chen is a consultant at Avanade, specializing in developing Web solutions using Microsoft technology. Xin also specializes in BizTalk Server and MSMQ technology. He has done most of his consultancy work for large financial institutions where he built web-centric applications with XML, BizTalk Server, and MSMQ. Xin is MCSD, MCSD, MCDBA certified.

Todd Mondor works as an independent trainer and consultant specializing in web-based application collaboration and integration, primarily using Microsoft technologies. Some of the world's largest organizations have hired him to produce worldwide developer frameworks that integrate their applications and reduce their costs. His current job entails building a new developer framework that integrates business processes with current web applications and legacy applications at Volvo using BizTalk Server.

Tomislav Rus works as a scientist at the Institut for Production Science at the University of Karlsruhe and as programmer at the BizTalk Competence Center Karlsruhe. Tomislav was speaker at Microsoft's XML in Action 2001 conference in Munich and has written several articles for scientific publications. Currently Tomislav is working on his Ph.D. at the University of Karlsruhe. Tomislav specializes in data exchange in the German automobile industry.

Ned Rynearson is a New York-based Solution Developer for Avanade, the leading global technology integrator for Microsoft solutions in the enterprise. As a Microsoft Certified Systems Engineer (MCSE), Microsoft Certified Solution Developer (MCSD), and Microsoft Certified Trainer (MCT) for more than five years, Rynearson is well steeped in Microsoft technology and has taken—and passed—more than 25 Microsoft exams during his career. Prior to joining Avanade, he was a consultant specializing in Microsoft servers and Internet security. Rynearson began his technology career while in the United States Air Force, where he worked for more than 14 years. His previous publications include three chapters for the book *Internet Security with NT*, and an article about SMS Installer for the magazine *InfoWorld*.

Ben Smith, MCSE+I and MCT, is an Instructional Software Design Engineer and Subject Matter Expert in E-Business currently developing courseware around BizTalk Server and business-to-business for Microsoft Training and Certification.

Steve Wright, MCSD, MCDBA, MCSE+I, is a Senior Architect with plaNet Consulting Inc., in Omaha, Nebraska. He has been developing mission-critical systems for over 13 years. He consulted for Microsoft in Redmond developing demonstration applications for BizTalk Server during the Technical Preview time frame. Steve is currently involved in developing and deploying EDI solutions based on BizTalk Server for clients in the chemical, automotive, healthcare, insurance, and transportation industries.

Tom Xu works as SAP Technical Advisor in the Getronics SAP Customer Competence Center. He provides consulting services for SAP R/3 system integration and development. Tom focuses on setting up universal interfaces for R/3 systems using BizTalk Server 2000 and researching on real-time data warehousing technology with SAP BW system.

Contents at a Glance

Contents

Part I

Getting Started with BizTalk Server

Part VI

Extending BizTalk Server

Part VII

BizTalk Server 2002 Enterprise Edition

Part VIII

Appendix

Acknowledgments

Many authors refer to the process of writing a book as "a labor of love", but working on *BizTalk Server: The Complete Reference* has led me to equate the effort more with "labor". The last nine months have seen my initial excitement give way to sleepless nights, unusual dietary habits, lower back pain, mood swings, and a wish that I had taken more time off work. However, to continue the analogy, nothing quite compares to the relief experienced when it's all over and to the pride felt when you can hold the fruits of your labor in your hands.

It was never my intention to write this book on my own, and it would have been foolhardy to try. I cannot express adequately my gratitude for the technical contributions from Tomislav Rus, Steve Wright, Xin Chen, Ned Rynearson, Tom Xu, Todd Mondor, and Ben Smith, who all made sure the book did not end up entitled "BizTalk Server: The Partial Reference". Ben jumped in at the very last moment to fill some final gaps and provided invaluable technical assistance, augmenting the great technical editing work done by Jeff Dalton who also caught many a bug and queried many an incorrect assumption. I also thank Bill Tyler for his contributions to what would become the final content outline for this ambitious project.

Special appreciation must go to Scott Woodgate, Technical Product Manager for BizTalk Server at Microsoft, who provided essential assistance at crucial points in the project, and was always willing to answer questions and offer whatever resources he could. Although I'm now employed by Microsoft, too, for most of the time I was writing this book I was privileged to work with the Centre for Advanced Technology Training in Dublin, Ireland. There, I was given much needed advice and support by Hilary Doyle, Gerry Whelan, and Anne O'Dwyer (among others)—the finest people you could ever hope to have on your side.

Of course, I must thank everyone at Osborne/McGraw-Hill for their guidance, assistance, and support throughout. In particular, Tracy Dunkelberger has been a fantastic Editorial Director, always making me feel like this was the only book on her mind, even though there were probably 20 others vying for her attention. Emma Acker did a tremendous job as Acquisitions Coordinator, gently reminding us all of each impending deadline to make sure everything stayed on target and always finding the solution to whatever problem was thrown at her. Also, special thanks must go to the Project Editor, Katie Conley, and her entire team of editors, who gave better grammar lessons than I had in school, and never got tired of correcting my spelling of the words "organisation" and "catalogue". I can now write in American almost as fluently as in English!

Lest I forget, thanks to my family—Harry, Barbara, Jeanette, and Carol Anne—and my friends—John and Gareth—for their support throughout the years, and of course to my dearly missed parents who made me the person I am. And if I'm going to give thanks and love to anyone, I should give it all to my girlfriend Naomi, who had to endure each of the symptoms mentioned in the first paragraph, but still gave me a smile every day to help me through.

David Lowe
Dublin, Ireland—September 2001

Introduction

Microsoft BizTalk Server represents the way forward for business-to-business trading, partner integration, and enterprise application integration over private and public networks. Since its release in late 2000, it has been implemented in a wide variety of organizations, such as Ford, Marks and Spencer, J.D. Edwards, Coca-Cola, and the United Kingdom government. Its success stems from its ability to provide integration for all manner of systems and applications existing on different platforms and using a range of transports and data formats. The routing and processing of disparate document formats and data structures is accomplished through its richly-featured services for messaging and business process orchestration.

As one of Microsoft's .NET Enterprise Servers, BizTalk Server emphasizes the importance of the Extensible Markup Language (XML) for the development of electronic business solutions. Apart from ground-breaking support for XML, BizTalk Server also includes built-in parsers and serializers for legacy file formats such as ANSI X12, UN/EDIFACT, and positional and delimited flat-files. It promotes the adoption of a loosely-coupled message-centric architecture to take advantage of both synchronous and asynchronous transports such as HTTP, SMTP, File, and Message Queuing. Through its own extensible application programming interfaces, it provides for the creation of further application integration components, parsers, and serializers to satisfy the most particular solution requirements.

What's In This Book?

This book attempts to cover all aspects of the development and deployment of BizTalk Server solutions. Although the information is presented sequentially, the topics have been segregated into discrete chapters that each discuss one specific feature. In turn, these chapters have been grouped into larger parts to emphasize the different sets of tasks that can be performed with the product, the varied roles of the individuals who will be working with the product, and the requisite skills each individual should possess to implement any specific facet of the technology.

Part I of the book covers Getting Started with BizTalk Server. This part is aimed at those new to the product, or developers and administrators who are already aware of what the product can do, but need to start actually building an implementation. The chapters in this part provide an overview of BizTalk Server, background information on XML, which is crucial to a proper appreciation of BizTalk Server's capabilities, and full instructions for how the product should be installed.

Part II, BizTalk Messaging Tools, gets straight into developing solutions using the BizTalk Messaging service and the tools provided to build messaging workflows. BizTalk Messaging depends on the definition of data formats and document structures, the transformation of those formats and structures, and the creation of messaging objects to represent the workflow. The tools provided to do this are, respectively, BizTalk Editor, BizTalk Mapper, and BizTalk Messaging Manager.

Part III, BizTalk Server Orchestration, discusses the tools and services which provide the business process automation functionality in BizTalk Server. Through the Visio-based interface in BizTalk Orchestration Designer, business processes can be designed and compiled into executable files. Advanced use of this tool provides for transaction handling, long-running business processes, and correlation of documents passed through BizTalk Messaging workflows.

Part IV covers managing BizTalk Server, and moves away from the development of BizTalk Server solutions to the administration and monitoring of those solutions. The features of the BizTalk Server Administration console with respect to individual servers and server groups are discussed. The sophisticated Document Tracking functionality is explained in detail, and methods for troubleshooting various aspects of BizTalk Server solutions are explored.

Part V, Deploying BizTalk Server, continues in the same vein, dealing with issues faced by administrators deploying small, medium, and large BizTalk Server enterprise solutions. In addition to planning and optimizing the deployment, it is necessary to secure the entire enterprise; best practices and recommendations are provided for all aspects of this. The integration of BizTalk Server with existing systems is also covered, with an example of how BizTalk Server and Commerce Server can work together for business-to-business integration, and how BizTalk Server can be adapted to communicate with an Enterprise Resource Planning system such as SAP for enterprise application integration.

Part VI of the book, Extending BizTalk Server, demonstrates how all is not lost if the functionality provided by the base product does not meet your needs. Sophisticated solutions can be programmatically created using the Messaging Configuration Object Model, and existing features can be extended through the creation of custom parser, serializer, preprocessor, functoid, and application integration components. Further, BizTalk Server can be made to take advantage of web services for increased compliance with Microsoft's .NET vision. The administration of BizTalk Server can also be handled programmatically using Windows Management Instrumentation (WMI), and new BizTalk Server Accelerators are being released to simplify the integration of the product into existing vertical markets.

Part VII, BizTalk Server 2002 Enterprise Edition, deals with the latest version of the product, to be released by late 2001. Almost everything covered earlier in the book applies to this new release, but there are some important differences to be found in existing features, and powerful new functionality provided by the SEED Wizard, along with improved integration with Microsoft Application Center 2000 and Microsoft Operations Manager 2000.

The final part, **Part VIII**, is an Appendix to the main body of the book, providing a reproduction of the BizTalk Framework 2.0, and information about the three CD-ROMs included with the book containing trial versions of BizTalk Server 2000, SQL Server 2000, and Visio 2000 to get you up-and-running even faster. Further detail on using these CD-ROMS can be found in the What's On The CDs section of this book.

Lastly, although we've tried not to make the book too code-heavy, there are certain topics where it's vital to include descriptive examples to illustrate the features for developers. To save your fingers, many of the code samples can be downloaded from the free code section on Osborne/McGraw-Hill's web site at http://www.osborne.com/.

Is This Book For You?

Regardless of whether you're an IT professional, a developer, or a business analyst, if your organization will be implementing BizTalk Server, there's something in this book for you. Each chapter is written to provide the basic background knowledge as well as the in-depth detail you'll need to implement each aspect of the product. However, this is not a Beginner's Guide, as we do not attempt to oversimplify everything or provide a running tutorial throughout the book. Similarly, we will assume that there are certain prerequisites already in place, such as a basic familiarity with Microsoft Visual Basic or Visual C++ in the developer chapters, or a fundamental knowledge of Windows 2000 and SQL Server 2000 in the administration chapters.

You may choose to read this book from start to finish, or after dispensing with the introduction chapters, you may decide to home in on specific topics of interest, such as those dealing with specific development or management tasks. However,

BizTalk Server is one of that new breed of products that requires experience on both sides of the IT fence to fully appreciate its complexities and subtleties, to allow you to become an expert in its implementation. If we've done our job, this book will be your Complete Reference for every task, but if you have any comments or complaints, please let us know at btstcr@osborne.com.

The
Complete
Reference

BizTalk Server

Part I

Getting Started with BizTalk Server

Chapter 1

Introduction to BizTalk Server

BizTalk Server is part of Microsoft's stated goal to provide tools, products, and services to allow organizations to implement business-to-business (B2B) electronic commerce (e-commerce) over the Internet. This goal is called the *BizTalk Initiative*, and it consists of three main activities: a proposed messaging standard called the BizTalk Framework, a not-for-profit web site (http://www.biztalk.org) containing resources for organizations, and the BizTalk Server product itself.

This book will tell you everything you need to know (and almost everything there is to know) about Microsoft BizTalk Server the product. In a nutshell, BizTalk Server provides a rich set of tools and services to enable not just B2B integration, but also Enterprise Application Integration (EAI), workflow management, and business process automation. However, before you can properly understand the product, it's important to appreciate its background and the larger picture surrounding its conception. Let's begin by taking a look at how the BizTalk Initiative came about.

Why BizTalk?

The whole idea behind BizTalk Server grew out of an earlier product—Microsoft Site Server 3.0 Commerce Edition. Just as Microsoft was making its initial foray into the realm of business-to-consumer (B2C) e-commerce with Site Server, many other Internet heavy-weights were taking a serious look at another aspect of this burgeoning industry. This aspect—business-to-business (B2B) e-commerce—was only lightly addressed by the Microsoft product, however, because companies were only starting to appreciate its potential. The reason why it would eventually become more lucrative than B2C e-commerce can be summed up in one statement: Businesses have more money to spend than consumers do. Nobody could accuse Microsoft of being blissfully ignorant of the potential of B2B e-commerce, however. Site Server Commerce Edition already had groundbreaking support for an emerging data interchange format known as the *Extensible Markup Language (XML)*, and it attempted to address the issues of B2B exchanges with its *Commerce Interchange Pipeline (CIP)* feature.

The CIP allowed businesses to package order information using this new XML format and to transport it to a trading partner. This trading partner might be responsible for sourcing parts for the customer order, providing warehousing facilities, or collecting and delivering the order itself. Normally, in this kind of relationship, there is a flow of information that begins with the customer's order. For example, if a customer places an order for a new PC on an e-commerce web site, the online store might have to contact its supplier to see whether the item is in stock. If it's not in stock, the supplier may need to contact the manufacturer. The manufacturer may not have all the parts in stock to build the product, such as memory chips or CD-ROM units. Therefore, it might have to contact a wholesaler. The wholesaler will also have its suppliers, and so on. This kind of flow is called a *supply chain*, or *value chain*, and it is this kind of process that Microsoft wished to address with the BizTalk Initiative.

The BizTalk Initiative

The BizTalk Initiative is made up of several parts. Foremost, Microsoft hoped to position BizTalk as a messaging framework for the various supply-chain documents that would be buzzing around the Internet. This framework would attempt to do over the Internet what Electronic Data Interchange (EDI) had already accomplished for business partners across proprietary value-added networks (VANs) during the previous 20 years. Moreover, the framework would take advantage of the increasingly popular XML data format, as opposed to the complicated flat-file formats used by EDI standards.

Although Microsoft has been the driving force behind this initiative, as with similar ventures, they have been supported or assisted by other leading players in the industry. In fact, the BizTalk Initiative was originally under the auspices of a BizTalk Steering Committee consisting of such diverse companies as Ariba, Boeing, CommerceOne, Compaq, Dell, J.D. Edwards, Reuters, RosettaNet, SAP, Siebel, UPS, and WebMethods. Many of these companies still partner with Microsoft today on BizTalk- and XML-related technologies.

The Framework

The BizTalk Framework was announced in March 1999 as a new cross-platform e-commerce framework for establishing a communication standard for companies and making it easy for businesses to integrate applications and conduct business over the Internet with their trading partners and customers. The BizTalk Framework sets the tone for how documents should be exchanged and is based on standard data structures called *XML Schemas* and an XML-based protocol for integrating disparate applications across distributed networks—the *Simple Object Access Protocol* (SOAP). These standards enable integration across industries and between business systems, regardless of platform, operating system, or underlying technology.

 A schema is an XML-based definition of the structure of an XML document. Schemas are discussed in more detail in Chapter 2.

The Web Site

After creating the BizTalk Framework, Microsoft (and the BizTalk Steering Committee) obviously wanted to publicize it in the hope that it would be adopted by the industry. To do this, they created a web site (BizTalk.org) that would serve as an online resource for anybody interested in the BizTalk Initiative. However, Microsoft often encounters skepticism when they try to promote an emerging technology as a standard. For this reason, they deliberately chose not to brand BizTalk.org as a Microsoft site, hoping instead that it would serve as a neutral playing field for concerned parties. On the site, they also created an online repository where organizations could upload XML schemas for the benefit of others, because it makes sense for people to use the same data structures whenever possible. Unfortunately, the site never really lived up to its potential, and although it still exists, Microsoft rebranded the site early in 2001 with a more traditional style and color scheme, as shown in Figure 1-1. However, neither this web site nor the BizTalk Framework is the jewel in the BizTalk Initiative crown.

The Product

Microsoft BizTalk Server is the product that directly addresses the primary goal of the BizTalk Initiative in a tangible way. BizTalk Server provides not only for business-to-business integration, but also for enterprise application integration. In fact, "integration" is the key point here. To successfully implement BizTalk Server in an enterprise, it should not be necessary to throw away systems; BizTalk Server complements legacy systems, allowing communication where none was possible before.

The product has undergone many dramatic changes since its conception, reflecting the evolution of the industry and the requirements of those who shape it. In September 1999,

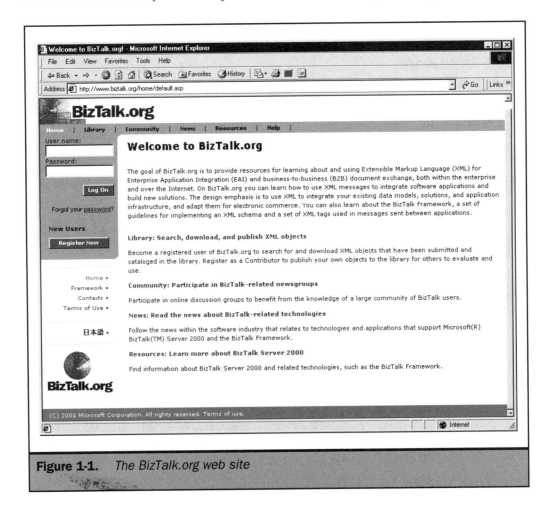

Figure 1-1.   *The BizTalk.org web site*

Microsoft released the BizTalk Jumpstart Kit—a collection of tools to help developers design BizTalk Framework 1.0–compliant schemas and to integrate XML into their applications. This was released simultaneously with the launch of the BizTalk.org web site. Version 2.0 of the toolkit followed in February 2000, and this release included a Software Development Kit (SDK) that would assist developers in the creation of adapters to allow XML-based data flow between applications. These would serve as the precursors to Application Integration Components (AICs), which still exist in the current version of the product to provide the various outbound transports.

In April 2000, the first version of BizTalk Server proper made its debut as the BizTalk Server Technology Preview. The final product was now starting to take shape. Graphical tools such as the BizTalk Editor and BizTalk Mapper made the creation of document specifications and the transformation of those specifications simple. The BizTalk Management Desk (now called BizTalk Messaging Manager) allowed the creation of partner agreements (channels) and pipelines (messaging ports) to effect the exchange of business documents with external trading partners. Out-of-the-box parsers provided support for common data formats such as ANSI X12 and EDIFACT, and application adapters (AICs) allowed the product to communicate with enterprise resource planning (ERP) systems such as SAP.

Over the next few months, excitement grew for the potential of the final product. One more milestone in the development cycle seemed to secure its success—the inclusion of BizTalk Orchestration in the first public beta of the product, released in July 2000. This new feature introduced the idea of business process automation, with a graphical interface based on the newly acquired Microsoft Visio. This interface, called the Application Designer (now the Orchestration Designer) allowed a business process to be graphically described, with each action implemented by a developer through technologies such as Component Object Model (COM) components and Message Queuing. This business process drawing could then be compiled into an executable program called an *XLANG schedule*, where XLANG is an XML-based language that defines how the process should run.

Finally, BizTalk Server 2000 was released to manufacturing in December 2000, boasting a complete infrastructure for business-to-business integration, enterprise application integration, workflow management, and business process automation. Before we get into detail on the services and tools provided by the product, however, let's take a step back to examine another aspect of the BizTalk Initiative. If you think about it, the only reason the product is called BizTalk Server in the first place is because it is fully compliant with the BizTalk Framework 2.0.

The BizTalk Framework

The Microsoft BizTalk Framework 2.0 is a framework based on the *Extensible Markup Language (XML) + Namespaces 1.0* and *Simple Object Access Protocol (SOAP) 1.1* specifications for application integration and e-commerce. It includes a design framework for implementing XML schemas and a set of predefined XML tags—called *BizTags*—that can be used to wrap documents sent between applications. These tags serve to provide descriptive and routing information not present in the document itself.

Schemas

Because the BizTalk Framework uses the recognized standard XML for describing documents, it makes it easier for other vendors and organizations to adopt the Framework and build on it. When the Framework was originally developed, Microsoft had also created a way of describing XML documents called *schemas*. Schemas describe the structure of an XML document using XML, if you can believe that. (No, this does not create a circular reference—you'll see how this works in Chapter 2.) However, while Microsoft was promoting its schema technology, called XML Data Reduced (XDR), the World Wide Web Consortium (W3C), a nonprofit organization devoted to the standardization of technologies for the Internet, was also working on a similar specification. The long wait for W3C schemas to appear is often cited as one reason why many companies held back from adopting the BizTalk Framework.

Either way, the intent was that interested software companies or industry standards bodies could use the BizTalk Framework to produce XML schemas that defined not only their business documents, but also how they should be processed. This processing, or routing, information is contained in the extra BizTags that envelop the document. The resulting envelope must comply with the SOAP 1.1 specification. SOAP is an XML-based syntax that defines an envelope for calls to methods exposed by an application and the data returned by those method calls. The SOAP 1.1 envelope forms the basis for the BizTalk Framework message structure shown in Figure 1-2.

The BizTalk Framework itself is not yet a standard, but the language used to define it—XML—is. One of the goals of the BizTalk Initiative is to accelerate the adoption of XML and XML schemas as the underlying data format and specification language for business document exchange. BizTalk Framework schemas, which are business documents and messages expressed using an extension of XML schemas, can be registered and stored on the BizTalk.org web site. Anyone can download the BizTalk Framework from this web site and use it to define their own XML schemas. As long as the schemas pass a validation test, they may be referred to as BizTalk Framework schemas. The BizTalk.org web site also provides an automated submission and validation process. Individuals or organizations can freely use XML schemas from the BizTalk.org web site within their applications for as long as the schema is published for public use. Businesses also have the option of publishing their schemas on the BizTalk.org web site in a secure area for private use between trading partners.

The full BizTalk Framework 2.0 specification is reproduced in Appendix A.

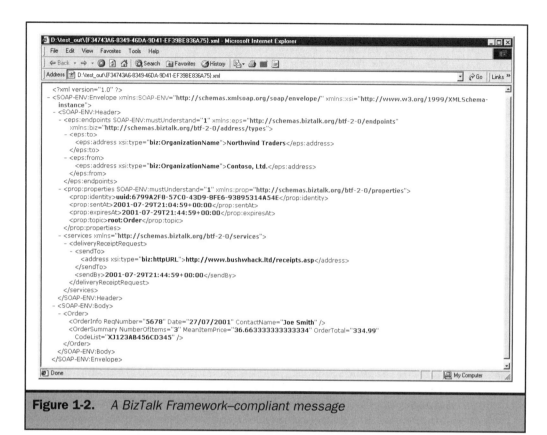

Figure 1-2.   *A BizTalk Framework–compliant message*

The end result is that the BizTalk Framework describes business documents as *BizTalk Messages*. BizTalk messages are an extension of SOAP documents, with additional BizTalk-specific tags referred to as BizTags. A server that implements the BizTalk Framework should utilize these BizTags as specified in the Framework. Microsoft BizTalk Server is, so far, the only publicly available BizTalk Framework–compliant software, although other companies are developing similar BizTalk server products.

Benefits

I must stress that you do not have to implement the BizTalk Framework to use Microsoft BizTalk Server. However, if your business and your trading partners are already using XML-based document structures, there are plenty of reasons why you should. Some of the benefits of using the BizTalk Framework are as follows:

- **Roadmap for consistent XML implementations**   Many companies report a strong interest in XML. XML, however, is so flexible that this is like expressing a strong interest in ASCII characters. XML enables advancements, but they are hard to achieve without a consistent framework for XML implementations. The BizTalk Framework implements a set of rules that makes it possible for a broad audience to adopt a common approach to using XML. As companies move beyond data modeling using XML and start automating business processes, BizTalk Framework messages define the necessary routing information for processing systems.

■ **Easier mapping across schemas**   By formalizing the process of expressing business process interchanges in a consistent and extensible format, the BizTalk Framework makes it easier for *Independent Software Vendors (ISVs)* and developers in a wide variety of industries to map from one business document structure to another. This promotes the adoption of electronic interchange using open standards such as XML.

■ **Design target for software vendors**   By establishing a critical mass of schemas implemented in a consistent format, the BizTalk Framework provides a clear design target for tools and infrastructure ISVs building the next generation of e-commerce and application integration products.

■ **Framework for standards bodies**   The BizTalk Framework provides a means for migrating an existing set of industry interchange standards to XML. This is especially useful for the Electronic Data Interchange (EDI) community.

■ **Repository for BizTalk schemas**   The BizTalk.org web site is an interactive place where industry groups and developers can publish their schemas. The web site allows public and private publication based on the decision of the publishing organization. Once a BizTalk Framework schema is accepted and published, the repository will provide versioning and specialization support for adoption and alteration. The repository will support dynamic detection of schemas, processes, and visualization maps connected to any given version of a BizTalk Framework schema.

■ **Showcase for the best practices in developing XML interchanges**   Many organizations involved in the standardization of business interchanges are more skilled in business process modeling than in systems programming and XML. These groups can use the BizTalk.org web site to discover best practices for implementing their own schemas or to discover other XML schemas they can use in their applications.

Microsoft has vowed to support the BizTalk Framework in its product line and will publish XML schemas to the BizTalk.org web site for public use. It has also promised to implement complete support for the W3C schema recommendation after it has been finalized. This recommendation was published in June 2001, and it is clear that future versions of the Framework, and BizTalk Server, will be compatible with these schema structures. In fact, Microsoft has provided the facility to upload W3C-compliant schemas to the BizTalk.org site since early in 2001. Other software vendors supporting the BizTalk Framework have also made this commitment.

BizTalk Framework Architecture Principles

The BizTalk Framework is designed to foster application integration and e-commerce through data interchange standards based on XML. It assumes that applications are distinct entities and that application integration takes place using a loosely coupled, asynchronous approach to pass messages. There is no need for a common object model, programming language, network protocol, database, or operating system for two applications to exchange XML messages formatted using the BizTalk Framework. The two applications simply need to be able to receive, parse, process, and transmit a standardized XML message.

Messages underlie the most significant contributions of the BizTalk Framework. A message flow between two or more applications is a means to integrate applications at the business-process level by defining a loosely coupled, request-based communication process. Since many business processes involve one party performing a service at the request of another party, the mapping of messages to requests is natural. Application solutions making tighter integration demands, such as those based on special programming languages or shared distributed computing "platforms," are highly appropriate to tightly connected applications on single machines or in controlled environments. They do not, however, adequately support distributed, loosely coupled, extensible business process integration. An XML-based messaging system with open, extensible wire formats captures the essentials of a business communication while allowing flexible implementations.

Microsoft anticipates that the vast majority of *interchanges* (messages containing one or more documents wrapped in an envelope) exchanged using the BizTalk Framework will use a simple HTTP (HyperText Transfer Protocol) post transport. But businesses can also use other transports including FTP (File Transfer Protocol) and messaging technologies, such as IBM's MQSeries, Microsoft Message Queuing 2.0, and SMTP (Simple Mail Transfer Protocol). As we will see in the next section, most of these transport methods enjoy out-of-the-box support in Microsoft BizTalk Server.

One other consideration is that since a limited (but growing) number of software applications provide support for XML, many businesses will need to implement specialized adapters to enable their existing applications to participate in the first generation of BizTalk Framework exchanges. For many applications, these adapters take an existing function call, translate it into an XML document, and route the document to a target destination, whether it is a trading partner or another application within a corporate intranet. As discussed earlier, these adapters may be implemented in Microsoft BizTalk Server as Application Integration Components (AICs).

If you would like to read the complete BizTalk Framework 2.0 specification, it is included as Appendix A, because it is a bit more in-depth than necessary for an introductory chapter such as this. Next up, we will examine in more detail how Microsoft BizTalk Server implements the BizTalk Framework and how it provides tools and services to simplify the integration of dissimilar systems.

BizTalk Server

As you're probably aware if you've read this far, BizTalk Server is a product from Microsoft that addresses the requirements of business-to-business integration, enterprise application integration, workflow management, and business process orchestration. To accomplish these feats, the product is built on core services and supporting tools to assist in the rapid development and deployment of BizTalk solutions. Before I discuss these tools and services, however, let's make sure we know what we mean by "enterprise application integration" and "business-to-business integration."

Enterprise Application Integration

Enterprise application integration may be defined as the cooperation of disparate systems and components to implement business rules in a distributed environment. Or, in less fancy words: different types of computer systems within an organization talking to each other. Although we can express the concept simply, its implementation can be far from simple. Getting different types of systems to talk to each other typically involves the following:

- The transportation of information between one or more applications, perhaps involving the transformation of data into a particular format
- Timing and sequencing rules that govern when and how the transportation and transformation take place
- Integrity constraints that determine the success or failure of the communication

For example, if my enterprise includes an enterprise resource planning (ERP) system, a customer relationship management (CRM) system, a web site, and a database, as shown in Figure 1-3, the business rules that govern my organization may require that orders arriving at my web site are first logged to my database. Some component, or *middleware*, will be necessary to effect this by ensuring that the order information is transformed into the correct hierarchy of records and fields that the database expects. The order may also need to be logged to the CRM system to be available for after-sales support queries, and again, the data will need to be in the correct format as expected by that system. The CRM system may also create an entry in the ERP system that provides information internally to accounting software and analysis tools. Once more, these systems will need to be able to communicate with each other for the smooth operation of the process. Typically, these pieces of software will have been developed separately in-house, or by a number of third parties, so it is extremely unlikely that they are designed to share information among themselves with no intervention.

Enterprise application integration may be achieved using one of three integration methods:

Method	Description
Application programming interfaces (APIs)	Programmatic interfaces provided by the software for synchronous communication

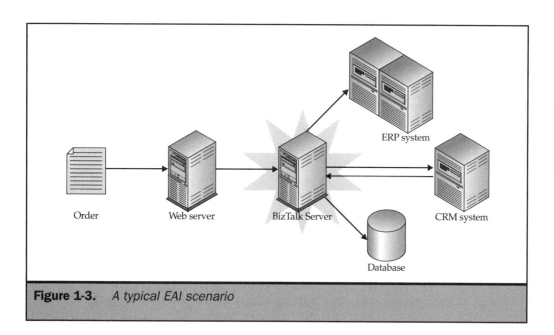

Figure 1-3.   *A typical EAI scenario*

Method	Description
Messaging	The asynchronous sending and receiving of messages between applications through an intermediary
File transfer	The importing and exporting of data to text or binary files in various formats

In each case, it may still be necessary to transform the data from one format to another as required by the interacting systems. Common data formats used by applications are as follows:

Format	Description
XML	Data encoded using the Extensible Markup Language (XML), which uses a hierarchical structure of elements, with each item of information described by tags.
EDI	Electronic Data Interchange (EDI) formats developed in the 1970s to define common business documents for transfer between trading partners. Two main standards are currently in use—ANSI X12, typically used in the United States, and UN/EDIFACT, used elsewhere.

Format	Description
Flat-file	Plain text in a simple hierarchical format, two or possibly three levels deep. There are two types—*positional*, where each item of data has a fixed length, and *delimited*, where special characters indicate the beginning or end of a data item.

Note   *These data formats will be discussed in more detail in Chapter 2.*

Furthermore, because these application systems may expect information to arrive by various means, enterprise application integration will also require the implementation of different transport mechanisms including, but not limited to, the following:

Transport	Description
DCOM	The Component Object Model (COM) provides a way for applications written using Visual Basic or Visual C++ to define public interfaces with methods that can be invoked programmatically for synchronous communication. Distributed COM (DCOM) describes such communication between remote networked applications.
HTTP	The HyperText Transfer Protocol (HTTP) defines a standard synchronous communication system between clients that make requests, and file or application servers that recognize, accept, and respond to those requests in a uniform way.
SMTP	The Simple Mail Transfer Protocol (SMTP) defines a standard asynchronous communication where specially formatted messages can be relayed across a network of servers.
Message Queuing	Message Queuing provides a way for disparate application systems to asynchronously communicate through the sending of messages that are stored for later retrieval. This can circumvent problems faced by distributed applications, such as availability and network connectivity.
File	Documents may be written to or read from a standard file folder on a local machine, or at a shared location on the network for asynchronous storage and retrieval.

Business-to-Business Integration

If enterprise application integration can greatly improve communication and increase efficiency for a single organization, extending the idea to encompass customers and trading partners can provide benefits for all. Because the same difficulties will arise in terms of disparate data formats, application architectures, and transport mechanisms, business-to-business integration is effectively nothing more than enterprise application integration conducted between multiple organizations, as opposed to within an organization.

In this context, business-to-business integration (and its sibling, business-to-consumer integration) should promote a seamless, consistent customer and supplier experience through real-time messaging workflow and automatic business process execution. I'm sure it seems obvious, but this is beneficial for a number of reasons. Traditional ways of doing business can be inefficient, even if both businesses claim to be electronically enabled, or *e-enabled*. For example, the lack of integration between systems can mean that an arriving purchase order must be manually converted into a corresponding invoice, and this reentry of information can sometimes lead to data errors. This involvement of human beings in the process also results in time delays between the arrival of a document and the transmission of an acknowledgement. By developing electronic business-to-business relationships where the processes are automated, companies can cut costs and overhead by taking the manual labor out of the loop.

Business-to-business integration can significantly improve your company's bottom line by promoting many of the key principles of business success. These include the following:

- Being faster to market with your products and services
- Providing a more efficient customer service
- Operating a smoother sales process
- Reducing operational, production, and inventory costs

In Chapter 2, we will see how businesses have attempted to address these problems in the past by implementing Electronic Data Interchange (EDI). EDI describes the process by which trading partners can exchange business documents and also describes the format of those documents. This sounds like a suitable solution, and to many organizations it is, but EDI systems can be costly to develop and maintain. One of the primary reasons for this is that EDI exchanges typically take place over value-added networks (VANs), which are expensive leased lines operated between business partners. Since the advent of the Internet, various consortia have tried to migrate EDI techniques to use public networks with varying degrees of success. Some of the industry groups involved in this work include RosettaNet (http://www.rosettanet.org), the Organization for the Advancement of Structured Information Standards (OASIS) (http://www.oasis-open.org), and the BizTalk Steering Committee mentioned earlier.

Today, a wide range of technologies, data formats, and transport mechanisms is in use for both enterprise application integration and business-to-business integration. It has become obvious that no one technology, data format, or transport will replace everything currently available, so integration is the key. That is why BizTalk Server provides tools and services to promote integration between disparate systems, rather than trying to take their place.

BizTalk Server Services

BizTalk Server provides two core services to address the issues discussed previously. These are BizTalk Messaging and BizTalk Orchestration. Parts II and III of this book will go into complete detail on these services, also covering the supporting tools that enable the implementation of these services.

BizTalk Messaging Service

In my discussions of both business-to-business integration and enterprise application integration, I described how various data formats, structures, and transport methods are involved when disparate systems attempt to communicate. BizTalk Messaging provides a means for the differences exposed by dissimilar systems to be reconciled. Let's look at a typical business-to-business example. Figure 1-4 shows a purchase order in an X12 format arriving from a remote trading partner via HTTP. Our business rules determine that an acknowledgement should be sent back using the same format as an e-mail, and that an invoice should be generated for the ordered goods and sent back to the trading partner's web site using HTTP. The purchase order should also be logged with our ERP system and a copy stored in a database. Obviously, the data required by our ERP system may not be in the same format or structure as the original message; likewise, some transformation will be necessary to insert the details into our database.

BizTalk Messaging can be configured to accept the purchase order submitted from the Active Server Page (ASP) on the web server. It will then parse the document from

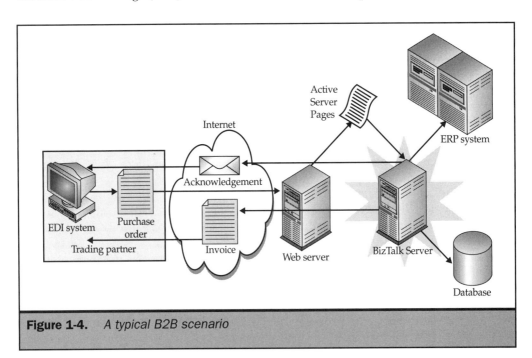

Figure 1-4. *A typical B2B scenario*

its original format into XML, transform the document as necessary using a special map file created with the Extensible Stylesheet Language for Transformation (XSLT), and serialize the XML data into the structure and format required by the ERP system. A custom Application Integration Component (AIC) can then be created to transport the data to the ERP system. Similarly, another AIC can be used to insert the information into the database. Finally, BizTalk Messaging can automatically construct both an acknowledgement and an invoice for return to the trading partner and can send them using SMTP and HTTP, respectively.

Although this example involves the programmatic submission of data from an ASP, this could also be achieved through programmatic submission from an Exchange Server script if the original purchase order had been sent using SMTP. Also, BizTalk Server provides File and Message Queuing receive functions to support those inbound protocols. Equally, although the example uses custom AICs to transport the transformed data to the ERP and database systems, SMTP to return the acknowledgement, and HTTP to return the invoice, BizTalk Messaging also provides out-of-the-box support for HTTPS, File, and Message Queuing transmission methods.

These workflows can be created using BizTalk Messaging Manager, a graphical utility shown in Figure 1-5. Using this application will be discussed in detail in Chapter 6. BizTalk Messaging Manager allows the creation and configuration of programmatic objects that represent the organizations and applications involved in a workflow, as well as the types of documents that are being processed, the transformations that might be needed for those documents, and the routing information necessary to deliver them to their final destinations.

BizTalk Orchestration

Many business processes are not just simple straight-through affairs such as those handled by BizTalk Messaging. Sometimes, a business process must be dynamic—capable of detecting different scenarios in real time and acting accordingly. A modern automated business process must be able to implement decision factors, perform tasks multiple times based on business rules, take account of transactions, and handle exceptions. For example, if a purchase request is generated by an intranet purchasing application, there may be expressly defined criteria that establish whether the request should be approved by a manager before it becomes an actual purchase order to be sent to a supplier. An automated business process should recognize these criteria and determine whether to seek approval, without the need for manual intervention. Similarly, an automated process must be able to detect errors that occur within the process and react accordingly, perhaps undoing previously completed tasks.

Transactions are business processes that must either succeed or fail as a whole. To use a common example, if a customer is transferring money from one bank account to another, there are two parts to the process—a withdrawal from the first account, and a deposit into the second account. If something goes wrong in the middle of this process, we must be careful not to leave the system in an inconsistent state. Bank customers tend to get upset if they try to transfer funds and the money just disappears, so

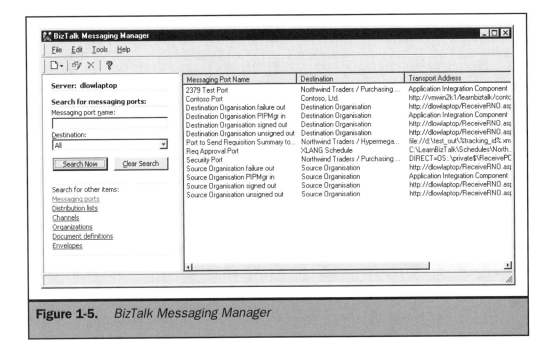

Figure 1-5.   *BizTalk Messaging Manager*

developers have to ensure either that the entire process completes successfully or that none of it takes place. Likewise, exceptions are errors that can occur in a business process, perhaps even within a transaction. For the process to be fully automated, these exceptions must be handled to ensure the system remains in a consistent state.

BizTalk Orchestration allows automated business processes defined using an XML-based language called XLANG to execute on a computer running BizTalk Server. These processes are defined in a graphical application called BizTalk Orchestration Designer, which is based on Microsoft Visio. As Figure 1-6 shows, by drawing the business process using flowchart shapes and by using implementation shapes representing various technologies to actually perform each action, a developer can describe the entire sequence of events and how each step will be carried out. BizTalk Orchestration Designer also allows developers to implement transactions in their business processes and to take remedial action in the event of an exception or a failed transaction.

BizTalk Server Tools

To implement the workflows and automated business processes supported by BizTalk Messaging and BizTalk Orchestration, BizTalk Server includes a number of tools that can be used to create the components used by these services. Both Microsoft and some third parties have also created other tools and utilities to simplify the creation of other types of processes. Chapter 19 will discuss some of the accelerators for BizTalk Server currently available.

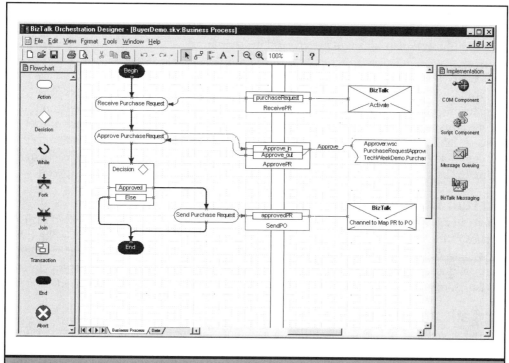

Figure 1-6.   *BizTalk Orchestration Designer*

BizTalk Editor

Because BizTalk Server primarily deals with business documents, it is important that
we can represent different types of document structure. This will be necessary for
BizTalk Server to parse incoming documents from their original format into XML and
to serialize outgoing documents from XML into the format they will be required to have
when they reach their destination. BizTalk Editor is a graphical utility for defining the
structure and format of business documents. These structures will be stored as XML
schemas, which will be discussed in Chapter 2. The creation of document specifications
using BizTalk Editor will be covered in Chapter 4.

BizTalk Mapper

We have seen that different organizations represent their business data in different
formats and different structures. Although the parsers and serializers included with
BizTalk Server enable the transformation of documents from one format to another, we
must also be able to restructure our business documents to reflect this diversity. BizTalk
Mapper is a graphical utility for creating the map files that will convert one document

structure to another. It does this by defining an XSLT stylesheet that effects the necessary transformation on the XML-encoded documents used internally by BizTalk Server. The creation of these map files will be covered in Chapter 5.

BizTalk Messaging Manager

As discussed, BizTalk Messaging allows the execution of workflows that accept, transform, and route documents between applications and organizations. Within the service, this is performed by programmatic objects that represent each aspect of the process. BizTalk Messaging Manager is a graphical HTML-based interface that simplifies the creation of these objects and the configuration of the workflows that involve them. Using BizTalk Messaging Manager to define these objects is dealt with in Chapter 6.

BizTalk Orchestration Designer

In Chapter 7, we will see how to use the Microsoft Visio–based application called BizTalk Orchestration Designer to create automated business processes called XLANG schedules. We will also see how these processes can take advantage of decision-making, looping, transactions, and exceptions. In Chapter 8, the integration of BizTalk Messaging and BizTalk Orchestration to create more sophisticated processes will be discussed.

BizTalk Administration

Although we have only discussed the deployment of a single BizTalk Server for various purposes in this introductory chapter, it is important to realize that multiple BizTalk Server computers can be clustered into server groups. The creation and management of these server groups, as well as the configuration of each individual server, is performed through the BizTalk Administration interface, which is a Microsoft Management Console. This console also allows the creation of the receive functions previously mentioned that provide a means for documents to be submitted to BizTalk Messaging. The use of this tool will be discussed in Chapter 9.

BizTalk Document Tracking

Because BizTalk Server can process hundreds or even thousands of documents a second, you might think that once a business document passes through BizTalk Messaging or through BizTalk Orchestration, all data pertaining to the interchange is destroyed. This would not make good business sense, however, as it is often necessary to call up previous documents to provide customer service or to settle legal disputes. By default, all documents processed by BizTalk Messaging are stored in a database for later retrieval. There is also a web-based application called BizTalk Document Tracking to allow you to search for and view these documents. The Document Tracking application and the management of the database that stores each interchange will be covered in Chapter 10.

We're almost ready to begin looking at each aspect of BizTalk Server in detail. Before we do, we should take a moment to see how BizTalk Server fits into the greater Microsoft plan. Like the BizTalk Initiative before it, Microsoft is now promoting another set of tools, technologies, and products that promise to change the way applications and businesses use the Internet to communicate. This initiative goes by the simple name of .NET.

The .NET Initiative

The .NET Initiative comprises a number of standards, technologies, and products. All serve to promote loosely coupled communication between distributed applications across the Internet. It is not the intention of this book to delve too deeply into the .NET Initiative or its technologies, but it is important to understand how it relates to BizTalk Server.

.NET is an evolving concept, and as such is perhaps too much of a moving target to address in this book. However, there are a couple of aspects that have been announced or are already available in one form or other. First, there are the .NET Enterprise Servers, of which BizTalk Server is one. Second, there is the .NET Framework, which describes a collection of services and classes that applications can use regardless of the language in which they are written or the operating system on which they run.

.NET Enterprise Servers

The .NET Enterprise Servers are the logical evolution of Microsoft BackOffice Servers for the Internet age. They are designed for interoperability and take advantage of open web standards such as XML. It is an important indication of Microsoft's commitment to the .NET Initiative that they have rebranded almost every product as a member of the .NET family, even if the brand fits some products better than others. Again, it is not the goal of this book to provide an in-depth analysis of each of these products, but because many of them will find a place in your enterprise alongside BizTalk Server, I will list them here with a brief description of their intended use.

Application Center 2000

Application Center 2000 is a deployment and management tool for high-availability distributed web applications built on the Windows 2000 or Windows.NET platform. It provides features such as component load-balancing and a health monitor for performance optimization. It also builds on the Content Replication Services originally provided by Site Server. Although it does not integrate directly with BizTalk Server, it could prove important in large solutions with multiple web servers that receive documents for BizTalk Server. In Chapter 12 we will see how Application Center can be used to provide load balancing for core products used by BizTalk Server 2000.

Commerce Server 2000

The successor to Site Server 3.0 Commerce Edition, Commerce Server 2000 provides key services and features to build an online business. It includes an extensible Business Desk application for the management of e-commerce web sites, ready-made solution sites to simplify the development process, and a full suite of analysis, prediction, profiling, and marketing tools. It integrates well with BizTalk Server to provide a complete value chain experience. In Chapter 14 we will explore how this integration can be achieved.

Content Management Server 2001

This is another recent acquisition by Microsoft that builds on the Content Management feature of Site Server 3.0 to provide document storage and retrieval facilities that again take advantage of XML. It integrates with SharePoint Portal Server to create complete collaboration solutions, and also with Commerce Server to simplify the publication of personalized content.

Exchange Server 2000

Exchange Server 2000 is an enterprise-level messaging and collaboration server, and it was the first of the .NET servers (though the term wasn't used at the time), coming hot on the heels of Windows 2000 and making full use of the Active Directory technology built into the platform. BizTalk Server can use its messaging features and its active scripting support to send and retrieve documents.

Host Integration Server 2000

Probably the most unlikely server product to bear the .NET name, Host Integration Server 2000 provides connectivity with legacy systems and mainframes. It is the successor to Systems Network Architecture (SNA) Server 4.0. BizTalk Server could use an AIC to communicate with such systems.

Internet Security and Acceleration Server 2000

A complete revamp of Proxy Server 2.0, Internet Security and Acceleration Server is a full-featured firewall, caching, and proxy server for enterprise security. This will often provide the required network security for a BizTalk Server deployment. The use of firewalls and proxy servers to secure BizTalk Server will be discussed in Chapter 13.

Mobile Information 2001 Server

One of the later additions to the fold, as its name suggests, Mobile Information Server 2001 provides a secure, extensible platform for the delivery of enterprise application data such as e-mail and intranet content to mobile employees using hand-held devices. BizTalk Server could potentially integrate with it to transform application content for delivery to portable devices in a variety of formats.

SharePoint Portal Server 2000

Another late addition, this was originally planned as Site Server version 4.0 and retains many of that product's features, such as Knowledge Management and Internet Crawl and Search. It provides a collaborative environment for companies, integrating heavily with Exchange Server 2000.

SQL Server 2000

Microsoft's enterprise-level database product, this provides important back-end support to BizTalk Server and Commerce Server among others. It includes groundbreaking XML support, as well as data warehousing and analysis services.

Windows.NET Server

On the desktop, the next version of Windows after Windows 2000 (code-named "Whistler" during development) will be Windows XP Home Edition (home use) or Windows XP Professional Edition (office use). In the enterprise, however, it will be Windows.NET Server or Advanced Server that provides the platform for y our applications, with full support for the .NET Framework. Windows.NET Server undoubtedly will be the platform of choice for later versions of the BizTalk Server product, such as BizTalk Server 2002 Enterprise Edition, which is discussed at the end of this book, and the next version of BizTalk Server currently in development, code-named "Mozart".

.NET Framework

The .NET Framework is the overall term used to describe services such as the Common Language Runtime (CLR), the Base Class Library, and the Common Type System that underlie applications written using the next generation of Microsoft's integrated development suite—Visual Studio.NET. One of the biggest problems in programming today is that it can be hard to be really productive because there are so many programming languages and technologies to learn. If you were, say, a Visual C++ developer, you might find it difficult to make an easy transition into Active Server Pages (ASP) development (or you may consider it beneath you). You would have to learn a whole new language (VBScript or JScript) and a whole new set of objects (the ASP intrinsic objects) to be able to create an ASP web application. One of the benefits of the .NET Framework will be to simplify the development process such that you will have a consistent set of objects and APIs available to you no matter what programming language or programming model you use.

One important goal of .NET is to simplify the development of distributed applications. By using open standards such as SOAP and HTTP, you can easily build distributed, disconnected, or stateless applications that are not tied into a specific platform or programming language. For example, you could build an application that resides on a Windows 2000 server and that communicates with an application on a Linux server. This is possible because .NET prefers standard protocols such as HTTP and SOAP instead of proprietary protocols like IIOP, CORBA, or DCOM.

To gain wide acceptance for the .NET Framework, Microsoft has submitted a subset of the .NET Framework called the *common language infrastructure*, and a new programming language called C# to ECMA (previously known as the European Computer Manufacturers Association, but now just an acronym!), which could lead to eventual multiplatform support. Indeed, there is already an open-source version of the .NET Framework in development for use with UNIX-based systems.

The core services in the .NET Framework are summarized here to give you an idea of the paradigm-shift that developers will face in becoming acquainted with these new technologies.

Common Language Runtime (CLR)

The CLR is one of the more compelling aspects of the .NET Framework. For example, through the CLR, developers will be able to create an interface containing object classes in C#, extend one of these classes using Visual Basic.NET (which now has true inheritance), and then make calls to it in an ASP application written in COBOL! This is because the CLR provides full language interoperability to any language that supports the .NET Framework. This is available not just at run time, as happens already today with COM components, but at design time as well. As mentioned, COBOL is but one of the supporting languages along with Perl, Python, Java, Pascal, Smalltalk, and a host of others. The CLR also provides important features useful to developers, such as exception handling, debugging, security, and garbage collection.

Base Class Library

This is a hierarchical system of classes and members similar to the Java class libraries included in the Java SDK that can be utilized by any .NET-compliant language. These classes are grouped into sets called *namespaces* (not related to XML namespaces) with System as its root. For example, a Visual Basic.NET developer could use the System.Windows.Forms namespace to create a button in a user interface or use the System.Data namespace to create a dataset containing information retrieved from a database.

Common Type System

This is a rationalization of the existing data type system in place across the different languages available in Visual Studio. Also, it is one of the fundamental aspects of the .NET Framework that must be supported by other compliant languages. The types include interfaces, classes, delegates, and value types, and conformance to the Common Type System provides much of the interoperability required by the CLR. One of the more interesting aspects is that for value types, the base is *object*, which means that even primitive data types such as string and integer can have properties, methods, and events.

BizTalk Server and .NET

So why would any of this be important to BizTalk Server? Although BizTalk Server is already fairly full-featured in its support for business-to-business integration and enterprise application integration, and although it already uses accepted standards such as XML and SOAP, and Internet transports such as HTTP and SMTP, there is always room for improvement. .NET promotes the use of special applications called *web services*. These are traditional applications, written using any type of architecture or programming language, that expose methods that can be called using SOAP across HTTP. In this way, an ASP application written in VBScript could include data provided from a Java application on a web server on the far side of the world. It doesn't matter that the applications can't communicate directly because SOAP acts as the go-between.

Obviously, BizTalk Server could make great use of this technology. As we will see in full detail in Chapter 7, one of the core features of BizTalk Server is BizTalk Orchestration, where automated business processes can call COM components on a local system or retrieve documents from a remote message queue. Taking this a step further, BizTalk Orchestration could benefit greatly if an XLANG schedule could call a web service to provide external processing of a document or supply real-time data. Although there is currently no web service implementation shape in the BizTalk Orchestration Designer, in Chapter 17, we will see how similar functionality might be implemented. Correspondingly, in the future, it will be possible to expose BizTalk Server itself as a web service, although again we can imitate this behavior now using a little ingenuity.

Before we get ahead of ourselves talking about future developments for BizTalk Server and Microsoft.NET, throughout this chapter you've probably noticed that three letters come up again and again. These three letters represent humanity's best hope for eventually agreeing on a standard data format for the transfer of information. These three letters are the cornerstone of both Microsoft's .NET Enterprise Servers and the whole .NET Initiative. In particular, these three letters are the way in which BizTalk Server represents data internally, regardless of its original or eventual formats as required by applications or trading partners. To be fully armed for a headlong odyssey through all that is BizTalk Server, you must become intimately familiar with those three letters—*X*, *M*, and *L*.

Chapter 2

BizTalk Server and XML

Since it first appeared on buzzword bingo cards a couple of years ago, XML has promised to change the way we communicate using computers. In books, journals, and the media, it is referred to as the *lingua franca* of the Internet—the language that will cross the boundaries of vendor, application, and trading partner. Now, with unprecedented support across the industry, it is starting to live up to its hype. For this reason, XML is the blood running through the veins of BizTalk Server.

By now, most people who know anything about the Internet have awoken from the misapprehension that XML is simply advanced HTML—a few extra tags to make your web site more "sticky," or another clutch of features supported by one browser but not the others. Slowly but surely, IT managers and developers everywhere are appreciating that XML is becoming the foundation of information transfer. The media are right when they say that XML is now the *de facto* standard for describing data.

Commercial organizations rely on data. Purchase orders, invoices, receipts, requisitions, and catalogs all contain valuable data. Within a company, each type of business document will have a structure, and these structures must be enforced to avoid misinterpretation. XML provides *Document Type Definitions (DTDs)* and *XML Schemas* to provide structure for electronic data, and BizTalk Server bases its own document specifications on XML Schemas.

When trading partners involved in business-to-business (B2B) e-commerce need to exchange data, it becomes more complicated, however. Electronic data comes in many different formats—some are recognized standards and some are proprietary representations. For trading partners to do business electronically, it is essential that the receiver explicitly understands every piece of data sent. Parsing documents to extract the relevant information can be a convoluted process and is by no means an exact science. Describing data using XML removes the uncertainty while also providing another benefit. The *Extensible Stylesheet Language for Transformation (XSLT)* allows XML data to be mapped from one structure to another. The BizTalk Server Messaging Engine employs XSLT to integrate disparate trading partners.

The Extensible Markup Language (XML)

XML is a set of syntactical rules that allow the creation of markup languages. These markup languages are completely extensible in that the tags they contain are not predetermined, as they are in something like HTML. As a result, authors can use XML to create their own markup tags to describe any aspect of the data they work with.

Why XML?

Since the inception of the World Wide Web, web designers and developers have striven to enrich the presentation of information across the Internet. As the following illustration shows, the earliest versions of the HyperText Markup Language (HTML), which is used to create web pages, included only basic formatting instructions such as bold, center, and horizontal rule, concentrating instead on providing textual links (hyperlinks) to related information.

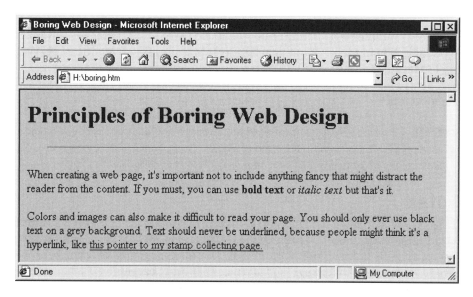

With the commercial success of browser software, vendors such as Microsoft and Netscape competed to add new formatting codes, or *tags,* to allow the rendition of images, tables, forms, and multimedia. As a standard, HTML formally accrued many of these tags to become a sophisticated publishing technology, but somewhere along the way the sheer wealth of information on the Web made it increasingly difficult for users to separate the wheat from the chaff. The data got lost in the presentation.

HTML provides no way for the author of a web page to describe the information contained in a page, to confer context, or to express relationships between data items. Search engines regularly return irrelevant results in response to queries because web pages lack the descriptive information to clarify what they contain.

Special tags called *meta-tags* can provide overall descriptions of a web page, but not the content itself. Imagine an HTML page that contains the minutes of a meeting. It would doubtless contain the names of various individuals present at or referred to in the meeting, but electronically searching the page for the name of the secretary who transcribed the minutes or the name of the person who seconded the motion that future meetings should be held in the bar across the street would be extremely difficult.

Note   *The term metadata means data that itself describes other data.*

To address this problem, members of the World Wide Web Consortium (W3C), the multivendor standards body that oversees the development of the Web itself, started looking at the roots of HTML, something called the Standard Generalized Markup Language (SGML). Despite its name, SGML is not actually a markup language, but instead is a syntax for defining markup languages.

SGML can be a fairly verbose, esoteric syntax that is not mastered easily, and the W3C did not want it to be difficult for people to create their own markup languages to describe the data in their documents. As a result, a simplified version of SGML, the Extensible Markup Language (XML), was proposed, refined, and eventually accepted. It has proven so stable that it is still at version 1.0 over two years since it became a W3C recommendation.

 HTML is a well-defined, bounded markup language, but it should not be thought of as a subset of SGML—it is an application of SGML. XML uses a simplified syntax to define markup languages to describe data, and as such, it is a subset of SGML.

XML Syntax

XML uses constructs called *elements* and *attributes* to contain data. If you are familiar with HTML, then you should recognize these constructs. However, no matter how careful you are, it is unlikely that your HTML would also qualify as XML, because there are much more stringent syntactical rules that must be followed when creating XML documents. Also, there are constructs used in XML, such as namespaces and processing instructions, that you will not have encountered before in HTML.

Elements

The basic unit of information in an XML document is an *element*. In fact, the only thing required of an XML document is that it contains at least one element. One single element must contain all other elements and data structures, and it is therefore called the *root element*. Elements consist of character data bounded by descriptive tags as in the following example:

```
<addressLine1>10 Burlington Street</addressLine1>
```

Notice that the *start-tag* and *end-tag* are enclosed in angle brackets, and the name of the end-tag is preceded by a forward slash. Tag names may contain a mixture of alphanumeric characters, but they should not begin with a numeric character. Also, XML is case-sensitive, so "<addressLine1>" and "</Addressline1>" would not match, and a parsing application would return an error. An XML document containing numerous elements and other data structures is shown in Figure 2-1.

Elements may also contain other elements, called *child elements*, which must be correctly nested, so

```
<bookRef><title>XML for Pre-School Infants</bookRef></title>
```

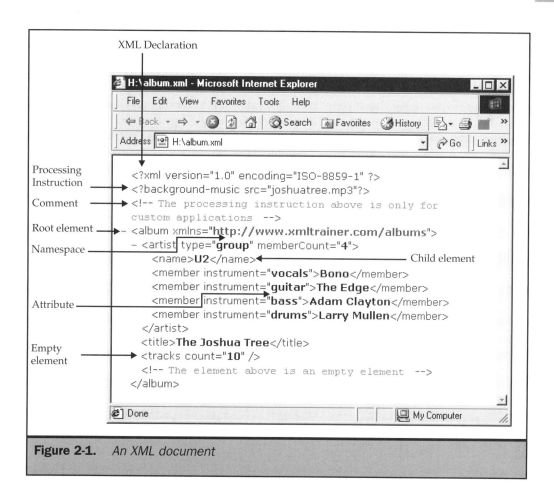

XML Declaration

Processing
Instruction

Comment

Root element

Namespace

Attribute

Empty
element

Child element

Figure 2-1.   *An XML document*

would be incorrect because the <title> tags are not completely nested within the
<bookRef> tags. Instead, it should be properly written as:

```
<bookRef><title>XML for Pre-School Infants</title></bookRef>
```

Every start-tag in an XML document must have a matching end-tag, even if the
element contains no data. Such elements are called *empty elements*, as in the following:

```
<qualifications></qualifications>
```

which may also be written using a shorthand notation:

```
<qualifications />
```

In Chapter 4, you will see that elements are used to represent data records in document specifications created with BizTalk Editor.

Attributes

Sometimes it is necessary to supply further information to modify an element, or to describe the purpose or semantics of an element, by providing supplemental data that does not warrant the creation of a child element. *Attributes* are used to modify elements in this way. Attributes are always name-value pairs, with the value enclosed in single or double quotes, inserted into a start-tag as follows:

```
<price currency="USD">199.99</price>
```

Multiple attributes may be included inside a single start-tag, but they must be unique for that element, for example:

```
<phoneNumber type="home" listed="yes" local="yes">555-1301</phoneNumber>
```

Notice that it would also be possible to describe the preceding information using nested child elements as follows:

```
<phoneNumber>
    <type>home</type>
    <listed>yes</listed>
    <local>yes</local>
    555-1301
</phoneNumber>
```

Neither representation is "more" correct. Using child elements will result in a larger file, but the information is easier to read. In many cases, it is simply a matter of personal preference, but some applications of XML require the use of one structure rather than the other. For example, the Simple Object Access Protocol (SOAP), which describes a way to invoke the methods of remote objects in a distributed application environment, uses an XML syntax that consists only of elements.

In Chapter 4, you will see how either attributes or child elements may be used to represent data fields in document specifications created with BizTalk Editor.

Namespaces

The beauty of XML is that its extensibility allows anyone to create his or her own markup language. Companies can create languages to describe their business documents, scientists can create languages to describe the structure of chemical compounds, and ice-cream vendors can create languages to describe their flavors and toppings, if they so desire.

However, many applications of XML could involve documents that consist of information merged from different sources, and so the possibility of a *collision* arises. For example, imagine an online purchasing system within a company. An intranet-based web application could create orders containing product information from a catalog combined with personnel details from the human resources database. A sample order might look like the following:

```
<order>
    <product>
        <title>Teach Yourself Social Skills in 24 Hours</title>
        <price>19.99</price>
    </product>
    <employee id="300772">
        <name>Arthur Dent</name>
        <title>Senior Vice President for Coffee Breaks</title>
    </employee>
</order>
```

If the online ordering system had to parse through the order looking for book titles to pass on to the supplier, it might get confused by the fact that there are two sets of <title> tags in the document, only one of which is a book title.

To address this problem, the W3C introduced the idea of a *namespace,* which is a collection of element and attribute names uniquely defined by a *Uniform Resource Identifier (URI)*. This URI may take the form of a *Uniform Resource Locator (URL), such* as http://www.xmltrainer.com/mynamespace, or a *Uniform Resource Name (URN),* such as urn:schemas-biztalk-org:yournamespace. In the former case, there is no requirement that the URL should be an actual location accessible on the Internet. It is simply an identifier that uses a recognizable format that can be kept unique.

Namespaces are declared using an attribute syntax with *xmlns* as the name and the URI as the value. When a namespace is declared on an element, that element and all children of that element are deemed to be part of that namespace, unless a different namespace is explicitly declared on any of the child elements. In that case, their children would take on the namespace declared on the parent element. Therefore, we could solve our earlier collision problem by applying namespace declarations as follows:

```
<order>
    <product xmlns="urn:ourproducts:catalog">
        <title>Teach Yourself Social Skills in 24 Hours</title>
        <price>19.99</price>
    </product>
    <employee id="300772" xmlns="http://intranet/hr/database">
        <name>Arthur Dent</name>
```

```
      <title>Senior Vice President for Coffee Breaks</title>
   </employee>
</order>
```

Now, the title of the book is defined on the namespace represented by *urn:ourproducts:catalog* and the employee's job title is defined on the namespace represented by *http://intranet/hr/database*. Because these namespaces are declared in such a way that they cascade down to the corresponding child elements automatically, they are called *default* namespace declarations.

However, if the document is not structured as to divide into neat sections as just described, we can provide prefixes to both the namespace declaration and the element name to more explicitly define the elements. For example:

```
<receipt xmlns:prod="urn:ourproducts:catalog"
         xmlns:hr="http://intranet/hr/database">
   <prod:title>Teach Yourself Social Skills in 24 Hours</prod:title>
   <hr:employee id="300772">Arthur Dent</hr:employee>
   <hr:title>Senior Vice President for Coffee Breaks</hr:title>
</receipt>
```

Here, we have declared both namespaces in the root element, and we have specified prefixes that can be applied to the element names as needed. Again, the title of the book is defined on the namespace represented by *urn:ourproducts:catalog*, because it is prefixed with *prod*, and the employee details are defined on the namespace represented by *http://intranet/hr/database*, because they are prefixed with *hr*. Notice that the root element, *receipt*, is not actually defined on any namespace because it has no prefix and there are no default namespace declarations.

In Chapter 4, you will see that document specifications created with BizTalk Editor make extensive use of namespaces to keep element and attribute names used internally by BizTalk Server separate from element names you create yourself.

Other Information Items

Although elements and attributes will contain most of the information in an XML document, there may be other information items as defined by the W3C in the *XML Information Set (Infoset)*. A complete discussion of the Infoset would be beyond the scope of this book, and there are numerous publications available if further detail is required, but the following are items you are likely to encounter while working with BizTalk Server.

XML Declaration   Most XML documents you see (certainly those created by BizTalk Server) will begin with a line similar to the following:

```
<?xml version="1.0" encoding="UTF-8" standalone="yes"?>
```

This is the *XML Declaration,* and this example states that what follows the declaration should be treated as an XML document conforming to version 1.0 of the specification, using 8-bit Unicode encoding (similar to ASCII), and that no other documents are required to render all of the information contained in it. You might encounter variations of the preceding, but only the version attribute is actually required. In fact, the XML Declaration itself is not mandatory for an XML document, but if it is included, it must occur before any other content.

Processing Instructions   Sometimes it will be necessary or desirable that further processing should be carried out on an XML document, and this may be provided by means of a *Processing Instruction.* Because XML itself is designed to describe information rather than present it, perhaps the most obvious example of the need for a Processing Instruction would be attaching formatting instructions to an XML document so that it may be displayed in a browser.

Processing Instructions have the following format:

```
<?target name1="value1" ... nameN="valueN"?>
```

where *target* represents the target application that should respond to the instruction. For the example given earlier, a Cascading Style Sheets (CSS) document containing formatting information could be attached to an XML document using a Processing Instruction similar to the following:

```
<?xml-stylesheet type="text/css" href="mystyles.css"?>
```

> **Note**   *Although the syntax for Processing Instructions is similar to the syntax for the XML Declaration, the XML Declaration should not be considered an example of a Processing Instruction.*

Comments   All software developers will be familiar with the concept of a *comment,* as inserting comments is usually the first thing programmers learn after printing "Hello world!" on the screen. Comments are meant not for machines, but for humans, to remind an author of why he or she wrote something a certain way, or to provide descriptive information to anyone else who reads the source code.

XML comments are constructed the same way as HTML comments, and they may be inserted anywhere in an XML document. Comments always begin with <!-- and end with --> and can contain absolutely anything except the string --, although you should not include anything that you want a parsing application to see, such as markup tags or processing instructions, because applications will (and should) completely ignore the contents of a comment. Here is an example of an XML document containing a comment:

```
<theorem>The equation [(x to the power of n) + (y to the power of n) =
(z to the power of n)] has no whole number solutions for n greater than 2 </theorem>
<!--I have a marvelous proof of this, which this comment is too small to contain-->
```

Well-Formed Documents

As mentioned earlier in this chapter, XML was derived not from HTML, but rather from SGML, a meta-language with its roots in documentation. The syntax of XML was deliberately designed to make it backwardly compatible with SGML while simultaneously making it easier for people to use and for machines to parse. To do this, it was necessary to tighten up some of the syntactical constraints for XML.

These constraints might seem a little harsh to anyone used to writing HTML for browsers that forgive syntactical misdemeanors and degrade gracefully without reporting errors to the hapless surfer. However, one of the reasons that browsers are able to gloss over missing tags, improperly nested elements, and missing quotation marks is because of the sheer amount of error-trapping built into them, adding megabytes of extra code that would not be required if HTML were more strict. One of the original design goals of XML was that "It shall be easy to write programs that process XML documents." Multivendor acceptance of the new standard could not be assured if the syntax were too flexible.

XML documents that meet all of the syntactical requirements in the XML 1.0 specification are said to be *well-formed*. The term "well-formed XML" is actually a double positive, because if a document were not well-formed, it would not be XML, and vice versa. The following is a brief summary of these requirements:

- Every XML document must contain at least one element.
- The root element of an XML document must be singular and unique.
- All start-tags must have corresponding end-tags.
- All markup should be case-consistent.
- All elements must be properly nested.
- Element names must not contain spaces or begin with numeric characters.

- Attribute names may not appear more than once in the same element.
- Attribute values must be enclosed in consistent single or double quotes.

Also, certain characters may cause parsing errors if included at certain locations, so escape characters are provided to avoid problems. For example, element content must not include the less-than sign (<), as it might be misconstrued as the beginning of a tag. The following table lists the characters that should be escaped in this way and their corresponding escape codes:

Character	Escape Code
<	<
>	>
'	'
"	"
&	&

Validating XML

As mentioned in the introduction to this chapter, business documents should have a consistent structure, particularly if they are to be processed automatically. Creating a markup language to describe the information in a document is only part of the process, as authors may subsequently use the elements and attributes defined in any order they like, or even create new tag names, resulting in documents that all have a different structure. An XML document that lacks a predefined structure is simply a collection of tags and attributes without any greater meaning, even if it is well-formed. Checking an XML document to ensure that it conforms to a predefined structure is called *validation.*

Well-Formed vs. Valid XML

To make XML documents useful, it is necessary to impose further constraints on the markup. These constraints may include but are not limited to the following:

- What elements must the document contain?
- What order must the elements follow?
- What content model should the elements have?
- What attributes are allowed in the document?
- What type of data should individual elements and attributes contain?

If a document is well-formed and conforms to such a predefined set of rules, we can say that it is *valid*. Consequently, validity is a stronger condition than well-formedness. All that's needed now is a way to express these rules.

Document Type Definitions

Because XML was derived from SGML, and was designed to be backwardly compatible, the authors of the XML specification chose to adopt the syntax already in existence for SGML to determine the validity of XML documents. SGML documents may contain or reference a Document Type Definition (DTD) that sets out the rules that the markup language used in the document must follow. An XML document that references a DTD is shown next:

```
<?xml version="1.0"?>
<!DOCTYPE employee SYSTEM "hr.dtd">
<employee SSN="1234-56-789">
    <name>Homer Simpson</name>
    <title>Safety Inspector</title>
    <sector>7G</sector>
</employee>
```

The line beginning *<!DOCTYPE* is called a *Document Type Declaration* (not to be confused with a Document Type Definition, to which it points), as it declares that there is a DTD in existence to which the structure of this document must conform. In this case, the DTD is a file called *hr.dtd*. The contents of this file are shown next:

```
<!ELEMENT employee (name, title, sector)>
<!ELEMENT name #PCDATA>
<!ELEMENT title #PCDATA>
<!ELEMENT sector #PCDATA>
<!ATTLIST employee SSN CDATA #REQUIRED>
```

If your first thought on reading the preceding document is "What's that all about?" you would not be alone. The syntax of a DTD can be quite difficult to follow, so creating one to describe your documents can be a tortuous process. In fact, not only are they tough to understand, but DTDs are often limited in their effectiveness by a number of factors. First, the syntax they use is not XML, so a separate parser must be written to interpret the DTD. Second, they support only a limited number of primitive data types, which are unwieldy and impractical for many situations. Third, because they were designed for SGML rather than XML, they have no support for XML-specific concepts such as namespaces.

As if that weren't enough, it is only possible to attach one DTD per document. However, we have already encountered scenarios where documents may contain data aggregated from multiple sources. We would probably want to make sure that the XML was valid for each fragment of the document.

Although DTDs will not solve all of our validity problems, they are already used in many environments, so they cannot be ignored. In Chapter 4, you will see how a DTD may be imported into BizTalk Editor to create a document specification.

XML Schemas

In the last couple of years, work has been ongoing to come up with an XML-based syntax that would overcome the limitations of DTDs. The first attempt to be submitted to the W3C came from Microsoft (and others), who proposed a syntax for defining document structures called *XML Data.* Although this never became a complete standard, it satisfied many of the requirements and served as a starting point for the XML Schema Working Group within the W3C.

While waiting for a final standard to emerge from the W3C, Microsoft implemented a limited version of their own proposal in their products, notably the MSXML parser included with Internet Explorer and BizTalk Server. This version, called XML Data Reduced (XDR), would give developers something to work with while the W3C finalized their standard, called XML Schema Definitions (XSD). This new XML Schema standard only became a full W3C Recommendation in May 2001.

Although this might seem to be leading developers astray, XDR Schemas do behave as a functional subset of XSD Schemas, and Microsoft has committed itself to supporting XSD in future releases. In fact, there is available already a technology preview of version 4.0 of the MSXML parser, and it supports the new standard. Also, Microsoft has released a tool to allow conversion between XDR and XSD Schemas. At the time of writing, both are available to download from the Microsoft Developer Network (MSDN) web site at http://msdn.microsoft.com/xml/. However, it is not yet possible to import an XSD Schema into BizTalk Editor, although such functionality will appear in a future update to the product.

In the next section, we will explore the syntax of XDR Schemas so that we may better understand BizTalk document specifications. It is not the purpose of this book to provide a comprehensive treatment of XDR, so we will only cover the basics. Also, because BizTalk Server does not currently support XSD, it is not as important (in this context) to discuss XSD syntax in any detail. In Chapter 4, you will see how an XDR Schema may be imported into BizTalk Editor to create a document specification. You will also see how BizTalk Server document specifications rely heavily on the XDR syntax.

XML Data Reduced

XML Schemas, whether written using XDR syntax or XSD syntax, are themselves XML documents. One of the first rules a well-formed XML document should follow is that it has a single, unique root element. In the case of XDR, the root element is called *Schema* (note the capital *S*), and it can be given a *name* attribute for identification purposes.

We have already seen that when there are elements and attributes in an XML document that may be considered part of a set with a specific purpose, we should emphasize their connection by declaring that they belong to a namespace. The namespace for elements and attributes used by XDR is defined by the URI *urn:schemas-microsoft-com:xml-data* and the set of data types used by XDR is defined by the URI *urn:schemas-microsoft-com:datatypes*. Thus, XDR schemas will typically have a root element similar to the following:

```
<Schema name="mySchemaName"
xmlns="urn:schemas-microsoft-com:xml-data"
xmlns:dt="urn:schemas-microsoft-com:datatypes">
    <!-- other definitions go here -->
</Schema>
```

What goes inside the *Schema* element is primarily a list of element and attribute type definitions, as shown in Figure 2-2. These definitions determine how a document

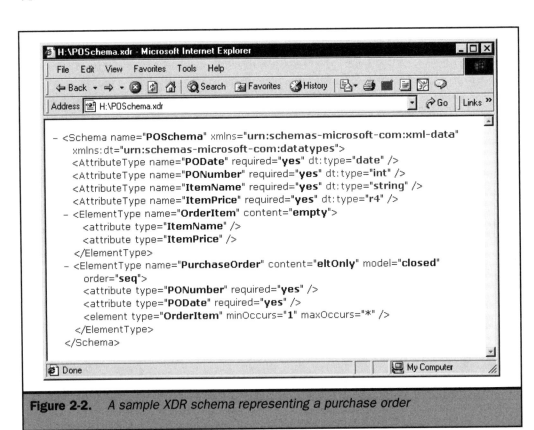

Figure 2-2. *A sample XDR schema representing a purchase order*

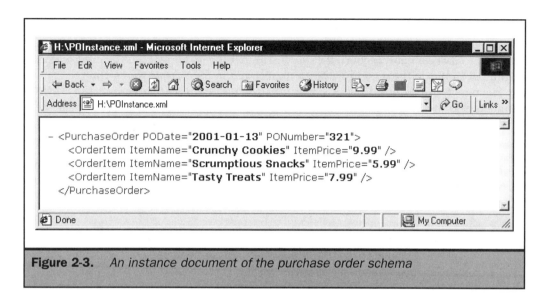

Figure 2-3. *An instance document of the purchase order schema*

that conforms to the schema must be structured. Any document satisfying these rules may be called an *instance document.* A sample instance document for the schema in Figure 2-2 is shown in Figure 2-3.

Element Types

To control which elements can appear in an instance document, we need to create *element type definitions.* This is achieved in XDR using the *ElementType* element. Each element type definition can specify what type of content an element should contain, whether this content is strictly or loosely defined, and whether any data that's present should conform to one of XDR's predefined data types. For example, the following element type definition describes a *book* element that will contain only child elements (no free-floating text), each of which must be defined in the same schema; furthermore, these child elements must appear in the sequence they appear in the schema:

```
<ElementType name="book" content="eltOnly" model="closed" order="seq">
    <!-- child elements are referenced here -->
</ElementType>
```

Another example could define a *title* element that will contain only text (no child elements) that will conform to the XDR *string* data type:

```
<ElementType name="title" content="textOnly" dt:type="string" />
```

There are a couple of things to note in this example. First, the *ElementType* element itself is an empty element in this case, because there will be no child elements or attributes attached to this element. Second, the *type* attribute is prefixed by *dt,* indicating that this attribute belongs to the second namespace declared in the *Schema* root element.

The next thing required in our schema is a way of defining the relationship between elements and their children. This is done using the *element* element, which appears as a child of *ElementType* elements to enforce the same relationship that should occur in instance documents. Each *element* element must reference a previously declared element type definition, as shown in Figure 2-2.

In the following schema fragment, two *element* elements are used to specify that each *book* element in the instance document should have one and only one *title* child element, but zero or more *author* child elements:

```
<ElementType name="book" content="eltOnly" model="closed" order="seq">
    <element type="title" minOccurs="1" maxOccurs="1" />
    <element type="author" minOccurs="0" maxOccurs="*" />
</ElementType>
```

 The default value for both minOccurs and maxOccurs is 1, so they may be safely omitted. The values are only included in the examples here for clarity.

Attribute Types

XDR schemas also allow us to specify that elements in instance documents should possess attributes. These attribute types are defined by name using the *AttributeType* element. We can further qualify an attribute type to say that it should conform to a particular data type or that the attribute must appear in the instance document, as in the following example:

```
<AttributeType name="ISBN" dt:type="string" required="yes" />
```

Attribute types may be declared either inside or outside element type definitions. If declared inside, they may only be referenced by that element or its children. If declared outside, the attribute type is said to have *global scope* and can be used anywhere in the document instance. Figure 2-2 shows a schema with multiple attribute type definitions, all of which have global scope.

After defining the attribute types, we then specify in which elements each attribute will appear using the *attribute* element. Similar to the *element* element, the *attribute* element appears as a child of *ElementType* elements for each element that should have that attribute. If you didn't quite catch that last sentence, don't worry—the following example should illustrate the idea:

```
<AttributeType name="currency" dt:type="string" required="yes" />
<ElementType name="price" content="textOnly" dt:type="r4">
```

```
        <attribute type="currency" />
</ElementType>
```

Here, we define an attribute type called *currency* and an element type called *price*. By inserting an *attribute* element referring to the *currency* attribute type definition inside the *price* element type definition, we are saying that document instances that conform to this schema must have a *price* element, and each *price* element must have a *currency* attribute, that is a string. The following would be a valid document instance for this schema fragment:

```
<price currency="Yen">500</price>
```

This is also demonstrated in Figure 2-2, where each predefined attribute type is referenced by an *attribute* element inside an element type definition.

In Chapter 4, you will see how BizTalk Editor's graphical user interface allows you to easily set the properties for element and attribute type definitions.

Data Types

So far we have looked at ways to validate the structure of business documents using XML schemas. However, it is also crucial that we are able to validate the type of data contained in an element or attribute.

For example, an application might have to make a mathematical calculation based on the value contained in a *price* element. We must ensure that the data type for that element constrains the value to be numeric in nature, or else our application will generate an error. Similarly, if we want to insert the contents of a business document into a database, we will need to make sure that the element and attribute data types correspond to the data types of the fields in our database tables. Assuming that an attribute called *PODate* actually contains a date could lead to disaster if the date specified is in a format that the database isn't expecting.

Originally, there were data types defined for DTDs, called *primitive* data types, and these could be used in XML documents, but most of them are esoteric constructions like *NMTOKENS* and *NOTATION*, unlikely to be used in everyday scenarios. The only useful data type available for attribute content is *CDATA*, or character data, and the only data type available for element content is *PCDATA*, or parsed character data, each of which effectively means a string of characters—in other words, anything you like!

On the other hand, XDR schemas provide a rich set of data types such as *int*, *date*, *float*, *char*, and *Boolean* from which to choose your element and attribute content. Be aware that XDR schemas can also use primitive data types for backward compatibility, but only useful types like *ENUMERATION* (which allows you to specify a list of values from which to choose, for example, the day of the week) find regular application in XML and BizTalk Server. The XDR data types available for use in document specifications created with BizTalk Editor are listed in Table 2-1.

Data Type	Description
Character	Single character
String	Any number of characters, including spaces and punctuation (except characters that must be escaped, like "<")
Number	Similar to Fixed Point 14.4, except without decimal place limits
Integer	Whole number with optional sign and no decimal places or exponent
Float	Real number with optional leading sign, decimal places, and an exponent, for example, $-3.056E+18$
Fixed Point 14.4	Number with no more than 14 digits to the left of the decimal point and no more than 4 digits to the right. Useful for currencies
Boolean	Either TRUE (1) or FALSE (0)
Date	Date in ISO 8601 format, for example, "1972-30-07"
Date Time	Date and time in ISO 8601 format, for example, "2001-02-27T12:30:00"
Date Time.tz	Date and time in ISO 8601 format, with optional time zone, for example, "1971-13-01T17:15:00-08:00"
Time	Similar to Date Time, except with no date information
Time.tz	Similar to Date Time.tz, except with no date information
Byte (i1)	Integer expressible in one byte
Word (i2)	Integer expressible in two bytes
Integer (i4)	Integer expressible in four bytes—same as Integer
Double Integer (i8)	Integer expressible in eight bytes
Unsigned Byte (ui1)	Unsigned integer expressible in one byte
Unsigned Word (ui2)	Unsigned integer expressible in two bytes
Unsigned Integer (ui4)	Unsigned integer expressible in four bytes
Double Unsigned Integer (ui8)	Unsigned integer expressible in eight bytes

Table 2-1.   *Data Types Supported in BizTalk Document Specifications*

Data Type	Description
Real (r4)	Real number with seven-digit decimal precision
Double Real (r8)	Same as Float—real number with 15-digit decimal precision
Universal Unique Identifier (uuid)	String of hexadecimal digits and optional hyphens, representing octets that may be used as a URI, for example, "e4f55cfc-0766-4558-a5a5-0652922752a9"
Uniform Resource Identifier (uri)	For example, "urn:schemas-biztalk-org:datatypes"
Binary (base64)	Binary encoding of binary text into characters
Binary (hex)	Binary hexadecimal digits that represent octets, for example, "0x0123D"
ID	Specifies that the field must act as a unique identifier within the document (like a primary key)
IDREF	Specifies that the field refers to an ID
IDREFS	Specifies that the field contains a space-separated list of ID references
ENUMERATION	Space-separated list of values referenced in a values data type, for example, "Mon Tue Wed Thu Fri Sat Sun"

Table 2-1.   *Data Types Supported in BizTalk Document Specifications* (continued)

In Chapter 4, you will see how these data types can be applied to fields in a document specification created using BizTalk Editor, to ensure the validity of documents created according to the specification.

Transforming XML

There are many advantages to expressing business documents as XML. The syntax is easily understood by humans and easily parsed by machines, it provides a hierarchical structure for data that reinforces the relationships between each data item, and it separates the meaning of the data from the presentation of the data. Also, the syntax is extensible so that anybody can create a markup language to express his or her information.

However, although XML is now an accepted standard for describing information, there are few agreed standards when it comes to the markup languages created with it.

Just because one company has used XML to create a structure for invoices doesn't mean that every other company in the world will adopt that same structure. In the world of B2B e-commerce, it is quite likely that trading partners will need to exchange documents that encode information differently, so we will need a mechanism to transform one XML structure into another. Such a technology now exists, although it emerged from an unlikely source.

Style Sheets

We know that XML is not concerned with the presentation of data, but that doesn't mean that XML data never needs to be presented. In fact, because XML emerged as a result of limitations with HTML, it is reasonable to imagine that there should be a way of displaying XML data in your favorite browser. This is accomplished using *style sheets*. Style sheets express how individual elements should be formatted for presentation purposes.

Cascading Style Sheets

HTML has many built-in formatting features. Apart from bold, italic, and underline, there are tables, horizontal rules, and heading levels, each of which have a predefined style. However, as the Web became more popular in the 1990s, authors and users alike craved diversity in the look and feel of page elements. While working to standardize HTML, the W3C were simultaneously putting together a language to give these authors complete flexibility in designing their sites. This language is the Cascading Style Sheets (CSS) specification.

CSS allows an author to define how a particular element in a web page should look, how all instances of that element in a page should look, or even how all instances of that element in an entire site should look. It does this through *selectors* that represent each element to which special formatting should be applied. For example, if I wanted every level one heading on my page to be red, italic, 36 points in size, and in the Tahoma font, I could use an *h1* selector to represent the <h1> tags on my page and provide the appropriate instructions as follows:

```
h1 {font-family : Tahoma ; font-size : 36pt ; font-style : italics ; color : red}
```

A full list of these instructions makes up a style sheet for my page or site. The same type of formatting can also be applied to XML documents. Again, we list selectors that represent the elements in our document and provide the appropriate formatting information. For example:

```
jobTitle {font-family : Verdana ; font-size : 14pt ; font-weight : bold}
```

specifies that the data in each *jobTitle* element in my XML document should be displayed as 14-point bold Verdana.

The only problem with CSS from an XML perspective is that the syntax is not itself XML, so another parser is needed to understand the styling information. Also, CSS was designed for use with flat HTML documents and does not properly address the hierarchical nature of XML or XML-specific concepts like namespaces, so really what is needed is an extensible style sheet language.

Extensible Style Sheet Language

To create a style sheet language for use with XML, the W3C went back to see if there was anything from SGML that could be leveraged. SGML uses the Document Style Semantic Specification Language (DSSSL) to define formatting semantics for SGML documents. Although the entire standard was too complicated to use completely, it would form the basis for a new XML-related specification.

Again, Microsoft played a part in pushing things forward, submitting a proposal for an Extensible Stylesheet Language (XSL) to the W3C in late 1997. There were three significant aspects to this submission that would lead to the creation of important new technologies. The first was that the language should be able to select elements and attributes from the document hierarchy using a pattern-matching syntax called *XSL Patterns*. Next, it should be possible to transform parts of XML documents into HTML for display in a browser. Finally, it should be possible for formatting instructions to be applied to each element in a similar way to CSS.

The XSL Working Group at the W3C quickly recognized that each of these aspects was important in its own right. As a result, XSL Patterns would later evolve into a full standard called the *XML Path Language (XPath)* to provide a means of addressing parts of an XML document at a granular level. The style sheet syntax itself would be enlarged and refined to create *XSL Formatting Objects (XSL FO)*, which has recently become a W3C recommendation. Finally, the transformation capabilities would turn out to have huge implications for B2B scenarios, because they effectively provided a means of changing the structure of an XML document into any other format—HTML, XML, or otherwise, and so the *Extensible Stylesheet Language for Transformation (XSLT)* was born.

XSLT

Although originally conceived as a style sheet syntax, XSLT is actually an event-driven programming language written in XML. As with any programming language, there is input, processing, and output. The input is the source XML document (or source tree), the processing is performed by special instructions, and the output is a result document (or result tree). There is support for variables, decision-making, repetitive processing, a host of built-in functions, and even a way of implementing reusable procedures.

Note   *The source and destination documents are called trees because of the hierarchical structure of XML. When we look at an XML document programmatically, we are considering a hierarchical set of elements, attributes, namespace declarations, comments, processing instructions, and so on. Each of these items can be considered a node in the tree. Similarly, collections of elements can be called a node-set.*

The instruction elements that comprise the language are grouped together in—you guessed it—a namespace, to avoid collision with elements and attributes that will form part of the result tree. The namespace URI defined in the specification is *http://www.w3.org/1999/XSL/Transform*. In most style sheets you encounter, this URI is mapped to the prefix *xsl* to further separate instruction elements from literal result elements. For example, the root element of an XSLT style sheet (and there must be one, because it's an XML document) is comprised of *<xsl:stylesheet>* start- and end-tags that contain the rest of the document.

The xsl:stylesheet root element can contain numerous attributes, but the only one that's required (other than the namespace declaration) is the version attribute, which has a value representing the version number of the technology, which is currently 1.0.

As before, a complete treatment of XSLT is beyond the scope of this book, so we will only introduce the main features of the language to give you a feel for what it looks like, how it works, and why it is used by BizTalk Server. In Chapter 5, you will see how XSLT is employed by BizTalk Mapper to transform document specifications.

Template Rules

Don't get carried away and think we meant to say "Templates Rule!"—actually, *template rules* are the foundation of XSLT, as they specify which parts of a source tree should be transformed, and what the result of the transformation should be. An XSLT style sheet containing template rules is shown in Figure 2-4. This stylesheet transforms the XML document from Figure 2-1 to HTML for display in a browser.

Each template rule contains a *match pattern,* expressed in XPath syntax, which selects the node or node-set in the source tree that should be transformed. For example, if we wanted to build a template that acted on an *author* element, located directly under a *book* element in a document, we would use the following:

```
<xsl:template match="book/author">
    <!-- output defined here -->
</xsl:template>
```

Similarly, a template that acts on the *ISBN* attribute of a book element would be written as follows (notice the use of the "@" sign to mean "attribute"):

```
<xsl:template match="book/@ISBN">
    <!-- output defined here -->
</xsl:template>
```

```
album.xsl - Notepad
File  Edit  Format  Help
<xsl:stylesheet version="1.0"
xmlns:xsl="http://www.w3.org/1999/XSL/Transform">

<xsl:template match="/">
        <html>
                <head>
                        <title>XML Document</title>
                </head>
                <body>
                        <xsl:apply-templates />
                </body>
        </html>
</xsl:template>

<xsl:template match="album">
        <h1><xsl:value-of select="artist/name" />
        <xsl:text> - </xsl:text>
        <xsl:value-of select="title" /></h1>
        <h3><xsl:value-of select="tracks/@count" /> tracks</h3>
        <xsl:apply-templates select="artist/member" />
</xsl:template>

<xsl:template match="member">
        <p><b><xsl:value-of select="text()" /></b>
        <xsl:text> - </xsl:text>
        <i><xsl:value-of select="@instrument" /></i></p>
</xsl:template>

</xsl:stylesheet>
```

Figure 2-4.   *An XSLT style sheet*

It's important to ensure that a result tree is actually created when a style sheet executes. We do this by always including a template that matches the *root node* of the source tree. Don't confuse the root node with the root element. The root node represents the root of the document itself, one level back from the root element. Thus, the XSLT style sheet in Figure 2-4 has a template with the following match pattern representing the root node:

```
<xsl:template match="/">
    <!-- result document begins here -->
</xsl:template>
```

This is the only template that will be processed automatically. To use multiple templates in a style sheet, we can invoke other templates recursively from the root template. For example, if we want our result document to have an *OrderList* root element, and contain the output of other templates in the style sheet, we should use the xsl:apply-templates instruction as follows:

```
<xsl:template match="/">
    <OrderList>
        <xsl:apply-templates select="book" />
    </OrderList>
</xsl:template>
```

Note that the *OrderList* element does not have the *xsl* prefix. This is because it is a *literal result element*, that is, there will literally be an *OrderList* element in the result document. Figure 2-4 also shows literal result elements that will be output by the template.

The xsl:apply-templates instruction can be used with a *select* attribute, as earlier, to specify which template should be executed next, or on its own. If used on its own, the instruction invokes templates that apply to the next level down in the source tree. In the preceding example , if we had not specified which template to invoke, the XSLT processor would look for templates that matched one level down from the current node. The current node in this case is the root node of the document, so one level down would be the root element. Similarly, the template for the root element could also have an xsl:apply-templates instruction to invoke templates one level further down or at any level by specifying a select pattern.

> **Tip** *Think of the style sheet as a static set of templates that sits in memory while the source tree is being read in one line at a time. As each node in the tree is encountered, the XSLT processor checks the style sheet for matching templates and executes them.*

In this way, templates can be applied recursively to transform each level of the source tree hierarchy into whatever format you want. We can also name templates and call them from anywhere at any time. In fact, developers can build up libraries of templates for different purposes and combine them as necessary using the xsl:include and xsl:import instruction elements. This could be considered the same as writing a class of object in an object-oriented programming language and invoking its properties and methods in many different programs. So when you think about it, templates do rule!

Instruction Elements

As we have seen, contained within each template rule, there may be literal result elements that should be output to the result tree. There also may be (and typically will be) further instruction elements. For example, we can use XSLT instruction elements to construct new elements or attributes dynamically, perform calculations, include data from the current node or some other node in the document, or sort the data based on one or more filters.

To illustrate this, here is another way to construct a new literal element in a result tree—by using the xsl:element instruction. Similarly, if we want to create a new attribute, there is an xsl:attribute instruction. In each case, we specify the name of the element or attribute we want to create and then supply the content, as in the following example:

```
<xsl:element name="car">
    <xsl:attribute name="make">Porsche</xsl:attribute>
    <xsl:attribute name="model">911</xsl:attribute>
</xsl:element>
```

This would cause the following to be created in the result tree:

```
<car make="Porsche" model="911" />
```

The next example shows how we could construct a result fragment for each *book* element in a document. The result will be a list of *OrderItem* elements, each possessing a *BookCode* attribute that contains the ISBN value for that book. Each *OrderItem* element will also have a child element called *AuthorName* that contains the full name of each author of the book (including a single space inserted between the first and last name), and these child elements will be sorted alphabetically by surname:

```
<xsl:template match="book">
    <OrderItem>
        <xsl:attribute name="BookCode">
            <xsl:value-of select="@ISBN">
        </xsl:attribute>
        <xsl:for-each select="author">
            <AuthorName>
                <xsl:sort select="lastname" />
                <xsl:value-of select="firstname" />
                <xsl:text> </xsl:text>
                <xsl:value-of select="lastname" />
            </AuthorName>
        </xsl:for-each>
    </OrderItem>
</xsl:template>
```

Notice how the *xsl:value-of* element is used to output the value of an element or attribute from the source tree so that it appears in the result tree. Using this method, we can create a brand-new result tree that has the same data as the source tree. The following illustration shows how the preceding template could be incorporated into a complete style sheet to transform a source tree into a result tree.

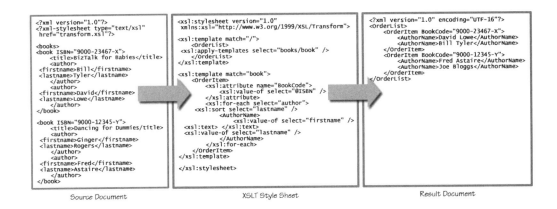

| Source Document | XSLT Style Sheet | Result Document |

We have now seen how XML and XSLT can be used to represent document structures and transform one structure into another, while retaining the data from the original. This is the idea behind BizTalk Server's document processing engine.

If we need to work with a type of business document, we refer to a document specification, encoded using XML, that matches the structure of the document. In Chapter 4, you will see how these specifications are created using BizTalk Editor.

If we need to send a document to a trading partner who uses a different data format, BizTalk Server uses XSLT to transform the document into the correct structure. In Chapter 5, you will see how BizTalk Mapper can create these transformations by writing the XSLT for you.

Caution   *BizTalk Server makes use of version 3 of the Microsoft XML parser (MSXML3). This parser is installed with BizTalk Server in "side-by-side mode." This means that components that make reference to older versions of the parser may still do so. It is also possible to install MSXML3 in "replace mode," but doing this will cause parts of BizTalk Server, such as BizTalk Editor and BizTalk Mapper, to fail. Similarly, you should not install later versions of the MSXML parser on a computer running BizTalk Server.*

The
Complete
Reference

Chapter 3

Installing BizTalk Server

53

L ike most things, installing BizTalk Server 2000 is easy if you know what you're doing. Preparation is the key, so it's important to know what's involved before jumping in. Certain hardware and software requirements must be met and certain settings must be configured to ensure the process goes without a hitch. Otherwise, you could run into unexpected problems and have to start over.

There are various configurations in which BizTalk Server can be installed. Enterprise deployment scenarios are discussed in Part V of this book, but there's nothing to stop you from straightaway getting up and running with BizTalk Server.

Before Installation

Although you will typically plan a full deployment strategy before installing BizTalk Server in a production environment, it is also likely that you will first install the product in a development environment. Either way, you will have to ensure that you have the appropriate hardware and software to proceed. BizTalk Server has different installation options, and each one will have differing hardware and software requirements. It will also be necessary to correctly configure Windows 2000 before continuing.

Installation Options

There are three different options available for installing BizTalk Server—*Complete, Tools,* and *Custom.* Complete is the method of choice if you are installing the software for development or single-server production purposes, as it gives you the core services (and thus the server functionality) as well as the XML and Orchestration tools. Installing a remote administration site will perhaps only require the BizTalk Administration management console, the editing tools, and the document tracking components, whereas installing the product on a server that will be part of a cluster or load-balanced system could require any combination of subfeatures:

Feature	Subfeatures
Core Services	BizTalk Messaging BizTalk Orchestration BizTalk Administration BizTalk Document Tracking WebDAV Repository
Tools	BizTalk Editor BizTalk Mapper BizTalk Orchestration Designer
Documentation	Help files SDK Tutorial

If you are installing the product as part of an existing BizTalk Server Group, however, you may only need certain components to be present on that system. BizTalk Server Groups will be discussed in more detail in Part IV. Similarly, if you will only be performing remote administration from the machine, you might only need the Tools and Document Tracking components.

Hardware Requirements

First of all, you should be prepared for the kind of hardware resources that BizTalk Server requires. BizTalk Server can only be installed on Windows 2000 Professional, Server, or Advanced Server, but the minimum requirements are slightly higher than those for Windows 2000. At the very least, you should make sure that your system meets the specifications in the following table:

Hardware	Requirement
Processor	Intel Pentium 300 MHz
Memory	128MB of RAM
Hard disk space	6GB
Monitor	VGA or Super VGA
Other	Network adapter, CD-ROM drive

Of course, these minimum requirements are just that—the bare minimum. If you're running Windows 2000 on 128MB of RAM, you've probably noticed that it can be a bit sluggish, particularly if you open up another application as well as Notepad. Here's a more realistic set of minimum requirements to help avoid frustration:

Hardware	Requirement
Processor	Intel Pentium 500 MHz
Memory	256MB of RAM
Hard disk space	8GB
Monitor	Super VGA (1024×768 resolution)
Other	Network adapter, CD-ROM drive

In a production environment, it is more likely that you will be using one of the recommended deployment options listed in Part V of this book, so your processor, memory, and disk space requirements will be different, depending on whether you're scaling *vertically* (increasing the specification of a server) or *horizontally* (adding more servers).

Software Requirements

Regardless of the environment in which you install BizTalk Server, you will want it to run without problems. Therefore, it is important to ensure that Windows 2000 is correctly configured before proceeding with the installation. Similarly, for complete functionality, you will need to install extra Windows 2000 services, or other software packages, such as SQL Server or Visio.

Windows 2000

As stated, BizTalk Server can be installed on anything as long as it's Windows 2000. However, you must have at least Windows 2000 Service Pack 1 installed with NTFS in place on the destination partition. In fact, it is highly recommended to install Windows 2000 Service Pack 2, as this includes hotfixes to address serious problems pertaining to BizTalk Server that were only discovered after the release of the product. The issues fixed include the following:

- **Q277660** Fix for COM+ Marshalling Bug
- **Q272501** Fix for Binding to XML-Based Windows Scripting Component
- **Q272502** Fix for FormatCurrency() Problem in BizTalk Mapper
- **Q272504** Fix for GetObject() Call to Return Rich Error Information
- **Q279130** Fix for MSMQ Bug on Single Transactional Messages
- **Q281462** Fix for Access Violation Error in MSMQ Under Heavy Loads
- **Q282769** Hotfix Package 6.1 for COM+ Memory Leak Problem

| Note |

These hotfixes are recommended for production servers that exhibit the specific problems mentioned in the articles referenced. Windows 2000 Service Pack 2 provides a complete set of these fixes, but you should always consult http://support.microsoft.com/ for the most up-to-date information before altering a working configuration.

Windows 2000 Service Pack 2 is officially recommended if you wish to install BizTalk Server Service Pack 1. Likewise, it is recommended—although not required—that you install Microsoft XML Parser (MSXML) 3.0 Service Pack 1 and either SQL Server 7.0 Service Pack 3 or SQL Server 2000 Service Pack 1. In general, it is probably a good idea to always keep your system up-to-date with the latest patches and service packs.

For complete functionality, there are also configuration changes you must make to a basic Windows 2000 install, regardless of the BizTalk Server installation type.

Internet Information Services

If you are using Windows 2000 Server or Advanced Server, Internet Information Services (IIS) are installed by default. If you are using Windows 2000 Professional,

IIS is not installed by default. You can quickly tell if IIS is present by checking for Internet Services Manager under Administrative Tools in the Start menu. IIS is required for BizTalk Messaging Manager and BizTalk Document Tracking. Perform the following steps to install it by using the Windows Component Wizard:

1. From the Control Panel, choose Add/Remove Programs.
2. Select Add/Remove Windows Components.
3. Select the Internet Information Services check box and click Next.
4. Click Finish when installation is complete.

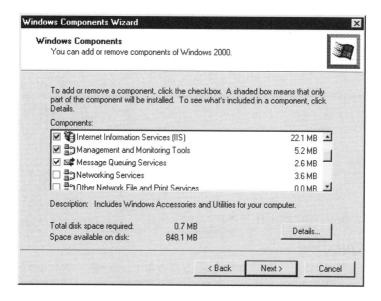

IIS is also used for the BizTalk Server Repository, which is accessed over the HyperText Transfer Protocol (HTTP) using *Web Distributed Authoring and Versioning (WebDAV)*. This repository is used to store document specifications, envelopes, and map files. WebDAV is a method of performing file input/output functions over HTTP. However, FrontPage Server Extensions, which are installed by default with IIS, also provide similar functionality using a different method, so it is important to disable these extensions using the following steps:

1. From the Start menu, choose Programs | Administrative Tools | Internet Services Manager.
2. Expand the My Computer node on the left side of the console.
3. Right-click Default Web Site and select Properties.

4. Select the Server Extensions tab (shown next) and clear the Enable Authoring check box.

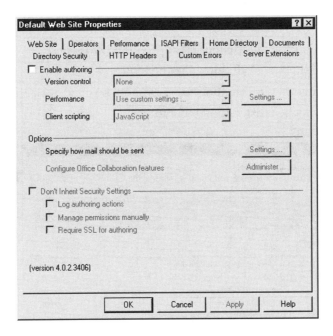

5. Click OK and close Internet Services Manager.

Message Queuing

BizTalk Server supports a loosely coupled architecture for application integration and asynchronous communication with trading partners. To put it a less fancy way, sometimes you will want BizTalk Server to communicate with applications or services (either your own or a trading partner's) that are not always available or cannot respond immediately. If you consider two Internet services—the Web and e-mail—it can help to understand the difference. When you send an HTTP request to a web server, it responds straightaway with the resource you asked for (synchronous communication). However, if you send an e-mail to friends or colleagues, it might be days before you get a reply (that's usually the case with my friends, anyway); the message sits in their Inbox until they log on, download it, read it, and have the time to reply (asynchronous communication).

The same type of asynchronous communication sometimes occurs when disparate applications try to send messages to each other across a network. It might not be possible for the application to respond straightaway (it might be temporarily stopped, there might be a network bottleneck, or it might be too busy, like my friends), so the message is stored at a predetermined location until it can be forwarded to the application. This store-and-forward mechanism is provided in Windows 2000 by

Microsoft Message Queuing (MSMQ) Services, which must be installed for BizTalk Server to function properly:

1. From the Control Panel, choose Add/Remove Programs.
2. Select Add/Remove Windows Components.
3. Select the Message Queuing Services check box and click Next.
4. Click Next to accept the defaults on subsequent pages.
5. Click Finish when installation is complete.

User Accounts

The installation of BizTalk Server adds new Windows 2000 services and changes certain system files, so you must be logged on as a member of the local Administrators group to set up the software. During installation, a *BizTalk Server Administrators* group is created, and the user who is logged on at the time is automatically added to this group along with the local Administrators group for the machine. You can add further users to it yourself later on. In Part IV, we will see which tasks the Administrators group and the BizTalk Server Administrators group can perform.

As shown in Figure 3-1, you will also be prompted during installation to specify the user account that the BizTalk Messaging Service should use. Services that interact

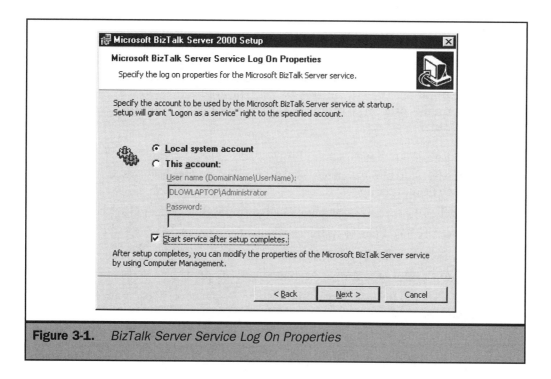

Figure 3-1. *BizTalk Server Service Log On Properties*

with the operating system require a valid *security context* to run, just as any user who wants to interact with the operating system must have a valid user account. Thus, system services impersonate user accounts in order to obtain a security context. You have the option of using the built-in Local System account (which is an extremely powerful account) or a user account you have already created manually. However, if you create an account yourself, you must ensure that it has the necessary permissions and rights that BizTalk Server will require during normal operation. For example, the account must have the appropriate NTFS permissions to read the contents of any folder you specify as a file receive location, or else BizTalk Server will not be able to use that function. To make your life easier, the installation process will automatically assign two important rights—Log On Locally and Act As Part Of The Operating System— to whatever user account you specify.

Similarly, there are a number of COM+ server applications created during the installation that also require a security context. These applications consist of groups of COM components that interoperate to form a single distributed application that can take advantage of Windows 2000 security, transaction, and queuing features. Unfortunately, when BizTalk Server is installed, it automatically configures these applications to execute under the security context of the interactive user, that is, whatever user is currently logged on. As a result, when the user logs off, the applications will not execute, and many BizTalk Server functions will not be operational.

One approach to avoid this is to lock the computer rather than to log off, leaving the applications free to run. However, there are security implications for having these applications run in the context of the interactive user. For example, if the Administrator is logged on, the application runs with the Administrator's credentials and consequently has more privileges than it might need or should be given.

The best way to circumvent this problem is to change the identity associated with the COM+ applications used by BizTalk Server. The applications for which you will have to perform this procedure are the BizTalk Server Interchange Application and the XLANG Scheduler:

1. From the Start menu, select Administrative Tools | Component Services.

2. On the left side of the console, expand the Component Services, Computers, and My Computer nodes.

3. Right-click the BizTalk Server Interchange Application node and select Properties.

4. On the Advanced tab, clear the check box for Allow Changes.

5. Click OK when the warning appears.

6. Click OK to close the Properties dialog box (Apply is disabled).

7. Right-click the BizTalk Server Interchange Application node again and select Properties.

8. On the Identity tab, select the option for This User, and either enter the user credentials manually, or click the Browse button to select a user.

9. Click OK to close the Properties dialog box.

10. Repeat the process for the XLANG Scheduler application.

SQL Server

A complete BizTalk Server system will need database storage for messaging, configuration, tracking, and orchestration information. SQL Server 7.0 with Service Pack 2 or SQL Server 2000 will be used to provide this storage, either on the same machine (in a development environment) or on another machine on the network (in an enterprise environment). If you plan to install BizTalk Server on Windows 2000 Professional, you will need to install SQL Server on a separate machine, as Windows 2000 Professional does not support SQL Server 2000 Standard or Enterprise Editions.

If you really need to install BizTalk Server and SQL Server 2000 on Windows 2000 Professional, and you will only be using the system for testing, you can use SQL Server 2000 Developer Edition. This supports the same features as the Enterprise Edition, except it is not licensed for use in a production environment.

Again, when you are installing SQL Server, you will need to choose an account for the MSSQLServer and SQLServerAgent services. If your database is part of a cluster or on a different machine than the BizTalk Server, you should choose a domain user account that has been created and configured with the appropriate permissions and rights. If SQL Server and BizTalk Server will reside on the same machine and SQL Server will not need to make contact with other machines on the network, the Local System account may be used for both services. Your account options are shown next.

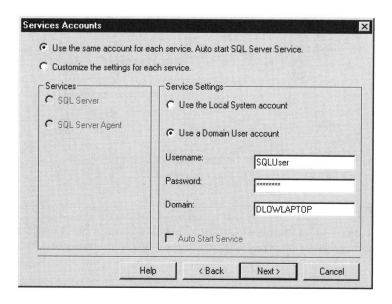

When BizTalk Server needs to retrieve configuration data or messaging data, it must log on to the database to do so. BizTalk Server uses SQL Server authentication rather than Windows authentication by default; so when you are installing SQL Server, you must specify Mixed Mode authentication, or BizTalk Server will not function correctly. If you have SQL Server already installed and you don't know what authentication method it is using, you can check using the following steps:

1. From the Start menu, select SQL Server | Enterprise Manager.

2. In SQL Server Enterprise Manager, expand Microsoft SQL Servers.

3. Expand SQL Server Group, right-click your computer, and select Properties.

4. In the Properties dialog box, click the Security tab.

5. On the Security tab (shown next), under Authentication, ensure SQL Server And Windows is selected.

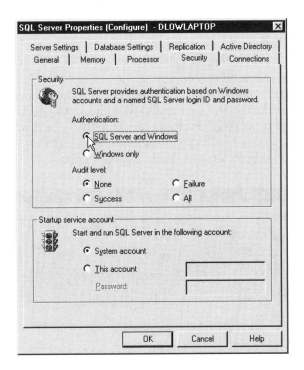

Visio 2000

One of the most powerful features built into BizTalk Server is Business Process Automation, or *Orchestration*. This feature allows a business analyst to create a visual representation of a business process in a graphical environment. A developer can then implement each step, or action, in the process using technologies such as Windows Scripting Components, COM Components, Message Queuing, and BizTalk Messaging. The finished drawing, complete with these implementations, is then compiled into an XLANG schedule that executes on the server. The graphical user interface that enables the creation of these drawings is based on Microsoft Visio 2000, which must be installed if this feature is to be used.

Note *XLANG is an XML-based language that defines the business process described in the drawing, including how each step should be implemented and how data flows through the process. A compiled XLANG schedule is executed by the XLANG scheduler application to invoke the business process. Orchestration and XLANG schedules will be discussed in Part III of this book.*

Either the Standard or Enterprise Edition of Visio 2000 will serve this purpose, although it is highly recommended that Service Release 1 (sometimes called SR-1A) of the product is installed to avoid problems. For example, if a version of Visio 2000 prior to SR-1A is installed, you might experience unexpected behavior if you try to open an XLANG Schedule Drawing file (with a .skv extension) directly without opening the Orchestration Designer first. Similarly, you may not be able to open more than one XLANG Schedule Drawing at a time.

Caution *Visio 2002 is not supported by BizTalk Server, or BizTalk Server Service Pack 1. A patch to allow you to install Visio 2002 should be available by the time you read this.*

If you have taken care to complete all steps listed earlier, you should be able to install BizTalk Server without issue.

Running the Setup Wizard

To install BizTalk Server, you should run setup.exe or the Microsoft BizTalk Server installer file (it will have a .msi extension) in the root directory of the CD or network location where the setup files reside. There is no real difference in the installation process whichever program you execute—the next thing you see will be the Microsoft BizTalk 2000 Setup Wizard. Click Next to advance past the opening screen.

You should then agree to the End-User License Agreement (you could choose not to agree if you like, but your days with BizTalk Server would be short-lived). Then click the Next button.

On the Customer Information page shown following, enter your name and company details, and fill in the product code that accompanied the CD. If you are using an evaluation version of the product, you may not have to enter this code. You should also choose whether BizTalk Server should be installed for all users or just the currently logged on user. For example, if you are developing solutions on a shared machine, you may only want BizTalk Server to be available when you are logged on. Click Next to continue.

The next page will ask you to select the destination folder for the product. The default installation location will be the Program Files directory on the drive where Windows 2000 is installed. You may accept this location, or change it by entering the path manually, or by clicking the Change button and browsing to a directory. Click Next when you are ready to continue.

On the next page, you can choose the setup type. The choices are Complete, Tools, and Custom. To install the complete product, including the core services, tools, documentation, and SDK, select the Complete option and click Next. To install only BizTalk Editor, BizTalk Mapper, and BizTalk Orchestration Designer, select Tools and click Next. To be presented with the complete list of components from which you can choose what to install, select Custom and click Next.

If you select the Custom option, you can individually select components and choose whether they should be included in the setup as shown. You can also select where each component should be installed. Click Next when you are satisfied with the components to be installed. If you selected either the Complete or Tools option, you will not see this page.

GETTING STARTED WITH
BIZTALK SERVER

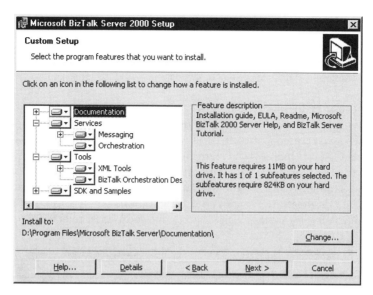

As mentioned earlier in this chapter, the installation process creates a BizTalk Server Administrators group and adds to this group the user account of the user who is logged on during setup. The built-in Administrators group for the machine is also added by default. The next page of the setup wizard allows you to change the name or description of this group as shown. This does not interfere with or alter the operation of the group. Click Next when you are done.

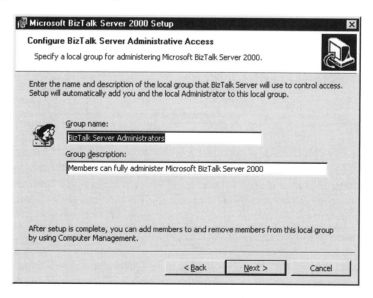

If you rename this group after setup has completed, you must also rename the value contained in the Registry key HKEY_LOCAL_MACHINE\Software\Microsoft\BizTalk Server\1.0\NTGroups\AdminGroupName.

It is then necessary to select the user account that will be used by the BizTalk Messaging Service. You have the option to use the built-in Local System account or an account you have created yourself. This account is assigned the Log On Locally and Act As Part Of The Operating System rights if they have not already been granted. You may also use the Start Service After Setup Completes option to choose whether the BizTalk Messaging Service should start automatically when the setup wizard is complete. BizTalk Orchestration is not controlled by this service and will be available when setup completes regardless. Click Next when you have selected an option.

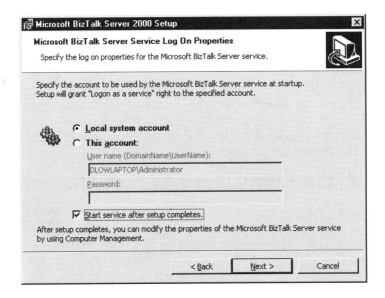

 Selecting this check box does not affect whether the BizTalk Server Messaging Service will start every time the computer is rebooted. By default, the service is configured to start automatically. To change this behavior—for example, if you need to perform some maintenance to a server in a group and you don't want the service to start when the computer reboots—you can use the Services snap-in in the Computer Management console under Administrative Tools.

 If you select an account other than the Local System account, you should make sure that it is a member of the local Administrators group. Otherwise, if you attempt to use S/MIME encryption from within BizTalk Messaging Manager, you will not be able to select a certificate.

You will then be presented with the list of components you have selected, along with a warning that Visio SR1 should be installed for BizTalk Orchestration Designer to run. You may choose to go back at this point if you wish to change any of the options. If all is well, click Next.

The setup wizard now begins to copy files and install components. However, before certain components and services can function, there must be databases in place to store the data they require. During the file copy process, depending on the components you chose to install, you will see the BizTalk Server 2000 Messaging Database Setup Wizard. Click Next to advance past the opening page.

In this wizard, you first have the option to create a new Messaging Management database or to point BizTalk Server at an existing database. If this is the first server of a new BizTalk Server group, you will need to create a new Messaging Management database. If this installation will be part of an existing BizTalk Server group, you will need to select an existing Messaging Management database for the group.

Note   *BizTalk Server groups allow you to share items such as databases, queues, receive functions, and components among multiple BizTalk Servers. They will be covered in detail in Part V of this book.*

You will need to know the name of the actual SQL Server computer on which the database will reside, the name of the database itself, and the user name and password that will be used to connect to this database. Enter this information as shown. Again, you should remember that BizTalk Server uses SQL Server authentication, so the user name and password you supply will not be from a Windows user account, but rather from an account configured specifically to access SQL Server. When you have entered the information, click Next.

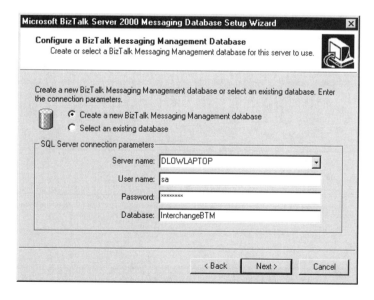

Caution   *If you choose to create a new Messaging Management database but the name you supply is the name of an existing database, BizTalk Server will attempt to use the database, reinitializing it and deleting existing data only if necessary. To avoid possible conflicts, you should delete the database content manually before reusing it as the Messaging Management database.*

Once the BizTalk Messaging Management database has been configured, you are prompted to create a new BizTalk Server group or join an existing one as shown. If you have created a new BizTalk Messaging Management database, then you will be creating a new group. However, if the details of the Messaging Management database you entered on the previous page match those of an existing database already in use by one or more BizTalk Server groups, you may choose to join one of those groups by selecting its name from the drop-down list, or to create another new BizTalk Server group. If there are no BizTalk Server groups in existence (that is, this is the first server to be installed on your network), you will only be able to create a new group. Click Next when you are done.

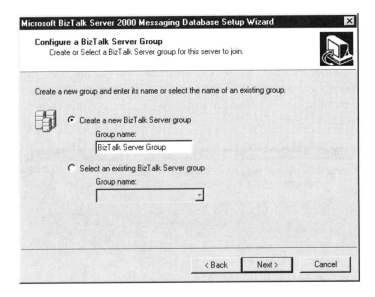

BizTalk Server group names should contain only alphanumeric, hyphen, underscore, and space characters.

If you chose to create a new BizTalk Server group, you will then be prompted for details for the Document Tracking database. Again you will need the name of the database server, the name of the database, and a SQL Server user name and password. If you chose to join an existing group, this step will be bypassed, as the group will already have a Document Tracking database. After entering the necessary data as shown, click Next.

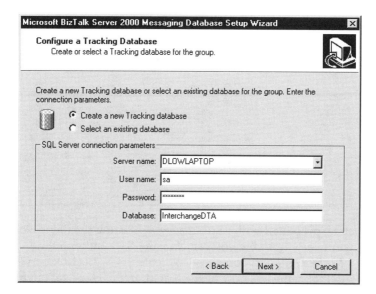

If you do not specify the SQL Server system administrator (sa) account at this point, it is important that you specify an account with administrative privileges on the database. The account specified in this wizard is not the actual account used to query the Document Tracking database. Instead, the account is used to create another SQL Server account (called dta_ui_login) that will be used by the Document Tracking tool. This is because the account will need to create another SQL server account (called dta_ui_login) that will be used by the Document Tracking tool. Of course, that account will also have to have the appropriate privileges to add, update, and delete records in the database as well.

If you chose to create a new BizTalk Server group, you will be prompted for information for the Shared Queue database and will again have to provide the server name, database name, and user account details as shown. If you chose to join an existing group, this step will be bypassed, because the group will already have a Shared Queue database. Click Next when you are done.

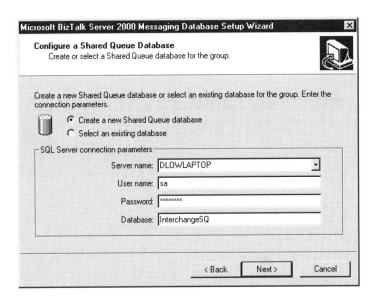

You will then be presented with a summary page listing the database and server group options you selected. Again, you can click the Back button in the dialog box to change any of the information. If you chose to create a new BizTalk Server group, an empty group with that name has now been created. If you chose to join an existing group, that name will be in the dialog box and the other servers that are members of that group will be listed on the right side. Click Next to continue.

The Messaging Database Setup Wizard reaches the last page. Click Finish to complete the process.

There is one final database that must be configured if you chose to install BizTalk Orchestration Services—the Orchestration Persistence database. This database will be used to store the state information for XLANG schedules that are waiting on messages rather than actually executing a process. The BizTalk Server 2000 Orchestration Persistence Database Setup Wizard guides you through the process. Click Next to advance past the opening page.

Note *If you click Cancel at this point, the installation of BizTalk Server will complete, but you will not have an Orchestration Persistence database. You will need to create this database at a later time if you plan to use BizTalk Orchestration. You can do this by running XLANGsetupDB.exe from \Program Files\Microsoft BizTalk Server\Setup.*

At this point, you can again choose an existing database or create a new one. However, if you opt to create a new database, and then enter the name of an existing one, BizTalk Server will delete all information in that database and reinitialize it. Make your selection as shown and click the Finish button to resume setup.

Note

You are not asked to type a user name and password in this wizard because a built-in SQL Server account called dbo is used instead. This user represents the owner of the database, and the login name and password of the user who is running the installation are mapped to it. Therefore, if you need to change the identity of the user account used by BizTalk Server to access this database, you will need to do it through SQL Server Enterprise Manager.

Caution

When you run the Messaging Database Setup Wizard, the server you select for the Messaging Management database is automatically used again as the default for the Tracking and Shared Queue databases, so you don't have to reselect it. However, the Orchestration Persistence Database Setup Wizard runs separately, and it does not use the default from the previous wizard, so make sure you don't select the wrong server accidentally.

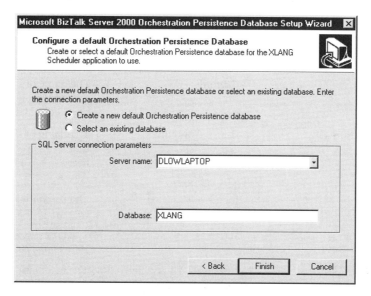

When the database configuration is complete, BizTalk Server Setup will finish copying the source files. It will then add the server to the new or existing server group, create the BizTalk Server Administrators group account, start the BizTalk Messaging Service, and register the COM+ applications. After this, the final page will appear, and you may click either the Finish button to end the setup or the View Readme button to read late-breaking information about the product. The readme.htm file is located in the documentation directory.

Silent Installation

Because BizTalk Server can be set up using a *Microsoft Installer* file (.msi), it is possible to execute the installation wizard from the command line, specifying various configuration options either as switches or using an initialization file (.ini).

For example, the following code typed at a command prompt will install a complete BizTalk Server from CD-ROM (drive D) to the Program Files\BizTalk folder on the E drive using an initialization file called mysettings.ini in the root of the C drive:

```
MSIEXEC /I "d:\Microsoft BizTalk Server.msi" "e:\Program Files\BizTalk"
INSTALLLEVEL=200 ALLUSERS=1 PIDKEY="abcde12345fghij67890klmno"
DSNCONFIG="c:\mysettings.ini"
```

Note   *Consult the BizTalk Server documentation for further generic Microsoft Installer switches that may be used.*

Table 3-1 lists the configurable command-line parameters for BizTalk Server and their default values.

Parameter	Default	Description
USERNAME	{LogonUser}	The name of the user that will appear in the licensee box under Help | About
COMPANYNAME	{LogonCompany}	The name of the company that will appear in the licensee box under Help | About
PIDKEY	{blank}	The 25-character product key without hyphens
INSTALLLEVEL	100	The type of install. 100=Tools; 200=Complete
INSTALLDIR	\Program Files\Microsoft BizTalk Server	The installation location for the product
BTS_GROUP_NAME	BTSAdmin	The name of the BizTalk Server Administrators group that will be created

Table 3-1.   *Configurable Command-Line Parameters for BizTalk Server and Their Default Values*

Parameter	Default	Description
BTS_GROUP_DESCRIPTION	Members can fully administer Microsoft BizTalk Server	The description that should appear alongside the BizTalk Server Administrators group
BTS_USERNAME	{blank}	The user account to be used for the BizTalk Messaging Service
BTS_PASSWORD	{blank}	The password for the user account configured for the BizTalk Messaging Service
BTS_SERVER	localhost	The name of the BizTalk Server to be administered in a Tools installation
BTS_SDK_SERVER	localhost	The name of the BizTalk Server to be used by COM+ in a Tools installation
DSNCONFIG	{blank}	The path and name of the initialization file that contains the settings for the Messaging Database Setup Wizard and the Orchestration Persistence Database Setup Wizard

Table 3-1.   *Configurable Command-Line Parameters for BizTalk Server and Their Default Values* (continued)

If either a complete installation or a custom installation requiring database support is selected, there must be an initialization file specified using the DSNCONFIG parameter. This file follows the format of other Windows initialization files, containing [section] identifiers, and name-value key pairs, as shown in the following example. The sample values are in italics:

```
[InterchangeBTM]
Server=MyBizTalkServer
Username=sa
Password=secretword
```

```
[Group]
GroupName=MyBizTalkGroup

[InterchangeDTA]
Server=MyBizTalkServer
Username=sa
Password=secretword

[InterchangeSQ]
Server=MyBizTalkServer
Username=sa
Password=secretword

[Orchestration]
Server=MyBizTalkServer
Database=XLANG
```

This sample is for a complete installation of BizTalk Server requiring all four databases (BizTalk Messaging, Document Tracking Activity, Shared Queue, and Orchestration Persistence). If your installation will not need certain databases, those sections may be safely left out.

If you specify an existing BizTalk Server group name in the [Group] section, the [InterchangeDTA] and [InterchangeSQ] sections will be ignored; the existing database settings for the group will be used instead.

Troubleshooting BizTalk Server Installation

The installation process for BizTalk Server is fairly straightforward, particularly if you have paid attention to the hardware and software prerequisites. For example, if you do not set SQL Server to use Mixed Authentication, you will receive an error during the BizTalk Server installation that helpfully explains that the BizTalk Messaging database could not be created due to a login failure. If this occurs, I've no sympathy for you, as I've already told you how to avoid this!

However, there are still times when things won't go according to plan, especially if you are working in a development environment, where you are trying out different configurations and installing and reinstalling the software many times. The following documented problems and their solutions should help you avoid the most troublesome situations.

Before/During Installation

First, you must be aware that BizTalk Server requires 25MB of hard disk space on the system drive (where the *winnt* folder is located) even if the product is installed to a different drive. Failure to make this space available can result in the following run-time error during installation:

```
Run-time error '-2147024784 (80070070)';
Method 'xx' of object 'xx' failed
```

If this error arises, cancel the installation, free up the necessary disk space, and run the setup wizard again.

A related problem occurs when you attempt to start the BizTalk Server Administration console only to be confronted with the message "Disk is full." This is, obviously enough, caused by the installation drive not having any space left.

An even less obvious but more frightening error can appear if you choose to cancel the installation process during the Database Setup Wizard. The message that appears is simply "Internal Server Error," which seems to indicate that all manner of things are going wrong inside your machine. However, it is simply a bug in the wizard, and after clicking the OK button, the installation is properly cancelled. Phew!

A last point to bear in mind is that although Windows 2000 features enhanced Domain Naming System (DNS) functionality, you should only use NetBIOS names when referring to SQL Servers or other BizTalk Servers during installation. Otherwise, you may encounter OLE DB errors, or the BizTalk Messaging Service may fail to start.

Uninstalling/Reinstalling

If you have removed BizTalk Server from your computer for whatever reason, certain issues may prevent you from returning your system to a clean state. After you uninstall BizTalk Server, you may notice that not all files have been removed. For example, the \Program Files\Microsoft BizTalk Server directory might still be present containing some files. This is because the uninstall process cannot remove files that are in use or have been changed during the process, perhaps by a running XLANG schedule or the BizTalk Messaging Service. After uninstalling BizTalk Server, you should manually delete the Microsoft BizTalk Server directory. Otherwise, if you attempt to reinstall the product, these remaining files might not be overwritten, causing the new installation to fail or exhibit unusual behavior.

One rather nasty situation that might arise is if your computer crashes during the installation process. This can lead to a partial installation where the BizTalk Messaging Service attempts to start when the system reboots but has not got all the information and files it needs. This causes the system to reboot repeatedly. As you can imagine, a problem of this type is a little trickier to fix and involves using the Windows 2000

Recovery Console available from your Windows 2000 installation CD. Perform the following steps to correct the fault:

1. Reboot your computer using the Windows 2000 CD-ROM or boot floppies if you have created them.

2. When the "Welcome to Setup" message appears, press R on the keyboard to enter repair mode.

3. In repair mode, press C on the keyboard to enter the Recovery Console.

4. When the Recovery Console appears, log on to the computer using the Administrator account.

5. At the command prompt, change to the \winnt\system32 folder on the system volume.

6. Type **disable btssvc** to disable the BizTalk Messaging Service.

7. Type **exit** at the console to reboot the machine.

Another problem can occur if you are uninstalling BizTalk Server and you are prompted to restart your computer. Depending on the configuration you are dismantling, you may receive this prompt or you may not. However, if it appears, you *must* reboot before attempting to reinstall the product. Otherwise, the removal process continues after the next restart, removing certain files necessary for BizTalk Server to function. Again, you should uninstall, reboot, and then reinstall to correct the fault.

Finally, if you uninstall and reinstall BizTalk Server and the Distributed Transaction Controller (MSDTC) service is not running during any part of the process, the XLANG COM+ applications may not be installed correctly and the XLANG scheduler service will fail to start. To repair such an installation, you should use Add/Remove Programs in the Control Panel to remove BizTalk Orchestration Services, and then add them back in again, making sure the MSDTC service is running before proceeding. A similar issue involving the XLANG COM+ applications is described next.

After Installation

Although not a direct result of the installation itself, there are some other issues that can arise to prevent you from using BizTalk Server. For example, changing the name of the computer after installation is disastrous. SQL Server, MSMQ, and BizTalk Server all rely heavily on the name of the computer as it was during installation to function correctly. There are numerous fiendishly difficult ways to solve this, but I have a favorite solution that is much easier to implement: pick a name before installation and stick to it.

Installation of other software or system configuration changes can also wreak havoc on a happy BizTalk Server. For example, Commerce Server 2000 seems like a good choice for interoperability with BizTalk Server, and there are indeed lots of ways these products can be integrated, as you will see in Chapter 14. However, installing Commerce Server 2000 on the same machine after BizTalk Server can lead to an issue whereby the XLANG scheduler COM+ application fails to start, and the XLANG tab is not available for other applications in the Component Services snap-in. To fix this problem, you need to install Windows 2000 Service Pack 2.

Similarly, uninstalling other software can also affect BizTalk Server adversely. For example, if Microsoft Office is on the same machine and is subsequently removed after the installation of BizTalk Server, it may no longer be possible to start the BizTalk Orchestration Designer application. If this happens, insert your Office 2000 CD-ROM, browse to CD_Drive:\Install\Bin\SP\VBA, and install the VBA6.msi file you find there. Likewise, it is possible that uninstalling Office 2000 will unregister the Office Web Components that are required by the BizTalk Document Tracking utility. To resolve this issue, search for msowc.dll and msowcf.dll on your system and re-register them using regsvr32.exe. Installing Office XP on a computer running BizTalk Server will also cause major problems. In particular, the WebDAV repository that is used to store document specifications and maps will cease to function. This issue—and many others—can be resolved by installing BizTalk Server Service Pack 1.

BizTalk Server Service Pack 1

As with all software, it's only when you get it out the door and your customers start to use it in real production environments, that problems can appear. To fix a number of problems that were encountered after the initial release of BizTalk Server, Microsoft has made available BizTalk Server Service Pack 1. To see the full list of bugs fixed by this service pack, consult http://support.microsoft.com/support/kb/articles/q297/4/45.asp?ID=297445. It is also recommended that you read the ReadMe that comes with the service pack. (That's why it's called a "ReadMe"!)

Installing Service Pack 1

Before installing BizTalk Server Service Pack 1, you should check the web address and ReadMe just mentioned to see if you actually need to install it. If your installation is running smoothly, then it might not be necessary (or recommended) to go fiddling with it. However, it is usually a good idea to keep your production software up-to-date with the latest patches and service packs. You should also bear in mind that all servers in a BizTalk server group must be running the same version of the software, so if you decide to install the service pack on one server, you must install it on all of them.

You can download, and run the service pack from a web site (such as the Microsoft BizTalk Server site), or from a local file on a CD-ROM, or hard drive. Either way, running the executable displays a warning as shown. Click Yes to begin the installation.

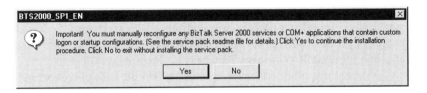

As the warning dialog box explains, you will lose any customizations you had made to the BizTalk Messaging Service and BizTalk COM+ applications. For example, if you have changed the credentials used by the BizTalk Messaging Service, or the XLANG COM+ application, you will need to make those modifications again after installing the service pack.

After acknowledgement of the warning, a command window will open, followed by the Microsoft BizTalk Server 2000 Setup Wizard. Click Next to continue. The installation of the service pack files will then begin on your computer. During this installation, you will be prompted for the original BizTalk Server source files. You must have these to continue. Either insert your BizTalk Server CD-ROM, or click Browse to search for locally installed source files. The installation of the service pack will then continue. Click Finish to exit the wizard and click Yes to restart your computer.

To verify that BizTalk Server Service Pack 1 has been successfully installed, browse to \Program Files\Microsoft BizTalk Server—or your installation directory, if different—right-click any of the .dll files there (except setupex.dll), and select Properties from the context menu. Click the Version tab, and check that the version listed is 2.1.1757.0.

Installing Service Pack 1 on a Server Group

Before you can install Service Pack 1 on the servers in a BizTalk Server group, you must ensure that all servers are stopped and that no work items are being processed. Although the administration of servers and server groups is covered in detail in Chapter 9, it won't hurt to walk through the necessary procedures here. The steps required are as follows:

- Stop the BizTalk Server COM+ applications on each server.
- Stop the BizTalk Server services on each server.
- Stop related services on each server.
- Install and execute the Shared Queue database stored procedure.

Stop the BizTalk Server COM+ Applications on Each Server   To stop the required applications: from the Start Menu, select Programs | Administrative Tools | Component Services. Expand the nodes for Component Services, Computers, My Computer, and COM+ Applications. On both the BizTalk Server Interchange Application node, and the XLANG scheduler node, right-click and select Shut Down from the context menu.

Stop the BizTalk Server Services on Each Server   To stop the required services: from the Start Menu, select Programs | Administrative Tools | Services. On both the entries for BizTalk Messaging Service, and XLANG Scheduler Restart Service, right-click and select Stop from the context menu.

Stop Related Services on Each Server   To stop the related services: open the Services console as before (if it's not still open). On both the entries for IIS Admin Service, and Windows Management Instrumentation Service, right-click and select Stop from the context menu.

Install and Execute the Shared Queue Database Stored Procedure   From the Start menu, select Programs | Microsoft SQL Server | Query Analyzer. In the Connect to SQL Server dialog box that appears, select the appropriate server from the SQL Server drop-down menu, and enter the corresponding authentication information. On the Query menu, select Change Database; select the Shared Queue database for the server group as shown, and click OK.

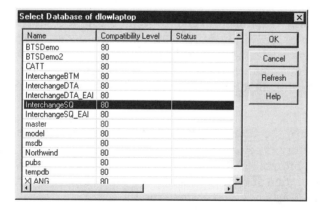

Select File | Open, browse to \Program Files\Microsoft BizTalk Server\Setup—or your installation location, if different—and select CleanQueuesPatch.sql. Click Open, and then choose Query | Execute to run the script.

Note   *All servers in a BizTalk server group must be running the same version of the software. Therefore, if you wish to add a new server to a group that has been updated with Service Pack 1, you must install Service Pack 1 on the new server before adding it to the group.*

Uninstalling Service Pack 1

If for some reason you need to revert to the original BizTalk Server installation, you can download a service pack uninstall utility from the Microsoft web site. Running it is straightforward; but if you are using the Document Tracking feature on any server, you must save the connection string information that allows you to access the Document Tracking web site. This process is detailed in the following section.

Uninstalling Service Pack 1 in a Server Group As with the installation process, you need to make sure that each server in your server group is running the same version of the software, so you will need to uninstall Service Pack 1 on every server in the group. Again, there are procedures that must be followed to do this correctly. You should perform the following steps:

■ Save the Document Tracking database connection information.

■ Stop the BizTalk Server COM+ applications on each server.

■ Stop the BizTalk Server services on each server.

■ Stop related services on each server.

■ Install and execute the Shared Queue database stored procedure.

The only steps that are different from those performed during the installation of the service pack are the first and last steps, so there's no need to go through the others again.

Save the Document Tracking Database Connection Information The user credentials required by the Document Tracking utility are kept in a file called connection.vb in the folder \Program Files\Microsoft BizTalk Server\BizTalkTracking\VBScripts. This file will be overwritten when the service pack is removed, so you should save a copy of it first in a different folder and then copy it back when the uninstall of Service Pack 1 is complete.

Install and Execute the Shared Queue Database Stored Procedure Start the Query Analyzer utility as before, and select the appropriate Shared Queue database. Select File | Open, browse to \Program Files\Microsoft BizTalk Server\Setup—or your installation location, if different—and select UndoCleanQueuesPatch.sql. Click Open, and then choose Query | Execute to run the script.

Using BizTalk Server with Active Directory

After installing BizTalk Server Service Pack 1, it is possible to publish BizTalk Server to an Active Directory installation so that other members of the directory can check the availability of BizTalk servers within an organization. To perform this action, open a Command Prompt window, and browse to the \Program Files\Microsoft BizTalk Server\Setup directory. Type the following at the command prompt:

```
cscript AD_registration.vbs
```

Press ENTER, and click OK in the confirmation dialog box.

Similarly, to remove BizTalk Server from Active Directory, open a Command Prompt window, and browse to the \Program Files\Microsoft BizTalk Server\Setup directory. Type the following at the command prompt:

```
cscript AD_registration.vbs /u
```

Press ENTER, and click OK in the confirmation dialog box.

The
Complete
Reference

Part II

BizTalk Messaging Tools

The
Complete
Reference

BizTalk
Server

Chapter 4

Using BizTalk Editor

One of the primary functions of BizTalk Server is to process business documents. The documents may be invoices, catalogs, scientific papers, stock quotes, procedural forms, or employee records. It doesn't really matter, as BizTalk Server is not restricted to purely commercial transactions. These documents can be received, acknowledged, routed, transformed, stored, and delivered by BizTalk Messaging Services or BizTalk Orchestration Services.

To make use of BizTalk Messaging Services, it is vital that a *specification* is created for each type of document that BizTalk Server will encounter. BizTalk Server cannot handle any type of document unless a corresponding specification exists. Document specifications are XML-based templates that define the structure of the documents to be processed, specifically allowing BizTalk Messaging to *parse* incoming files and *serialize* outgoing files. Parsing is the first step in a document's life cycle after it has been received by the software. BizTalk Server uses X12, EDIFACT, Flat-File, and XML parsers to convert the original document into an intermediate XML format for processing by the server. The information contained in the document specification is crucial to this step. Remember that all internal routing, tracking, and transformation within BizTalk Server is done through XML, regardless of the original file format. Serializing is what happens at the other end, when a document needs to be converted from its intermediate XML format into the format required by the application or trading partner to which it will be sent. Again, a specification is used to assist the serializer in creating the correct structure for the outgoing document.

BizTalk Editor is a graphical application in BizTalk Server that is used to create document specifications. These specifications will later be used to create document definitions in BizTalk Messaging, so that the software can tell what type of documents are coming in, how they are structured, how they may need to be transformed, and how they will need to be formatted before being sent to an application or trading partner. The specifications are XML files that may be stored to disk, or in the BizTalk Server Repository, which is a WebDAV repository accessible through HTTP.

Document Specifications

Business documents are usually linear or hierarchical in nature. An example of a *linear structure* would be a comma-separated values file. This type of file is called a *flat-file* because there is only a single level of depth. Each line of the file can be thought of as a record (similar to a row in a database table), and each distinct item of data in the record can be thought of as a field (similar to a column in a database table). More complicated document structures may involve records nested within other records to many levels, until finally there are records that contain fields of data as before. For obvious reasons, these structures are called *hierarchical*.

In BizTalk Editor, the linear or hierarchical structure of a business document is mapped as records and fields in a document specification. Each record and field has a number of configurable properties depending on the document format. For example, we will need to determine if a record is allowed to repeat, in what order the fields should appear, or what type of data each field should contain. By creating document specifications in BizTalk Editor, we are laying down the rules for each type of document that will be processed by the server.

Before going any further, let's be clear on one important point—document specifications are not documents. Document specifications do not contain actual business data, but instead model the structure of a document. We have already seen that XML can be used to describe the data in a document using markup tags and attributes. Now imagine that we're going to use XML to describe those tags and attributes—what they're called, how they're ordered, and what type of data they will hold—without worrying too much about the data itself. That's a document specification.

If the preceding paragraph reminds you of XML schemas, then give yourself a prize. XML schemas (using the XDR syntax) form the basis of BizTalk Editor document specifications. That syntax provides most of the descriptive information required to model many business document formats. BizTalk Editor adds in anything else that XDR schemas can't handle. XDR schemas were covered in Chapter 2, and you should really have a good understanding of what they are to properly get to grips with document specifications and BizTalk Editor.

Supported Standards

Fortunately or unfortunately, there is no global standard document format. The world would probably be a lot less interesting if such a thing existed. At the very least it is unlikely that XML or BizTalk Server would ever have been invented, so we should be grateful for such diversity! Documents may be flat or have hierarchical structures, they may contain easily identifiable fields of data, or they may be a morass of information. One of the goals of BizTalk document specifications is to apply order to this chaos. As mentioned in Chapter 1, one of the original parts of the BizTalk Initiative was the BizTalk.Org web site, where organizations could store XML schemas to act as document specifications for their business data. Similar initiatives include the RosettaNet Dictionaries and Partner Interface Processes (PIPs), and the XML.Org registry operated by the Organization for the Advancement of Structured Information Standards (OASIS).

Tip *You can find out more about the RosettaNet initiatives at http://www.rosettanet.org/ and more about OASIS at http://www.oasis-open.org/ and http://www.xml.org/.*

We have already seen in Chapter 2 how data may be represented using XML. We have learned that XML affords many advantages over other data formats, not least through its self-describing properties and the ease by which it may be transformed from one structure to another. However, we have also seen that XML is a relatively new technology and one that is only now gaining wide acceptance.

Electronic Data Interchange

Before XML, companies and organizations had to find other methods of structuring data in some standard way. Data records were represented in flat-files that were either *positional* or *delimited*. More complicated data structures could be represented as hierarchical and relational data tables. Slowly but surely, business documents converged into a few accepted formats, particularly when trading partners attempted to automate the transfer of these documents.

One such set of formats that emerged from the need to transfer trading documents such as invoices and purchase orders is Electronic Data Interchange (EDI). This evolved from attempts in the 1970s by the shipping and transportation industries to send business documents via electronic means. The idea soon caught on, with retailers and suppliers each using their own EDI formats. Over the next few years, many groups sought to integrate the various disparate formats that were in use; and in 1979, the Accredited Standards Committee (ASC) X12 was chartered by the American National Standards Institute (ANSI) to develop uniform standards for interindustry electronic communication. These standards thus became known as ANSI X12 EDI (or just X12).

Soon after, the United Nations developed another set of standards, called Electronic Data Interchange for Administration, Commerce and Transport (UN/EDIFACT or just EDIFACT), which was adopted by the International Organization for Standardization (ISO) in 1987. These new standards were also accepted by the ASC X12 committee, but many businesses in North America still use the older ANSI X12 standards.

BizTalk Editor has built-in support for many ANSI X12 (Table 4-1) and EDIFACT (Table 4-2) document standards. As we will see later, these ready-made document specifications may be modified to suit your own business requirements.

Code	Description	2040	3010	3060	4010
810	Invoice	*	*	*	*
832	Price / Sales Catalog	*	*	*	*
846	Inventory Inquiry / Advice	*	*	*	*
850	Purchase Order	*	*	*	*
852	Product Activity Data		*	*	*
855	Purchase Order Acknowledgement	*	*	*	*
856	Ship Notice / Manifest	*	*	*	*
861	Receiving Advice	*	*	*	*
864	Text Message	*	*	*	*

Table 4-1.   *X12 Versions Included with BizTalk Server*

Code	Description	2040	3010	3060	4010
867	Product Transfer and Resale Report	*	*	*	*
940	Warehouse Shipping Order			*	*
944	Warehouse Stock Transfer Receipt Advice			*	*
997	Functional Acknowledgement	*	*	*	*

Table 4-1. *X12 Versions Included with BizTalk Server* (continued)

Note The versions included with BizTalk Server do not comprise a complete set. New versions of X12 are released annually. Versions 2040, 3010, 3060, and 4010 are included with BizTalk Server; but other sub-versions, such as 3072, a precursor to the Year 2000–compliant 4010 version, exist. Similarly, there are other versions of EDIFACT available. The United Nations Trade Data Interchange Directories (UNTDIDs) are updated at least once a year, so other directories such as D96a and D96b may also be in use.

Code	Description	d93A	d95A	d95B	d97B	d98A	d98B
DESADV	Dispatch Advice Message	*	*	*	*	*	*
INVOIC	Invoice Message	*	*	*	*	*	*
INVRPT	Inventory Report Message	*	*	*	*	*	*
ORDERS	Purchase Order Message	*	*	*	*	*	*
ORDRSP	Purchase Order Response Message	*	*	*	*	*	*
PARTIN	Party Information Message	*	*	*	*	*	*
PAYEXT	Extended Payment Order Message	*	*	*	*	*	*

Table 4-2. *EDIFACT Versions Included with BizTalk Server*

BIZTALK MESSAGING TOOLS

Code	Description	d93A	d95A	d95B	d97B	d98A	d98B
PRICAT	Price / Sales Catalog Message	*	*	*	*	*	*
SLSRPT	Sales Data Report Message	*	*	*	*	*	*
APERAK	Application Error and Acknowledgement Message		*	*	*	*	*
PRODAT	Product Data Message				*	*	*
RECADV	Receiving Advice Message				*	*	*
CONTRL	Syntax and Service Report Message					*	*

Table 4-2.   *EDIFACT Versions Included with BizTalk Server* (continued)

XML

Although many companies are still using the various EDI standards to transmit business documents to their trading partners, many organizations coming on board with BizTalk Server may wish to use XML equivalents to simplify the process. BizTalk Editor includes a number of document specifications that are ready to use for various purposes. These specifications may be used as they are, or modified to suit your business needs. For example, there are Common Invoice, Common Purchase Order, Common Purchase Order Acknowledgement, and Common Price Catalog specifications available in the BizTalk Server WebDAV Repository under the Microsoft folder.

Custom Formats

EDI and XML formats may account for a large proportion of business documents, but many organizations will still use custom formats produced by legacy database management systems or proprietary applications. By their very nature, these formats do not necessarily follow any standard structure, so BizTalk Server does not include ready-made document specifications. As a result, creating specifications to match your own document formats is a bit more involved. For simple flat-files, BizTalk Editor allows you to set properties that conform to positional or delimited formats. For anything more complicated, you may need to consult the Software Development Kit (SDK) included with the product documentation to see how to build custom parser and serializer components.

Flat-Files

Flat-file formats are either delimited or positional. *Delimited files* consist of records and fields that are separated by predetermined characters. A common example of this is a comma-separated values file (typically saved with a .csv file extension), as shown in Figure 4-1, in which each record is delimited by a carriage return and each field is delimited by a comma. To circumvent situations in which an actual comma might be encountered in the data itself, text qualifiers—such as quote characters—are often used to bound the data. BizTalk Server has a built-in parser that can recognize incoming documents that are delimited in nature, but we still have to tell the parser what delimiters and text qualifiers to expect, and how the document should be mapped to XML. This is what the document specification is for. Later in this chapter, we will see how properties can be configured in BizTalk Editor to create delimited document specifications.

Positional files consist of records and fields that have a predetermined length. This might be because they have been exported from a database for which each field has a set character width, and this is reflected in the file format. Or it may be because of a custom transport mechanism that is used to transmit the documents in fixed chunks. Either way, there is a regular structure that BizTalk Server's built-in parser can recognize. Again, there must be a document specification to assist BizTalk Server to transform the document into the interim XML format. Later in this chapter, we will see how properties can be configured in BizTalk Editor to create positional document specifications. Usually, positional files will also be delimited, as shown in Figure 4-2. Each field will have a fixed length, but each record will be delimited, for example, by a carriage return.

Other Formats

It is conceivable that the formats of the business documents used in your company do not follow simple positional or delimited flat-file structures. Similarly, they may not be easily expressible as XML, or at the very least, BizTalk Editor might not be able to represent the structure satisfactorily. Also, BizTalk Server only supports ASCII text documents, whereas your file format may contain binary information. If this is the case, then you will need to develop custom parser and serializer components to handle these

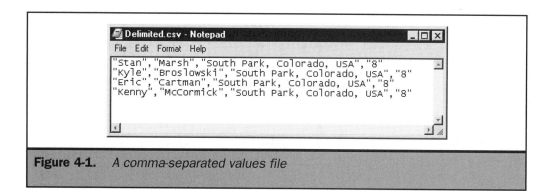

Figure 4-1. *A comma-separated values file*

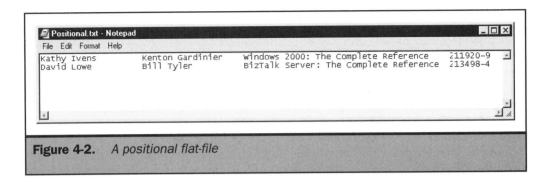

Figure 4-2.   *A positional flat-file*

documents as they enter and leave your BizTalk Server system. In Chapter 16, we will
explore the creation of these custom components.

Envelopes

There is a special type of specification that can be created with BizTalk Editor, except
it's not a document specification—it's an *envelope specification*. Like ordinary envelopes
we use in the real world, BizTalk Server envelopes are used to enclose single or multiple
documents, called *interchanges*, and can also supply source and destination details, or
further information about the envelope contents. As we will see in Chapter 6, BizTalk
Messaging Manager allows us to create envelope objects. These are virtual objects that
are used to help BizTalk Messaging handle documents. The types of envelope included
are X12, EDIFACT, Flat-File, Custom, Reliable, and Custom XML. Depending on the
type of envelope in use, it will either exist on its own, or point to an envelope
specification that has been created with BizTalk Editor.

When a document is submitted to BizTalk Server, the type of envelope that contains
it is extremely important, as this tells the parser what type of document to expect. Unlike
real-world envelopes, BizTalk envelopes are not multipurpose items. Each envelope
needs to match the type of document it contains. In this way, envelopes assist BizTalk
Server in selecting the parser that should be used to process an incoming document
interchange. Once determined, the parser can then set about converting the document
to XML using the rules in the appropriate document specification. Sometimes, the
envelope will also point to an actual envelope specification. If so, and if this specification
contains routing information, then the parser will extract these values, and use them
to determine how BizTalk Messaging should handle the document.

Note   *Although envelope specifications are usually used to contain routing
information, document specifications may also contain this kind of data.*

When a document is being delivered by BizTalk Messaging to an application or
trading partner, the properties in the document specification can be used to determine

which serializer should be used to convert the document from the internal XML format used by BizTalk Server. However, an envelope is still required at this stage to wrap the document and provide any additional header information before delivery. If the envelope points to an envelope specification, this will be used to explicitly tell the serializer how to package the outgoing document interchange.

Using Envelopes

Although envelopes will be discussed in greater detail in Chapter 6, let's look at the situations in which they are required. In the following paragraphs, when we refer to an *envelope*, we mean an envelope object as created in BizTalk Messaging Manager. When we refer to an *envelope specification*, we mean a specification created in BizTalk Editor that represents the structure of an actual envelope. Remember that in each case, the format of the envelope must match the type of document it contains. We will see how a document specification can be configured as an envelope specification later in this chapter.

XML Formats   Inbound documents conforming to the built-in XML document specifications do not require an envelope, as they already contain enough descriptive information for BizTalk Messaging Services to determine how each document should be processed. However, if your inbound documents use a custom XML document specification, then you should also create an envelope with the same format.

For outbound documents, an appropriate XML envelope should be created, or else the document will be sent as XML without any header or footer. You should also create an envelope specification in the same format; otherwise the document will be encapsulated in the Reliable envelope format. A Reliable envelope conforms to the BizTalk Framework 2.0 specification. BizTalk Framework-compliant documents are always enclosed in an envelope, as they are required to specify routing and receipt information. The envelope type is called Reliable because documents sent in this way will be retried indefinitely until a receipt is received to acknowledge delivery of the document.

EDI Formats   Inbound X12 and EDIFACT documents do not explicitly require envelopes. BizTalk Server is already aware of the structure of these documents and their corresponding headers, so it is able to select a specification accordingly.

For outbound interchanges, a corresponding X12 or EDIFACT envelope must be used, but it does not need to point to an envelope specification. Instead, we will specify an interchange control number and the delimiters used by the document. These properties will be discussed in more detail in Chapter 6.

Custom Formats   Inbound document interchanges that use a custom flat-file format will always require an envelope, and the envelope must point to an envelope specification with the same format. However, the actual flat-file document specification can be used as the envelope specification if each interchange will only contain a single document with no extra header or footer information. Outbound flat-file interchanges will also need to use an envelope, but it does not need to point to a specification, as only one document at a time is sent in an outgoing interchange.

Remember that another possibility is that your business documents may require custom parser and serializer components to be properly processed. In this case, you will have to use a Custom envelope. The envelope may or may not need an envelope specification to correctly parse incoming documents, but it will probably need an envelope specification to help the serializer package outgoing documents. Building custom parser and serializer components will be covered in Chapter 16.

Creating New Specifications

BizTalk Editor is a graphical environment in which you can create or modify document specifications. Although these specifications are enhanced XML schemas, BizTalk Editor writes all the XML for you. A document specification is a hierarchical tree of nodes corresponding to the records and fields in a document, so it is important that you are able to express the structure of your documents in this fashion.

BizTalk Editor Environment

The BizTalk Editor interface is shown in Figure 4-3. The pane on the left displays the collapsible hierarchy of nodes that represent the records and fields of the document. The right pane has six tabs on which you can configure specific properties for each record and field depending on the type of specification you are creating. We will

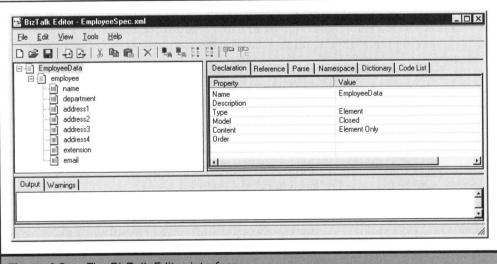

Figure 4-3. *The BizTalk Editor interface*

see the various properties that are available on these tabs later in this chapter as we explore the different formats supported by BizTalk Editor. The bottom pane has an Output tab that displays sample document instances created by the program and a Warnings tab that displays any errors encountered while compiling a specification or validating an instance document.

The standard toolbar allows you to create a new specification, open an existing one, or save the current one to the local hard disk; store specifications to or retrieve specifications from the WebDAV Repository; cut, copy, paste, or delete nodes; create a new record or field; insert a record or field; and expand or collapse the node hierarchy in the left pane. These buttons all have associated commands in the menu bar along with other tasks, such as to import existing schemas or document instances or to call up the BizTalk Server documentation.

When you opt to create a new specification in BizTalk Editor, the New Document Specification dialog box, shown next, appears. You can choose the type of specification you wish to create. If you choose X12, EDIFACT, or XML, you will see a list of available specification types. You can then modify these to suit your own purposes by adding or removing records and fields, or changing the properties of existing records and fields. If you choose Blank Specification, you are starting from scratch and will have to create and configure each record and field manually.

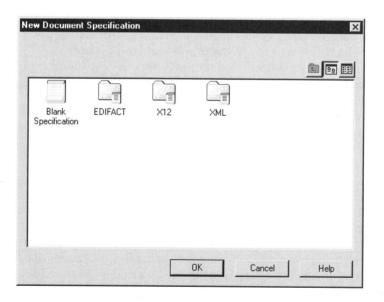

Tip *The built-in specifications are stored at \Program Files\Microsoft BizTalk Server\ XML Tools\Templates. If you have your own templates that you wish to use to create document specifications, you can create subfolders at this location containing your templates, and they will appear in the New Document Specification dialog box.*

Creating Records and Fields

Records are used in document specifications to group related fields together. Fields are used to contain data. There are a number of ways to create a new record or field. You can click the Create Record, Insert Record, Create Field, or Insert Field buttons on the toolbar; you can use the New Record, New Field, Insert Record, or Insert Field commands on the Edit menu; or you can right-click an existing record or field and choose one of the New Record, Insert Record, New Field, or Insert Field commands on the context menu. Choosing New Record places the new record as a child of the selected node, whereas choosing Insert Record places the record immediately after the selected node as a sibling. Likewise, selecting a record and choosing New Field places a field at the end of the existing fields, while selecting a field and choosing Insert Field places a field immediately after the current field.

To delete a record or field, simply select the record or field, and then use the Delete Specification Node button on the toolbar; choose Edit | Delete; or right-click the node and select Delete from the context menu. You can even press DELETE on the keyboard. For brevity, throughout this chapter we will use the commands available on the context menu, as it is probably the quickest way to perform tasks.

Creating the Root Node

When you create a blank specification, it is not really blank. There is always a record at the root of the node hierarchy, called *BlankSpecification*. This cannot be deleted, but you can (and should) rename it to match the purpose of your document.

The term *root node* as it is used here should not be confused with the root node of an XML document as defined by the W3C *Document Object Model (DOM)*. The DOM is an interface definition language that defines each part of an XML document as an object with associated properties and methods. As a result, any aspect of the document may be configured or manipulated programmatically through an object-based or object-oriented programming language in conjunction with a DOM-compliant parser such as MSXML. The base object in the DOM is the Node object, and the root node of a document is equivalent to the document itself. The root element (called the document element in the DOM) of an XML document is thus the singular child of the root node that must exist for the XML to be well-formed. In contrast, the *root node* of a BizTalk Server document specification is actually a definition of the root element of the XML-based document that BizTalk Server will use internally after an incoming document has been parsed. This use of terminology may be confusing, but as the BizTalk Server documentation uses the term *root node* to refer to the root record in a document specification, we will do the same.

The name that you give to the root node (or any other record or field) must not contain any spaces, and you should also follow the rules associated with naming XML elements and attributes that were outlined in Chapter 2. This is because this name will be used as the name of the root element of the XML document that BizTalk Server uses internally to represent the actual business document.

The root node can act as a record in that it can contain fields, but the properties of the root node are different from those for any other record in the specification, as we will see.

Creating Child Records

It is often confusing to decide whether to use a record or a field when creating a new specification from scratch. To make your decision easier, there are a couple of simple guidelines you can follow. I must stress that these are only guidelines, as each scenario will impose its own requirements and restrictions.

- If a document item will have multiple or complex properties that contain actual data, it should be created as a record with each property defined as a field of that record.

- If a document item will only contain actual data and not have complex properties, it should be created as a field.

For example, suppose we wanted to create a document that described an office building. We would first need to consider the properties of the building that we wanted to include. These might be address, dimensions, resident companies, and the building manager. If we consider each of these items in turn, we can decide how they would need to be represented. First, the address might seem like a simple property that would lend itself to being represented as a field. This might be true if the only purpose of the address field were to print a mailing label. However, if it became necessary to differentiate between or to group buildings based on the country, state, city, or street in which they were located, then having the address as a single field would not be sufficient. It would make more sense to create an address record containing fields for street, city, state, and country.

Second, let's consider the building dimensions. If the document is to serve in an official capacity, there might be several different items of data that need to be included. If the document will just contain summary information, then specifying the area it occupies and the number of floors should be sufficient. Again, we could use a record to represent the building dimensions, and fields for the area and the number of floors.

Third, it is likely that there will be multiple companies located in the building. If we only needed the name of the company, we might think that a field would be sufficient. However, here we have to consider how the information will actually be stored as XML. One of the things we saw in Chapter 2 was that an element can have multiple attributes, but that each attribute must be unique. By default, BizTalk Editor stores records as XML elements and fields as attributes, so having multiple fields called "Company" would not be possible within the same record.

Note *We can change any given field in a specification to be stored as an XML child element rather than an attribute, by changing the properties of the field on the Declaration tab. Although it is not illegal in XML to have multiple child elements with the same name (in fact, it is quite common), BizTalk Editor does not allow two fields of the same record to have the same name even if they are configured as elements. It does allow two fields to have the same name if one is configured as an element and the other is configured as an attribute, but that is an exceptionally bad design. If you really must have repeated simple fields with a single property, then you should create them as records and set the value of their Content property to Text Only on the Declaration tab.*

As a result, we will represent each company as a separate record containing a single field that stores the company name. This is a much more flexible arrangement, anyway, because it is likely that we will wish to store further information about each company: for example, the number of offices it has, the number of people employed, the contact person for the company, and so on. In fact, we might even decide to make some or all of these items records if we feel that further information might be required in each case.

Finally, the document will contain information about the building manager. Again, depending on the amount and type of information we need to store, we could choose records or fields. In this example, we'll be happy with just the name of the building manager, so a simple field will suffice. Figure 4-4 shows how this information might be represented in a BizTalk Editor document specification.

To create a child record, simply select the record (or root node) that you wish the record to be a child of, right-click, and select New Record (shown next). If you wish to insert a child record immediately following an existing record, select that record,

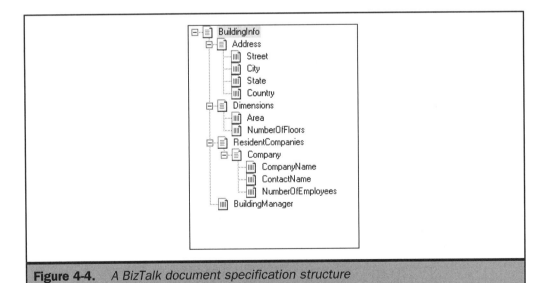

Figure 4-4. *A BizTalk document specification structure*

right-click, and select Insert Record. You can then name the new record or rename it at any time by right-clicking and selecting Rename.

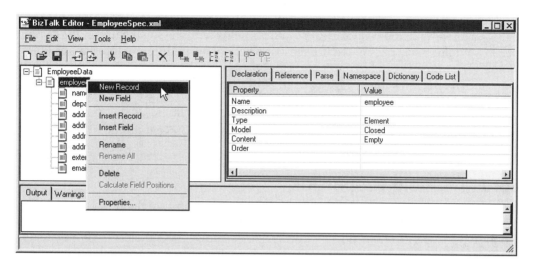

Be aware that if you create a record and give it the same name as an existing record, the new record will instantly adopt the structure and properties of the existing record, including child records and fields. This is not a bug—it is by design and has to do with how elements are defined in XDR schemas. In XDR, an element may only be defined once (by an *ElementType* element), even though XML documents may legally contain similarly named elements in different locations with different structures. For example, in our building specification, if we needed to create a new record that held the address information for the Building Manager, we would simply create a new record called *Address* under *BuildingManager*, and it would automatically have *Street*, *City*, *State*, and *Country* fields.

Remember, just because something is allowed in XML, doesn't make it a good idea. Avoid creating documents that use the same element names if they should have different purposes.

Creating Fields

As mentioned, document fields contain actual data, and they can exist either immediately below the root node or grouped under records. By default, fields are created as XML attributes, but it is possible to change the default in the Tools | Options dialog box. It is also possible to manually change a field type from attribute to element on the Declaration tab. In general, it is probably sufficient to stick with the default. But as our building specification example showed, you might encounter a situation where you need to have repeated items with the same name, in which case they must be configured as text-only records or as a record containing a single text field that is allowed to appear multiple times, repeating records each containing a single text field.

To create a field, simply select the record (or root node) that will contain the field, right-click, and select New Field. If you wish to insert a field after an existing field, select that field, right-click, and select Insert Field. You can give the field a name immediately after creation and rename it at any time by right-clicking and selecting Rename.

Remember that you cannot create multiple fields with the same name in the same record, although it is possible to use the same field name in different locations as long as the Type property is set to Attribute. This is because XDR schemas allow you to define attributes (using an *AttributeType* element) within element definitions such that they only hold scope within that element, and BizTalk Editor follows this behavior. However, if you try to create a field as an element and there already exists a field of type *element* with the same name somewhere else in the specification, BizTalk Editor will gently remind you that this is not supported.

Record and Field Properties

BizTalk Editor has six different tabs on which you can configure the properties of the specification or individual records and fields. Not all of these tabs are relevant, depending on the type of specification you are creating. For example, the Code List tab is only used if you are creating an X12- or EDIFACT-based specification. Some of these properties directly relate to the XDR schema syntax that BizTalk Editor uses, while some of the properties are BizTalk Server specific.

Declaration Tab

The Declaration tab, shown next, contains properties that are used to declare each record and field used in the specification. Depending on whether you have selected a record or field, the properties will be different. These properties relate directly to the XDR schema syntax discussed in Chapter 2.

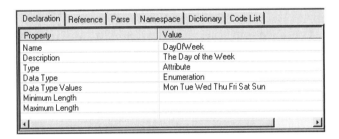

Name   The value of the Name property is the name of the record or field. This corresponds to the *name* attribute on an *ElementType* or *AttributeType* definition in an XDR schema, and it will appear as an actual element or attribute name when BizTalk Server converts a document instance to XML. As a result, its format is limited to that of an XML element or attribute.

Note *The value of the Name property that is configured for the root node will also appear as the value of the Specification Name property on the Reference tab. If you change the name of the root node, this property will also change, unless you have explicitly set the value of the Specification Name property.*

Description   The value of the Description property is a free-text description of the purpose of the record or field. This corresponds to a *Description* element within an *ElementType* or *AttributeType* definition in an XDR schema. It does not have any real function other than to annotate the record or field for humans.

Tip *You can also add descriptive information to any record or field by right-clicking the node and choosing Properties from the context menu. On the Note tab, simply enter the description and it will be saved with the specification.*

Type   The value of the Type property determines whether the record or field will be represented by an element or attribute when the instance document is converted to XML by BizTalk Server. This corresponds to using either an *ElementType* or *AttributeType* definition in an XDR schema. For a record, the value of the Type property must be set to Element. For a field, the value of the Type property can be set to Element or Attribute.

Note *If you configure a field to be declared as an element, the value of the Content property will automatically be set to Text Only, and it will not be possible to specify a default value. However, it will be possible to set the value of the Model property to Open so that further custom properties may appear as attributes or child elements in an actual document instance. Again, although this is possible, it is not recommended, as a data field should only contain textual data, and not other properties.*

Model   The value of the Model property can only be set for a record, or for a field whose Type property has been set to *element*. This value determines whether extra fields are allowed to appear in a document instance, and it corresponds to the *model* attribute on an *ElementType* definition in an XDR schema. If the value of the Model property is set to Closed, then only fields that are declared in the specification will be allowed. The presence of any other fields will cause a validation error. This property should not be changed from the default for fields configured as elements.

If the value of the Model property is set to Open, elements in a document instance may contain extra attributes or child elements as long as those attributes or child elements belong to a different namespace. Therefore, within the document instance, any custom fields must have a prefix in front of their name, and this prefix must map to a namespace that is in scope for the record containing that field.

Note *If the value of the Model property for a record is set to Open, then the Content property of that record may be set to Element Only, even if that record does not have any child records or fields. This is valid XML, but there is no sane reason why you would want to do that.*

Content   The value of the Content property can only be set for a record. It determines whether the record will contain other records, fields, or actual data. This corresponds to the *content* attribute on an *ElementType* definition in an XDR schema. For a record without fields or child records, or a record that contains only fields that are configured as attributes, you can set the value of the Content property to Element Only, Empty, or Text Only. However, if you add a child record or a field that is configured as an element, the value of the Content property for the parent record will automatically be set to Element Only. If you are familiar with XDR syntax, you might be aware that there is a fourth possible value for the *content* attribute—Mixed. This value means that a record may contain a mixture of both free text and named child elements. This value is not supported by BizTalk Editor because it is not considered good practice to use this type of structure for business documents.

Note   *Setting the value of the Content property for a record to Text Only implies that the record may contain data that is not defined as a field. This is not good practice. This value is only made available because it is also possible to define a field as an element. In this case the Content property will appear on the Declaration tab for that field, but it will be automatically set to the value Text Only.*

Order   The value of the Order property can only be set for a record. It determines how child records or fields must appear in an instance document. This corresponds to the *order* attribute on an *ElementType* definition in an XDR schema. The Order property can take the values Many, One, or Sequence. If the value is set to Many, the named child records and fields may be included in any order, any number of times (including zero), in an instance document. If the value is set to One, then any child records or fields configured as elements defined on this record are mutually exclusive. That is, only one of them can appear in that location in an instance document. For example, there may be a child record for Billing Address or Shipping Address, but not both. If the value is set to Sequence, the named child records or fields must appear in an instance document once and only once in the same order as they appear in the specification. Hopefully, it will be obvious to you why Sequence is the default value, why One is only used in specific scenarios, and why Many should be avoided.

Note   *Another reason to avoid Many is that even if a child record is configured to appear a maximum of one time on the Reference tab, it may validly appear any number of times in the instance document if the Order property of its parent is set to Many.*

Data Type   The value of the Data Type property can only be set for a field. It is used to restrict the type of data that can appear in that field in a document instance. The values it can take are listed in Table 4-3. For example, we would probably want to prevent somebody from typing "XYZ" into an Age field, or we might need to check that a field called OrderDate contains an actual date that has been formatted correctly so that our application can use it intelligently. This corresponds to the *dt:type* attribute on an *ElementType*, *AttributeType*, or *datatype* definition in an XDR schema.

Data Type	Description
Character	Single character
String	Any number of characters, including spaces and punctuation (except characters that must be escaped, like "<")
Number	Similar to Fixed Point 14.4, except without decimal place limits
Integer	Whole number with optional sign and no decimal places or exponent
Float	Real number with optional leading sign, decimal places, and an exponent, for example, –3.056E+18
Fixed Point 14.4	Number with no more than 14 digits to the left of the decimal point and no more than 4 digits to the right. Useful for currencies
Boolean	Either TRUE (1) or FALSE (0)
Date	Date in ISO 8601 format, for example, "1972-30-07"
Date Time	Date and time in ISO 8601 format, for example, "2001-02-27T12:30:00"
Date Time.tz	Date and time in ISO 8601 format, with optional time zone, for example, "1971-13-01T17:15:00-08:00"
Time	Similar to Date Time, except with no date information
Time.tz	Similar to Date Time.tz, except with no date information
Byte (i1)	Integer expressible in one byte
Word (i2)	Integer expressible in two bytes
Integer (i4)	Integer expressible in four bytes—same as Integer
Double Integer (i8)	Integer expressible in eight bytes
Unsigned Byte (ui1)	Unsigned integer expressible in one byte
Unsigned Word (ui2)	Unsigned integer expressible in two bytes
Unsigned Integer (ui4)	Unsigned integer expressible in four bytes

Table 4-3.   *Available Data Types in BizTalk Editor*

Data Type	Description
Double Unsigned Integer (ui8)	Unsigned integer expressible in eight bytes
Real (r4)	Real number with seven-digit decimal precision
Double Real (r8)	Same as float—real number with 15-digit decimal precision
Universal Unique Identifier (uuid)	String of hexadecimal digits and optional hyphens, representing octets that may be used as a URI, for example, "e4f55cfc-0766-4558-a5a5-0652922752a9"
Uniform Resource Identifier (uri)	For example, "urn:schemas-biztalk-org:datatypes"
Binary (base64)	Binary encoding of binary text into characters
Binary (hex)	Binary hexadecimal digits that represent octets, for example, 0x0123D
ID	Specifies that the field must act as a unique identifier within the document (like a primary key)
IDREF	Specifies that the field refers to an ID
IDREFS	Specifies that the field contains a space-separated list of ID references
ENUMERATION	Space-separated list of values referenced in a values data type, for example, "Mon Tue Wed Thu Fri Sat Sun"

Table 4-3. *Available Data Types in BizTalk Editor* (continued)

You can also create custom data types within X12, EDIFACT, and custom formats by setting the value of the Custom Data Type property on the Parse tab. If the Data Type property on the Declaration tab has been set, setting the Custom Data Type property on the Parse tab will clear it, and vice versa.

In Chapter 6, we will see how to configure document definitions in BizTalk Messaging Manager so that individual fields are tracked for later analysis using the Document Tracking feature of BizTalk Server. If you will need to explicitly track a field as an integer, real, or date data type, you must set the value of the Data Type property appropriately. Otherwise, you will only be able to track the value as text or custom data. Similarly, we will also see how to configure a channel in BizTalk Messaging Manager to filter documents based on the values of individual fields. To do this, the field by which you want to filter the documents must have a value set for the Data Type property.

Note *If you set the value of the Data Type property to IDREF or IDREFS for any field in a specification, there must exist at least one other field where the Data Type property has been set to ID.*

Data Type Values The value of the Data Type Values property can only be set for a field that has its Data Type property set to Enumeration. It is used to list the possible values that this field may contain in a document instance. The list of values must be separated by spaces. This corresponds to the *dt:values* attribute on an *ElementType*, *AttributeType*, or *datatype* definition in an XDR schema that has a *dt:type* attribute with a value of *enumeration*.

Minimum Length The value of the Minimum Length property can only be set for a field that has its Data Type property set to String, Number, Binary (base64), or Binary (hex). It is used to set a lower limit on the value that this field may contain in a document instance. This corresponds to the *dt:minLength* attribute on an *ElementType*, *AttributeType*, or *datatype* definition in an XDR schema that has a *dt:type* attribute with a value of *string*, *number*, *bin.base64*, or *bin.hex*.

Maximum Length The value of the Maximum Length property can only be set for a field that has its Data Type property set to String, Number, Binary (base64), or Binary (hex). It is used to set an upper limit on the value that this field may contain in a document instance. This corresponds to the *dt:maxLength* attribute on an *ElementType*, *AttributeType*, or *datatype* definition in an XDR schema that has a *dt:type* attribute with a value of *string*, *number*, *bin.base64*, or *bin.hex*.

Default Value The value of the Default Value property can only be set for a field that is configured as an attribute, and then only in an XML specification. It is used to provide a value for document instances that do not explicitly contain this field when the value of the Required property on the Reference tab is set to No. It can also be used to provide a required value for all document instances if the value of the Required property on the Reference tab is set to Yes. This does not correspond to the default attribute on an *AttributeType* definition in an XDR schema, but rather to the *default* attribute on an *attribute* reference in an XDR schema. This is because default values can be set on a per-instance basis for each field, even if multiple fields with the same name exist in a specification.

Cycle Count The Cycle Count property is only available for record nodes in XML specifications where the record is a child of a record of the same name. The value of the property is used to set the maximum number of recursions for a cyclical reference. We have already seen that when a record is created with the same name as an existing record, it takes on all of the properties of that record because each depends on a single *ElementType* definition in the XDR schema contained in the specification. To take this a step further, if the new record is created as a child of the first record, it sets up a cyclical reference, meaning that the entire record structure will be nested inside the first, like a set of Russian dolls nested inside each other. This cycle can only nest to a depth of seven levels, so the value of the Cycle Count property must be a number between 1 and 7.

Caution *For a cyclical node, the value of the Minimum Occurrences property on the Reference tab must be set to 0 to prevent an infinite loop.*

For example, consider a document that contains information about an employee. The document might have personal data and information about the company the employee works for. The record containing the company details will have a certain structure in terms of the fields that it incorporates. If you wished to also supply information about a previous employer, you might decide to use the same record structure for the details of that company, and so you could use a cyclical reference. A specification created in this way is shown in Figure 4-5. Notice that the repeating node, Company, has an icon with a curved arrow to indicate that it is part of a cyclical reference. A document instance that conforms to this specification is shown in Figure 4-6.

Note *Records and fields that form a cyclical node cannot be dragged and dropped. Also, if you change the content of a cyclical node, you may see a warning displayed on the Warnings tab. This is only a warning, and validating the specification will clear it unless there is a more serious error.*

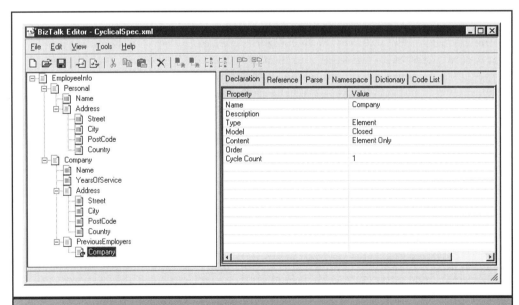

Figure 4-5. *A document specification containing a cyclical reference*

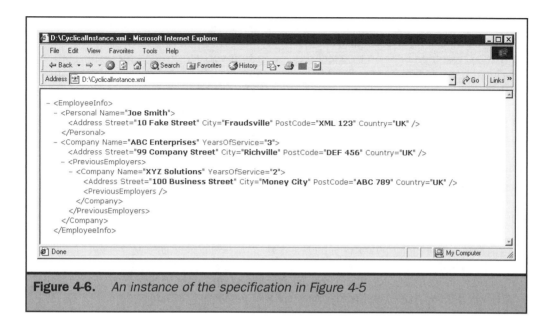

Figure 4-6. *An instance of the specification in Figure 4-5*

Custom Annotations   If your document specification represents data retrieved from a SQL Server 2000 database, it is possible to annotate the XDR schema in the specification to map the elements and attributes to their corresponding records and fields in the database. This annotated XDR schema, called a *mapping schema*, can then be queried to return data. This differs from a typical query in that the XML Path language (XPath) will be used to query the database rather than SQL, and the data will be returned as an XML document conforming to the specification rather than as a normal SQL result set. These annotations can be added on either the Declaration tab or Reference tab depending on the annotation being used.

For example, to specify that a record called *employee* in a document specification will contain data from a SQL Server table called *Employees*, you can add the *sql:relation* annotation to this record on the Declaration tab with its value set to Employees. This adds the attribute *sql:relation="Employees"* to the *ElementType* definition for that record in the XDR schema used in the specification. Similarly, to indicate that a field called *address1* in a specification will contain data from a database column called *Street Address*, you can add the *sql:field* annotation to this field on the Reference tab with its value set to Street Address. This adds the attribute *sql:field="Street Address"* to the *attribute* reference in the XDR schema within the specification. If you are wondering if the use of the *sql:* prefix indicates that a namespace is employed, give yourself another prize. The namespace URI represented by this prefix is urn:schemas-microsoft-com:xml-sql. It is added automatically to the list of namespaces on the Namespace tab in BizTalk Editor if one of these annotations is used.

To add a SQL annotation, double-click any blank property field on the Declaration tab or Reference tab. A drop-down menu of available SQL annotations, as shown in Figure 4-7, can then be used to select the annotation you require. As these annotations involve the use of SQL Server 2000 features rather than BizTalk Server features, any further discussion of them is beyond the scope of this book.

You can also add custom annotations by double-clicking in a blank property field on the Declaration tab and typing the name of the property, including its namespace prefix. This namespace prefix must be mapped to a corresponding URI on the Namespace tab. These properties will not have any specific function as far as BizTalk Server is concerned, unless used by a custom parser, but their creation will not interfere with the operation of the specification.

In general, the Declaration tab is concerned with the definition of records and fields. In other words, properties set on this tab apply to all instances of that record or field. Therefore, annotations created on this tab will have global scope. On the other hand, the Reference tab is used to set properties for each individual record or field. That is, they will only apply to that particular instance of the record or field. Therefore, annotations created on the Reference tab will only have local scope.

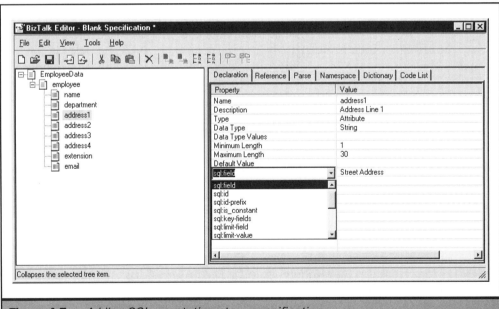

Figure 4-7.   *Adding SQL annotations to a specification*

Reference Tab

The Reference tab, shown next, allows you to configure properties that determine the format of the specification. In particular, you can choose whether you will be creating an XML, EDI, or CUSTOM specification. Depending on the standard you select, the properties that are available will vary. Unless otherwise stated, the properties configured here are custom BizTalk Server parameters, because they cannot be easily represented (if at all) using XDR schema syntax.

Property	Value
Declaration Reference Parse Namespace Dictionary Code List	
Specification Name	EmployeeInfo
Standard	CUSTOM
Standards Version	
Document Type	
Version	
Default Record Delimiter	CR (0xd)
Default Field Delimiter	, (0x2c)
Default Subfield Delimiter	
Default Escape Character	
Code Page	
Receipt	
Envelope	
Target Namespace	

Specification Name   The Specification Name property is only available for the root node. The value of this is used to name the specification (as if you hadn't guessed). It corresponds directly to the *name* attribute of the *Schema* root element in an XDR schema. Its value usually reflects the Name property of the root node on the Declaration tab, but it can be explicitly set here.

Standard   The Standard property is only available for the root node. The value of this property is used to configure the overall format for the specification. The available values are XML, X12, EDIFACT, and CUSTOM. You may also type in a value if you are using a custom parser component, but this will not have any observable effect over using the CUSTOM setting. Depending on the value you choose for this property, other properties will appear or disappear on the Reference tab.

Standards Version   The Standards Version property is only available for the root node. The value of this property is primarily used to determine the version of EDI (X12 or EDIFACT) on which the specification is based. As discussed previously, the X12 specifications supplied with BizTalk Server come in four different versions, and there are six different directories for EDIFACT. You may also type in a custom value here if you are creating a CUSTOM specification, but it will have no observable effect unless a custom parser component has been programmed to make use of it.

Document Type The Document Type property is only available for the root node. The value of this is again used to determine the type of EDI document on which the specification is based. For example, a Document Type value of 850 for an X12 specification would indicate that the specification was modeling a Purchase Order. Similarly, a Document Type value of SLSRPT for an EDIFACT specification would indicate that the specification referred to a Sales Report. Once again, a custom value may be typed here, but it will only be useful if a custom parser component is looking for it.

This property should not be confused with a Document Type Declaration that may appear at the beginning of an XML document (using the <!DOCTYPE … > syntax) or the Document Type Definition (DTD) to which it refers.

Version The Version property is only available for the root node. The value of this property is used to set the version number of the specification. Although it may be used with any type of specification, this property is mainly used with EDI document formats (X12 and EDIFACT) to differentiate specifications that may have undergone revision.

Default Record Delimiter The Default Record Delimiter property is only available for the root node of a specification where the Standard property has been set to CUSTOM. The value of this property is used to determine a default character that marks the end of a record in a flat-file document. This default character may then be referenced by the Delimiter Type property on the Parse tab for multiple records without having to be explicitly defined each time. The characters that are directly available are listed in Table 4-4. If another character is typed in the combo box, it will appear alongside its hex equivalent. Only single characters are allowed. If you have entered a value accidentally and wish to clear it, right-click the property value and select Clear Property.

Character	Code (Hex)	Character	Code (Hex)
TAB	0x9	,	0x2C
LF	0xA	.	0x2E
CR	0xD	0	0x30
SPACE	0x20	;	0x3B
*	0x2A	?	0x3F
+	0x2b			0x7C
~	0x7E	NULL	0x0

Table 4-4. *Built-In Characters Available as Record and Field Delimiters*

If you choose a NULL character by pressing BACKSPACE *or* DELETE, *it will appear in BizTalk Editor as a question mark (?) alongside the hex value 0x0. This is not the same as using a literal question mark, which has a hex value 0x3F.*

Default Field Delimiter   The Default Field Delimiter property is only available for the root node of a specification where the Standard property has been set to CUSTOM. The value of this property is used to determine a default character that marks the beginning or end of a field in a flat-file document where the Structure property on the Parse tab has been set to Delimited. This default character may then be referenced by the Delimiter Type property on the Parse tab for multiple records without having to be explicitly defined each time. The characters that are directly available are listed in Table 4-4. If another character is typed in the combo box, it will appear alongside its hex equivalent. Only single characters are allowed. If you have entered a value accidentally and wish to clear it, right-click the property value and select Clear Property.

Default Subfield Delimiter   The Default Subfield Delimiter property is only available for the root node of a specification where the Standard property has been set to CUSTOM. The value of this property is used to determine a default character that marks the beginning or end of a subfield in a flat-file document where the Structure property on the Parse tab has been set to Delimited. Sometimes, when a document has records that are delimited, a field may actually contain multiple items of data. If that is the case, then each individual data component can be called a subfield. For example, if we wanted to store the name, telephone number, and date of birth of a customer, we might encode the information in a delimited text field as follows:

```
CUSTFred Smith, 555 2121, 10-05-1965
CUSTNaomi Turner, 555 3232, 30-07-1972
```

In the preceding data, we are using a carriage return (CR) as the record delimiter, and a comma (,) as the field delimiter with an *infix* field order. That is, the delimiter appears only between the fields, rather than before or after each field. To separate out the individual parts of the date of birth, we can store it as a self-contained record within each customer record, and then store the day, month, and year of the date of birth as subfields, using a hyphen (-) as the subfield delimiter with an infix field order. Creating the specification in BizTalk Editor and testing the preceding sample data produces the output shown in Figure 4-8.

Once set, the default subfield delimiter character may then be referenced by the Delimiter Type property on the Parse tab for multiple records without having to be explicitly defined each time. The characters that are directly available are listed in Table 4-4. If another character is typed in the combo box, it will appear alongside its hex equivalent. Only single characters are allowed. If you have entered a value accidentally and wish to clear it, right-click the property value and select Clear Property.

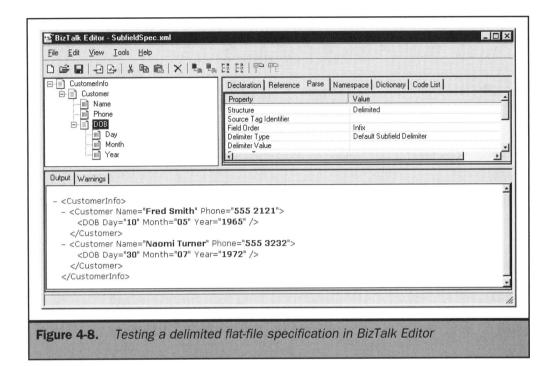

Figure 4-8. *Testing a delimited flat-file specification in BizTalk Editor*

Default Escape Character   The Default Escape Character property is only available for the root node of a specification where the Standard property has been set to CUSTOM. The value of this property is used to determine a character that prevents a literal character in the data from being incorrectly parsed as a delimiter. For example, if we had a comma-delimited flat-file containing contact information, it might contain a record like the following, with Name, Address, and Telephone fields:

```
Bill Gates, Big House?, Big Lake?, Seattle?, Washington?, USA,425-555-1212
```

In this case, the commas within the address are prefixed with a question mark because they should be treated as part of the data and not as delimiters.

This default character may then be referenced by the Escape Type property on the Parse tab for multiple records without having to be explicitly defined each time. The characters that are directly available are listed in Table 4-4. If another character is typed in the combo box, it will appear alongside its hex equivalent. Only single characters are allowed. If you have entered a value accidentally and wish to clear it, right-click the property value and select Clear Property.

Code Page   The Code Page property is only available for the root node of a specification where the Standard property has been set to CUSTOM. The value of this property is used to determine the character set in use within the document. BizTalk Server supports the following Unicode formats (UTF-16 only):

- Arabic (1256)
- Baltic (1257)
- Central-European (1250)
- Cyrillic (1251)
- Greek (1253)
- Hebrew (1255)
- Japanese-Shift-JIS (932)
- Korean (949)
- Little-Endian-UTF16 (1200)
- Simplified-Chinese-GBK (936)
- Thai (874)
- Traditional-Chinese-Big5 (950)
- Turkish (1254)
- Vietnamese (1258)
- Western-European (1252)

If no value is specified for the Code Page property, Western-European (1252) is assumed.

Receipt   The value of the Receipt property is used to indicate if the specification represents an inbound document generated automatically by a trading partner in response to an outbound document previously sent, or an outbound receipt that will be sent automatically in response to an inbound interchange from a trading partner. If the value of the Standard property on the Reference tab is set to X12, EDIFACT, or CUSTOM and the specification represents a receipt, then the value should be set to Yes.

If the value of the Standard property on the Reference tab is set to XML and the specification represents a receipt, then the value should be set to No. In this case, the *CanonicalReceipt* specification available in the WebDAV repository should be used, or a specification should be created based on it. Receiving and generating receipts will be covered in more detail in Chapters 6 and 8.

Envelope   The value of the Envelope property is used to indicate whether the specification will be used as a wrapper for an inbound or outbound interchange. Document interchanges that use a CUSTOM XML, FLATFILE, or CUSTOM envelope require an envelope specification. If an incoming interchange could contain multiple messages, then a separate envelope specification should be created, and the value of the Envelope property for that specification should be set to Yes. If every interchange will be a single document, then the document specification can be used for the envelope, and this property can be left at its default setting, No. Envelopes will be covered in more detail in Chapter 6.

Target Namespace   The value of the Target Namespace property is used to specify the default namespace for each document instance. This is typically used for documents contained in the body of a BizTalk Framework message. This property must be set to the actual namespace used in the document. It is important that this namespace should not begin with "x-schema:". Otherwise, the parser might attempt to validate the document by downloading an actual schema from the location specified after "x-schema:", which could cause the instance to fail validation.

Note   *Namespaces were discussed in Chapter 2.*

Minimum Occurrences   The Minimum Occurrences property is available for any record node, and the value entered is used to determine the minimum number of times that a record must appear (in that location) in an instance document. It corresponds to the *minOccurs* attribute on an *element* reference in an XDR schema. Because of its use in XDR, the only values it can contain are 0 and 1.

Caution   *When you create a new field, its value is set to 0; but if the value is cleared in the specification, it will default to 1.*

Maximum Occurrences   The Maximum Occurrences property is available for any record node, and the value entered is used to determine the maximum number of times that a record can appear (in that location) in an instance document. It corresponds to the *maxOccurs* attribute on an *element* reference in an XDR schema. Because of its use in XDR, the only values it can contain are 1 and *, where * represents multiple occurrences.

Caution   *When you create a new field, its value is set to 1; but if the value is cleared in the specification, it will still default to 1.*

Required   The Required property is available for any field node, and the value entered is used to determine whether that field must exist in an instance document. If the Type property for the field has been set to Attribute on the Declaration tab, the Required property corresponds to the *required* attribute on an *attribute* reference in an XDR schema. If the Type property for the field has been set to Element on the Declaration tab, the Required property corresponds to *minOccurs="1"* and *maxOccurs="1"* attributes on an *element* reference in an XDR schema.

The possible values for the Required property are Yes and No, and the property behaves differently depending on how the Type property of the field has been set. If the field is configured as an attribute, and the value of the Required property is set to Yes, then any value specified in the Default property on the Declaration tab is the value that must be present in that field for all document instances. If the property is set to No, then the field does not have to be present in a document instance, but any value specified in the Default property on the Declaration tab will be inserted into each document instance that does not explicitly contain that field. If the field is configured as an element, there is no Default property available on the Reference tab, so it is a simple case of whether the field should be present or not.

Start Position   The Start Position property is only available for field nodes in a specification where the Structure property of the parent record has been set to Positional on the Parse tab. The value of this property is used to indicate the character position of the beginning of a data field within a positional record.

End Position   The End Position property is only available for field nodes in a specification where the Structure property of the parent record has been set to Positional on the Parse tab. The value of this property is used to indicate the character position of the end of a data field within a positional record.

Calculate Field Positions   Calculate Field Positions is not a property—rather it is a command that is available on the context menu of a record where the Structure property on the Parse tab has been set to Positional. It is used to ease the process of entering Start Position and End Position values on the Reference tab by figuring out where each start and end character needs to be, based on the Maximum Length property configured on the Declaration tab. To calculate field positions automatically, do the following:

1. For each field in the positional record, set the value of the Maximum Length property on the Declaration tab to the length of the field.

2. When the value has been entered for every field in the record, right-click the record and select Calculate Field Positions.

3. Now click the Reference tab—the appropriate values have been added to the Start Position and End Position properties for each field.

Note   *If a positional record contains a number of fields and a positional child record, the start and end positions of the fields in the child record are also calculated. However, the start and end positions of any fields that occur after the child record are not calculated.*

> **Note**   *If the Source Tag Identifier and Source Tag Position properties on the Parse tab have been set, the length and position of the source tag for the record will be taken into account when calculating the field positions. For example, if the value of the Source Tag Identifier property is ABC and the value of the Source Tag Position property is 1, then the Start Position property of the first record will be set to 4 and all other positions will be calculated based on that.*

Parse Tab

The Parse tab, shown next, is used to set properties for flat-file specifications that have the value of the Standard property on the Reference tab set to X12, EDIFACT, or CUSTOM. These properties are used by the X12, EDIFACT, or Flat-File parser to correctly extract the records and fields from incoming documents, or by the corresponding serializer to construct outgoing documents. All of these properties are BizTalk Server specific, having no equivalent representation in XDR.

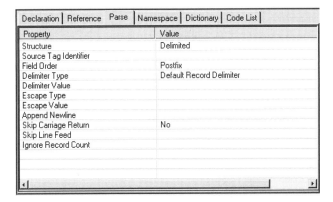

Structure   The Structure property is available for the root node and all record nodes. The value of this property determines the format of the corresponding record in a flat-file document instance. If the Standard property on the Reference tab is set to CUSTOM, then the available values are Delimited and Positional, but the value may only be set to Delimited for a record if the value of the Structure property for the parent record is also set to Delimited. If the Standard property on the Reference tab is set to X12 or EDIFACT, then the Structure property defaults to Delimited and cannot be changed.

Source Tag Identifier   The Source Tag Identifier property is available for the root node and all record nodes. The value of this property determines the characters that indicate the beginning of the record. These values are typically used in EDI documents, but you may also need them for a custom flat-file specification. For example, in the following line from an X12 850 Purchase Order, "DTM" indicates the beginning of the Date/Time Reference record, so "DTM" should be set as the value of the Source Tag Identifier property.

```
DTM*999*20010422~
```

> **Note** *The value of this property is case sensitive.*

Source Tag Position   The Source Tag Position property is available for the root node and all record nodes where the Structure property has been set to Positional. The value of this property indicates where the characters that indicate the beginning of the record may be found. If this property is required, its value will typically be set to 1. However, there may be situations where these characters will be found in the middle of a positional record, and the position will have to be set accordingly.

Field Order   The Field Order property is available for the root node and all record nodes where the Structure property has been set to Delimited. The value of this property determines the location of the delimiter characters. The values available are Prefix, Postfix, and Infix. *Prefix* means the delimiter appears before the record or field, *postfix* means it appears after the record or field, and *infix* means that the delimiter only appears in between records or fields.

For example, both EDIFACT and X12 documents use a delimited structure, so the first record in an X12 850 Purchase Order might be the following:

```
BEG*00*SA*6682946X**20010113~
```

Here, BEG is the source tag identifier, and * is the delimiter that occurs before each field, so we would set the value of the Field Order property to be Prefix for each BEG record. In the example, the second-last field is empty, so there are two asterisks in front of the final field (representing the date). At the end of each line, there is a tilde character (~), which is used to delimit each record, so we would set the value of the Field Order property to be Postfix for the root node.

Comma-separated values files provide an example of infix delimiters. In the following example, the comma character (,) does not prefix each field nor does it postfix each field—it occurs between the three fields, so we would set the value of the Field Order property to be Infix for each record:

```
"Ted Crilly", "Craggy Island Parochial House", "Craggy Island"
```

Delimiter Type   The Delimiter Type property is available for the root node and all record nodes where the Structure property has been set to Delimited. The value of this property indicates what type of delimiter to use for the records or fields contained by this record. For EDI-based specifications, the values available are Default Record Delimiter, Default Field Delimiter, and Default Subfield Delimiter, although it is strongly recommended that you do not change the delimiter type from its default when creating an EDI specification. Whichever value the property is set to, the value of the corresponding property as configured on the Reference tab will be used. For specifications where the Standard property on the Declaration tab is set to CUSTOM, the value Character is also available. If this is selected, then the actual delimiter character will also need to be selected using the Delimiter Value property directly underneath.

Delimiter Value   The Delimiter Value property is available for the root node and all record nodes where the Structure property has been set to Delimited and the Standard property on the Declaration tab has been set to CUSTOM. The value of this property should be set if the value of the Delimiter Type property is set to Character. It determines the character to use to delimit the records and fields contained by this record. The values that are directly available are listed in Table 4-4, although any single character can be typed into the field.

Escape Type   The Escape Type property is available for the root node and all record nodes where the Structure property has been set to Delimited, and the Standard property on the Declaration tab has been set to CUSTOM or EDIFACT. The value of this property determines a character that may occur in the data to indicate that the character immediately following it should be treated as data rather than as a delimiter. For custom flat-file specifications, the available values are Character and Default Escape Character. If the value is set to Character, then the character that will be used will need to be selected using the Escape Value property directly underneath. For EDIFACT documents, the only available value is Default Escape Character, so you might wonder why they included it at all for these specifications.

Escape Value   The Escape Value property is available for the root node and all record nodes where the Structure property has been set to Delimited and the Standard property on the Declaration tab has been set to CUSTOM. The value of this property should be set if the value of the Escape Type property has been set to Character. It determines the character to use to indicate that the immediately following character should be treated as data rather than as a delimiter. The values that are directly available are listed in Table 4-4, although any single character can be typed into the field.

Append Newline   The Append Newline property is available for the root node and all record nodes. It is used by the serializer to determine whether a line feed character (0x0A) should be placed at the end of each record when constructing an outgoing document. The available values are Yes and No, and the default value is No.

Skip Carriage Return   The Skip Carriage Return property is available for the root node and all record nodes. It is used by the parser to determine whether carriage-return characters found in incoming interchanges should be ignored. Often, carriage returns are inserted into documents for legibility but serve no other purpose. The available values are Yes and No, and the default value is Yes.

Note   *If you are creating a custom flat-file specification that uses carriage returns as record delimiters, you must set the value of this property to No, or else your record delimiters will not be recognized.*

Skip Line Feed   The Skip Line Feed property is available for the root node and all record nodes. It is used by the parser to determine whether line-feed characters found in incoming interchanges should be ignored. Again, line feeds are sometimes inserted to improve legibility, and they can be safely skipped unless used explicitly as a delimiter. Also, Windows-based applications sometimes insert a carriage-return line-feed combination rather than just a carriage return, so this may also cause spurious line-feed characters. The available values are Yes and No, and the default value is Yes.

Ignore Record Count   The Ignore Record Count property is available for the root node and all record nodes. It is used by the parser to determine whether this record should not be included in the total number of records. The available values are Yes and No, and the default value is Yes. The number of records in a document instance should always match the number of records in the specification, or else the document might be considered invalid. For example, if a record in a document itself contains records that may occur multiple times, such as an Item record, then the Ignore Record Count property should be set to Yes, as each item should not contribute to the overall record total.

Custom Data Type   The Custom Data Type property is available for all field nodes. It is used to specify the type of data that the field will contain. If the value of the Standard property on the Declaration tab is set to X12 or CUSTOM, then the following values are available:

Data Type	Description
String (AN)	Alphanumeric string
String (ID)	String for identification
Date (CY)	Date for four-digit fields
Date (DT)	Date
Time (TM)	Time
Number (D0–D4)	Decimal number with 0 to 4 decimal places
Number (N)	Integer
Number (N0–N9)	Decimal number with 0 to 9 decimal places where decimal point is implied
Number (R)	Real number
Number (R0–R9)	Real number with 0 to 9 decimal places
Binary Hexadecimal (B)	Binary data expressed in hexadecimal

If the value of the Standard property on the Declaration tab is set to EDIFACT, then only the String (AN) and Number (N) values are available. If the value of the Custom Data Type property is set to Date (CY), Date (DT), or Time (TM), then the format for the data must be selected using the Custom Date/Time Format property immediately following.

Custom Date/Time Format   The Custom Date/Time Format property is available for all field nodes. It is used to specify the format for dates or times that will appear in the field if the value of the Custom Data Type property is set to Date (CY), Date (DT), or Time (TM).

Caution

BizTalk Server Service Pack 1 must be installed if you need to represent fractions of a second in a field containing time information in an X12 document. In this case, the supported time format for X12 documents is HHMMSSDD, where HH represents hours between 00 and 23, MM represents minutes between 00 and 59, SS represents seconds between 00 and 59, and DD represents either tenths of a second between 0 and 9, or hundredths of a second between 00 and 99. If you use the HHMMSSss format, or any of its variations, you will receive a validation error with X12 documents that use fractions of a second. This custom time format is actually stored as a string, because XML does not support fractions of a second for time formats.

Justification   The Justification property is available for all field nodes. The value of this property is typically used in positional files to indicate whether the data in the field is to be found at the left or right of the field if the number of characters that form the data is less than the minimum length. It may also be used in delimited files for the same purpose, but this would not be as common. The available values are Left and Right, and the default value is Left. If the number of characters in the data is less than the minimum field length, a pad character is typically employed to fill the remaining field spaces.

Pad Character   The Pad Character property is available for all field nodes. The value of this property is used to indicate a character that may exist in a field only to bring the total number of characters up to a certain minimum length. In this way, the parser can ignore these characters in incoming documents, and the serializer can insert them for outgoing documents. The values that are directly available are listed in Table 4-4, although any single character can be typed into the field. If this value is required for a particular type of document, it will also be important to specify whether the data will be found at the left or right of the field by setting the value of the Justification property.

Wrap Character   The Wrap Character property is available for all field nodes where the value of the Structure property for the parent record has been set to Delimited. The value of this property is used to indicate the character that will appear immediately before and immediately after the data in the field. In this way, it is possible to use a delimiter character as an actual data character without the parser misinterpreting it. For example, if we had a comma-separated values file containing the following record,

```
"Bill Gates","Big House, Big Lake, Seattle, Washington, USA","425-555-1212"
```

the double quote would serve as the wrap character, ensuring that the commas within the address field were treated as data rather than as delimiters. The values that are directly available are listed in Table 4-4, although any single character can be typed into the field.

Note *If a field contains a character that has been configured as a wrap character for the field, it must itself be wrapped in another pair of wrap characters. For example, "Bill """Microsoft""" Gates" would be required to represent "Bill "Microsoft" Gates."*

Minimum Length with Pad Character   The Minimum Length with Pad Character property is available for all field nodes where the value of the Structure property for the parent record has been set to Delimited. The value of this property is used to indicate how many pad characters should be inserted into an outgoing document by the serializer when the number of data characters in the field is less than a certain value. For example, in a delimited file, we might have the constraint that the data in the telephone number field needs to be at least seven characters. However, there might be another constraint imposed by the receiving application that the field itself must consist of ten characters. In this case, we could set the Minimum Length with Pad Character property to 10 to tell the serializer to insert three pad characters to fulfill this criterion. A value cannot be entered into the Minimum Length with Pad Character property until the value of the Pad Character property has been set.

Custom Maximum Length   The Custom Maximum Length property is available for all field nodes where the value of the Standard property on the Reference tab is set to X12, and the value of the Custom Data Type on the Parse tab is set to Number (N), Number (Nx), Number (R), or Number (Rx). The value of this property is used to indicate how many characters a numeric field can have in an X12 document. This is important because some newer X12 specification types allow characters such as plus signs (+) or decimal points (.) to be included in a numeric field, but those characters should not be treated as numeric digits. For example, if a field should only contain six digits, but there may also be a minus sign and a decimal point in the data, you should set the value of this property to be 8.

Note *This property is only available in BizTalk Editor if BizTalk Server Service Pack 1 is installed.*

Namespace Tab

The Namespace tab, shown next, contains references to namespaces used in the specification. By default, three namespaces are already declared:

Prefix	URI
(default)	urn:schemas-microsoft-com:xml-data
b	urn:schemas-microsoft-com:BizTalkServer
d	urn:schemas-microsoft-com:datatypes

Earlier I mentioned that custom annotations could be added to records and fields on the Declaration or Reference tabs. These custom annotations must exist in a namespace separate from those used by BizTalk Server, so this namespace must be declared on the Namespace tab, like the one that follows. If you add a custom annotation, the namespace prefix you use will be added to the list on the Namespace tab so that you only have to add the URI. If a SQL annotation is added to a record or field, then the prefix "sql" is added to the Namespace tab, complete with a URI of urn:schemas-microsoft-com:xml-sql.

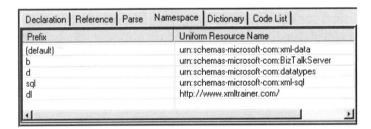

Dictionary Tab

The Dictionary tab is used to set routing properties within a document specification. Whenever a document is submitted to BizTalk Server, the Messaging Service needs to know how the document should be processed. This is done by creating a messaging channel that will determine the source organization from which the document came, the type of document received, how that document should be transformed, and the *messaging port* that should be used to deliver the document to its destination.

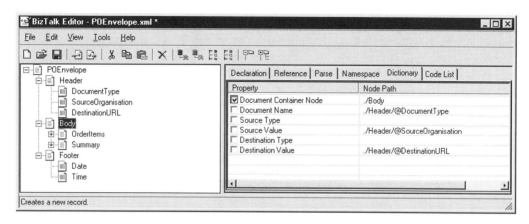

There are a number of different ways in which a document may be submitted to BizTalk Server. It can be done programmatically from an application or an Active Server Page (ASP), from a file or message queuing receive function, or from an Orchestration schedule. In each case we can specify the name of the channel to use, so this is called *static routing*, as the same channel will always be used for the same type of document.

Note	*Configuring messaging channels and ports will be covered in Chapter 6, submitting documents from an Orchestration schedule will be covered in Chapter 7, creating and managing receive functions will be covered in Chapter 9, and submitting documents programmatically will be covered in Chapter 16.*

However, sometimes we will want a document to be processed differently depending on the organization from which it was received, the organization to which it will be sent, or the type of document it is. If each document is to be considered individually, then the information we need must be present in the document itself or the envelope in which the document is wrapped, so the document is called *self-routing*. For a self-routing document, we cannot know in advance which channel will be used to process the document, so whichever method we use to submit the document, we will not specify the name of a channel. Only by looking inside the document can BizTalk Server decide which channel should be used. As a result, it must know where to look in the document for this routing information. Each property on the Dictionary tab (no, I don't know why it was called that, either) can be associated with a particular record or field in the document specification. Dictionary properties can only be set for specifications where the Standard property on the Reference tab has been set to XML or CUSTOM.

Document Container Node   The Document Container Node property can only be selected for the root node or a record node. It is used to specify the part of an incoming document instance that actually represents business data. It is possible that when a document is submitted to BizTalk Server, it is wrapped in an envelope that also contains header or footer information that is used for routing purposes or to provide metadata. By selecting the Document Container Node property for a particular record, we are telling BizTalk Server where to find the actual document within the envelope. This is done by setting the value of the node to an XPath expression representing the position of the record within the document. Luckily, we don't have to type the XPath expression ourselves. Simply selecting the check box causes the XPath expression for that record to be entered into the Node Path field automatically.

Although the property is available for all specification types, setting the Document Container Node property has no effect for specifications where the value of the Standard property on the Reference tab is set to CUSTOM. It is provided in case it is required by specifications used with custom parser components.

Document Name   The Document Name property can only be selected for a field. It is used to specify which field in a document instance contains the name of a BizTalk Messaging document definition. A *document definition* is an object created in BizTalk Messaging Manager to represent a type of document that will be sent or received by BizTalk Server. The creation and use of document definitions will be covered in Chapter 6. Selecting the Document Name check box (shown next) will cause the XPath expression representing the position of that field in the document to be entered into the Node Path field.

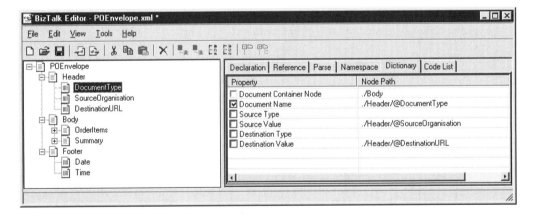

Source Type   The Source Type property can only be selected for a field. It is used to specify the field in a document instance that will contain the type of identifier that BizTalk Server should use to select the Organization from which the document came. In BizTalk Messaging, it is possible to create Organizations that represent your trading partners. These Organizations can be identified in a number of ways. The default is to use the name of the Organization, which is a property called OrganizationName. If this is the case, OrganizationName is called the *Identifier Qualifier*, meaning the type of identifier. Whatever the identifier is set equal to will be the *Identifier Value*.

We will see in Chapter 6 that it is possible to use other types of identifier, such a Dun & Bradstreet number or a telephone number. Either way, the Identifier Qualifier is the type of identifier in use, and the Identifier Value is the value of that identifier. If we wish to define a field in our document that contains the Identifier Qualifier that signifies the organization from which the document was sent, we should select the Source Type check box for that field. This causes the XPath expression representing the position of that field in the document to be entered into the Node Path field.

Source Value   The Source Value property (shown next) can only be selected for a field. It is used to specify the field in a document instance that will contain the Identifier Value corresponding to the Identifier Qualifier referenced by the Source Type property. Selecting this property causes the XPath expression representing the position of that field in the document to be entered into the Node Path. If a field has this property selected, but there is no field for which the Source Type property is selected, then it is assumed that the OrganizationName qualifier is being used.

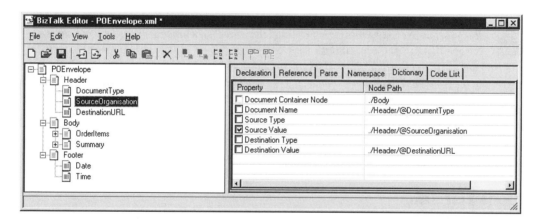

Destination Type   The Destination Type property can only be selected for a field. It is used to specify the field in a document instance that will contain the Identifier Qualifier that BizTalk Server should use to select the destination organization. The value of the identifier will then be in the Destination Value property. If a field has this property selected, the XPath expression corresponding to the position of that field in the document is entered into the Node Path.

Destination Value   The Destination Value property (shown next) can only be selected for a field. It is used to specify the field in a document instance that will contain the Identifier Value corresponding to the Identifier Qualifier referenced by the Destination Type property. Selecting this property for a field causes the XPath expression corresponding to the position of that field to be entered into the Node Path. If a field has this property selected, but there is no field for which the Destination Type property is selected, then it is assumed that the OrganizationName qualifier is being used.

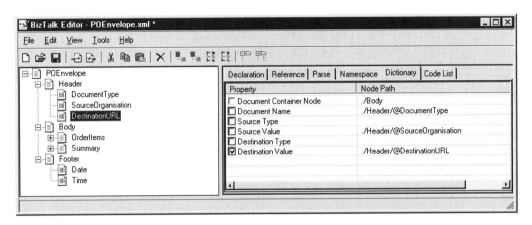

Note

It is possible to create a messaging channel that directs documents toward a port that has been configured as Open. In this case, the destination and transport information is not configured explicitly in the port, but is provided instead when the document is submitted or in the document itself. For example, if a document is self-routing such that it has fields that identify a source organization and a document type, this should be enough to select the appropriate channel. If that channel in turn uses an open port, then the Destination Value property can be used to select a field in the document that contains a URL with the destination details. The URL (by definition) will contain both the transport method to be used (for example, HTTP) and the location to which it should be sent.

Code List Tab

The Code List tab, shown next, is only used with EDI specifications. When an X12 or EDIFACT specification is open in BizTalk Editor, selecting certain fields in the specification causes the list of available codes for that field to be displayed on the Code List tab. Not all codes can be used in all fields, so the list of codes is different depending on the type of document specification you are creating and the field you have selected. If you want to constrain an EDI specification, you can select certain codes for a given field, so that only documents whose fields contain values selected on the Code List tab will validate.

Setting a code property for a given field will cause the value of the Data Type property on the Declaration tab to be set to Enumeration. Also, the Data Type Values property will contain a space-separated list of the codes that have been selected. The full set of available codes for each field in each specification version is available as a Microsoft Access database at \Program Files\Microsoft BizTalk Server\XML Tools\Databases\CodeLists\CodeListsX12a.mdb.

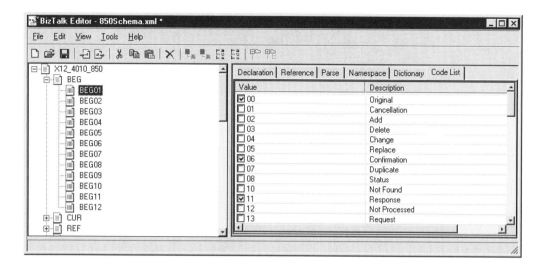

Importing, Exporting, and Testing Specifications

As we have seen, depending on the complexity of the specification you are building, there are plenty of properties that may need to be configured when you are creating a blank specification from scratch. If you are creating a new XML, X12, or EDIFACT specification, you will typically be deleting nodes you don't need or changing the properties of the ones you do need. However, it is also possible to create a specification by importing an existing file. The type of file you import can be a well-formed XML document instance, a DTD, or an XDR schema, as shown in Figure 4-9. You can also export a specification as an XDR schema, create a sample document instance, or validate an existing document instance.

Importing Files

To ease the process of creating a specification, you can import an existing file. This may be because you already have an example of the type of file that the specification should represent, or because you have an existing DTD or schema that contains the structure you are trying to model.

Importing Well-Formed XML Instances

To create a specification based on an instance document, choose Tools | Import. This will call up the Select Import Module dialog box, shown in Figure 4-9. Select Well-Formed XML Instance and click OK. If the document is indeed well-formed, the specification tree will appear in the left pane showing the structure of the document. This can then be saved or stored to the WebDAV repository in the normal way.

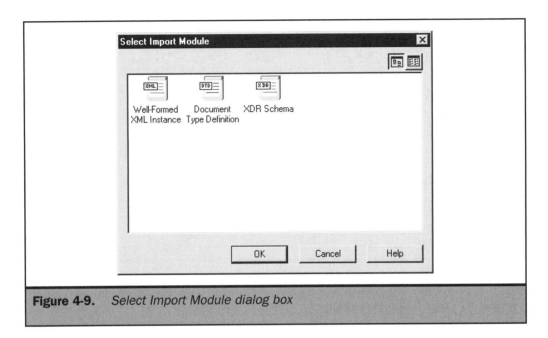

Figure 4-9. *Select Import Module dialog box*

There are some limitations to the way BizTalk Editor imports well-formed XML. First, if the instance contains elements or attributes that have namespace prefixes, the namespace prefixes are converted to text characters separated from the local name of the element or attribute by an underscore. Second, if the instance has any elements that have both child elements and child text nodes, the child text nodes are discarded. This is because BizTalk Editor does not support the Mixed content model.

> **Note** *If the document instance has a default namespace declared on the root element, that namespace is entered into the value of the Target Namespace property on the Reference tab.*

Importing DTDs

To create a specification based on an existing DTD, choose Tools | Import. Select Document Type Definition in the Select Import Module dialog box and click OK. The document specification can then be saved or stored as normal.

Again, there are limitations to the way BizTalk Editor imports DTDs. First, if the DTD contains comments within element definitions, the DTD cannot be imported. You will need to edit the DTD to remove these comments first. Second, if the DTD contains attributes of type ENTITY, ENTITIES, NMTOKEN, or NMTOKENS, the Data Type property on the Declaration tab will not be set for those fields. Finally, if the DTD contains attributes of type NOTATION, the value of the Data Type property on the Declaration tab will be set to Enumeration.

Importing XDR Schemas

To create a specification based on an existing XDR schema, choose Tools | Import. Select XDR Schema in the Select Import Module dialog box and click OK. The document specification can then be saved or stored as normal.

If the XDR schema contains attributes of type ENTITY, ENTITIES, or NOTATION, the schemas cannot be imported. Similarly, if the schema contains attributes of type NMTOKEN or NMTOKENS, the value of the Data Type property on the Declaration tab will not be set for these fields.

Exporting Files

When you have created your specification, you can export it as an XDR schema for use in an XML-based application or as a document instance to test how the specification functions when used in BizTalk Messaging. Because BizTalk specifications are themselves XDR schemas with extra information, exporting a specification based on an X12, EDIFACT, or CUSTOM standard will not retain all the configuration details.

Exporting an XDR Schema

To export an XDR schema, simply select Tools | Export XDR Schema. In the dialog box that appears (shown next) type a filename and an encoding scheme and click Save.

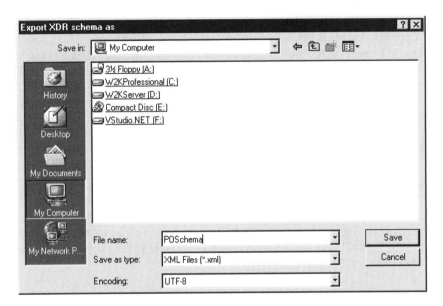

Creating a Document Instance

To create an instance of a specification, simply select Tools | Create XML Instance. Type a filename for the instance and click Save.

Testing Specifications

After you have created a specification, it is important to test it before deploying it in a production environment. You can validate the specification itself to see whether there are any errors, such as incorrectly configured properties or undeclared namespaces, and you can validate an instance document to see whether the specification corresponds to the type of documents it's meant to represent.

Validating Specifications

To test a specification, simply press F5 on the keyboard or select Tools | Validate Specification. Any warnings or errors generated will be displayed on the Warnings tab.

Double-clicking an error on the Warnings tab (shown next) will highlight the node that contains the error in red.

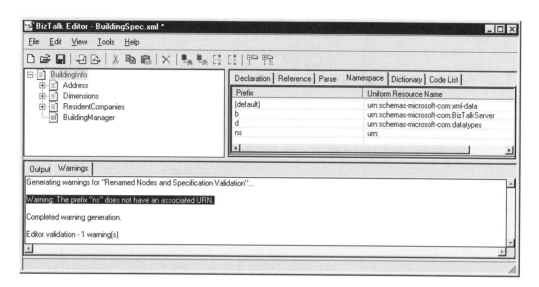

Validating Document Instances

To test a document instance to see whether it conforms to the structure laid out in a specification, select Tools | Validate Document Instance, and browse for the file you wish to validate. If the specification is based on X12 or EDIFACT, the Document Delimiters dialog box will appear, as shown in Figure 4-10.

Note   *If you are validating an instance of an EDIFACT specification, the Document Delimiters dialog box will also contain a field in which you can select the Default Escape Character.*

For each delimiter type, select an appropriate delimiter from the drop-down menu, or type it into the field. Click OK to test the document instance. If the specification is based on an XML or CUSTOM standard, the Document Delimiters dialog box will not be displayed.

If there is a problem with the document instance, the errors will be displayed on the Warnings tab. If the document instance successfully validates, the XML format to which it has been converted will be displayed on the Output tab. Figure 4-11 shows an X12 Purchase Order specification instance in BizTalk Editor after it has been successfully validated.

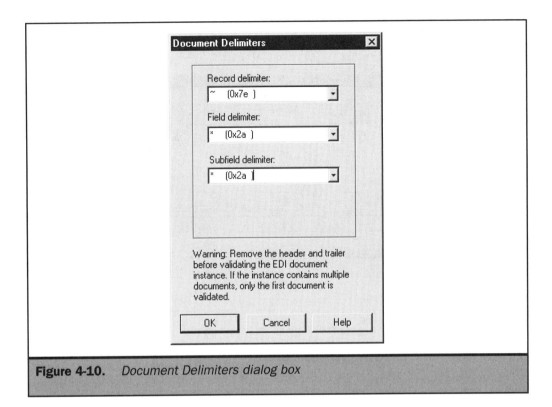

Figure 4-10. *Document Delimiters dialog box*

Note *If you attempt to validate an XML document instance that has a schema attached using the xmlns attribute with a value beginning "x-schema", the instance will be validated against the schema specified in the attribute rather than against the specification.*

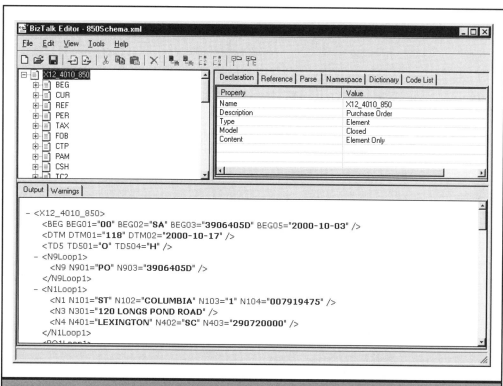

Figure 4-11.   *An X12 850 document instance validated in BizTalk Editor*

Caution   *To validate X12 or EDIFACT instances, you must first remove any interchange, group, or envelope records from the header and footer of the document.*

Chapter 5

Using BizTalk Mapper

izTalk Server facilitates business-to-business (B2B) e-commerce by allowing
trading partners to exchange documents even if they use different standards and
formats. In the previous chapter, we saw that BizTalk Editor represents each type
of document as a *specification,* which is a set of rules that allows a document structure to
be represented as XML. This is important, because BizTalk Server converts everything to
XML for internal use, regardless of the types of document being exchanged. Incoming
documents are converted to XML after they have been received by BizTalk Server, and
outgoing documents are converted from XML into the format required by an application
or trading partner. It should be obvious, therefore, that we will need some way of
mapping one XML syntax to another if these structures don't match.

In Chapter 2, we saw that one of the main advantages of XML is that documents can
be transformed from one structure to another using the Extensible Stylesheet Language
for Transformation (XSLT). This language is designed to convert between different
XML syntaxes in a clear and unambiguous manner while retaining as much or as little
of the original data as required. For our business interchanges, we will therefore need
appropriate stylesheets to transform different document specifications. BizTalk Mapper
is a graphical, extensible application that simplifies the process of creating these stylesheets
by linking records and fields between source and destination specifications. The
stylesheet, or map, produced in this way can then be used by BizTalk Messaging to
transform document specifications, regardless of the disparities between them.

Creating Specification Maps

When BizTalk Server receives incoming documents, they are parsed into XML using a
document specification. When outgoing documents are being sent, they are serialized
from XML into the format required by the destination organization. If the structures of
the documents being exchanged do not match, then the internal XML representations
also will not match. For example, Figure 5-1 shows what happens if BizTalk Server
accepts an EDI X12 purchase order, but needs to send out a flat-file invoice. Because
the internal XML structures that BizTalk Server uses to model these formats will be
completely different, a map is needed to determine how one structure is transformed
into another.

BizTalk Mapper is an application that allows you to transform one document
format into another by creating links between the records and fields in the corresponding
document specifications. When you have created links between records and fields in
the source and destination specifications, you can compile the links into a map file
that contains an XSLT stylesheet, and store the map file in the BizTalk Server WebDAV
Repository. When incoming documents need to be restructured before sending them
to an application or external trading partner, the map can be invoked by BizTalk
Messaging to effect the transformation.

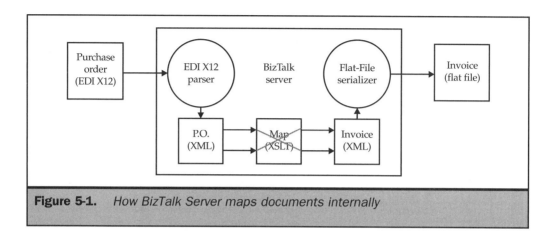

Figure 5-1.   *How BizTalk Server maps documents internally*

BizTalk Mapper Concepts

You create a BizTalk map file by linking records and fields in a source specification to corresponding records and fields in a destination specification. The complete map file contains information about each specification, as well as the XSLT stylesheet needed to transform a document instance. Because the data will usually be found in the fields of the document, most of the links you create will be field-to-field links. The map file will usually take care of transforming the parent records automatically, but for more sophisticated mappings, you may also need to create record-to-record links.

Map Structure

Figure 5-2 shows a BizTalk map file opened in Internet Explorer. It's quite a big file, and some of the nodes have been collapsed to allow it to fit inside a browser window, but the important parts of the structure are still visible. The first thing that you should notice is that it is an XML document. As we have said, everything BizTalk Server does internally uses XML where possible, and a map file is no exception. Table 5-1 lists the elements that are visible and their purposes. Because BizTalk Mapper creates map files automatically, it is not necessary to discuss the structure in too much detail, as you should never have to directly edit a map file yourself.

One element that is not visible in Figure 5-2, but is used frequently in map files, is msxsl:script. This element is not part of the official XSLT language, but instead is an extension from Microsoft that allows VBScript to be embedded in the map. In this way, anything that can be done in VBScript, including creating and using COM objects, is possible within a map. We will see later how this is used to add powerful transformation features to the map.

Transforming Specifications

Every document specification consists of a hierarchy of records and fields. The fields are grouped within records, which may, in turn, be grouped within other records, and

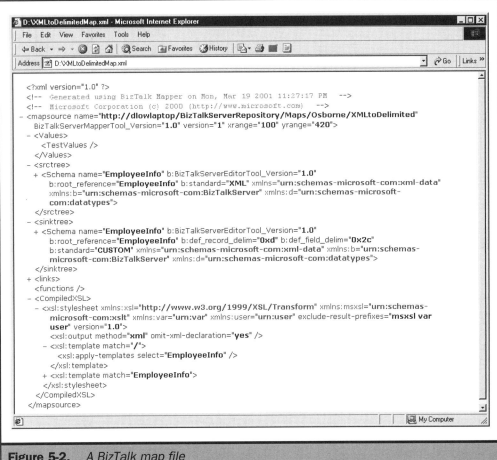

Figure 5-2. A BizTalk map file

Element	Description
mapsource	The *mapsource* element is the root element of the map file, within which every other element is contained. It specifies name and version information.

Table 5-1. The Main Elements in a BizTalk Map File

Element	Description
Values	The *Values* element contains any values that have been directly entered into the source specification in BizTalk Mapper for testing purposes.
srctree	The *srctree* element acts as a container for the source specification, i.e., the specification that determines the format of an incoming document.
Schema	The *Schema* element is the root element of a document specification. An instance of this element will appear directly underneath both the *srctree* and *sinktree* elements, as that is where the specification data is saved.
sinktree	The *sinktree* element acts as a container for the destination specification, i.e., the specification that determines the format of an outgoing document.
links	The *links* element contains a list of all the links that have been established between the records and fields in the specifications. Links to functoids are also listed, but compiler links are not.
functions	The *functions* element contains a list of the functoids that are used in the map, if any. Each *function* child element contains information about a particular functoid, such as type and parameter values.
CompiledXSL	The *CompiledXSL* element acts as a container for the XSLT stylesheet that actually implements the transformation.
xsl:stylesheet	The xsl:stylesheet element is the root element of an XSLT stylesheet. It contains the required XSLT namespace and *version* attribute, along with BizTalk-specific namespaces used to define functoids.
xsl:template	The xsl:template element defines a stylesheet template. Each template has a *match* attribute containing an XPath expression, such that the template will be invoked if the XPath expression is satisfied by the source document. The first template will always contain a *match* attribute consisting of a single forward slash (/) to represent the root of the source document.

Table 5-1.   *The Main Elements in a BizTalk Map File* (continued)

Element	Description
xsl:apply-templates	The xsl:apply-templates element invokes other templates that match nodes relative to the current context, as specified by the *select* attribute. The template invoked for the matching node-set will typically contain further *xsl:apply-templates* instructions that recursively map the rest of the source document.

Table 5-1.   *The Main Elements in a BizTalk Map File* (continued)

so on, up to the root node of the specification. In the specification hierarchy shown in Figure 5-3, there is a root node called *EmployeeInfo* containing a record called *Details*, which itself contains fields called *Name, Department, Email,* and *Extension.* Each of these fields will hold data. If we want the value contained in each field to be mapped to the fields called *EmpName, EmpEmailAlias, EmpPhone,* and *EmpDivision* in the specification shown in Figure 5-4, we will need to create links from each source field to each destination field.

The destination specification in Figure 5-4 also has a containing record called *EmpInfo,* and it, in turn, is contained in a root node called *EmpData.* However, although we require that a root node called *EmpData* should exist in the destination document and that there should be a record called *EmpInfo* for each *Details* record in the source document, we do not need to explicitly map the root nodes or the containing records.

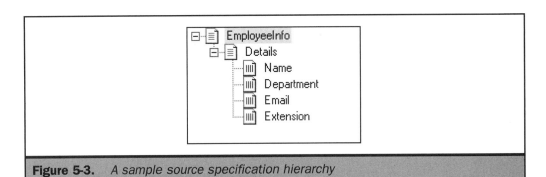

Figure 5-3.   *A sample source specification hierarchy*

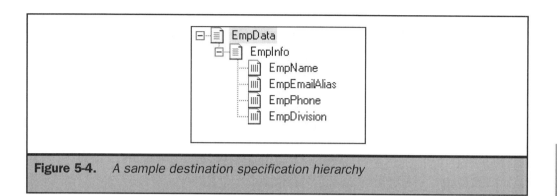

Figure 5-4. *A sample destination specification hierarchy*

As we will see, BizTalk Mapper understands the hierarchy of nodes that must exist and creates these links automatically. Figure 5-5 shows how the links created manually in BizTalk Mapper are shown as solid lines, and the links created by the application are shown as dotted lines.

BizTalk Mapper Environment

When you are working with a map in BizTalk Mapper, you can see both the source and destination specifications, and a mapping grid where the links between records and fields are displayed graphically. You can also view a subset of the properties of each specification and the output generated when the map is compiled or tested. The BizTalk Mapper interface is shown in Figure 5-6.

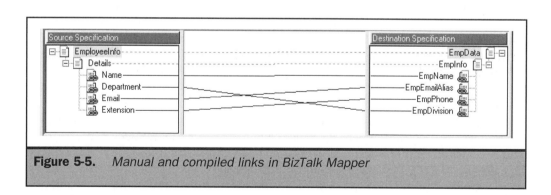

Figure 5-5. *Manual and compiled links in BizTalk Mapper*

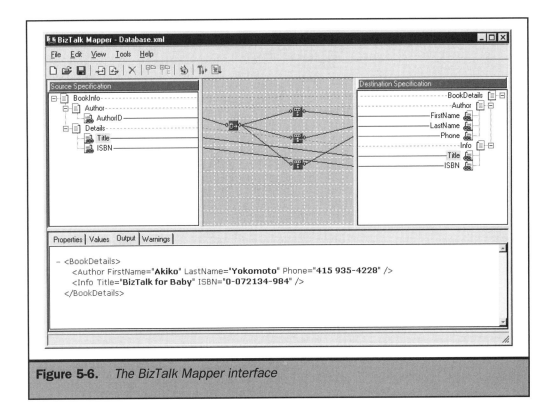

Figure 5-6. *The BizTalk Mapper interface*

Specification Panes

To create a new map in BizTalk Mapper, you will need two specifications—a *source* specification and a *destination* specification. Each of these is visible in Figure 5-6. The source specification always appears on the left and the destination specification, on the right. The structure of each specification looks exactly as it did in BizTalk Editor, as a collapsible hierarchy of records and fields.

Mapping Grid

The gray rectangle between the specifications is known as the *mapping grid*. This area is where links between fields will be displayed, showing how the source document structure will be transformed into a destination document structure. This is also the region where *functoids* are placed. As we will see later, functoids allow more complex actions to be performed rather than just direct field-to-field mapping. For example, we might wish to concatenate the values of two or more fields in a source document and store the result in a single field in the destination document.

The mapping grid is actually an extremely large area, and what is visible on the screen at any one time is only a small portion of it. If you move the mouse toward any edge of the grid, the cursor will turn into a large white arrow (shown next). Holding down the mouse button will cause the mapping grid to pan in the selected direction. You can also zoom out and see the entire mapping grid by selecting View | Grid Preview. This can be useful if you are working with a complicated map that uses many different types of functoids that are linked together, or *cascaded*. The Grid Preview dialog box allows you to see the grid on a smaller scale, including any functoids that are present, and to jump quickly to another section of the mapping grid.

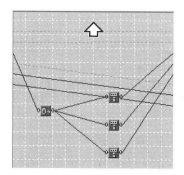

Mapper Tabs

At the bottom of the BizTalk Mapper interface, there are four tabs that can display information about a specification or a map, or that can allow you to enter values for the purpose of testing a compiled map.

Properties Tab   The Properties tab shows a list of properties that have been configured on the Declaration, Reference, and Parse tabs in BizTalk Editor. As a result, the properties displayed will vary, depending on the type of specification being viewed and the node that is currently selected. Note that it is not possible to edit the values displayed for any given property. If you wish to change any property, you will have to open the specification in BizTalk Editor and then reload it into BizTalk Mapper.

Values Tab   The Values tab allows you to enter test values for a source specification so that you can determine how a completed map will work. However, BizTalk Mapper does not have the functionality whereby you can load an instance of a document to see how it will be transformed (although so many people have complained about this, I imagine it will make an appearance in a service pack or future release). We will discuss testing a map later in this chapter.

Similarly, if there are fields in the destination specification that require constant values, these values may also be entered on the Values tab. This is not just for testing purposes, however. The values you enter here will actually be used by BizTalk Messaging when a map is invoked. This can be useful if you already know certain values in a document, such as the type of document it is or the source organization information (which may be your own organization).

Output Tab   The Output tab functions similarly to the Output tab in BizTalk Editor, showing the results of a compiled map or the transformation of test values. When you use the Compile Map command, the Output tab will show the XSLT stylesheet that was created to effect the transformation. As mentioned earlier, the XSLT stylesheet is only one part of a complete map file, but it is the only part displayed here. If you use the Test Map command, you will see the results of the transformation as applied to any test values entered on the Values tab, as BizTalk Mapper builds a sample destination document. Compiling and testing maps will be discussed in more detail later in the chapter.

Warnings Tab   The Warnings tab shows any warnings generated during the testing or compilation of a map. Typically, this may occur as a result of a mismatch between the data types of source and destination fields, or a functoid that does not have all the necessary inputs or outputs. In the former case, these warnings may not affect the actual use of the map; but in the latter case, the warning could be considered a fatal error because the map will not function correctly without the specified information.

Toolbars, Menus, and Options

The standard toolbar and menus contain the commands that you will work with as you create or modify a map. Most of the commands need no discussion as they are self-explanatory, or they will be discussed in further detail later in the chapter. On the standard toolbar, there are commands to create a new map, open an existing map, or save the current map. There are also commands to store a map to or retrieve a map from the WebDAV Repository. In addition, you can delete a selected link or functoid, expand or collapse a specification tree, and compile or test the map. There is also a button to bring up the *functoid palette,* which contains all built-in and custom functoids for use in a map. Functoids are discussed in depth later in this chapter.

The options in the various menus reflect the commands available on the toolbar, along with commands to replace source or destination specifications, change the viewing parameters, or display the entire mapping grid. The Tools menu also offers an Options command, which opens the BizTalk Mapper Options dialog box. The dialog box has two tabs—General and Colors.

General Tab   The General tab allows you to customize certain aspects of the behavior of BizTalk Mapper. The options and descriptions of their use are listed in Table 5-2.

Colors Tab   The Colors tab, shown after Table 5-2, allows you to set the colors used by BizTalk Mapper for various objects, links, and the grid. You can also reset the colors to the default.

Option	Default Setting	Description
Warnings for simple linking errors	Enabled	Displays a dialog box when a link between fields of differing data types is created.
View compiler links	Enabled	Shows links that BizTalk Mapper automatically generates between the parent records of linked fields. Turn this off if you are working with a large complicated map.
Clear compiler links after user action	Disabled	Removes compiler links (assuming the previous option is enabled) after a user action. Turn this on if you want to see compiler links after compilation, but not all the time.
Allow record content links	Disabled	Normally, only document fields will contain data, so you will only want to link fields to each other. However, if a document contains data in a record, you may need to turn this on. There are also functoids that make use of record links, but they will operate regardless of the setting of this option.
Allow multiple inputs to destination tree nodes	Disabled	Fields are usually linked in a one-to-one fashion, so a field in the destination specification should not need to accept multiple values. However, if there are fields in a source specification that are mutually exclusive, you should turn on this option to allow the value of whichever field is present to be passed to the destination.
Prompt to save before testing the map	Enabled	If you test a map by entering sample values, you will be asked to save changes to the map each time. Turn off this option to disable this behavior.

Table 5-2.   *Options on the General Tab of the BizTalk Mapper Options Dialog Box*

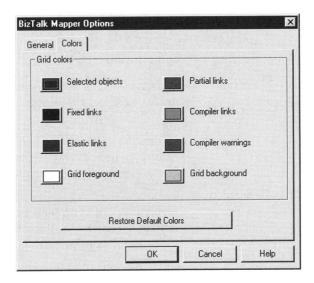

Creating a New Map

To create a new map, click the New button on the standard toolbar or choose File |
New. If you click the Open button on the toolbar or choose File | Open, you can open
a previously created map. Attempting to open a document specification, or any other
type of XML file, at this point will result in an error. If you are creating a new map,
you will be prompted to select the source specification you wish to transform, and the
destination specification to which it will be mapped.

Opening Specifications

After choosing to create a new map, you will be presented with the Select Source
Specification Type and Select Destination Specification Type dialog boxes. In each
dialog box, you can choose to open a specification from Local Files, which would be
any hard drive or network drive accessible from your computer; from Templates,
which will show a list of the XML and EDI formats shipped with BizTalk Server;
or from WebDAV Files, which is the BizTalk Server WebDAV Repository.

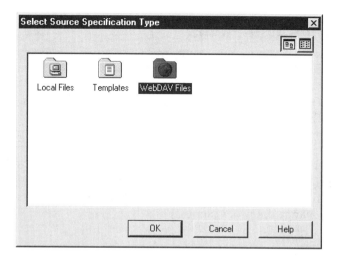

After you have opened each specification, the source specification will be displayed on the left, and the destination specification will be displayed on the right, as shown earlier in Figure 5-6.

Replacing Specifications

As mentioned, although parts of the BizTalk Mapper interface look similar to that of BizTalk Editor, it is not possible to make changes to a specification within the Mapper tool. If, during the course of creating a map, you realize that you need to make a change to the source or destination specifications (perhaps to rectify a mismatch between data types for linked fields), you will have to reopen the specification in BizTalk Editor and modify it there.

You do not need to close BizTalk Mapper or the map file itself to make the swap. After you have made the changes, simply right-click any node in the specification that has changed and select Replace Specification. This will open either the Select Source Specification Type or Select Destination Specification Type dialog box, depending on which specification you wish to replace. Simply browse to the new version, and it will be loaded in place of the existing one. If the changes made to the specification were minor, the map will be successfully re-created with the new specification. If fields were deleted or renamed, a warning will be displayed, and you may need to re-create certain links.

Any changes made to specifications in BizTalk Editor are not reflected automatically by BizTalk Mapper. Each map file contains an actual copy of the source and destination specifications as they existed when the map was originally created, so you will have to manually replace the specifications and recompile the map for changes to take effect.

Mapping Records and Fields

The whole purpose of mapping documents from one specification to another is to recast the data in a different format, as may be required by an application or trading partner. In most cases, the data will not change during the mapping. It will simply appear at a different location, or in a field with a different name. This can be done easily by linking the necessary fields or records.

Once you have opened the specifications that will be mapped, you can effect the transformation by linking the fields and records in the source specification to the corresponding fields in the destination specification. The values will usually be stored in document fields, so your links will be field to field; however, you will need occasionally to map from record to record, or even from record to field. In certain scenarios, you may also need to change the properties of a link.

Linking Fields

To link the value in a source specification field to a destination specification field, simply click the mouse on the source field and drag across the mapping grid to the destination field. When you release the mouse button, the link is saved and is displayed on the mapping grid.

You can repeat the process as necessary to link each source field with its corresponding destination field. In each case, when the map is in use, BizTalk Messaging will extract the value in that location in the source document and place it in the correct location in the destination document. No processing or manipulation of the data will take place in the case of these simple field-to-field links. A map with some simple links defined between specification fields is shown in Figure 5-7.

Linking Records

To link a record to another record, a record to a field, or vice versa, you must have enabled the option Allow Record Content Links in the BizTalk Mapper Options dialog box. Even then, although you will be able to drag a link from a record in the source specification to a record or field in the destination specification, it's a really bad idea, unless the specifications you are dealing with involve records with data embedded directly, rather than in fields.

For example, Figure 5-8 shows what happens in a map where the field called *empFirstName* in the source specification has been linked to a record called *POHeader* in the destination specification. This record has been configured in BizTalk Editor such that its Content property has been set to Element Only. Apart from displaying a warning, BizTalk Mapper lets the link take place and even compiles without error. However, as the Output tab shows, the value ("Joe") of the *empFirstName* field (which is an XML attribute) has now been placed directly into the *POHeader* record (which is an XML element) when the internal XML representations are mapped. This results in an element that's only supposed to contain other elements, having a free-floating text node as well. Recall that in Chapter 4, when we discussed the different types of content that an element could have in an XML document, we said that such a mixture was

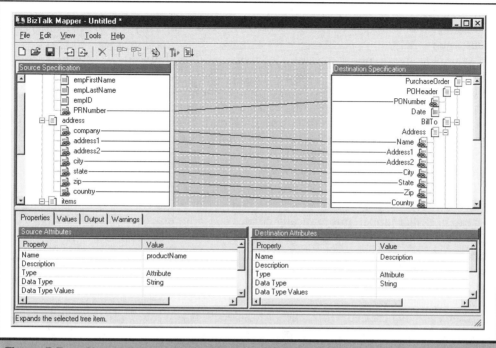

Figure 5-7.   *Simple links between fields in a map*

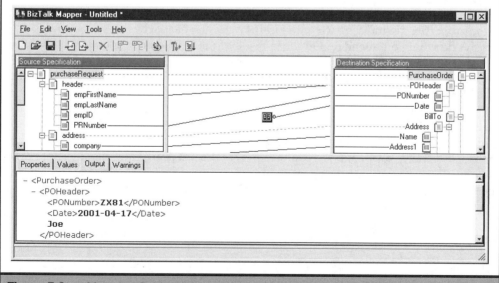

Figure 5-8.   *Mapping field data to a record*

really bad practice. In fact, the *Mixed* content model, although acceptable in XML in general, is not supported by BizTalk Editor, as it has no real place in business documents.

Again you should notice in Figure 5-8 that faint dotted lines have appeared alongside the solid lines created when we manually linked the fields. These are compiler links that are generated when a map is compiled or tested. As mentioned previously, they are there to ensure that if a field is supposed to exist in a destination specification, then its parent record—and indeed all its ancestors up to and including the root node—must also exist. This is another reason we don't need to create record-to-record links; BizTalk Mapper does it automatically. The option is disabled by default, so you should probably leave it that way.

Setting Link Properties

Because BizTalk Mapper automatically creates compiler links between the parent records of fields when a map is compiled, you must be aware of how this process works, as it can produce unexpected results if your specifications contain many nested records. Although this is getting into quite advanced stuff, there may be times when you will need to edit the properties of the links that you create to ensure that this hierarchy is respected.

After you have created a link, click it to select it. If you then right-click and select Properties from the context menu, you will be presented with the Link Properties dialog box, which has two tabs. The General tab is shown in Figure 5-9. It shows the XPath expressions that correspond to the source and destination ends of the link. These expressions are always read-only, so you might wonder why this tab was included at all, other than to help people learn XPath.

The Compiler tab is shown in Figure 5-10 and is not read-only. In fact, although these properties are hidden away, they can save you a headache when your map doesn't do what you intended. On the left side of the tab, you can specify whether the link should cause the value of the source node or the name of the node to be copied to the destination. This can be useful in scenarios in which the names of the fields can be considered valuable data.

On the right side of the tab, you can configure how BizTalk Mapper should treat hierarchical record structures when compiling a map. The options are best illustrated with a simple example. Suppose we were an e-commerce portal site that sold products on behalf of many suppliers. We could represent our list of product catalogs as an XML document, where each supplier's products were grouped within a *Catalog* element. In the following sample, the first catalog is for kitchen appliances, and the second catalog is for furniture.

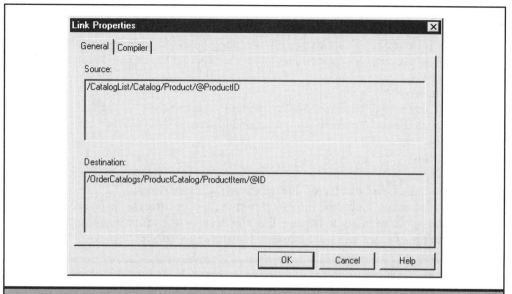

Figure 5-9. *The General tab of the Link Properties dialog box*

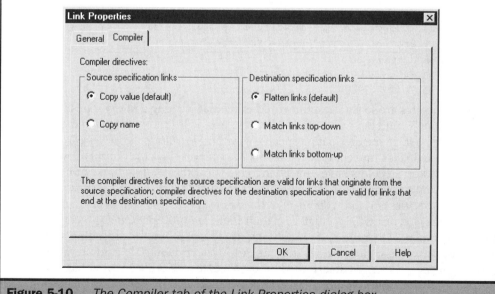

Figure 5-10. *The Compiler tab of the Link Properties dialog box*

```
<CatalogList>
    <Catalog>
        <Product ProductID="X5" ProductName="Waffle Iron" />
        <Product ProductID="X6" ProductName="Electric Toaster" />
    <Catalog>
    <Catalog>
        <Product ProductID="Y2" ProductName="Coffee Table" />
        <Product ProductID="Y4" ProductName="Bookshelf" />
    <Catalog>
</CatalogList>
```

If we needed to send our list of catalogs to a trading partner, say a foreign subsidiary, they may require the information in a different structure. To keep the example simple, we're going to assume that the destination structure should be the same, but that the record and field names (element and attribute names) are different:

```
<OrderCatalogs>
    <ProductCatalog>
        <Product ID="X5" Name="Waffle Iron" />
        <Product ID="X6" Name="Electric Toaster" />
    <ProductCatalog>
    <ProductCatalog>
        <Product ID="Y2" Name="Coffee Table" />
        <Product ID="Y4" Name="Bookshelf" />
    <ProductCatalog>
</OrderCatalogs>
```

The structures are so similar, you would think that creating a map for this transformation would be child's play. All we have to do is link *ProductID* in the source specification to *ID* in the destination specification, and *ProductName* to *Name* in the same fashion. If we do that, and compile it, BizTalk Mapper displays the output shown in Figure 5-11 (the grid colors have been changed to show the compiler links more clearly).

Notice that the compiler has created links from both *Catalog* and *Product* in the source specification to *ProductItem* in the destination. This means that a single *ProductCatalog* record will be created, even if there are multiple *Catalog* records in the source document. To prove it, if we actually use this map on our preceding sample data in BizTalk Messaging, we see that the output document only contains a single *ProductCatalog* element, as determined by the links that BizTalk Mapper has compiled. Consequently, our foreign subsidiary will think that we only have a single catalog, consisting of both kitchen appliances and living room furniture, as shown next.

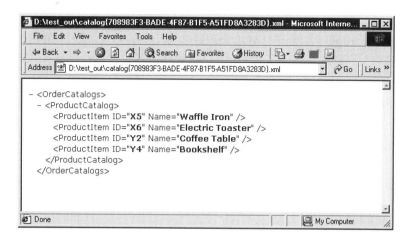

BIZTALK MESSAGING
TOOLS

Note *Those of you more familiar with XSLT will find a further clue to what's happening on the Output tab of Figure 5-11. Notice that a single OrderCatalogs element will be created, containing a single ProductCatalog element, which will then contain multiple ProductItem elements, one "for each" Product in each Catalog.*

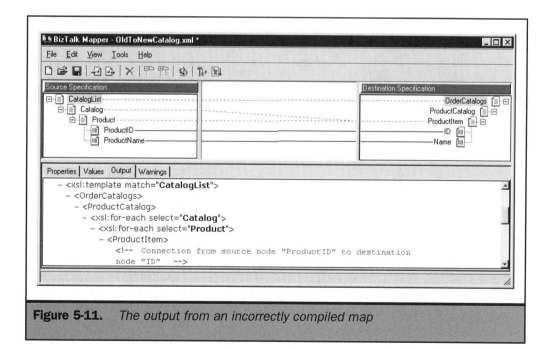

Figure 5-11.   *The output from an incorrectly compiled map*

To rectify the problem, we need to inform BizTalk Mapper not to flatten our rich source hierarchy into a single record in the destination specification, but instead to map each level in the record hierarchy in the source specification with the corresponding level in the destination hierarchy. There are two options available for the order in which this should occur, as shown earlier in the dialog box in Figure 5-10. We can choose the links to be mapped downward, from the top level of the hierarchy to the parent of the field being linked, or we can choose to map the links from the bottom up, that is, from the field being linked back up to the top of the hierarchy.

In our simple example, it doesn't matter which order we choose, as both the source and destination specifications have the same number of levels. However, in a scenario where the depth of the hierarchy was different on each side, the order of the mappings would reflect that difference. If we select the top-down option and recompile our map, we get the output shown in Figure 5-12. Notice that the compiler links join the parent records in a one-to-one fashion.

XSLT experts will see from the Output tab in Figure 5-12 that the XSLT will now create a ProductCatalog element "for each" Catalog element in the source document.

Using this map in BizTalk Messaging produces the following output, which is, of course, what we intended.

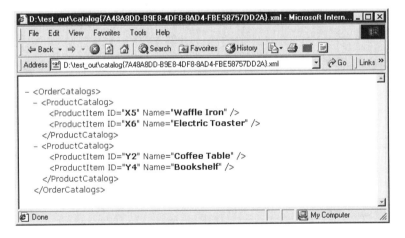

It is possible to set different compiler options for multiple fields that share the same parent record. This is not recommended. If a combination of all three options is set for links to sibling fields, or a combination of Match Links Top-Down and Match Links Bottom-Up directives is used, the compiler will build the map using the default Flatten Links directive. If the Flatten Links directive is combined with one of either the Match Links Top-Down, or the Match Links Bottom-Up directives, the Flatten Links directive will be lost, and the compiler will build the map using whichever Match Links directive was also selected.

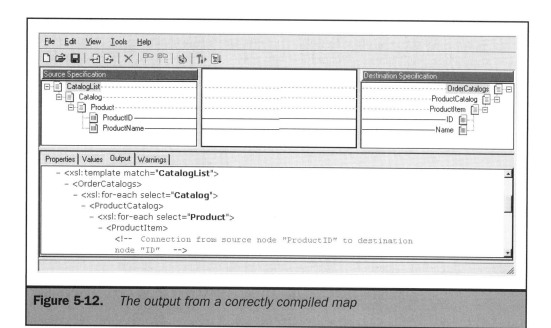

Figure 5-12. *The output from a correctly compiled map*

Implementing Functoids

Linking from a field in a source specification to a field in the destination specification is quick and easy if all you need to do is copy the exact value from one place to another. However, that's not always enough, and sometimes you need to process the data in the source field before mapping it to the destination. For this reason, BizTalk Mapper provides *functoids*. Functoids are effectively pieces of VBScript that can be used to implement a number of calculations or processes that would not normally be possible using simple linking.

There are over 60 functoids built into BizTalk Mapper, and a couple of different ways to implement your own. In fact, if you want to see how any given functoid works, you can view the VBScript on the Script tab in the Properties dialog box for that functoid. If you do this, you will see that a functoid is essentially one or more functions that behave overall as a single function. A functoid takes one or more input parameters, performs some processing, and returns a value that can then be copied to the destination specification or act as input to another, *cascaded* functoid.

To use a functoid in a map, simply drag it from the functoid palette to the mapping grid. Using the mouse, click and drag one or more source specification fields or records to the left side of the functoid to specify the input parameter(s), and then click-and-drag from the functoid to the field in the destination specification where the output should go. If two or more functoids will be cascaded, simply drag from one to the next, remembering that functoid operations must always run from left to right, that is, from source to destination.

In some cases, one or more parameters used by a functoid will be fixed values, rather than values retrieved from a field. To configure a functoid to use a constant value, right-click the functoid after it has been placed on the mapping grid, and select Properties from the context menu. On the General tab, click the Insert New Parameter button, and type in the value you require.

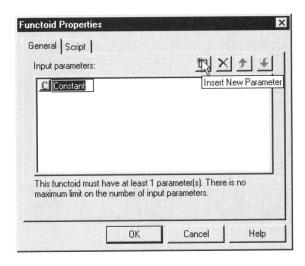

When multiple parameters are used, you can change the order in which they are interpreted using the Move Up Selected Parameter button or the Move Down Selected Parameter button. This is extremely important in many cases, as each parameter might have a different purpose.

Built-In Functoids

The built-in functoids shipped with BizTalk Mapper can perform a wide range of tasks, from concatenating multiple values to performing a database lookup and returning a recordset. To make it easier to find the one you need, the functoid palette has nine tabs, with each tab containing related functoids. In the following section, examples are not given for every single functoid, as this may insult the intelligence of the reader!

String Tab

The String tab contains functoids that can be used to manipulate string values stored in one or more fields in the source specification. In each case, there will be a single output that can be mapped to a field in the destination specification or used as the input for another functoid. The input parameters in all cases may be field values or constants as required.

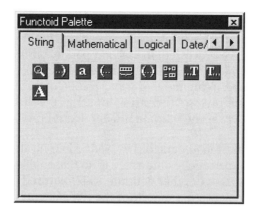

String Find   The String Find functoid is used to search one string for the presence of another and to return the position at which it was found. It takes two input parameters. The first parameter is the string being searched, and the second is the string for which you are searching. The output is a string representation of the position at which the string occurs. If the string is not found, the output is zero. For example, supplying "Test string" as the first parameter and "string" as the second parameter would produce the output "6".

String Left   The String Left functoid is used to return a specified number of characters from the beginning of a string. It takes two input parameters. The first parameter is the string to be processed, and the second parameter is an integer specifying how many characters from the left of the string to return. For example, supplying "Test string" as the first parameter and "8" as the second parameter would produce the output "Test str".

Lowercase   The Lowercase functoid is used to convert a string to all lowercase characters. It takes one input parameter, which is the string to be converted.

String Right   The String Right functoid is used to return a specified number of characters from the end of a string. It takes two input parameters. The first parameter is the string to be processed, and the second parameter is an integer specifying how many characters from the right of the string to return. For example, supplying "Test string" as the first parameter and "4" as the second parameter would produce the output "ring".

String Length   The String Length functoid is used to return the length of a string. It takes one input parameter, which is the string to be examined.

String Extract   The String Extract functoid is used to return a substring beginning and ending at specified character positions. It takes three input parameters. The first parameter is the string to be processed, the second parameter is an integer specifying the character position of the beginning of the string to be extracted, and the third parameter is an integer specifying the character position of the end of the string to be extracted. For example, supplying "Test string input" as the first parameter, "8" as the second parameter, and "14" as the third parameter, would produce the output "ring in".

Concatenate   The Concatenate functoid is used to join multiple strings together. It takes at least one input parameter, and there is no reasonable limit on the number of inputs it can have. If spaces or other delimiters are required, they must be manually added as constant parameters. An example of the Concatenate functoid being used is shown in Figure 5-13.

String Left Trim   The String Left Trim functoid is used to remove leading spaces from an input string. It takes one input parameter, which is the string to be trimmed.

String Right Trim   The String Right Trim functoid is used to remove trailing spaces from an input string. It takes one input parameter, which is the string to be trimmed.

Uppercase   The Uppercase functoid is used to convert a string to all uppercase characters. It takes one input parameter, which is the string to be converted.

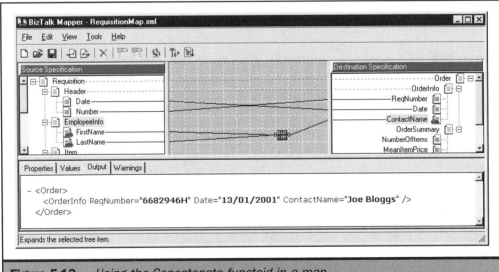

Figure 5-13.   *Using the Concatenate functoid in a map*

Mathematical Tab

The Mathematical tab, shown next, contains functoids that can be used to manipulate numeric values stored in one or more fields in the source specification. In each case, there will be a single output that can be mapped to a field in the destination specification or used as the input for another functoid. The input parameters in all cases may be field values or constants, as required.

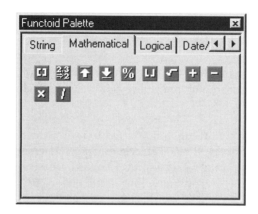

Absolute Value   The Absolute Value functoid is used to convert a number to its absolute (positive) value regardless of whether the input is positive or negative. It takes one input parameter, which is the number to be converted.

Integer   The Integer functoid is used to truncate a real number by removing the decimal portion. It takes one input parameter, which is the number to be truncated. For example, supplying "14.8" as the parameter would produce the result "14".

Maximum Value   The Maximum Value functoid is used to return the highest value (farthest from negative infinity) from a set of numbers. It takes at least one input parameter, and there is no reasonable limit on the number of parameters it can have.

Minimum Value   The Minimum Value functoid is used to return the lowest value (farthest from positive infinity) from a set of numbers. It takes at least one input parameter, and there is no reasonable limit on the number of parameters it can have.

Modulo   The Modulo functoid is used to return the integer remainder after one number has been divided by another. It takes two input parameters. The first parameter is the number to be divided, and the second parameter is the divisor. Note that the remainder will be rounded up or down based on the value of the most significant decimal digit. If the digit is 5 or greater, the number will be rounded up. For example, supplying "47" as the first parameter and "10" as the second parameter would produce the output "7".

Round The Round functoid is used to truncate a number to a certain number of decimal places. It takes two input parameters. The first parameter is the number to be truncated, and the second parameter determines the number of decimal places that should be retained. Note that the original number will be rounded up or down based on the value of the most significant decimal digit to be removed. If the digit is 5 or greater, the number will be rounded up. For example, supplying "14.888" as the first parameter and "2" as the second parameter would produce the output "14.89".

Square Root The Square Root functoid is used to return the square root of a number. It takes one input parameter.

Addition The Addition functoid is used to return the sum of a set of numbers. It takes at least one input parameter, and there is no reasonable limit on the number of parameters it can have.

Subtraction The Subtraction functoid is used to return the result of successive subtraction of a set of numbers. It takes at least one parameter, and there is no reasonable limit on the number of parameters it can have. Each successive parameter is subtracted from the first. For example, supplying values in the order "10", "20", and "–35", would produce the output "25".

Multiplication The Multiplication functoid is used to return the product of a set of numbers. It takes at least one parameter, and there is no reasonable limit on the number of parameters it can have.

Division The Division functoid is used to return the result of dividing one number by another. It takes two parameters. The first parameter is the number to be divided, and the second parameter is the divisor.

Logical Tab

The Logical tab contains functoids that can be used to compare values stored in one or more fields in the source specification. It also contains functoids to test the type of value stored in a field or perform logical operations. In each case, there will be a single output containing either a Boolean "true" or Boolean "false" value. These values may not be mapped to a field in the destination specification. Instead, they are mapped to records in the destination specification to determine whether that record exists in the output or not. The values may also be used as input for certain advanced functoids. The input parameters in all cases may be field values or constants as required.

The logical functoids are case-sensitive, so comparing "String" with "string" would return a Boolean "false". However, all variations of characters that spell "true"—such as "True", "TRUE", or "tRuE"—are treated as equivalents. The same holds for any combination of characters that spells "false".

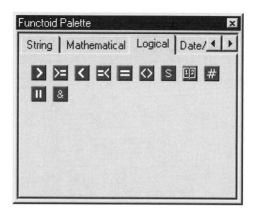

Greater Than   The Greater Than functoid is used to test whether one value is greater (closer to positive infinity) than another value. It takes two input parameters. A Boolean "true" value is returned if the first parameter is greater than the second parameter.

Greater Than or Equal To   The Greater Than or Equal To functoid is used to test whether one value is greater (closer to positive infinity) than or numerically equivalent to another value. It takes two input parameters. A Boolean "true" value is returned if the first parameter is greater than or equal to the second parameter.

Less Than   The Less Than functoid is used to test whether one value is less (closer to negative infinity) than another value. It takes two input parameters. A Boolean "true" value is returned if the first parameter is less than the second parameter.

Less Than or Equal To   The Less Than or Equal To functoid is used to test whether one value is less (closer to negative infinity) than or numerically equivalent to another value. It takes two input parameters. A Boolean "true" value is returned if the first parameter is less than or equal to the second parameter.

Equal   The Equal functoid is used to test whether one value is numerically equivalent to another value. It takes two input parameters. A Boolean "true" value is returned if the first parameter is equal to the second. For example, Figure 5-14 shows a map in which the destination document will only contain a record called "Spouse" if the value of the MaritalStatus field is equal to "Married". The functoid properties are shown in Figure 5-15.

Not Equal   The Not Equal functoid is used to test whether one value is numerically different from another value. It takes two input parameters. A Boolean "true" value is returned if the first parameter is not equal to the second parameter.

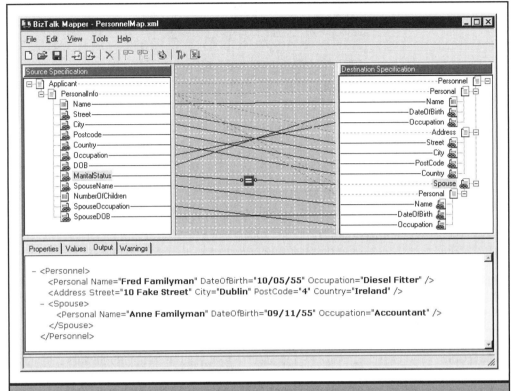

Figure 5-14. *Using the Equal functoid in a map*

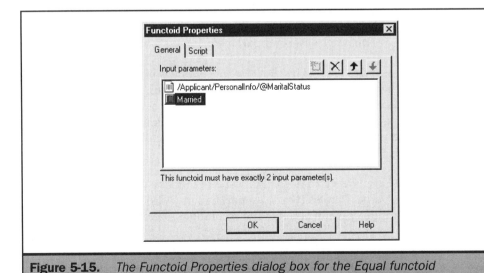

Figure 5-15. *The Functoid Properties dialog box for the Equal functoid*

Logical String   The Logical String functoid is used to test whether a value is a string. A string expression is any value that can be converted to a non-empty string. It takes one input parameter and returns a Boolean "true" value if the parameter is a string.

Logical Date   The Logical Date functoid is used to test whether a value is a valid date. A date expression is limited to numbers or strings, in any combination, that can represent a date from January 1, 100, to December 31, 9999, inclusive. It takes one input parameter and returns a Boolean "true" value if the parameter is a date.

Logical Numeric   The Logical Numeric functoid is used to test whether a value is a number. A numeric expression is any expression that can be recognized entirely as a number. It takes one input parameter and returns a Boolean "true" value if the parameter is a number. For example, supplying "34" as the parameter would produce the output "true", but supplying "34 days" as the parameter would not.

Logical OR   The Logical OR functoid is used to return the outcome of a Boolean OR operation on two values. It takes two parameters. Both parameters will be converted to Boolean values before the operation. A Boolean "true" value is returned if at least one of the parameters also equates to a Boolean "true".

Logical AND   The Logical AND functoid is used to return the outcome of a Boolean AND operation on two values. It takes two parameters. Both parameters will be converted to Boolean values before the operation. A Boolean "true" value is returned only if both parameters equate to a Boolean "true".

Date/Time Tab

The Date/Time tab, shown next, contains functoids that can be used to return date and time information, or to add days to a given date. In each case, there will be a single output that can be mapped to a field in the destination specification or used as the input for another functoid. All Date/Time functoids except the Add Days functoid require no input parameters. The input parameters for the Add Days functoid may be field values or constants as required.

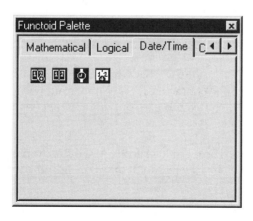

Add Days   The Add Days functoid is used to return a date that has been incremented by an integer number of days. It takes two input parameters. The first parameter must be recognizable as a date, and the second parameter must be an integer. The output will be in the ISO 8601 format YYYY-MM-DD.

Date   The Date functoid is used to return the current date. It takes no input parameters, and the output will be in the ISO 8601 format YYYY-MM-DD.

Time   The Time functoid is used to return the current time. It takes no input parameters, and the output will be in the ISO 8601 format HH:MM:SS.

Date and Time   The Date and Time functoid is used to return the current date and time. It takes no input parameters, and the output will be in the ISO 8601 format YYYY-MM-DDTHH:MM:SS, where T is a literal character.

Conversion Tab

The Conversion tab, shown next, contains functoids that can be used to perform standard character or numeric conversions. In each case, there will be a single output that can be mapped to a field in the destination specification or used as the input for another functoid. The input parameters in all cases may be field values or constants as required.

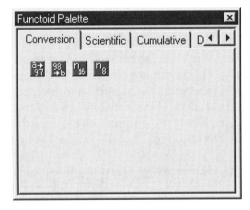

ASCII from Character   The ASCII from Character functoid is used to return the ASCII code for a given single character. It takes one input parameter, which is the character to be converted. For example, supplying "A" as the parameter would produce the output "65".

Character from ASCII   The Character from ASCII functoid is used to return a single character, given an ASCII character code. It takes one input parameter, which is the character code to be converted. For example, supplying the parameter "120" would produce the output "x".

Hexadecimal   The Hexadecimal functoid is used to return a hexadecimal integer value, given a decimal number. It takes one input parameter, which is the number to be converted. Note that any real number will be rounded up or down, depending on the most significant decimal digit, before conversion.

Octal   The Octal functoid is used to return an octal integer value, given a decimal number. It takes one input parameter, which is the number to be converted. Note that any real number will be rounded up or down, depending on the most significant decimal digit, before conversion.

Scientific Tab

The Scientific tab, shown next, contains functoids that can be used in scientific or mathematical equations. There are trigonometric, logarithmic, and other transcendental functions available. In each case, there will be a single output that can be mapped to a field in the destination specification or used as the input for another functoid. The input parameters in all cases may be field values or constants as required.

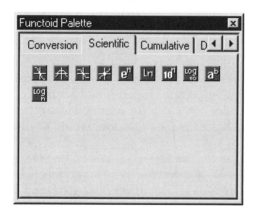

Arc Tangent   The Arc Tangent functoid is used to return the result of performing the Arc Tangent trigonometric operation. It takes one input parameter, which is the value in radians on which to operate.

 If you can't remember this from school, a radian is an alternative unit of measure for an angle. On this scale, zero is still zero, 90 degrees is $\pi/2$, and 360 degrees is 2π.

Cosine   The Cosine functoid is used to return the result of performing the Cosine trigonometric operation. It takes one input parameter, which is the value in radians on which to operate.

Sine   The Sine functoid is used to return the result of performing the Sine trigonometric operation. It takes one input parameter, which is the value in radians on which to operate.

Tangent   The Tangent functoid is used to return the result of performing the Tangent trigonometric operation. It takes one input parameter, which is the value in radians on which to operate.

Natural Exponentiation Function   The Natural Exponentiation Function functoid is used to return the result of performing a natural exponentiation operation. It takes one input parameter, which is the power to which *e* should be raised.

> **Note**   *You might not remember this from school either, but e is the base of natural logarithms and has a value approximating 2.71828.*

Natural Logarithm   The Natural Logarithm functoid is used to return the result of calculating the natural logarithm of a number. It takes one input parameter, which is the value for which the natural logarithm should be calculated.

10^X   The 10^X functoid is used to return the result of performing a decimal exponentiation operation. It takes one input parameter, which is the power to which 10 should be raised. For example, supplying "4" as the parameter would produce the output "10000".

Common Logarithm   The Common Logarithm functoid is used to return the result of calculating the common, or decimal, logarithm of a number. It takes one input parameter, which is the value for which the common logarithm should be calculated. For example, supplying "10000" as the parameter would produce the output "4".

> **Note**   *There is a slight bug in BizTalk Server, such that taking the log of 1000 gives a result of "2.9999999999999995", as opposed to "3". This appears to be due to the way BizTalk Server handles the precision of real numbers. The good news is that other powers of 10 seem to work fine.*

X^Y   The X^Y functoid is used to return the result of performing an exponentiation of one number by another number. It takes two input parameters. The first parameter is the value to be raised, and the second parameter is the exponent by which it should be raised. For example, supplying "16" as the first parameter and "3" as the second parameter would produce the output "4096".

Base-Specified Logarithm   The Base-Specified Logarithm functoid is used to return the result of calculating the logarithm of a number using a specific base. It takes two input parameters. The first parameter is the value for which the logarithm should be calculated, and the second parameter is the base, or counting system to use, such as 16 for hexadecimal.

Cumulative Tab

The Cumulative tab, shown next, contains functoids that can be used to return the result of an operation repeated over the number of occurrences of the parent record, such as a cumulative sum, or cumulative mean. Obviously, these functoids are only really applicable to fields in the source specification that have a parent record for which the Maximum Occurrences property is set to "*", although BizTalk Mapper will not prevent you from using them with non-repeating records. In each case, there will be a single output that can be mapped to a field in the destination specification or used as the input for another functoid.

The left side of each cumulative functoid can be connected either to a field in the source specification or to the right side of a functoid, which, in turn, is connected to a field in the source specification. In either case, the functoid will operate based on the number of occurrences of the parent record of the field in the source specification.

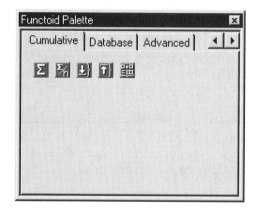

Cumulative Sum   The Cumulative Sum functoid is used to calculate the aggregate value of a particular field whose parent record occurs multiple times. It takes one input parameter, which is the value that should be totaled for each instance of the parent record. Figure 5-16 shows the Cumulative Sum functoid used to calculate the order total for a requisition, after the price of each item has been calculated by multiplying the unit price by the quantity.

Cumulative Average   The Cumulative Average functoid is used to calculate the mean value of a particular field whose parent record occurs multiple times. It takes one input parameter, which is the value that should be averaged for each instance of the parent record. Figure 5-17 shows the Cumulative Average functoid (selected) used to calculate the average unit price of each item in a requisition.

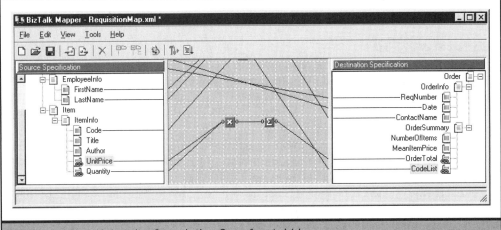

Figure 5-16.   *Using the Cumulative Sum functoid in a map*

Cumulative Minimum   The Cumulative Minimum functoid is used to calculate the smallest value (closest to negative infinity) in a particular field whose parent record occurs multiple times. It takes one input parameter, which is the value that should be checked for each instance of the parent record.

Cumulative Maximum   The Cumulative Maximum functoid is used to calculate the largest value (closest to positive infinity) in a particular field whose parent record occurs multiple times. It takes one input parameter, which is the value that should be checked for each instance of the parent record.

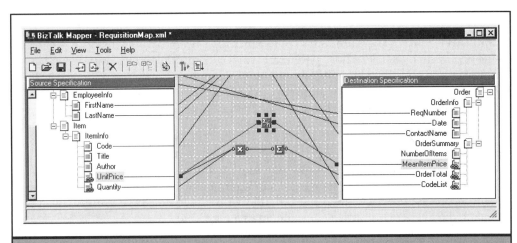

Figure 5-17.   *Using the Cumulative Average functoid in a map*

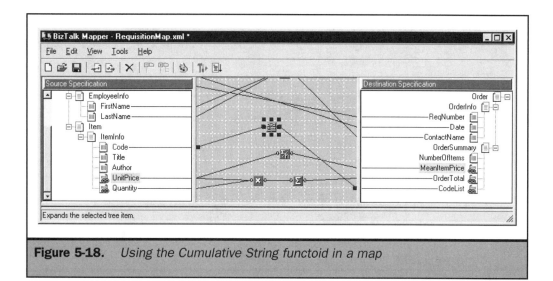

Figure 5-18.   *Using the Cumulative String functoid in a map*

Cumulative String   The Cumulative String functoid is used to concatenate the values of a field whose parent record occurs multiple times. It takes one input parameter, which is the field whose value should be added to the string for each instance of the parent record. Figure 5-18 shows the Cumulative String functoid (selected) used to concatenate code values for each book in a requisition into a single string.

Database Tab

The Database tab, shown next, contains functoids that can be used in conjunction with one another to query a database based on values supplied from a source document, and to return a recordset for that query. Column values from the recordset can then be retrieved and mapped to fields in the destination document.

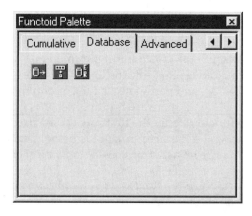

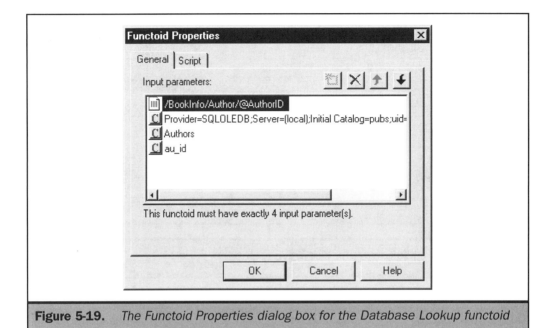

Figure 5-19. *The Functoid Properties dialog box for the Database Lookup functoid*

Database Lookup   The Database Lookup functoid is used to execute a simple query against a database. It takes four input parameters, as shown in Figure 5-19. The first parameter is the value for which to search in the database. The second parameter is the connection string to the database and may contain information on the database provider, data source name, user ID, and password, if required. The third parameter is the table in which to search for the data, and the fourth parameter is the column in which to search for the data. The output from this functoid cannot be mapped to a field or record in the destination specification. The output is an ActiveX Data Objects (ADO) recordset object that can serve only as the input for the Value Extractor or Error Return database functoids.

Value Extractor   The Value Extractor functoid is used to retrieve the value of a column in an ADO recordset. It takes two input parameters. The first parameter must be a Database Lookup functoid, as that returns the ADO recordset from which the value will be extracted. The second parameter is the column in the recordset from which to extract the value. Even if there are multiple records in the recordset returned by the Database Lookup functoid, only the first row can be used. Figure 5-20 shows the Database Lookup and Value Extractor functoids being used to retrieve personal information about an author from a database using only an ID number.

Error Return   The Error Return functoid is used to retrieve any Open Database Connectivity (ODBC) error messages that are returned by a database operation. It takes

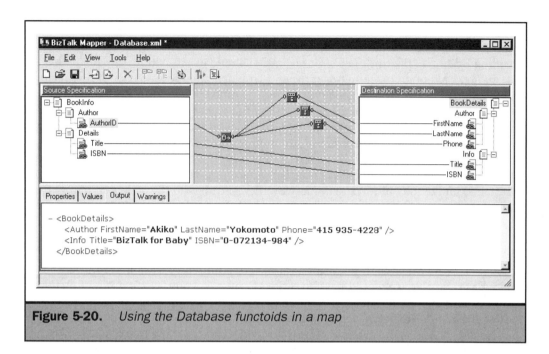

Figure 5-20.   *Using the Database functoids in a map*

one input parameter, which must be a Database Lookup functoid. The value returned by the functoid can be useful in troubleshooting database queries.

Advanced Tab

The Advanced tab, shown next, contains functoids that can be used to perform a variety of tasks that don't really fit into any of the other categories. These include a Scriptor functoid that can be used to implement practically any custom task by simply adding the necessary VBScript.

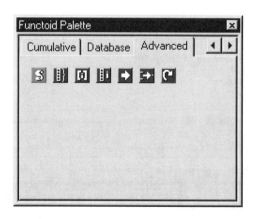

Scripting   The Scripting functoid is used to implement some user-defined functionality through the addition of custom script, which must be written using Visual Basic Scripting Edition (VBScript). The script is implemented as a function, initially called *MyFunction0,* although the numeral at the end will increment for each Scripting functoid added to the map, and you can always rename the functions. The number of input parameters will be specified by the number of parameters defined for the function. The type of output will also be user defined, so it may or may not be valid for mapping to a field in the destination specification, or another functoid.

To use a Scripting functoid, drag it onto the mapping grid, right-click it, and select Properties from the context menu. On the Script tab, you will see that the functoid script is editable, unlike the built-in functoids. You then simply add the code that makes the functoid work. You define the parameters, variables, additional functions—whatever is needed.

For example, suppose a source requisition document supplied a date in the format YYYY/MM/DD and we need to convert it into the format DD/MM/YYYY for a destination order document. There are no functoids built into BizTalk Mapper to perform this task, so we would have to write our own. A complete Scripting functoid to do this is shown in Figure 5-21. Note that we chose to rename the function from the default in order to better demonstrate its purpose.

The code converts the incoming data to a string, checks to see that it's the correct format, performs the conversion, and returns the result. If the incoming data is not in

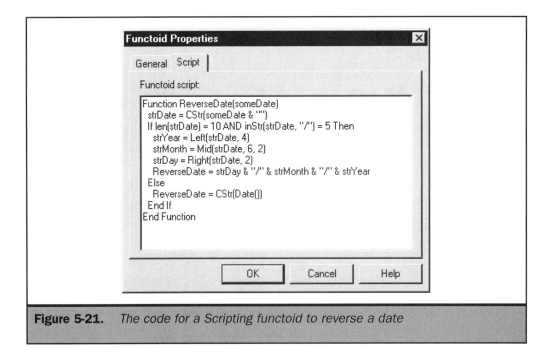

Figure 5-21.   *The code for a Scripting functoid to reverse a date*

the correct format, today's date is returned instead. Of course, a different type of error handling could have been implemented, if we wished. You're only limited by your imagination and your scripting skill. Testing the functoid (selected) with a sample value of 2001/01/13 produces the output shown in Figure 5-22.

Record Count   The Record Count functoid is used to return the total number of times a given record is repeated in a source document instance. It takes one input parameter, which is the record to be counted, and the value returned may be mapped to a field in the destination specification or used as the input for another functoid. Again, the Record Count functoid is only really applicable when the input record in the source specification has its Maximum Occurrences property set to *, but BizTalk Mapper will not prevent you from using it with non-repeating records. For example, Figure 5-23 shows how we can count the number of items ordered in our requisition document using the Record Count functoid (selected). Note that the functoid is connected to the *ItemInfo* record in the source specification, even though it is the *Item* record that is configured to repeat. That's no problem, because each repeating *Item* record will still contain an *ItemInfo* record, and the functoid will count each one.

Index   The Index functoid is used to select a field from a particular iteration of a repeating record in a source document instance. It takes at least two input parameters, depending on how deep the repeating record is nested. The first input parameter is the field whose value should be mapped. The second and any subsequent parameters refer

BIZTALK MESSAGING TOOLS

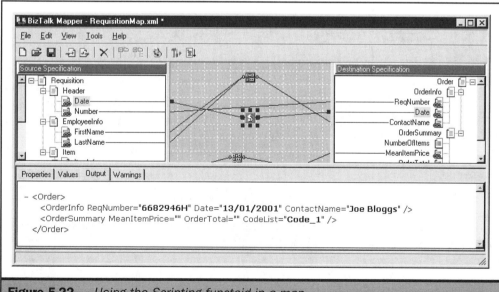

Figure 5-22.   *Using the Scripting functoid in a map*

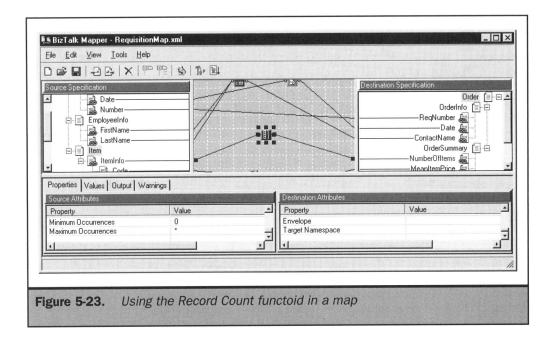

Figure 5-23. *Using the Record Count functoid in a map*

to the position of the record within the document hierarchy. The best way to show how the Index functoid works is with an example. The following illustrations show a sample football league table represented in XML.

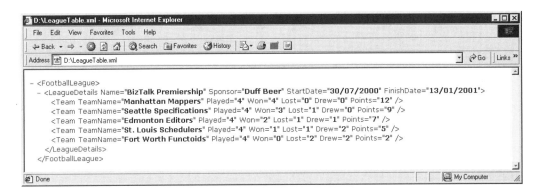

If we create a specification in BizTalk Editor to represent the structure of this league table, it would look like the following illustration:

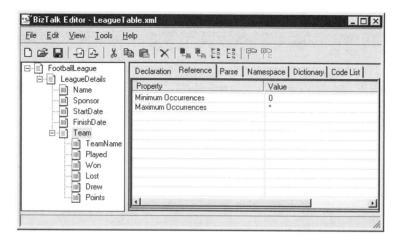

Now, let's say we would like to create a map that only selected the first two teams in the list (assuming they had already been sorted by the number of points) and converted the data into a document showing the league results. This league results document could have the following structure:

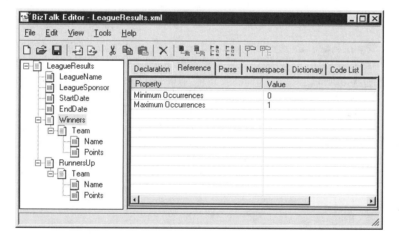

Therefore, we decide to use Index functoids to select the values of the *TeamName* and *Points* fields for the first Team record and place the data under the *Winners* record in the destination, and then take the same details for the second *Team* record and place the data under the *RunnersUp* record in the destination. We can link the corresponding fields to each functoid, as shown in Figure 5-24.

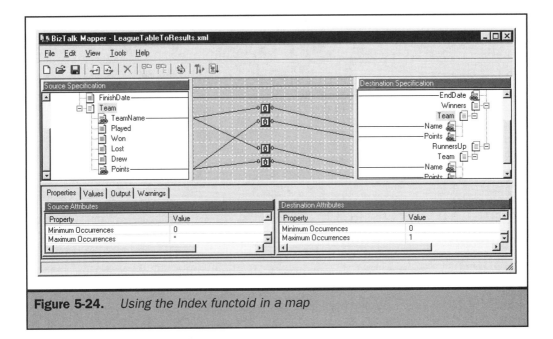

Figure 5-24. *Using the Index functoid in a map*

To make it work, we need to know how to index each record. Because there are two parent records, *Team* and *LeagueDetails,* between each field and the root node, we will need two index values. The first index value refers to the iteration number of the *Team* record, and the second index value refers to the iteration number of the *LeagueDetails* record. For the winning team, the value of the first index is 1, as it is the first iteration of the *Team* record. The value of the second index is also 1 (in fact, the value of the second index will always be 1, as the *LeagueDetails* record is non-repeating). For the runner-up team, the value of the first index is 2, and the value of the second index is again 1. The following illustration shows how the Index functoid would be configured for the name of the winning team.

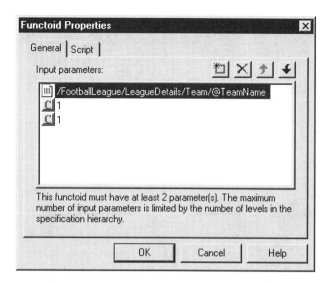

When the map from Figure 5-24 is used by BizTalk Messaging, the output shows how only the details from the first two Team records have been mapped to the destination document.

Iteration   The Iteration functoid is used to return the iteration number of a repeating record in a source document instance. It takes one input parameter, which is the record to be counted; and the value returned will typically be stored in a field in a similarly repeating record in the destination, although it may also be used in conjunction with the Logical functoids to make comparisons. For example, Figure 5-25 shows the

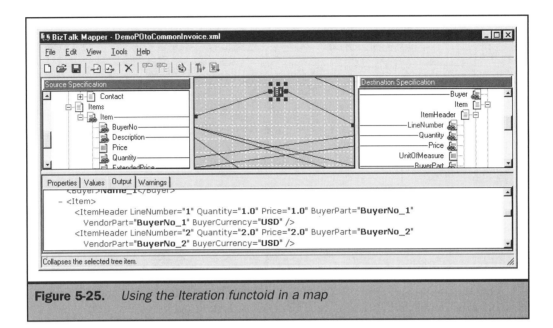

Figure 5-25. *Using the Iteration functoid in a map*

Iteration functoid used to map the iteration number of the *Item* record in the source to the *LineNumber* field in the destination.

Value Mapping The Value Mapping functoid is used to return the value of a field in a source document instance if another parameter evaluates to a Boolean "true". Although this functoid can be used in a variety of ways, its main purpose is to restructure source documents where the name of a field or record is stored as a data value, and to create destination documents where the value has become the actual field or record name. For example, a database might produce a product catalog, as shown in Figure 5-26.

As Figure 5-26 shows, the category name for each product is stored as an actual data value for each record. However, we might need to restructure the catalog so that there are records called *ElectricalAppliances, Furniture,* and *GardenAccessories* that each contain the appropriate product records. Therefore, what we need to do is test the value of the *Category* field against one of these record names, and if it is the same, map the *ItemID* and *Name* values to the corresponding record. We can use the Logical Equals functoid to perform the comparison, configured as shown next. That will yield a Boolean "true" value if the parameters are equivalent, and a Boolean "true" value is just what we need as the first parameter of our Value Mapping functoid.

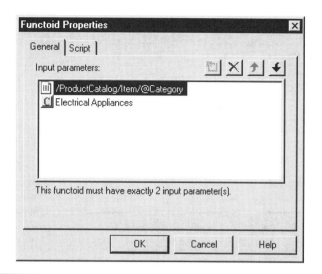

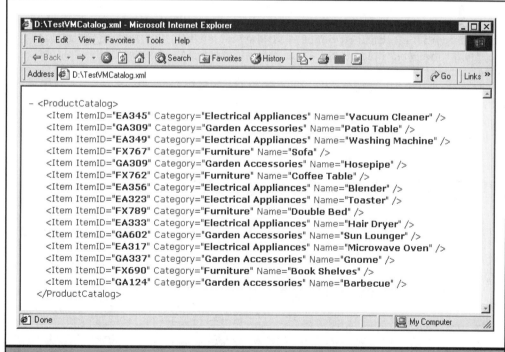

Figure 5-26.   *A sample product catalog converted to XML*

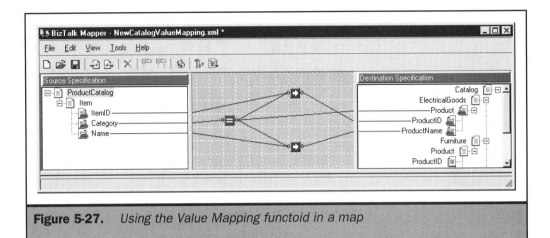

Figure 5-27.   *Using the Value Mapping functoid in a map*

Figure 5-27 shows the functoids in place for the first category. In this case, we are comparing the value of the *Category* field for each repeating record in the source document with "Electrical Appliances". If they match, we are mapping the values of the *ItemID* and *Name* fields to the *ProductID* and *ProductName* fields in the *Product* record under the *ElectricalGoods* record.

To ensure that blank records are not created when the category name doesn't match, we are also linking the Equals functoid to the corresponding *Product* record. Thus, the record will only be created when the values match. We can then repeat the process for the other two categories to create the complete map shown in Figure 5-28.

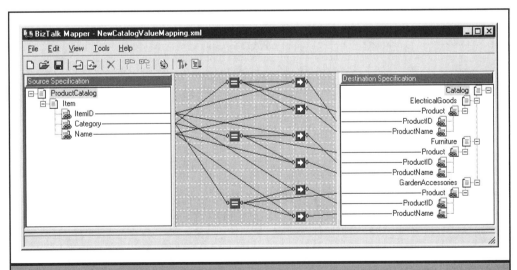

Figure 5-28.   *The complete map using multiple Value Mapping functoids*

When the map in Figure 5-28 is used by BizTalk Messaging with the sample
product catalog shown in Figure 5-26, it yields the following output:

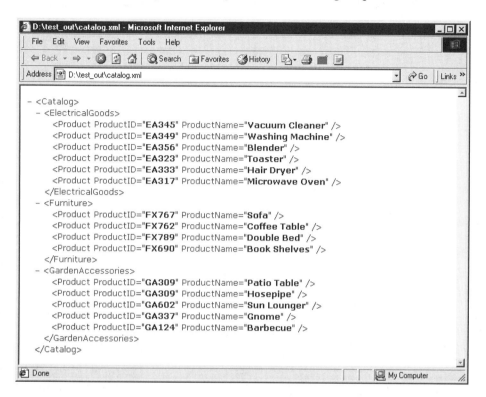

Value Mapping (Flattening)   The Value Mapping (Flattening) functoid is also used
to return the value of a particular field if another parameter evaluates to a Boolean
"true". The difference between this functoid and the Value Mapping functoid is that
this functoid attempts to flatten a source document structure by removing nested records.
This is particularly useful with certain types of catalogs, such as those used by Commerce
Server 2000, that store product property names as field values, as well as the values of
those properties themselves. Figure 5-29 shows sample data retrieved from a Commerce
Server 2000 catalog. The properties for each product have been given more descriptive
names to properly illustrate how the property names are stored.

If we now need to send our catalog to trading partners who use a more traditional
means of structuring their product information, we can use the Value Mapping (Flattening)
functoid. As before, we will use an Equals functoid to compare the value of the *fieldID*
field against each of our field names. The Value Mapping (Flattening) functoid can
then be used to map the data from the sibling fields to the appropriate field in the
destination specification. The complete map is shown in Figure 5-30—the grid
background color has been changed to make the links a little easier to distinguish.

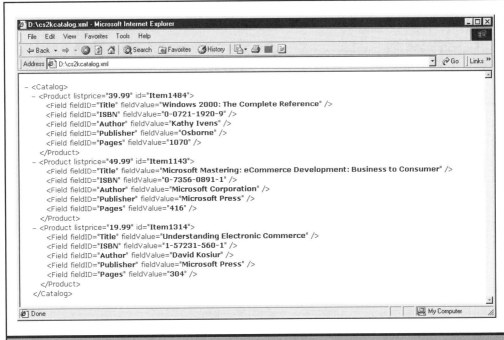

Figure 5-29. *A sample Commerce Server 2000 catalog*

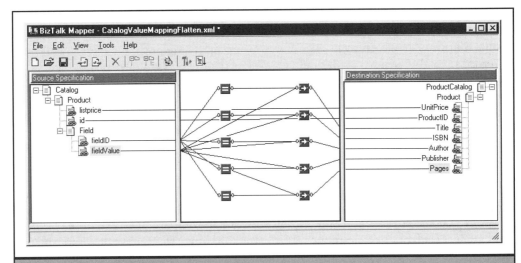

Figure 5-30. *Using Multiple Value Mapping (Flattening) functoids in a map*

When the map in Figure 5-30 is used by BizTalk Messaging with the sample product catalog shown in Figure 5-29, it yields the following output:

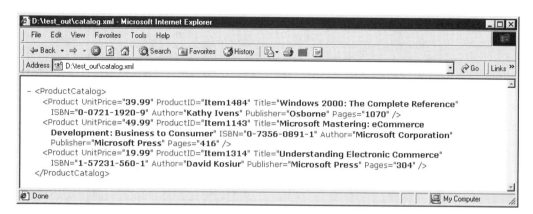

Looping Functoid   The Looping functoid is used to combine data from different records or fields in a source document instance into a repeating record in a destination document instance. This is done by creating an instance of the destination record for each different input. The Looping functoid can thus be used to perform the inverse of the Value Mapping (Flattening) functoid, to transform a catalog into the format used by Commerce Server 2000.

Examine the map shown in Figure 5-31. The text size has been increased to space out the fields. In this map, the source specification on the left represents the type of custom catalog that was the destination for the Value Mapping (Flattening) functoid map. Some of the fields have been omitted to make it easier to read, but the overall structure is the same. The destination specification on the right represents the type of catalog we would wish to import into Commerce Server 2000, with the *id* field removed.

The only functoid necessary in this case is a single Looping functoid. Notice that each of the *Title, ISBN,* and *Author* fields is linked to the functoid. This means that for every occurrence of each field, a record called *Field* will be created in the destination document. So each occurrence of a *Product* record in the source document instance will cause three *Field* records to be created in the destination. However, to complete the conversion, some clever link manipulation is required. We know that the *fieldID* field in a Commerce Server catalog should contain the name of the property, so we create a link from the *Title* field, for example, to the *fieldID* field. It's not the value of the Title field we require, though, so we have to configure the properties of the link by changing the compiler directive to copy the name of the field rather than the value.

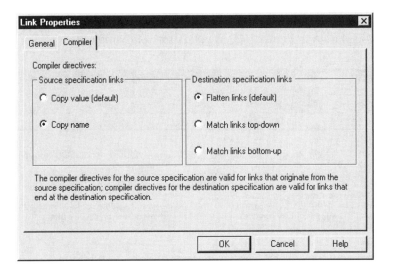

We also need the value of the field mapped to the *fieldValue* field in the destination, however; so we need to create a second link from *Title* to that field in the destination—but this time we will use the default compiler properties. To make sure that a *Field* record will be created for each field in the source document, we repeat the process for each of the *ISBN* and *Author* fields. This will require multiple links going into the *fieldID* and *fieldValue* fields, which is not usually allowed, so we will need to open the BizTalk Mapper Options dialog box from the Tools menu; and select Allow Multiple Inputs

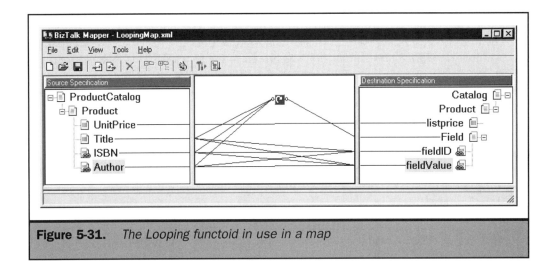

Figure 5-31.   *The Looping functoid in use in a map*

To Destination Tree Nodes on the General tab. After the map has been completed, using it in BizTalk Messaging produces the following output:

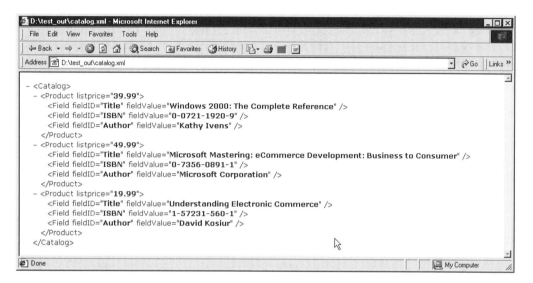

Custom Functoids

Although there are many built-in functoids available in BizTalk Mapper, by no means do they cover all possible tasks that you would ever want to perform in a map. Yes, there is also the Scripting functoid on the Advanced tab to allow you to create a custom script; but if you need to use a custom functoid frequently, or on multiple machines, re-creating it each time can be time-consuming and awkward.

The BizTalk SDK provides an example of how to build and register your own custom functoid using Visual Basic, by implementing the *CannedFunctoid* class. These custom components can also be created in Visual C++ using the *IFunctoid* interface. Once configured to implement the required class in the Windows Registry, the functoid will appear on the palette inside BizTalk Mapper on whatever tab you specify to allow ease of reuse. Chapter 17 will discuss the steps necessary to create a custom functoid in full detail.

Compiling Maps

When you have created your map by linking all the records and fields, and adding all the functoids you need, you must compile the map and save it. You can save it to a location on the hard disk, but if you want to use it in BizTalk Messaging, you will need to store it in the BizTalk WebDAV Repository. As we will see, you can also choose to export only the XSLT portion of the map or to supply sample values for testing purposes.

Adding Test Values and Constants

One of the features that's sorely missing in BizTalk Mapper is the ability to load up a sample document instance and see how it will be transformed by the map. In fact, its omission is so glaringly conspicuous by its absence, I reckon they did actually go to the trouble of building it; but they were in such a hurry to get the product out before the end of 2000, they forgot to put it in.

You can still check certain aspects of your maps, however, by supplying values for fields in the source specification and using Tools | Test Map. Unfortunately, there's no way to enter multiple field values for a repeating record, so the only proper way to test it is to plug it into BizTalk Messaging and give it a real document to work with. In the next chapter, we will see how BizTalk Messaging uses map files.

One other thing that you can do, which really has nothing to do with testing but everything to do with implementation, is to add constant values for the destination specification. Often when you are creating links for a map, you will find that the fields do not directly correspond between the specifications. If there are fields in the source specification that have no matching place in the destination, that data simply won't get mapped. However, if there are fields in the destination that don't have corresponding fields in the source, you will end up with empty fields in your outgoing documents. We can add in constant values on the Values tab to circumvent this problem.

Adding Test Values

If you want to see how your map will work with real data, you can enter test values for fields in the source specification on the Values tab, shown next. BizTalk Mapper does not check to make sure that the value you enter conforms to the data type for that field, however, so don't be surprised if you enter funny values and get a funny result.

To add a test value, simply select the field in the source specification by clicking it, and then type the value into the box on the Values tab. These values are saved with the map to make it easier for you to test the map at a later stage, if you need to make some modifications.

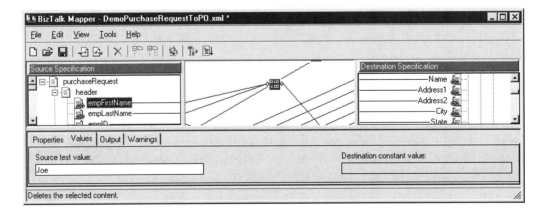

Adding Constants

As mentioned, there are many scenarios in which your source document will not contain all the data needed for the outgoing document. For example, if a company is using BizTalk Server to automatically generate an invoice from a purchase order that arrives, it might be necessary for that invoice to contain the name of the person in the company who is responsible for sending out invoices (perhaps in a *Contact* field). That information is only provided at the time the invoice is generated, however—it will not come from the purchase order. Therefore, we would need to insert the name of the financial administration employee into the relevant field in the invoice as a constant.

To add a constant value, simply select the field in the destination specification by clicking it, and then type the value into the box on the Values tab, shown next. Again, these values are saved with the map, as they will be necessary when the map is deployed for production.

  If you have added a constant value to a destination specification in a map, BizTalk Mapper will not allow you to create a link to that field either from a field in the source specification or a functoid. Similarly, if there already exists a link to a field in the destination specification, you will not be able to add a constant value for that field.

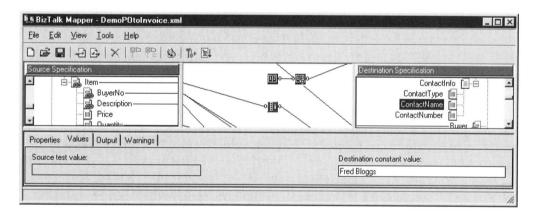

Compiling a Map

BizTalk Mapper automatically generates the XSLT and VBScript functions necessary to implement the map you created visually in the application. This process is therefore called *compiling* the map. It's not actually necessary to explicitly compile a map before using it, because BizTalk Mapper always compiles it before saving it to the hard disk, storing it to the WebDAV repository, or testing it with dummy values.

Compiling a map can be useful, though, if you want to do a quick check to see whether a new functoid has been properly configured or whether links are being mapped in the correct order. The compiler will generate warnings if there are any problems with the map, such as a functoid with not enough inputs or outputs, or data types that don't match between linked fields. It can be easier to troubleshoot these issues without having to plug in sample values.

To compile a map, choose Tools | Compile Map, or click the Compile Map button on the toolbar. The XSLT for the map will be displayed on the Output tab, and any problems encountered during compilation will be displayed on the Warnings tab.

Testing a Map

As we have seen, before you deploy a finished map, you may want to test it to see how certain records and fields are transformed. Although we cannot supply a complete document instance, we do have the capability of entering individual values on the Values tab. Even if we don't provide sample values, BizTalk Mapper will do it for us when we test the map.

To test a map, choose Tools | Test Map or click the Test Map button on the toolbar. You will be asked to save the file, but it is not necessary to do this to run the test. BizTalk Mapper will then compile the map. Again, if any errors were found, they will be displayed on the Warnings tab. Unlike the compilation process, though, the Output tab will display a sample destination document instance using the dummy data for the source specification.

As mentioned, there are limitations with the testing process, as data type validation is not performed on the sample values you enter, and any repeating records in the source specification are only represented by two records in the test document instance. This may be enough for certain types of maps, but for anything advanced, you will need to give the map a proper test by using it in a BizTalk Messaging implementation.

Exporting a Map

At the beginning of this chapter, we discussed the structure of a BizTalk Mapper map file. We saw how it contained both the source and destination specifications, the XSLT necessary to transform one to another, any test values or constants that were entered, and configuration information for each link and functoid used.

Because BizTalk Mapper generates clean, standards-conformant XSLT 1.0, we can probably envisage other uses for the tool, or other ways in which the XSLT can be applied. For example, there may be a need to use the stylesheet in an Active Server Page, or in an application other than BizTalk Server, for transforming document structures. For very simple structures, it might be even possible to map an XML document structure to an HTML document structure in order to build a stylesheet that will display the XML document in a browser. However, don't get too carried away with that idea. BizTalk Mapper was not designed to create XML stylesheets, and it's not very good at it. Maybe in the future, Microsoft or another company will make available functoids or other add-ons to do just that.

In the meantime, if you do need to use the XSLT in another way, BizTalk Mapper has an option to save it on its own. It does not save all the source and destination information—just the XSLT. To export the XSLT only, choose File | Save Compiled Map As, type in a filename, and click Save.

Chapter 6

Using BizTalk Messaging Manager

In the previous two chapters, we saw how an organization's electronic document structures could be represented as XML by creating document specifications using BizTalk Editor, and how one type of document could be transformed into another by creating a map using BizTalk Mapper. In this chapter, we will see how specifications and maps are used by one of the core features of BizTalk Server—BizTalk Messaging.

BizTalk Messaging is essentially a service that runs in the background on a BizTalk Server, constantly monitoring for the arrival of electronic documents. Documents can arrive into BizTalk Messaging in a number of ways. They can be posted using HTTP or SMTP to an Active Server Page or Exchange script. They can also be dropped off to a physical directory or message queue, where they will be picked up by a *receive function*. A COM-aware application can even submit documents directly using a COM interface. It is also possible to integrate BizTalk Messaging with the other core service in BizTalk Server—Orchestration—so that a document may be submitted from an XLANG schedule.

How documents are delivered to BizTalk Messaging is not covered in this chapter, as it doesn't really affect how they are processed. Integrating Orchestration with BizTalk Messaging will be covered in Chapters 7 and 8; receive functions will be covered in Chapter 9; and using the Interchange object to submit documents programmatically will be covered in Chapter 16. In this chapter, you will see how to configure BizTalk Messaging to receive, transform, package, deliver, and track documents by creating virtual objects that represent each step in an automated process. These objects are created and modified using a graphical application called BizTalk Messaging Manager.

This chapter is divided into two main sections. The first section introduces BizTalk Messaging concepts and is targeted at those new to BizTalk Server. The second section covers the creation of BizTalk Messaging objects using the BizTalk Messaging Manager. If you are already familiar with Messaging concepts, you may find it more useful to go straight to the second half of this chapter.

Messaging Concepts

Every electronic business process involves the interaction of a number of physical entities. Figure 6-1 shows a typical process, where an organization, perhaps our own company or business, has a purpose-built EDI application that extracts order information from a database, encodes it as multiple X12 documents, and sends the packaged documents to a web page on a trading partner's extranet site using HTTP. The trading partner organization would then retrieve the information, extract the individual documents by examining the predetermined format, create invoices based on each order using a set of transformation rules, and return those invoices to us in an e-mail using SMTP. Simultaneously, they could keep a copy of each in their own database.

In this example, the important entities in the process are our organization, our application, our document definitions, the transport mechanism we use to send the information, the location to which they are sent, the trading partner organization to

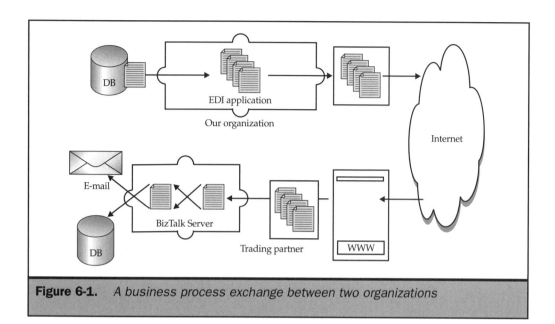

Figure 6-1.   *A business process exchange between two organizations*

which they are sent, their document definitions, their mapping rules, their transport mechanism for returning the data, and the location to which they will be returned. To automate this type of process, we—and perhaps our trading partner—would need to create a *workflow* that encompasses each step. If one or both parties are using BizTalk Server, the workflow could be implemented using BizTalk Messaging. In that case, an object representing each of these entities can be created and configured using a web-based application called BizTalk Messaging Manager. Once each object exists and the appropriate connections have been made between them, the BizTalk Messaging service will look after the actual processing when documents arrive.

Overview of BizTalk Messaging Objects

Figure 6-2 shows how the various objects created in BizTalk Messaging work together to create a business process. The terms appearing in bold in the following discussion refer to the corresponding objects in that diagram. After a document or *interchange* arrives at BizTalk Server, the appropriate **parser** is selected based on the **envelope** in which the interchange is contained. If there is further information available about the **application** or **organization** from which the document originated, that will assist BizTalk Server in selecting the correct **channel** to process the document, although the actual name of the application or organization configured for the channel will only really be used for tracking purposes. Each channel will be configured for a specific type of incoming document, identified by a **document definition**, which will

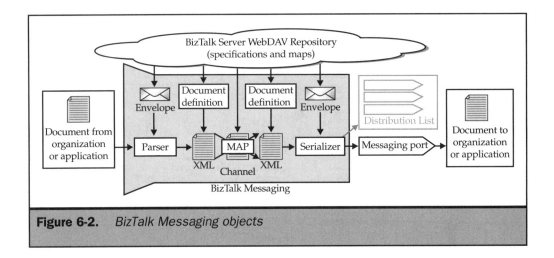

Figure 6-2.   *BizTalk Messaging objects*

normally contain a reference to a particular specification stored in the **BizTalk Server WebDAV Repository**.

An interchange is a unit of data that is submitted to BizTalk Server or transmitted by BizTalk Server. Incoming interchanges may consist of multiple documents, but outgoing interchanges will only ever consist of a single document. In either case, there may also be header and footer information. Interchanges will be discussed in more detail later in the chapter.

As discussed in Chapter 3, this specification will help the parser convert the document from its original format into XML. The channel can then convert this internal XML structure into another XML structure that corresponds to the format required by the document's eventual destination. This format is determined by a second **document definition**, whose corresponding specification and the **map** file needed to complete the transformation are chosen from the BizTalk Server WebDAV Repository. However, these items will be stored in the BizTalk Messaging Management database for use at run time. After the conversion is complete, the document can then be transported to its destination.

Every channel must feed either into a single **messaging port** or into a single **distribution list** that consists of multiple messaging ports. Each messaging port will be configured with a destination address and an appropriate transport mechanism to get the document to that destination. The messaging port will also use an **envelope** to instruct the **serializer** how to package the data before it is sent on its way. Again, we will typically configure a messaging port with information about the destination **application** or **organization**, but this information is mainly used for document tracking.

Note *The name of the application or organization can also have a more important function. We can specify the name of the source or destination organization for a document either at the time the document is submitted or in the actual document itself. In this case, the channel or messaging port used is only determined when the document arrives. Consequently, we would say that the document is self-routing. This will be discussed later in the chapter.*

In the following section, we will discuss each type of object and how it fits into the process. In the second half of this chapter we will see how to use BizTalk Messaging Manager to create and modify each object. When referring to items in BizTalk Messaging Manager such as organizations or applications, understand that we are not creating physical entities, but rather virtual objects that represent these entities.

Note *All of these objects are in fact entries in the BizTalk Messaging Management database. When a document definition (or envelope) that points to a specification is created, that specification is actually loaded into the database for later use by BizTalk Messaging.*

Organizations and Applications

In our scenario in Figure 6-1, two organizations were interacting—our organization and the organization that is one of our trading partners. In an automated process, the actual sending and receiving of the documents will typically be performed not by entire organizations, but by individual computer applications within those organizations, such as server software, dynamic web pages, or database management systems.

If we were a company configuring the first half of the process, we would need to know which of our applications were sending the data and to which organization it was being sent. We might not be overly concerned with which application our trading partner actually uses to process the data, though, as that is their business. Similarly, if we were a company configuring the second half of the process, we would need to know from which trading partner the documents arrived and which of our applications would handle them. Again, we typically would not worry about which of our trading partner's applications actually sent the documents.

BizTalk Messaging Manager allows us to create *organization* and *application* objects that represent each end of a business process interaction. We will see that we can easily configure objects that represent our own internal applications, but we will not usually create applications for a trading partner organization, unless we create them programmatically using the BizTalk Messaging Configuration Object Model.

Note *Using the BizTalk Messaging Configuration Object Model to create messaging objects programmatically will be covered in Chapter 16.*

Organizations

When BizTalk Server is installed, a Home Organization is automatically created to represent our own department, company, conglomerate, or whatever. As shown in the following illustration, BizTalk Messaging Manager allows us to modify the properties of the Home Organization, such as its name, but we cannot delete it. We can also create various other organizations, to represent our trading partners. If we are using BizTalk Server Standard Edition, we are limited to five trading partner organizations; the Enterprise and Developer editions have no such restrictions.

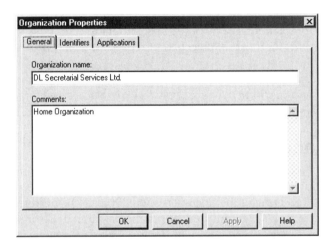

Organization Identifiers   When we communicate with an organization, we often identify them by name. For example, we might be sending an invoice to Bushwhack Fruit Distributors Ltd. However, in electronic business, there are various ways to identify an organization. We might refer to them by their web site address, their telephone number, their Dun & Bradstreet number, or we might use another method that's meaningful or relevant to us. BizTalk Messaging Manager allows us to create any number of standard or custom identifiers to do this.

The type of identifier used by BizTalk Server is called an *Identifier Qualifier*, and its value is called an *Identifier Value*; so in the preceding example, the Identifier Qualifier is "OrganizationName", and the Identifier Value is "Bushwhack Fruit Distributors Ltd". If we wanted to identify the company by its telephone number, the Identifier Qualifier would be "12", and the Identifier Value might be "555 7878". Hold on a second, you're thinking—where did "12" come from? As mentioned, there are a number of standard identifiers built into BizTalk Messaging Manager. These are identifiers that are commonly used in EDI transactions and have short qualifier codes associated with them. It just happens that "12" represents "Telephone Number".

Note   *These standard identifiers are defined by ISO6523.*

When configuring organization identifiers, there is also a more friendly way to reference each identifier, called Identifier Name. The Identifier Name acts only as a description of the identifier for humans. BizTalk Server always uses the Identifier Qualifier instead. Table 6-1 lists a number of commonly used standard organization identifiers available in BizTalk Messaging Manager. There are many others, but space prohibits listing them all.

Name	Qualifier
DUNS (Dun & Bradstreet)	01
Federal Maritime Commission	02
IATA (International Air Transport Association)	04
Drug Enforcement Administration	11
Telephone Number	12
American Bankers Association	17
AIAG (Automotive Industry Action Group)	18
Health Industry Number	20
ISO 6523: Organization Identification	30
DIN (Deutsches Institut fuer Normung)	31
U.S. Federal Employee Identification Number	32
NHS (National Health Service)	80
Swiss Chamber of Commerce	85
SITA (Societe Internationale de Telecommunications)	90

Table 6-1.   *Standard Organization Identifiers*

Note   *When BizTalk Server is installed, the home organization is automatically configured with two identifiers. The first is Organization, which has an identifier qualifier of OrganizationName and an identifier value of Home Organization. The second is Reliable Messaging Acknowledgement SMTP From Address, which has an identifier qualifier of SMTP and a blank value. The first can be changed or deleted, but the second should only be modified if BizTalk Framework messages will be used with an SMTP transport. In this case, we would supply the e-mail address that should appear in the From field for the MIME-encoded message. This is not the same, however, as the Reliable Messaging Reply-To Address, which is configured within BizTalk Administration.*

We can also create custom identifiers, as shown in the following illustration, that correspond to how we might wish to refer to an organization. For example, we could create an identifier that represents a company by its web site address:

Identifier Name	Identifier Qualifier	Identifier Value
Web Site	URL	http://www.bushwhack.ltd/

Again, remember that BizTalk Server would use the Identifier Qualifier and Identifier Value, and the Identifier Name is just a friendly name for humans.

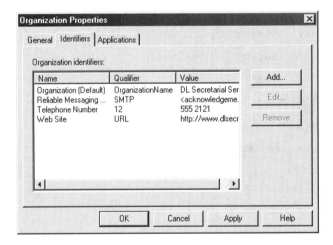

Caution   *If you are creating identifiers for organizations that will send or receive X12 documents, the identifier qualifier must be 4 or fewer characters, and the identifier value must be 35 or fewer characters. Similarly, for organizations that will send or receive EDIFACT documents, the identifier qualifier must be 2 or fewer characters, and the identifier value must be 15 or fewer characters. Normally, you will use standard identifiers in such cases, and the standard identifiers satisfy these requirements.*

Applications

Configuring our own end of a business process will usually involve identifying which application should send or receive a document. On the other hand, we are unlikely to have in-depth knowledge of our trading partner's internal applications. BizTalk Messaging Manager allows us to create applications as shown within the Home Organization to represent our own application processes.

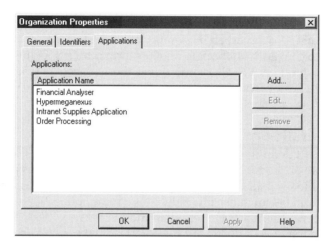

The applications we create for the Home Organization are simply virtual endpoints for our workflow. They allow us to organize our processes by saying that purchase orders should go to the application called "Order Processing", for example. It doesn't matter if "Order Processing" represents a third-party software package, a page on our web site, or the sad guy in the financial department who doesn't get out much. Similarly, we could say that sales receipts get sent from the "Hypermeganexus" application, which is really a 20-year-old legacy system written in COBOL.

It should be obvious, therefore, that configuring some application called, say, "Financial Analyzer" in BizTalk Messaging Manager does not magically create an executable program that will actually do our tax returns and come up with expenditure reports. It only creates an entry in the BizTalk Messaging database that we can refer to when configuring our workflow processes or tracking the flow of documents using the BizTalk Document Tracking feature. In fact, there's nothing to stop us from creating three different applications under the Home Organization that all refer to the same Active Server Page (ASP) on our web site, just to make it easier for us to track different kinds of documents that might get sent to that page. Also, just creating the application does not tell BizTalk Server anything about that application, or how documents should be submitted to it. That will be configured later on, when we specify the transport method in the messaging port.

Document Definitions and Envelopes

After we've established the organization objects that represent our trading partners and ourselves, we will need to create objects that represent the different types of documents that will be exchanged between these various organizations. These are called *documents definitions*, and we will usually link each one to an actual document specification created using BizTalk Editor.

The documents we exchange will come in different formats, such as EDI, XML, and Flat-File. Thus, we will also need an object that assists BizTalk Messaging in selecting the appropriate parser to convert an incoming document to XML, or in choosing the correct serializer to convert XML back to another format for packaging and eventual transport to its destination. We also came across these objects in Chapter 3, when discussing BizTalk Editor. They're called *envelopes*, and they're crucial to a proper understanding of BizTalk Messaging.

Document Definitions

Creating a document definition in BizTalk Messaging Manager does not actually create an invoice template or product catalog. As before with organizations and applications, a document definition is really only another entry in the BizTalk Messaging database. However, it wouldn't be much use if it didn't have some connection to a real document structure; so when we create a document definition in BizTalk Messaging Manager, we will also configure the type of document the object represents. We do this by pointing to a physical document specification stored in the BizTalk Server WebDAV Repository. In this way, when BizTalk Messaging needs to parse an incoming document into an internal XML format for processing, the source document definition will direct it to the specification created using BizTalk Editor, which contains all the information needed for the conversion.

Note	*It is not necessary to select a specification for a document definition if there is no requirement for the incoming data to be translated into XML, validated against a predefined structure, or transformed into a different format. This would be the case if BizTalk Server were processing a binary file.*

As we have mentioned, when a document is passing through a BizTalk Messaging channel, the document definition—and, consequently, a document specification—is used to parse the data into XML. The channel will also perform a transformation that maps this internal XML into a different structure that corresponds to the format that the document will be required to have when it leaves BizTalk Server. This new structure is also XML since the transformation is performed using a map file created with BizTalk Mapper, and we know that these maps are only used to convert XML to XML.

As a result, to convert this second XML structure into a file format such as X12 or CSV, we will again need to know what type of document it's supposed to be. This information is provided in a channel by a second document definition, which also points to a specification, as shown next. This specification will have been created using BizTalk Editor. As before, the document structure laid out in the specification will provide all the information required for a serializer component to turn the internal XML into this new format. Not only that, BizTalk Messaging handles all of these conversions and transformations automatically once the appropriate specifications and maps have been created.

```
┌─ New Document Definition ─────────────────────────────────[×]─┐
│                                                               │
│  General │ Global Tracking │ Selection Criteria │            │
│                                                               │
│  Document definition name:                                    │
│  ┌─────────────────────────────────────────────────────────┐ │
│  │Common Purchase Order                                     │ │
│  └─────────────────────────────────────────────────────────┘ │
│                                                               │
│  ☑ Document specification:                                    │
│     WebDAV repository reference:                              │
│     ┌───────────────────────────────────────┐  ┌──────────┐  │
│     │http://DLOWLAPTOP/BizTalkServerReposito…│  │ Browse...│  │
│     └───────────────────────────────────────┘  └──────────┘  │
│     Document type:              850                           │
│     Version:                    4010                          │
│                                                               │
│                                                               │
│         ┌──────┐   ┌────────┐   ┌───────┐   ┌──────┐         │
│         │  OK  │   │ Cancel │   │ Apply │   │ Help │         │
│         └──────┘   └────────┘   └───────┘   └──────┘         │
└───────────────────────────────────────────────────────────────┘
```

Global Tracking Fields   In Chapter 10, we will see that BizTalk Server has a feature called *Document Tracking* that allows us to query a Document Tracking Activity (DTA) database for information about incoming or outgoing exchanges. One of the ways we can query this database is to search for documents where the values stored in individual document fields match certain Boolean expressions. For example, we might wish to search for invoices where the value of the *Total* field is greater than 50,000, or search for acknowledgement messages where the name in the *Recipient* field is Mary Smith.

It would be inefficient for BizTalk Server to keep track of the value of every field in every document that it processes, just in case we might ever want to query that information. Consequently, this functionality is not available by default. If you will need to track certain fields for a particular type of document, you must preconfigure the corresponding document definition, as shown next. BizTalk Messaging Manager allows us to do this for each document definition we create. However, the schema of the DTA database is limited so that we can only track two integer fields, two real number fields, two date fields, and two text fields. We can also track any number of custom fields that are stored as a concatenated string in the database.

To track a field as an explicit data type, you must ensure that the field has been configured with that data type in the document specification.

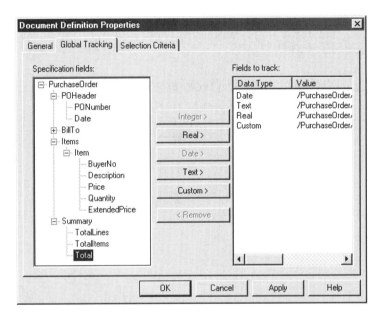

 The structure of the DTA database will be discussed in Chapter 10.

If we decide to track these fields by configuring the document definition, they will be tracked for all instances of that type of document, regardless of from where they arrived or to where they are being sent. As a result, they are called *global tracking fields*. Later in this chapter, we will see how to track fields for documents that are processed by a particular channel only.

Selection Criteria   There are various ways in which documents can be submitted to BizTalk Server. Though we will not go into detail on these methods in this chapter, it is enough to know that depending on the method you use, it is possible to provide extra information that allows BizTalk Server to identify the appropriate channel to process the document. For example, if we submit a document programmatically using the Submit method of the Interchange object, we can specify the name of the document definition and identifiers for the source or destination organization. We could even provide the actual name of the channel explicitly.

As I have mentioned, it is also common for BizTalk Server to select a channel by extracting information contained in the document itself after it has arrived. Such documents are called self-routing, and their specifications will identify particular fields that contain the routing information. This is done using the Dictionary tab in BizTalk Editor. However, EDI documents do not have fields that can be used for this purpose,

Criterion Name	X12 Field
functional_identifier	GS01
application_sender_code	GS02
application_receiver_code	GS03
standards_version	GS08

Table 6-2. *Selection Criteria for X12 Document Definitions*

so it is impossible to specify routing information, such as the name of the document or the source or destination organization, within the document itself. All is not lost, though, as EDI interchanges consist of more than just the raw document data; there are interchange headers as well, and they do contain this data. Specifically, an EDI X12 interchange stores such information in fields within the functional group header, and EDIFACT interchanges can store it in either the functional group header or the interchange header. Therefore, BizTalk Server will be able to match incoming EDI documents to a particular document definition by examining these fields and comparing them with values set within each document definition. These values are called *selection criteria*.

The selection criteria that can be specified for an EDI X12 document and the fields in which this data can be found are listed in Table 6-2. The names of the criteria must be entered exactly as written, or they will not work. The selection criteria that can be specified for an EDIFACT document and the fields in which the data can be found are listed in Table 6-3. Note that the values may be in the functional group header (the

Criterion Name	EDIFACT Field (UNG)	EDIFACT Field (UNH)
functional_identifier	S009, 0065	0038
application_sender_code	Not Used	S006, 0040
application_receiver_code	Not Used	S007, 0044
standards_version_type	S009, 0052	S008, 0052
standards_version_value	S009, 0054	S008, 0054

Table 6-3. *Selection Criteria for EDIFACT Document Definitions*

UNG record) or the interchange header (the UNH record). Again, the names must be typed exactly as shown.

For example, an incoming EDI X12 document may have the following functional group header:

```
GS*PO*503812*556462*20010423*1615*711*X*003060~
```

Using the information in Table 6-1, we can see that the type of document is a purchase order, because the first field (after the GS identifier tag) is "PO", and that field corresponds to the functional identifier. Similarly, we can see that the sender code is "503812", the receiver code is "556462", and the standards version is "003060". Therefore, if we wanted BizTalk Server to be able to handle documents with this particular functional group header automatically, we would create a document definition and set the selection criteria as listed in Table 6-1 to have these values. The following illustration demonstrates this. When the documents arrive, BizTalk Server will examine the fields in the header and compare them with the selection criteria values configured for each document definition. If it finds a match, it will know to select a channel that has this particular document definition configured as the inbound document type. Needless to say, it is important to ensure that the selection criteria are unique for each document definition.

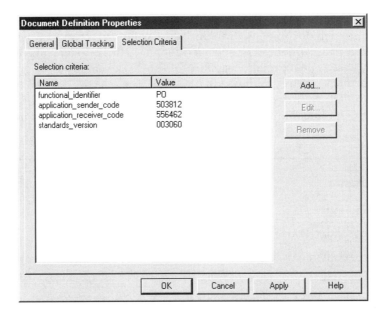

Selection criteria are also important for outgoing EDI documents. Because BizTalk Server will need to create an interchange containing a functional group header for every EDI document it transmits, it will have to know what information to put into the fields in the header. Therefore, it will be necessary to set the selection criteria for any EDI document definitions that will be used as an outgoing document type in a channel.

Envelopes

Before BizTalk Server can perform any processing on a document, it must convert it to XML. As discussed, this is done by a parser component in conjunction with a predefined document specification. For this to happen, however, BizTalk Server must know which parser to use. Four parsers ship with the product by default, and it is also possible to create and install further custom components. Similarly, when BizTalk Server is sending out a document, it will be converting a document from XML to a different file format using one of at least four serializer components. Selecting the appropriate parser or serializer to use is accomplished by means of an envelope. There are six envelope formats available for use in BizTalk Messaging—ANSI X12, EDIFACT, Flat-File, Custom XML, Custom, and Reliable.

> **Note**   *Custom parser and serializer components will be covered in Chapter 16.*

Envelope objects in BizTalk Messaging correspond to their real-world counterparts in that they will contain one or more transmitted documents. However, whereas you could use the same envelope in the real world to enclose an invoice written in English, a receipt written in Greek, or a love letter written in French, in BizTalk Messaging, the format of an envelope must match the format of the document(s) it contains. So, XML documents must be enclosed in an XML envelope, and custom flat-file documents must come in a flat-file envelope. In fact, you could imagine that the format is written on the outside of the envelope, so that when BizTalk Messaging receives a document, it can look at the accompanying envelope to see the file format and thus select the appropriate parser.

An envelope may simply define the file format, such as X12 or Flat-File, for the purpose of selecting a parser. Or, as the following illustration shows, an envelope may point explicitly to a special type of specification that determines the exact structure of an interchange. This will be necessary when multiple documents arrive together or when extra information is present apart from the document itself. Because there may be multiple documents contained in data received by BizTalk Messaging, or routing information supplied in a header or footer, we will often refer to interchanges, rather than documents.

Interchanges   When we submit data to BizTalk Server, we can package one or more documents together in an interchange. The interchange may consist of a single document, a single document with accompanying header and footer information, or multiple documents with accompanying header and footer information. In the latter two cases, BizTalk Messaging will need to be able to extract the actual document data from the interchange, so it will need to know where any header ends, where the document begins, and also perhaps where the document ends and the footer begins. To make this possible, depending on the file format, we will need to tell BizTalk Messaging how the header and footer information is structured and where the document can be found. You do this by using an envelope that points to a specification created by BizTalk Editor.

For inbound interchanges, the type of document being submitted to BizTalk Server determines the type of envelope that must accompany the document. Depending on the format, however, it may or may not be necessary to configure the envelope to point to an envelope specification. In fact, for certain inbound interchange formats, an envelope is not necessary at all. Table 6-4 summarizes the possible scenarios.

For outbound document interchanges, it is always necessary to configure an envelope. Otherwise, the document will not be converted from the internal XML format used by BizTalk Messaging. Specifying an envelope for outbound interchanges is done during configuration of the corresponding messaging port. This may seem contrary to what we have learned already, but the serializer cannot build the outgoing document interchange without referring to an envelope with the corresponding format.

Note   *Although the envelope is selected during the configuration of the messaging port, the corresponding serializer is actually used at the end of an associated channel.*

Document Format	Envelope Required	Specification Required
ANSI X12	No	No
EDIFACT	No	No
Custom XML	Yes*	No
Flat-File	Yes	Yes
Custom	Yes	Yes**
Reliable	No	No

* Although an envelope must be created to allow BizTalk Server to open inbound interchanges in a Custom XML format, it is not necessary to provide the name of the envelope during submission. BizTalk Server will able to locate the correct envelope itself.

** The need for a specification will be determined by the custom parser component. A custom parser must be created to handle inbound interchanges in any format not directly supported by BizTalk Server.

Table 6-4.   *Scenarios in Which Inbound Envelopes Are Required*

It is true that the outbound document definition configured in a channel will instruct BizTalk Server how to convert the XML to the intended format, but the envelope will allow the serializer to build a complete outgoing interchange, including any required header and footer information. Therefore, if the envelope is not present, although the serializer could guess from the outgoing document specification what the format of the file should be, it's not able to build a complete interchange without an envelope that explicitly declares the required format. For example, there would be no way for the serializer to know whether an outbound document should be packaged in a custom XML or Reliable envelope just by looking at a document specification that uses the XML standard. Similarly, a custom flat-file specification might use the same delimiters as an X12 specification, but a flat-file document should not be packaged with X12 functional group headers.

ANSI X12 / EDIFACT Envelopes   Both EDI formats employ a delimited flat-file format, but inbound EDI interchanges will also specify functional group or interchange headers. As a result, although EDI X12 interchanges will actually be in a delimited flat-file format, we would want BizTalk Messaging to use its built-in X12 parser to convert an X12 document, rather than the more generic (and thus less efficient) flat-file parser.

Luckily, out-of-the-box X12 and EDIFACT support was considered so crucial to BizTalk Server when it was being developed that Microsoft hard-coded the structure of these file formats into the product for greater speed. As a result, BizTalk Messaging is able to recognize incoming EDI interchanges without having to look at an envelope. It quickly establishes that an X12 or EDIFACT interchange has arrived and is able to extract the documents from within the headers and pass them on to the appropriate X12 or EDIFACT parser. As discussed, the values contained in these headers may be examined and compared against the selection criteria configured for each document definition in order to select the appropriate channel. After that, the specification associated with the inbound document definition for the channel is used to convert the document into XML.

For outbound interchanges, however, we must specify an appropriate X12 or EDIFACT envelope when configuring the associated messaging port. Otherwise, the serializer will not be able to build the required functional group or interchange headers. Also, when we configure an X12 or EDIFACT envelope in a messaging port, we must specify the delimiters that will be used in the document and an *interchange control number* that will be used to track the document.

The delimiters need to be specified so that the interchange and functional group headers can be built in the correct format, and the dialog box allows you to enter the component element, element, and segment separators, which correspond to the subfield, field, and record delimiters for that type of specification. The interchange control number that you specify simply has to be a number greater than zero that will act as a unique identifier for the interchange. This number will be added to the interchange header and footer by the serializer, and it will increase by one automatically each time that particular messaging port is used.

One last thing that must be configured if you intend to use an X12 or EDIFACT envelope is a *group control number*. When EDI interchanges are submitted to BizTalk Server, they may contain several documents. In EDI, these documents are called *transaction sets*. If there are multiple transaction sets within a functional group, BizTalk Server will extract each one as a single document and process it separately. However, we will need to ensure that the documents are marked as part of the same functional group, so we use a group control number. This is similar to an interchange control number in that the number will automatically increment for each document instance, but it is entered into the Functional Group header and footer, rather than the Interchange header and footer. One other significant difference is that it is not configured in a messaging port. Instead, it is configured in a channel, even though it will not be used until the serializer is building the outgoing interchange. If you select an X12 or EDIFACT envelope in a messaging port, you will need to ensure that this information is entered into the corresponding channel, or you will receive an error.

Custom XML and Reliable Envelopes   If the documents being submitted to BizTalk Messaging are in an XML format, they will typically be contained in an interchange that also specifies routing information, such as the destination organization or the type of document. BizTalk Messaging is again able to recognize XML interchanges instantly because of hard-coded support, but only the Reliable envelope format is readily available. The Reliable format conforms to the BizTalk Framework 2.0. It's called Reliable because incoming documents must always generate a receipt as acknowledgement. Thus, if a sending application (such as BizTalk Server) does not receive an acknowledgement in an allotted timeframe, it will resend the document as necessary. In that way, we can rely on the document arriving at its destination. An example of the Reliable messaging format is shown in Figure 6-3.

If an inbound XML interchange does not use the Reliable format, then it is considered to be a Custom XML format, and an appropriate envelope needs to be created. However, the name of the envelope does not need to be explicitly declared when the document is being submitted, as BizTalk Server is able to locate the appropriate envelope. If the interchange only consists of the document, with no extra routing or receipt information, then the envelope does not need to be associated with a particular specification. But if there is extraneous header or footer information, an envelope specification will have to be created using BizTalk Editor and attached to the envelope in BizTalk Messaging Manager.

For outbound XML interchanges, if an envelope is not specified, the raw internal XML data will be sent. If a Reliable envelope is specified, that format will be used for the outgoing data. If a Custom XML envelope is specified, an envelope specification must also be selected, or the data will be sent using the Reliable format.

Flat-File Envelopes   As discussed, flat-file formats are positional, or delimited, in nature. To allow BizTalk Server to select the correct parser when a flat-file interchange

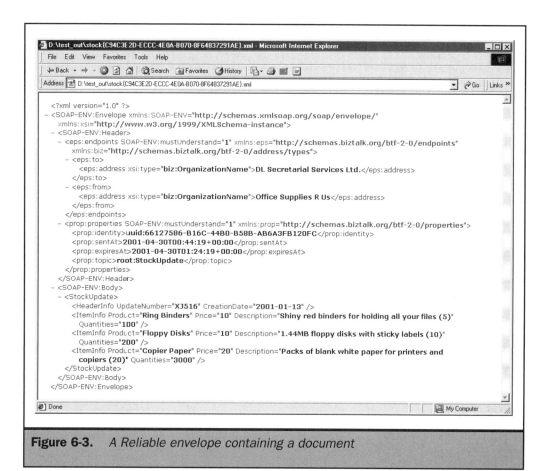

```
D:\test_out\stock{C94C3E2D-ECCC-4E0A-B070-8F64837291AE}.xml - Microsoft Internet Explorer    _ □ ×
File  Edit  View  Favorites  Tools  Help
← Back  →  ·  ⊗ 🔄 🏠  🔍 Search  📰 Favorites  ⏱ History  🔄· 🖨 🖅 🖃
Address 🔄 D:\test_out\stock{C94C3E2D-ECCC-4E0A-B070-8F64837291AE}.xml          ▼  ⮕ Go  Links »

  <?xml version="1.0" ?>
- <SOAP-ENV:Envelope xmlns:SOAP-ENV="http://schemas.xmlsoap.org/soap/envelope/"
    xmlns:xsi="http://www.w3.org/1999/XMLSchema-instance">
  - <SOAP-ENV:Header>
    - <eps:endpoints SOAP-ENV:mustUnderstand="1" xmlns:eps="http://schemas.biztalk.org/btf-2-0/endpoints"
        xmlns:biz="http://schemas.biztalk.org/btf-2-0/address/types">
      - <eps:to>
          <eps:address xsi:type="biz:OrganizationName">DL Secretarial Services Ltd.</eps:address>
        </eps:to>
      - <eps:from>
          <eps:address xsi:type="biz:OrganizationName">Office Supplies R Us</eps:address>
        </eps:from>
      </eps:endpoints>
    - <prop:properties SOAP-ENV:mustUnderstand="1" xmlns:prop="http://schemas.biztalk.org/btf-2-0/properties">
        <prop:identity>uuid:66127586-B16C-44B0-B58B-AB6A3FB120FC</prop:identity>
        <prop:sentAt>2001-04-30T00:44:19+00:00</prop:sentAt>
        <prop:expiresAt>2001-04-30T01:24:19+00:00</prop:expiresAt>
        <prop:topic>root:StockUpdate</prop:topic>
      </prop:properties>
    </SOAP-ENV:Header>
  - <SOAP-ENV:Body>
    - <StockUpdate>
        <HeaderInfo UpdateNumber="XJ516" CreationDate="2001-01-13" />
        <ItemInfo Product="Ring Binders" Price="10" Description="Shiny red binders for holding all your files (5)"
          Quantities="100" />
        <ItemInfo Product="Floppy Disks" Price="10" Description="1.44MB floppy disks with sticky labels (10)"
          Quantities="200" />
        <ItemInfo Product="Copier Paper" Price="20" Description="Packs of blank white paper for printers and
          copiers (20)" Quantities="3000" />
      </StockUpdate>
    </SOAP-ENV:Body>
  </SOAP-ENV:Envelope>

🔄 Done                                                        🖳 My Computer
```

Figure 6-3. *A Reliable envelope containing a document*

is submitted, it is necessary to create an envelope with a Flat-File format. This envelope must also be configured to point to a specification created with BizTalk Editor. If the interchange will only consist of a single document, then the document specification for the flat-file document can also be used as the envelope specification. If the interchange will contain multiple documents or extra header or footer information, then an appropriate specification needs to be created in BizTalk Editor, and the envelope must point to this specification.

For outbound documents it is also necessary to use a Flat-File envelope, but it is not necessary for the envelope to point to a specification, as BizTalk Messaging does not support batching multiple files together into an outbound interchange, even if the documents arrived as part of the same incoming interchange.

Custom Envelopes   A Custom envelope is required when the format of an incoming or outgoing document is one that is not directly supported by BizTalk Server. In this case, it will be necessary to create custom parser and serializer components to process the data. So that BizTalk Messaging can select the appropriate parser when an inbound interchange arrives, it will be necessary to create an envelope. Whether a specification will also be required will depend on the custom parser component. Similarly, outgoing documents will also need to specify an envelope of type Custom, and again, the need for a specification will be determined by the custom serializer component.

Messaging Ports and Distribution Lists

There isn't much point in allowing documents to be submitted to BizTalk Messaging and performing fancy XSLT transformations on the information unless we intend to do something with the finished data. In a B2B scenario, that could mean posting the data to a trading partner using a particular transport method. In an Enterprise Application Integration (EAI) scenario, it could involve sending the data to an internal application by again specifying a location and the appropriate transport method to get it there.

BizTalk Messaging supports HTTP, HTTPS, SMTP, File, Message Queuing, and Loopback as preconfigured transports. For custom transport methods, it is possible to build an Application Integration Component (AIC), which is a special type of COM component. As an enterprise-level piece of software, BizTalk Server also supports the encryption and signing of outgoing data. All of this information is specified in BizTalk Messaging by creating a messaging port. For scenarios where multiple destinations are required, BizTalk Messaging allows you to group messaging ports together to form a Distribution List.

Note	*Application Integration Components will be discussed in detail in Chapter 17.*

Messaging Ports

BizTalk Messaging Manager allows you to specify how a document should be sent by creating a messaging port. Although the first thing a document encounters when it is submitted to BizTalk Messaging is a channel, we cannot create a channel without first creating the messaging port or distribution list that into which the channel will feed.

To configure the various aspects of a messaging port, BizTalk Messaging Manager provides the New Messaging Port wizard. This is invoked once you decide whether the messaging port should point to an organization or an application. There is no real difference between the two types, except that a messaging port to an organization allows you to set an open destination, and a messaging port to an application provides you with the option to send the document directly to an *XLANG schedule*. An XLANG schedule is an automated process that runs in a COM+ application called the *XLANG Scheduler*. These schedules are created using the BizTalk Orchestration Designer tool.

Creating XLANG schedules using BizTalk Orchestration Designer will be covered in Chapter 7.

To an Organization   If you decide to create a messaging port to an organization, the first page of the wizard allows you to specify the organization to which the document will be sent. The organization you specify (or more correctly, the organization identifier qualifier and organization identifier value) will be used to help BizTalk Messaging select a channel when a document arrives. It is always necessary for BizTalk Server to have enough information about a document to know the type of document it is, the source organization from which it came, and the destination organization to which it should be sent. Armed with these details, BizTalk Server will look for channel-messaging port pairs that match this information, and thus will select the appropriate channel to process an inbound document.

Note   *It is not possible to specify the Home Organization as the destination for a messaging port through BizTalk Messaging Manager. Instead, you must create a messaging port to one of the applications configured for the Home Organization. Similarly, a messaging port to an application can only point to the Home Organization.*

A document that contains enough information to determine how it should be processed, without those details having to be explicitly declared during submission, is called "self-routing" for obvious reasons. When a document is not self-routing, then the source and destination organization information will need to be provided explicitly during submission. We will see later that all submission methods rely on the Submit and SubmitSync methods of the BizTalk Interchange object, and each method allows this information to be defined when the method is called. As a result, supplying the necessary source and destination information during submission is termed *call-based routing*. Either way, the information will be used to select an appropriate channel-messaging port pair.

The other purpose of the organization information provided in either a channel or a messaging port is to act as a label that can be used by the Document Tracking feature. This is also true if a channel is configured from an application, or a messaging port is configured to an application. The Home Organization is used as the label in such cases.

On the same page as you configure the destination organization, you also select the primary—and optionally, a backup—transport, as shown next. The available transports of AIC, File, HTTP, HTTPS, Loopback, Message Queuing, and SMTP will be covered later, when we discuss creating messaging ports in detail. We can also specify a service window, which is a timeframe during which the messaging port should be operational, as defined using the Universal Time Convention (UTC) on the server.

BIZTALK MESSAGING TOOLS

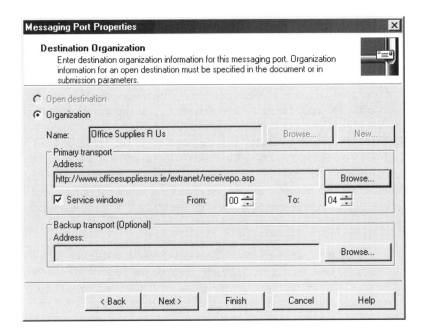

Open Destination Another possibility is to specify that the messaging port should have an open destination. In this case, the transport and destination properties are not configured explicitly. Instead, the information will be present in a particular field in the document instance. For this to happen, it is necessary that the specification for the incoming document definition, or the specification for the envelope in which it is contained, has the Destination Value property set for the appropriate field on the Dictionary tab in BizTalk Editor.

It is also possible to configure an open messaging port by providing the destination as a parameter when calling the Submit or SubmitSync method of the BizTalk Interchange object. It is not possible to specify this information in a receive function, however. Submitting documents to BizTalk Server programmatically will be covered in Chapter 16, and creating receive functions will be covered in Chapter 9.

If you create a messaging port with an open destination, it is not possible to specify any transport information within the messaging port, as that information will be contained in the document. An open destination is a valid setting, however, that can be declared when the document is being submitted, so that BizTalk Server will look for a channel-messaging port pair where the messaging port is open. Also, it is not possible to create a channel-messaging port pair where both the channel and the messaging port are open.

Because EDI documents cannot contain explicit destination information, they cannot be used with open destination messaging ports. Also, BizTalk Messaging requires both the source and destination identifiers to build an X12 or EDIFACT envelope; but again, this information is not available for an open destination messaging port.

To an Application If you decide to create a messaging port to an application, then you won't be specifying a destination organization. Instead, you have the option to send the document to an internal application configured on the Home Organization or to an XLANG schedule. In the case of an internal application, you will still need to specify the transport method(s) to be used and the actual destination address.

If your document will be going to an XLANG schedule, there are two options—a new XLANG schedule that will be instantiated by BizTalk Messaging, or an already running schedule. In the former case, you will need to specify the path to the schedule file, which has a .skx file extension, and also the name of a port in the schedule (usually the first port bound to an action) where the document should arrive.

| Note | *The term "port" used in connection with BizTalk Orchestration should not be confused with the term "messaging port" as used by BizTalk Messaging. An orchestration port represents a binding between a process action and the means by which that action will be implemented, such as a COM component or a Message Queuing interface. Unfortunately, this seems to have confused someone on the BizTalk Server product team, because failing to enter a value in this field gives the message "Enter a valid messaging port name", when it is the name of an orchestration port that is, in fact, missing.* |

The latter case is a bit more complicated, and we only provide an overview here. Sometimes, an XLANG schedule will make use of BizTalk Messaging to send a document, and the schedule will continue running until it receives a reply. For example, sending a purchase order from an XLANG schedule to a trading partner may require a purchase order acknowledgement to be sent back from the trading partner. In such a scenario, it is vital that the XLANG schedule that receives the acknowledgement is the same one that sent the document, because a BizTalk Server running at full stretch in an enterprise environment will typically have multiple instances of the same schedule running at the same time.

To ensure that the correct schedule picks up the return document, a unique message queue is created for each running schedule. When the original document is sent to the trading partner, it will contain information about the location to which the acknowledgement should be returned. For example, the return location may be an Active Server Page containing script necessary to correctly route the document. This is done by ensuring that the trading partner passes the unique identifier from the original document into the return document. The Active Server Page will then be able to extract the identifier because it will be sent back as part of the URL. It will also be sent back in the document itself as the value of a predefined field. When the Active Server Page receives the acknowledgement, it is also able to extract the name of a channel in the same way. This channel will be configured to feed into a messaging port that points to a running XLANG schedule. The unique queue identifier inside the document is then used by BizTalk Messaging to figure out the schedule instance into which to place the acknowledgement.

As you can probably guess from the last two paragraphs, using BizTalk Messaging to select the correct XLANG instance into which to place a return document is quite advanced stuff. This process, called correlation, will be given a more in-depth discussion in Chapter 8.

Other Messaging Port Properties   Regardless of which type of messaging port you choose, the remaining pages are pretty much the same. As discussed, you need to choose an envelope to determine which serializer component will be used to create the outbound interchange, and the type of envelope you choose must match the format of the outgoing document itself.

The final page of the wizard, shown following, allows you to set encoding and encryption information. The available encoding is None, MIME, or Custom. Because most business documents will consist of simple ASCII plain text, it is usually fine to leave this setting as None. You should only change it to MIME to ensure that binary documents are correctly encoded or if you are sending a document using SMTP. The content type for the document can be configured in the advanced properties for the transport when you are creating an associated channel. If you will need to encrypt the outgoing document for extra security, you should select that option here and choose the appropriate trading partner's certificate from the BizTalk store. It is also possible to digitally sign the outgoing document to prove its authenticity; and although the option is available on this page of the messaging port wizard, the digital certificate used to sign the outgoing data will actually be chosen during the configuration of the channel.

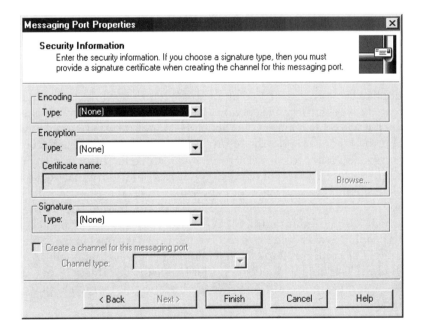

> **Note** *Securing BizTalk Server communications will be covered in more detail in Chapter 13.*

Distribution Lists

Sometimes it will be necessary to perform multiple actions on an outgoing document. For example, in the scenario presented in the beginning of this chapter, it was necessary for the trading partner to send the invoices back via SMTP while also saving a copy of the documents in their database. It is not possible for a single messaging port to handle both transports, but it is possible to combine multiple messaging ports together into a distribution list.

When we choose to create a distribution list from existing messaging ports, we are effectively creating multiple output scenarios for a single channel. In this way, we can send an invoice using HTTP, use an application integration component to update a database, and send an acknowledgement via e-mail all at the same time, by creating a messaging port for each transport and adding them to a new distribution list. After we create at least one channel that feeds into the list, any document picked up for processing by that channel will invoke all three messaging ports.

However, when we use a channel to invoke a distribution list that consists of multiple messaging ports, if any of the individual messaging ports is also associated with a channel, those channels will not be invoked. If you need a single inbound document transformed more than once into different output formats and then sent to multiple destinations, you will need to create multiple channels with the same source, destination, and inbound document properties and to ensure that these parameters are specified when the document is submitted. When a document that matches multiple channels is received, BizTalk Server invokes each matching channel.

> **Note** *You cannot add a messaging port that points to an XLANG schedule to a distribution list. However, you could configure a messaging port to point to an AIC and have that AIC submit the document to the XLANG schedule. Also, you cannot include open messaging ports in a distribution list. This is because it would be inconsistent to have a document that is both self-routing and non-self-routing. In addition, it would make little sense to have multiple open messaging ports combined together (because they would all end up using the same transport as specified in the document).*

Channels

The final component required to complete a BizTalk Messaging workflow is a *channel*. Ironically, although a channel will be typically the last object we create with BizTalk Messaging Manager, it still represents one of the earliest stages in the overall process. A channel might determine how a document is processed after it first arrives, but it will need to be created after organizations, applications, document definitions, messaging ports, and distribution lists, because its configuration will usually refer to each of these objects.

In particular, before you create a channel, you must create at least one messaging port. With a messaging port or distribution list selected, you can then choose to create a channel from an organization or from an application. Either option will cause the New Channel wizard to start, although the first page of the wizard will vary depending on the option you choose. As with messaging ports, you should create a channel from an organization if the document will come from a trading partner or if you need to create a channel where the source information is specified in the document itself. If the latter is the case, you will be creating something called an *open channel*. You should create a channel from an application if the document originates within your own organization, or if it will arrive from an XLANG schedule.

To better understand when to use organizations or applications for channels and messaging ports, you should consider the various environments in which BizTalk Server will be employed. In a typical B2B situation, we will send a document from an internal application to an external organization that is our trading partner. Likewise, an organization that is our trading partner could send a document to us, such that when it is received, we pass it off to an internal application. However, B2B solutions are not the only scenarios in which BizTalk Messaging can be used. For example, many electronic business transactions take place through online trading portals called *marketplaces*. If a company providing marketplace services were to use BizTalk Server, many of the exchanges would only pass through the marketplace, so that the source of the document would be an external organization, and the destination would be another organization. Creating a channel-messaging port pair in BizTalk Messaging where both the source and destination are external organizations is perfectly acceptable.

Similarly, we know that BizTalk Server is not just for B2B transactions. We know that BizTalk Server is also an extremely powerful way to implement EAI solutions. For example, if we have a customer-relationship management (CRM) system that delivers a report in a custom flat-file format, and we need to pass it to an enterprise resource processing (ERP) system that expects XML, we can use BizTalk Messaging to handle the receipt, transformation, and delivery of each message. Obviously, in such situations the original document will come from an internal application, but the final destination for the document will also be an internal application. Again, it is quite reasonable that BizTalk Messaging should support such a configuration, and it does.

Either way, when we are creating a channel, the first page of the wizard will ask us to enter a name for the object and also to specify whether the channel should act as a receipt channel. Before we get into receipts, however, which are part of a slightly more advanced topic, let's consider the rest of the things we need to know about the configuration of a channel.

From an Organization

When we opt to create a channel from an organization, the first page of the New Channel wizard will ask us to choose the source organization for the document, as shown. We can pick a specific organization from the list of organizations configured in BizTalk Messaging Manager, or we can choose to create an open source channel. Just like with messaging ports, if we create a channel where the source organization is not specified explicitly, it will be necessary for that information to be present in the document itself. If a document is submitted to BizTalk Server without expressing the organization explicitly, BizTalk Messaging will look for channels that have been created as open source. As long as the destination information and document type are specified in the document or in the submission call, BizTalk Server will still be able to select the appropriate channel-messaging port pair corresponding to these parameters.

> **Note** *Although a self-routing document will usually contain both source and destination information, it is not possible to create an open source channel that feeds into an open destination messaging port. If you think about it, the lack of any organization information in the channel-messaging port pair would mean that all documents of a particular type would match every pair, even if other channels and messaging ports were specifically required for that document type.*

From an Application

If we choose to create a channel from an application, we will have two different options available, as shown. The first option is to configure the source to be an internal application as referenced by an application of the home organization, while the second option is to configure an XLANG schedule as the source application. If we configure the source to be an internal application, that label will serve no real purpose other than to allow us to track documents that have passed through this channel. If we specify an XLANG schedule, however, we will later need to configure a BizTalk Messaging implementation shape in BizTalk Orchestration Designer to point to this particular channel or else it won't get used. As mentioned earlier, messages sent from BizTalk Orchestration through BizTalk Messaging may need to be correlated with their original schedule instance to ensure the consistency of those schedules. This will be covered in more detail in Chapter 8.

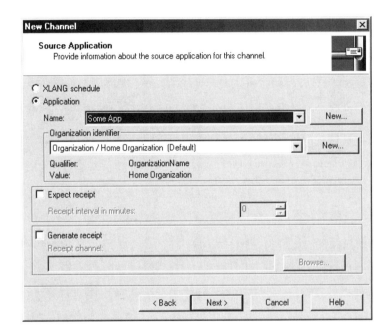

Other Channel Properties

After we have selected the source organization or application, we can choose to generate a receipt, or expect a receipt, which we will discuss shortly. On the next page of the wizard, we select the inbound document definition. As mentioned, the inbound document definition will usually point to a specification stored in the WebDAV Repository. This specification will be used by the appropriate parser to convert the incoming document into an intermediate XML representation. If the incoming document has been encrypted using a copy of our digital certificate, we can decrypt it at this point by browsing the private store for our digital certificate. Documents coming from trading partners will be encrypted using the public key that we make available through our digital certificate, so we will need a copy of our private key for decryption. Similarly, if a trading partner digitally signed the incoming document using their private key, we can browse the BizTalk store for a copy of that partner's digital certificate, as it will contain the necessary public key to verify the digital signature. Securing BizTalk Server transactions and digital signatures will be covered fully in Chapter 13.

On this page, we can also choose to track or filter documents passing through this particular channel. We saw earlier how to track all instances of a document by configuring the global tracking fields in the document definition. Here we can do the same thing, but only documents that are processed by this channel will have their values stored in the tracking database. If an inbound document definition specifies fields to be tracked that do not agree with the configuration of the global tracking fields set for the document definition, the settings for the channel will override those of the document definition.

Filtering To filter a document, we can create a special type of expression that will be used to determine whether the channel should be invoked. This can be based on the presence of a field or its value. These are *XPath expressions*, as they are built using the XML Path Language (XPath), which is a W3C recommendation for navigating XML documents and selecting single or multiple nodes. Although this sounds rather complicated, XPath expressions can look very much like file paths in a directory structure. For example, if we have an XML document as follows, we may wish to test the value of the *invoiceTotal* field.

```
<ContosoInvoice>
    <Header invoiceNumber="XJ501" referenceNumber="ZX13"
        PONumber="52"created="2001-12-12T00:00:00-00:00"
        invoiceTotal="100"/>
    <BillTo name="Joe Bloggs" address="10 Fake Street"
        city="Fraudsville"state="CA" zip="90210" country="US"/>
</ContosoInvoice>
```

To navigate to this field, we start at the root of the document and move down through the *ContosoInvoice* root element, down through the *Header* child element, until we reach the *invoiceTotal* attribute. The path to this field is thus:

```
/ContosoInvoice/Header/@invoiceTotal
```

Notice that we preface the *invoiceTotal* field with an "@" sign because it is an attribute. In XPath terminology, we have just created a *location path*. Needless to say, location paths can get much more involved, but we'll usually only need to use simple expressions. This kind of expression would allow us to select the *invoiceTotal* field, but we want to do more than just select that field. We want to test the value of the field, so we'll also have to use something called a *predicate*. Predicates are filters enclosed in square brackets that can appear in XPath expressions. Every step in a location path (that is, from one forward slash to the next) can have zero or more predicates to filter the node-set selected at each step. In our example, we would want to put a predicate on the location step that selects the *Header* child element, so that we can test it for an attribute called *invoiceTotal* having a certain value. This XPath expression would look like this:

```
/ContosoInvoice/Header[@invoiceTotal = 500]
```

We can enter that expression into the Channel Filtering Expressions dialog box during the configuration of a channel. With this filtering expression in place, the channel will only be invoked if the *invoiceTotal* field has a value of 500.

To use channel filtering on a particular field, that field must be configured with a data type in the specification created in BizTalk Editor. This is done on the Declaration tab for that field. Creating specifications with BizTalk Editor was covered in Chapter 3.

 If a field has been configured to use a Boolean data type, the XPath expression must test for the values –1 or 0 rather than "true" or "false".

Receipts

BizTalk Messaging provides a mechanism for the automatic handling and processing of receipts if EDI or Reliable messaging is being used. If a B2B scenario involves the sending of a document to a trading partner, we will often require that trading partner to send us a receipt to act as an acknowledgement of the sent document. Similarly, if our organization receives a document from a trading partner, it may be necessary for us to send a receipt back to them. Receipts can sometimes be as important as the original document to which they are sent as a response. Sometimes, a company's international standards accreditations may even depend on the way in which they handle incoming and outgoing receipts.

Let us consider the latter case first. If our trading partner has sent us an X12 purchase order, we will need to process the document as normal, but we will also need to send an X12 receipt. We know that to send any kind of document requires a channel-messaging port pair, and a receipt is no different. Therefore, when we create the channel to receive the original purchase order, we will need to select the check box to generate a receipt, as shown in the following illustration, and to specify the name of a receipt channel. We can either create the receipt channel first and then select it when configuring the channel for the purchase order, or we can create the purchase order channel first, create the receipt channel, and then go back and reconfigure the original channel to generate a receipt using this receipt channel.

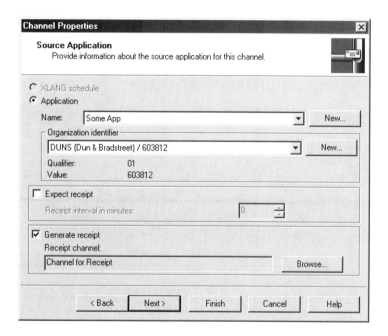

Handling EDI Receipts   When we create the receipt channel, we will specify that it is a receipt channel, as shown, and this will allow us to select that channel when configuring the channel for the original document. Normally, when we configure a channel, we will have to specify manually the document definitions that correspond to the incoming and outgoing document types. For receipt channels, however, BizTalk Messaging provides the BizTalk Canonical Receipt document definition, and this is automatically configured as both the incoming and outgoing document definition when the receipt channel is created. It is not possible to just change the outgoing document definition in this case. If we need to send the receipt in a different format, we will first have to configure the inbound document properties of the channel to use a document definition that points to the Canonical Receipt specification found in the WebDAV Repository. Then we will be allowed to select a different outbound definition and the appropriate map to convert the canonical receipt into the format required.

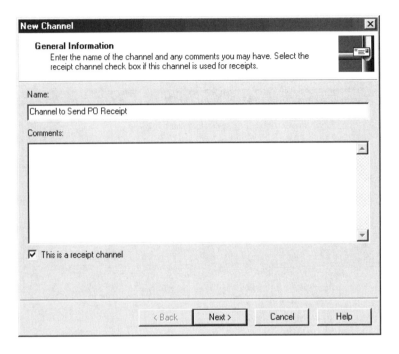

 As with all document definitions used in EDI exchanges, you will need to configure the selection criteria for the outgoing receipt document definition if it is in either an X12 or EDIFACT format. You will also need to select the appropriate envelope in the messaging port and set the delimiters corresponding to that format.

The other scenario involves us sending an X12 or EDIFACT document to a trading partner and getting a receipt document in the corresponding format in return. In this case, when we configure the channel to process the original document that we will be sending, we can specify that a receipt should be expected, as shown. We can also enter a value in minutes for the time interval in which the receipt should arrive after the original document has been sent. When BizTalk Server receives this receipt, it will be correlated with the original document by comparing the interchange header information.

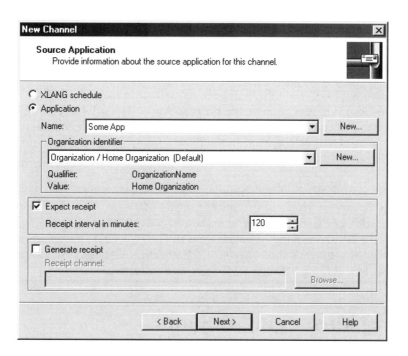

Note   *If you are using a custom document format rather than X12 or EDIFACT, you can still generate and expect receipts. However, you will need to create a custom correlation component that compares the receipts received with the outgoing documents to validate those receipts.*

Handling Reliable Receipts   BizTalk Server 2000—as its name suggests—is a BizTalk Framework 2.0–compliant server, capable of automatically processing documents sent using the Reliable XML format. As a result, when an organization sends out a document that uses a Reliable envelope, if it is sent to another BizTalk Framework–compliant server, that server will automatically return a receipt. It is not even necessary to create a channel and messaging port to process the returned receipt, as the original document will contain a URL to which all receipts should be sent, and the trading partner's server should return the receipt to this address. The address is called the *Reliable Messaging Reply-To URL*, and it is configured for the BizTalk Server Group in BizTalk Administration. It will typically point to an Active Server Page on the server that will store the receipts in a directory or database. Of course, if extra processing of the receipts is required, that ASP could feed the receipts back into BizTalk Server to be handled by BizTalk Messaging or BizTalk Orchestration.

Similarly, if your BizTalk Server receives documents that use the Reliable format, it will automatically generate receipts and send them back to the URL specified in those documents with no configuration necessary. The only exception to this is if SMTP has been used as the transport address to send a document to your server. In that case, the Reliable Messaging Reply-To URL will be an e-mail address, and it will be necessary to configure the Home Organization on the BizTalk Server that will be sending the receipt, so that its Reliable Messaging SMTP From Address identifier has a valid e-mail address. This e-mail address will then appear in the *From* field on the e-mail containing the receipt that is sent back to the trading partner.

The automatic generation and sending of receipts is done using hidden messaging objects that are not shown in BizTalk Messaging Manager. These objects consist of a channel called "Reliable Messaging Acknowledgement Channel", a messaging port called "Reliable Messaging Acknowledgement Port", and a document definition called "Reliable Messaging Acknowledgement". If you attempt to use these names for objects you create in BizTalk Messaging Manager, you will receive an error.

Creating Messaging Objects

Once you understand the concepts behind BizTalk Messaging and appreciate how all the various objects interact to produce a complete workflow, you are ready to create those objects in BizTalk Messaging Manager. This section assumes you are familiar with the basics discussed in the first half of the chapter, so repetition of these topics will be avoided where possible.

BizTalk Messaging Manager Interface

The BizTalk Messaging Manager interface is shown in Figure 6-4. It is actually an HTML application that queries and manipulates the InterchangeBTM database and displays the data as a web page. As a result, the World Wide Web service must be running on the BizTalk Server on which the Messaging Manager application is installed. A standard toolbar and a menu bar give you access to the commands. The File menu contains commands to create new objects, edit existing objects, delete existing objects, and exit the application. The Edit menu contains commands to find channels associated with a selected messaging port, find messaging ports or distribution lists associated with a selected channel, or select all visible objects. The Tools menu contains a single command to change the application options, and the Help menu displays the BizTalk Server help files (as if you hadn't guessed).

The first time you open BizTalk Messaging Manager, it will display a dialog box presenting a limited number of common choices, as shown. It is unlikely that every

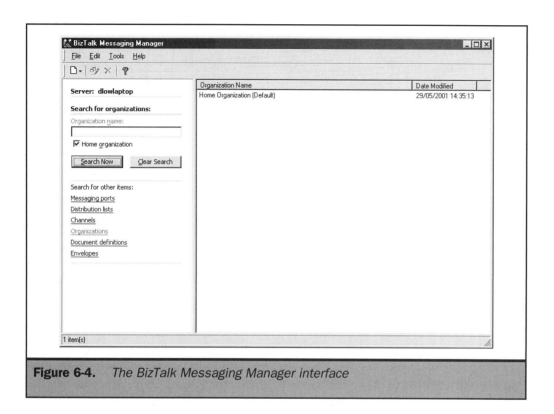

Figure 6-4. *The BizTalk Messaging Manager interface*

time you open the utility, you will want to perform one of these four tasks, as there are so many other tasks to perform that are just as important.

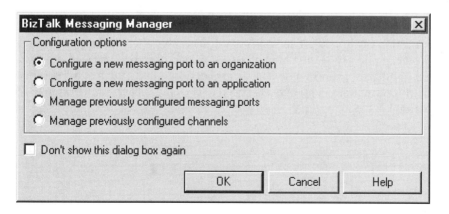

I would recommend selecting the box that prevents the dialog box from appearing in the future. If you feel the need to, you can cause it to be displayed again by accessing Tools | Options. The Options dialog box, shown here, also allows you to set the maximum number of objects to be listed when you run a search, the name of the server to connect to, and the timeout value that BizTalk Server should use when trying to connect to that server.

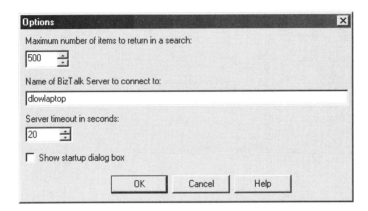

The main window consists of two panes. The left pane allows you to perform searches for existing objects, and the right pane shows the objects returned by a search. You can edit any object in the right pane by clicking the Edit button on the main toolbar or by choosing File | Edit. You can also edit an object by double-clicking it, by far the easiest method.

To create a messaging object, you can use the File | New command or use the New button on the main toolbar. To search for existing objects, you can select a category by clicking on a hyperlink on the left and clicking the Search Now button. Depending on the category you click, there may be other options available to narrow your search. For example, there is always a text box in which you can type a name, or an SQL wildcard expression, such as "Port%". You conduct the search by then clicking the Search Now button. You can often type the name of an associated object, such as an organization or document definition, as shown next. The application retains the last thing typed into the box during searches, so you may also need to click the Clear Search button to reset the search parameters.

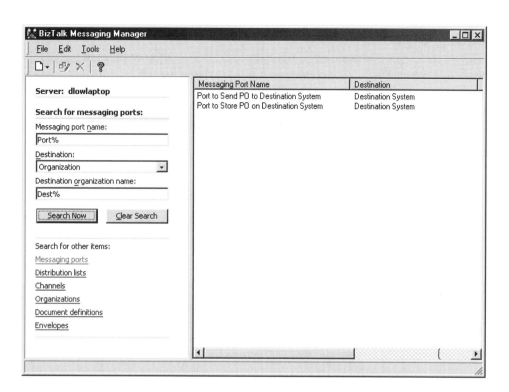

Creating Organizations and Applications

Each end of a BizTalk Messaging workflow consists of an organization or an application. The Home Organization is created automatically when BizTalk Server is installed, and it represents your company, division, or agency. You can add applications to this organization to represent your internal applications. You will not use the Home Organization itself as an endpoint for a workflow, however; you will use these internal applications instead. You can also create other organizations to represent your trading partners, but it is not possible to add applications to these other organizations through BizTalk Messaging Manager, as these organizations will themselves serve as endpoints.

Creating Organizations

When you choose to create a new organization, the New Organization dialog box appears, as shown. You will need to type a unique name for the organization, and you can also type a comment.

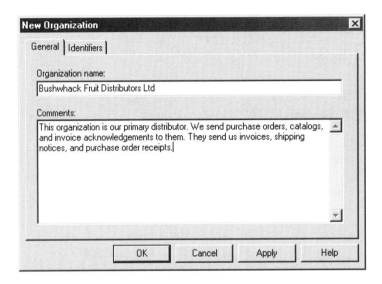

Creating Identifiers   On the Identifiers tab you can add other identifiers for the organization. There is always a default identifier qualifier called "OrganizationName" that will have as its value the name given to the organization, but you can add, edit, or remove further standard or custom identifiers. In each case, the identifier qualifier and identifier value must form a unique pair across all organizations. There are multiple standard identifiers you can choose, as shown, or else you can create a custom identifier that suits your needs. After you have created another identifier, you can choose to set that identifier as the default for that organization. This is useful, for example, if you are constantly exchanging EDI documents with organizations that will use a Dun & Bradstreet number as an identifier, as opposed to an organization name.

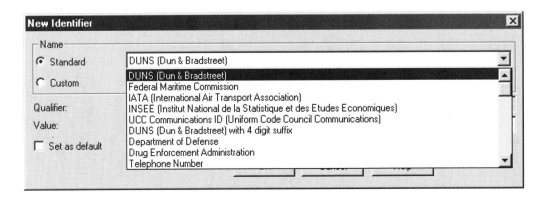

Creating Applications

For the Home Organization, you can also create applications that represent your own internal applications. This is another important way to distinguish different types of documents sent from your organization or received by your organization when you use the Documents Tracking feature. To create a new application on the Home Organization, edit the Home Organization object, and click the Add button on the Applications tab, as shown. It is only necessary to provide the name of the application, as there is no other configurable information.

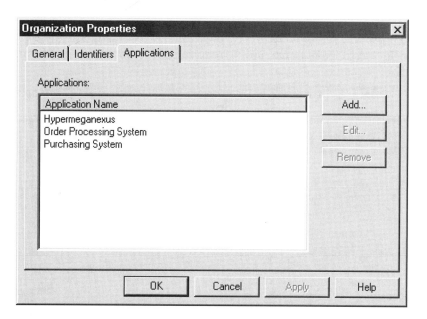

Creating Document Definitions and Envelopes

Although every workflow you create in BizTalk Messaging will use a variety of objects, possibly the most important object from a conceptual point of view is a document definition, as it represents the actual data that will flow between organizations and applications. These document definitions will almost always represent a particular business document structure by referencing a document specification that was previously created with BizTalk Editor, and which is stored in the WebDAV Repository.

Because BizTalk Server can handle multiple document formats, multiple parser components exist to convert incoming documents to BizTalk Server's internal XML format. Similarly, there are multiple serializer components that take an internal XML representation of a document and convert it to a particular format, as might be required by another organization or application. To aid BizTalk Server in the selection of an appropriate parser for an incoming document or an appropriate serializer for an outgoing document, we will need to create envelopes.

Creating Document Definitions

There are multiple properties to be configured when creating a document definition. This is done using the New Document Definition dialog box, shown following. First, it will be necessary to provide a name, which must again be unique. Second, we will typically select a document specification to which this document definition should point, as stored in the WebDAV Repository. This specification, created using BizTalk Editor, enables the appropriate parser to convert the document to or from the internal XML representation used by BizTalk Messaging. The only time we will not need to reference a document specification is when a document definition will represent a document that should not be parsed, validated, transformed, or tracked. This would be the case if BizTalk Server were processing a binary document. The other properties we can configure will be optional or only required for certain document formats.

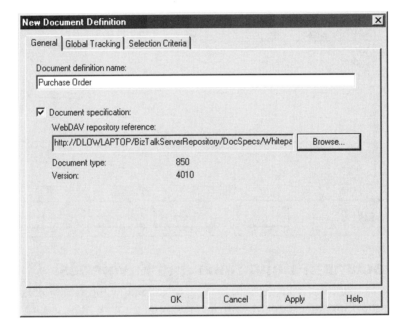

 As previously mentioned, document definitions and their associated document specifications are actually stored in the BizTalk Messaging Management database after creation. Thus, if you make a change to a document specification, you will need to edit the document definition and reselect the specification to load the new file into the database.

Configuring Global Tracking Fields   The Global Tracking tab allows us to specify that the values of certain fields should be explicitly tracked and stored in the InterchangeDTA database for later querying using the Document Tracking tool. As shown in the following illustration, we can select two fields to be tracked as integers, two fields to be tracked as real numbers, two fields to be tracked as dates, two fields to be tracked as text, and any number of fields to be tracked as a custom data type. Be aware, however, that we will only be able to track fields using the integer, real, and date data types if those fields have been configured with the appropriate data types in BizTalk Editor. The fields are called *global tracking fields* because they are tracked for all instances of that document type, as opposed to tracking fields configured within a channel, which are only tracked for documents processed by that channel.

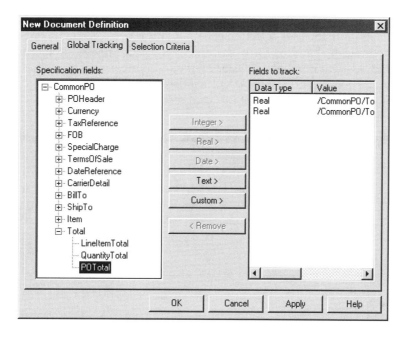

Caution   *Tracking fields in either a document definition or a channel will only work if document tracking has been enabled for the BizTalk Server group to which the server belongs. It is enabled by default, but it may be turned off using the BizTalk Administration utility. BizTalk Administration will be covered in Chapter 9.*

Configuring Selection Criteria   The Selection Criteria tab is important if we are creating document definitions that represent ANSI X12 or UN/EDIFACT documents. They are used to assist BizTalk Server in the selection of a channel-messaging port pair for incoming self-routing documents and to populate interchange header information for outgoing documents. For self-routing documents that use other formats, it is possible to specify the fields that will contain the routing information using the Dictionary tab in BizTalk Editor. However, X12 and EDIFACT document specifications do not have fields that can be used to store this information; instead, the routing information is always present in particular fields in the interchange header.

For example, if there is a channel that has an X12 3060/850 purchase order configured as the inbound document definition, and we need to ensure that this channel is selected when such a document is submitted to BizTalk Server, we will configure the selection criteria for the document definition to match the values contained in the interchange header for the inbound interchange. Similarly, if the outbound document definition configured in a channel was an X12 4010/810 invoice, we would also need to make sure that the appropriate selection criteria were configured for that document definition. Otherwise, BizTalk Server would not be able to create the outgoing interchange header.

You can add, edit, and remove selection criteria on the Selection Criteria tab. In the following illustration, the four selection criteria required by X12 documents have been configured to indicate that the type of document is a "PO", the sending organization has a Dun & Bradstreet number of "503812", the receiving organization has a Dun & Bradstreet number of "556462", and the X12 standards version is 3060. Refer to the section on selection criteria in the first half of this chapter for further details.

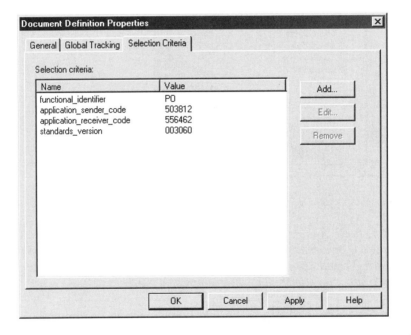

 Each criterion is a name-value pair, and it is important to specify the names exactly. For X12 documents, they are "functional_identifier", "application_sender_code", "application_receiver_code", and "standards_version". For EDIFACT documents, they are "functional_identifier", "application_sender_code", "application_receiver_code", "standards_version_type", and "standards_version_value".

Creating Envelopes

As discussed, envelopes are objects that help BizTalk Server select the appropriate parser for incoming documents or the appropriate serializer for outgoing documents. In either case, when we create an envelope object, we will need to specify the envelope format, which will be one of Custom XML, X12, EDIFACT, Flat-File, Custom, or Reliable. Depending on the format and whether we're dealing with inbound or outbound documents, it may be also necessary to point the envelope at an envelope specification that has been created with BizTalk Editor and is stored in the WebDAV Repository.

Creating an envelope is done in the New Envelope dialog box, as shown in the first half of this chapter. We must provide a unique name for the envelope and an appropriate format that will correspond to the type of document the envelope will contain. As discussed in the first half of this chapter, an envelope specification is always required for inbound flat-file interchanges, and they may possibly be required for custom interchanges, depending on the custom parser component used. For outbound interchanges, specifications are only required for custom XML and possibly other custom document types, although this will again depend on the custom serializer component used.

Creating Messaging Ports and Distribution Lists

To configure where an outgoing document should be sent after processing and the transport mechanism that should be used to get it there, we create messaging ports. If a document needs to be sent to multiple destinations using multiple transports, we can combine messaging ports into a distribution list. Although the creation of distribution lists is very straightforward, each messaging port is defined using a wizard. Many different properties need to be configured, and different scenarios will involve the discussion of these properties in detail.

Creating Messaging Ports

Unlike organizations, applications, document definitions, and envelopes, which are created and configured using simple dialog boxes, messaging ports and channels are created using wizards. There is quite a number of options that need to be configured, and some of these options will determine the availability of other properties. In fact, before we even start up the wizard, we need to decide which type of messaging port we wish to create. This will depend on the scenario in which the messaging port will be used.

For example, if we are sending a document to a trading partner, we will be transporting the document outside our own organization, so it will be necessary to create a messaging port *to an organization*. This will also be true even if the document itself contains the information about its destination and how it should get there. These self-routing documents could end up practically anywhere, including an actual application within our own organization, so we will again create a messaging port to an organization, but we will specify the destination as *open*.

In a different scenario, if a document needs to be delivered specifically to one of our internal applications for processing, we will wish to create a messaging port *to an application*. This will also be the case if we wish to deliver a document for further processing to an XLANG schedule created with BizTalk Orchestration Designer, because XLANG schedules are executable files, so they also count as applications.

The wizards used to create each type of messaging port are almost the same. Only the destination information page is different, so we will first discuss the differences between available on that page for each messaging port type before discussing the remaining options that are common to both types.

Creating a Messaging Port to an Organization
When creating a new messaging port to an organization, the General Information page of the New Messaging Port wizard asks you to enter a unique name and optional comments, as shown. You should be as descriptive as possible with the name of the messaging port, as it will make it easier to figure out which is which later on.

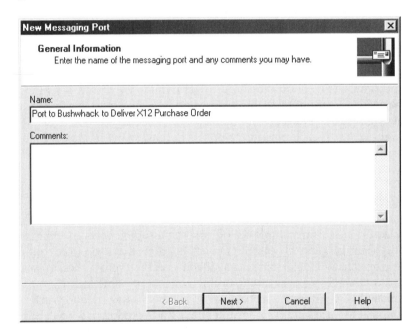

Clicking Next brings you to the Destination Organization page, where you provide information about the organization to which the document should be sent. If the document will be self-routing, you should specify Open destination. As discussed in the first half of this chapter, the destination transport and location for a self-routing document must be available in a field in the document itself. Consequently, if you choose to configure an open destination messaging port, the primary and backup transport fields are not available on this page, the organization identifier information is not configurable on the next page, and it will not be possible to encrypt the document using a digital certificate on the final page of the wizard.

Even if a document does not contain the necessary destination information itself, it is still possible to use an open messaging port. If the document is being submitted programmatically using the Submit or SubmitSync method of the Interchange object, you can provide the destination identifier as a parameter to the method call.

If you will be manually configuring the destination information, you should select the Organization option, as shown, and click Browse to choose an organization by name. Later in the wizard, you will be able to select a different identifier for that organization if required. On this page, however, you will also need to select a primary transport and destination, and, optionally, a backup transport and destination. As these properties are shared with messaging ports configured to an application, the available transports will be discussed after we cover the initial creation of this other type of messaging port.

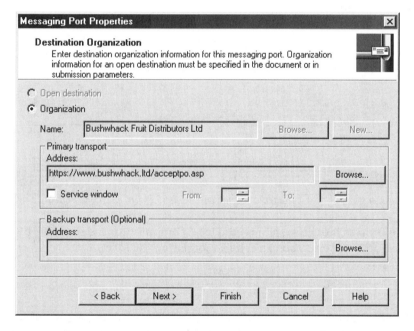

Creating a Messaging Port to an Application   When creating a new messaging port to an application, the General Information page of the New Messaging Port wizard is the same as for an organization, in that you must provide a unique name and an optional comment. On the Destination Application page, you then have the option to select an application of the Home Organization, a new XLANG schedule, or a running XLANG schedule. Specifying an application of the Home Organization actually results in the identifier qualifier-value pair for the Home Organization being configured as the destination, but the application name chosen can be later used to query documents that were sent using this messaging port in the Document Tracking utility. Again, it is possible to select different identifiers for the Home Organization later in the wizard.

If you select a new XLANG schedule as the destination, you will have to provide the path to the .skx file that represents the XLANG schedule, and the name of an orchestration port, as shown. This uses the XLANG *moniker* syntax that begins with "sked://".

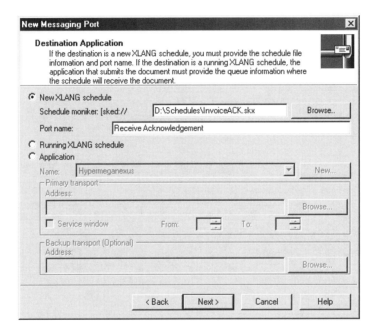

 Caution   *The maximum size of a document that can be sent to an XLANG schedule is 2MB.*

You can browse the file system on the local computer for the schedule by clicking the Browse button, or else you can type a moniker in the form,

```
sked://localhost!applicationName/path\filename.skx
```

where *filename*.skx is the name of the file, *path* is the local path to the file, *applicationName* is the name of the COM+ application that will host the schedule instance (this name is case-sensitive), and *localhost* is either the name of the local computer or else the actual string "localhost". If you are using the default XLANG Scheduler application, only the path and filename are required. Unfortunately, it will be necessary for the schedule to run on the same machine as BizTalk Messaging, so Microsoft's goal of loosely coupled application integration breaks down here. You will also have to specify the name of an orchestration port in the schedule that is bound to a BizTalk Messaging implementation. This port should be joined to the first action in the schedule, and it must be the only port bound to a BizTalk implementation that is configured to activate a new schedule instance when a message arrives.

> **Note**   *An orchestration port is a uniquely named location in an XLANG schedule that represents the binding between a workflow action and the technology by which it will be implemented. It also serves as the logical point through which messages flow into and out of the schedule.*

You will only choose to send the document to a running XLANG schedule instance if you are integrating BizTalk Messaging and Orchestration services. In such a scenario, an XLANG schedule will use BizTalk Messaging to send a document to another location, perhaps a trading partner. However, the XLANG schedule will not finish executing at that point; it will wait for a response. When an acknowledgement or related message is returned to BizTalk Server, it must be sent to a specially configured Active Server Page (ASP) or Message Queue. The ASP will extract the name of a channel, which should have been embedded in the document before it was sent.

The document will then be submitted programmatically to that channel, which, in turn, will feed it into a messaging port to an application, where the destination is the still-running XLANG schedule. Unique identifying information that is also embedded in the document and extracted by the ASP will allow BizTalk Server to select the correct instance of the XLANG schedule. Further details on how to set up an integrated process will be given in Chapter 8.

> **Note**   *If the destination of the document is an XLANG schedule, either new or existing, it will not be possible to encrypt the document. Microsoft says this is by design, as it should not be necessary to encrypt a document traveling between BizTalk Messaging and BizTalk Orchestration within an organization.*

Once the destination information has been decided upon, the remainder of the wizard is the same, regardless of whether the messaging port is going to an application or an organization. The next thing we have to configure is the transport information. BizTalk Server provides seven transport methods—Application Integration Component, HTTP, HTTPS, File, Loopback, Message Queuing, and SMTP. We can set both a primary and a backup transport method. If the primary transport fails a set number of times (the retry count), the backup transport will be used. We can also set a service window for the primary transport, which is a timeframe specified using the Universal Time Convention (UTC). Select the Service Window check box to enable it, and select the start and end hours between which this messaging port should attempt to use the primary transport to send the document.

You cannot set a service window for open messaging ports or for messaging ports that use the Loopback transport.

Using Application Integration Components   Application Integration Components (AICs) are COM components that implement the IPipelineComponent and IPipeline ComponentAdmin interfaces, or else the IBTSAppIntegration interface. These components allow you to create custom transport methods to extend BizTalk Server. The IBTSAppIntegration interface is a very simple interface with a single method—ProcessMessage—that takes a single parameter representing the document. The IPipelineComponent interface is more complicated in that it uses a special type of object called a *Dictionary* object to store the document and related data. This data can be configured at design time by using the methods of the IPipelineComponentAdmin interface. If these interfaces sound familiar to you, it's because they are also used to create pipeline components for Microsoft Commerce Server.

For example, if you wished to create an AIC that stored a document in a database, you might want to be able to reuse that component in a number of different scenarios. As a result, it would make more sense to allow the database details to be provided at design time, rather than hard-coding the information into the component itself. Setting design-time configuration information for an AIC is actually done in the New Channel wizard and will be discussed later in the section dealing with creating channels. The actual creation of AICs and their associated design-time configuration pages will be covered in Chapter 17.

You select an AIC by clicking the Browse button in the Primary (or Backup) Transport dialog box, as shown. Because these components use particular interfaces, they need to be registered as AICs before they will appear in the Select A Component dialog box. This can be done by adding the component to a COM+ application, or by *registering affinity* for the components. This also will be covered in Chapter 17.

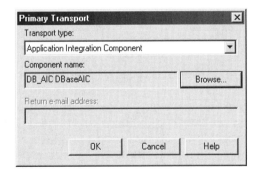

Using the HTTP Transport   If you choose the HTTP transport in a messaging port, you are electing to transport the document to a page or script on a web server. Obviously, that web server must be accessible to BizTalk Server, either directly or via a proxy server. Default proxy server information can be specified in the BizTalk Administration utility, but if you need to provide different proxy server details for a specific messaging port, you can do so by overriding the messaging port defaults during the configuration of an associated channel. At this point, you can also specify a user name and password if required by the web server. Overriding these defaults will be discussed in the section dealing with creating channels.

It is not enough just to specify the name of an HTTP server when configuring the transport; the full URL to the script or executable that will accept the data must be provided, for example, "http://www.bushwhack.ltd/receivepo.asp". You must also ensure that this is the actual path to the script, as BizTalk Server does not support redirection. Redirection occurs if a web server sends an HTTP 302 status code to the client along with a new URL or if the location of the file has moved. It can also occur on some UNIX-based web servers. Their filenames are case-sensitive, so that if the incorrect case is used in the URL, the web server will automatically redirect the request to the correct location.

Using the HTTPS Transport   The configuration for the HTTPS transport is the same as for the HTTP transport, except that a secure connection will be established with the web server before the data is sent. The initiated connection will cause the web server to send a digital certificate containing its public key to BizTalk Server, which will then encrypt information using that key. The web server may also request a client certificate from the BizTalk Server for authentication. The appropriate client certificate can be selected during the creation of an associated channel by overriding the defaults for the HTTPS transport. Again, this will be discussed in the section dealing with channel creation.

Using the File Transport   Although BizTalk Server does not support sending documents via FTP to an organization or application, it does support the File protocol for delivering documents to the local file system. Again, it is not enough to specify the directory to which the file should be delivered; you must also specify the filename. If you specify a single filename, each new document that arrives in the directory will be appended to that file. If you wish to ensure that each document is saved with a unique filename, you must use the *%tracking_id%* symbol within the filename. This generates a Global Unique Identifier (GUID) that will be inserted into the filename at the specified position. For example, a valid address for the File transport would be

```
file://c:\purchaseorders\po%tracking_id%.xml
```

You can also specify a Universal Naming Convention (UNC) path of the form
\\servername\sharename\filename.ext to output the file to a network share. To do
this, you will need to ensure that the user account being used by the BizTalk Messaging
service has the appropriate permissions on both the share and the file system.

It is also possible, by overriding the transport defaults in an associated channel, to change the behavior from append to overwrite. However, take care that documents are retrieved from the directory before they are overwritten, or the data will be lost.

You can also use the special symbols *%datetime%*, *%document_name%*, and *%server%*, which will insert the date and time in GMT milliseconds, the name of the document definition, or the name of the BizTalk Server, respectively. In each case, it is possible that non-unique filenames could be created. Similarly, there is a final symbol—*%uid%*—that inserts a time-based counter in milliseconds, but this counter is reset if the BizTalk Server is restarted, so again the possibility of non-unique filenames arises.

With BizTalk Server Service Pack 1 installed, the dictionary properties *src_filepath* and *src_filename* are also available for use in the destination file path. For example, specifying *file://c:\invoices\%src_filename%.xml* as the path would use the original name of a file that had been submitted to BizTalk Server as its destination name. This information only exists, however, if the *filename* parameter is used in the Submit or SubmitSync method call, or if the interchange was submitted using a file receive function. These methods will be discussed in Chapter 16.

Note *These dictionary properties are not available if a file is submitted with the pass-through flag set to true, as the transport dictionary object is not populated by BizTalk Server in this case.*

Using the Loopback Transport   You would be forgiven for thinking that the Loopback transport is simply for testing a configuration. "Loopback" is a term often used in networking troubleshooting, such as "loopback address" or "loopback adapter." However, the Loopback transport has a very specific use in BizTalk Server. But first, I must make a confession. At the beginning of the chapter, I stated that the method by which a document arrives at BizTalk Server does not affect how BizTalk Messaging processes it. Actually, I lied a little. When documents are submitted programmatically using the Interchange object, there are two methods available— Submit and SubmitSync. Although we won't go into too much detail on using these methods until Chapter 16, it is enough to know now that the method we use can actually affect how the document is processed.

The Submit method sends a document asynchronously to BizTalk Server. This means that the application doing the submission doesn't hang around waiting for a reply. Once the document has been delivered, its job is done. The SubmitSync method, however, sends a document synchronously and waits for a response before completing. This response can be another document or the same document in a different format. BizTalk Messaging bumps these submissions up to the top of the queue to ensure they are given preferential treatment. The Loopback transport method allows the document that is output by the channel to be fed back to the SubmitSync method call as an immediate response. No further configuration is necessary. The application that invoked this method call will then typically perform extra processing on the returned document, for example, storing it in a database. Also, we could create a distribution list consisting of two messaging ports. The first messaging port could use the Loopback transport to return a response, while the second could send the document somewhere else.

It is not possible to use a Reliable envelope with the Loopback transport. This is because Reliable envelopes are used to set routing information and to cause an acknowledgement to be generated. Neither feature should be used with the Loopback transport.

Using the Message Queuing Transport   A brief discussion on message queues was given in Chapter 2. If you will be using the message queuing transport in BizTalk Messaging, it is assumed you know what message queues are for. When you select the message queuing transport method, again, you must specify the complete path to the queue, as shown. However, a prefix is not automatically inserted for you. This is because the prefix can vary depending on the type of message queue to which you will be sending the document.

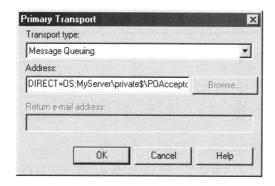

First of all, the "queue://" prefix should not be used. Examples of valid message queue paths are shown in the following table.

Path Type	Syntax
Direct	DIRECT=OS:MyServer\private$\POAcceptor DIRECT=TCP:192.168.0.100\ReceiveInvoice
Private	PRIVATE=67452301-AB89-EFCD-0123-456789ABCDEF\0000000D
Public	PUBLIC=12345678-90AB-CDEF-1234-567890ABCDEF

The maximum size of a document transported using a message queue is 2MB. If an envelope is used, the size of the combined interchange must not exceed 4MB.

Using the SMTP Transport   The SMTP transport method can be used to send documents via e-mail to trading partners or to SMTP servers that can process messages, such as Microsoft Exchange Server. As before, you must provide a valid address, which is in the format *mailto:alias@domain*, as shown. Obviously, an SMTP server must be available to send the document. The name of the SMTP server is configured for a BizTalk Server Group in the BizTalk Administration utility. You must also provide a return e-mail address that will be placed in the From field of the outgoing e-mail.

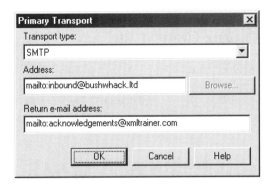

If an open messaging port is configured to use SMTP as its transport, then the value specified in the Reliable Messaging Acknowledgement SMTP From Address organization identifier is used as the From address for the e-mail. Also, the Subject line is automatically set to the tracking ID unless BizTalk Server Service Pack 1 is installed, in which case it is set to the document definition name followed by the tracking ID.

Setting Envelope and Identifier Properties As discussed earlier in the chapter, it will always be necessary to select an envelope in a messaging port, or the internal XML format will be used as the outgoing format. You can select an existing envelope from the menu or click the New button to create a new envelope in the required format. If you select an X12 or EDIFACT envelope to wrap an outgoing EDI document, it will be also necessary to specify the document delimiters. Click the Delimiters button, and enter the component element, element, and segment delimiter characters, as appropriate for the format. For example, typical X12 delimiters are ">" for component element, "*" for element, and "~" for segment terminators. You will also have to enter an interchange control number for EDI envelope formats. This is a unique identifier that will be used to track outgoing EDI interchanges. Simply enter a nonzero number in the field. BizTalk Server will place this number into the outgoing interchange header, and the number will be incremented each time the messaging port is used.

The component element delimiter will always be found at position 105 in the interchange header; the element delimiter will always be found at position 4 in the interchange header; and the segment delimiter will always be found at position 106.

On this page of the wizard, you can also select the identifier qualifier and value to use for the destination organization. If the messaging port is to an application, you can set the identifiers to be used for the Home Organization, unless the messaging port is configured to send the document to a new or existing XLANG schedule.

Setting Encoding and Encryption Properties   The final page of the wizard allows you to specify encoding and encryption information for the outgoing document. First, you can select an encoding method. Most documents will be ASCII text documents, so you can usually leave the default setting of None. The other option available is MIME, which might be used if you were sending a binary document to an application or trading partner, and you needed to set the content type of the document. Setting the content type is done in the channel wizard by overriding the messaging port properties. It is also possible to use a custom encoding component, but this can only be set through programmatic manipulation of BizTalk Messaging, which will be covered in Chapter 16.

To encrypt the outgoing data, select S/MIME from the menu. You will need a certificate from the trading partner or application to which the data will be sent. These certificates should be kept in the BizTalk Store. To manage these certificates, create a Microsoft Management Console (MMC) tool, and add a Certificates snap-in configured to manage the computer account on the local computer. From here, you can import certificates as necessary. Clicking the Browse button in BizTalk Messaging Manager will then allow you to select a certificate for encryption, as shown here.

The final thing to be configured for a messaging port is whether the document should be digitally signed. This will prove that a particular party sent the message and that the document has not been tampered with. Together, these properties also provide non-repudiation so that the sending party cannot later claim that it did not send the document or that it sent a different document. Again, this will require a digital certificate, although the digital certificate itself will only be selected when the associated channel is created.

At this point, the configuration of the messagsing port is complete, and you can either accept the default, which is to create an associated channel after clicking the Finish button, or you can clear the check box to create a channel for the messaging port later. If you are creating a messaging port to an organization, the menu will default to creating a channel from an application; and if you are creating a messaging port to an application, the menu will default to creating a channel from an organization. The defaults will be suitable for many scenarios, but you are free to select either option in each case.

Creating Distribution Lists

It is only possible to configure a single transport and address in a messaging port. If you need to send a document to multiple locations using different methods, you will need to create a distribution list. These are sometimes called "port groups" in the documentation, as that was the name by which they were previously known.

When you choose to create a distribution list, you will be presented with a list of available messaging ports to add to the list, as shown. Select the appropriate messaging ports, and click the OK button. The distribution list can then be used to create an associated channel from an organization or from an application.

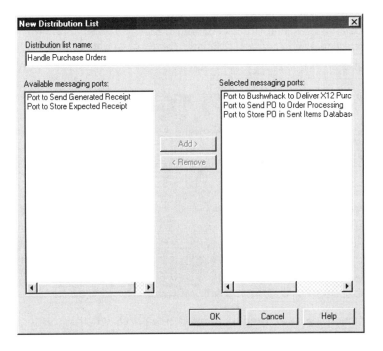

Distribution lists cannot contain open messaging ports or messaging ports that send documents to XLANG schedules.

Creating Channels

Channels are objects that involve the configuration of multiple properties, so their creation is likewise performed using a wizard. Reflecting the scenarios in which BizTalk Messaging can be used, channels can be created for a single messaging port or for a distribution list. To reuse already configured transport methods, many different channels can feed into a single messaging port or into a single distribution list. Also, channels can be created from an organization or from an application. In either case, the first page of the wizard requests general information consisting of a required unique name and an optional comment. On this first page, we can also choose to create a *receipt channel*, which we will discuss after the more generic types. We will first deal with the different information required by each type and then discuss the properties common to both.

Creating a Channel from an Organization

If a document will arrive from a trading partner for processing by BizTalk Server, or if we are not sure from where the document will come because the information will be contained within the document itself, we will create a channel from an organization. In contrast to messaging ports, the first page requires information about the source organization rather than the destination, but again we have the option to create an open source channel if the document will be self-routing and will contain this information within.

Note   *If you choose open source, the options to expect and to generate a receipt are disabled.*

If you do not choose Open source, you must specify the source organization by clicking the Browse button. Although the organization will be selected by name, you can choose a different organization identifier for the channel to use, as shown. You can also create a new organization or create a new identifier for an existing organization on this page. Below the organization information are options to expect or generate a receipt. Receipt channels will be discussed later.

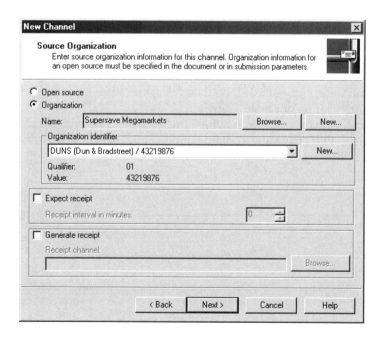

Creating a Channel from an Application

If the document to be processed by the channel will originate from an internal application or from an XLANG schedule, you should create a channel from an application. The opening page of the wizard is the same as for a channel from an organization, but the next page asks you to provide source application information. Here you can specify that the document will come from an internal application of the Home Organization or an XLANG schedule.

Note *If you choose XLANG schedule, the options to expect and to generate a receipt are disabled.*

If your channel will accept a document coming from BizTalk Orchestration, you will need to have an XLANG schedule that contains a port bound to a BizTalk Messaging implementation. That implementation must be configured to send a document. When you are integrating BizTalk Messaging and BizTalk Orchestration services, there are two possible scenarios. If you will be the organization that sends a document by implementing BizTalk Messaging, your channel will be configured from an application with XLANG schedule specified as the source. This channel must not feed into an open messaging port. The name of the organization must be explicitly defined. On the other hand, if you will be the organization that receives such a document and uses BizTalk Messaging to send back a response, you will also need to create an XLANG schedule to process the initial document and to extract unique identifier information about the XLANG schedule that originally sent it. Your XLANG schedule will also use a BizTalk Messaging implementation to return the response; but in this case, the channel you create to accept the response from the XLANG schedule must feed into an open messaging port, because it will point to a URL that is contained within the document.

Note *Integrating Orchestration and Messaging services will be covered in Chapter 8.*

If your application is not an XLANG schedule, you can choose an existing application of the home organization or create a new one. Either way, the home organization will act as the source, but you can specify which organization identifier should be used, as shown next. Again, this page also contains options to generate or to expect a receipt, but these will be discussed later.

Setting Inbound Document Properties

All options from this point on are common to channels both from an organization and an application. The next page of the wizard in each case asks you to specify information about the incoming document. You will need to select a document definition from the BizTalk Server repository or create a new definition. This definition represents the type of document arriving at the channel. The associated document specification, if present, will be used to parse the document from its original format into XML.

> **Note**   *If the inbound document definition is not associated with a document specification, the options to track and to filter the document will be disabled. Nor will you be able to select a different outbound format or map on the next page of the wizard.*

After the inbound document definition has been selected, you can choose to select a certificate to decrypt the data, if it has been encrypted by an application or trading partner. To do this, you will need to browse the local certificate store for certificates belonging to your organization, because the application or trading partner who sent it would have used your public key to perform the encryption. You can also verify a digital signature if the document was digitally signed before being sent to you. Verification of the digital signature will require a certificate from the application or trading partner that did the signing. Clicking this Browse button will therefore bring you to the BizTalk certificate store, where certificates from other parties are kept. It is possible (and indeed likely in a secure B2B environment) that the document has been both encrypted and digitally signed, so that you will need to select both options on this page, as shown here.

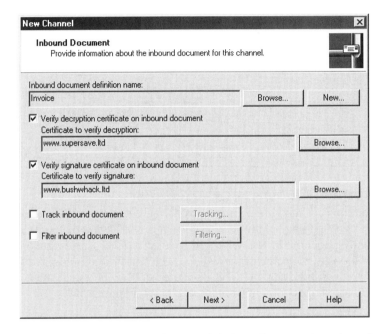

Earlier, we saw that we could configure global tracking options in a document definition to select fields whose values would be tracked for all instances of that document. If we want to track fields for document instances that only pass through a certain channel, or if we want to override the global tracking options, we can do it here. Select the Track Inbound Document check box, and click the Tracking button to bring up the Tracking For Inbound Document dialog box, shown next. In this box, select the fields whose values you wish to track. As with global tracking fields, you can only track two integer fields, two real number fields, two date fields, two text fields, and any number of custom fields that will be stored as a concatenated string in the database. Also, the fields to track must have been configured with the appropriate data type when the specification was created in BizTalk Editor.

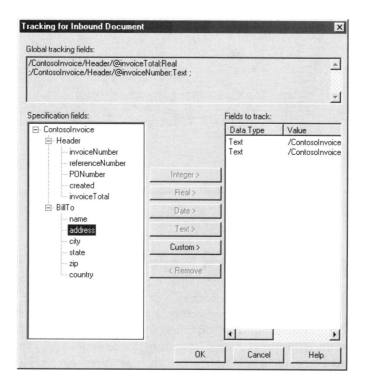

We can also add filtering expressions to the channel to limit the documents that are processed. To do this, select the Filter Inbound Document check box, and click the Filtering button. This will bring up the Channel Filtering Expressions dialog box, shown next. In this box, you can select the field you wish to filter by and click the Add button to create an expression using this value. Alternatively, if you are familiar with XPath syntax, you can add the expression manually by typing in the Expressions field. You can add multiple conditions to further refine the filter.

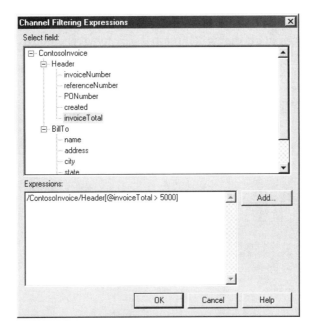

Setting Outbound Document Properties

After you have specified all of the information required for the incoming document, you will need to provide details of how the document should be transformed into a new document format, as may be required by a trading partner or application. This is done by selecting an outbound document definition from the BizTalk Repository and by choosing the appropriate map to transform the internal XML created from the inbound document data into a new XML structure that will correspond to this outbound data format. This stage does not actually convert the XML into a different format such as EDI X12 or Flat-File—only the structure is changed. Serialization into a different format is done after this depending on the type of envelope that was selected at the end of the associated messaging port.

If the inbound and outbound document definitions match, it will not be necessary to select a map file, as no transformation is required. Otherwise, the Map Inbound Document To Outbound Document check box is selected. Click the Browse button to choose a map from the BizTalk Repository. The path to the map will be displayed in the wizard after you click OK.

There is one important point that I want to emphasize here, although I've mentioned it previously in this chapter. When you select a map or document definition during the creation of a channel, the current version of the associated specification is loaded from the BizTalk Repository into the BizTalk Messaging Management database. These specifications are not automatically reloaded if they are edited in BizTalk Editor or BizTalk Mapper. You will need to reload the document specification in the document definition and reselect the map file in the channel before the modifications will become

active. Also, the following script, which makes use of the BizTalk Messaging
Configuration Object Model, can be used to automatically refresh the objects in
BizTalk Messaging Manager.

```
Dim objConfig, objEnvelope, objDocument, objChannel
Dim rsEnvelopes, rsDocuments, rsChannels

Set objConfig = CreateObject("BizTalk.BizTalkConfig")
Set objDocument = objConfig.CreateDocument
Set objEnvelope = objConfig.CreateEnvelope
Set objChannel = objConfig.CreateChannel
Set rsDocuments = objConfig.Documents

While Not rsDocuments.EOF
    objDocument.Load(rsDocuments("id"))
    objDocument.Reference = objDocument.Reference
    objDocument.Save
    rsDocuments.MoveNext
WEnd

Set rsEnvelopes = objConfig.Envelopes
While Not rsEnvelopes.EOF
    objEnvelope.Load(rsEnvelopes("id"))
    objEnvelope.Reference = objEnvelope.Reference
    objEnvelope.Save
    rsEnvelopes.MoveNext
WEnd

Set rsChannels = objConfig.Channels
While Not rsChannels.EOF
    objChannel.Load(rsChannels("id"))
    objChannel.MapReference = objChannel.MapReference
    objChannel.Save
    rsChannels.MoveNext
WEnd

Set rsDocuments = Nothing
Set rsEnvelopes = Nothing
Set rsChannels = Nothing
Set objChannel = Nothing
Set objEnvelope = Nothing
Set objDocument = Nothing
Set objConfig = Nothing
```

You can also choose to digitally sign the outgoing document at this stage by selecting the check box, as shown next, and clicking Browse to choose a digital certificate from the local store. This digital certificate will belong to your organization.

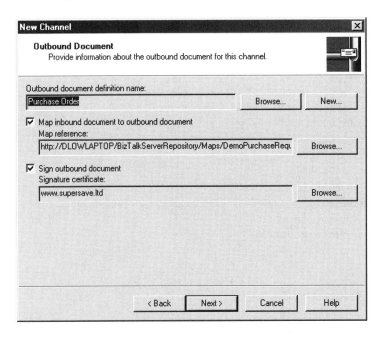

 If you are creating a channel that feeds into a messaging port for which the signature type is set to S/MIME, the Sign Outbound Document check box will already be selected. You must choose a digital certificate or else you will receive an error.

Setting Document Logging Properties

In Chapter 10, you will learn about the Document Tracking feature of BizTalk Server. This feature allows you to view information about interchanges that have passed through BizTalk Messaging. When using this feature, you will normally be able to view the original interchange data. As mentioned, inbound interchanges will sometimes contain multiple documents, but each individual document is extracted and processed separately by BizTalk Server. As a result, you may wish to be able to view individual document instances within the Document Tracking interface, assuming that document tracking has been enabled for the BizTalk Server group.

You can configure how each document processed by a channel will be logged to the InterchangeDTA database. By default, every inbound document will be logged in its native format, meaning its original format after it is extracted from an interchange, but before it is converted to XML. The four check boxes on the Document Logging page in the New Channel wizard allow you to specify other methods for how the document should be stored. You can choose to log the inbound document in its internal XML format after it has been parsed. You also can choose whether the outbound document should be logged in its XML format after it has been transformed by the map but before it has been serialized, or in its native format after it has been serialized.

Setting Advanced Configuration Properties

The final page of the New Channel wizard from an application or from an organization allows you to set advanced configuration properties that will often be left alone. These properties may need modification if you are using EDI formats or if you need to set or override the properties of the associated messaging port.

The first property on the page is group control number, and it must be set for channels that have an EDI format configured as the outbound document format. As discussed earlier, when the outbound document format is ANSI X12 or UN/EDIFACT, BizTalk Server must create an interchange that is wrapped around the document. This interchange header will contain an *interchange control number*, which is a numeric identifier for each interchange that can be used to track the interchange. This is set in the messaging port. However, outbound EDI interchanges must also contain a group control number. This is because EDI documents are often submitted in groups, but BizTalk Server will extract and process each document individually. To track documents that arrived at BizTalk Server in a group but leave one by one, we use a group control number. In this way, we can query the Document Tracking interface for EDI documents that have the same group control number to see those documents that were submitted as part of the same interchange. Again, the group control number is a nonzero numeric value that will be inserted into the functional group segment of an outbound EDI interchange header.

Another setting you can configure on the final page of the wizard is the number of times BizTalk Server should attempt to use the transport(s) specified in the messaging port. The interval between each attempt in minutes can also be set. If the messaging port does not succeed in sending the document the first time using the primary transport, the document will be placed on the retry queue until the specified interval has elapsed. It will then be retried up to the number of times specified in the channel, waiting in the retry queue until the interval has elapsed. If all retry attempts fail, BizTalk Messaging will attempt to use the backup transport using the same retry settings. If that also fails, the document will be moved to the suspended queue.

Note   *Managing BizTalk Server queues will be covered in Chapter 9.*

The final properties that can be set in the New Channel wizard involve the transport methods and envelope format set during the configuration of the associated messaging port. Some advanced properties can be set here, or the existing properties for the port can be overridden for just this particular channel. To access these properties, click the Advanced button. As the properties will vary for each transport type and envelope format used, I will discuss each one in detail in the following sections.

Setting AIC Properties   If your messaging port uses an AIC as its primary or backup transport, and if the AIC was created using the IPipelineComponent and IPipeline ComponentAdmin interfaces, you may set the properties of the AIC in the Override Messaging Port Defaults dialog box. AICs created using the IBTSAppIntegration interface do not support design-time configuration. For example, if you have created an AIC to store the outbound information in a database, you may wish to reuse that AIC for different messaging ports that will save the data to different databases. As a result, the AIC could allow the configuration of the database parameters at design time. In the Override Messaging Port Defaults dialog box, clicking the Properties button for the transport method configured as AIC might bring up a dialog box like the following.

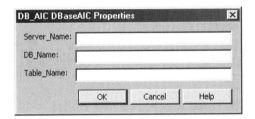

The available properties will vary for each AIC created. This is because the construction of an AIC also involves building two Active Server Pages that will be used to collect the design-time parameters. These pages must be stored in the Program Files\ Microsoft BizTalk Server\Messaging Manager\Pipeline folder on the server. Creating AICs and associated property pages will be covered in Chapter 17.

Overriding File Transport Properties   If the messaging port into which your channel feeds uses the File transport, you can override the transport settings by clicking the Properties button on the relevant tab of the Override Messaging Port Defaults dialog box. This will open the BizTalk SendLocalFile Properties dialog box, shown next. In this box, you can configure a user name and password if the destination directory requires authentication as a result of NTFS permissions, and also choose how the file should be saved. You cannot, however, change the file path or filename. The three save options are Overwrite File, Append To File (default), and Create A New File. If you choose to create a new file, you must make sure that the filename is unique for each instance, or BizTalk Server will return an error. This can be ensured by using the *%tracking_id%* variable in the filename.

Note *You may also receive errors or experience unusual behavior if there is antivirus software on your server, or if you are using Reliable envelopes, and BizTalk Server attempts to write two files with the same name to the same directory at the same time. You can work around this by including the %tracking_id% variable in the filename.*

Overriding HTTP and HTTPS Properties   If your messaging port uses HTTP as a transport, you can override those settings in the BizTalk SendHTTPX Properties dialog box, shown next. Note that the same dialog box is used for both HTTP and HTTPS transports. As with the File transport, the URL cannot be changed here. You can, however, specify a user name and password if the web server to which the document will be sent requires authentication.

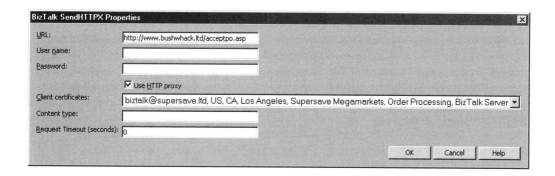

BizTalk Messaging supports neither NTLM/Windows Integrated authentication, nor digest authentication. You must ensure that the web server to which the document will be transported uses either no authentication or basic authentication. For additional security, HTTPS should be used.

If there is an HTTP proxy configured for the BizTalk Server Group, but it is not required for this particular exchange, it can be deselected here. You can further specify the content type for any outgoing interchanges that will be MIME encoded and enter the request timeout in seconds before the transmission attempt fails.

 When BizTalk Server Service Pack 1 is installed, there is also the option to specify a user name and password to provide authentication to a proxy server.

The final configurable option is Client Certificates. This menu shows the available client certificates that can be used with the HTTPS transport. If BizTalk Server uses HTTPS to send a document to a trading partner, the web server will often ask for a client certificate as a means of authentication. These certificates must be created for the sole purpose of client authentication, and they must be available in the local store for the local computer, rather than for the current user.

 When you apply for a client certificate for use with BizTalk Server, it is important not to specify private key protection. If you do, then every time BizTalk Server attempts to use the certificate, a dialog box will appear asking if it is all right for the private key to be accessed. BizTalk Server cannot answer these dialog boxes, so an error will occur.

Overriding Message Queuing Properties If your messaging port is configured to drop a document into a message queue, there are also properties that can be set within an associated channel, as shown next. Many of these properties are involved with authentication. First, you can specify a user name and password if one is required to write to the message queue. You can also choose the authentication level that BizTalk Server will use when communicating with the message queuing server. The authentication level allows the sending application—in this case, BizTalk Server—to identify itself and also to verify the integrity of the message.

BizTalk SendMSMQ Properties

Message queue name:	DIRECT=OS:BTServer\private$\receivePO
User name:	
Password:	
Message label:	%document_name%
Priority:	3

Authentication level:
- ⦿ None
- ○ Always
- ○ MSMQ 1.0 signature
- ○ MSMQ 2.0 signature

Delivery type:
- ⦿ Recoverable
- ○ Express

[OK]   [Cancel]   [Help]

By default, message queuing servers will try to authenticate the sending application. In this case, BizTalk Server will need to attach a digital signature to the document before it is sent.

If set to None, BizTalk Server will not attempt to provide authentication to the message queuing server before sending a document. This will cause the message queuing server to forego authentication, unless the queue is explicitly marked as Authenticated. If set to Always, BizTalk Server will always attach a digital signature before sending a document. If the message queuing server is not in a Windows 2000 domain, we should set the level to MSMQ 1.0. In this case, BizTalk Server will use an external certificate to authenticate itself, as the message queuing server will not have access to an Active Directory from which to retrieve certificate information. If set to MSMQ 2.0, BizTalk Server will provide authentication to the message queuing server by providing a *sender identifier (SID)* and a digital certificate. In this case, the message queuing server will be running on Windows 2000, and the sender can be authenticated using Kerberos. In the Message Queuing Control Panel, you can choose which digital certificate to register in Active Directory for use with message queuing servers.

Apart from authentication, there are further properties to set in this dialog box. You can choose the label that should be used for the message when viewed in the queue. By default, this is set to %document_name%. You can also set the message priority for the document. When combined with the base priority of a public queue, this determines the order in which documents are sent by BizTalk Server to message queues. Messages with a higher total priority are sent first. If multiple messages have the same total priority, those that have a higher base priority are sent first.

You can only set a base priority for public message queues. For messages sent to private queues, BizTalk Server just uses the message priority.

Finally, you can choose the delivery type. The options are Express and Recoverable. Express messages, as their name suggests, are delivered faster, but they are only stored in memory, so they will be lost if the message queuing server fails. Recoverable messages are persisted to disk, so they can be recovered no matter which computer fails. Obviously, recoverable messages use more resources and are slower.

Overriding SMTP Properties   The SMTP transport properties can also be overridden in the BizTalk SendSMTP Properties dialog box, which is accessible through the Advanced configuration page of the New Channel wizard. The available options are shown in the following illustration. First, you can set the authentication method— Anonymous, Basic, or NTLM—that should be used by the SMTP server to authenticate BizTalk Server. If you set it to Basic, you can also specify a user name and password with permission to use the SMTP server.

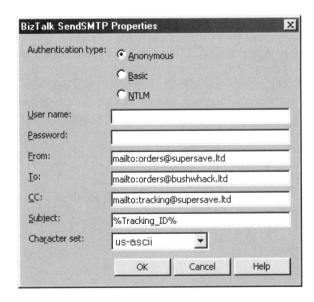

You can also set properties for the e-mail itself, including providing a carbon copy (CC) address or changing the subject line, which is set to %tracking_id% by default. You cannot change the From or To addresses here, however. Finally, you can set the encoding that should be used for the e-mail. The default is "us-ascii".

Overriding Envelope Properties   In addition to tabs for overriding the properties of the primary and backup transports, there is also a tab to set custom properties for certain envelope types. The envelope types that allow configuration are X12 and EDIFACT, although a custom serializer component may also require extra configuration.

The properties that can be set in the X12 and EDIFACT envelopes are values that will be inserted into the interchange headers for those formats. Changing any of these values requires extensive knowledge of EDI interchange header elements, and we will not go into that detail here. The following illustration shows the available properties if an X12 envelope is being used. Table 6-5 lists the interchange header elements into which each property value will be inserted. For example, the Security Information element acts as a kind of password to authenticate the interchange, by specifying information that's not general public knowledge. Similarly, the Acknowledgement Required property determines whether a TA3 Interchange Acknowledgement document should be sent. Finally, the Usage Indicator element specifies whether the document is for testing or production, and takes a value of "T" or "P" accordingly.

Property Name	Element
Authorization information qualifier	ISA01
Authorization information	ISA02
Security information qualifier	ISA03
Security information	ISA04
Interchange control standards identifier	ISA11
Interchange control version number	ISA12
Acknowledgement required	ISA14
Usage indicator	ISA15

Table 6-5. *ANSI X12 Interchange Header Properties*

The following illustration shows the available properties for EDIFACT envelopes. Again, these should only be changed if you know exactly what you're doing.

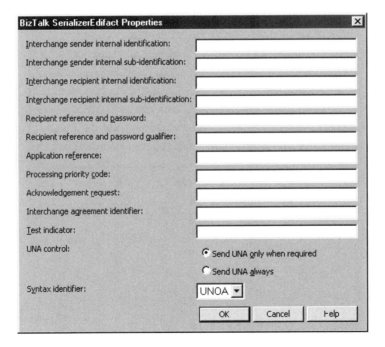

Overriding Distribution List Defaults   If you are creating a channel that will feed into a distribution list, there are multiple messaging ports that can be overridden. Clicking the Advanced button on the final page of the New Channel wizard will give you the Override Distribution List Defaults dialog box, as shown. In this box, you can override the properties for each individual messaging port as before.

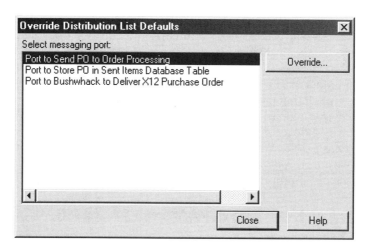

Receipt Channels

The concepts behind receipt channels were discussed in the first half of this chapter, so this section will concentrate on the configuration of these objects. As mentioned, it is only necessary to provide configuration for EDI receipts, as Reliable receipts will be processed automatically by BizTalk Server.

Generating Receipts   If it will be necessary for us to send a receipt to a trading partner in response to a document, we will need to create a receipt channel. First, we should create the accompanying messaging port that will be used to transport the receipt to the trading partner. This should not be an open messaging port, but should have the organization explicitly declared. Also, because it will be used to transport an X12 or EDIFACT receipt, it must have an appropriate envelope selected, and the correct delimiters and interchange control number specified. We can then create an associated channel from an application bound to that messaging port. On the opening page of the New Channel wizard, we should select the check box to specify that it is a receipt channel. For the source application, we might choose an internal application that has been created for the sole purpose of acting as the receipt generator.

When we get to the Inbound document page of the wizard, we will notice that the BizTalk Canonical Receipt specification is already listed. This is an internal document definition used by BizTalk Server for Reliable messaging. If we are creating a receipt channel for EDI documents, we should create a document definition that points to the

CanonicalReceipt.xml document specification in the BizTalk Repository and set that as the inbound document type for the channel. We could then create a document specification for an X12 997 Functional Acknowledgement or EDIFACT CONTRL Service Report, store it in the BizTalk Server Repository, and create another document definition pointing to it. This document definition would then be used as the outbound document type for the channel. Because the document types are different, we will need to specify a map. BizTalk Server supplies a map in the BizTalk Repository for the purpose of transforming a canonical receipt into an X12 4010 997. Similarly, if EDIFACT documents are being exchanged, there is a map for translating a canonical receipt into a D98B CONTRL.

Finally, on the last page of the New Channel wizard, we should enter a nonzero group control number, and click Finish. Our receipt channel is now ready for use.

To use a receipt channel, we configure another channel that will be receiving a document from a trading partner to generate a receipt, as shown next. Clicking the Browse button will show us a list of available receipt channels where the associated messaging port has a destination organization that matches the source organization of the channel we are currently creating. We can then continue setting the rest of the channel properties as appropriate.

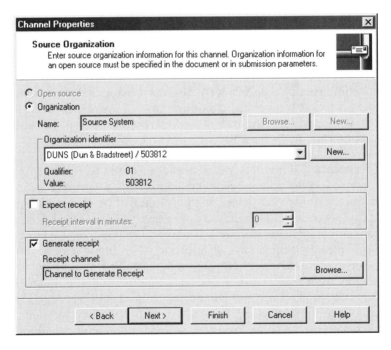

Expecting Receipts   If we are sending a document to a trading partner that will also be using BizTalk Server or other software capable of sending receipts in the appropriate format, we can configure the channel that processes that document to expect a receipt. We will also need to create a receipt channel to receive the receipt.

This should be configured as before, with an inbound document type matching the receipt format and an outbound document type of whatever we require. It will feed into an associated messaging port as before, and that messaging port will be configured to send the receipt to some internal application, perhaps even to an XLANG schedule.

When we are sending the document to our trading partner, we will create a channel as normal. But on the Destination organization page, we will select the Expect receipt check box, as shown, and specify in minutes the interval during which we expect the receipt to arrive. When it does arrive, BizTalk Messaging will examine the document and organization identifiers, and correlate it with the original document. If the receipt does not arrive within the specified interval, an error will be generated.

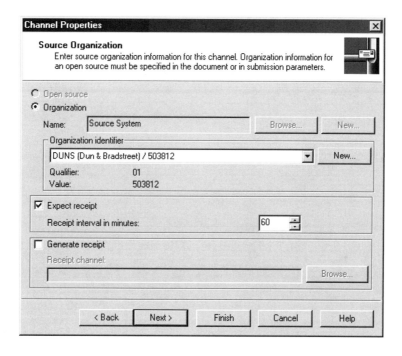

The Complete Reference

Part III

BizTalk Server Orchestration

The
Complete
Reference

Chapter 7

Using BizTalk Orchestration Designer

W ith the BizTalk Orchestration Designer, you can create schedules to control your business process workflow. However, the schedules alone do not enable a workflow. They must be connected with implementation technology like COM, HTTP, MSMQ, or BizTalk Messaging. In this chapter, you will learn how to create an orchestration schedule and how to connect communication components with your business process workflow. Chapter 8 discusses advanced features of orchestration and includes examples of some very interesting features of orchestration.

Orchestration Concepts

The business process defines a workflow process or a business logic that may involve message exchange between trade partners, or rather between the applications of the partners, through use of a set of rules. The mechanism that controls the exchange of messages between the different applications is called *orchestration*. The BizTalk Orchestration Designer specifies the business process in a document called an *XLANG schedule drawing* (.skv files). XLANG schedule drawings are later compiled to well-formatted XML documents called *XLANG schedules* (.skx files). A *business process* in the BizTalk Orchestration Designer is a logical sequence of actions. The *XLANG schedule drawing* is a visual representation of business logic. The exchange of messages is coordinated by connecting actions with the corresponding implementation technology, like COM, MSMQ, script components, or BizTalk Messaging.

Therefore, orchestration revolves around the development and execution of B2B and EAI interactions, which, in time, will extend across companies' borders, their applications, and the Internet. BizTalk Orchestration—roughly speaking—is a service for coordinating business processes through messages, and communicating with other business processes or applications through messages. BizTalk Orchestration performs the following key functions:

- Separation of process definition from implementation
- Integration of communication
- Long-running transactions
- Integration of concurrency

Separation of Process Definition from Implementation

The exchange of messages between companies or the implementation of business logic requires the definition of a business process as well as the integration of software components and applications to execute the process. Previously, applications often united both the process and its implementation in one application. A disadvantage of this practice was that when the process or the implementation technology was modified, the entire code for the application had to be adapted to it. This was a very difficult task.

Further problems arose when new business partners or new internal systems were supposed to be integrated into the business process, because the application had to be adapted to them, too. This led to business processes being inappropriately developed.

BizTalk Server's objective is the explicit separation of process definition from the implementation. BizTalk Orchestration provides a complete semantic for describing processes. For processes to coordinate an external application, a mechanism is provided to connect applications, protocols, transports, and so on, with processes. Thus, different external applications can communicate with one another through orchestration in a loosely coupled way. Figure 7-1 shows the separation of the business process model from the software implementation in the BizTalk Orchestration Designer. The business process is defined on the left side and then connected with the software implementation on the right side.

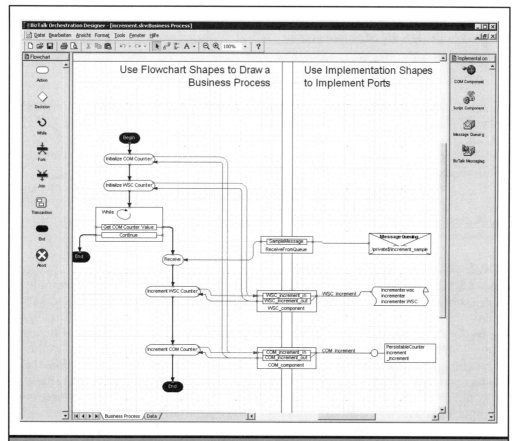

Figure 7-1.   *The BizTalk Orchestration Designer user interface*

The separation of process definition and software implementation has several advantages that allow companies and IT experts, as well as developers, to concentrate on their core competences. This enables the development of optimal processes and optimal implementations. The process is easier to maintain and modify since the applications are only loosely coupled via the BizTalk Server. The business process can easily integrate further elements and participants.

Integration of Communication

Business processes must be able to communicate with software. While it is necessary to separate the definition of a process from the software implementation, it is also essential to be able to communicate with the process. BizTalk Orchestration possesses an open connection architecture; this means that any component may be connected at run time. BizTalk Server 2000 provides connections to the following communication components:

- COM Components
- Windows Script Components
- Microsoft Message Queuing
- BizTalk Messaging Service (HTTP, SMTP, MSMQ, and so on)

BizTalk Orchestration Services, together with BizTalk Messaging Services, makes it possible to exchange messages via the Internet by means of HTTP, SMTP, and MSMQ. BizTalk Orchestration enables the linking of synchronous communication via COM or Windows Script Components for processes requiring a high performance that are also relatively close to implementation.

Due to its open connection architecture, BizTalk Orchestration enables synchronous and asynchronous coupling of applications in distributed structures. BizTalk Orchestration provides a mechanism to connect applications, protocols, and transports with business processes.

Long-Running Transactions

One of BizTalk Server's main strengths lies in the option to implement long-running business processes and transactions with loosely coupled, asynchronous interactions. Today, the term *transaction* is always associated with closely coupled, synchronous interactions between database systems and components. A typical example of such an interaction is withdrawing an amount from a bank account. If for any reason the transaction should fail, the state of the system is restored to its initial state before the interaction through use of a mechanism called a *rollback*. When considering business processes more closely, you will notice that few processes are actually short lived—for example, databank transactions. Under normal circumstances, a matter of weeks or months could pass between order arrival and order confirmation, receipt, invoicing, and so forth.

BizTalk Orchestration provides a function allowing loosely coupled, long-running business processes to be managed as a single, closely coupled transaction. To realize long-running transactions, the current state of the business process is written into the Orchestration Persistence database, which has been created during the installation of BizTalk Server 2000. If a long-running transaction should fail, it is possible to execute the compensation code by using BizTalk Orchestration. BizTalk Server 2000 is equally capable of short-lived DTC-style transactions, as well as a combination of short-lived transactions with long-running transactions. In Chapter 8, transactions in XLANG schedules are discussed in detail.

Integration of Concurrency

When running business processes, you may need to execute processes simultaneously— that is, in parallel. If several pieces of information are required at a particular time, the necessary send and receive processes can be arranged in several different flows, allowing the processes to run in parallel. It would be inefficient to execute these processes one after the other. For example, if you receive a customer order containing several elements that you have to order from your suppliers, it would be impractical to have to wait until each order is confirmed before the next order is given to the suppliers. BizTalk Orchestration supports the description and execution of simultaneous subprocesses. Simultaneously executed processes should be reunited at a particular time, that is, *synchronized*. Continuing with the aforementioned example: Your customer can only be sent an order confirmation once all your suppliers have been given an order. BizTalk Orchestration guarantees that all the orders are first sent to the suppliers before a confirmation of the order is sent to your customer. BizTalk Orchestration coordinates simultaneous processes and guarantees the synchronization of the processes that follow.

BizTalk Orchestration Designer

The BizTalk Orchestration Designer tool can map business processes and transform them into XLANG syntax so that they can be executed from the XLANG Scheduler Engine. The business process is mapped on a surface based on Microsoft Visio 2000 SR1, which is the installation requirement for the BizTalk Orchestration Designer. Figure 7-1 portrays the user interface of the BizTalk Orchestration Designer.

The BizTalk Orchestration Designer provides two stencils. On the left is the *flowchart* stencil, which shows the flowchart shapes that can be used in the business process. On the right is the *implementation* stencil, which contains shapes representing communication to the outer world. The shapes presented on the stencils are the only shapes that you may use to model your business process. If the stencils are not visible, choose View | Stencils.

After the BizTalk Orchestration Designer has been opened, it creates an empty Business Process page. The only shape on the page is the Begin shape. In addition to the Business Process page, the BizTalk Orchestration Designer also creates the data page. Strictly speaking, only the logical sequence of actions and their connection to implementation shapes are configured on the Business Process page. The data flow that is fundamentally for BizTalk Orchestration is configured on the data page. While you model your process flow on the Business Process page, the BizTalk Orchestration Designer designs all the shapes for the data page. Every message and port created on the Business Process page leads to a shape on the data page. After the Business Process diagram has been designed on the data page, the flow of the messages is configured. The data page will be also be discussed in the section "Data Flow", later in this chapter. Figure 7-2 portrays the data flow on a data page.

If you consider the Business Process shown in Figure 7-1, you will notice that the Business Process page has been divided into two sections. On the left is an area titled "Use Flowchart Shapes to Draw a Business Process". On the right the area is titled "Use Implementation Shapes to Implement Ports". This separation corresponds to the BizTalk concept of separating business process definition and implementation.

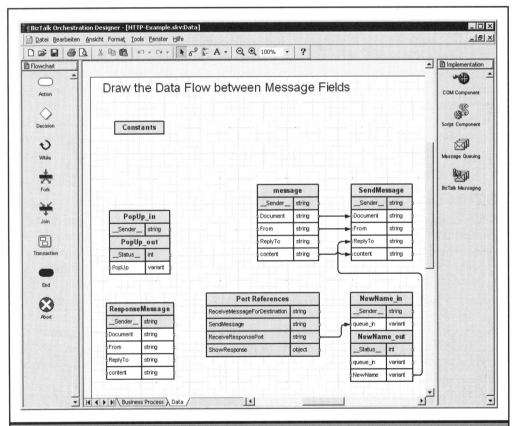

Figure 7-2.   *The data page of the BizTalk Orchestration Designer*

Deleting the headings "Use Flowchart Shapes to Draw a Business Process" and "Use Implementation Shapes to Implement Ports" will prevent the XLANG drawing from being complied into well-formatted XML documents.

Creating business process drawings is a joint task of business analysts and developers. Where business analysts analyze the status quo of a live business process to optimize and find a process definition, it's up to developers to implement BizTalk Orchestration according to goals defined by the analysts. The flowchart diagram consists of a logical sequence of action shapes complemented by decision or loop shapes. On the right side, a developer—familiar with the BizTalk Messaging and the organization of the applications—should specify the messaging implementation.

XLANG Schedules

After the business process has been graphically modeled and the actions have been connected with the outside world via the orchestration ports, the XLANG schedule must be created from the flowchart, which can be processed from the BizTalk workflow engine—the XLANG Scheduler Engine. This task is taken over by the BizTalk Orchestration Designer. Choose File | Make XLANG <*filename*>.skx to create an XLANG schedule. The XLANG Scheduler Engine is the service that looks after the activation, execution, dehydration, and rehydration of schedules. The XLANG schedule implements the orchestration logic and is executed via the XLANG Scheduler Engine. Since communication between applications is implemented by XLANG schedules, an XLANG schedule contains the communication type and information regarding the orchestration ports, connected with the actions. Once the XLANG schedule drawing is compiled to an XLANG schedule, you can open the .skx files with notepad.exe and examine the XML document that the XLANG Scheduler Engine will execute.

Dehydration and Rehydration of XLANG Schedules

In a production environment, hundreds or maybe thousands of XLANG schedules could run in parallel over a long period. Retaining the schedules in memory could cause massive scaling problems. To prevent these scaling problems, the XLANG Scheduler uses two processes: dehydration and rehydration. If instantiated schedules are not immediately required at any one time, the XLANG Scheduler writes their status in the XLANG Persistence database (Orchestration Persistence database), thus freeing resources. This procedure is called *dehydration*. As soon as the schedule is required again, the XLANG Scheduler reloads the schedule in the main memory, with the same status it had at the time of dehydration. This procedure is called *rehydration*.

The Orchestration Persistence database stores the structures of XLANG schedules, the progress of activated XLANG schedule instances, and messages that are sent by or received from a running XLANG schedule instance. The Orchestration Persistence database enables some core features of BizTalk Server, such as the dehydration and rehydration of long-running schedules, and the rollback of long-running transactions.

Actions, Ports, and Messages

As in a classic flowchart diagram for business processes, the XLANG schedule symbols have the Begin and End shapes that represent the beginning and completion of the flowchart. The XLANG schedules also contain symbols identifying action and decision rules. In contrast to other flowchart diagrams, the action shapes in the XLANG schedule drawings do not represent codes to be executed, but rather the exchange of messages. When the flow in the XLANG schedule reaches an Action shape, it sends a message to another application and waits for a message to arrive. This is the only Action within an XLANG schedule that can be executed in addition to the standard flow control. Indeed, designing an Action shape alone is not sufficient for sending and receiving messages.

To connect the actions of an XLANG schedule with the BizTalk Messaging Service, orchestration ports are implemented to which the action can be bound. The orchestration port represents the connection between the action shape and the implementation infrastructure. The binding of actions with the orchestration ports is supported via binding wizards for each transport type. At this point, it is useful to identify the differences between orchestration and messaging ports, so that you can correctly comprehend BizTalk.

In the BizTalk Orchestration Service a *port* is a named location in an XLANG schedule. Here, the port implements a technology—for example, COM or Windows Script Components, MSMQ, or BizTalk Messaging—in order to send and receive messages. A port can synchronously or asynchronously implement communication and is used either to send messages to or to receive messages from an XLANG schedule.

Ports are also used in the BizTalk Messaging Service. Messaging ports and orchestration ports are completely different and have nothing to do with each other. A *messaging port* is a set of characteristics that instructs the BizTalk Server 2000 to transport a message to a specific destination. A messaging port provides only the destination of a message and must always be associated with a channel. A *channel* defines the origin of a message and instructs the BizTalk Server 2000 as to what should be done (mapping, validation against schema, and so on) before a message is transferred to a port.

Thus, BizTalk Orchestration Services and BizTalk Messaging Services have direct contact with one another only if an *orchestration port*, which is bound to BizTalk Messaging, is implemented in an XLANG schedule. In this case, the messages that have been sent to an orchestration port implementing the BizTalk Messaging technology are sent to a channel. If an orchestration port should receive the messages, they are transferred to the XLANG schedule via a messaging port. With the BizTalk Messaging Services, ports can be defined to send messages to a particular orchestration port in an XLANG schedule. For a complete discussion of channels and ports, refer to Chapter 6.

Creating XLANG Schedule Drawings

The BizTalk Orchestration Designer uses a Visio interface. If you are already familiar with Visio, creating XLANG schedules will certainly appear very easy to begin with. The BizTalk Orchestration Designer integrates the visual design and configuration processes in a unified designed environment. Instead of analyzing the business process and then coding it separately, as formerly practiced, everything occurs here in one unified environment with a drawing surface and implementation tools.

Flowchart Shapes

The flowchart shapes are the elements available to you for modeling, on the left side of the page, your business process diagram. You cannot use any other shapes. Moreover, the shape names you create for your business process drawings must abide by the following conventions:

- The name must be a valid XML token name.
- The name must not begin with an underscore (_).
- The name must not include colons (:).
- The name is allowed a maximum of 32 characters.
- The name of constants or messages must not begin with a number.

Begin   The Begin shape is the only shape that is not incorporated into the flowchart stencil. It is automatically inserted at the top of every design page. Begin shapes cannot be deleted, and more Begin shapes cannot be added.

Action   An Action shape is used to receive a message via a port from an external source or to send a message from an XLANG schedule.

Decision   A Decision shape represents a process analogous to the If-Then-Else statement that sequentially processes rules. The rules consist of a VBScript expression.

While   The While shape contains a rule repeated until the rule evaluates to "true". If the rule evaluates to "false", the continued flow follows. This construct is analogous to the While-Do statement.

Fork   A Fork shape branches out its process flow into a maximum of 64 concurrent flows. Each flow is concurrently executed. All process flows must be reunited in a Join shape following a Fork shape.

Join   The Join shape synchronizes concurrent process flows that have come from the Fork shape. Join shapes are also used to join branches from a Decision shape.

Transaction   The Transaction shape can combine several flowchart shapes in a transaction. All actions within the Transaction shape must be completed successfully; otherwise, the transaction will fail.

End   The End shape represents the completion of the process flow. The XLANG schedule can contain several End shapes.

Abort   The Abort shape is used to terminate a transaction so that corrective measures may be initiated.

ImplementationShapes

The Implementation shape represents the technologies provided by the BizTalk Orchestration Designer to effect communication with the implementation infrastructure.

COM Component   COM Components can be integrated into the XLANG schedule. The COM Component shape is used to implement a port in order to synchronously send or receive messages via a method call. Drag the shape onto the right side of the separator bar to start the COM Component Binding Wizard. You can read more about this in the section "Implementing COM Components", later in this chapter.

Script Component   Script components can be integrated in the XLANG schedule. The Script Component shape is used to implement a port in order to synchronously send or receive messages via a method call. Drag the shape onto the right side of the separator bar to start the Script Component Binding Wizard. You can read more about this in the section "Implementing Script Components", later in this chapter.

Message Queuing   The Message Queuing service is used to send and receive messages asynchronously from message queues. Drag the Message Queuing Implementation shape onto the right side of the separator bar to start the Message Queuing Binding Wizard. You can read more about this in the section "Implementing Message Queuing", later in this chapter.

BizTalk Messaging   The BizTalk Messaging Service is used to send and receive messages using BizTalk Server Messaging components. Drag the BizTalk Messaging Implementation shape onto the right side of the separator bar to start the BizTalk Messaging Binding Wizard. You can read more about this in the section "Implementing BizTalk Messaging", later in this chapter.

Creating Actions

An action is used either to receive a message via a port from an external source or to send from the XLANG schedule. The Send or Receive action may be synchronous or asynchronous, depending on the implementation that is connected with the port. However, it is only in connection with the binding of an orchestration port that an Action shape can actually implement actions. An Action shape looks like the following:

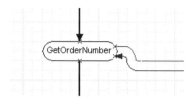

To position an Action shape in the flowchart, click an Action shape on the flowchart stencil, and drag it onto the design page. Action shapes have only names as a characteristic, and these can be configured by right-clicking the Action shape and opening the Edit Properties dialog box. Here, the name of the Action shape can be entered. Make sure to give the Action shape a logical name that clearly describes its function.

Making Decisions

You can add rules to the BizTalk Orchestration flowchart. Rules can use the individual field values of a message to form the basis of a decision, and depending on this decision, they can modify the flow within their schedules. Decision shapes look like the following:

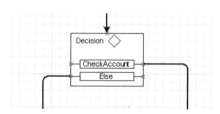

A rule consists of a VBScript expression that returns a Boolean value, "true" or "false", thus making use of the incoming values. If the rule returns the value "true", the flow of the rule connection follows; otherwise, the "else" connection follows. A Decision shape is created by means of the following method:

1. Drag the Decision shape from the flowchart stencil onto the design page.

2. Right-click the decision shape and select Properties.

3. Click the Add button to add a condition to the decision.

4. Enter a name in the Rule Name field. Optionally, enter a description for the rule in the Rule Description field.

5. In the Script Expression field, enter the rule as a VBScript expression. The Expression Assistant may be used for this purpose. A condition for the created expression must be added, which could, for example, resemble the following: *price.total < 500.*

6. Click OK to proceed.

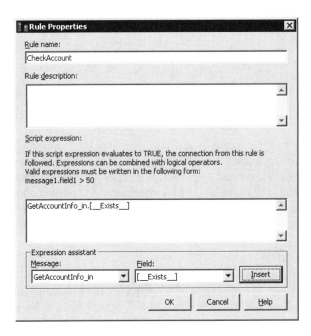

The Expression Assistant allows you to quickly select the available fields from the existing messages. To do this, proceed as follows:

1. In the Expression Assistant field, select the Message and the Field that are to be used in the rule, and click Insert.

2. The Expression Assistant now inserts the expression in the Script Expression field. If necessary, the expression must then be completed.

You can only see real document fields if you use a message that has been associated with a document specification in the XML Communication Wizard.

The Expression Assistant field is activated once the mouse has been used to click in the Script Expression field. In addition to the Message field, the XLANG Scheduler provides other further fields, as shown next.

Field	Description
__Exists__	Indicates whether a message exists. With messages that already exist, the value is "true".
__Sender__	Indicates the origin of the message—the sender.
__Status__	Returns the HRESULT value of a COM call.

The fields additionally provided by the XLANG Scheduler are inserted into the expression in square brackets, as follows:

```
Message1.[__Exists__]
```

Right-clicking the Decision shape opens the context menu. Select Properties and the Decision Properties dialog box opens, as shown here.

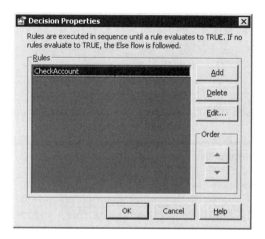

Click Add to add rules. The marked rules in the Rules field can be deleted via the Delete button. You can open the Rule Properties dialog box by clicking the Edit button and, as already described, change the characteristics of the rule.

Decision shapes can contain more than one rule. In this case, the rules are viewed sequentially, from top to bottom. The branching of the first rule, returning the value "true", is followed. If none of the rules returns the value "true", the process flow of the Else branching is followed. The order of the rules in the Decision shapes can be specified in the Order field. You can compare the way the decision shapes walk through the rules with the switch statement in C++, Perl, and Java, or with the select/case statement in Visual Basic.

Implementing While Loops

With the While loop shapes, a rule is iteratively passed until the rule returns the value "false", at which point the process flows from the Continue branching. The While loop is repeated as long as the rule returns the value "true", corresponding to the While rule at programming. A While shape looks like the following:

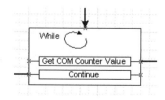

Rules can be added at While loops in the same way they are added at Decision shapes, as described earlier in the chapter. In contrast to Decision shapes, While loops have only one rule that can be passed. Right-click the While loop shape to open the context menu. Select Properties and the While Properties dialog box opens:

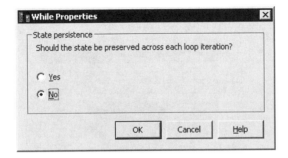

The state persistence of the While loop can be specified in the While Properties dialog box. In the State Persistence field, choose between the following options:

- **Yes** All the messages that are passed through an iterative loop are saved in the XLANG schedule state. If the While loop component is a transaction, then in the event of the failure of a transaction, either the code of an On Failure Of page or a Compensation page is executed for *every* saved message.

- **No** Only the last message that is passed through an iterative loop is saved in the XLANG schedule state. If the While loop component is a transaction, then either the code of an On Failure Of page or a Compensation page is executed, but only for the *last* saved message.

To use the data created during an iteration outside the While loop, select Yes in the While Properties dialog box.

Implementing Concurrency

Concurrent (parallel) process flows can be realized through using the BizTalk Orchestration Designer. Fork and Join shapes are available for the implementation of concurrent process flows in XLANG schedules. To implement concurrent process flows, drag the Fork shape symbol onto the design page. In contrast to the Join shape, the Fork shape does not have any further properties. Right-click the Join shape, and the context menu opens. Select Properties, and the Join Properties dialog box appears. For the Join shapes, the following options are available:

- **AND** The XLANG schedule waits to implement the following action until all the process flows have reached the Join shape.

- **OR** The XLANG schedule executes the following action as soon as one process flow reaches the Join shape.

The Fork and Join shapes look like the following:

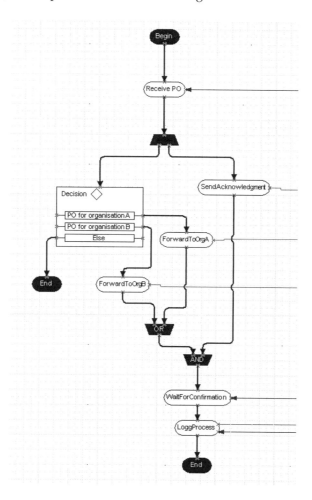

The following guidelines should be taken into consideration when implementing Fork and Join shapes for concurrent process flows:

■ Fork shapes can implement only one incoming and a maximum of 64 outgoing connections.

■ Join shapes can implement a maximum of 64 incoming and one outgoing connection.

■ All forked process flows either end in an End shape or are synchronized through a Join shape.

■ When several concurrent process flows are synchronized with an Or Join shape, then the concurrent process flows can include only one action.

- Every Fork shape has a one-to-one relationship with exactly one Join shape. This means that a Join shape cannot synchronize concurrent process flows of different Forks.

- Actions cannot communicate with one another in concurrent process flows. This means that a message cannot be sent to a message queue, and this message cannot be received by another concurrent action. If this happens, nevertheless, the XLANG schedule fails at run time without displaying an error message.

Implementing Transactions

A *transaction* is a series of operations that is processed as a single action. A transaction ensures that two users who are trying to access and modify the same data see each other's changes only when these modifications have been completely carried out. Transactions also guarantee that data alterations of a transaction are either completely executed or not at all. Therefore, a transaction always transfers data from one consistent state into a new consistent state.

To implement transactions in the XLANG schedule, drag the Transaction shape symbol from the flowchart stencil, and drop it over the actions to be grouped in a transaction. Action shapes can also be inserted in Transaction shapes at a later time. Transaction shapes look like the following:

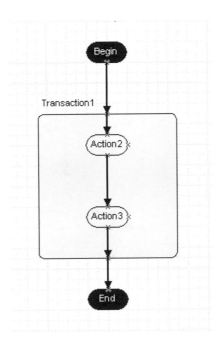

In XLANG schedules, three types of transactions can be configured: timed, short-lived, and long-running transactions. By double-clicking or right-clicking the Transaction shape and selecting Properties, the Transaction Properties dialog box appears, as shown next. In the Name field, enter the name of the transaction, which is shown on the design page. In the Type field, choose Timed Transaction; Short-Lived, DTC-Style; or Long-Running. Every selected option can be further configured in the Transaction Options field. The characteristics of transactions are presented on the design page by means of the following colors:

- **Blue**   Timed transactions.
- **Beige**   Long-running transactions.
- **Gray**   Short-lived, DTC-style transactions. This is the default setting.

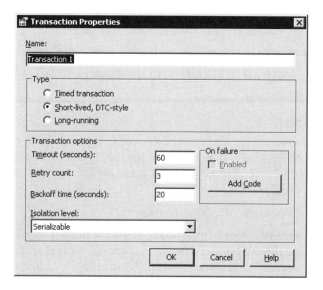

Further characteristics of transactions are summarized in the Transaction Options field. Timeout indicates the time in seconds that the transaction may run before it is automatically aborted. Retry Count specifies how often a transaction commit may be attempted before a transaction is finally aborted. Backoff Time (seconds) specifies the time between the individual attempts. The interval increases with the Exponent Retry Count ($B^{**}R$; B = Backoff time, R = Retry Count). The option Isolation Level specifies the visibility of data for other transactions processed in the transaction.

Failure handling is the standout feature of transactions. Transactions follow the principle "everything or nothing": all the actions within a transaction must be successful so that the transaction commits or else the transaction fails. When the transaction fails, then the original state of the data from the transaction is restored through a mechanism called a *rollback*. This mechanism can be used only for the short-lived, DTC-style transaction type. Timed and long-running transactions, however, have their own mechanism for handling failures. You can click on Add Code in the On Failure field of the Transaction Properties dialog box, and BizTalk Orchestration Designer provides an additional design page, On Failure Of *<transaction name>*, for failure handling. If the transaction fails, the code of the On Failure Of *<transaction name>* page is automatically executed. Click Delete Code to remove the additional design page.

When creating transactions, consider the following design guidelines:

- Every Flowchart shape or flow that is completely within the boundaries of the Transaction shape becomes a part of the transaction.

- Flowchart shapes that are not completely contained within a Transaction shape are not a part of the transaction.

- External shapes cannot be directly connected with shapes within the transaction. The external shape must initially be connected to the Transaction shape and subsequently connected to the internal shape.

- A transaction has exactly one entrance and one exit.

- If a transaction containing shapes is deleted, then the shapes are also deleted.

Chapter 8 discusses in detail the subject of transactions and explains their practical use by means of examples.

Connecting Shapes

With the BizTalk Orchestration Designer, there are two possibilities of connecting shapes with one another; one way is by use of the Connector tool, and the other way is by use of the Pointer tool. To connect shapes on the business process diagram with the Connector tool, proceed as follows:

1. Click the Connector Tool toolbar button.

2. Drag the mouse pointer over the shape to be connected with another shape. As soon as the mouse pointer is over a control handle, it will be framed with a small, red square. This shows that the handle has been activated.

3. Click and hold the left mouse button to establish the connection to the destination shape, until the pointer is over the shape to be connected.

4. After reaching the destination shape, release the mouse button to establish the connection.

To connect shapes on the business process diagram without using the Connector tool, proceed as follows:

1. Click the Pointer Tool toolbar button.

2. Select the shape to be connected with another shape. The shape has a green border, and the control handle is activated (symbolized by small green squares on the edge of the shapes).

3. Drag the activated control handle to the connection point of the destination shape.

4. When the connection point is activated (symbolized by the appearance of a small, red square), release the mouse button to establish the connection.

BizTalk Orchestration Designer Menu Options

Some menu options need to be discussed in detail. In the BizTalk Orchestration Designer, the Tools menu offers the following options:

- **Delete Unused Ports And Messages**   This option deletes all unused ports on the business process page and their corresponding port references, as well as all unused messages on the data page of the XLANG schedule drawing.

- **Delete Unused Rules**   This option simply deletes all rules that are not currently used in a Decision or While shape from the business process page of the XLANG schedule drawing.

- **Refresh Method Signatures**   Use this option if you are creating COM Components at the same time you are creating your XLANG schedule. When changing the COM interface, a refresh of the available method parameters in the XLANG schedule is recommended. When recompiling the XLANG schedule, a refresh of the method signatures is run automatically.

- **Shut Down All Running XLANG Schedule Instances**   This option shuts down all running instances of the schedule. When using COM Components in the XLANG schedule, it is not possible to modify the COM Components as long as instances of the XLANG schedule are running. This option unlocks the file containing the COM Component, so that changes can be made.

Implementing Business Processes

The Implementation stencil lists four implementation technologies that can be used to implement the orchestration ports. The BizTalk Orchestration Designer supports the following implementation technologies:

- COM Components
- Windows Script Components
- Message Queuing Services
- BizTalk Messaging Services

The process of connecting the implementation technologies in the XLANG schedule occurs in two steps. In the first step, the orchestration port is connected to an implementation technology. In the second step, an action is connected to an orchestration port. These processes specify the type of location to which the port is bound and the schemata of the messages that are sent or received via the port.

Business process implementation always leads to the definition of orchestration ports. Ports are named locations that use a specific implementation. In BizTalk Orchestration Designer, a port is defined via the location to which a message is sent or from which a message is received, in connection with the technology enabling communication. There are two types of orchestration ports—*static* and *dynamic* ports.

- **Static ports**   To implement static ports, the user must have all the information ready at design time. Thus, at design time, the designer must know where the messages are to be sent or from where the messages will be received, as well as the technology enabling communication.

- **Dynamic ports**   When implementing dynamic ports, the XLANG Scheduler Engine receives all the necessary data for defining the ports at run time. The necessary information at run time for the XLANG Scheduler Engine is contained within the message. This means that the location of a dynamic port is transferred via the message to the port reference. Nevertheless, the message must arrive beforehand at a known point in the process flow of the XLANG schedule before it can be sent via a dynamic port.

The following sections describe how integrating Implementation shapes in the XLANG schedule can enable communication with the outer world.

Implementing COM Components

The XLANG Scheduler Engine can send messages to and receive messages from a COM Component. The COM Component Implementation shape offers the possibility of integrating COM Components or applications in the XLANG schedule. Communication between an Action shape and the COM Component is *synchronous*, meaning that the flow of messages is always bidirectional; this contrasts with *asynchronous communication*, where the flow of messages is only unidirectional (e.g., MSMQ). For every method call, the BizTalk Server waits for a message to return.

The COM Component Binding Wizard opens after the COM Implementation shape is dragged onto the diagram and dropped on the BizTalk design page. On the first page of the COM Component Binding Wizard, a new port must be defined. A COM Component Implementation shape cannot be connected with an already existing port, since the port of a COM Component Implementation shape is attached to the interface of the COM Component.

Static or Dynamic Communication   It is possible on the Static or Dynamic Communication page to specify how the XLANG Scheduler Engine should instantiate the component. The following three options are available:

- **Static**   XLANG creates a COM Component instance. Choose this option when the XLANG Scheduler Engine can already be provided with all the information (necessary for implementation) at design time.

- **Dynamic**   An application other than the XLANG Scheduler Engine instantiates the COM Component. Select this option when the XLANG Scheduler Engine requires additional information at run time in order to complete the implementation.

■ **No Instantiation**   Use this option only when the XLANG schedule should receive data via a method call without activating the component. This means that the XLANG Scheduler Engine neither instantiates the component nor executes a method call.

Next, a COM Component must be chosen so that the XLANG Scheduler Engine knows what it must do. If Static has not been chosen, ignore the following steps and proceed to the "Interface Information" section.

Class Information   If the Static instantiation was chosen in the preceding step for the COM Component, then the following Class Information page appears in the COM Component Binding Wizard.

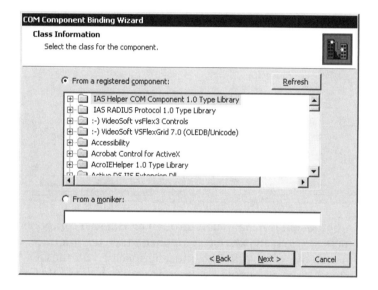

The COM Component Binding Wizard enables COM Components to be directly referenced or a COM moniker to be specified. The options are as follows:

■ **From A Registered Component**   The tree control shows all the registered COM Components on the system. Select the component to communicate with the XLANG schedule from the tree control. Enlarge the folder and define the class to be used.

■ **From A Moniker**   In this field, enter the standard COM moniker that specifies the location of the COM Component. If this option is chosen, the COM

Component cannot participate in any communications used within a transaction in the XLANG schedule. A COM moniker looks like the following example:

```
sked://MyComputer!XLANG Scheduler/C:\MySchedules\example3.skx
```

Interface Information   If either the Dynamic or the No Instantiation option was chosen in the preceding step, then the Interface Information page should appear in the COM Component Binding Wizard, as shown.

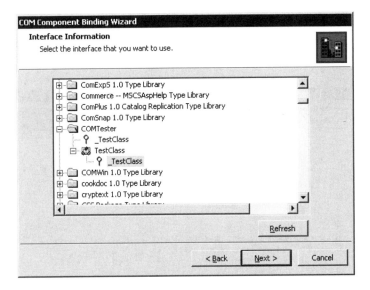

If the COM Component is instantiated through an external component or must receive a message from an external component, then the interface, which the XLANG Scheduler Engine can work with, must be specified for the COM Component implemented in the XLANG schedule. Ignore this section if the COM Component has only one interface.

After the COM Component and, if necessary, the interface for the XLANG Scheduler Engine, have been determined, we can now proceed with the next step, which is the same for all COM Components.

Method Information   After having defined how the COM Component should be instantiated, let's turn our attention to the penultimate step: selecting the methods that the COM Components should provide for the XLANG schedule. The Method Information page lists all the methods that the COM Component has implemented:

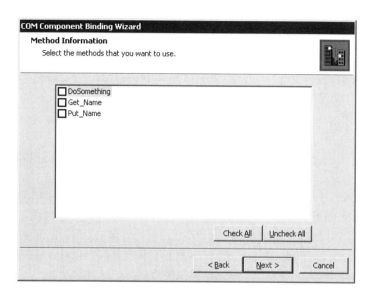

Select at least one method to be used. If only one method is applicable to the COM Component, this window should be ignored.

Advanced Port Properties   The last dialog box of the COM Component Binding Wizard is the Advanced Port Properties page. Here, security, transaction support, state management support, and error handling are configured:

The sender identity settings are defined in the Security area. With the COM Component shape, the authenticated user information of received messages can be queried to determine whether a message should be processed or rejected by the XLANG Scheduler. The information is contained in the field __Sender__ on the Data View page. The following three options are available:

- **Not Required**   Select this option when the XLANG schedule should receive a message without knowing the identity of the sender.

- **Optional**   Select this option when the XLANG schedule should identify the sender of the message if the information is available.

- **Required**   Select this option when the XLANG schedule should not receive messages from a sender whose identity is not known.

When a COM+ component is bound to a transaction shape in the XLANG schedule, it can be determined, via the transaction support in the COM Component Binding Wizard, how the COM Component participates in the transactions. The options in the Transaction Support field are similar to those of the COM+ properties of the Microsoft Transaction Server (MTS). The following describes the settings of the transaction support:

- **Disabled**   This option specifies that the component will ignore COM+ transaction management. This option is suitable for all non-COM+ components.

- **Not Supported**   This option specifies that the component will not participate in COM+ transactions or will not transmit the transactions of other COM+ components. This option only applies to COM+ components.

- **Supported**   This option specifies that the component will support transactions. If the component is associated with a transaction via an orchestration port, the component will be included in the transaction. When the creator is not executed within a transaction, the component will also be instantiated without transaction support. This option only applies to COM+ components.

- **Required**   This option specifies that the component will support transactions. If the component is associated with a transaction via an orchestration port, the component will be included in the transaction. When the generator is not executed in a transaction, then the component will, nevertheless, be instantiated in a new transaction. This option only applies to COM+ components.

- **Requires New**   This option specifies that a new transaction will always be created for a component. This option only applies to COM+ components.

Flowcharts for long-running business processes can be created using the BizTalk Orchestration Designer. When using COM Components in a long-running business process, only COM Components may be used whose state can be saved when the XLANG schedule is dehydrated. For this purpose, the components must have implemented the interfaces IPersistStream or IPersistStreamInit. Using components whose state cannot be saved will result in the component instance being destroyed when the XLANG Schedule is dehydrated and a new component instance being produced again at rehydration. In the State Management Support field, the following options are available:

- **Holds No State**   Select this option to use a stateless component that must not retain information between method calls. In this case the XLANG Scheduler Engine will terminate the component instance when the XLANG Schedule is dehydrated. The XLANG Scheduler Engine will create a new component instance as soon as the XLANG schedule is rehydrated.

- **Holds State, But Doesn't Support Persistence**   This option causes the XLANG Scheduler Engine to allow the COM Component to continue as soon as the XLANG schedule is dehydrated.

- **Holds State And Does Support Persistence**   If the status of the component is to be maintained following dehydration of the XLANG schedule, the interfaces IPersistStream or IPersistStreamInit must be implemented in the component. When the XLANG schedule is rehydrated again, the component's status at the time of dehydration will be restored again.

Every COM Component returns a value specifying whether the COM Component has been successfully completed or closed with an error. HRESULT is the COM standard return value, which returns the value 0 (NULL) only when a successful completion has been achieved. All other values imply that an error has occurred. By selecting Abort Transaction If The Method Returns A Failure HRESULT in the Error Handling field, the XLANG Scheduler Engine can be instructed to abort a transaction if the COM Component returns a failure. This option must be chosen when the XLANG Scheduler Engine should execute the error-recovery process code on the On Failure Of *<transaction>* or Compensation For *<transaction>* at the termination of a transaction.

COM Binding Example   In the following example, we implement a process flow with some user interaction. A message box should appear and ask the user whether he or she wants to create a new account. If the user decides to do so, another message box will appear where he or she can type in some information that will then be displayed in

another message box to prove that the information was transported to the XLANG
schedule. The example should demonstrate the use of COM Components in XLANG
schedules and the message flow between COM Components and XLANG schedules.
The following illustration depicts the business process used in this example:

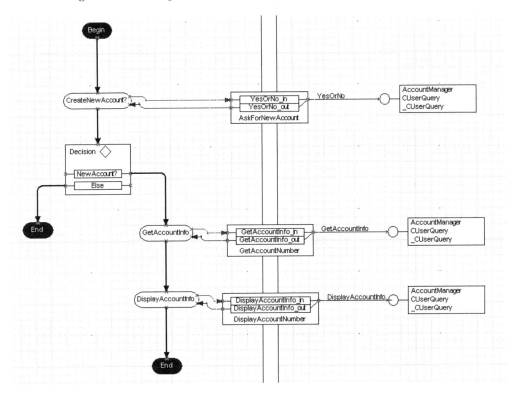

To create a simple VB COM Component for the example, follow these steps:

1. Open Visual Basic and create a new ActiveX DLL.

2. The project name used in this scenario is **AccountManager**, and the class name
   is **CUserQuery**.

3. Create a form called **Form1** with a text box called **Text1**. We need that form
   to get the user information in our schedule. Don't forget to add a button to the
   form that executes the following sub:

```
Sub Command1_Click()
    Me.Hide
End Sub
```

4. Now add the following functions to the class CUserQuery:

```
Function YesOrNo()
    YesOrNo = MsgBox("Create new account?", vbYesNo, "AccountManagerDemo")
```

```
End Function

Function GetAccountInfo() As String
    Dim f As Form1
    Set f = New Form1
      f.Show (1)
      GetAccountInfo = f.Text1.Text
    Set f = Nothing
End Function

Sub DisplayAccountInfo(ByVal info As String)
    MsgBox ("Account Number typed in: " & info)
End Sub
```

5. When compiling the ActiveX DLL, Visual Basic will automatically register the COM Component.

The function YesOrNo displays a VB message box showing Yes and No buttons. The return values are vbYes for clicking Yes and vbNo for clicking No. The function GetAccountInfo displays the form Form1 and returns the text input of the user. The sub DisplayAccountInfo simply shows the value of the user input in a VB message box.

Let's walk through the creation of the XLANG schedule. The first action, "CreateNewAccount?", calls the method YesOrNo of the COM Component. To open the COM Component Binding Wizard, drag the COM Implementation shape on the implementation page (on the right side of the separator bar). The dialog box settings of the COM Component Binding Wizard are summarized in the following table:

Page	Settings
Welcome to the COM Component Binding Wizard	Type in the orchestration port name for that component.
Static or Dynamic Communication	Select Static.
Class Information	Expand AccountManager and select CUserQuery.
Method Information	Check the select box at YesOrNo.
Advanced Properties	Click Finish.

After you finish the wizard, the named port appears on the separator bar connected to the COM implementation shape. When connecting the action "CreateNewAccount?" with the just-created orchestration port using the Arrow or Connector tool, the Method Communication Wizard appears. On the first page, select Initiate A Synchronous Method Call, and click Next to proceed to the Method Specification Information page. Because we implemented only one method in the COM Component Binding Wizard before, we have only the method YesOrNo to select. Click Finish to complete the configuration. Let's follow the message flow to the decision shape.

The Decision shape contains a rule to check which button was clicked. To add a rule to the decision shape, right-click the shape and select Add Rule from the context menu. The Rules Properties dialog box appears. You can use the Expression Assistant to create the rule or type the following into the Script Expression text area:

```
YesOrNo_out.YesOrNo = vbYes
```

The rule checks the return value of the implemented COM Component. If the return value is vbYes, the decision evaluates "true", and the process flow is following the right branch. If the user selected No in the message box, the rule evaluates "false", and the process ends at the End shape.

Now configure the remaining actions like the "CreateNewAccount?" action. We'll use the same COM Component, but other methods. Instead of using one COM component that implements all the methods we need for our orchestration, we could implement several single COM Components. In the example, I used the same names for the action shapes and the method names of the COM Component; this is not necessary, but helps with the configuration in bigger projects.

After configuring the actions and COM Components, proceed to the Data View page. Here, you have to make only one connection between two messages. The typed-in account information should be displayed in a message box, and therefore we have to configure the transport of this piece of information from the communication shape GetAccountInfo_out to the communication shape DisplayAccountInfo_in.

Here is the data view of account.skv:

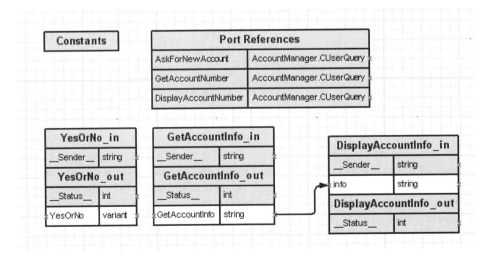

Now start the schedule to test the configuration using the XLANG Event Monitor. You can find the tool at Program Files\Microsoft BizTalk Server\SDK\XLANG Tools\XLANGMon.exe. Start the tool and run the XLANG schedule by selecting Instance | Run on the menu. Type in the full path to your XLANG schedule in the message box that appears. If you configured the example well, a message box should appear asking you whether you want to create a new account.

Implementing Script Components

Windows Script Components can be implemented in the XLANG schedule through using the Script Component shape. Script components are dealt with in the same way as COM Components; thus, the implementation of the Script Component Implementation shape is similar to the COM Component Implementation shape. Script components use the script engine of the operation system and are treated similarly to COM Components. Every action connected with a port to a script component sends a message via a method call, and then the component returns a result. The XLANG Scheduler Engine waits for a reply from the script component before it proceeds with the business process.

The Script Component Binding Wizard first opens when the Script Component Implementation shape is dragged in the diagram. On the first page of the Script Component Binding Wizard, a new port must be determined. A Script Component Implementation shape cannot be connected with an already existing port, since the port of a Script Component Implementation shape is fixed to the interface of the script component.

Static or Dynamic Communication   On the Static or Dynamic Communication page, you can specify how the XLANG Scheduler Engine should instantiate the script component. These settings are identical to those of the COM Component. Thus, if you already know how to implement COM Components, proceed to the next section. The following three options are available:

- **Static**   The XLANG creates a script component instance. Choose this option when the XLANG Scheduler Engine can already be provided with all the information (necessary for implementation) at design time.

- **Dynamic**   An application other than the XLANG Scheduler Engine instantiates the script component. Select this option when the XLANG Scheduler Engine requires additional information at run time in order to complete implementation.

- **No Instantiation**   Use this option only when the XLANG schedule should receive data via a method call without activating the component. This means that the XLANG Scheduler Engine neither instantiates the script component nor executes a method call.

At this point, a script component must be chosen so that the XLANG Scheduler Engine knows what it must do.

Specify the Script File In this dialog box, the XLANG Scheduler Engine specifies which file contains the script component code. The path of the file can be immediately entered, or the Field dialog box can be opened, where the files can be immediately browsed. If selecting the Windows Script Components, consider the following:

- Parameters must be passed on by value, not by reference.
- VB subroutines are not supported, only functions.
- Multiple components within the source code of the Windows Script Component cannot be used. Each WSC file is only allowed to contain one component.

After selecting the script component file, the XLANG Scheduler Engine must be told how it should instantiate the script component. However, this only applies if Static is chosen in the preceding step. If another option is chosen, ignore the dialog box and proceed directly to the Method Information page, since script components only have one dispatch interface.

Component Instantiation Information Proceed with this step if you previously selected the option specifying that the XLANG Scheduler Engine instantiates the script component. The XLANG Scheduler Engine instantiates a script component either via a moniker or via the Prog ID of the script component, as shown.

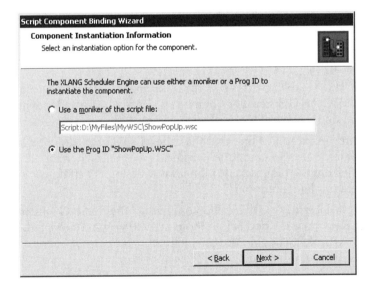

The instantiation options are as follows:

- **Use A Moniker Of The Script File**   The moniker for script components is made up of the fully qualified path name of the script file, with the expression "Script:" placed in front. The moniker for script components could, for example, look like the following:

```
Script:C:\MyComponents\MyScriptComponent.wsc
```

- **Use The Prog ID**   A ProgID (programmatic identifier) is a unique name mapped to the Windows Registry by a COM application to uniquely identify an object. When selecting this option, the ProgID itself should already be blended in the dialog box. The Script Component Binding Wizard checks the Registry information and appropriately inserts the ProgID. If no ProgID is available, check whether the script component was correctly registered.

Method Information   Now let's turn our attention to selecting the methods that the script components should provide for the XLANG schedule. Select at least one method to be used. If only one method is applicable to the script component, this dialog box should be ignored. This step corresponds to the implementation of COM Components.

Advanced Port Properties   The last dialog box of the Script Component Binding Wizard is the Advanced Port Properties page. Here, security, transaction support, and error handling are configured. This step corresponds to that of the COM Components, with the exception that script components do not have state management support, because script components support only the IDispatch interface. There is no possibility of implementing the interfaces IPersistStream and IPersistStreamInit. Therefore, Windows Script Components cannot be serialized and will be destroyed when the XLANG schedule is dehydrating. This means that Windows Script Components must remain in memory for their lifetime. Consequently, Windows Script Components should not be used in long-running business processes, except when they are used within a short-lived transaction nested within a long-running business transaction.

The sender identity settings are determined in the security area. With the Script Component shape, the authenticated user information of received messages can be queried, and it can be determined whether a message should be processed or rejected by the XLANG Scheduler. The information is contained in the field __Sender__ on the Data View page. The following three options are available:

- **Not Required**   Select this option when the XLANG schedule should receive a message without knowing the identity of the sender.

- **Optional**   Select this option when the XLANG schedule should identify the sender of a message if the information is available.

- **Required**   Select this option when the XLANG schedule should not receive a sender's message whose identity is not known.

When a script component is bound to a transaction shape in the XLANG schedule, it can be determined, via the transaction support in the Script Component Binding Wizard, how the script component participates in the transactions. The options in the Transaction Support field are similar to those that the COM+ programmer already knows from the Microsoft Transaction Server (MTS). The following are the settings of the Transaction Support field:

- **Disabled**   This option specifies that the script component will ignore COM transaction management.

- **Not Supported**   This option specifies that the script component will not participate in COM+ transactions or transmit the transactions of other COM+ components. This feature is available only when the script component is installed as a COM+ component.

- **Supported**   This option specifies that the script component will support transactions. If the component is associated with a transaction via an orchestration port, the component will be included in the transaction. When the generator is not executed in a transaction, then the component will also be instantiated without the transaction. This feature is available only when the script component is installed as a COM+ component.

- **Required**   This option specifies that the component will support transactions. If the component is associated with a transaction via an orchestration port, the component will be included in the transaction. When the generator is not executed in a transaction, then the component will, nevertheless, be instantiated in a new transaction. This feature is only available when the script component is installed as a COM+ component.

- **Requires New**   This option specifies that a new transaction will always be created for a script component. This feature is available only when the script component is installed as a COM+ component.

Every COM Component returns a value specifying whether the COM Component has been successfully completed or closed with an error. HRESULT is the COM standard return value, which returns a value only once a successful completion has been achieved. All other values imply that an error has occurred. If you select Abort Transaction If The Method Returns A Failure HRESULT in the Error Handling field, the XLANG Scheduler Engine can be instructed to abort a transaction if the script component returns a failure. This option must be chosen when the XLANG Scheduler Engine should execute the error-recovery process code on the On Failure Of *<transaction>* or Compensation For *<transaction>* at the termination of a transaction.

Creating a Script Component   Script components are extremely useful to quickly get a component up and running for testing purposes before creating a compiled COM Component. You can use script components as middle-tier business logic, to access a database, or to simply create a pop-up window. The Windows Script Component technology consists of a script component run time (Scrobj.dll), an interface handler, and your script component file (WSC file). The script component implements only the functionality of the COM Component; you need no deeper understanding of COM to create a script component.

To easily create a Windows Script Component, you can download the Windows Script Component Wizard from the MSDN home page at http://msdn.microsoft.com/scripting/scriptlets/wz10en.exe. The following example will show how to create a Windows Script Component using the Windows Script Component Wizard. The example component will receive a value and display it in a simple message box. To create a script component, follow these steps:

1. Start the Windows Script Component Wizard.

2. On the Define Windows Script Component Object page, fill in the name, filename, Prog ID, version, and location where the script component will be stored and click Next. The filename used in this example is simply test.WSC.

3. On the Specify Characteristics page, select the script language you want to use. The supported script languages are JScript, VBScript, PERLscript, PScript, and Python. Also select the option Special Implements Support if you want DHTML behavior or Active Server Pages Support. Error checking and debugging support can also be set on this page. Click Next to proceed.

4. The Add Windows Script properties page prompts for properties you want to expose and creates the necessary elements in the scripting language you specify. Click Next to proceed.

5. The Add Windows Script methods page prompts for methods you want to expose and creates the necessary elements in the scripting language you specify. Click Next to proceed. The example uses one method named Show_Popup, and one parameter, *content*. If you want to use more than one parameter within one method, just type the parameters into the Parameters field separated by commas.

6. The Add Windows Script Events page prompts for events that the script component can fire and creates the skeleton event elements.

The WSC file created by the Script Component Wizard looks like the following:

```
<?xml version="1.0"?>
<component>
<registration
      description="test"
      progid="test.WSC"
      version="1.00"
      classid="{a5508fd2-8ffe-4cf4-8991-343753e4b4b9}"
>
</registration>
```

```
<public>
      <method name="Show_Popup">
            <PARAMETER name="content"/>
      </method>
</public>
<script language="VBScript">
<![CDATA[
function Show_Popup(content)
      Show_Popup = "Temporary Value"
end function
]]>
</script>
</component>
```

Script component files are—as you may recognize—XML (Extensible Markup Language) files. The file contains all information that is needed to create a COM Component.

As a next step, you have to insert the script functionality that you want into the WSC file. To show a message box containing a message received through a method call, replace the code Show_Popup = "Temporary Value" with this short line of code:

```
MsgBox (content)
```

Before you can insert a script component implementation into your XLANG schedule drawing, the script component has to be registered. This is much simpler than it may sound. Just browse to the location where you saved your script component, right-click the WSC file to display the context menu, and select Register. A message box will appear confirming that the registration has succeeded, depending on whether the script has no errors. That's it. Now the script component is ready for use in an XLANG schedule.

Implementing Message Queuing

Microsoft Message Queuing (MSMQ) can be used to realize asynchronous communication between your XLANG schedule and other XLANG schedules or an application. Messages are filed in message queues in order to be read sometime by an application or an XLANG schedule. When a port is connected with a Message Queue Implementation shape, it is also connected with a message queue, so that no extra BizTalk messaging port has to be implemented to send a message from an XLANG schedule to a message queue. A port can be connected with an existing known message queue or a per-instance message queue.

To connect a Message Queue Implementation shape with your port, drag the Message Queue Implementation shape symbol from the stencil, and drop it on the design page. The first page of the Message Queuing Binding Wizard appears. You can use it to create a new port for the message queue binding or to bind an existing unbound port with the message queue.

Static or Dynamic Queue Information   Here, you can specify whether a message queue should already be available at design time or whether it should be created at run time. The following two options are available in the dialog box:

- **Static Queue**   Choose this option when you have enough information at design time concerning the message queue to be used.

- **Dynamic Queue**   If this option is chosen, the XLANG Scheduler Engine requires additional information in order to assign a message queue at run time. On the Data View page, the Port Reference field must be connected to a message field that transfers the necessary information onto the port at design time.

If you have chosen the Dynamic Queue, ignore the following step and proceed to the Advanced Port Properties dialog box.

Queue Information   If you chose Static Queue in the previous section, you now have to specify the message queue to be used. You can either create a new message queue for every XLANG schedule instance, or you may resort to an already existing message queue. The dialog box should look like the following:

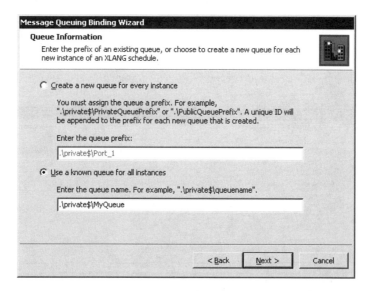

If the first option—Create A New Queue For Every Instance—is chosen, the XLANG Scheduler Engine creates a new per-instance message queue at run time for every instance of an XLANG schedule. The name of the message queue is expanded by the prefix, and a Global Unique Identifier (GUID) is appended for every instance. The Message Binding Wizard provides a default prefix for the message queue, which can be changed. To share the name of the newly created queue in order to enable someone to reply to this port, a reference to this port must be sent in a message. To achieve this, connect the message field containing the reference to the port reference shape of the port on the Data View page. This is one way in message correlation to guarantee that a message sent by an XLANG schedule can return to the right XLANG schedule instance. Message correlation is discussed in detail in Chapter 8. The per-instance message queue is terminated as soon as the XLANG schedule has ended.

However, the second option—Use A Known Queue For All Instances—will usually be selected. Here, only the path name of the preexisting message queue needs to be entered. The XLANG Scheduler will deliver all messages for every instance of an XLANG schedule in this message queue. If you want to set up a queue for use by another application, a known queue for all instances will be the preferred configuration. An example queue name for a preexisting message queue is the following:

```
.\private$\MessageQueueName
```

We have now reached the final step before completing the configuration of the MSMQ message binding. Since message queues as an element of windows resources are an element of security systems, message queues can impose security restrictions.

Advanced Port Properties   The sender identity settings are determined in the Security area, as shown next. At message queues, the sender of a message can be identified. The XLANG Scheduler Engine can query this information, which is then contained in the __Sender__ field on the Data View page.

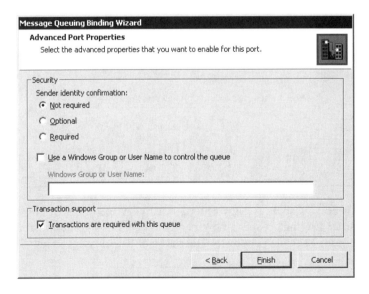

At this point, the following three options are available:

- **Not Required**   Select this option when the XLANG schedule should receive a message without knowing the identity of the sender.
- **Optional**   Select this option when the XLANG schedule should identify the sender of the message if the information is available.
- **Required**   Select this option when the XLANG schedule should not receive messages from a sender whose identity is not known.

The read/write access on the message queue can also be controlled by selecting the check box Use A Windows Group Or User Name To Control The Queue. The user or group name that will be permitted access to the queue must then be entered in the field. This option is only available with static message queues.

When using a transactional message queue, you must select the Transactions Are Required With This Queue check box. It is important that the XLANG Scheduler Engine can define whether a message queue is transactional or not, in order to implement the correct MSMQ API calls. If the port binding was configured with Transactions Are Required With This Queue and the message queue is not transactional, the XLANG schedule will fail.

Implementing BizTalk Messaging

The BizTalk Messaging Implementation shape enables you to exchange messages between your XLANG schedule and the BizTalk Messaging Service. When sending messages through BizTalk Messaging, you can use any transport type that BizTalk Messaging provides, such as HTTP, SMTP, Loopback, or AIC. When receiving a message from BizTalk Messaging, you must specify an HTTP address at which to receive messages. But for static activation of an XLANG schedule by BizTalk Messaging, the message can arrive at BizTalk Messaging (File or MSMQ receive function, ASP using Interchange.Submit, and so on). To create a new BizTalk Messaging binding, drag the BizTalk Messaging shape symbol from the implementation stencil, and drop it on the BizTalk design page.

Communication Direction   Selecting the communication direction causes further dialog boxes to divide into two separate branches at the BizTalk Messaging Binding Wizard. If you would like to send a message, click Send and then click Next. The next step is discussed in the following section, "Static or Dynamic Channel Information."

If you would like to receive messages, click Receive and then Next. Then proceed to the next step, "XLANG Schedule Activation Information".

Static or Dynamic Channel Information   The following illustration portrays the Static Or Dynamic Channel Information page. If Static Channel is selected, you must specify the name of an already existing BizTalk Messaging channel. As mentioned earlier, when sending messages through BizTalk Messaging, every transport type for sending messages from BizTalk Messaging Service is provided. The only thing to configure here is to name the messaging channel where the XLANG Scheduler Engine has to deliver the messages.

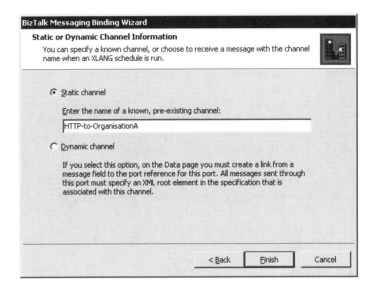

The second option permits the use of dynamic routing. *Dynamic routing* means that the port must be configured so that it can accept the additional information provided by the BizTalk Messaging Service at run time. As a result, the port can identify the name of the channel. If Dynamic Channel is chosen, a field in the message, containing information regarding the name of the channel, must be connected to the port reference. Additional information on dynamic routing can be found in Chapter 6. Dynamic routing is also a core point of correlating messages back to the right XLANG schedule instance, which will be discussed in Chapter 8.

At this point, the configuration for sending messages through BizTalk Messaging is done. The following sections cover how XLANG schedules receive messages through BizTalk Messaging.

XLANG Schedule Activation Information   When receiving messages, you can select from two options on the XLANG Activation page, depending on whether you want to create a new instance of an XLANG schedule upon arrival of a new message. If you do not want to create a new instance, select No and click Next. This transfers you to the next section, "Channel Information".

If you have selected Yes in the dialog box, the XLANG Scheduler creates a new instance of the XLANG schedule for every message arriving at this orchestration port. The BizTalk Messaging Implementation shape has the label "Activate" to symbolize the orchestration port that activates the XLANG schedule upon arrival of a message. When implementing an orchestration port to activate the XLANG schedule, the following restrictions must be taken into consideration:

- Only one port can be used to activate the XLANG schedule upon arrival of a message.

- Only a single action can be connected to this port to receive messages.

- The action receiving messages through this port is not allowed to be in a loop body. If the action were within a loop, the XLANG Scheduler could not decide in which iteration of the loop it should begin.

- No data flow connection between the port reference for this port and another communication shape on the Data View page can be created.

If the Yes option is chosen, the configuration of the port binding is now complete, and you can click Finish. However, if No is selected, then proceed with the following step to define a channel, via which the message shall reach the messaging port that delivers the message to the schedule.

Channel Information   At this point, enter the channel and the HTTP URL address that are used by the BizTalk Messaging Service to receive messages. In this case, the receive function of BizTalk Server 2000 is a dynamic web page, upon which a script is executed (for example, ASP). The web page receives the message with a script that can process the HTTP POST. This script transfers the data to BizTalk Server 2000 with the Submit( ) method. You can read more about this in Chapter 8.

Data Flow

Every XLANG schedule has a data page, upon which the data flow within an XLANG schedule is described. The data flow is represented by arrows connecting the Source Message shape with the Destination Message shape. While you are configuring the message flow between the orchestration ports and the actions on the Business Process page with the XML Communication Wizard, the BizTalk Orchestration Designer is busy designing a Communication shape for every message entering or leaving the XLANG schedule. The XML Communication Wizard starts upon connection of an action to an orchestration port. The following sections describe in detail the procedure for connecting actions to orchestration ports. As a final point, a description details how to configure the data flow on the data page.

Connecting Actions to BizTalk or MSMQ Implementations

After defining your action and configuring the implementation port, the Action shape will now be connected to the Port shape. Using the Arrow or Connector tool and starting with the action, connect the two shapes to one another. After completing this first step, the XML Communication Wizard starts. The following dialog boxes for connecting actions with BizTalk Messaging and MS Message Queuing are identical. On the first page of the XML Communication Wizard, you will see the following:

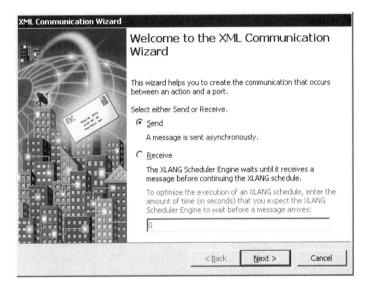

Depending on whether you have configured the implementation shape for sending or receiving messages, the options, indicating the communication direction, will have already been selected or disabled. If, for example, you have configured the implementation shape to receive messages, the communication direction for receiving has already been determined, and this cannot be influenced through the XML Communication Wizard. If you have connected the action to the unbound port of a port bound to MSMQ Implementation, the communication direction may be chosen.

If Receive has been chosen, you can specify in the field how many seconds the XLANG Scheduler Engine should wait for the incoming messages. With values above 180 seconds, the XLANG schedule instance is immediately dehydrated. The value 0 signifies that the arrival of a message is immediately expected.

On the page shown next, specify to the Orchestration Designer the type of message that should be transferred via the port.

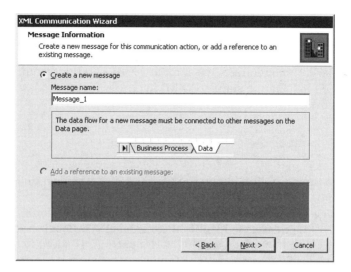

On the Message Information page, you have the option to either create a new message or refer a message that you have already created for the XLANG Schedule. The messages that have already been created are listed in the lower list box. When you create a new message, a new communication shape also appears on the Data View page for this message. Following specification of the message information, you are transferred to the XML Translation Information page:

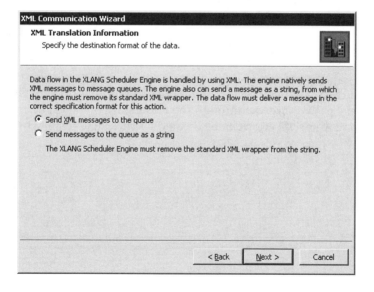

On the XML Translation Information page, you must specify whether a message should be sent or received as XML or a text string. The XLANG Scheduler Engine, internally, works exclusively with XML. If you have chosen to send text strings, the XLANG Scheduler Engine removes the standard XML wrapper from the messages. The XLANG Scheduler Engine standard XML wrapper for string data looks like the following:

```
<?xml version="1.0" ?><StringData></StringData>
```

You must choose this option if working with flat files. The next dialog box is the Message Type Information page.

On the Message Type Information page, specify the label for your messages that the XLANG Scheduler Engine uses to identify the messages. The label chosen for the message is used to allocate the message to the right action. To identify the messages, the XLANG Scheduler Engine proceeds as follows:

- The XLANG Scheduler Engine compares the message type information to the message label in the message queue. When using MSMQ, the message type information should correspond to the label of the message in the message queue; otherwise, the message is ignored. This enables the MSMQ port implementation to deliver various messages to several actions.

- When using BizTalk Messaging, the XLANG Scheduler Engine attempts to equalize the message label with the document element of the message.

When sending a message as XML, the Message Specification Information page follows. Otherwise, you have already completed this section and may click Finish.

On the Message Specification Information page, shown next, enter the path to a message specification that you have already created with the BizTalk Editor. You can either type in the path or browse through the folders. If you have still not created a specification, a new specification can be created by clicking Create, which opens the BizTalk Editor.

If you select the Validate Messages Against The Specification check box, messages that are arriving or leaving can be validated against specifications. Click Add in the area Message field, and the Field Selection dialog box appears:

In the Field Selection dialog box, you can select individual Document Specification fields by expanding the tree view and clicking a field in the Select Node tree. The field name is automatically inserted in the Field Name box. You can also manually process the name and the node path that you want to insert. The fields selected in the Field Selection dialog box appear on the Data View page as fields of communication shapes, which are automatically created by the BizTalk Orchestration Designer.

Connecting Actions to COM or Script Component Implementations

To create a message flow between an action and a COM Component or a script component implementation, use the Arrow or Connector tool to connect the action with the port bound to a COM Component Implementation shape. When these shapes have been connected, the Method Communication Wizard appears with the following dialog box:

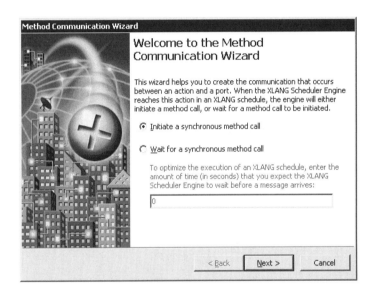

On the first page of the Method Communication Wizard, you can specify whether the XLANG Scheduler Engine will call a method or wait for a method call. In the first case, a COM Component or a script component is called; in the second case, the XLANG schedule is running and waits for a method to be called by another application or component. If the option to Wait For A Synchronous Method Call has been chosen, you can specify in the lower text field how many seconds the XLANG Scheduler Engine should wait for an incoming message. If the time chosen is above 180 seconds, the XLANG schedule instance is immediately dehydrated. The standard value for this option is 0, which signifies that the arrival of a message is immediately expected.

On the Message Information page, shown next, specify whether you want to create a new message or to refer to a message pair that is already used in the XLANG schedule drawing. If you want to reference an already-existing message, you can select a message from the lower list field.

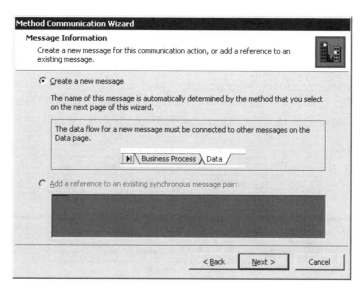

If the message you want to use is not listed, you can create a new message. The name of the message that appears on the Data View page depends upon the method chosen on the Message Specification Information page, shown next.

The Methods list box contains all the methods that you have already chosen at the COM Component port implementation. Select the method you want to use. The lists below the In Fields and Out Fields of the method, as well as the corresponding types, appear. Following selection of the method, click Finish to complete the configuration for message exchanges.

Communication Shapes

During the configuration for connecting actions with the orchestration ports, the BizTalk Orchestration Designer busily inserted communication shapes on the Data View page. The following illustration portrays a screen shot with communication messages.

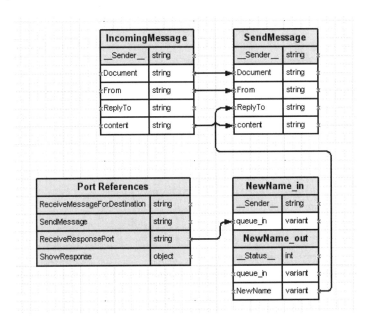

The Port References, Constants, and Message shapes are displayed on the Data View page. The Port shape, on the other hand, is displayed on the Business Process page. On the Data View page, the data of the messages is represented through the Communication shapes. Data flow will be discussed in more detail in the section "Configuring Data Flow", later in the chapter.

Ports   Ports are defined locations where messages are received or from which they are sent. Your XLANG schedule can insert an unbound port. Right-click the separator bar, and then select Add New Port from the context menu. Every port has a corresponding message that appears on the Data View page.

Port References   The Port Reference message contains all the ports that have been created on the Business Process page. The Port Reference message has a field for every port that contains information regarding the origin of the port. For every new port, a new reference in the message is automatically created. Every instance of an XLANG schedule is identified by a Global Unique Identifier (GUID), and this GUID is part of the port reference string. The port reference shape cannot be deleted.

The port reference to a COM port binding may look like the following:

```
sked://MyComputer!XLANG Scheduler/{b7be0403-49a2-46a2-8747-
16b09c65c10e}/MyOrchestrationPortName
```

In this case, the port reference contains a COM moniker of a running XLANG schedule instance. For more information about COM monikers, see the later section "Moniker Syntax".

A port reference to a message queue port binding the port reference has, of course, another look:

```
MyComputer\private$\MyQueue{b7be0403-49a2-46a2-8747-16b09c65c10e}
```

The port reference field is used when a message is allotted to a running instance of an XLANG schedule. In a production environment, if several instances of one XLANG schedule are running, the port reference can be used to correlate messages back to their original XLANG schedule instance. If you are using a COM implementation with the option No Instantiation selected, the port is utilized to connect to a running XLANG schedule using the moniker of the instance, but the GUID of the XLANG schedule instance is not known before the instance is run. The port reference field gives the opportunity to pass the GUID within the port reference string to a message, so that an external COM Component processing this message can create a moniker to point to the COM binding port implemented with the No Instantiation option set.

Constants   The Constants message contains—as the name suggests—constant data. Constants can be inserted by right-clicking the Constant shape and selecting Properties in the context menu, or by double-clicking the Constant shape. The Constant Message Properties dialog box appears. Click Add to insert a further field into the Constant shape. This shape cannot be deleted.

Messages   The Message shape portrays the field of the message to be received or sent via a port.

System Fields   Message shapes contain fields that are automatically inserted by the BizTalk Orchestration Designer. The System field can contain descriptive information about the messages. Table 7-1 shows the System fields.

System Field	Description
__Exists__	This field specifies whether a message exists. This field is not shown in the Communication shapes on the Data View page, but only with the Decision and While shapes.
__Sender__	This field contains the identity of the sender of a message, but only if the sender of the message is recognized. This field is shown on the Data View page.
__Status__	This field returns the status of a COM method call. The return value is the HRESULT. The field is only shown in connection with COM component or script component implementations on the Data View page.
Document	This field contains a message in the form of a string. The message is always an XML message. This field is only shown in connection with MSMQ and BizTalk Messaging implementations on the Data View page.

Table 7-1. *System Fields of Communication Shapes*

Configuring Data Flow

Every XLANG schedule has a data page upon which the data flow is configured. The data page contains the following:

- A Message shape for every message, which is either sent to or received from an XLANG schedule

- A Constant Message shape

- A Port Reference shape containing a field for every orchestration port in the XLANG schedule

Every message consists of a clearly named set of fields. The fields contain a data element with a specific data type. Every Message shape is shown on the data page as a table with all the message fields. System fields not requiring data flow have a yellow background. User and System fields requiring data flow, however, have a white background.

On the data page, data flow connections go from the right side—the exit—to the left side of the message field—the entrance. This connection specifies that the data from the Source field will be delivered to the Destination field. At run time, the XLANG Scheduler copies the data from the Resource Message field into the Destination Message field. An XLANG schedule is not compiled until all the fields of the messages to be sent have been specified.

Draw Flow Between Messages   If you would like to connect Message fields, proceed as follows:

1. On the BizTalk Orchestration Designer data page, click in the source message field from which you would like to establish a data flow connection to a destination message field. On the right side of the message field, a small green square appears.

2. Drag the green square to the left side of the destination message field to which you would like to connect. When a red square appears on the left side of the Destination Message field, release the mouse button.

The BizTalk Orchestration Designer works, internally, exclusively with XML. All non-XML messages are surrounded with the XLANG Scheduler standard XML wrapper. If you do want to send or receive non-XML messages in connection with message queuing, use the following guidelines.

Send Non-XML Messages to a Message Queue   If you would like to send messages as non-XML to a message queue, go to the XML Communication Wizard. Select the option Send Message To The Queue As A String on the XML Translation page. The Message shape on the data page then contains an additional StringData field in this configuration. To send the data as a string to a message queue, you need the XLANG Scheduler Engine XML standard wrapper for string data. In this case, the wrapper is not automatically created, so a standard wrapper must be manually created. The procedure is the following:

1. Create a new constant with any name, but the data type must be string.

2. Now enter the following standard wrapper as a value of the constant:

```
<?xml version="1.0" ?><StringData></StringData>
```

3. Draw a data flow connection between the Constant field and the Document field of the message.

4. Draw a data flow connection between the field containing the string message and the StringData field of the message, which should be sent to the message queue.

5. The following illustration clarifies the connection:

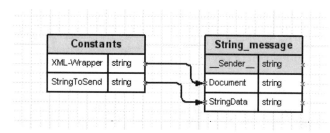

Receive Non-XML Message from a Message Queue   If you would like to receive non-XML messages from a message queue, go to the XML Translation Wizard and select the option Receive String Message From A Queue. The string message will be surrounded with the XLANG Scheduler Engine standard XML wrapper for the string data type. The data is contained in the message field StringData.

The XLANG Scheduler COM+ Application

When installing the BizTalk Orchestration Designer, a set of COM+ applications is installed. The XLANG Scheduler is the COM+ application that hosts XLANG schedules. This application hosts a default instance of the XLANG Scheduler Engine. After the installation, every new created COM+ application has an additional XLANG tab in the Properties dialog box.

Persistency

When an XLANG schedule is dehydrated waiting for a message to arrive on an orchestration port, the XLANG Scheduler Engine has to restore the state of the XLANG schedule to its state before dehydration to perform a correct rehydration, so that the XLANG schedule can continue to operate correctly. During the lifetime of an XLANG schedule, various events can take place, such as

- Starting, completing, or aborting transactions
- Sending or receiving messages, or waiting to receive messages
- Executing decisions or While loops

All these events can modify the state of an XLANG schedule. Therefore, the state of any XLANG schedule at any time of the XLANG schedule's life is stored in the Orchestration Persistence database by the XLANG Scheduler Engine. The Orchestration Persistence database—also named XLANG Persistence database—is created at the installation of BizTalk Server 2000. The Orchestration Persistence database enables the core features of BizTalk Orchestration: dehydration, rehydration, and long-running transactions.

Of course, the state of XLANG schedules will not be stored to the Orchestration Persistence database in a permanent stream of data, but only when events occur that modify the state of XLANG schedules. The XLANG Scheduler Engine stores the structure of XLANG schedules, the progress of running XLANG schedule instances, and messages that are received from a running XLANG schedule instance. Additionally, the state of XLANG schedules will be persisted at the beginning and the end of a transaction, to enable retries of a transaction if an error occurs and the rollback of long-running transactions after an abort or a failure.

When XLANG schedules wait for an extended time without any activity, the XLANG Scheduler Engine can dehydrate the XLANG schedule instance into the Orchestration Persistence database. Dehydration is removing all instance-specific data from memory and saving it into the Orchestration Persistence database. However, persisting information to a database is like logging the history of an XLANG schedule instance's state to be able to restore an older XLANG schedule state—for example, after an aborted transaction.

Using Persistent COM Components

When using COM or Windows Script Components that hold state, problems with scalability and performance in long-running business processes may occur in high-volume production environments. The XLANG Scheduler must keep the COM components that hold state in memory if they don't support persistence. The state management support of COM Component settings in the COM Component Binding Wizard tells the XLANG Scheduler how to treat the components that are bound to the XLANG schedule.

BizTalk Orchestration Designer leads you through the implementation of a COM component with the COM Component Binding Wizard. On the Advanced Properties page in the State Management Support field, the following options can be selected to describe the state management of the COM Component that is implemented:

- **Holds No State**   Select this option to use a stateless component that must not retain information between method calls. In this case, the XLANG Scheduler Engine will terminate the component instance when the XLANG Schedule is dehydrated. The XLANG Scheduler Engine will create a new component instance as soon as the XLANG schedule is rehydrated.

- **Holds State, But Doesn't Support Persistence**   This option causes the XLANG Scheduler Engine to allow the COM Component to continue as soon as the XLANG schedule is dehydrated.

- **Holds State And Does Support Persistence**   If the status of the component is to be maintained following dehydration of the XLANG schedule, the interfaces IPersistStream or IPersistStreamInit must be implemented in the component. When the XLANG schedule is rehydrated again, the component's status at the time of dehydration will be restored again.

The first option is the one that causes no problems at all. If a COM Component doesn't keep state, the COM Component will be destroyed when the XLANG schedule is dehydrated and then re-created when the XLANG schedule rehydrates. Although these components do not affect the execution of XLANG schedules, they will affect the performance of the system.

The second option must be used carefully. COM Components that hold state but do not support persistence will remain in memory when the XLANG schedule instance is dehydrated, because the XLANG Scheduler cannot persist their current state. In a production environment where possibly hundreds of XLANG schedules are running at the same time, this option will lead to a massive scalability problem. Even worse, if a system error were to occur, or the system were to be rebooted, the current state of the components could not be restored. Therefore, the XLANG schedule instances depending on the correct state of these components could not be restored to their full and correct state. The XLANG schedule instance then will fail to complete their business process.

The last option can only be used with COM Components that support the IPersist interface. The state of these COM Components will be serialized in the Orchestration Persistence database when the XLANG schedule is dehydrated. When the XLANG schedule is rehydrating, the XLANG Scheduler Engine creates a new instance of the COM Component. The serialized data in the Orchestration Persistence database is then passed to the COM Component to configure itself to the state before dehydration.

Persistable COM Component Example The following example will demonstrate persistency and the use of persistable Visual Basic COM Components in XLANG schedules. The business process depicted in the following illustration continuously polls the message queue .\private$\increment_sample and counts the incoming messages. The implementation of the message queue in the XLANG schedule is used in this example to make the XLANG schedule dehydrate when the business process reaches the Receive action. For this example, no configuration on the data page is necessary.

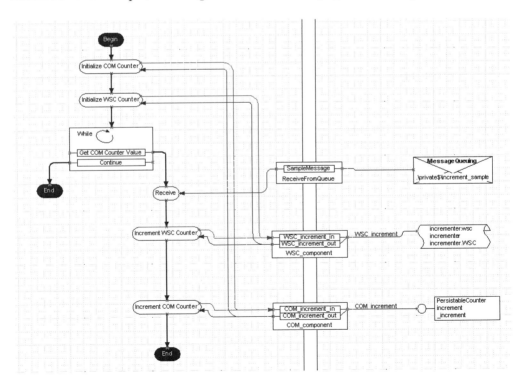

When the XLANG schedule is started, the actions Initialize COM Counter and Initialize WSC Counter are executed. For each COM Component, a message box will be displayed showing the current counter status. In this example, two different COM Components are used purposely. Windows Script Components do not support the IPersist interface, and therefore cannot be serialized to the Orchestration Persistence database when the XLANG schedule dehydrates. The other COM Component that is used supports persistency. How to achieve persistency with Visual Basic COM Components is described later in this section. When adding the COM implementation shape, the option Holds State, And Does Support Persistence has to be selected on the Advanced Port Properties page of the COM Component Binding Wizard.

The following While shape checks the value of the counter in the rule "Get COM counter value". The condition COM_increment_out.COM_increment < 3 checks whether the counter value of the persistable COM Component is smaller than 3. If the rule evaluates "true", then the right branch will be executed, or else, the left branch and the XLANG schedule end. (If you want to infinitely poll the message queue, insert a condition that always evaluates "true", like 1 = 1.) The output value COM_increment_out.COM_increment of the COM Component PersistableCounter must contain a value before the process flow leads into the While shape, or the XLANG schedule will fail because the VB script expression cannot make a reference to nonexisting objects. To check whether COM_increment_out.COM_increment exists with [__exists__] will also lead to a failure. Thus, the counter of the COM component is increased once before the message flow leads into the While shape; and, therefore, the variables "inc" are initialized with the value –1.

When the rule of the While shape evaluates "true", the process flow reaches the Receive action, where the XLANG schedule waits for incoming messages in the message queue. When connecting the Receive action with the orchestration port ReceiveFromQueue on the first page of the XML Communication Wizard, select Receive and enter an amount of time greater than 180 seconds. This will make the XLANG Scheduler Engine immediately dehydrate the XLANG schedule instance into the Orchestration Persistence database when the business process reaches the Receive action shape. When a message arrives at the message queue, the XLANG schedule instance will be rehydrated. Choosing a value smaller than 180 seconds will not lead to an immediate dehydration, and a value of 0 (Null) will lead to no dehydration of the XLANG schedule.

After the Receive action shape waits for messages from the message queue, the COM Components increase the counter value and display the value in a message box. When connecting the COM and the Windows Script Component with their corresponding action shapes on the second page of the XML Communication Wizard, create a reference to the existing message that is used to initialize the components. Both components have a global variable that stores the counter value over the While loops. In case of a dehydration of the XLANG schedule instance, the Windows Script Component will be destroyed, and so will the global variable storing the value of the iteration loop.

The persistable COM Component will keep the state over each iteration loop even if the XLANG schedule dehydrates. Let's examine the Visual Basic code for the persistable COM Component that is used in this example.

```
Private inc As Integer

Private Sub Class_Initialize()
    inc = -1
End Sub

Private Sub Class_ReadProperties(PropBag As PropertyBag)
    inc = PropBag.ReadProperty("counter", inc)
End Sub

Private Sub Class_WriteProperties(PropBag As PropertyBag)
    PropBag.WriteProperty "counter", inc
End Sub

Function COM_increment() As Integer
    inc = inc + 1
    COM_increment = inc
    MsgBox ("Visual Basic Component: while loop " & inc)
End Function
```

Visual Basic provides the functionality to create persistable COM Components. In the Properties window of the Visual Basic user interface, change the property Persistable from 0 – NotPersistable to 1 – Persistable. After the property Persistable is set to 1 – Persistable, the events InitProperties, ReadProperties, and WriteProperties are added to the class. When selecting the events from the drop-down menu in the code editor window, the subs Class_WriteProperties and Class_ReadProperties will be automatically added to the source code. The persistable COM Component uses the PropertyBag object to save and restore information across the iteration loops. A PropertyBag object is passed into an object through the ReadProperties event and the WriteProperties event in order to save and restore the state of an object. In the example code, the PropertyBag named "counter" is used to save and restore the information from the variable *inc*. If you need to save and restore more than one variable, just use more PropertyBag objects, and name them individually. The function COM_increment increases the value of the variable *inc* in every method call. Now that we have discussed the code of the persistable COM Component, let's examine the code of the Windows Script Component used in this example:

```
<?xml version="1.0"?>
<component>
```

```
<?component error="true" debug="true"?>
<registration
    description="incrementer"
    progid="incrementer.WSC"
    version="1.00"
    classid="{33769ee2-9e68-4994-b885-9cca3bf0f6a2}"
>
</registration>
<public>
<method name="WSC_increment">
    </method>
</public>
<script language="VBScript">
<![CDATA[

Dim inc
inc = -1

function WSC_increment()
    inc = inc + 1
    wsc_increment = inc
    MsgBox ("Windows Script Component: while loop " & inc)
end function
]]>
</script>
</component>
```

BIZTALK SERVER
ORCHESTRATION

The Windows Script Component uses a global variable *inc* to store the counter's value. The function WSC_increment increases the counter and displays the value in a message box.

When running the XLANG schedule, the message boxes that appear are showing the counter values of the COM Component and the Windows Script Component; both values are 0 (Null) at the beginning. Then the XLANG schedule is dehydrated, waiting for a message to arrive at the message queue. When a message is dropped into the message queue, the XLANG schedule is rehydrated, and the component's message boxes pop up showing the counter's values. (Chapter 8 provides a Visual Basic Script for putting XML files into a message queue.) Not surprisingly, the Windows Script Component is still showing a counter value of 0 (Null), while the persistent COM Component is showing the right value. The Windows Script Component was destroyed when the XLANG schedule was dehydrated, and the counter value disappeared. To evaluate the scenario, you can change the configuration of the message queue implementation in the XLANG schedule by setting the amount of time the XLANG schedule is expected to wait for an arriving message on the message queue to 0 (Null). This will keep the XLANG schedule from dehydrating. Running the XLANG schedule now, the Windows Script Component and the COM Component are both showing the right counter values, because both components and the XLANG schedule remain in memory. This setting is not recommended for a production environment, where hundreds or more XLANG schedules could be running concurrently. The conclusion from this example is that if you use COM Components, they should either be stateless or support persistence.

Maintaining the Orchestration Persistence Database

It is recommended that at least BizTalk Service Pack 1a be installed on the computer on which BizTalk Server is installed. The installation of BizTalk SP1a provides some additional utilities to maintain the Orchestration Persistence database. After the installation of the service pack, the utilities can be found at \Program Files\Microsoft BizTalk Server\Setup. To apply the utilities, you have to execute the stored procedure XLANG_Purge_Script.sql with the Query Analyzer of your Microsoft SQL Server installation.

The stored procedure can be used to delete records of the Orchestration Persistence database. For detailed usage of the stored procedure, read the associated Readme.htm of BizTalk Service Pack 1a.

Manage the XLANG Scheduler COM+ Application

When you install BizTalk Server, the XLANG Scheduler and the Orchestration Persistence database will be installed with default settings. The information will help you manage the Persistence database and the COM+ application that hosts the XLANG schedules.

Change Identity of a COM+ Application   It is recommended that you change the identity of the XLANG COM+ application from Interactive User to a unique user account, because COM+ applications that use Interactive User can only be used when the user is logged onto the computer. For example, if you are working with Microsoft Windows 2000 Terminal Services, the instantiation of an XLANG schedule will fail as long as the XLANG Scheduler identity is configured to Interactive User. To change the identity of a COM+ application, proceed with the following:

1. Open the Component Service with Start | Programs | Administrative Tools | Component Service.

2. Browse through the console tree to Console Root | Component Service | Computers | My Computer | COM+ Applications, and select XLANG Scheduler.

3. On the Advanced tab, deselect the Disable Changes check box. A message appears; click Yes to proceed. The XLANG Scheduler Properties dialog box closes. Open the XLANG Scheduler Properties dialog box as described in step 2, and proceed to step 4.

4. On the Identity tab, select This User and type in the required user information. Click OK. A message box appears; click OK.

From now on, XLANG Scheduler Engine will run in the specified user account.

Change Orchestration Persistence Database Settings   The Orchestration Persistence database has default settings when you install BizTalk Server 2000. The Orchestration Persistence database is located in your Microsoft SQL server. To change settings of the database, use the Enterprise Manager, by selecting Start | Programs | Microsoft SQL Server.

For more information about Microsoft SQL Server, see the associated help files or visit the Microsoft SQL server web site at http://www.microsoft.com/sql/default.asp.

Shut Down All Running Applications   When you execute a controlled shutdown for all XLANG schedules, the current state of all XLANG schedule instances will be stored in the XLANG Persistence database. An uncontrolled shutdown through right-clicking the XLANG Scheduler COM+ application and selecting Shut Down will cause transactions to abort and data to be lost when schedules are not fully transactional. To perform a controlled shutdown of all XLANG Schedule instances, do the following:

1. Open the Component Service by choosing Start | Programs | Administrative Tools | Component Service.

2. Browse through the console tree to Console Root | Component Service | Computers | My Computer | COM+ Applications, and select XLANG Scheduler.

3. On the XLANG tab, in the Controlled Shutdown area, click the All XLANG Applications button.

Restart Dehydrated XLANG Application   This action will restart all dehydrated XLANG schedule instances:

1. Open the Component Service by selecting Start | Programs | Administrative Tools | Component Service.

2. Browse through the console tree to Console Root | Component Service | Computers | My Computer | COM+ Applications, and select XLANG Scheduler.

3. On the XLANG tab, in the Restart Dehydrated XLANG Applications area, click the All XLANG Applications button.

Create an XLANG Schedule Host Application   To create an XLANG host application, you'll have to create a new empty COM+ application and a new database that will be the new Persistence database for the XLANG host application. After creating a new database, you'll have to configure the DSN settings for the new empty COM+ application, and then finally initialize the XLANG Persistence database. Proceed using the following configuration instructions:

1. Open the Component Service by choosing Start | Programs | Administrative Tools | Component Service.

2. Browse through the console tree to Console Root | Component Service | Computers | My Computer | COM+ Applications, and select it.

BIZTALK SERVER ORCHESTRATION

3. *After* you select COM+ Applications, right-click it and select New from the context menu. (If COM+ Applications is not selected first, the New option will not be available on the context menu.) The COM Application Install Wizard opens. To proceed, click Next.

4. On the Install Or Create A New Application page, click Create An Empty Application.

5. On the Create An Empty Application page, type in a name for the host application. Select the option Server Application and click Next to proceed.

6. On the Set Application Identity page, select an account for the application identity. It's recommended that you create a new service account for the COM+ applications that host the XLANG application.

7. Click Next to proceed to the last page of the wizard, and click Finish.

Now that the new COM+ application is created, create a new database in your SQL server. Open the Enterprise Manager of your SQL server installation, and browse through the console tree to your local SQL server. Expand the tree, and right-click Databases to open the context menu and select New Database. Type in the database name and click Finish. Now that you have created a new database, you have to configure the new COM+ application and set the DSN settings to the new database. Open the component service, right-click the new empty COM+ application to open the context menu, and select Properties. Now proceed as follows:

1. Select the XLANG tab and click Create New DSN. The Database Required alert box appears; don't worry, we have already created one. In the Create New Data Source dialog box, select the type of data source and click Next.

2. Select the SQL driver and click Next.

3. Give the DSN a name and click Finish. The name of the DSN and the COM+ application must be the same.

4. The Create A New Data Source To SQL Server dialog box appears. Insert the required authentication information and click Next. On the next page, change the default database to the new database created like described in the paragraph above. Click Next, click Finish, and the DSN configuration is done.

Before you can use the COM+ application as a host application for XLANG schedules, you have to initialize the database. Click Initialize Tables. This action will destroy all existing data in the database and create all tables that are required in an XLANG Persistence database. For more information about configuring a DSN using the ODBC data sources, click Help in the ODBC Data Source Administrator dialog box.

Starting XLANG Schedules

XLANG schedules can be started through BizTalk Messaging. BizTalk Messaging Service and BizTalk Orchestration Service are configured to activate and run a new instance of an XLANG Schedule. Starting XLANG schedules at message arrival is discussed in detail in Chapter 8. An XLANG schedule can also be started through an instantiating application like an ASP page or a COM Component.

The following sections will discuss the moniker syntax and the COM interfaces that are needed to programmatically run an XLANG schedule instance, and will show in an example application how to start an XLANG schedule programmatically.

Moniker Syntax

A *moniker* is used to explicitly identify an object in the COM+ run-time system. Monikers determine which COM+ application will host the XLANG schedule instance.

```
sked://[HostName] [!GroupManager] [/FilePath] [/PortName]
sked://[HostName] [!GroupManager] [/{GUIDRunningInstance}] [/PortName]
```

Each segment of the moniker is optional. The moniker syntax segments are described in the following:

- **HostName**   HostName is the name of the computer running the XLANG Scheduler Engine. HostName is an optional string value. If no name is provided, **localhost** will be set as the default value. The name of a host application for a moniker could look like this:

  ```
  sked://MyComputer/C:\MySchedules\example1.skx
  sked:///C:\MySchedules\example2.skx
  ```

- **GroupManager**   The XLANG Scheduler Engine group manager is used to manage instances of an XLANG schedule. GroupManager is an optional string value. If no name is provided, **XLANG Scheduler** will be set as default value. An example moniker could look like the following:

  ```
  sked://MyComputer!XLANG Scheduler/C:\MySchedules\example3.skx
  ```

- **FilePath**   FilePath is the full path name to a compiled XLANG schedule file to be activated.

- **PortName**   This moniker can name an orchestration port of an XLANG schedule that is bound to a COM or Windows Script Component. Note the forward slash in the following syntax example between FilePath (example5.skx) and PortName (PortA):

  ```
  sked:///C:\MySchedules\example5.skx/PortA
  ```

■ **GUIDRunningInstance**   This moniker syntax segment is only used to refer to a *running* schedule instance, which is identified by its unique GUID. The following shows an example moniker to refer to an existing XLANG schedule instance:

```
sked://MyComputer/{6FCA955D-6EC2-41E3-9D07-E481DFD665AF}
```

You can use monikers to run new XLANG schedule instances, to establish a communication to an XLANG schedule's port, or to make a reference to a running XLANG schedule instance.

The COM Interfaces IWFWorkflowInstance and IWFProxy

The interfaces IWFWorkflowInstance and IWFProxy are implemented in skedcore.dll, which is installed with BizTalk Server. When using the DLL in a Visual Basic project, refer to the XLANG Scheduler Runtime Type Library.

IWFWorkflowInstance Interface   When you want to launch a new XLANG schedule programmatically, you have to call GetObject (CoGetObject in C++) with an XLANG schedule moniker. Then, the COM+ run time passes a reference to an IWFWorkflowInterface interface. Use this interface to navigate to known ports of an existing XLANG schedule instance, check the completion status, and get other information about running XLANG schedule instances. The properties of the IWFWorkflowInstance interface provide information about launched XLANG schedules and some information to navigate to XLANG schedule ports (see Table 7-2). You can navigate only to known XLANG schedule ports, because there's no way to enumerate the existing ports.

The IWFWorkflowInstance interface has a single method, shown in the following table. The WaitForCompletion method is used to determine whether the current XLANG schedule instance has completed executing.

Method	Description
WaitForCompletion	Blocks and does not return until the schedule instance completes. Return value is HRESULT.

IWFProxy Interface   The IWFProxy interface contains information about ports in a running XLANG schedule. This interface can only be used in conjunction with a COM message port binding. The IWFProxy provides the following properties:

Property	Type	Description
FullyQualifiedName	BSTR	The fully qualified name of a COM-bound port
WorkflowInstance	IWFWorkflowInstance	The current schedule instance

Property	Type	Description
Completion Status	Long	Return value denotes completion of the XLANG schedule instance. Return value zero denotes successful completion.
FullPortName	BSTR	Returns full name of a port depending on the underlying transport protocol. A COM port returns a moniker, and an MSMQ port binding returns a queue name.
FullyQualifiedName	BSTR	Returns the fully qualified name of the XLANG schedule (COM moniker).
InstanceID	BSTR	Returns the GUID associated with the XLANG schedule instance.
IsCompleted	VARIANT_BOOL	Returns a Boolean value, whether or not the XLANG schedule instance has completed. FALSE is for still-running instances.
ModuleID	BSTR	Returns the GUID of the XML module that contains the schedule binding information associated with the current XLANG schedule instance.
ModuleName	BSTR	Returns the module name of the XML module that contains the schedule binding information associated with the current XLANG schedule instance.
ParentInstanceID	BSTR	Returns the GUID of the parent schedule instance.
Port	IUnknown	Returns the IWFProxy reference information of the current XLANG schedule instance. This can only be used in conjunction with a COM port binding.

Table 7-2.   *IWFWorkflowInstance Properties*

BIZTALK SERVER
ORCHESTRATION

Example Application   The sample application is a VB COM Component that starts an XLANG schedule. Let's have a closer look:

```
Function Start_Schedule(ByVal sked_url as String)
    Dim sked As IWFWorkflowInstance
    Dim sked_url As String
        On Error GoTo failure
            Set sked = GetObject(sked_url)
    Exit Sub
failure:
    Err.Raise
End Function
```

As you can see, the implementation of an application that starts an XLANG schedule is quite simple. The moniker will be passed by a string into the function. The application then passes the moniker for the completed XLANG schedule file (.skx) to the XLANG Scheduler Engine using the COM function GetObject. You can use this example COM Component to start a new XLANG schedule instance from another running XLANG schedule.

XLANG Event Monitor

Microsoft provides a tool with the BizTalk Server installation to examine and manage running schedules. The XLANG Event Monitor displays the XLANG Scheduler Engine working in real time. You can use the XLANG Event Monitor, shown next, to run, suspend, or terminate XLANG schedule instances and to examine the events in real time, which can be very useful when you're debugging your XLANG schedule. The XLANG Event Monitor tool (XLANGMon.exe) can be found at \Program Files\ Microsoft BizTalk Server\SDK\XLANG Tools.

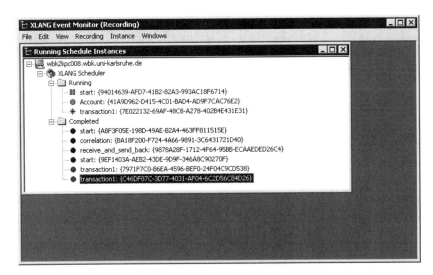

The several states of an XLANG schedule instance are represented through icons and the associated folders in the main window of the XLANG Event Monitor. The following list describes the icons representing the XLANG schedule instance states:

- The *green dot* represents a running XLANG schedule.
- The *black dot* represents a successfully completed XLANG schedule.
- *Red dots* represent XLANG schedules that completed with an error.
- *Blue snowflakes* represent dehydrated XLANG schedule instances.
- *Blue lines* represent a suspended or paused XLANG schedule instance.

Running New XLANG Schedule Instances   You can create new instances of XLANG schedules with the XLANG Event Monitor in two ways. One way is to use the main menu; the other way is to simply drag an .skx file from the shell into the COM+ application within the main window. When using the menu, select the COM+ application in the main window first. Then, on the Instance menu, click Run. Type in the full path to the .skx file, for example, C:\MySchedules\Order.skx. The XLANG Event Monitor will add the prefix to the file path according to what COM+ application you select for hosting the schedule instance, for example, sked://MyComputer!XLANG Scheduler/.

After the XLANG schedule is activated, you can see the XLANG schedule instance state in the Running folder of the COM+ application that hosts the XLANG schedule. Each XLANG schedule instance has a GUID appended to the name to identify different instances of the same XLANG schedule. When an XLANG schedule instance completes or is terminated, it appears in the Completed folder of the COM+ application that hosts that XLANG schedule instance.

Controlling XLANG Schedule Instances   You can suspend or terminate schedule instances and examine events of a schedule's instances with the XLANG Event Monitor.

- To terminate an instance of an XLANG schedule, select that instance on the main window. On the Instance menu, click Terminate.
- To suspend an instance of an XLANG schedule, select that instance on the main window. On the Instance menu, click Suspend. The XLANG schedule will be suspended before the next action will be executed. On the Instance menu, click Resume to resume the XLANG schedule instance. Suspension does not dehydrate the XLANG schedule instances.
- To examine an event of an XLANG schedule instance, double-click the instance you want to view; the Events For *<instance_name{GUID}>* list appears. Clicking an event in the top pane of the window shows the details in the bottom pane.

For additional information on the XLANG Event Monitor, see the associated Readme.htm file in the installation directory.

The
Complete
Reference

Chapter 8

Advanced Orchestration

329

This chapter puts together what was discussed in Chapter 7. We will combine the flexible possibilities of designing business processes using the BizTalk Orchestration Designer with the possibilities of the BizTalk Messaging Services. After reading this chapter, you will have learned the following:

- How to secure an application with transactions
- What you should do to respond to an error
- How to make use of the integration of BizTalk Orchestration with BizTalk Messaging
- How to start XLANG schedules at message arrival
- How messages can be correlated again with the correct XLANG schedule instance

Implementing Transactions

Long transactions can control complex business processes, even over a long period. The persistence of messages is achieved by saving data on the XLANG Persistence database. Moreover, many users generally want access to data at the same time. To guarantee the persistence of data being concurrently accessed, software-developers use the concept of the transaction. A *transaction* ensures that two users who are trying to access and modify the same data only see each other's changes when these modifications have been completely carried out. Transactions also guarantee that data alterations of a transaction are either completely executed or not at all. Therefore, a transaction always transfers data from one consistent state into a new state.

Fundamentals of Transactions

A *transaction* is a series of operations processed as a single action. A common example of a transaction is withdrawing money from a bank account via a cash dispenser. During this transaction, the personal identification number (PIN) must be checked, the customer must be paid the requested amount, and this amount must be debited, or rather, withdrawn, from the customer's account. Imagine if a transaction were to be unsuccessful: a customer would be delighted if his or her bank dispensed money without debiting the sum from his or her account. Moreover, the bank would be very annoyed if this money were missing.

A transaction must fulfill the following four conditions: it must be atomic, consistent, isolated, and durable. These four characteristics are known as the ACID rules:

- **Atomicity**   This is a transaction that either occurs as a whole (all) or does not occur as a whole (nothing). All or none of the data should be actualized.

- **Consistency**   Individual operations within a transaction can cause the data to have a specific status that damages the integrity defaults of the system. For example, a database might enforce uniqueness on a particular field.

- **Isolation**   One transaction cannot perceive the incomplete modifications of another transaction. This means that the unsaved changes of a transaction must be isolated from all other transactions.

- **Durability**   When a transaction is carried out, all participating data sources must permanently save the completed changes, which must be able to be restored in the case of a system error.

When an application has completely executed all the modifications of a transaction, it stores the transaction. This is necessary, since the data source must be able to store accounts of all the changes, even in the event of a system error. Thus, the transaction becomes consistent.

If an application cannot completely execute the modification of a transaction, the transaction must be canceled. In this case, the application instructs the data source to cancel the changes that have been executed thus far. Accordingly, the data source must offer the possibility of restoring unsaved changes back into their initial state. In general, DBMS systems record all changes on a database and execute the required restoration by canceling all the modifications up to the last recorded event. This mechanism is referred to as a *rollback*. Following a rollback, the data source acquires a status as if the (unsuccessful) transaction had never occurred. In this manner, the transaction becomes atomic.

Specific integrity limitations are normally defined for data in a system. These limitations guarantee that the data in the system remains in an acceptable state; for example, a limitation could stipulate that the balance of a customer's data record must never exceed the credit limit. Consequently, transactions should only be stored when the consistent state of the database can be guaranteed.

Why must transactions be isolated? Imagine the following scenario: Transaction A has access to the data, which has been modified within transaction B. Transaction A fails and the DBMS attempts to carry out a rollback. Unfortunately, transaction B also failed previously, and the database has already been transformed into its former state. As a result, transaction A can no longer access the data that was modified within transaction B. Accordingly, the rollback of transaction A will fail, and the data source can no longer be left in a consistent state.

For a transaction to be durable, the results of a realized transaction must continue even in the case of a complete system failure. For example, a customer is invoiced for an order, and before the order can be saved on the database tables, the system crashes. For this transaction to be durable, the system upon restarting must either credit the amount back to the customer's credit card (rolling back), or add the order information to the database and execute the transaction. The chosen procedure depends on the state of the transaction; however, durability is normally managed by the database.

Microsoft's Transaction Manager is called the Distributed Transaction Coordinator (DTC). This product was originally delivered with the SQL Server 6.5 and is already a component of additional Microsoft products such as MS Message Queuing (MSMQ) and COM+. The BizTalk XLANG Scheduler is a COM+ application. It doesn't introduce any new features to those of the DTC, and is thus based on the transactional characteristics of COM+.

COM+ provides five transaction levels:

- **Disabled**   A component will ignore COM+ transaction management.

- **Not Supported**   This option specifies that the component will not support COM+ transactions or transmit the transactions of other components.

- **Supported**   A component will participate in a COM+ transaction if one exists. The component will not initiate a transaction.

- **Required**   A component will participate in a COM+ transaction if one exists. If not, a new transaction will be created for the component.

- **Requires New**   A new COM+ transaction will always be created for a component.

The following sections will discuss in detail the possibilities provided by the BizTalk Orchestration Services with reference to transactions.

Transaction Properties of XLANG Schedules

The transaction model of an XLANG schedule can be set up in the Begin Properties dialog box, shown next, which is opened by right-clicking the Begin shape. The way the XLANG schedule participates in the transactions is determined by selecting a transaction model.

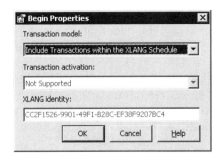

The Begin Properties dialog box provides two possibilities for defining the characteristics of the XLANG schedule:

- **Include Transactions within the XLANG Schedule**   Choose this option to work with transaction shapes within schedules.
- **Treat the XLANG Schedule as COM+ Component**   Choose this option to call up the schedule from a COM+ transaction.

The BizTalk Orchestration Service permits, via selecting Treat The XLANG Schedule As COM+ Component, XLANG schedules to be managed as transactional COM+ components. An XLANG schedule becomes instantiated through a COM+ component. (The XLANG engine is a COM+ application.) For that reason, the schedules support the transaction in a similar manner to COM+ components. The levels of transaction activation can be described as follows:

- **Not Supported**   This option indicates that the schedules will not participate in COM+ transactions. This is the default option.
- **Supported**   This option indicates that the schedules will participate in COM+ transactions, if a transaction context exists.
- **Required**   This option specifies that the schedules require COM+ transactions and won't start if a transaction context does not exist.
- **Requires New**   This option specifies that schedules require COM+ transactions in which they are to be executed.

Via the preceding described use of the transaction model, the XLANG engine provides business process automation in an individual COM+ component. This means that the entire schedule functions as a COM+ component and, as a result, supports the COM+ transactions, as described earlier.

 If a schedule is used as a component, the XLANG schedule cannot contain any transaction shapes. Consequently, the XLANG schedule will not be compiled, and an error will be returned.

The option Include Transactions Within The XLANG Schedule offers the possibility of defining transactions in a business process diagram.

Transactions Within XLANG Schedules

The default option for an XLANG schedule transaction model is Include Transactions Within The XLANG Schedule. To add the schedule transactions, drag the Transaction shape from the flowchart palette, and position it over the actions that are to be grouped together in one transaction, as shown next.

BIZTALK SERVER ORCHESTRATION

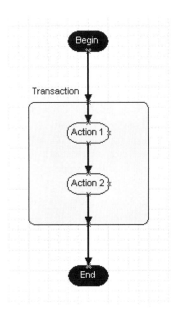

Right-clicking a Transaction shape in a business process diagram opens the Transaction Properties dialog box , as shown in Figure 8-1.

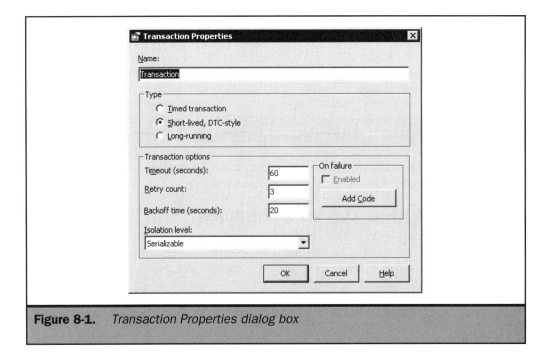

Figure 8-1. *Transaction Properties dialog box*

In the Transaction Properties dialog box, the following characteristics can be configured:

Type   The default option is Short-Lived, DTC-Style.

Timed Transaction   With this option, long-running transactions can be aborted after a specific time if they have not yet been completed. This option is not available for long-running transactions.

Short-Lived, DTC-Style   This option manages a group of actions as a unit, which complies with the ACID rules for transactions. It is available for nested and stand-alone transactions, but not, however, for external transactions from nested transactions.

Long-Running   This option combines a group of actions into an indefinite long-running transaction and is available for all transaction types. Long-running transactions do not conform to the ACID rules.

Timeout   This option indicates how long a transaction may run before it is automatically aborted or attempted again. This feature is only available for timed and short-lived transactions.

Retry Count   This option specifies how often a process can be repeated within a short-lived transaction if the process should not yet be completed. With every further attempt, the process will begin at the process starting point within the transaction. This feature is only available for short-lived transactions.

Backoff Time   This option specifies the interval between every further transaction attempt. The backoff time is employed together with the retry count to determine the time before the next transaction attempt. The value of the backoff time is calculated as backoff time with the exponent retry count ($B^{**}R$, with B = backoff time and R = retry count). If the backoff time is greater than 180 seconds, the schedule is dehydrated.

Isolation Level   When a transaction runs independently, conforming to the ACID set of rules (meaning that all concurrent transactions must wait until a transaction releases a data record), transaction isolation can have a negative effect on data throughput and parallelism. When a transaction reads a data element, the data element is locked for all other transactions. To improve transaction performance, so-called isolation levels have been introduced. When the isolation level is defined, data entries can be free to read, even before the end of a transaction. This option is available for short-lived, DTC-style transactions. The four isolation levels are as follows.

- **Read Uncommitted**   The transaction can read all data elements, regardless of whether the data element has an outstanding write protection or not. However, the transaction does not accept a read protection. This isolation level provides the fastest access, but is extremely susceptible to inconsistent data.

■ **Read Committed** This level exclusively reads saved data elements. A transaction that has been executed on this isolation level must wait until the write protection has been released before it can have access to the data elements. If a transaction is to be executed without MTS, this is the default isolation level from MSSQL server and ADO.

■ **Repeatable Read** This level corresponds to the Read Committed level, with the exception of one factor—namely, that all read protection must be maintained for the duration of the transaction. All data that is read from the transaction must remain unchanged until a rollback for the transaction has been executed or until the transaction has been saved.

■ **Serializable** This level corresponds to the Repeatable Read level. However, it offers an additional qualification: a request that is repeatedly carried out in a serializable transaction should always achieve the same result. For example, if a transaction that is carried out on this isolation level determines the number of data records in a table, another transaction cannot insert data records into the same table. This transaction must wait until the first transaction has been completed. This level is the most restrictive of the four isolation levels.

Every isolation level except Serializable has a negative effect on isolation in order to improve data throughput and performance. When using the isolation level Serializable, the transaction manager prefers consistency and isolation at the expense of parallelism and performance.

On Failure

If you click Add Code, BizTalk Orchestration Designer creates the page On Failure Of *<transaction name>*. On this page an alternative business process can be designed to compensate for the transaction error. This option is available for all types of transactions.

Deleting the heading text "Use Flowchart Shapes to Draw a Business Process" and "Use Implementation Shapes to Implement Ports" will prevent the XLANG drawing from being complied into well-formatted XML documents.

Compensation

This option only appears at nested transactions in the characteristic dialog box. If you click Add Code, the BizTalk Orchestration Designer creates the compensation page for *<transaction name>*. On this page an alternative business process can be designed to compensate for the interleaved transaction error.

Why Transactions Fail

Transactions are not only executed until an error occurs, but also, under certain circumstances, transactions can start from the beginning again after a rollback. This depends on the characteristic retry count, which can be configured in the Transaction Properties dialog box. However, if a transaction is still aborted, the following causes should be taken into consideration.

Explicit Abort Shape   A transaction will abort if it encounters the Abort shape in an XLANG workflow schedule.

COM+ Component Failure   An implemented COM+ component returning an error (HRESULT) can lead to a cancellation of the schedule if the error handling has been activated in the Component Binding Wizard. On the other hand, in a transactional COM+ component, the component transactions will also be unsuccessful if the implementation port does not support the transaction level of the component. The COM+ transaction level must be explicitly defined in the Orchestration Designer, as shown in Figure 8-2. Moreover, it must be given the same value that was used to compile the component. The XLANG Scheduler Engine is a COM+ application itself, which executes instances from XLANG schedules. A DTC error could cause, for example, the transactions of an XLANG schedule instance to be aborted.

Binding Technology Failure   A short-lived transaction can be unsuccessful via a failed commit on a transactional resource within a transaction. For example, if the MSMQ messaging implementation fails to send a message on to a queue because the XLANG schedule did not have write authorizations for a specific message queue, the transaction will abort.

Pausing a Schedule   Pausing the XLANG Scheduler can cause all the transactions within the schedule to be aborted.

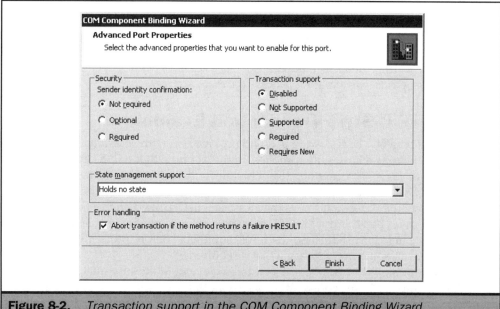

Figure 8-2.   *Transaction support in the COM Component Binding Wizard*

Transaction Timeout   A transaction may exceed the timeout specified in the Transaction Properties dialog box.

When any errors occur, the XLANG Scheduler hands over control to the On Failure Of *<transaction name>* page. The transaction error can then be solved by using the code acquired from the page, on failure.

Short-Lived Transactions

All transaction shapes in an XLANG schedule have, as a default, the feature short-lived, DTC-style. In the case of a transaction failure, every transactional resource based on DTC can be rolled back within the transaction. A short-lived, DTC-style transaction within an XLANG schedule uses the same rollback mechanisms as DTC. However, the schedule's transaction type depends on the subordinate transaction support of the COM+ or MSDTC.

Although the characteristics of the transaction shapes are configured in the dialog box, the characteristics of the schedule transaction also depend on the implementation of the ports, which are connected to the actions. The characteristics of the schedule transaction are also dependent on the transaction characteristics of the components, the script, or the message queue that is referenced with the port. Accordingly, for a transaction to successfully restore the state of a transaction through a rollback, the actions grouped in a transaction must be connected via ports with COM+ components or scripts that are marked as being transaction capable, or with transactional message queues. Actions that are not referenced with a transaction-capable resource can certainly be grouped together as a transaction in a schedule. However, the rollback cannot be successfully executed for this resource. This means that the resource retains its state at the time the transaction broke off and cannot be restored to its original state before the transaction. (For example, BizTalk Messaging is a nontransactional implementation shape.) For cases of transaction break off, a business process diagram can be designed (in the Transaction Properties dialog box by clicking Add Code) that can execute a series of actions to correct the error or to send messages to participating process partners.

Short-Lived, DTC-Style Transaction Example

Practice makes perfect! The following text will provide you with an example so that you can put your theoretical basics into practice. In the example that will be explained next, an MSMQ message will be passed on to a schedule. In the schedule, the message will be validated in a Decision shape. If the contents of the MSMQ message correspond to the rule specified in the Decision shape, the message will be passed on to a further message queue. On the other hand, if the MSMQ message does not satisfy the rule, the schedule is broken off via an Abort shape and the transaction fails. Before proceeding with the example, however, some preparatory work is required.

First, two private message queues need to be created. Make sure that the message queues are marked as transactional at preparation. In the example, the message queues have been called transaction_in and transaction_out (not particularly imaginative!).

1. With the BizTalk Editor, create a simple document specification to be used in the example. The given example uses a simple XML file as a message:

```
<price>
   <total>1000<total/>
<price/>
```

2. As a next step, a couple of test messages are required to test the schedule.

3. To get the message in the MSMQ, a small program has been prepared, which conveniently enables messages to be sent to the message queue.

4. Write a small script for the Windows Scripting Host, which will be displayed in a pop-up window in the case of an unsuccessful transaction. This step is optional.

5. A business process diagram must also be designed, data streams must be configured in the data sheet, and the schedule must be compiled.

Once everything is finished, the schedule can be tested.

Getting Documents into the Message Queue

Somehow, documents must get into the message queue. To send messages to the message queue, a small command-line tool, xml2queue.vbs, has been written in Visual Basic Script that is very easy to work with. It is rather rudimentary and can be extended according to personal requirements.

The following short source code describes the actual functionality to move XML files into a specific message queue:

```
'Access modes
const MQ_RECEIVE_ACCESS      = 1
const MQ_SEND_ACCESS         = 2
const MQ_PEEK_ACCESS         = 32

'Sharing modes
const MQ_DENY_NONE           = 0
const MQ_DENY_RECEIVE_SHARE  = 1

'Transaction Options
const MQ_NO_TRANSACTION      = 0
const MQ_MTS_TRANSACTION     = 1
const MQ_XA_TRANSACTION      = 2
const MQ_SINGLE_MESSAGE      = 3
```

```
dim qinfo, qSend, mSend, xmlDoc
dim sPath, sFile, sMesg, sInFileName

'Input file name
sInFileName = WScript.Arguments(0)
QUEUE_PATH = WScript.Arguments(1)
qLabel = WScript.Arguments(2)

'Create queue
set qinfo = CreateObject("MSMQ.MSMQQueueInfo")
qinfo.PathName = QUEUE_PATH

' Open queue with SEND access.
Set qSend = qinfo.Open(MQ_SEND_ACCESS, MQ_DENY_NONE)

' Put file into message.
sPath = WScript.ScriptFullName
sPath = Mid(sPath, 1, InStrRev(sPath, "\"))
sFile = sPath & sInFileName

set xmlDoc = CreateObject("MSXML.DOMDocument")
xmlDoc.load sFile

set mSend = CreateObject("MSMQ.MSMQMessage")
mSend.Body = xmlDoc.xml
mSend.Label = qLabel

' Send message to queue.
mSend.Send qSend, MQ_SINGLE_MESSAGE
msgbox "File """ & sInFileName & """ sent to queue """ & QUEUE_PATH

' Close queue.
qSend.Close
```

To move an XML file into a message queue, open the command prompt and type the following command:

```
xml2queue.vbs <file path> <queue path> <queue label>
```

An example command line would be

```
xml2queue.vbs c:\MyFiles\invoice.xml .\private$\incoming invoice
```

This command will put the XML file invoice.xml into the message queue .\private$\incoming with the message label "invoice". When the command is executed successfully, a message box appears, which confirms the execution.

Designing a Business Process Diagram

To design a business process diagram as illustrated in Figure 8-3 you'll need to do the following.

The Receive Message action is connected to the MSMQ port TestMessageIN, which connects the static message queue, .\private$\transaction_in (which has already been created), with the schedule. On the Message Specification Information page of the XML Communication Wizard, add the message field "total", because you will need

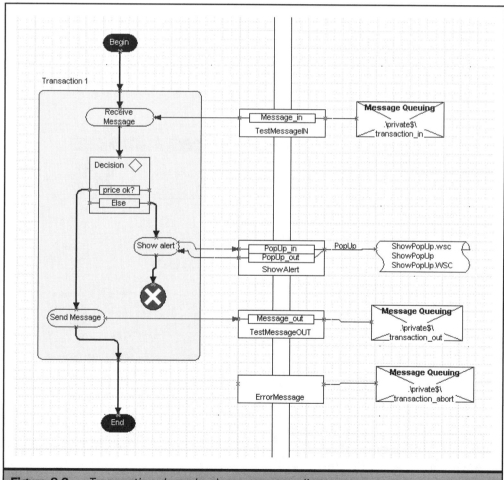

Figure 8-3. *Transaction demo business process diagram*

that field to check whether the price is lower than $500. Make sure that the message queue is private and that transactions are required. The transaction support is activated during the configuration of the message queue in the Message Queuing Binding Wizard, as portrayed in Figure 8-4. Proceeding in the same manner, now configure the Send Message Action shape, and connect it to the TestMessageOUT orchestration port.

Insert a Decision shape. In the example, only messages should be accepted whose price is less than $500. At this point, any action can be included to cause the failure of the transaction. In this example a rule has been chosen—first, because a rule is simple to create; and second, because its function is easy to understand. Create a corresponding rule by right-clicking the Decision shape; and then click Add Rule to arrive at the Rule Properties dialog box, where a rule can be added. In the example this would be

```
Message_in.total < 500
```

Insert an Action shape and call it **Show Alert**. With this Action shape connect the port to the script component, which will be displayed in a pop-up window in the case of an unsuccessful transaction. Connect the Action shape to the Abort shape. This step is optional; the Rule shape can also be directly connected to the Abort shape,

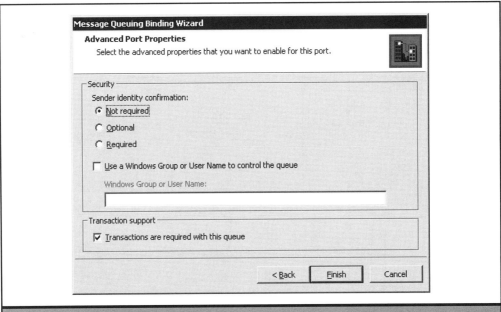

Figure 8-4.   *MSMQ implementation of transaction support in the Message Queue Binding Wizard*

or, at this stage, an error message can be sent to a corresponding message queue. Error handling of the transaction will be dealt with in more detail in the next section. The source code of the script component could be as follows:

```
<?xml version="1.0"?>
<component>
<?component error="true" debug="true"?>
<registration
 description="ShowPopUp"
 progid="ShowPopUp.WSC"
 version="1.00"
 classid="{2d2235fd-0d65-4985-a8eb-a4adb6f20ed4}"
>
</registration>
<public>
 <method name="PopUp">
 </method>
</public>
<script language="VBScript">
<![CDATA[
function PopUp()
 MsgBox ("Transaction failed!")
end function
]]>
</script>
</component>
```

Connect the Action shapes Receive Message, Send Message, the Decision shape, the Show alert, and the Abort shape, as depicted earlier in Figure 8-3.

Now place a Transaction shape over the connected action shapes, as shown in Figure 8-3. Right-clicking the Transaction shape will open the dialog box Transaction Properties in which you can select the transaction type Short-Lived, DTC-Style. In the Transaction Properties dialog box, set the Retry Count to 1.

At last we have to configure the data flow on the data page. For that reason, connect the document fields from the messages message_in to message_out using the Pointer or the Connector tool.

Following the successful compilation of the XLANG schedule, we can go on to test configuration. First, send a message, which has been created for the example, into the message queue. Then start the XLANG Event Monitor (described in more detail at the end of this chapter in the section "Testing the Configuration"), start a new schedule via Instance | Run, and simply type in the dialog box the complete path to the XLANG schedule.

When an XML file corresponding to the rule in the Decision shape has been sent to the message queue, nothing will happen, except that now the corresponding message appears in the message queue .\private$\transaction_out.

However, if an XML file that doesn't correspond to the rule in the Decision shape has been sent to the message queue, the alert window from the Windows Scripting Component appears because the transaction has failed (Abort shape). After some time, the alert window appears once again; this is because we set the Retry count of the transaction properties to the value 1. The message we sent to the message queue remains in the queue .\private$\transaction_in.

If the components have not been integrated, nothing happens. In this case, a subtle and unnoticed mistake has occurred. In fact, this is the rule for BizTalk Server 2000: the business process should run automatically. For that reason, aborted or failed transactions can be dealt with through using the business process diagram On Failure Of *<transaction shape name>*, where several actions can be initiated to counteract the error. The message, sent to the message queue .\private$\transaction_in, can still be found in this queue since the transaction has been completely rolled back. However, if the Receive Message Action shape had not been included in the transaction, the message would have been lost.

The transaction error could, of course, be aborted directly after the Decision shape, instead of waiting for an alert window to appear. In the main, implemented COM+ objects are combined with short-lived, DTC-style transactions in order to handle COM+ transaction failures.

Transaction Failure Handling

The handling of a failed transaction can be aborted with a further schedule, the On Failure Of *<transaction name>*. To design such an XLANG schedule, proceed with the following:

1. Open the Transaction Properties dialog box by right-clicking the Transaction shape.

2. In the group, On Failure, click Add Code and select the Enabled check box. Click OK.

3. The Orchestration Designer has now designed a further business process diagram. All the implemented message ports have already been included in the business diagram, as well as the Begin and End shapes.

Now design a business process diagram on the page On Failure Of *<transaction name>*, as depicted in Figure 8-5. This procedure corresponds to the previous procedure for executing actions and transactional messaging ports:

1. Create a new private message queue, for example, .\private$\transaction_abort.

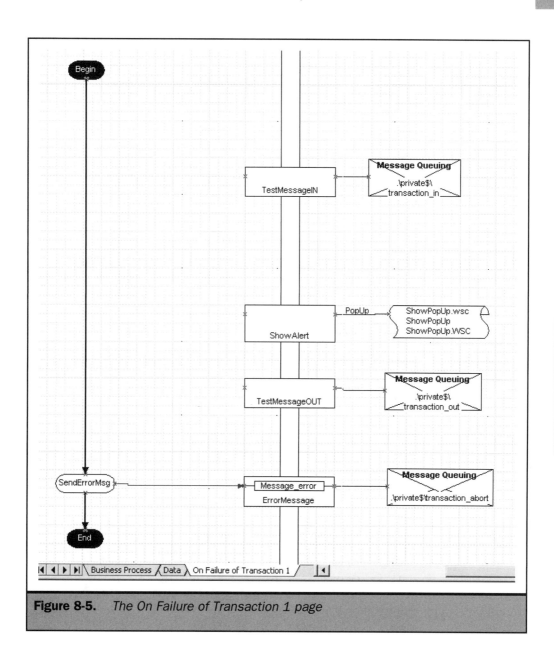

Figure 8-5.   *The On Failure of Transaction 1 page*

2. Using BizTalk Editor, create an error message like the following:

```
<error><message schedule="transaction_2"/></error>
```

3. Design a new Action shape and label it, for example, SendErrorMsg.

4. Following this, connect the Action shape with the Begin and End shapes, as well as with the messaging port of the message queue.

5. Create a message queue implementation on the On Failure Of Transaction 1 page to the message queue created previously.

6. Connect the Action shape with the orchestration port implementing the message queue.

7. On the Data View page, create a new string constant called **ErrorMessage** containing the string

```
<error><message schedule="transaction_2"/></error>
```

8. Connect the constant message field with the document message field of the Message_error message.

Following successful compilation of the schedule, it can now be tested to determine what happens when an XML message is delivered to the schedule that is rejected by the Decision shape. If all goes according to plan, an error message appears to have been delivered to the transaction_abort queue. To monitor the transaction, an application can be designed that checks message queues and determines where error messages are located.

Long-Running Transactions

Classical business processes across company boundaries generally last longer than normal database transactions. The short-lived, DTC-style transactions are unsuitable for a long-running business process. The reason for this is that short-lived transactions occupy unnecessary system resources through idle XLANG schedules. With several thousand parallel-running business processes, this would certainly cause scaling problems. To prevent such scaling problems, the XLANG Scheduler uses *dehydration* and *rehydration*. If instantiated schedules are not immediately required at any one time, the XLANG Scheduler writes their status in the XLANG Persistence database, thus freeing resources. This procedure is called dehydration. As soon as the schedule is required again, the XLANG Scheduler reloads the schedule in the main memory with the exact same status it had at the time of dehydration. This procedure is call rehydration.

A consequence of the hydration process is that in long-running business processes the data records must be blocked over a specific time if the transactions are to be oriented toward the ACID rules. If a dehydrated schedule blocked data records for concurrent transactions at indefinite times, the performance of the system would be impaired. Subsequently, this means that the long-running transaction cannot have DTC at its disposal for transaction rollbacks. For example, if during a long-running transaction all the rows of a table were to be included in a process, the entire table would have to be blocked. The reason transactions must be isolated is that up to the point where the transaction commits or fails, the result of the transaction is not yet known. Due to data that could change without isolation during the transaction, concurrent transactions cannot guarantee the restoration of the initial state following a rollback.

Consequently, long-running transactions follow the ACID rules apart from one exception, isolation. This means that other transactions can see which data is being used in a long-running transaction. Since DTC is not available for long-running transactions, the user must specify how to execute a rollback when a transaction has failed. The transaction shown in Figure 8-6 illustrates two message queue operations and the function of a BizTalk messaging port, which, for example, can be configured to receive the message via HTTP. At the Join shape, the schedule waits for the message from a transactional resource, the message queue, and the message from a nontransactional resource. The business process will continue only after both the messages have arrived. A rollback for this transaction, as with short-lived, DTC-style transactions, is not possible, since an HTTP resource cannot be integrated into a DTC rollback.

Long-running transactions fail for the same reasons as DTC-style transactions. The On Failure Of <*transaction_name*> page is also available here to respond to transaction cancellations. The main difference between long-running transactions and short-lived,

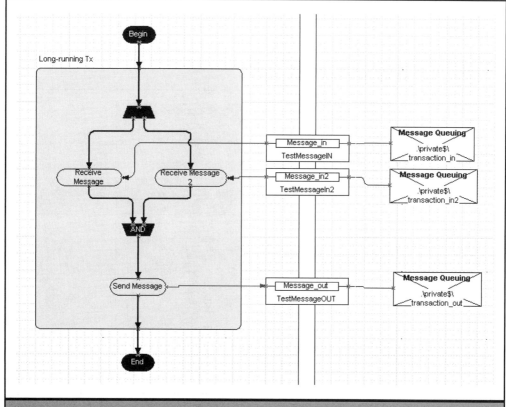

Figure 8-6.   *Long-running transaction demo business diagram*

DTC-style transactions is the degree of automation, since aborted long-running transactions cannot be rolled back via the DTC. This means, however, that when a long-running transaction fails, the only possibility of responding to this transaction cancellation is via the On Failure Of *<transaction_name>* page. Accordingly, in the example, this would mean that one business partner who communicates with another organization via HTTP would have to be sent a message regarding the transaction failure on their page. This would enable them to initiate the appropriate measures on their page to respond to the error with the necessary requirements.

Nested Transactions

The BizTalk Orchestration Designer enables nesting of transactions through placing the Transaction shapes over one another. Nested transactions are particularly useful when consecutive actions are dependent on successful preceding actions.

In nesting a transaction within a long-running transaction for the first time, notice that when you open the Transaction Properties dialog box for the internal transaction, the Compensation field appears (see Figure 8-7). It hasn't been enlarged—it has appeared. It wasn't there before in the DTC Transaction Properties dialog box.

The problem with nested transactions is the following: What should you do when the internal short-lived, DTC-style transaction commits, but the external transaction

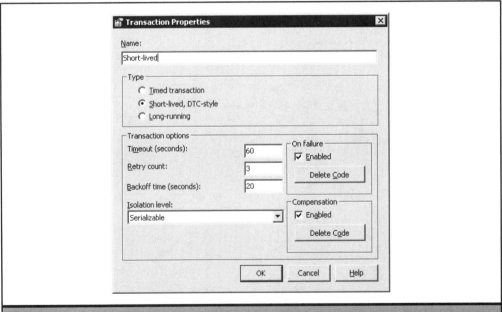

Figure 8-7. *Transaction Properties dialog box for internal (short-lived) transactions*

fails? In this case, the DTC rollback mechanism is not available for the internal short-lived, DTC transaction, because this transaction has *not* failed. On the contrary, it has already been successfully committed. Short-lived, DTC-style transactions that have been successfully committed cannot be rolled back via DTC. Consequently, the Orchestration Designer provides a further option, namely, the execution of actions on the compensation page (see Figure 8-8), in order to respond to successfully completed short-lived, DTC-style transactions within failed external transactions. The actions on the compensation page are, therefore, only executed when the internal transaction has already been successfully completed. If the internal transaction fails, then the page, on failure, is called up as normal.

Bear in mind that every time the internal transaction fails, the external transaction will also fail.

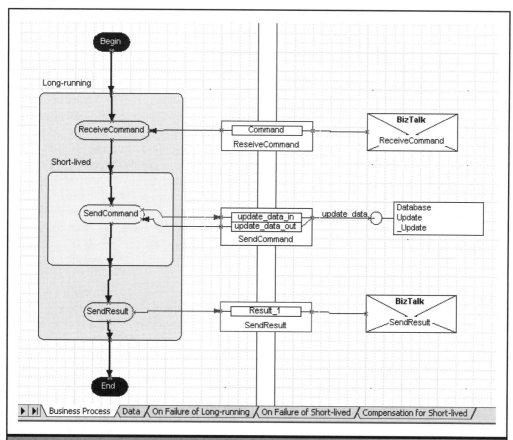

Figure 8-8. *The Orchestration Designer business process page showing the short-lived transaction nested inside a long-running transaction*

BIZTALK SERVER ORCHESTRATION

Failure of the Internal Short-Lived, DTC-Style Transaction   In this case, the On Failure Of Short-Lived page is activated, which can respond to the transaction error. Transactional resources are rolled back using DTC.

Successful Internal Transaction, Failure of External Transaction   In this case, the On Failure Of Long-Running page is activated. However, in the example, the internal transaction has already committed, resulting in DTC not being available for transaction rollback. In this case, the Compensation For Short-Lived page is activated, and a sequence of actions can be executed to counteract the already-committed action. Another option, for example, is to save the initial status of the internal transaction before the transaction is executed. This initial status can then be restored, if needed.

Timed Transactions

Timed transactions are normally used when a sequence of actions can have a definite time until their completion. For example, a business partner has a very slow and unreliable network link, or an answer is expected at a specific time—or not at all. To assure that system resources are not occupied with a never-ending transaction because that business partner's message will probably never arrive, timed transactions can be employed. The duration of a transaction is quite difficult to estimate. However, before a transaction starts to be processed endlessly, testing can often reveal the averages and extremes, which can be used as benchmarks.

In the orchestration business process, the type can be set to Timed transaction in the Transaction Properties dialog box. The maximum duration in seconds of a transaction can be defined using the Timeout field. Timed transactions are also long-running transactions; thus, there is no isolation here, and the same consequences apply. Therefore, the rollback mechanism of the DTC is not accessible if a timed transaction must be aborted. Within a timed transaction, nested short-lived, DTC-style transactions that have already committed the cancellation of an external timed transaction cannot be rolled back via DTC. Instead, the compensation code must be employed, as already explained in the previous section concerning nested transactions.

Figure 8-9 portrays an XLANG schedule waiting for a message to arrive after another message has been sent via the BizTalk Messaging Services. If any errors were to occur at the destination source, the XLANG schedule, without the transaction, would wait eternally for the acknowledgement message to arrive, and thus unnecessarily occupy resources.

Remember the Transaction Properties dialog box? When configuring DTC transactions, you can cancel a transaction after a specific time via the Timeout option. As a result, a long-running, DTC-style transaction can be configured that incorporates all the advantages of DTC. However, this option doesn't have the possibility of interleaving further transactions, since the external transaction cannot be a short-lived, DTC-style transaction.

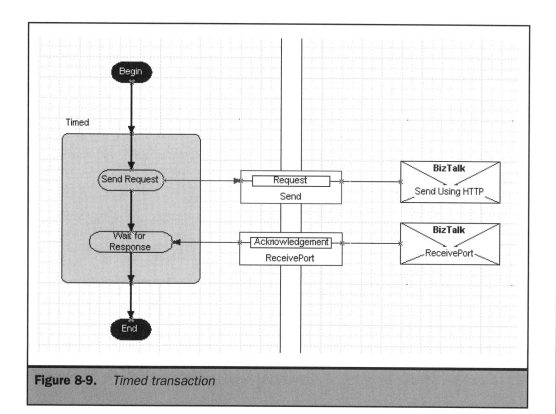

Figure 8-9.   *Timed transaction*

Integrating Orchestration with BizTalk Messaging

The integration of BizTalk Orchestration Services and BizTalk Messaging Services offers the possibility of exchanging messages between trading partners and within their internal informational technology systems. Moreover, the user gains support from different transport possibilities such as HTTP, SMTP, and MS Message Queuing.

Integration means that not only does the user have control over very complex and long-running business processes through the advantages offered by the BizTalk Orchestration Service, but, moreover, that the user has the functions of the BizTalk Messaging Service at his or her disposal. These features include secure delivery of messages, validation of a message against a schema, and the mapping of data, data security and integrity through coding, as well as support for receipt generation and correlation.

This chapter is concerned about the integration of BizTalk Messaging Services and the BizTalk Orchestration Services, and demonstrates how to start a new business process on message arrival, send messages from XLANG to BizTalk Orchestration Service, and return messages to a running business process.

Starting a New Business Process on Message Arrival

The following example describes a business process that simply receives and sends a single message. This example discusses the mode of operation for the Orchestration Activation instantiation of an XLANG schedule after receiving a message:

- A message is dropped into a folder or message queue.
- The BizTalk Messaging Service polls the folder or the message queue, and as soon as a message arrives, delivers it to a channel.
- The message reaches the messaging port via the messaging channel.
- The messaging port has been configured so that it can instantiate a new XLANG schedule upon arrival of a message and deliver the message to a particular orchestration port of the running XLANG schedule.
- The message is written in a message queue, and thus completes the business process.

The orchestration schedule to be used in the example should resemble that shown in Figure 8-10.

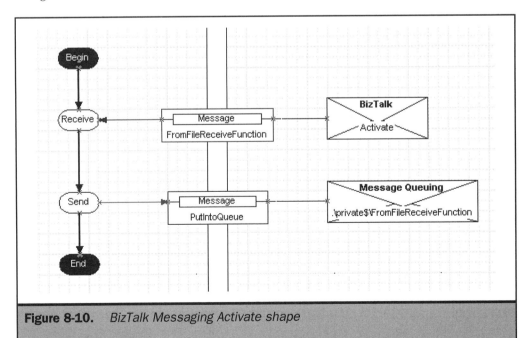

Figure 8-10. *BizTalk Messaging Activate shape*

To configure BizTalk Messaging Services and BizTalk Orchestration Services for the demonstrated orchestration activation, proceed with the following:

1. Using the BizTalk Orchestration Designer, create an XLANG schedule on the business process page, as shown in Figure 8-10.

2. Add the schedule to a BizTalk messaging port.

3. In the BizTalk Message Binding Wizard on the Communication Direction page, click Receive and then click Next.

4. On the XLANG Schedule Activation Information page (see Figure 8-11), select Yes and then click Finish.

Configure the message queue in which to send the message, and implement the binding as described in Chapter 7.

If the port has been configured correctly, a BizTalk Messaging shape should appear on the design page with the word "Activate". This means that a message will be delivered to this port, and the XLANG schedule will be activated. For messages to be delivered to this port, a messaging port must be configured that, upon receipt of a message, instantiates a new XLANG schedule. Accordingly, proceed with the following steps:

1. Open the BizTalk Messaging Manager, and create a new messaging port to an application. Enter a Name and click Next.

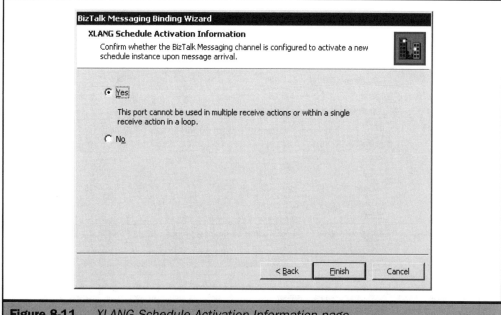

Figure 8-11.   *XLANG Schedule Activation Information page*

2. On the Destination Application page, activate the option New XLANG Schedule. Browse through to the compiled XLANG schedule on the hard disk.

3. In the Port Name field, enter the name of the orchestration ports for the XLANG schedule (see Figure 8-12). Now click Finish.

4. With the BizTalk Messaging Manager, create the messaging channel to an application.

After configuring the messaging ports and messaging channels, a received function must be configured that polls a specific message queue or data directory, and that upon message arrival, sends the message to the recently configured channel. To define a File receive function, proceed with the following:

1. Open the BizTalk Server Administration tool.

2. In the left pane select Receive Functions.

3. Right-click the Receive Functions icon and select New. Here, either File Receive Function or Message Queuing Receive Function can be selected. In both cases, the procedures are very similar.

4. Enter a Name for the receive function. Comments are optional.

5. Determine a Server on which the Receive Function will run.

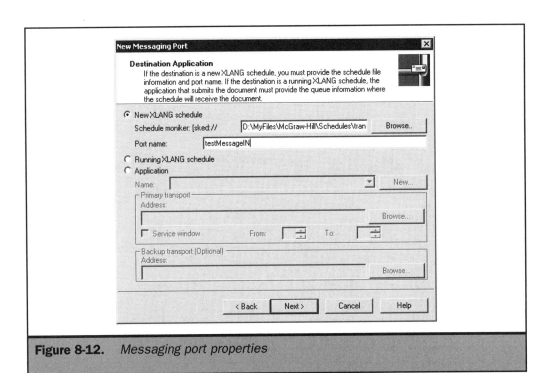

Figure 8-12. *Messaging port properties*

6. To configure a File receive function, a server must now be identified, along with which File Types To Poll For—for example, *.xml or *.nada.

7. At the Polling Location, the physical directory path to the directory must be specified via the File receive function. At Message Queuing Receive Function, the queue must be identified that will be polled. At Message Queuing, enter the path to the selected queue using the following syntax:

```
DIRECT=OS:MyServer\private$\MyQueue
```

8. At this point, click Advanced. The Advanced File Receive Options dialog box appears.

9. In the Channel Name drop-down box, select the messaging channel that corresponds to the application.

Figure 8-13 depicts the Add A File Receive Function dialog box from the BizTalk Server Administrator tool.

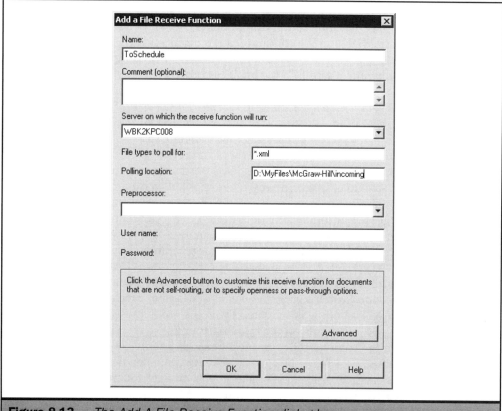

Figure 8-13. *The Add A File Receive Function dialog box*

Once the File receive function has been configured, the file to be sent to the XLANG schedule can now be dropped in the directory, which is monitored by the receive function. After a certain period, the file will disappear from the directory. If everything has been correctly executed, the file should now be found in the message queue that was implemented in the orchestration on the design page. For more information on receive functions, see Chapter 9.

Return a Message to a Running Business Process

When exchanging messages with a business partner, the business process mostly flows according to the following pattern. A purchase order is sent to the business partner. After the purchase order has been processed in their system, the business partner will return a purchase order confirmation. This purchase order confirmation, returned from the business partner, must now be allocated the correct purchase order in your ERP system. In general, an ERP system can execute such a task automatically by connecting a number that has been assigned to both the messages, for example, a purchase order number, a vendor number, a vendor item number, or a date. This process of connecting messages correctly with one another is called *correlation*. Many large suppliers of ERP systems are already offering Application Integration Components (AICs), which permit a simple integration of the ERP system in the communication infrastructure. The AICs can be connected to the XLANG orchestration schedule via the BizTalk Messaging Services, and thus can be simply integrated into the business process.

 Application Integration Components (AIC) are also known as BizTalk adapters. A number of application and technology adapters are available at http://www.microsoft.com/biztalk/evaluation/adapters.asp.

The previous section explained how a business partner's incoming message could activate an XLANG schedule. In a company where possibly a hundred to a thousand business partners' messages are arriving, the XLANG schedule instances that are waiting for incoming messages are automatically dehydrated to avoid scaling problems and to maintain the system's performance. Upon arrival of a message, the XLANG schedule instance is rehydrated again. At this point, it must be guaranteed that the message also arrives at the correct XLANG schedule instance. For this reason, XLANG schedules have a Global Unique Identifier (GUID) to make them clearly addressable.

The following section explains how to develop a message correlation scenario. In the scenario, an XLANG schedule is activated by an incoming message and then sends a message to the XLANG schedule on the trade partner's system via HTTP. The destination organization receives the message and sends a reply confirmation back to the source organization. To restore the correlation between an arrived message and the XLANG schedule instance, the destination organization's message must contain information regarding its source, for example, the GUID of the XLANG instance. The destination system can only do this, however, when this information is contained in the source system's message. For this reason, the BizTalk Messaging Services, which manage the sending and receiving of messages, and BizTalk Orchestration Services, which administer the XLANG schedule instances, are closely connected to one another. The close integration of the two services provides a mechanism that enables the correlation of XLANG schedule messages—the dynamic port binding.

The *dynamic port binding* is a mechanism that enables messages to be sent via an open destination message port. Open messaging ports, which do not have a protocol-specific destination address, can be implemented with the Orchestration Designer. The XLANG Scheduler determines the endpoint of the message at the moment it attempts to send a message via a dynamic port. However, this can only succeed if the message has a field with the corresponding destination address. The mechanism of the dynamic binding will be explored in more detail in the following chapters. First, let's recap what the source system must inform the destination system in a message:

- The reply address, the address to which a message should be returned, must be contained in the message.

- Both communication partners should know the schemata of the messages that are exchanged. This includes knowledge of the message field, which contains the reply address.

- If the transport does not occur via HTTP, the format name of a pre-instanced message queue must be contained in the message.

The next section will take a closer look at the following:

- Implementation of HTTP in the business process with BizTalk Messaging Services to communicate across the company's borders

- The mode of operation of the dynamic port binding mechanism

- Correlation of messages with the correct XLANG schedule instance, via HTTP and non-HTTP transport protocols

With regard to the implementation of HTTP and non-HTTP transport protocol for communication via BizTalk Messaging Services, sending and receiving a message will both be discussed in more detail. The configuration of BizTalk Server 2000 by the message correlation distinguishes whether a message is sent via the HTTP transport protocol or via a non-HTTP transport protocol, for example, SMTP or MSMQ. Within the framework of an example, the individual points, important when configuring HTTP and correlation, will be discussed step by step.

Implementing HTTP Messaging

This section deals with the implementation of HTTP for sending and receiving messages via BizTalk Messaging Service. Although the correlation of messages will be discussed in a later section in more detail, a first step for correlating messages is already carried out in this section. More about that later. To begin with, let's consider the circumstances of the example that is portrayed next.

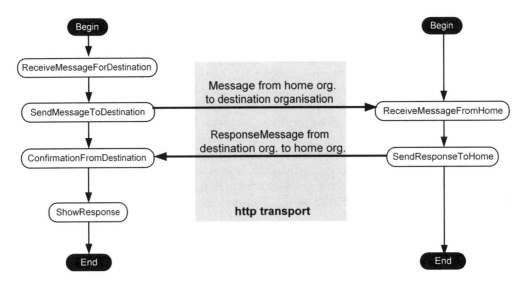

The example scenario we are going to develop will be as simple as possible, without any extra features that could draw attention away from the core problem. In this scenario the system is configured to do the following:

- A message is received that is activated in an XLANG schedule.

- This message is then sent to the destination organization via an HTTP transport. With reference to this, see "Configuration of the Source System to Send and Receive Messages via HTTP", where this will be discussed in detail.

- The destination XLANG schedule is activated through a message that is incoming via HTTP transport. With reference to this, see "Configuration of the Destination System for HTTP Transport", where this will be discussed in detail.

- The destination XLANG schedule then sends a reply message to the correlated XLANG schedule of the source system.

- The source system receives the reply message of the destination system and must then deliver the message to the correct XLANG schedule instance. With reference to this, see "Configuration of the Source System to Send and Receive Messages via HTTP".

Using HTTP Transport

The BizTalk Messaging Service provides a simple option for sending messages via HTTP posts. When configuring the BizTalk messaging port, only the destination address of the receiver must be entered. For this, proceed as follows:

1. Open the BizTalk Messaging Manager and then, via File | New | Messaging Port | To An Organization, open the New Messaging Port dialog box.

2. Enter the name of the port and then click Next.

3. On the Destination Organization page, select an organization to send the message to.

4. In the Primary Transport field, click Browse. The Primary Transport dialog box should then open.

5. Select HTTP from the Transport Type drop-down menu. In the Address field, enter the destination address and click OK.

6. Click Next two times.

7. On the Security Information page, select the Option box. Create a channel for this messaging port, and select From An Application. The New Channel dialog box appears.

8. Enter the name of the channel and click Next.

9. On the Source Application page, select the XLANG schedule and click Next.

10. On the following two pages, enter the inbound and outbound documents.

11. On the Document Logging page, select the preferred option and click Next.

12. On the Channel Properties page, click Finish.

The Messaging Port and Messaging Channel have now been configured for sending messages via HTTP transport. Make sure that a valid destination address has been entered. The address must always specify a dynamic web site, and thus resemble the following:

```
http://MyTradingPartnersWebsite/receivescript.asp
```

It is not absolutely necessary to install a BizTalk Server 2000 in order to receive its HTTP messages. The only requirement is a web-based receive mechanism that can accept HTTP POST, such as ASP, ISAPI, Java Server Pages (JSP), Servlets, PHP, and so on, to receive the data and process it in any way. However, if a message is to be forwarded to BizTalk Server 2000, the task is much simpler, because the installation directory, under .\Microsoft BizTalk Server\SDK\Messaging Samples\ReceiveScripts, contains the complete ASP script ReceiveResponse.asp, which can be used to deliver incoming messages to BizTalk Server 2000. To exactly understand the functions of the mechanism that is required in the script, let's examine the following source text from the ReceiveResponse.asp:

```
queuepath = Request.QueryString("qpath")
queuepath = "queue://Direct=OS:" & queuepath
channelname = Request.QueryString("channel")

Set interchange = CreateObject( "BizTalk.Interchange" )
```

```
call interchange.submit (4,PostedDocument,,,,,queuepath,channelname)
Set interchange = Nothing
```

Configuration of the Source System to Send and Receive Messages via HTTP

This section explains how to configure BizTalk Messaging Services and BizTalk Orchestration Services in order to be able to send messages to the destination process via HTTP transport in our scenario.

Designing a Messaging Document   Use the BizTalk Editor to create a document specification. Make sure the specification contains a reply-to field, so that the message can be later correlated again with the correct XLANG Scheduler instance. Save the specification in WebDAV, and create an XML instance for the specification that is to be later sent as a message from the home organization to the destination organization. The XML instance could look like the following:

```
<message>
<header replyto="me" from="home.org"/><body content="Please send me back!"/>
</message>
```

The fields can be given any values, since they will be given other values during the business process.

Before creating the orchestration schedule, create a new document definition in BizTalk Messaging Manager.

Creating an XLANG Schedule   An example has been prepared to demonstrate the data flow in connection with the actions. Figure 8-14 shows the XLANG schedule of the home organization.

XLANG Schedule Activation   The earlier-created message is supposed to activate a schedule. Now proceed accordingly, as described in the section "Starting a New Business Process on Message Arrival", earlier in the chapter. Design a File Receive function that will be used later to start the example scenario.

XLANG Schedule for the Configuration of the HTTP Transport   In the XLANG schedule, the orchestration ports must be configured for the HTTP transport. To configure

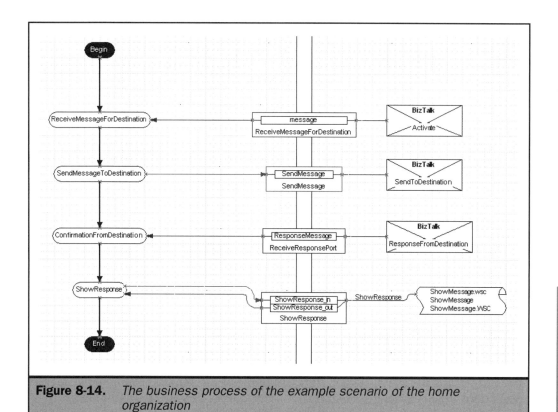

Figure 8-14. *The business process of the example scenario of the home organization*

the SendMessage ports by which the message is to be sent to the destination organization, proceed with the following:

1. Use the BizTalk Messaging Implementation shape to create a new port.

2. The BizTalk Messaging Binding Wizard appears. Enter the name at Create A New Port, and then click Next.

3. On the Communication Direction page, select Send and click Next.

4. On the Static Or Dynamic Channel page, select the Static Channel and enter the name of the channel. If a channel has not yet been created, enter the name that will later belong to the messaging channel, which will send the message via HTTP transport to the destination system.

Every time a message is sent through this port, a new instance of the XLANG schedule will be created.

To configure the port ReceiveResponseMessage that will receive the message back from the destination organization, proceed with the following:

1. Use the BizTalk Messaging Implementation shape to create a new port.

2. The BizTalk Messaging Binding Wizard appears. Enter the name at Create A New Port, and then click Next.

3. Select Receive as the Communication Direction, and click Next.

4. On the XLANG Activation Information page, select No and click Next.

5. On the Static Or Dynamic Channel page, select Dynamic Channel and enter the name of the channel.

6. Enter the URL of the destination web site and click Finish.

An important point at the implementation of these ports is selecting No on the XLANG Schedule Information page of the BizTalk Messaging Binding Wizard. If Yes were selected, the XLANG Scheduler would create a new instance for the orchestration schedule, and the incoming message could no longer be correlated with the original XLANG schedule instance, because it would arrive at some other XLANG instance—a new XLANG schedule instance.

Inserting Scripting Component   The following small scripting component can be inserted for a data exchange between two organizations to be visually displayed:

```
<?xml version="1.0"?>
<component>
<?component error="true" debug="true"?>
<registration
    description="ShowPopUp"
    progid="ShowPopUp.WSC"
    version="1.00"
    classid="{92bbdfbd-1ec0-46a1-875b-e4713f52af81}"
>
</registration>
<public>
    <method name="PopUp">
    </method>
</public>
<script language="VBScript">
<![CDATA[
```

```
function PopUp(From, ReplyTo, Content)
MsgBox("From: " & From & " - ReplyTo: " & Replyto & " - Content: " & Content)
end function
]]>
</script>
</component>
```

When a data exchange has been successful, a VBScript Message box appears.

The actions on the business process page have now been configured. At this point, let's concentrate on the correct data flow on the data page.

Data View Page   Figure 8-15 shows the complete data flow of the scenario. First, let's consider the data flow for sending messages. The important communication shapes for the data flow are message, SendMessage, and Port References.

The communication shape that is important later for message correlation is the Port References shape. The Port References shape contains information regarding the origin of all port locations. In the example scenario, a message, correlated with the XLANG schedule instance, will later arrive at the port ReceiveResponsePort. Connect the port's field (here, ReceiveResponsePort) to the field for the reply-to address of the message to be sent (here, SendMessage). Connect the fields of the Message Communication shape, to which the outgoing message will be sent, to the SendMessage Communication shape. The message that creates the Communication shape SendMessage should resemble the following:

```
<message>
<Header
replyto="http://MyServer/demo/homeorg/receiveresponse.asp?channel=r
esponsefromdestination&qpath=MyServer\private$\responsefromdestinat
ion{b7be0403-49a2-46a2-8747-16b09c65c10e} from="home.org"/>
<body content = "Please send me back"/>
</message>
```

As you can see, the attribute *replyto* contains the URL of the reply address to the home organization. The URL consists of the address of the dynamic web site, the channel of the source organization, and the unique queue path of a per-instanced message queue.

When the message arrives from the destination organization, the action ShowResponse starts the scripting component and the Communication shape ResponseMessage delivers to it the data in the fields as a parameter.

The configuration of the XLANG schedule for sending messages via HTTP transport has now been completed. Now let's consider the integration of BizTalk Messaging Services.

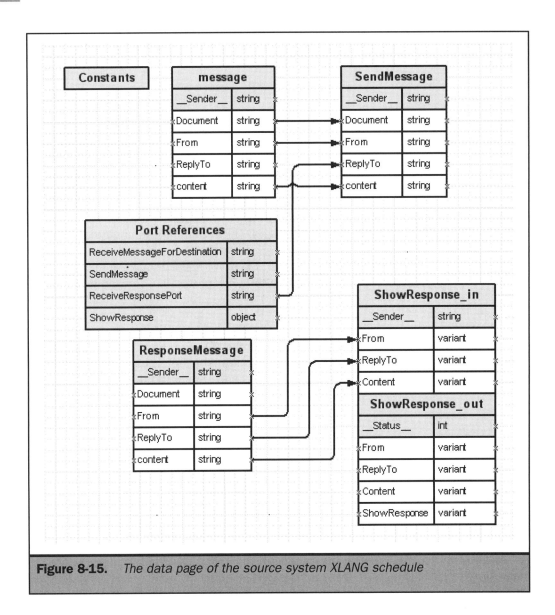

Figure 8-15.   *The data page of the source system XLANG schedule*

Configuration of Messaging Ports and Channels for Sending via HTTP   Use the BizTalk Messaging Manager to integrate the XLANG schedule with the BizTalk Messaging Service, and create a new port to an organization. Accordingly, proceed as already described in the section "Using HTTP Transport". The following table provides a brief overview:

Port Settings	Value
Port to	Organization
Name	Name of port
Organization	Select destination organization
Primary transport	Select HTTP and enter the destination address

Following configuration of the ports, create a new channel to an application with the following values:

Channel Settings	Value
Name	Enter the channel name that was determined in the BizTalk Messaging Binding Wizard when implementing the port to send messages.
Source	XLANG schedule.
Inbound document definition name	Enter the document definition of the inbound message.
Outbound document definition name	Enter the document definition of the outbound message.

The configuration for sending messages is thus complete. Now, let's consider the more extensive configuration for receiving messages.

Preparing the Source System to Receive Messages

As already shown in the section "Using HTTP Transport", the BizTalk Server 2000 uses HTTP POST when messages are supposed to be sent via HTTP transport. To receive messages, use a dynamic web site, which has an HTTP receive mechanism. This could also be a non-Microsoft IIS–based web server, which uses script languages such as JSP, Servlets, or PHP. However, for this example, it is presumed that you have installed a Microsoft IIS.

To design a dynamic web application, follow these steps:

1. Design a new directory on the hard disk that should contain the web site.

2. Copy the file ReceiveResponse.asp from the directory .\Program Files\ Microsoft BizTalk Server\ SDK\Messaging Samples\ReceiveScripts into the new directory.

3. Open the Internet Services Manager from Start | Programs | Administrative Tools.

4. Select the default web site and select Action | New | Virtual Directory.

5. Enter the alias of the virtual directory and click Next.

6. Browse to the path of the directory where the ReceiveResponse.asp file has been saved.

7. Select the Run Scripts check box, so that the ASP scripts can be executed there.

8. Click Finish.

Please take into account that a fully functional web site has been created. Further options for web sites—like security—can be taken from Microsoft Windows 2000 Server Documentation.

Configuration of Messaging Ports and Channels for Message Correlation   The next table provides a brief overview:

Port Settings	Value
Port To	Application
Name	Enter the name of the port
Destination Application	Running XLANG schedule

Following configuration of the port, create a new channel to an organization with the values shown in the following table:

Channel Settings	Value
Name	Enter the same name of the channel that was entered when implementing the orchestration port. It is important that a messaging port exists, with the name specified in the orchestration schedule, because the incoming message will refer to this channel.
Inbound document definition name	Enter the document definition of the inbound message.
Outbound document definition name	Enter the document definition of the outbound message.

Following configuration of the source system to send messages via HTTP, let's now turn our attention to the configuration of the destination system.

Configuration of the Destination System for HTTP Transport

This section configures the XLANG schedule for receiving and sending messages. The configuration for sending messages is of particular interest here, since the system for sending messages will be configured via an open destination port.

Preparing the Destination System for Receiving Messages   As with the source system, a dynamic web site is required here to receive messages. However, before proceeding, a small modification must be made to the script. Replace the openness parameter and the name of the channel in ReceiveResponse.asp with the code shown in boldface in the following example:

```
call interchange.submit
(1,PostedDocument,,,,,queuepath,"MyChannel")
```

Make sure to replace MyChannel with the name of the channel delivering the message to the messaging port that activates the XLANG schedule. Submitting documents to BizTalk Server is discussed in detail in Chapter 17.

Creating a Messaging Document   Use the BizTalk Editor to create a messaging document. Make sure that the specification contains a ReplyTo field, so that the message can be later correlated again with the correct XLANG Scheduler instance. Save the specification in the WebDAV, and create a new document specification in the BizTalk Messaging Manager.

Creating an XLANG Schedule   Figure 8-16 shows the XLANG schedule for the example scenario. The schedule is activated via an incoming message via the orchestration port ReceiveMessageFromHome, and sends a reply message via the orchestration port SendResponseToHome back to the home organization. You can also see a BizTalk Messaging shape with a shadow and with the name "Dynamic". These shapes represent open destination ports. Open destination ports are used when the destination of the message is not known at design time. This implies that the destination has to be provided at run time. The Figure 8-16 depicts the XLANG schedule of the destination organization.

To implement an orchestration port that has a binding to an open destination port, follow these steps:

1. Implement a new orchestration port by dragging the BizTalk Messaging shape onto the Implementation page.

2. The BizTalk Messaging Binding Wizard now opens. Enter the name of the orchestration port and click Next.

3. On the Communication Direction page, select Send and click Next to proceed.

4. On the Static Or Dynamic Channel Information page, select Dynamic and click Finish.

An orchestration port has now been created without having to enter the destination at design time. The port first gets a destination through an incoming message, which contains a ReplyTo field with the necessary information. The following section describes how this can be achieved.

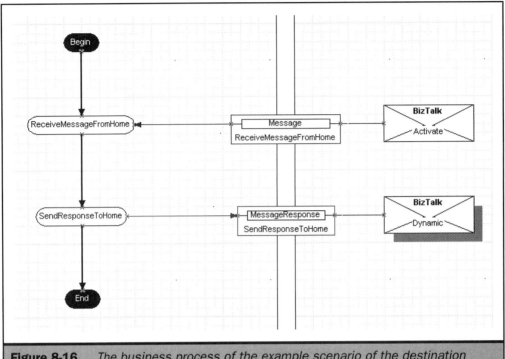

Figure 8-16. *The business process of the example scenario of the destination organization*

Data View Page   Let's examine the data page of our example scenario in more detail, as depicted in Figure 8-17.

The incoming message has a ReplyTo field, which is connected to the field SendResponseToHome of the Port Reference shape. The information that is contained within these fields is delivered to the dynamic port, so that the port can now have a destination. The message ResponseMessage, which is supposed to be sent, will be filled with values via the Constants shape and then sent via the port SendMessageToHome. This mechanism—dynamic port binding—has already been described in a previous section.

XLANG Schedule Activation   To configure the messaging ports, proceed as described earlier in the section "Starting a New Business Process on Message Arrival".

Configuration of an Open Destination Messaging Port   Use the BizTalk Messaging Manager to integrate the XLANG schedule with the BizTalk Messaging Service. Create a new port to an organization. Proceed in the same way as described earlier in the section "Using HTTP Transport". The table that follows provides a brief overview:

Port Settings	Value
Port to	Organization
Name	Port name
Destination organization	Open destination

Following configuration of the port, create a new channel to an application with the values shown in the table that follows:

Channel Settings	Value
Name	Your channel's name.
Source	XLANG schedule.
Inbound document definition name	Enter the document definition of the inbound message.
Outbound document definition name	Enter the document definition of the outbound message.

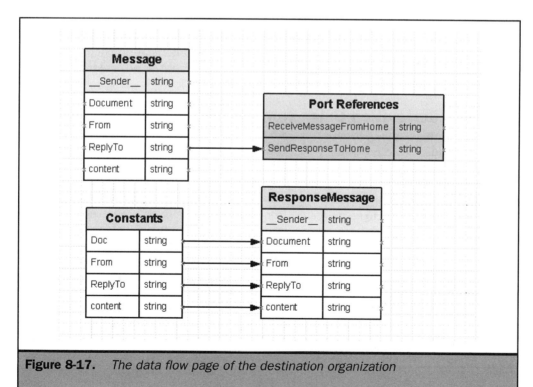

Figure 8-17.   *The data flow page of the destination organization*

After configuring the destination organization, the configuration for the example scenario has now been completed. Accordingly, to test the configuration, proceed with the section "Testing the Configuration", at the end of the chapter.

Implementation of Non-HTTP Transport

The implementation of non-HTTP transport–based message correlation is more difficult to create than with HTTP transport, since the dynamic orchestration port and the Orchestration BizTalk Messaging receive port only support HTTP transport. As shown in the previous section, the source organization delivers a ReplyTo address, contained in the message, to the destination organization. However, with non-HTTP transport for the correlation of messages, this is both necessary and important. The port reference at MSMQ transport, given to the message in the ReplyTo field, looks like the following:

```
MyServer\private$\responsefromdestination{b7be0403-49a2-46a2-8747-16b09c65c10e}
```

With the HTTP transport, the destination organization returns a message, based on the delivered reply-to address, to the source organization via an open destination port. However, this mechanism is not accessible with the non-HTTP transport. Consequently, a message has to be sent from the destination organization page to a fixed address in the source organization. In contrast to HTTP transport, the address of the per-instance message queue must now be given to the message, so that it may be correlated again with the correct XLANG schedule instance on the source organization page.

The following section presents an example that demonstrates the essential points for message correlation using non-HTTP transport.

Message Correlation Using Non-HTTP Transport

All that is required for a destination system message to be correlated again with the XLANG schedule instance is a single path to the pre-instanced message queue, where the message can then be delivered. With non-HTTP transport, the incoming message is not delivered with Submit( ) in the ASP Script to BizTalk Server 2000. The message is probably saved in a message queue, in a mailbox at SMTP, or in a folder at FTP transport. The message only needs to be delivered from here to the pre-instanced message queue, regardless of which transport system is used. At this point, a further XLANG schedule could be created, which could receive the message and allocate it to the correct source XLANG schedule instance. Or a simpler method can be employed, namely, using another mechanism called *self-routing of documents*. Self-routing has been described in detail in Chapter 6.

Configuration of the destination organization is very simple: all that is required is an XLANG schedule, which reads an incoming message from a message queue or folder and then saves this message in another message queue or file. The procedure for configuring the home organization is as follows:

1. The path of the per-instance message queue must be given to the outgoing document.

2. The specifications of the document must be prepared so that it can be received again for self-routing.

3. A receive function for incoming messages must be configured.

4. Ports and channels must be configured.

The XLANG schedule should look like that shown in Figure 8-18.

Per-Instance Message Queue Information   At this point, let's turn our attention to the address of the per-instance message queue, to which the message will be given. The address, containing information required for this example, should resemble the following:

```
queue://Direct=OS:MyServer\private$\responsefromdestination{b7be040
3-49a2-46a2-8747-16b09c65c10e}
```

The port reference address is unfortunately incomplete, because only the path name is available and not the format name of the message queue. Thus, the address string

BIZTALK SERVER ORCHESTRATION

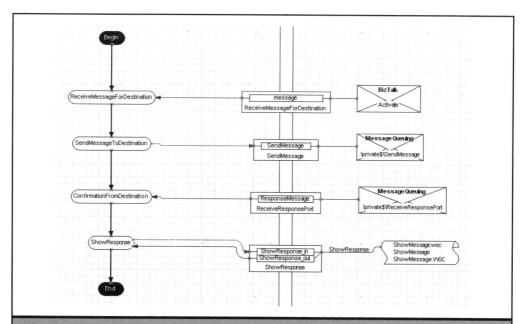

Figure 8-18.   *XLANG schedule of home organization implementing non-HTTP transport*

"queue://DIRECT=OS:" must be added in front. Create a small Windows Script Component CreateQueuePath.WSC, and add it to your schedule containing the following code:

```
<?xml version="1.0"?>
<component>
<?component error="true" debug="true"?>
<registration
    description="CreateQueuePath"
    progid="CreateQueuePath.WSC"
    version="1.00"
    classid="{77307757-2e03-4e76-b96e-2d97bd4f1440}"
>
</registration>
<public>
    <method name="NewName">
        <PARAMETER name="queue_in"/>
    </method>
</public>
<script language="VBScript">
<![CDATA[
function NewName(queue_in)
    Dim qname
    qname = "queue://DIRECT=OS:" & queue_in
    NewName = qname
end function
]]>
</script>
</component>
```

Connect the communication shapes of the XLANG schedule of the source organization as presented in Figure 8-19:

The conversion of the message queue path name into the format name must occur on the source organization schedule, before sending the message, since it cannot be expected or guaranteed that the destination organization will carry out the task.

Document Specification for Self-Routing Documents   Self-routing documents contain information that is required by the BizTalk Messaging Service for routing. To use self-routing of documents, a small modification to the message specification must be made.

1. Open the document specification of the reply message with the BizTalk Editor.

2. Mark the field, which should contain the reply-to information.

3. Open the Dictionary tab, as shown in Figure 8-20, and select the Destination Value field check box.

4. Save the specification to WebDAV.

Note   *Further information on the subject of self-routing documents can be found in Chapter 6.*

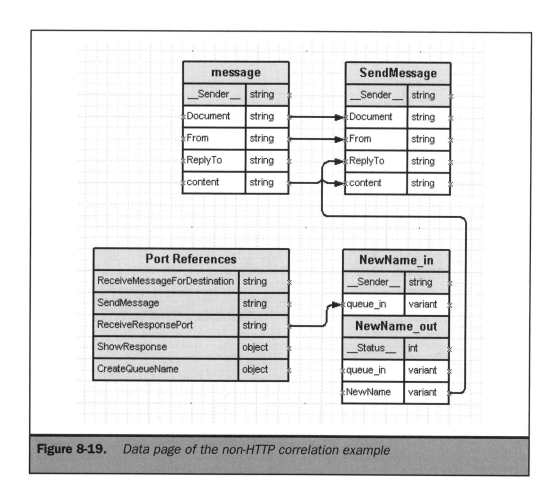

Figure 8-19.   *Data page of the non-HTTP correlation example*

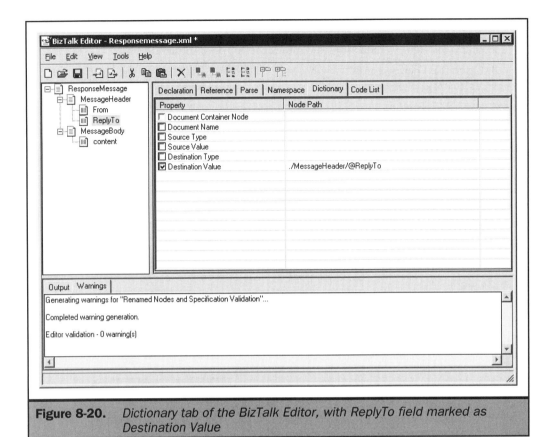

Figure 8-20. Dictionary tab of the BizTalk Editor, with ReplyTo field marked as Destination Value

Messaging Port and Messaging Channel Configuration Create an open messaging port with the following settings:

Port Settings	Value
Port to	Organization.
Name	Give the port a logical name.
Destination organization	Open destination.

Create a channel from an application with the following settings:

Channel Settings	Value
Name	Give the channel a logical name.
Source	XLANG schedule.
Inbound document definition	Enter the document obtained from the destination organization.
Outbound document definition	Enter the document processed in the source organization, and, if required, carry out a mapping.

Receive Function Configuration   Depending on the transport that is being used, create a receive function to MSMQ or file. Accordingly, use the following settings:

Receive Function Settings	Value
Name	Enter a name.
Polling location	Enter the file directory of the MSMQ that should be polled.
Openness	Open destination.
Channel name	Enter the channel that was defined earlier.

With this configuration, the receive function is particularly important. A self-routing document has been defined so that when it is received by the receive function, due to the Openness setting, the receive function will parse the document according to a destination value. The document is then sent to this destination. The format name of the message's per-instance message queue has already been entered in a field, which has already been marked as the destination value in BizTalk Editor. Thus, the message is delivered to the correct queue and, consequently, also to the correct XLANG schedule instance. The correlation of the message has been achieved. Further information on the subject of routing can be found in Chapter 6, and with reference to receive functions, in Chapter 9.

Testing the Configuration

After you execute your configured XLANG schedule, usually nothing happens. If an error occurs, neither a message box appears nor are other messages created by BizTalk Server 2000. If your XLANG schedule doesn't execute as expected, you have different sources to get information on what went wrong in your configuration:

- BizTalk Server Administration should always be the first choice of where to find information that can help you solve your problems.
- XLANG Event Monitor displays events of XLANG Scheduler.

BizTalk Server 2000 provides a tool that allows you to monitor events and progress of XLANG schedules. The XLANG Event Monitor is part of the BizTalk Server 2000 installation and can be found in the directory .\Program Files\Microsoft BizTalk Server\ SDK\XLANG Tools. The XLANG Monitor can help you troubleshoot your XLANG schedules by identifying the current state of the instanced XLANG schedules on your BizTalk Server 2000 machine. An XLANG schedule instance can have the following states, represented by symbols in the XLANG Event Monitor main window:

- **Running**   Represented by a green dot
- **Successfully completed**   Represented by a black dot
- **Completed with errors**   Represented by a red dot
- **Dehydrated**   Represented by a blue snowflake
- **Suspended**   Represented by two blue vertical lines (like a pause symbol)

Figure 8-21 shows the XLANG Event Monitor window recording events of XLANG schedule instances.

For more information on deploying and debugging your configuration, refer to Chapter 12.

Consider the XLANG schedule of the home organization in the HTTP transport scenario. After sending the message to the destination organization, the schedule waits for the arrival of the correlated message. If an error should occur at the destination organization, the home organization will not notice it. If an error seems to have emerged in the demo configuration, use timed schedules to abort the schedules after a specific time. If the scenario has been executed on a local computer, 15 to 30 seconds is a realistic value for the Timeout option in the Transaction Properties dialog box.

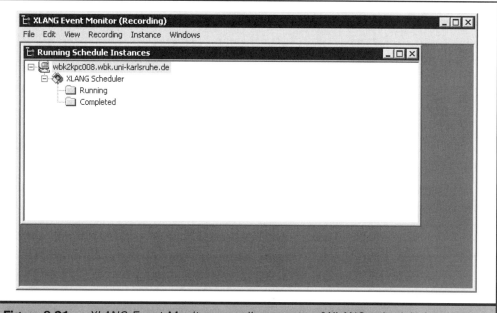

Figure 8-21.   *XLANG Event Monitor recording events of XLANG schedule instances*

The
Complete
Reference

Part IV

BizTalk Server Administration

Chapter 9

Managing BizTalk Server

BizTalk Server provides an administrative interface for IT professionals to configure properties related to the overall management of individual BizTalk servers, as well as BizTalk Server groups, work-item queues, and receive functions. *BizTalk Server groups* allow multiple servers to act as a single unit, sharing resources such as databases, receive functions, and queues. *Work-item queues* hold documents and interchanges submitted to BizTalk Server as they pass through the various stages of BizTalk Messaging. *Receive functions* provide a way for applications that don't support component object model (COM) interfaces to submit documents to BizTalk Messaging. All of these items can be managed through the BizTalk Administration interface, which is a Microsoft Management Console (MMC).

The administrative utility allows servers to be stopped or restarted. It also provides a means to add new servers to, or remove existing servers from, BizTalk Server groups. Properties can be set to improve performance; work-item queues can be monitored and managed; and file and message queuing receive functions can be created, configured, or deleted.

BizTalk Server Administration Console

The BizTalk Server Administration utility is a set of tools within a Microsoft Management Console (MMC). The console is preconfigured with the Microsoft BizTalk Server 2000 snap-in and the Windows 2000 Event Viewer snap-in. Each snap-in contains items to assist in the administration of BizTalk Server, and you can add further snap-ins to extend the capabilities of the tool.

 It is also possible to programmatically administer BizTalk Server using the Windows Management Instrumentation (WMI) interfaces. This will be covered in Chapter 18.

BizTalk Server Administration Interface

The BizTalk Server Administration console is shown in Figure 9-1. When the utility is started, it contains the Microsoft BizTalk Server snap-in, as well as the snap-in for the Windows 2000 Event Viewer. The Microsoft BizTalk Server 2000 snap-in expands to show one or more BizTalk Server Group nodes. Within each of these nodes, there is a Queues node showing the four work-item queues that are stored in the Shared Queue database. There is also a Receive Functions node showing each configured File and Message Queuing receive function. Finally, there will be one or more nodes for each server in that particular group. These nodes do not expand further.

Clicking any node will show summary information in the results pane on the right. If available, properties for a node can be viewed by double-clicking the node in the results pane, or by selecting the node and choosing Action | Properties. To perform most tasks, however, you will right-click the node and select a command from the context menu that appears. The commands in the context menu reflect those in the Action menu in the menu bar. There is also a View submenu on the context menu that reflects the commands in the View menu in the menu bar.

The rightmost portion of the menu bar in an MMC is known as a *rebar*. The rebar will always contain toolbar buttons that reflect the tasks that can be performed on a particular

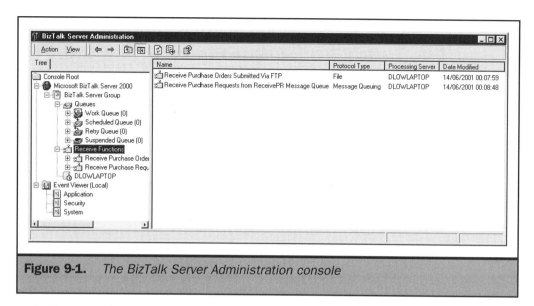

Figure 9-1. *The BizTalk Server Administration console*

node. For example, with the Microsoft BizTalk Server 2000 node selected as shown, the rebar contains buttons to get the properties of the node, refresh the contents of the node, or export the information below the node as a text file. The button to display help information is always present.

On the other hand, with a receive function node selected as shown, the rebar contains buttons to delete the node, display the properties of the node, refresh the contents of the node, or export the information below the node as a text file.

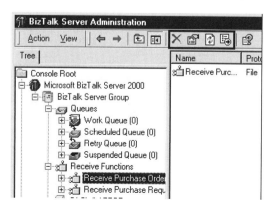

Modifying the Administration Console

When BizTalk Server Administration is started after a default installation, it opens in an MMC window that has been set to "User mode—limited access, single window." This means that it is not possible to modify the existing interface, for example, by adding new snap-ins. However, it is often useful to be able to see other tools in the same window. Table 9-1 lists other snap-ins that may be suitable for use during the administration of BizTalk servers.

As with all MMC windows, it is straightforward enough to change the available snap-ins if you are logged on as an Administrator. Simply open up a blank console by typing **mmc** in the Run dialog box available from the Start menu, and then choose Console | Open. Browse to \Program Files\Microsoft BizTalk Server—or your installation location, if different—and select btsmmc.msc. You can then choose Console | Options to change the console to author mode, or you can choose Console | Add/Remove Snap-In to add other snap-ins to the console.

If you save the console in author mode, you will be able to make changes whenever you like. However, if you add a new snap-in and then save the console as is, you will need to go through the process just described each time you want to make changes.

Managing Server Groups

Every BizTalk Server needs certain external resources to function. For example, SQL Server databases hold work items that are being processed, track document data from inbound or outbound messages, orchestrate schedule state information, and configure information for messaging objects. Similarly, external file folders or message queues

Snap-In	Purpose
SQL Server Enterprise Manager	Performs administrative tasks on the BizTalk Server databases
Component Services	Creates and configures COM+ applications to host AICs or XLANG schedule instances
Computer Management	Accesses services, message queuing, and local users and groups to configure security options or to create message queues

Table 9-1. *Suggested Snap-Ins to Add to BizTalk Server Administration*

can act as drop-off points for applications to deliver interchanges for submission to BizTalk Messaging.

Although BizTalk Server is capable of processing hundreds or thousands of documents at a time, it is often infeasible to expect a single server to cope with a constant stream of documents on its own. For load balancing and fault tolerance, many enterprises will use multiple BizTalk Servers to handle large numbers of documents. In such cases, it makes sense to allow these servers to share the external resources, rather than duplicating them. This built-in load balancing is made possible through the automatic creation of BizTalk Server groups, which are managed through the BizTalk Administration tool.

BizTalk Server Groups

When BizTalk Server is installed for the first time, a single default server group is created, and the properties of this group are stored in the adm_Group table in the Messaging Management database. This server group contains one server—the server that has just been installed. The server configuration—including the name of the group to which it belongs—is stored in the adm_Server table in the same database. If an enterprise needs multiple BizTalk servers to handle high volumes of documents, we can add any subsequently installed servers to this same initial group.

Regardless of how many server groups we require, we will typically store the configuration information for each group—and each server in each group—in a single Messaging Management database. Also, servers in a BizTalk Server group specifically share two other databases—the Document Tracking Activity database and the Shared Queue database. The servers also share any configured receive functions and collectively process submitted work items.

| Note | *When BizTalk Server is installed on a computer, and BizTalk Orchestration will be used, it is necessary to specify a database to store dehydrated XLANG schedules—that is, long-running schedules that are currently not required in memory. This Orchestration Persistence database is not automatically shared by servers in a single group, although we will usually configure it this way when installing each server in the group.* |

Adding and Removing Server Groups

In very large enterprises, it may be necessary to create multiple server groups; each is configured to handle different areas of a business. For example, we may have one server group devoted to Enterprise Application Integration (EAI), which will only process documents traveling within the internal network, and one group devoted to business-to-business (B2B) exchanges, which handles documents coming in from and going out to the Internet. In such scenarios, we can create further groups whose details will be stored in the same Messaging Management database. In this database, the table called adm_Group contains the properties of each server group. This database holds relatively static information and would rarely grow to an unmanageable size, so it makes sense for a single database to be shared in this way. Obviously, if reconfiguration is later necessary, it is also possible to remove server groups.

 There are many different scenarios in which server groups may be required, and many different configurations in which they can be deployed. These deployment scenarios are covered in Chapter 12.

Adding Server Groups

To add a new server group to the database, right-click the Microsoft BizTalk Server 2000 node, and select New | Group from the context menu. You will then be presented with the New Group dialog box, as shown here.

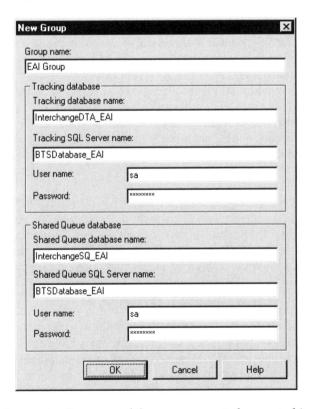

In this dialog box, enter the name of the new group to be created in the Group Name field. This must be a unique name. Under Tracking Database, provide the name of the database that should be used to store document-tracking data, the name of the server on which the database resides, and the user name and password to access that database. Then provide similar information under Shared Queue Database and click OK. Obviously, the server specified must exist and be reachable in each case. If databases with the specified names do not already exist on the server(s), you will be prompted to create new databases. The new group will then be created and will appear as a new node in the BizTalk Administration tool. As shown, the new group will contain no servers, and at least one server (that does not already belong to another group) will have to be added before it becomes functional.

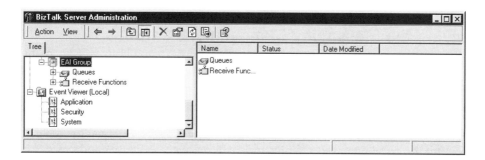

Note

This process will not create an Orchestration Persistence database. In fact, although a single Orchestration Persistence database can be shared by multiple servers hosting XLANG schedules, it should not be considered a function of a server group. To create a new database for XLANG schedule state information, run XLANGSetupDB.exe from the \Program Files\ Microsoft BizTalk Server\Setup folder. This is the same wizard that is run at the end of the BizTalk Server installation process, as discussed in Chapter 3. After the database has been created, any COM+ applications that are configured as hosts for XLANG schedules, and which should use this database, must be appropriately configured using the Component Services utility, as discussed in Chapter 7.

When installing BizTalk Server on a computer that should become a member of this new server group, the name of the server group should be specified during the installation process, as discussed in Chapter 3. However, if BizTalk Server has already been installed on a computer, and that server is configured as a member of another server group, it will be necessary to remove it from that server group before adding it to a newly created group. Adding servers to and removing servers from a group will be covered later in the chapter.

Removing Server Groups

To remove an existing server group, it first will be necessary to stop each BizTalk server that is currently a member of that group. Although this process is covered later in the chapter, it's generally a simple matter of right-clicking the server in the BizTalk

Server Administration tool and choosing the Stop command. Once all servers have been successfully stopped, right-clicking the server group and choosing Delete from the context menu will remove the server group. Any servers that were members of the deleted group will have to be added to another group before they can be operational again.

 Removing a server group does not automatically remove the Document Tracking and Shared Queue databases that were created for the group. They must be manually deleted using SQL Server Enterprise Manager.

Changing the Messaging Management Database

As mentioned, multiple server groups within an organization will typically share the same Messaging Management database. For this reason, it usually should not be necessary to change the database used by the BizTalk Server Administration utility. However, good practice will determine that the Messaging Management database should be replicated to avoid catastrophe, and every so often it may be necessary to take down the primary database for maintenance. In such cases, we can point the Administration utility at the secondary database for the duration of this maintenance. Alternatively, because good practice also may determine that you change the security credentials on your databases from time to time, you may need to change these credentials in the Administration utility to ensure that the utility will still be able to access the database.

To change the Messaging Management database information, you first must ensure that all servers in all server groups controlled by the database are stopped. You also must stop the BizTalk Server Interchange Application through the Component Services MMC. When this has been done, right-click the Microsoft BizTalk Server 2000 node and select Properties. This will bring up the Microsoft BizTalk Server 2000 Properties dialog box, shown next. Enter the database name, server name, user name, and password, and then click OK. This will cause the Administration utility to use the new database. You may then restart all servers in each group.

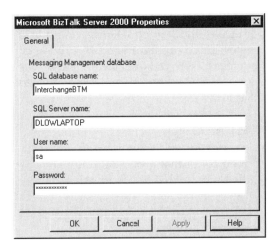

Do not change the name of the server or database unless the group and server information in the new database is an exact replica of the original database. If there are profound differences, you will be prevented from doing so; but if the differences are minor, you may be able to successfully complete the procedure. These differences can then cause serious problems to your BizTalk Server installation.

Many MMC tools allow you to administer a remote computer, as opposed to the local computer. The BizTalk Server Administration utility does not allow you to do this, as it is recommended that only one Messaging Management database is used, even for multiple server groups. On every server that is a member of a server group whose configuration is stored in the Messaging Management database, the name of the database server will be written to a value called MgmtDbServer, and the name of the database will be written to a value called MgmtDbName under the key

 `HKEY_LOCAL_MACHINE\SOFTWARE\Microsoft\BizTalk Server\1.0\Administration`

in the Registry on that computer. This value is used by BizTalk Server Administration to determine from which database the tool should retrieve configuration data for groups and servers. As discussed, changing the details of the Messaging Management database in the Microsoft BizTalk Server 2000 Properties dialog box should only be done to switch to a replicated database. Attempting to choose a database that contains different groups and servers will fail.

Adding and Removing Servers

Each server group in your enterprise can contain zero or more BizTalk servers. As mentioned, however, a group cannot function until at least one server has been added, and sometimes we will need to add servers to or remove servers from a group. Each of these tasks can be performed through the BizTalk Server Administration interface.

Adding Servers to a Group

Adding a BizTalk server to a server group is normally done during the installation of BizTalk Server on that computer. As covered in Chapter 3, we can opt to select an existing server group that the new installation should join. However, reorganizing an enterprise deployment often will require moving servers between groups after installation. For example, in the scenario presented earlier, suppose we had three servers in a group handling EAI exchanges and six servers in another group handling B2B exchanges. The introduction of a new internal application or the loss of a trading partner might require that we remove a server from the B2B group and add it to the

EAI group. Adding a new server can only be performed if that server does not belong already to another group.

To add a server to a group, right-click the node for the server group to which the server should be added, and choose Add | Server from the context menu. The Add A BizTalk Server dialog box will appear, as shown next, and the name of the server to add should be entered in the BizTalk Server Name field. Click OK and the server will appear as a member of the group.

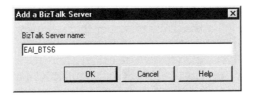

Removing Servers from a Group

To remove a BizTalk server from a group, you must first stop the server. If any interchanges were being processed by that server when it was stopped, they will get stuck in the Work Queue waiting for processing to complete, and will therefore need to be freed from the Work Queue. This will make the interchanges available to the remaining servers in the group. To do this, right-click the server that has been stopped, and choose All Tasks | Free Interchanges from the context menu. After the interchanges have been redistributed, we can right-click the server and choose Delete from the context menu. The server will not function again until it has been added back to a group.

You will also need to remove any receive functions that are associated with a particular server before deleting it from the group. Removing receive functions will be discussed later in the chapter.

Moving Servers Between Messaging Management Databases

On rare occasions, if your enterprise uses so many BizTalk servers that it is necessary to maintain separate Messaging Management databases, you may need to remove a server from a group in one Messaging Management database and add it to a group that is stored in another Messaging Management database. To do this, you will need to run BTSsetupDB.exe from the \Program Files\Microsoft BizTalk Server\Setup folder. This is the wizard that is run during the installation of BizTalk Server, and it will allow you to specify the name of the Messaging Management database with which the server should now be associated. When asked to specify the server group that the server should join, you then will be able to enter the name of a server group whose details are stored in that database.

Tip

You can also run BTSSetupDB.exe to add a server to an empty server group that is the only group in a particular Messaging Management database. In such a scenario, there would be no servers whatsoever in that database, so there would be no server on which to use the BizTalk Server Administration utility to connect to that database. Admittedly, you could also edit the Registry on a server to force the issue, but that is definitely not recommended, because it does not produce consistent behavior.

Modifying Server Group Properties

As mentioned, each BizTalk server group shares resources such as databases, receive functions, and parsers. Although there may be many servers in a group, the sharing of resources and work-item queues allows them to act as a single server by also sharing the processing of inbound interchanges. For this reason, we can set properties that affect the whole group, not just an individual server.

To modify server group properties, right-click the Server Group node in the BizTalk Administration tool, and select Properties from the context menu. The BizTalk Server Group Properties dialog box will appear. The dialog box has four tabs, allowing you to configure general parameters, database connection parameters, document tracking parameters, and available parsers.

Modifying General Properties

The General tab of the BizTalk Server Group Properties dialog box, shown following, displays the name of the server group being modified. Beneath that, we can specify the hostname of the SMTP server that should be used if BizTalk Server will be expected to send e-mails. This will be the case, for example, if SMTP has been chosen as the transport method for a messaging port.

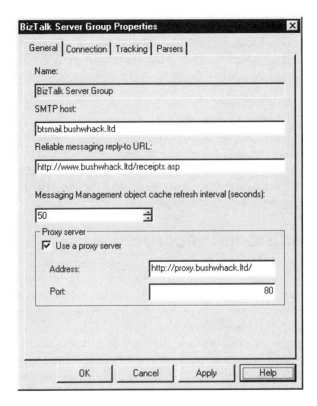

We can also specify the Reliable Messaging Reply-To URL, which is the address to which other BizTalk Framework–compliant servers should send receipts if we are using Reliable messaging. At this location there will be an Active Server Page (if HTTP is used) or Exchange Server script (if SMTP is used) that programmatically submits receipts posted to that location to BizTalk Server. It is also possible to specify a file folder (using the "file://" prefix), or a message queue (using the "queue://" prefix), as long as there is a corresponding receive function created to pick up any receipts arriving at that location.

Below that is a control to select the Messaging Management object cache refresh interval in seconds. As the name suggests, this is the time interval between calls to the Messaging Management database to refresh cached messaging objects. The default is 50 seconds, but you should increase it if there are not many items in your Messaging Management database, and these objects do not change often.

Finally, you can also opt to have BizTalk Server use a proxy server when attempting to connect over the Internet. Select the Use A Proxy Server check box to enable this, and type in the Address and Port number used by the proxy server. Earlier, we gave an example of two server groups—one that processed EAI exchanges, and hence would not need to use a proxy server, and one that processed B2B exchanges, which may need to use a proxy server to communicate with trading partners.

Modifying Connection Properties

The Connection tab of the BizTalk Server Group Properties dialog box, shown following, allows you to point your BizTalk Server group at different Document Tracking and Shared Queue databases or database servers. You can also change the credentials used to access each database.

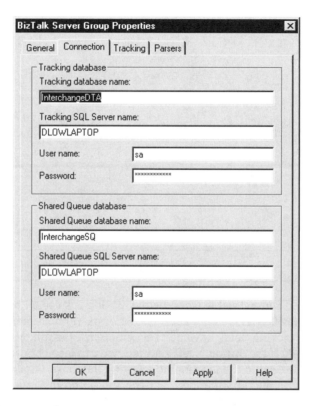

As discussed previously, we sometimes will need to take down a database for maintenance, in which case we could change the properties of the server group to point to a secondary server containing replicated data. Similarly, for security reasons we may need to change the user name and/or password used to access the databases. Either way, we could modify the properties of the Document Tracking and Shared Queue databases on the Connections tab.

Modifying Tracking Properties

In Chapter 10, we will discuss the Document Tracking feature provided by BizTalk Server. On the Tracking tab of the BizTalk Server Group Properties dialog box, shown following, we can configure which information should be accessible through this interface.

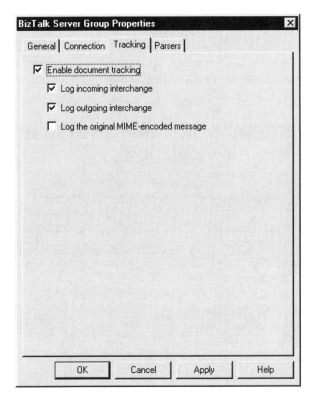

First of all, the option to Enable Document Tracking is selected by default when BizTalk Server is installed. If we deselect this check box, no document tracking will take place, even if tracking fields have been specified in a BizTalk Messaging document definition or channel. If the option is left selected, we can also choose which document formats should be logged to the Document Tracking database. Again, by default, we will normally log both the inbound interchanges and outbound interchanges, but we can also choose to Log The Original MIME-Encoded Message, if that particular encoding was used on submitted documents.

Note *Once document tracking is enabled, we can choose to log the inbound and outbound interchanges. During the configuration of a BizTalk Messaging channel, we can specify whether the documents contained in each interchange should also be tracked in their native and/or internal XML formats. This was covered in Chapter 6.*

Modifying Parser Order

On the Parsers tab of the BizTalk Server Group Properties dialog box, shown following, we can choose the order in which BizTalk Server should apply its document parsers to test incoming interchanges. As discussed in Chapter 6, document parsers are used to extract documents from inbound interchanges and to convert those documents into BizTalk Server's intermediate XML format for processing.

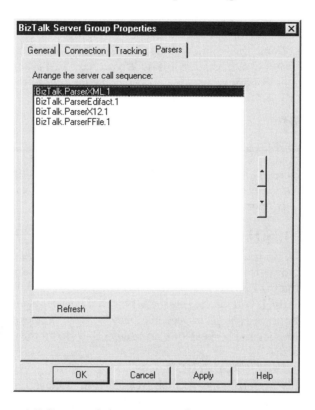

Also in Chapter 6, I discussed the creation of messaging objects called *envelopes*, which are used to help BizTalk Server determine which parser to use for inbound interchanges and which serializer to use for outbound interchanges. However, we saw that BizTalk Server is usually able to handle inbound interchanges that have an XML, EDIFACT, or X12 format, even if no envelope is specified, because the format of these interchanges has been hard-coded into the product.

As a result, when an interchange arrives, BizTalk Server tries each of its parsers in turn to determine the type of document that has been submitted. Because flat-file documents should always be contained in an envelope when submitted, that parser is last on the list, being the least likely to match when no envelope is present. The XML parser is first on the list by default, followed by the EDIFACT parser, and then the X12 parser. However, if you know that most of the interchanges that your server group will be accepting are in an X12 format, you should bump that parser up to the top of the list, to ensure that BizTalk Server finds the appropriate parser as quickly as possible. This can greatly improve the performance of BizTalk Messaging.

Of course, it is possible that there will also be custom parsers on the list. Likewise, they can be moved up or down as appropriate. If you have just added a custom parser component, but it does not appear in the list, you can click the Refresh button.

Managing Servers

As well as managing server groups, the BizTalk Server Administration utility allows you to manage individual servers. There are not many things that you can do with each server, as most properties are shared across server groups. However, you can stop and start individual servers, configure a server not to take part in work-item processing, and set performance properties.

Stopping and Starting Servers

This topic is a bit of a no-brainer. You may need to stop a server before removing it from a server group or before configuring its properties. To do this, simply right-click the server node in the BizTalk Server Administration utility, and select Stop from the context menu. Similarly, if you need to start a server that has just been added to a server group, or on which the service has either been manually stopped, or unexpectedly terminated, you can simply right-click the server node and select Start from the context menu.

Configuring Server Properties

There is only a single property page available for each BizTalk server in a group, as shown in Figure 9-2. This property page is accessed by right-clicking the server node and selecting Properties from the context menu. Before changing any of the properties, however, we will need to decide whether this particular BizTalk server should be used primarily as a host on which receive functions will execute, or as a server that actively participates in the processing of documents using BizTalk Messaging. Of course, it is possible for each server to do both, although that might not be the most efficient use of each server if there are multiple servers in the group.

Note   *Designing BizTalk Server groups and the factors that will help you determine the assignment of each server in a group will be covered in Chapter 12.*

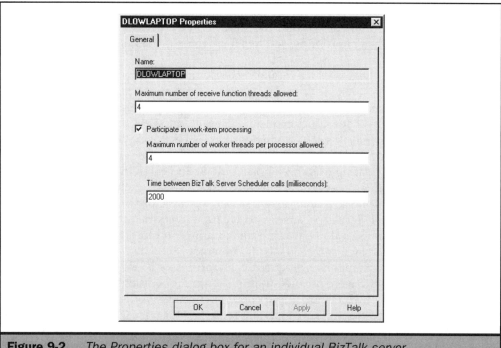

Figure 9-2. *The Properties dialog box for an individual BizTalk server*

In this dialog box, you can set properties to optimize the performance of receive functions or to specify that a particular server should not participate in the processing of items in the Work Queue. However, if a server will process work items—the default setting—you can also configure the maximum number of worker threads per processor for that server, and the time between BizTalk Server Scheduler calls.

The first property is the Maximum number of receive function threads allowed. If the server hosts receive functions, then you can set this value to determine the maximum number of threads—as opposed to the actual number of threads—that each processor will be allowed to create for those receive functions. The value can be between 1 and 128. Increasing the value causes more processing time to be given over to the handling of documents that arrive through the configured receive functions. If the server only handles receive functions, and does not process documents in the BizTalk Messaging Work Queue, then you should definitely increase the value from its default setting of 4. However, setting the value too high could cause problems for any other services running on the server. Setting the value too low could cause a bottleneck if your receive functions process a large number of interchanges. There is no specific recommended value, as it will depend on whether the server is only used for receive functions and on the power of the processor in question. Testing different values and examining the behavior of various BizTalk counters in the Performance monitoring utility can help establish appropriate settings for a given installation.

Note *Optimizing BizTalk Server and tuning performance will be covered in Chapter 12.*

Second, you can choose that the server should not participate in work-item Processing. This means that as documents are submitted to BizTalk Server and are placed in the Work Queue, this server will not process them using BizTalk Messaging. Often, it is appropriate to dedicate at least one server in a server group to handling receive functions, so clearing this check box would be indicated in that situation. If a BizTalk server has to process work items as well as receive functions, then there will be a loss of performance due to *context switching*, as the processor switches from one thread to the other. This is because a receive function thread that is processing input/output operations could be waiting for an input/output operation to complete, so the processor would switch threads to an in-memory BizTalk Messaging operation. When this switching is happening frequently, the processor is not operating as efficiently as it could if it were devoted to input/output operations.

Another scenario in which you might choose to turn off work-item processing is if the BizTalk server is also a Message Queuing server. In this case, BizTalk Server will be reading messages from a local queue. This is preferable, as Message Queuing 2.0 only supports local transactional reads, meaning that transactions would not be supported if BizTalk Server were reading documents from a message queue on a separate server. However, transactional queues require more resources, so you would want to ensure that the performance of the server was not compromised by the presence of BizTalk Messaging as well.

Note *The ability to use transactional private message queues with BizTalk Server groups was added with BizTalk Server Service Pack 1.*

If the BizTalk server will participate in work-item processing, then you can also configure two additional properties. The first property is the Maximum number of worker threads per processor allowed. This is similar to the earlier property that was configured for receive functions. Here, we want to ensure that enough processing time is given over to BizTalk Messaging, so we should again increase this value from the default setting of 4. However, if the server will also be used for receive functions or to host BizTalk Orchestration XLANG schedules, then setting this value too high could be detrimental to the performance of the other tasks.

Note   *Even if your server will not process items in the Work Queue, you should not set this value to zero. Instead, you should clear the Participate in work-item processing check box.*

The final property allows us to specify how often BizTalk Server should check to see whether there is an item in the Work Queue that it can process. By default, the value is 2000 milliseconds, although we can set this property to anything between 1 and 4,294,967,295 milliseconds. If your BizTalk Server installation processes a lot of documents, you should decrease the value to ensure that items are not backing up in the Shared Queue database. However, because each scheduled call uses up resources on both BizTalk Server and SQL Server, if your installation does not process a high volume of documents, you should increase the interval, to save these resources.

Managing Server Queues

Earlier in this chapter, we discussed the fact that servers in a BizTalk Server group share a number of databases, and that the Document Tracking and Shared Queue databases must be explicitly shared by a server group. However, we have not mentioned exactly what goes on in the Shared Queue database, or indeed what these shared queues are. There are four main queues contained in this database, and they can be viewed in the BizTalk Administration interface. We can also move documents between selected queues, and in many cases, view information about an interchange or document.

We have already seen that multiple BizTalk servers can operate together in a single group, sharing the load of receiving and processing documents. The processing of documents by BizTalk Messaging across multiple servers is made possible by the fact that as each document arrives, it is stored in a SQL Server database table, and as it proceeds through other processing stages, it is moved from one table to another. Each of these tables represents a queue, because that is how it behaves—documents are written to a table along with relevant processing information, and BizTalk Messaging removes each document sequentially in a database transaction to perform the necessary processing.

Specifically, there are four tables in the Shared Queue database that are treated as queues in this way. The table names and the queues they represent are shown in the following table.

Table Name	Queue Name
cs_WorkQ	Work Queue
cs_ScheduledQ	Scheduled Queue
cs_RetryQ	Retry Queue
cs_SuspendedQ	Suspended Queue

There is also a table—cs_SuspendedQErrorStrings—that stores the error messages that are displayed in the BizTalk Administration interface for documents in the Suspended Queue.

For each queue, BizTalk Administration shows the first 15,000 documents or interchanges in the queue. Because the queues operate on a first-in, first-out basis, in extreme cases where there are more than 15,000 documents or interchanges in the queue, it may be necessary to wait or to move items to the Suspended Queue to see new arrivals.

Managing the Work Queue

The Work Queue is the table into which documents are placed as they are submitted to BizTalk Messaging. Because this queue contains items that are currently being processed, the BizTalk Administration interface will normally show no items present, unless there is a backlog of items, as may be the case with a high volume of documents.

If any documents or interchanges are visible in the Work Queue, as shown next, we can see information about that document or interchange in the BizTalk Administration interface. The queue shows the Timestamp when the document was received, the name of the Source and Destination organizations involved in the exchange, the name of the Document being processed, and the Server that is currently processing it. In the State column, we can also see the current state of the document. In the Work Queue, this will always show the state as Processing. If we can see a document or interchange in the Work Queue, it is possible to prevent BizTalk Server from completing the processing, by right-clicking the document and selecting All Tasks | Move To Suspended Queue from the context menu.

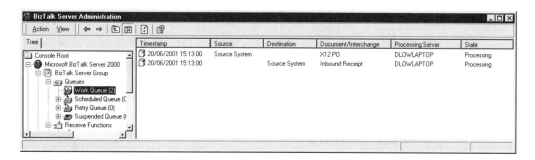

   If BizTalk Server with Service Pack 1 is processing a document, and a failure occurs—such as a lost connection to the Shared Queue database, or a SQL Server timeout or deadlock—it will stop processing and roll back the Shared Queue database transaction. This rollback will occur if the document is still in the Work Queue, even it has been transmitted. This can lead to a situation in which the document is processed a second time, except in cases in which transactional message queues or Reliable messaging is being used. Note that this behavior only occurs when Service Pack 1 has been installed.

Managing the Scheduled Queue

The Scheduled Queue is the table into which documents are placed if they are not due for transmission until a later time. This happens when a messaging port has been configured with a service window. As shown in the following illustration, the BizTalk Administration utility shows similar information for these items as those in the Work Queue, including the service window during which the document will be sent. Again, it is possible to right-click any document visible in the Scheduled Queue and choose All Tasks | Move To Suspended Queue from the context menu to prevent the transmission of the document.

BIZTALK SERVER ADMINISTRATION

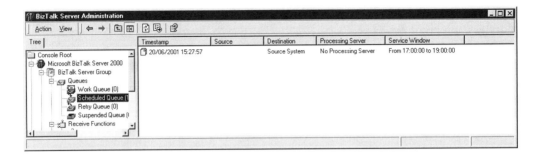

Managing the Retry Queue

If a transmission attempt for a document fails, the document will be sent to the table representing the Retry Queue. Here it will sit until a specified interval has elapsed, at which time the transmission will be retried. For example, network conditions or a crashed web server could cause a temporary problem for BizTalk Messaging to send a document. When we configure a channel in BizTalk Messaging, we specify the retry interval as shown. By default, BizTalk Server will retry three times, at intervals of five minutes, to resend a document.

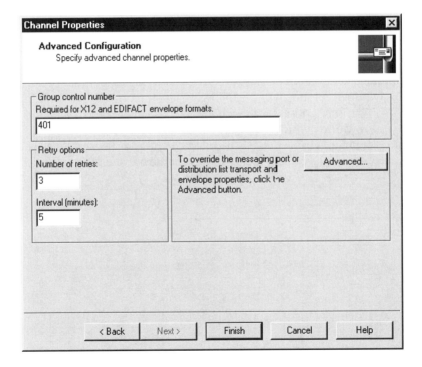

Documents may also appear in the Retry Queue if they are awaiting a Reliable Messaging receipt from a BizTalk Framework–compliant server. The following illustration shows two documents in the Retry Queue. The first document is there because the web server to which the document is being sent is unavailable. The second document is waiting for a Reliable Messaging receipt. As you can see, there is no way to tell just by looking at the Retry Queue why a document is there. However, if we were to examine the Application Log under the Event Viewer snap-in in BizTalk Administration, we would see an entry for the document whose transmission attempt failed. We would not see any entry for the document awaiting the receipt, because that is not an error condition.

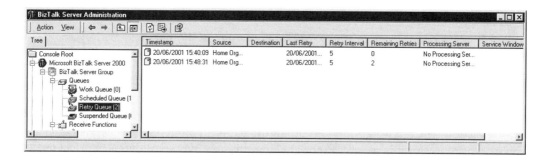

Managing the Suspended Queue

If BizTalk Server fails to process a document for whatever reason, including the exhaustion of numerous retry attempts, the document will end up in the Suspended Queue. Here, we can see information about why the document failed to process, and view the interchange or document data to help troubleshoot the problem. The information available here, in conjunction with the more detailed reasons given in the Windows 2000 Event Viewer Application and System logs, can usually reveal the source of the problem.

When a document or interchange is being processed by BizTalk Messaging, it passes through a number of states. Problems may be encountered at any one of these stages. Regardless of when the error occurs, you can right-click an item in the Suspended Queue in the BizTalk Administration utility and select View Error Description from the context menu. Depending on the state at which processing stopped, you can also choose View Interchange or View Document from the context menu. The various states through which an interchange or document will pass, and the problems that may be encountered at each stage, are listed in the following sections.

BIZTALK SERVER ADMINISTRATION

Note   *Troubleshooting BizTalk Server will be covered in full detail in Chapter 11.*

Initial State

The Initial state represents the actual submission of the interchange, before BizTalk Server has even had a chance to parse the data. For example, if a call to the Submit method of the Interchange object specified a channel that did not exist, the interchange would appear in the Suspended Queue in the Initial state. The first item visible in Figure 9-3 shows an interchange in the Suspended Queue that failed at the initial stage because of such an error. Right-clicking this item would allow us to select the View Interchange command from the context menu.

Parsing State

When an interchange is submitted to BizTalk Messaging, it must be parsed by an appropriate parser component to extract the relevant documents from the interchange and convert them to the intermediate XML format used by BizTalk Messaging. If there is a discrepancy between any of the documents and the specifications that govern the structure of those documents, an error will occur when the document is in the Parsing state. For example, the XML parser would not be able to parse an XML document that was not well-formed. The second item in Figure 9-3 is an interchange that has failed at the parsing stage for this reason. Right-clicking this item would allow us to select the View Interchange command from the context menu.

Document Validation State

Even if a parser successfully extracts documents from an inbound interchange and converts them to XML, there may be further constraints imposed in a document specification to which the document will not conform. For example, a field may contain data that does not match the data type for that field as configured in the specification. The third item in Figure 9-3 is a document that has failed at the document validation stage. Right-clicking this item would allow us to select the View Document command from the context menu.

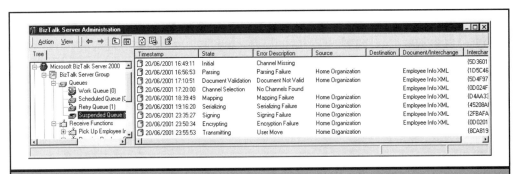

Figure 9-3.   *Items placed in the Suspended Queue for various reasons*

Channel Selection State

When an interchange is submitted to BizTalk Server, it is possible to specify the name of a channel explicitly or to let BizTalk Messaging select the channel based on parameters supplied in the method call or in fields within the document. If BizTalk Messaging cannot find an appropriate channel-messaging port pair, processing will fail in the Channel Selection state. For example, a self-routing document may contain an identifier for the destination organization, but there may be no channel available that feeds into a messaging port configured for that organization. The fourth item in Figure 9-3 is a document that has failed at the channel selection stage. Right-clicking this item would allow us to select the View Document command from the context menu.

Field Tracking State

We saw in Chapter 6 that it was possible to track the values of individual fields with a document as it passes through BizTalk Messaging. This part of the process is pretty resilient to failure. If the data type specified in the channel does not match the data type in the specification, the document will still be processed, but the field value will not be stored in the Document Tracking database. In fact, even if a channel is configured to track a field, and the document specification is later modified so that the field no longer exists, the document will still be successfully processed. Again, no field value will be tracked. About the only thing that will cause a document to end up in the Suspended Queue in relation to the Field Tracking state is if the Document Tracking database were to become corrupt during processing. BizTalk Server Service Pack 1 contains stored procedures for this database to help prevent such failures.

 Document Tracking and the stored procedures available with BizTalk Server Service Pack 1 to purge and archive the Document Tracking database will be covered in Chapter 10.

Mapping State

During the processing of a document by a channel, the internal XML data representing the inbound document structure may need to be transformed into a different XML document representing the structure of the outbound document. Needless to say, if the map file specified does not correctly transform one document structure into the other, then the document will fail processing in the Mapping state. For example, a map file may use a functoid that outputs a string into a field of data type *integer*. The fifth item in Figure 9-3 is a document that has failed processing at the mapping stage. Right-clicking this item would allow us to select the View Document command from the context menu.

Serializing State

After a document has been through the mapping stage of BizTalk Messaging, it will then be serialized into the outgoing format required by an application or trading partner. The format is specified during the configuration of a messaging port, where we select an envelope in the same format as the outgoing document. If the format of the envelope and the outbound specification don't match, it could cause a serialization error. Even if they do match, there may be constraints placed on fields in the interchange header or footer that cause the interchange to become invalid. For example, an X12 interchange header has a maximum field length of 15 characters for an organization identifier, so trying to place a value longer than that will cause the document to fail in the Serializing state. The sixth item in Figure 9-3 is a document that has failed processing for this reason. Right-clicking this item would allow us to select the View Document command from the context menu.

Encoding State

During the configuration of a messaging port, we can also choose to apply MIME or custom encoding to an outbound document. If a custom encoding component reports an error during this phase, then processing fails in the Encoding state.

Signing State

As we saw in Chapter 6, it is possible to digitally sign outgoing documents using a digital certificate that is kept in the Personal store. However, digital certificates have a finite lifespan, as they expire after a certain period. They may also be revoked at any time for a number of reasons, for example, if it were reported that the private key for the certificate had been compromised. The Certificate Authority that issued the certificate maintains a Certificate Revocation List (CRL) that is viewable using the Certificates MMC snap-in for the BizTalk Messaging Service. If BizTalk Messaging attempts to sign an outgoing document with a certificate that has been revoked, has expired, or is no longer available, processing fails in the Signing state. The seventh item in Figure 9-3 is an interchange that has failed processing at the signing stage. Right-clicking this item would allow us to select the View Interchange command from the context menu.

Encrypting State

We can also use a digital certificate to encrypt an outgoing document, although this is done using a trading partner's certificate, which will be kept in the BizTalk store. Again, this certificate can be revoked or expire, so it is possible for processing to fail in the Encrypting state. The eighth item in Figure 9-3 is an interchange that failed processing at the encryption stage. Right-clicking this item would allow us to select the View Interchange command from the context menu.

Transmitting State

When an interchange has been serialized, and possibly signed and encrypted, it is ready to be sent to its final destination. Of course, network connectivity problems, typing errors, and application errors can all come into play at this point. If a document cannot be sent to its destination, processing will fail in the Transmitting state. This may also occur if a BizTalk Framework document has a "receiptRequiredBy" timestamp and that time has passed. Indeed, it is also possible for documents in other queues to be moved to the Suspended Queue. The ninth and final item in Figure 9-3 shows an interchange that has been manually moved to the Suspended Queue by an administrator. Right-clicking this item would allow us to select the View Interchange command from the context menu.

Custom Component State

BizTalk Server can make use of many different types of custom components to provide additional functionality. Two types of components that can be used with BizTalk Messaging are parsers/serializers and preprocessors. The creation of these components will be discussed in Chapter 16. If one of these components reports an error to BizTalk Messaging, then processing will fail in the Custom Component state.

Correlating State

One last state in which documents may find themselves is the Correlating state. This occurs when a document has been sent to a server that is expected to return a receipt. When this receipt arrives at BizTalk Messaging, it is possible to have a custom correlation component that checks the data in the receipt against the original message. If they do not match, then the receipt will be moved to the Suspended Queue in the Correlating state.

Managing Receive Functions

We saw in Chapter 7 that BizTalk Orchestration could be used to submit documents to BizTalk Messaging. In Chapter 16, we will also see that there is a programmatic interface called IInterchange that is exposed by the BizTalk Server API. The Interchange object has two methods—Submit and SubmitSync—that allow applications to pass documents to BizTalk Messaging for processing. However, this assumes that the applications in question support COM interfaces, or can make use of Distributed COM (DCOM) to submit documents across a network. For applications that cannot make use of these programmatic methods, BizTalk Server provides receive functions.

Even if your applications support the submission of documents to BizTalk Server using DCOM, Microsoft recommends using receive functions in distributed scenarios to avoid context switching with other I/O threads.

Receive functions allow us to specify accessible locations into which documents can be dropped by an application. Once they've arrived, the receive function will itself use the Submit method of the Interchange object, along with any parameters we specify during the configuration of the receive function, to pass the document to BizTalk Messaging. There are two types of receive function—file and message queuing. Each type can be created using the BizTalk Administration utility. They can also be created programmatically using the Windows Management Instrumentation (WMI) interfaces that will be discussed in Chapter 18.

File Receive Functions

File receive functions allow us to create a folder on a local hard drive, or shared network location, into which an application or trading partner can drop a document for submission to BizTalk Messaging. For example, we could configure a receive function to monitor a directory that was located on an FTP server. As documents are uploaded to the relevant directory on the server, the receive function is informed and picks them up from that location. Multiple receive functions can be created, each monitoring the same location for different file types, or monitoring different locations for similar file types. In a BizTalk Server group, each receive function belongs to a particular server, but the documents retrieved by it can be processed by any server in the group.

Creating a File Receive Function

To create a new file receive function, right-click the Receive Functions node in the left pane of the BizTalk Administration interface, and select New | File Receive Function from the context menu. This will bring up the Add a File Receive Function dialog box, as shown in Figure 9-4. There are many different parameters that can be set in this dialog box, and also in the Advanced Receive Function Options dialog box that appears when the Advanced button is clicked.

The first thing to do is to give the receive function a Name. As with messaging ports and channels in BizTalk Messaging, the more descriptive a name is, the easier it will be to figure out what one particular receive function does when you've built up a collection of tens or hundreds of them. You can also provide a descriptive Comment in the box underneath. You will then have to choose the server on which the receive function will run. This is because there may be many servers in your server group, and each receive function is tied to a particular server. Select the appropriate server from the drop-down menu. As discussed earlier in the chapter, you may decide to keep all of your receive functions running on a server that does not participate in BizTalk Messaging work-item processing for increased performance.

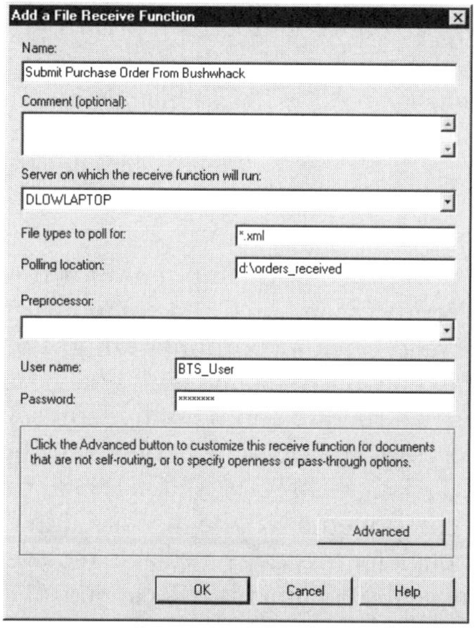

Figure 9-4.   *Add A File Receive Function dialog box*

As shown in Figure 9-4, the next things to specify are the type of file for which this receive function should poll and the file location in which it should look. Although this is the terminology used in the product documentation, it can be misleading to think of the receive function "polling" that particular directory to see whether a new document has arrived. What actually happens is that the receive function is notified by the Windows 2000 File System (NTFS) that a new file has appeared in the directory. For this reason, it is not possible to change how frequently documents will be picked up from the location by configuring BizTalk Server.

In the File types to poll for field, enter a filtering expression as if you were searching for files on your hard drive. For example, type ***.xml** if you want the receive function to pick up all files with an .xml file extension; type ***.x?l** if you want to pick up files with an .xml, .xsl, or .xql file extension; or type **x12*.edi** if you want the receive function to pick up files whose names begin with x12 and that have an .edi file extension. In the Polling location field, enter the path to the directory in which the documents will be dropped. This may be a local directory, such as **c:\invoices**, or a shared folder on the local area network, such as **\\publicserver\invoiceshare**. If the location is protected using NTFS permissions or shared folder permissions, you may also need to enter the name and password of a user account with the appropriate rights on that folder.

Because the receive function removes the file from the directory, you must ensure that files delivered to this location do not have their read-only attribute set. Also, this means that the user account credentials provided must have permission to delete files from the directory.

You can also choose a preprocessor component for the receive function, if there are any available. Preprocessors are COM components that implement the IBTSCustomProcess interface. Such a component might be used in a situation in which a document used an encoding scheme with which BizTalk Server was not familiar, or if the document's structure could not be represented easily using BizTalk Editor. For custom preprocessor components to be visible here, they must implement the category CATID_ BIZTALK_ CUSTOM_PROCESS in the Registry. The creation and registration of these components will be discussed in Chapter 16.

These settings will be enough for a receive function to retrieve and submit self-routing text-based documents. That is, the documents will contain all the necessary information for BizTalk Messaging to select the appropriate channel-messaging port pair to process the document. If the documents are missing some or all of this information, you must click the Advanced button to bring up the Advanced Receive Function Options dialog box. Because these properties are common to both file and message queuing receive functions, I'll discuss them after covering the creation of message queuing receive functions.

A very quick and easy way to test a new BizTalk Messaging workflow is to set up a file receive function that feeds into the channel you've just created and to configure the messaging port you've just created to transport the outgoing document to another file folder. Then simply drop a sample document into the pickup folder, wait a few seconds until it disappears, and have a look in the destination folder. If the document is not there, a quick check of the Event Viewer Application Log should reveal the problem.

Message Queuing Receive Functions

In Chapter 3, I introduced message queues as a way for applications to communicate asynchronously. That is, one application can drop a message into a message queue for retrieval by another application at some later time. Therefore, when an application uses a message queue to send data, it does not expect an immediate response. The messages are stored in the queue until the receiving application is ready to accept them, at which point they are forwarded to that application.

We have already seen that both BizTalk Messaging and BizTalk Orchestration can send documents to message queues, and that BizTalk Orchestration can receive documents submitted to a message queue. To complete the picture, we can also create message queuing receive functions to allow applications to submit documents to BizTalk Messaging. This is important for BizTalk Server's stated goal of supporting loosely coupled applications—where the communicating systems do not have to depend on or connect directly to each other to successfully exchange data.

Creating a Message Queuing Receive Function

To create a message queuing receive function, right-click the Receive Functions node in the left pane of the BizTalk Server Administration utility, and select New | Message Queuing Receive Function. This will bring up the Add a Message Queuing Receive Function dialog box, as shown in Figure 9-5. This dialog box is almost identical to the Add a File Receive Function dialog box shown in Figure 9-4, so it is only necessary to discuss the differences.

In fact, there are only two real differences. First, because documents placed into a message queue are not stored in the same way as those stored in a file system, we cannot differentiate between file types based on the name or extension of the file. Thus, we must be sure to create a message queue for each type of document we expect to receive. These can be public message queues accessible from outside our organization, or private message queues located on a message queuing server within our organization.

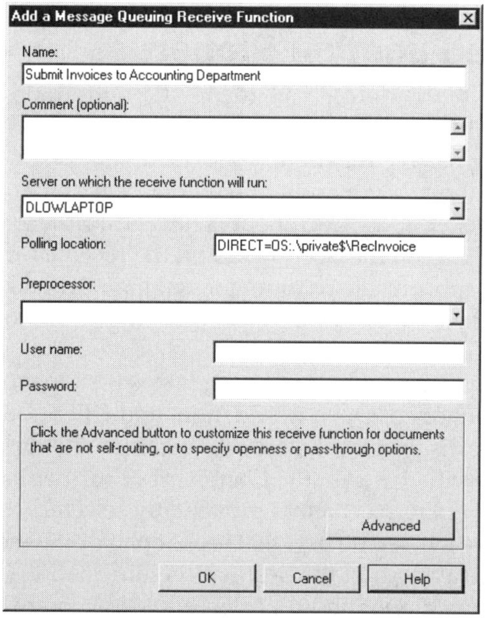

Figure 9-5.   *Add A Message Queuing Receive Function dialog box*

BIZTALK SERVER
ADMINISTRATION

To use private message queues, BizTalk Server must be installed on the message queuing server. However, BizTalk Server Service Pack 1 allows private queues to be shared among servers in a BizTalk Server group.

The second difference is the format of the Polling Location. As with message queues configured within a messaging port, there are various ways to specify a queue, depending on its type. For example, we might type **DIRECT=OS:\.private$\RecInvoice** to specify a private queue called RecInvoice on the local machine, or we might type **DIRECT=TCP:172.168.10.10\Drop** to specify a queue called Drop on the machine with an IP address of 172.168.10.10.

All other parameters set on this page correspond to those discussed for file receive functions, but again we can set advanced properties by clicking the Advanced button. The parameters configured in the Advanced Receive Function Options dialog box are common to both types of receive functions.

You can configure multiple receive functions on different servers to retrieve documents from the same file or message queue location (with the caveat that transactional reads are not supported from remote message queues unless BizTalk Server Service Pack 1 is installed). However, you must always ensure that each receive function for a server group has a unique name.

Advanced Receive Function Properties

Figure 9-6 shows the Advanced Receive Function Options dialog box. In this dialog box, you can configure how a document will be routed once it has been picked up by a file or message queuing receive function. If the document is self-routing and contains both source and destination information, it may not be necessary to configure any of these parameters. However, if the document is not self-routing, there must be enough information available between the document and the receive function to allow BizTalk Messaging to select an appropriate channel-messaging port pair. All of the parameters configured here correspond to the parameters passed in a call to the Submit method of the Interchange object.

The first property you can set in this dialog box is the Openness property. The available options are Not open, Open destination, and Open source. If the property is set to Not open, this means that the source organization and destination organization identifiers are either specified within the document or further down in the dialog box. It can also be set to Not open if a channel is explicitly selected, this channel is not open source, and it feeds into a messaging port that is not open destination. If Open destination is selected, then we are saying that the destination information (including transport type) is present in the document and that BizTalk Messaging should use a channel-messaging port pair where the messaging port is set to open destination. If Open source is selected, then we are saying that the source organization information is contained within the document, and that BizTalk Messaging should use a channel-

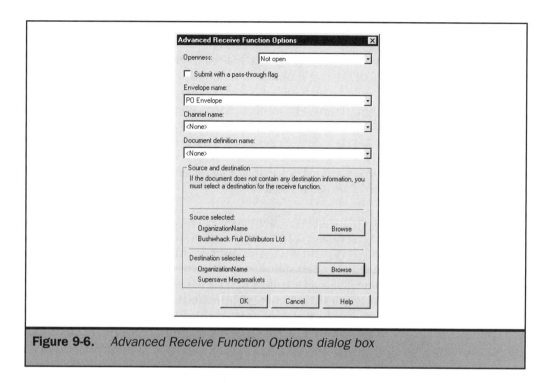

Figure 9-6. *Advanced Receive Function Options dialog box*

messaging port pair where the channel is set to Open source. We can also set this property to Open Source and select the source organization identifier further down in the dialog box.

The next property we can set is whether the document should be submitted with a pass-through flag. If we select this check box, the inbound document will not be parsed, decrypted, validated against a document specification, mapped, signed, or encrypted. This option is only used to submit binary documents or business documents that need to be transported in their original format.

Note *If either Open destination or Open source is selected, the Submit with a pass-through flag check box is not available.*

As discussed in Chapter 6, the type of document being submitted may require an envelope. This will enable BizTalk Server to select the appropriate parser and to extract the document from any interchange headers or footers that may be present. In general, XML and EDI formats don't require an envelope, except in the case of a Custom XML envelope. This should have been created already in BizTalk Messaging Manager, but it's not actually necessary to specify it here because BizTalk Server is able to select the appropriate one. However, if a flat-file or custom format document is being submitted, then a previously created envelope in the same format should be chosen from the drop-down menu.

If our document is not self-routing, we need to make sure that BizTalk Messaging knows what kind of document is being submitted, from what organization it originates, and to what destination it should be sent. Each piece of information can be set individually, but a channel comes preconfigured with those details. If an appropriate channel to process the document exists, it can be selected from the Channel Name drop-down menu.

If a channel is selected from the Channel name drop-down menu, the Document definition name drop-down menu and the Browse buttons in the Source selected and Destination selected areas are not available.

If we are not sure which channel may end up processing the document, we will need to select some of those details explicitly. The first item that BizTalk Messaging needs to know is the type of inbound document we're submitting. This can be compared against all existing channels to find a match. Second, we can choose the source organization from which the document has come. This will also help BizTalk Messaging select the appropriate channel(s). To do this, we can click the Browser button in the Source selected area, to bring up the Select source dialog box, shown next. In this dialog box, we can choose the appropriate organization identifier qualifier and value that corresponds to the source organization.

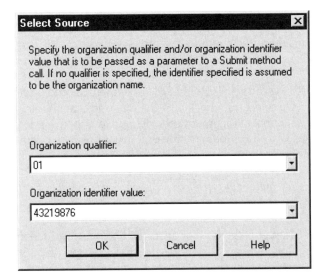

Finally, we can click the Browse button in the Destination selected area, to bring up a similar dialog box from which we can choose the destination organization identifier qualifier and value. If we would like the document to be submitted to a channel that feeds into a distribution list, we can choose GROUP in the Organization qualifier drop-down menu in the Select destination dialog box, as shown next, and then choose an available distribution list from the Organization identifier value drop-down menu.

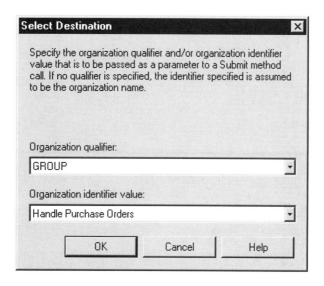

Removing Receive Functions

Earlier, I mentioned that it is possible to remove BizTalk servers from a server group, but that it is necessary to remove any receive functions that are associated with the server before doing so. Luckily, this procedure does not require too much mental or manual dexterity. In the BizTalk Administration interface, simply right-click the node for the receive function in question, and choose Delete on the context menu. The User Action Confirmation dialog box will appear, so click Yes if you really want to delete it.

Chapter 10

Tracking Documents

We have seen how BizTalk Server can integrate systems within an organization for enterprise application integration (EAI) and how it can support communication with external trading partner organizations for business-to-business (B2B) transactions. We have also seen that each scenario can make use of BizTalk Server's core features—BizTalk Messaging and BizTalk Orchestration. Regardless of how we implement the details, we could say that the primary function of BizTalk Server is to transport and manipulate business data. This data is the currency of our B2B and EAI transactions, and in the same way that we need a statement of financial transactions from our bank or credit card company, we will often need a statement of data transactions from BizTalk Server. This is provided by the document tracking features that are built into the product.

We may need this information for a variety of reasons. It may be for legal or tax purposes; it may be to meet certain international procedural standards; it may be to provide customers with better service; or it may be to analyze our business data for trends and summaries. During the development of a BizTalk Messaging solution, the ability to see how an interchange was processed and how each individual document was parsed, mapped, and serialized can be invaluable for troubleshooting. Similarly, for BizTalk Orchestration, a record of the documents that passed through XLANG schedule instances and of the events fired by those instances can provide even greater detail. In both development and production environments, we can enable various degrees of document tracking, we can use a richly featured interface to query tracking details, and we can examine and maintain the database that stores those details.

Enabling Document Tracking

By default, the document tracking capability of BizTalk Server is enabled. All servers in a server group that process interchanges using BizTalk Messaging will store information about those interchanges in the Document Tracking Activity database (InterchangeDTA if you accepted the default database name). For each of those interchanges, the raw data will be logged in both incoming and outgoing formats. Similarly, for each inbound interchange, the contents of each contained document will also be logged in its native format. Each of these options can be changed. We can even choose to track individual fields for a given type of document or only for documents processed by a particular channel.

Setting Server Group Tracking Properties

Document tracking is configured at a server group level through the BizTalk Administration interface, and the settings chosen will apply to all servers in that group. In this interface, you have the option to track all inbound and outbound interchanges as shown, and also to log the inbound interchange in its original MIME format if available. If you so desire, you can even specify that document tracking should be globally disabled for all interchanges, regardless of how they are processed, but this is probably not a good idea.

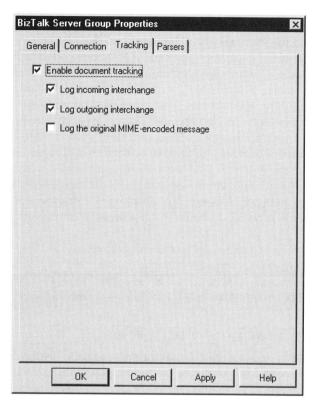

You should not disable document tracking at this level. Otherwise, no interchange or document data will be written to the database, even if it has been configured at a lower level, such as in a channel or document definition. The exception to this is if your business handles extremely large XML interchanges (greater than 20MB) or flat-file interchanges (greater than 10MB). In such cases, you should disable document tracking at the server group level to avoid a dramatic drop in performance. In fact, the document tracking database cannot handle documents in excess of 20MB.

The configuration shown in the illustration is the default setting after BizTalk Server is installed. This means that metadata for all inbound and outbound interchanges will be logged automatically without any input on the part of an administrator. As a result, you instantly have a record of all interchanges processed by BizTalk Server; this can prove adequate for many commercial uses, such as proof of transmission and nonrepudiation (that is, proving that a document was received or that it contained particular information). This metadata is stored in the dta_interchange_details table and consists of information such as the interchange format (XML, X12, and so on), the date and time received or sent, the source organization or application, the destination organization or application, and the number of documents contained in the interchange.

If you have MIME-encoded documents arriving at BizTalk Server via SMTP, you can also choose to log the interchanges in that format, although that would be unnecessary in most cases. The only time logging the original MIME-encoded interchanges might be important is if you are receiving S/MIME-encrypted or -signed documents, and you wish to save the original data as further proof of the contents of an original interchange. For example, if a digitally signed document is sent to you by a trading partner, the interchange will consist of the document and a summary of the document encrypted using the trading partner's private key. This summary, or *hash*, can only be generated by the trading partner. So if that trading partner tried to accuse you of manipulating your document tracking database to show a document they claim they never sent, you could call up the original interchange and show that the hash could only have been generated for that particular document. With Public Key Infrastructure (PKI) technology there's no way you could have forged the hash without their private key.

 If you clear the check boxes beside Log Incoming Interchange and Log Outgoing Interchange, then only the metadata pertaining to the interchange will not be saved to the database. You can still choose to log individual documents, or data fields in a channel or document definition, as long as the Enable Document Tracking check box remains selected.

Setting Channel Tracking Properties

As long as document tracking is enabled at the server group level, you can also choose to track individual documents contained within an interchange. The documents can be logged in either their native format or in the XML format used internally by BizTalk Server. This is the format into which all documents are parsed after they have been submitted to BizTalk Server, and it is the format from which all outgoing documents are serialized before they are sent. This logging is configured during the creation or modification of a channel in BizTalk Messaging Manager, as shown next.

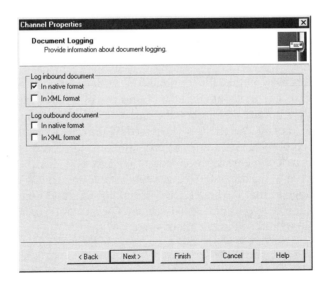

Note   *Creating and configuring channels was covered in Chapter 6.*

By default, BizTalk Server will log each inbound document processed by a channel in its native format. (All documents passing though BizTalk Messaging must be processed by at least one channel.) The native format is the original format of the document when it was extracted from the inbound interchange. However, either during the creation of a channel, or through editing the properties of an existing channel in BizTalk Messaging Manager, you can also opt to log the inbound document in the internal XML format. Similarly, you can choose to log the outbound document resulting from the channel in its native format—that is, the format into which it will be serialized—or in the internal XML format.

Caution   *If your business handles extremely large XML documents (greater than 20MB) or flat-file documents (greater than 10MB), you should disable document logging in BizTalk Messaging Manager to avoid a dramatic drop in performance.*

If you think about it, these defaults are adequate for most scenarios. BizTalk Server supports the processing of batched inbound documents, so if an interchange arriving at BizTalk Server contains multiple documents, you would probably want to track each document separately from the original interchange. However, BizTalk Server does not support the batching of outbound documents, so there is no need to track outbound documents in their native format. We already will be tracking the outbound interchange (assuming we haven't changed the server group defaults), and this will only contain that single document. Therefore, we will always have a record of each individual outbound document anyway, even if it is contained in an interchange. Similarly, there is usually no need to track the XML format used internally by BizTalk Server, because it will never contain anything extra that was not in the original document or that will not be in the final document. Selecting these check boxes is generally only called for during the troubleshooting of an errant map file.

Setting Field Tracking Properties

There is another thing for which BizTalk Document Tracking is incredibly useful—business analysis. For example, if we quickly needed to see how many invoices sent to different trading partners during the month of January were worth more than $1000, it would be beneficial to be able to query BizTalk Server for this information. After all, if every one of these invoices passed through BizTalk Server, the data must be present somewhere. We should not have to query BizTalk Server for all invoices and then have to select those with an appropriate total. This information should be readily accessible; with some configuration, it is.

Global Field Tracking

In our example, we wished to find out how many invoices greater than a certain amount were sent to all of our trading partners. Assuming that the invoices we generate internally are of the same format, regardless of the format they will be in when sent to each trading partner, we will have a single document definition in BizTalk Messaging Manager representing the structure of our invoice. In this case, we can configure global field tracking for that document type. This means that for every instance of an invoice that is submitted to BizTalk Messaging, the values of certain fields will be extracted and stored in the document tracking database for easy retrieval later.

Note *Creating and configuring document definitions was covered in Chapter 6.*

Before we can do this, however, we will need to ensure that BizTalk Server is able to extract this data in the correct format. For example, if we wish to track the date of a purchase order, we will need to establish that a certain field within a document is indeed a date. Similarly, to track the total of an invoice, we will need to be sure that the field in the document that contains that data is a numeric data field. Because document definitions rely on document specifications created using BizTalk Editor to parse and validate incoming documents, it is in BizTalk Editor that this information needs to be configured. For any specific field that we will wish to track within a document, we should set the appropriate data type for that field during the creation of the document specification, as shown in Figure 10-1.

Note *The creation of document specifications using BizTalk Editor was covered in Chapter 4.*

After the appropriate data types have been set in BizTalk Editor, we are ready to use BizTalk Messaging Manager to track those fields. During the creation or modification

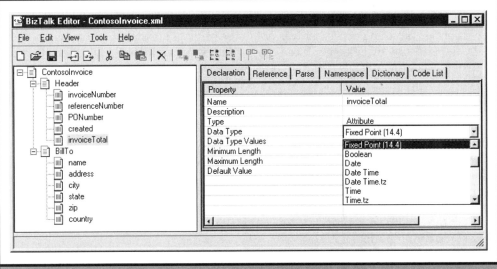

Figure 10-1. *Selecting the data type of a field in BizTalk Editor*

of a document definition, we can access the Global Tracking tab, as shown next, and select the fields that should be explicitly tracked in the database. In the illustration, we have selected the *invoiceTotal* field to be tracked as a real number.

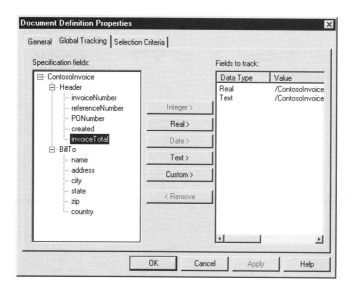

In this interface, it is possible to track two fields as integers, two fields as real numbers, two fields as dates, two fields as strings, or, indeed, any number of fields in any format using the Custom option. However, the Custom option should only be used to track other data types that are not supported explicitly (for example, Boolean values), or if it is necessary to track more than two integers, real numbers, dates, or strings. This is because the values tracked for explicit data types are stored in columns in the document tracking database that have matching data types, making it much more efficient to search for that data. However, Custom data values are stored as a concatenated XML string in a single field in the database, which is not as efficient to search. Later in this chapter, we will see how to search for documents based on the values of these global tracking fields.

Channel Field Tracking

If the scenario in our example were slightly different—for example, that we would only ever want to query BizTalk Server for invoices worth more than $1000 that had come from a single trading partner—we could choose to turn on field tracking for documents that had passed only through the relevant channel. While it is still possible to use the document tracking interface to query for documents with a particular field value that have come from a specific organization, if we log the fields as global tracking fields, we will still be storing that information for documents coming from all organizations. This might be more than our business purposes require, because we may only ever need to analyze data for certain trading partners. Obviously, that is neither as efficient nor as performance friendly as only storing the data we need. For this reason, we can use BizTalk Messaging Manager to track fields for documents that only pass through individual channels. We do this during the creation or modification of a channel, by opting to track fields in the inbound document, as shown in the following illustration.

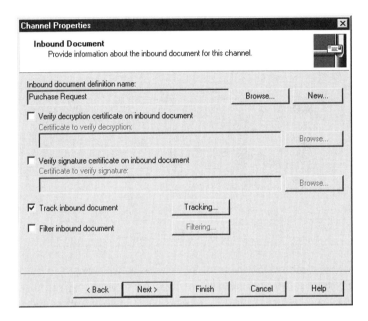

Clicking the Tracking button will then open the Tracking For Inbound Document dialog box, shown in Figure 10-2.

The interface shown in Figure 10-2 is similar to that used to configure global tracking fields, but again, we should remember that fields selected here for tracking will only be tracked for documents that pass through this specific channel. However, if the document definition in question has already been configured for global tracking fields, they will appear at the top of the dialog box. In this way, we can choose to track certain fields for all document instances and then select further fields that should only be tracked for a particular channel. Figure 10-2 shows a purchase request for which the *empID* and *total* fields will be tracked in all cases, and for which the *productID* field will only be tracked within this channel.

Note   *The syntax used to select the fields is the XML Path language (XPath). As you can see in Figure 10-2, the syntax is very similar to that used for MS-DOS or UNIX file paths. In the path /purchaseRequest/header/@empID, the first forward slash (/) represents the root of the document, followed by the purchaseRequest record, the header record beneath that, and finally the empID field within that record. The at sign (@) is used because the empID field is stored as an XML attribute, while the records are stored as elements.*

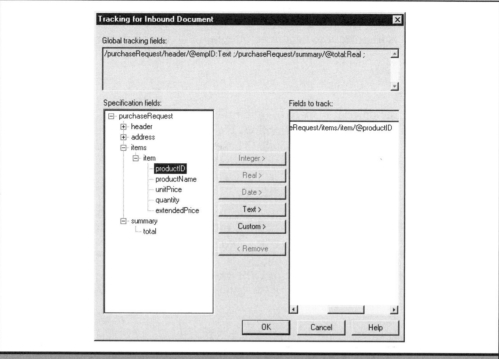

Figure 10-2.   *The Tracking For Inbound Document dialog box*

BizTalk Document Tracking Database

As documents pass through BizTalk Messaging, they are logged to a database known as the Document Tracking Activity (DTA) database. This database is called InterchangeDTA if you accepted the default name during the installation of BizTalk Server. A number of core, or primary tables in this database store the actual tracking information. There are also secondary tables that store metadata for the primary tables. It is not necessary to understand the schema of this database to enable document tracking, nor is it necessary to be familiar with each table to be able to query that tracking information using the web-based interface discussed later. However, it can be useful to examine how each interchange and document is logged—particularly if you need to customize the Document Tracking client interface, or if you need to build a custom tracking application.

We have seen that interchange tracking is enabled by default for a BizTalk server group and that each incoming and outgoing interchange will be logged to the database. We have also seen that the default for each configured channel is to log each inbound document in its native format. Not only that, but we can choose to log further information for each interchange or document, including the values of individual fields. As you can

BIZTALK SERVER ADMINISTRATION

probably imagine, a busy BizTalk server group could track hundreds or even thousands of documents per hour, causing enormous growth in the document tracking database. For this reason, it is important to be able to maintain the database, purging unneeded data regularly.

Primary Tables

In the document tracking database, a number of core, or primary, tables are used to hold interchange and document information. These tables are dta_interchange_details, dta_indoc_details, and dta_outdoc_details. These tables, and the relationships between them and other important secondary tables, are shown in Figure 10-3.

dta_interchange_details Table

The dta_interchange_details table contains one record for each interchange submitted to BizTalk Server. As Figure 10-3 shows, it has one-to-many relationships with the tables dta_indoc_details, dta_outdoc_details and dta_group_details, and a many-to-one relationship with the table dta_interchange_data. Although not shown in Figure 10-3, there are also many-to-one relationships with the tables dta_direction_values, dta_error_message, and dta_transport_type_values. Table 10-1 describes each field in this table.

Field	Description
nInterchangeKey	Unique interchange identifier (primary key).
nInterchangeDataKey	Identifier for each record stored in the dta_interchange_data table (foreign key).
nResponseDocDataKey	Identifier for response documents (receipts or responses to a SubmitSync method call) stored in the dta_document_data table (foreign key).
uidInterchangeGUID	Global tracking identifier for each interchange processed by BizTalk Messaging.
uidSubmissionGUID	Identifier returned during initial submission of interchange—also used to identify corresponding MIME data in dta_MIME_details table.
dtProcessedTimeStamp	Date and time the record was created.

Table 10-1. *Structure of the dta_interchange_details Table*

Field	Description
nvcSyntax	The data format of the interchange, for example, X12 or CUSTOM XML. This will be UNKNOWN if no envelope was specified, if parsing failed, or if the pass-through flag was enabled.
nvcVersion	The version of the data format, if specified.
nvcControlID	Unique interchange control number. This will be a positive integer if used for EDI formats, or a UUID if used for Reliable messaging formats.
nDirection	Possible values are 1 for inbound documents, or 0 for outbound documents.
dtTimeSent	Date and time of the outgoing transmission.
nError	Identifier for error message returned by unsuccessfully processed interchanges and stored in dta_error_message table (foreign key).
nTestMode	Reserved.
nvcSrcAliasQualifier	Identifier qualifier for source organization.
nvcSrcAliasID	Identifier value for source organization.
nvcSrcAppName	Identifier for source application extracted from interchange. Note that this is not the source application as specified in a channel.
nvcDestAliasQualifier	Identifier qualifier for destination organization.
nvcDestAliasID	Identifier value for destination organization.
nvcDestAppName	Identifier for destination application extracted from interchange. Note that this is not the destination application as specified in a messaging port.
nAckStatus	Identifier for receipt status message stored in dta_ack_status_values table (foreign key).
nvcSMTPMessageID	Reserved.

Table 10-1. *Structure of the dta_interchange_details Table* (continued)

Field	Description
nDocumentsAccepted	Number of documents from the interchange that were accepted for processing.
nDocumentsRejected	Number of documents from the interchange that were rejected for processing.
nTransportType	Identifier for transport protocol stored in dta_transport_type table (foreign key).
nvcTransportAddress	Destination for the outbound interchange as specified in a messaging port or in a self-routing document.
nvcServerName	Name of BizTalk server that processed the interchange.
nNumberOfBytes	Size of the interchange in bytes.
nNumOfTransmitAttempts	Number of attempts before successful transmission.

Table 10-1. *Structure of the dta_interchange_details Table* (continued)

dta_indoc_details Table

The dta_indoc_details table contains one record for each document extracted from an inbound interchange submitted to BizTalk Server. As Figure 10-3 shows, it has a one-to-many relationship with the dta_outdoc_details table, many-to-one relationships with the dta_group_details and dta_interchange_details tables, and one-to-one relationships with the dta_document_data and dta_debugdoc_data tables. Although not shown in Figure 10-3, there are also many-to-one relationships with the tables dta_error_message and dta_validity_values. Table 10-2 describes each field in this table.

dta_outdoc_details Table

The dta_outdoc_details table contains one record for each outbound document processed by BizTalk Server. As Figure 10-3 shows, it has a many-to-one relationship with the dta_indoc_details, dta_interchange_details, dta_group_details, dta_routing_details, dta_custom_field_names, and dta_debugdoc_data tables, and a one-to-one relationship with the dta_document_data table. Although not shown in Figure 10-3, there are also many-to-one relationships with the tables dta_error_message,

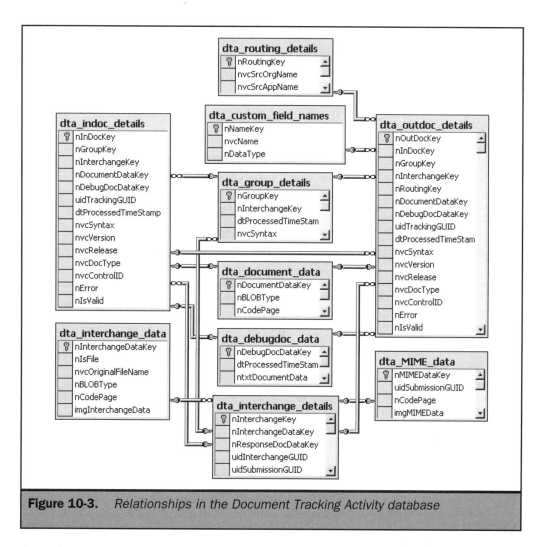

Figure 10-3. *Relationships in the Document Tracking Activity database*

dta_ack_status_values, dta_data_level_values, and dta_validity_values. Table 10-3 describes each field in this table.

Secondary Tables

Along with the primary tables used to store interchange and document data, there are also seven secondary tables that store related information. These secondary tables are dta_interchange_data, dta_document_data, dta_routing_details, dta_custom_field_names, dta_group_details, dta_debugdoc_data, and dta_MIME_data. They are also shown in Figure 10-3, along with their relationships to the primary tables.

Field	Description
nInDocKey	Unique document identifier (primary key).
nDocumentDataKey	Identifier for each record stored in the dta_document_data table (foreign key).
nDebugDocDataKey	Identifier for each record stored in the dta_debugdoc_data table (foreign key).
nGroupKey	Identifier for each record stored in the dta_group_details table (foreign key).
nInterchangeKey	Identifier for each record stored in the dta_interchange_details table (foreign key).
uidTrackingGUID	Unique identifier for each document within the tracking database.
dtProcessedTimeStamp	Date and time the record was created.
nvcSyntax	The data format of the document, for example, X12 or CUSTOM XML. This will be UNKNOWN if no envelope was specified, or if parsing failed.
nvcVersion	The version of the data format, if specified.
nvcRelease	The release number of the data format, if specified.
nvcDocType	Document type or transaction set identifier, if specified.
nvcControlID	Unique interchange control number. This will be a positive integer if used for EDI formats, or a UUID if used for Reliable messaging formats.
nIsValid	Possible values are 0 if document is valid, 1 if document is not valid, or 2 if pass-through flag was set on submission.
nError	Identifier for error message returned by unsuccessfully processed documents and stored in dta_error_message table (foreign key).

Table 10-2.   *The Structure of the dta_indoc_details Table*

Field	Description
nOutDocKey	Unique document identifier (primary key).
nInDocKey	Identifier for each corresponding record stored in the dta_indoc_data table (foreign key).
nDocumentDataKey	Identifier for each record stored in the dta_document_data table (foreign key).
nDebugDocDataKey	Identifier for each record stored in the dta_debugdoc_data table (foreign key).
nGroupKey	Identifier for each record stored in the dta_group_details table (foreign key).
nInterchangeKey	Identifier for each record stored in the dta_interchange_details table (foreign key).
uidTrackingGUID	Unique identifier for each document within the tracking database.
dtProcessedTimeStamp	Date and time the record was created.
nvcSyntax	The data format of the document, for example, X12 or CUSTOM XML. This will be UNKNOWN if no envelope was specified or if parsing failed.
nvcVersion	The version of the data format, if specified.
nvcRelease	The release number of the data format, if specified.
nvcDocType	Document type or transaction set identifier, if specified.
nvcControlID	Set to 1 to indicate that an EDI document is part of a functional group.
nIsValid	Possible values are 0 if document is valid, 1 if document is not valid, or 2 if pass-through flag was set on submission.
nError	Identifier for error message returned by unsuccessfully processed documents and stored in dta_error_message table (foreign key).

Table 10-3. *The Structure of the dta_outdoc_details Table*

Field	Description
nAckStatus	Identifier for each receipt status message stored in the dta_ack_status_values table (foreign key).
nRoutingKey	Identifier for each record in the dta_routing_details table, which contains a copy of the relevant messaging port information from the Messaging Management database.
nReceiptFlag	Possible values are 1 if a receipt corresponds to an entry in dta_interchange_details, 2 if a receipt corresponds to an entry in dta_group_details, 4 if a receipt corresponds to an entry in dta_indoc_details, or 8 if a receipt corresponds to an entry in dta_outdoc_details. Identifier for values held in dta_data_level_values (foreign key).
nReceiptKey	Unique identifier for a receipt document.
dtReceiptDueBy	Date and time by which a receipt is expected.
nRealName1	Identifier for the first tracked real number field as stored in dta_custom_field_names (foreign key).
rlRealValue1	Value of the first tracked real number field.
nRealName2	Identifier for the second tracked real number field as stored in dta_custom_field_names (foreign key).
rlRealValue2	Value of the second tracked real number field.
nIntName1	Identifier for the first tracked integer field as stored in dta_custom_field_names (foreign key).
nIntValue1	Value of the first tracked integer field.
nIntName2	Identifier for the second tracked integer field as stored in dta_custom_field_names (foreign key).
nIntValue2	Value of the second tracked integer field.
nDateName1	Identifier for the first tracked date field as stored in dta_custom_field_names (foreign key).
dtDateValue1	Value of the first tracked date field.

Table 10-3.   *The Structure of the dta_outdoc_details Table* (continued)

Field	Description
nDateName2	Identifier for the second tracked date field as stored in dta_custom_field_names (foreign key).
dtDateValue2	Value of the second tracked date field.
nStrName1	Identifier for the first tracked string field as stored in dta_custom_field_names (foreign key).
nvcStrValue1	Value of the first tracked string field.
nStrName2	Identifier for the second tracked string field as stored in dta_custom_field_names (foreign key).
nvcStrValue2	Value of the second tracked string field.
nvcCustomSearch	XML-encoded string containing concatenated custom tracked fields.

Table 10-3. *The Structure of the dta_outdoc_details Table* (continued)

dta_interchange_data Table

The dta_interchange_data table contains one record for each interchange processed by BizTalk Messaging, including any response documents returned by calls to the SubmitSync method of the Interchange object. As Figure 10-3 shows, it has a one-to-many relationship with the dta_interchange_details table. Although not shown in Figure 10-3, it also has many-to-one relationships with the dta_blobtype_values and dta_ui_codepage_charset tables. Table 10-4 describes each field in this table.

dta_document_data Table

The dta_document_data table contains one record for each individual document processed by BizTalk Messaging. As Figure 10-3 shows, it has one-to-one relationships with the dta_indoc_details and dta_outdoc_details tables. Although not shown in Figure 10-3, it also has a many-to-one relationship with the dta_blobtype_data table. Table 10-5 describes each field in this table.

dta_routing_details Table

The dta_routing_details table contains a record for each distinct source-destination pair, including organization and application details. As Figure 10-3 shows, it has a one-to-many relationship with the dta_outdoc_details table. Table 10-6 describes each field in this table.

Field	Description
nInterchangeDataKey	Unique interchange identifier (primary key).
nCodePage	The code page used by the interchange, for example, 1252 for ISO-8859-1, 65001 for UTF-8, or −1 if code page information is unavailable.
nIsFile	Possible values are 0 if the document did not come from a file, or 1 if the document was submitted from the file system.
nvcOriginalFileName	The local or network path- and filename, if nIsFile is 1.
nBLOBType	Possible values are 0 for unknown binary type or 1 if the binary object could be loaded into an XML DOM object.
imgInterchangeData	The actual interchange stored as a binary large object.

Table 10-4.   *The Structure of the dta_interchange_data Table*

Field	Description
nDocumentDataKey	Unique document identifier (primary key).
nCodePage	The code page used by the document, for example, 1200 for Unicode, 65000 for UTF-7, or −1 if code page information is unavailable.
nBLOBType	Possible values are 0 for unknown binary type or 1 if the binary object could be loaded into an XML DOM object.
imgDocumentData	The actual document stored as a binary large object.
nNumberOfBytes	The size of the document in bytes.
nNumberOfRecords	The number of records or segments in the document.

Table 10-5.   *The Structure of the dta_document_data Table*

Field	Description
nRoutingKey	Unique identifier for the record (primary key).
nvcSrcOrgName	Name of the source organization in the pair. The value is <OPEN SOURCE> for self-routing documents.
nvcSrcAppName	Name of the source application, if applicable.
nvcDestOrgName	Name of the destination organization in the pair. The value is <OPEN DESTINATION> for self-routing documents.
nvcDestAppName	Name of the destination application, if applicable.
nvcDistributionName	Name of the distribution list used, if applicable.
uidChannelGUID	Unique identifier for the channel as stored in the table bts_channel in the Messaging Management database.
uidPortGUID	Unique identifier for the messaging port as stored in the table bts_port in the Messaging Management database.

Table 10-6.   *The Structure of the dta_routing_details Table*

dta_custom_field_names Table

The dta_custom_field_names table contains a record for each configured tracked field as specified in a document definition or channel. As Figure 10-3 shows, it has a one-to-many relationship with the dta_outdoc_details table. Table 10-7 describes each field in this table.

Field	Description
nNameKey	Unique identifier for the tracked field (primary key).
nvcName	XPath expression representing the path to the field within the document structure.
nDataType	Possible values are 1 for real, 2 for integer, 3 for date, or 4 for text.

Table 10-7.   *The Structure of the dta_custom_field_names Table*

dta_group_details Table

The dta_group_details table contains a record for each functional group encountered in an inbound or outbound interchange. As Figure 10-3 shows, it has a one-to-many relationship with the dta_indoc_details and dta_outdoc_details tables, and a many-to-one relationship with the dta_interchange_details table. This is because an EDI interchange can contain multiple functional groups, and each functional group can contain multiple documents. Although not shown in Figure 10-3, there are also many-to-one relationships with the dta_ack_status_values and dta_direction_values tables. Table 10-8 describes each field in this table.

Field	Description
nGroupKey	Unique identifier for each functional group (primary key).
nInterchangeKey	Identifier for the corresponding parent interchange record in the dta_interchange_details table (foreign key).
dtProcessedTimeStamp	Date and time the record was created.
nvcSyntax	The data format of the interchange, for example, X12.
nvcVersion	The version of the data format, as specified in the functional group header.
nvcRelease	The release number of the data format, if specified.
nvcFunctionalGroupID	Code representing the type of document contained in this functional group.
nvcControlID	Unique control number for this functional group as specified in the functional group header for inbound interchanges, or as set by BizTalk Messaging for outbound interchanges.
nvcSrcAppName	Identifier value for the source organization, as specified in BizTalk Messaging.
nvcDestAppName	Identifier value for the destination organization, as specified in BizTalk Messaging.
nAckStatus	Identifier for receipt status message stored in dta_ack_status_values table (foreign key).

Table 10-8. *The Structure of the dta_group_details Table*

Field	Description
nDirection	Possible values are 1 for inbound documents or 0 for outbound documents.
nDocumentsAccepted	Number of documents from the interchange that were accepted for processing.
nDocumentsRejected	Number of documents from the interchange that were rejected for processing.
nNumberOfBytes	Size of the interchange in bytes.

Table 10-8. *The Structure of the dta_group_details Table* (continued)

dta_debugdoc_data Table

The dta_debugdoc_data table contains a record for each document tracked in the BizTalk Server internal XML format. As Figure 10-3 shows, it has a one-to-one relationship with the dta_indoc_details table, and a one-to-many relationship with the dta_outdoc_details table, because a single inbound document may result in multiple outbound documents. Table 10-9 describes each field in this table.

dta_MIME_data Table

The dta_MIME_data table contains a record for each interchange logged in its original MIME-encoded format. As Figure 10-3 shows, this field has a one-to-one relationship with the dta_interchange_details table, in that the value of the uidSubmissionGUID field in one table can be used to retrieve related data from the other. Table 10-10 describes each field in this table.

Field	Description
nDebugDocKey	Unique identifier for each document (primary key)
ntxtDocumentData	The actual document stored as a Unicode binary large object
nNumberOfBytes	Size of the interchange in bytes
dtProcessedTimeStamp	Date and time the record was created

Table 10-9. *The Structure of the dta_debugdoc_data Table*

Field	Description
nMIMEDataKey	Unique identifier for each MIME-encoded interchange (primary key)
uidSubmissionGUID	Global unique identifier returned on submission of an interchange to BizTalk Messaging
nCodePage	The code page used by the interchange, for example, 1200 for Unicode or 1252 for ASCII
imgMIMEData	The actual interchange stored as a binary large object

Table 10-10. *The Structure of the dta_MIME_data Table*

Supporting Tables

As well as the primary and secondary tables used in document tracking, a number of tables contain other supporting data. Most of these tables contain static data, such as error messages, direction values, or status codes that are used by the Document Tracking client interface. It is not necessary to discuss the structure of these tables in detail, but Table 10-11 describes the main features of each.

Table	Description	Used By
dta_ack_status_values	Contains the status codes used for receipt processing. There are six possible values: None, Pending, Overdue, Accepted, Accepted With Errors, or Rejected.	dta_interchange_details dta_outdoc_details dta_group_details
dta_blobtype_values	Contains the values for the types of binary large objects. There are two possible values: Unknown and XMLDOM Loadable.	dta_interchange_data dta_document_data

Table 10-11. *Supporting Tables Used by Document Tracking*

Table	Description	Used By
dta_data_level_values	Contains the values for the types of receipt and where they should be stored. Possible values are Interchange, Group, Incoming Document, and Outgoing Document.	dta_outdoc_details
dta_direction_values	Contains the values used to specify the direction of interchanges and documents. Possible values are Outgoing and Incoming.	dta_interchange_details dta_group_details
dta_error_message	Contains the messages used to indicate the error encountered by a document or interchange.	dta_interchange_details dta_indoc_details dta_outdoc_details
dta_group_correlation_keys	Contains correlation identifiers that are dynamically generated for functional groups that expect receipts.	
dta_interchange_correlation_keys	Contains correlation identifiers that are dynamically generated for interchanges that expect receipts.	
dt_transport_type_values	Contains the types of transport used for outgoing interchanges.	dta_interchange_details
dta_ui_codepage_charset	Contains the system identifiers for different character sets. These will be used to display document and interchange data in the client interface.	dta_interchange_data dta_document_data

Table 10-11.   *Supporting Tables Used by Document Tracking* (continued)

Table	Description	Used By
dta_ui_user_ queries	Contains the advanced queries that have been created and saved in the client interface.	
dta_validity_ values	Contains the values representing the result of document validation.	dta_indoc_details dta_outdoc_details

Table 10-11. *Supporting Tables Used by Document Tracking* (continued)

Maintaining the Document Tracking Database

As I'm sure is obvious from the last few sections, there is an awful lot of data stored in the document tracking database. Every time a single interchange arrives at BizTalk Server, there could be multiple records inserted into various tables, representing the inbound interchange, the functional groups it contains, the documents each functional group contains, the outgoing documents generated from these, the interchange in which each outgoing document is wrapped, the routing information retrieved, and so on. As a result, even with only the default tracking options enabled, a BizTalk Server installation will generate a huge amount of information. Some of it is valuable, but some of it only serves to enlarge the database and to potentially affect its performance.

When BizTalk Server was originally released, a sample SQL script was provided in the SDK to create two stored procedures to assist in the management of the document tracking database. However, these procedures are mainly provided as unsupported samples, and they don't go nearly far enough to address the complexity of managing a database of this size. It was not until BizTalk Server Service Pack 1 that further utilities for managing the database were provided.

Using the Sample Jobs

There are two stored procedures included with the base BizTalk Server product. The script for generating these procedures can be found at \Program Files\Microsoft BizTalk Server\SDK\Messaging Samples\SQLServerAgentJobs. The first is dta_job_purge_ extra_rows, which ensures that the dta_debugdoc_data table is kept to a maximum of 25,000 rows. It does this by removing the oldest records in the table, according to the value of the dtProcessedTimeStamp field. The second is dta_job_mark_expired_outdocs, which marks any entries in the dta_outdoc_details table where a receipt is expected but the time at which it was expected has passed. It does this by checking the value of the dtReceiptDueBy field against the current time (in GMT format), and setting the value of the nAckStatus field from 1 (pending) to 2 (overdue) if the receipt has not arrived in time.

In addition to the stored procedures, the script also creates SQL Server Agent jobs to run the procedures every 30 minutes. These jobs are called dtaJob_purge_database_ DBName and dtaJob_receipt_monitor_DBName, where DBName is the name of the document tracking database. To install the two stored procedures and their corresponding jobs, follow these steps:

1. From the Start menu, open Programs | Microsoft SQL Server | Query Analyzer.

2. In the Connect To SQL Server dialog box, select your server from the drop-down menu, choose the SQL Server authentication option, and enter the login name and password for the server.

3. In the drop-down menu in the standard toolbar, choose the name of your document tracking database.

4. Choose File | Open, browse to \Program Files\Microsoft BizTalk Server\SDK\ Messaging Samples\SQLServerAgentJobs, and select DTA_SampleJobs.sql.

5. Select Edit | Replace, and in the Replace dialog box, type **%interchangeDTA%** in the Find field, and type the name of your document tracking database in the Replace With field.

6. Click the Replace All button.

7. Select Query | Execute. This will install the stored procedures on the database.

Unfortunately, the dta_job_mark_expired_outdocs stored procedure calls another stored procedure called dta_getgmt_time, which does not exist in the database! Therefore, you will also need to create this stored procedure, which simply returns the current time as GMT. To do this, open Query Analyzer as before, selecting the appropriate database, and type the following into the query window:

```
CREATE PROCEDURE [dbo].[dta_getgmt_time]
@dtGMTTime DATETIME OUTPUT
AS
        DECLARE @mins INT
        EXEC master.dbo.xp_regread 'HKEY_LOCAL_MACHINE',
        'SYSTEM\CurrentControlSet\Control\TimeZoneInformation',
        'ActiveTimeBias', @param = @mins OUTPUT
        SET @dtGMTTime = DATEADD(mi, @mins, GETDATE())
GO
```

Select Query | Execute, and the jobs created to execute the stored procedures will have all they need. By default, the jobs are scheduled to run every 30 minutes, but you can change the frequency at any time through SQL Server Enterprise Manager.

BIZTALK SERVER ADMINISTRATION

Using the Service Pack 1 Jobs

BizTalk Server Service Pack 1 also comes with SQL scripts to create stored procedures on the document tracking database. Again, these need to be installed before they can be used. Not only that, but because the jobs purge records from the active document tracking database and archive them to another database, you will need to create this archive database, create the appropriate schema, and configure it as a SQL linked server.

To Create the Archive Database   You will generally want to keep an archive of the document tracking records you purge from the database using the stored procedures included in BizTalk Server Service Pack 1. If you only wish to purge the original tracking database and do not wish to archive the information, you won't need to complete this task. However, if you do wish to keep an archive, the steps needed to create the archive database that will hold the purged records are as follows:

1. From the Start menu, select Programs | Microsoft SQL Server | Enterprise Manager.
2. Expand the Microsoft SQL Servers, SQL Server Group, and ServerName nodes, where ServerName is the name of your server.
3. Right-click the node for the server on which you want to create the database, and from the context menu, select New | Database.
4. In the Database Properties dialog box, type a name for the database, for example, InterchangeDTA_Archive, and click OK.
5. Open the SQL Server Query Analyzer as before, ensuring that you connect to the SQL Server computer on which you've just created the archive database, and select that database in the drop-down menu in the standard toolbar.
6. Select File | Open, browse to \Program Files\Microsoft BizTalk Server\Setup, and select BTS_Tracking_ArchiveDB_Schema.sql.
7. Select Query | Execute to create the schema.

 Make sure to execute this script on the new blank archive database, not the original tracking database.

To Link the Archive Database to the Tracking Database   After the archive database has been created, it needs to be linked to the original tracking database. This is because the records from the original database will need to be directly inserted into the archive by the stored procedures when they're installed. Again, if you only wish to purge the original tracking database and do not wish to archive the information, you won't need to complete this task. Otherwise, the steps needed to link the databases are as follows:

1. Open SQL Server Query Analyzer if it is not already open.
2. If your archive is on the same SQL Server computer, you can proceed to step 4. Otherwise, choose File | Disconnect, and then File | Connect.

3. In the Connect To SQL Server dialog box, select the server that holds the original tracking database from the drop-down menu, choose the SQL Server Authentication option, and enter the login name and password for the server.

4. In the drop-down menu on the standard toolbar, choose the name of your document tracking database. Note that this should be the original database—not the archive.

5. In the query pane, type the following:

```
EXEC sp_addLinkedServer N'MyRemoteServer', N'SQL Server'
```

where *MyRemoteServer* is the name of the SQL Server computer on which the archive database will reside, and *SQL Server* is a literal value representing the name of the product to which we're linking. (This will always be "SQL Server".)

6. If the authentication information between the two SQL Server computers is different, you should also type the following line:

```
EXEC sp_addLinkedSrvLogin 'MyRemoteServer', 'FALSE', 'sa', 'sa', 'myPass1'
```

where *MyRemoteServer* is again the name of the SQL Server computer on which the archive database will reside, the first *sa* is the name of the administrator account on the local server, the second *sa* is the administrator account on the remote server, and *myPass1* is the password for the administrator account on the remote server.

7. Select Query | Execute to link the database servers.

To Install the Stored Procedures   Even if you chose not to create a linked server containing an archive database, you can still install the stored procedures to purge old records from the tracking database. The steps to do this are as follows:

1. Open SQL Server Query Analyzer if it is not already open, and ensure that you are connected to the server that contains the original tracking database. Also, ensure that the original tracking database is selected in the drop-down menu in the standard toolbar.

2. Select File | Open, browse to \Program Files\Microsoft BizTalk Server\Setup, and select BTS_Tracking_Archive_Purge_Script.sql.

3. Select Edit | Replace, and in the Replace dialog box, type **InterchangeDTA** in the Find field, and type the name of your document tracking database in the Replace With field. Obviously, this step is not required if the name of your tracking database already is InterchangeDTA.

4. Click the Replace All button.

5. Select Query | Execute to install the stored procedures.

The stored procedure that's installed is called dta_purge_old_records, along with a SQL Server Agent job called "Archive and Purge BizTalk Tracking Database: DBName", where DBName is the name of your tracking database. This job is disabled by default. If you wish to use it (and why else would you have come this far?), you'll need to enable it through SQL Server Enterprise Manager and execute it with the appropriate parameters.

To Execute the Archive and Purge Job   The steps to execute the archive and purge job you created in the last task are as follows:

1. In SQL Server Enterprise Manager, expand the Microsoft SQL Servers, SQL Server Group, ServerName, Management, and SQL Server Agent nodes, where ServerName is the name of your server.

2. Click Jobs, and in the details pane, right-click Archive And Purge BizTalk Tracking Database: DBName, and select properties from the context menu.

3. On the Steps tab, select the single step and click Edit.

4. In the Command field, edit the sample procedure call to purge and/or archive the document tracking database as discussed after these steps, and click OK.

5. By default, the job is set up to run at midnight every day. If you want to change this behavior, click the Schedules tab, select the single schedule, and click Edit. In the Edit Job Schedule dialog box, select an option, or click Change to modify the existing recurring schedule.

6. Make any further changes as necessary and click OK.

7. Right-click the job in the details pane, and select Enable Job from the context menu. The job will now execute as scheduled using the parameters specified.

Obviously, it's important to correctly configure the appropriate parameters for this job to avoid purging records without archiving them or removing records within the wrong timeframe. The syntax for the dta_purge_old_records stored procedure is as follows, and the parameters for the procedure are explained in Table 10-12.

```
EXEC dta_purge_old_records nPurgeType, nPurgeValue, nCompleteOnly,
nArchive, nvcArchiveServer, nvcArchiveDB
```

Parameter	Description
nPurgeType	Set this parameter to 1 to purge records by timestamp, or 2 to purge a set number of records.

Table 10-12.   *Parameters for the dta_purge_old_records Stored Procedure*

Parameter	Description
nPurgeValue	If nPurgeType is set to 1, nPurgeValue is the number of hours records must have been in the database before they will be purged. If nPurgeType is set to 2, this is the number of interchanges that should be left in the database after purging.
nCompleteOnly	Set this parameter to 0 to purge interchanges regardless of whether they have finished processing, or 1 to only purge interchanges that are complete.
nArchive	Set this parameter to 0 to purge interchanges without archiving them, or 1 to archive interchanges in the archive database before purging them from the original tracking database.
nvcArchiveServer	Set this optional parameter to the name of the server on which the archive database resides if the nArchive flag is set to 1.
nvcArchiveDB	Set this optional parameter to the name of the archive database if the nArchive flag is set to 1.

Table 10-12. *Parameters for the dta_purge_old_records Stored Procedure* (continued)

Using the Document Tracking Interface

Now that you're armed with the details of the document tracking database schema, the developer in you probably wants to go off and write an application that can retrieve and display all that data. However, BizTalk Server already provides a rich web-based user interface to access the document tracking information. Because it is a web application, document tracking and analysis can be done from a remote machine, even if BizTalk Server isn't installed on that computer. In fact, you can even access BizTalk Document Tracking from Windows 9x, as long as you're running Internet Explorer 5 Service Pack 1 or later.

Running the BizTalk Document Tracking Application

To access the BizTalk Document Tracking application, the document tracking feature must be installed on at least one BizTalk server in your server group. If your server is called BTServer, then you can access the Document Tracking application through http://BTServer/BizTalkTracking/. If this is the first time the web site has been accessed from that machine, you will be asked to install some ActiveX components that allow the site to function. Depending on the operating system you're using, you will be asked to install one or more of the following:

- Microsoft Windows Common Controls
- Microsoft Windows Common Controls 2
- Microsoft Windows Common Dialog
- BizTalk Document Tracking Installation Control

You will also be presented with the following warning, asking you whether it's okay for Internet Explorer to access data on a different domain. Click Yes in this dialog box, and then add http://BTServer/ to the list of trusted sites on the Security tab of the Internet Explorer Options dialog box to prevent the message appearing again.

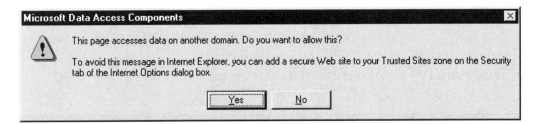

If it occurs to you that having your business data accessible to anyone with a web browser presents a possible security risk, you'll be glad to know that the physical directory (\Program Files\Microsoft BizTalk Server\BizTalkTracking) corresponding to the virtual directory in which the BizTalk Document Tracking interface resides is protected by NTFS permissions, such that only members of the BizTalk Server Report Users group have access. The BizTalk Server Report Users group is created during the installation of BizTalk Server if the Document Tracking feature is selected. By default, the only members of this group are the user who was logged on when BizTalk Server was installed and the local Administrators group.

As a result, if you browse to the Document Tracking site from a remote computer, you will be asked to enter a user name and password. This is submitted using Basic Authentication, so although it will work across a proxy server or firewall, the authentication details will also be sent in clear text (actually Base64 encoded, which is as good as clear text). The best way to protect your data from network sniffers, therefore, is to install a certificate on your web server and only allow users to access it using HTTPS.

Another more dangerous security breach could arise if remote users have direct access to the SQL Server computer on which the document tracking database resides. This is because the user account created to access the document tracking database is a SQL account called dta_ui_login. This account is created during the installation process, and it's given a blank password by default. That's right—a blank password! To correct this oversight, use SQL Server Enterprise Manager to change the password for the user account to something a bit less obvious. To allow the Document Tracking web application to access the database, you will then need to edit the connection string contained in the file \Program Files\Microsoft BizTalk Server\BizTalkTracking\VBScripts\Connection.vb.

Executing Queries

After all the necessary ActiveX controls have been installed, and the security issues have been taken care of, the Document Tracking interface appears, as shown in Figure 10-4. As you can see, you can determine the information you wish to track in a number of areas on the page. After you've chosen your search criteria in these areas, you can click the Query button at the bottom of the window. Each of the different areas is called a *nugget* in the script for the page, so that's how I'll refer to them here. There are six nuggets on the page—Date Range, Source Selection, Destination Selection, Document Type Selection, Sort Control, and Advanced Query—and I'll deal with each one in turn.

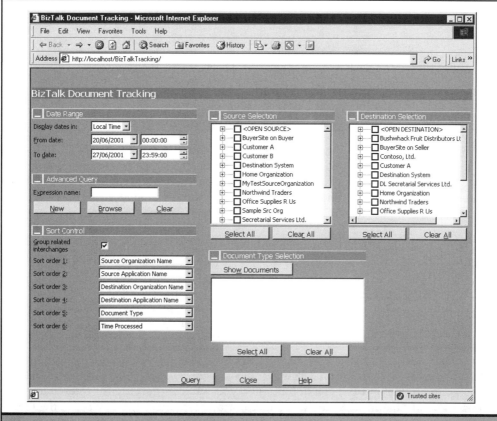

Figure 10-4. *The Document Tracking client interface*

Date Range

First, you can select a range of dates during which the interchanges or documents you seek were processed. In the Date Range nugget, you can choose to display the dates in local time or using the Universal Time Convention (UTC). By default, the date in the From Date field is set to midnight (00:00) seven days before the current date, and the date in the To Date field is set to one minute before midnight (23:59) on the current date. If you wish to change either of the dates, you can type them directly, or click the drop-down arrow to display a calendar control, as shown. Similarly, you can type a new time value directly, or select the hours, minutes, or seconds value, and use the wheel control to adjust the value.

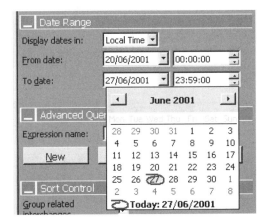

After you have selected the relevant dates, you can click the Query button at the bottom of the window. This will search for all interchanges coming from, or going to, any organization within those dates. This can place a great load on the server, so unless you specifically need to search for different types of interchange within a particular timeframe, you should use the other nuggets to further refine your search.

Source and Destination Selection

To be more specific about the interchanges returned by your query, you should specify source and destination information. In the Source Selection nugget, you can choose those organizations that were configured as the source in a channel or within a self-routing document. Similarly, in the Destination Selection nugget, you can choose those organizations that were configured as the destination of a messaging port or within a self-routing document.

In either case, if you select the Home Organization, you are actually selecting all of the applications of the Home Organization as well. Thus, if you select the Home Organization in the Source Selection nugget, you will be querying for interchanges processed by all channels created from an application. Similarly, if you select the Home Organization in the Destination Selection nugget, you will be querying for interchanges processed by all messaging ports created on an application. To further refine the query, you can expand the Home Organization node and select or clear individual applications, depending on whether they should be included. For example, the following illustration shows that we wish to search for interchanges that originated within our own organization (called Northwind Traders here), but only from the Backoffice CRM System and Messaging System applications, and also interchanges that came from the Office Supplies R Us trading partner organization. Furthermore, we will filter for those interchanges that were sent to the Backoffice ERP System, Purchasing App, or TaxCalc applications within the Home Organization.

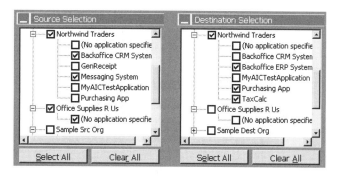

Note *If you create messaging configurations programmatically using the BizTalk Messaging Configuration Object Model as discussed in Chapter 17, you can also create applications under trading partner organizations. If an interchange is processed going from or to any of those applications, the applications will also appear under their parent organizations in the document tracking interface.*

Of course, you can also click the Select All button or Clear All button in either nugget to select all organizations and applications, or none at all. Either way, if you click the Query button at the bottom of the window, you will execute a query for all interchanges that have the selected organizations or applications as source and destination endpoints and that were processed within the timeframe specified in the Date Range nugget.

Note *Although it seems to contradict basic logic, the Select All and Clear All buttons actually have the same effect, because if no organizations or applications are explicitly specified, then interchanges matching all source and destination organizations are returned. The best use of the Select All button is if you have a large number of organizations, and you want to select most but not all of them. It's much easier to select them all first and then clear the ones you don't want. Similarly, use the Clear All button if you have a large number of organizations selected, but you only want a few of them for your next query. Click the Clear All button first to remove the selections.*

Document Type Selection

After you've selected the appropriate date range, and the source and destination for the interchanges in which you are interested, you can click the Show Documents button in the Document Type Selection nugget, to show the documents that satisfy those criteria. Of course, there may be interchanges containing different types of document traveling between those organizations, and you may only be interested in a subset of them. Using the SHIFT and CTRL keys, you can choose contiguous or noncontiguous subsets of those documents as shown, before executing the final query.

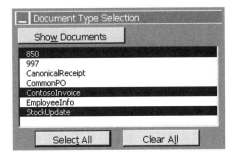

As with the Source Selection and Destination Selection nuggets, selecting no documents has the same effect as selecting all of them.

Sort Control

When you execute a query by clicking the Query button at the bottom of the Document Tracking window, you may receive a larger set of results than you expected. To make it easier to find the interchanges in which you are interested, you can choose a number of sort keys in the Sort Control nugget, as shown.

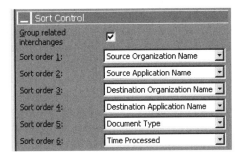

The first thing to do is select the Group Related Interchanges check box. This ensures that outgoing interchanges are listed immediately after the incoming interchanges to which they are related. Most of the time, you will want to see both the incoming and outgoing interchanges together in the Query Results window, but clear this check box if you don't. Below that check box, there are six drop-down menus in which you can select sort keys to determine how the interchanges should be listed. The available options choices are Source Organization Name, Source Application Name, Destination Organization Name, Destination Application Name, Document Type, and Time Processed.

Constructing Advanced Queries

As illustrated, the Advanced Query nugget in the upper left of the BizTalk Document Tracking window allows you to select interchanges containing documents for which individual fields have been tracked. The advanced queries can combine different criteria using Boolean operators, and the queries can be saved for later use. The queries are saved in the dta_ui_user_queries table.

Creating New Queries

To create a new advanced query, click the New button in the Advanced Query nugget. This will open the Advanced Query Builder window, which is shown in Figure 10-5. In this window, you can select the criteria for your advanced search.

First, select a tracked field from the Source Selection drop-down menu. This contains a list of all the tracked fields stored in the dta_outdoc_details table. Each field is associated with a data type because of the way document fields are tracked. You can then select an operator in the Operators drop-down menu. The available operators are less than (<), greater than (>), equal to (=), and not equal to (!=). Depending on the data type of the tracked field, the Value field in the window will be either a simple text box (for integer, real, and string data types), or a control in which you can select a date and time (for date data types). Type or select the value that the field should be compared with.

If you chose to track fields using the Custom option—in either a document definition or channel in BizTalk Messaging Manager—those fields are stored as XML in the nvcCustomSearch field in the dta_outdoc_details table. To search for values in those fields, you should select the <CustomSearch> option in the drop-down menu. The Operators drop-down menu is then redrawn with two options—Contains and Does Not Contain. Select the appropriate operator, and type the value you're searching for in the Value text box.

Note *If you have not configured any tracked fields in BizTalk Messaging Manager, only the <CustomSearch> option will be available. However, because no fields were tracked, this query will return no results.*

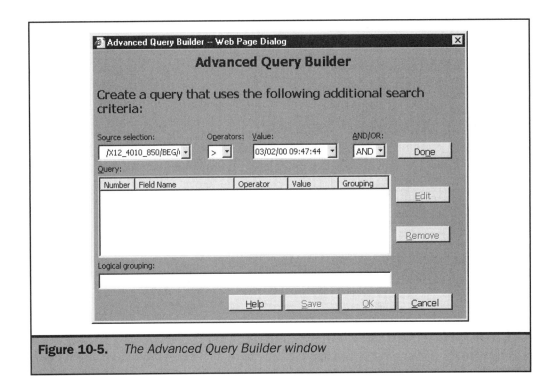

Figure 10-5. *The Advanced Query Builder window*

After you've entered the details for your search criterion, you can combine it with further search clauses. To do this, select a Boolean operator from the AND/OR drop-down list. As you can probably guess, this decides whether both conditions will need to be true, or if only one condition need be satisfied. When you have selected an operator, click the Done button. This will cause the criterion to appear in the Query field underneath, and the Done button to change into a New button. Click New to add the next condition to the expression. Obviously, if your expression will only contain a single expression, it doesn't matter which Boolean operator you pick—just click Done to finish.

If you combine criteria using different Boolean operators, the interface will automatically group them for you. For example, if you entered condition number 1 with the Boolean operator set to OR, and then entered condition number 2 with the Boolean operator set to AND, and then entered condition number 3 with any value for the Boolean operator, the expression would appear in the Logical grouping field as "(1 OR 2) AND 3" as shown, meaning that condition 3 must be satisfied, but satisfying either condition 1 or condition 2 will do.

Number	Field Name	Value	Grouping
1	/X12_4010_850/PO1Loop1/PO1/@PO102 (Integer)	99	OR
2	/X12_4010_850/BEG/@BEG01 (String)	00	AND
3	/X12_4010_850/BEG/@BEG05 (Date)	3/2/2000...	AND

Logical grouping:

(1 OR 2) AND 3

Using Saved Queries

If this all sounds like hard work, you'll be glad to hear that you can save the complete expressions after you've added all the appropriate criteria. Just click the Save button, and you will be asked to enter a name for the expression. Click OK and then click OK in the Advanced Query Builder window to return to the main interface. The name you entered for the expression will appear in the Expression Name field in the Advanced Query area. If you need to call up another saved expression, click the Browse button. This will bring up the Advanced Queries window, as shown next, containing a list of expressions from which to choose. You can also click the Edit button to redefine an expression or the Delete button to delete it.

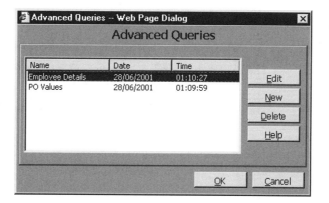

Once an expression has been either retrieved or created in the Advanced Queries nugget, it can be combined with the selection criteria specified in the other nuggets to further refine your search. When you click the Query button, the results will be displayed in the Query Results window.

Examining Query Results

After you have selected the criteria for your query and applied the appropriate filters to refine the search, clicking the Query button opens the Query Results window, as shown in Figure 10-6. This window shows the list of interchanges that matched the query parameters. For each interchange there is also a plus button located to the left of the interchange records. Clicking this expands the interchange record to show the documents contained.

Examining Interchange Data

For each interchange there is a set of properties displayed, as described in Table 10-13.

Property	Description
Data	Clicking the icon shows the raw interchange data.
Schedule	Clicking the icon shows the XLANG schedule information.
Direction	Incoming or outgoing.
Error	The text of any errors that were encountered.
Source Organization	The source organization specified for the interchange.
Source Application	The source application specified for the interchange.
Destination Organization	The destination organization specified for the interchange.
Destination Application	The destination application specified for the interchange.
Document Type	The type of document contained in the interchange or <Multiple> if there are many different types.
Document Count	The number of documents contained in the interchange.
Control ID	The interchange identifier. This is a positive integer for EDI interchanges or a UUID for reliable interchanges.

Table 10-13. *Query Results Properties for Interchanges*

Property	Description
Receipt Status	The status of any accompanying receipts.
Time Processed	The date and time the interchange record was created.
Time Sent	The date and time the outgoing interchange was transmitted.
Source ID Qualifier	The identifier qualifier for the source organization.
Source Identifier	The identifier value for the source organization.
Destination ID Qualifier	The identifier qualifier for the destination organization.
Destination Identifier	The identifier value for the destination organization.

Table 10-13.   *Query Results Properties for Interchanges* (continued)

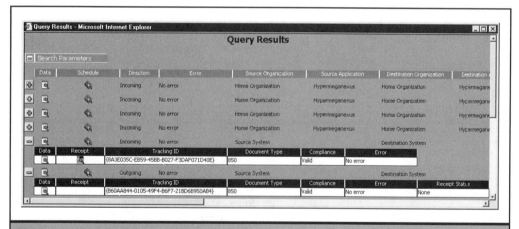

Figure 10-6.   *The Query Results window*

If you click the data icon for an interchange, the View Interchange Data window appears, containing the interchange, as shown next. This window has a Save As button, so that you can save the interchange data to a file if required.

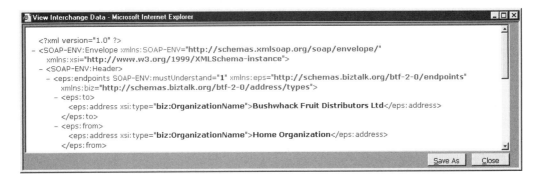

If you click the schedule icon for an interchange, the View XLANG Schedule Summary window appears, containing data for related XLANG schedules, as shown. This data is only available using the WorkFlowAuditClient application that will be discussed later in this chapter.

Event Name	Attribute Name	Attribute Value
OnBTASinkEnter	ActionTag	Receive Purchase Request
OnBTASinkEnter	ShapeId	0!5
OnBTASinkEnter	PortId	ReceivePR
OnBTASinkEnter	MsgType	ElementType_purchaseRequest
OnBTAMSMQReceive	PortId	ReceivePR
OnBTAMSMQReceive	ChannelId	ReceivePR;QN:bts://&ReceivePR&.\private$\ReceivePR{455D48EB-84ED-41BA-8123-8A0F7217B1A3}
OnBTAMSMQReceive	CorrelationId	{C2EDF5C2-5C1E-41E4-B4A0-A30357FABC8A}-00000000
OnBTAMSMQReceive	MsgType	ElementType_purchaseRequest
OnBTAMSMQReceive	MsgId	purchaseRequest
OnBTASinkLeave	ActionTag	Receive Purchase Request
OnBTASinkLeave	ShapeId	0!5
OnBTASinkLeave	PortId	ReceivePR
OnBTASourceEnter	ActionTag	Approve Purchase Request

Examining Document Data

As shown in Figure 10-6, if you click the plus button beside an interchange, the record will expand to show the documents contained. For each document within the interchange, there is a set of properties displayed, as described in Table 10-14.

Property	Description
Data	Clicking this icon shows the document data.
Receipt	Clicking this icon shows the related receipt interchange in a separate Query Results window.
TrackingID	The unique identifier for the document.
DocumentType	The type of document, such as 850 or PurchaseOrder. Note that this is the name of the root element of an XML document, not the name of the document definition.
Compliance	Valid, Not Valid, or Pass Through.
Error	The text of any errors that were encountered.
Receipt Status*	The status of any receipts that have yet to arrive.
Real 1*, Real 2*	The values of the two fields tracked as real numbers.
Integer 1*, Integer 2*	The values of the two fields tracked as integers.
Date 1*, Date 2*	The values of the two fields tracked as dates.
String 1*, String 2*	The values of the two fields tracked as strings.
Custom Search*	Clicking this icon shows the custom fields tracked for this document.

* This property only appears for outgoing documents.

Table 10-14. *Query Results Properties for Documents*

If you click the data icon for a document, the View Document Instance Data window appears, containing the document, as shown next. There are two possible views for the document—native view and XML view. However, if you have left the document logging options at their defaults when configuring the corresponding channel in BizTalk Messaging Manager, only the native format will be available. In this window, there is also a Save As button, so that you can save the document data to a file if required.

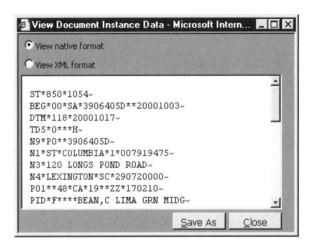

If you click the custom search icon for a document, the View Custom Search Field Data window appears, containing the data for which you searched. This is the value of the nvcCustomSearch field in the dta_outdoc_details table. As the illustration shows, the custom search data is XML encoded, even if the incoming and outgoing data formats are not XML. This window also has a Save As button, so that you can save the document data to a file if required.

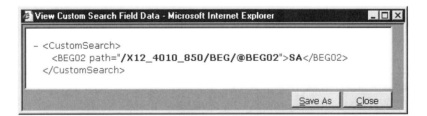

Displaying Orchestration Data

The final set of information that can be tracked for a workflow is data related to the execution of an XLANG schedule. However, this data is not persisted by default, and the sample application provided to log the data is provided more as an example of what can be done, rather than a complete solution, so I'll only cover it briefly here.

Installing the WorkFlowAudit Application

Under \Program Files\Microsoft BizTalk Server\SDK\XLANG Samples\
WorkFlowAudit\Bin, you will find WorkFlowAudit.dll. This is the application that
needs to be installed to enable XLANG schedule data to be persisted to the document
tracking database. Use regsvr32.exe to register the DLL, and install the application. The
application subscribes to XLANG schedule events, and it has two methods—Install and
Uninstall. The Install method installs the subscription into the COM+ catalog. This
allows a client application to trap XLANG schedule events. The parameters of the
Install method are listed in Table 10-15. The Uninstall method is called to remove the
subscription from the COM+ catalog and should be called before any client application
exits to prevent an orphaned subscription from hanging around in memory.

Running the WorkFlowAuditClient Application

With the DLL installed, it is possible to subscribe to XLANG schedule events and to
persist them to the document tracking database. There are two tables provided in the
database for this purpose: dta_wf_workflow_event and dta_wf_eventdata. For each
event trapped by a client application, a record is created in dta_wf_workflow_event,
and one or more records pertaining to the properties of each event are created in
dta_wf_eventdata. These are the tables queried by the Document Tracking application
when a schedule icon is clicked for an interchange in the Query Results window.

The BizTalk Server SDK also contains a sample client application to demonstrate
how the DLL can trap events for running XLANG schedules. This sample is located at
\Program Files\Microsoft BizTalk Server\SDK\XLANG Samples\WorkFlowAuditClient

Parameter	Description
ServerName	The name of the server on which the tracking database resides.
DBName	The name of the tracking database.
UserName	The user name required to access the tracking database.
Password	The password required to access the tracking database.
ApplicationFilter	The name of the COM+ application into which to install the subscription. This parameter is optional.
EventFilter	The types of event to trap. This parameter is optional and defaults to a value of egAllEvents.

Table 10-15. *The Parameters of the Install Method*

and is called WorkflowAuditClient.exe. Double-click this file to execute the client application, which will appear as shown here.

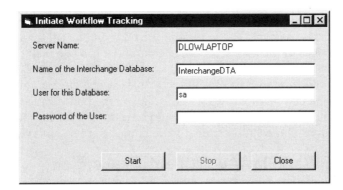

As you can see, it's a simple Visual Basic form that uses the BizTalk WMI provider to populate fields with the names of the document tracking server, database, and user name. To run the application, enter the password for the document tracking database, and click Start. While the application is running, any XLANG events that occur will be logged to the document tracking database. Obviously, it's not really workable to have an interactive application running on a server, so in a production environment, you could edit the client application (with the source code provided) to connect to the database and start trapping events automatically. The application could then be installed as a noninteractive service on Windows 2000, running silently in the background.

As shown earlier in the chapter, while the client application is running, any XLANG schedule events that fire will be stored in the database. Clicking the schedule icon for an interchange in the Query Results window in BizTalk Document Tracking will show the trapped data in the View Interchange Data window.

Chapter 11

Troubleshooting BizTalk Server

461

This chapter presents one of the most challenging aspects of mastering BizTalk Server 2000. Troubleshooting requires a thorough understanding of how and why BizTalk Server operates as it does. We will look at the most common areas that cause problems when using BizTalk Server. We will also concentrate on ways to make these problems manageable or even preventable.

BizTalk Server not only is a very complex product in its own right, but it also contains many technologies and processes that are significant enough to be valid stand-alone products. Specifically, BizTalk Server's dual personalities of Messaging and Orchestration present very different challenges to the professional trying to make everything run smoothly. Given the need to install the product and keep it running, the task of maintaining a stable system seems daunting.

Unfortunately, BizTalk Server's troubleshooting tools are a bit primitive in this first release. It is usually necessary to look in two or more places to gather all of the information necessary to diagnose a problem in BizTalk Server. The BizTalk Server SDK is a valuable addition to your toolkit. While technically not part of the product, the tools and samples in the SDK provide critical insights into BizTalk Server.

Scared yet? Don't be. The reality is that BizTalk Server's learning curve is steep but short. While many of the concepts associated with BizTalk Server are new to most people, there aren't that many of them. Once you master a few basic debugging skills, solving problems with these components is simple. More good news is that, based on the first months of the product's life, BizTalk Server seems to be a very stable piece of software. Therefore, you won't spend a lot of time chasing minor glitches that make your system crash and that then disappear for no apparent reason.

This chapter will take a process-by-process approach to troubleshooting. We will examine each of the major areas of the product: Messaging, Orchestration, Installation, and Operations Support. Within each of these areas we will examine the processes that go on and what can cause them to fail. We will also examine the tools that are available to help us diagnose and correct problems as we encounter them.

Troubleshooting Messaging

BizTalk Messaging contains many elements that must work in unison to move and transform information. We are going to examine the tools used to explore messaging problems. We will walk through the messaging pipeline to examine what problems look like at each stage of processing and to see how best to collect the information necessary to correct these problems. A priority will be to identify problem areas that can be avoided through proper planning.

Debugging Tools

As noted before, the tools used to diagnose problems with BizTalk Messaging are still underdeveloped. The key tools we will be using are the BizTalk Server Administration console and the Windows 2000 Application Event Log. In general, we will look in the

BizTalk Server Administration console to determine which interchanges have failed and why. Unfortunately, the messages generated are very vague in most cases. Next we will dig into the Event Log to find the details of the problem. We will also look at how we can use the Document Tracking database as a debugging tool. The BizTalk Server SDK, which is installed with the BizTalk Server product, will provide some useful tools as well.

BizTalk Server Administration

Chapter 9 presented a detailed walk-through of the BizTalk Server Administration console. In this chapter, we will concentrate on using this application to debug problems that occur during the processing of documents.

The first task is to successfully start BizTalk Server Administration. During installation, a Windows 2000 group is created for BizTalk Server Administration. By default, this group is named BizTalk Server Administrators. To use BizTalk Server Administration, the user must be a member of this group. In addition, the console must be configured with the proper credentials to connect to the BizTalk Management Database. If the password used to connect to this database changes, the console will need to be updated by right-clicking the BizTalk Server 2000 node of the console tree and selecting Properties to display the dialog box shown in Figure 11-1.

The BizTalk Server Administration console contains three types of information. The first section, Queues, provides a window into the queue database shared by all BizTalk Servers in the server group. This gives the user a quick overview of the processing that

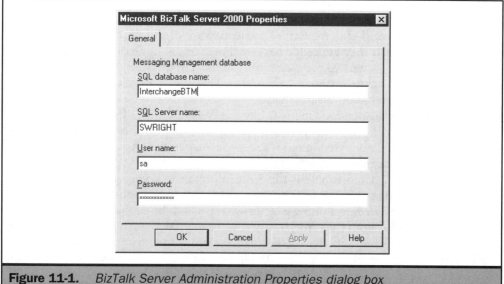

Figure 11-1.   *BizTalk Server Administration Properties dialog box*

is currently happening (or not happening) in the group. For troubleshooting purposes, the most important queues are the Retry and Suspended queues.

The Retry Queue contains documents that, for some reason, were not successfully delivered to their final destination. The fact that they are in the Retry Queue indicates that BizTalk Server plans to retry the action that failed before. The most common reasons for a document to be in the Retry Queue are a connectivity problem or the failure of an Application Integration Component (AIC). It is also possible for documents to reside in the Retry Queue when they are awaiting a receipt. This occurs when using Reliable Messaging with the BizTalk Framework.

If the document is to be delivered via SMTP, the mail server was most likely down. If the document is to be delivered via HTTPS, the web server may not have responded or may have been unreachable from the BizTalk Server. File and queued deliveries commonly fail because the destination was not available from the system that attempted to complete the delivery. It is important to remember that delivery may be attempted from any server in the server group. If you are running multiple servers, they must all be able to access the delivery location. Another common reason for file deliveries to fail is a permission problem. The BizTalk Server service must have rights to create a file in the directory to which your document is being delivered. MSMQ deliveries also fail for security reasons. The BizTalk Server service must have the right to send messages over the queue to which the document is being delivered. In any of these cases, the best place to look for diagnostic information is in the Event Log.

For a more detailed discussion of the security requirements associated with BizTalk Server, refer to Chapter 14.

BizTalk Server considers a user-defined Application Integration Component (AIC) to be just another type of transport protocol like HTTP or SMTP. If the component returns an exception, BizTalk Server interprets this as a failure to deliver the document. Therefore, the document is forwarded to the Retry Queue. Beware of situations where your AIC is updating a database. It may get called several times for the same document if your AIC throws an exception. Defensive programming is a must in this case. Encapsulating your database changes in a transaction is a good idea. This allows the changes to be cleanly rolled back before later attempts are made.

BizTalk Server's Suspended Queue is like the Postal Service's Dead Letter Office. This is where BizTalk Server documents go when BizTalk Server can no longer handle them automatically. Once a document reaches the Suspended Queue, we can retrieve error information, the interchange identifier, and even the contents of the document, as shown in Figure 11-2. Unfortunately, the error information is very generic in most cases. A common error message is "The server is unable to continue parsing this data." This isn't very useful in determining exactly what caused the problem. To find the detailed information about the error, it is necessary to view the Application Event Log. We will examine this tool shortly. The key to correlating an entry in the Suspended Queue with an entry in the Event Log is the Interchange ID that is listed to the extreme right of the Suspended Queue list. This ID will appear in the Event Log entry associated with this error.

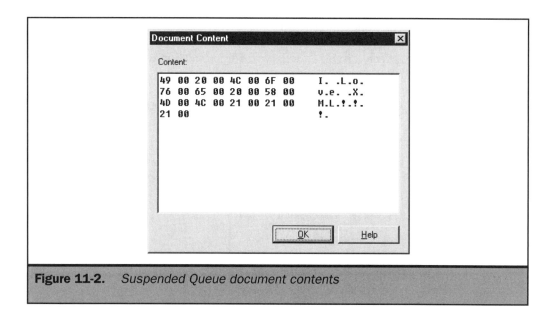

Figure 11-2.   *Suspended Queue document contents*

The next section of the BizTalk Server Administration console is for receive functions. In addition to defining receive functions, you can also check on their status. When there is a problem with a receive function that BizTalk Server cannot correct, BizTalk Server quietly disables it. Typical problems would include invalid permissions, user rights assignments, and invalid paths or queue names. When this occurs, the receive function is shown in BizTalk Server Administration with a red X through it, as in the following illustration. The cause of the problem is logged in the Event Log.

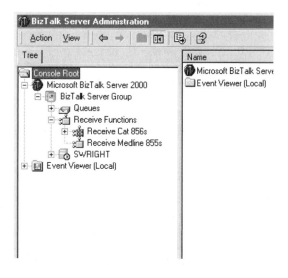

The last part of the BizTalk Server Administration console is a listing of the servers in the server group and their statuses. Just as in the case of receive functions, when a server has failed, it is reflected in BizTalk Server Administration with a red square on the server's icon, as shown next.

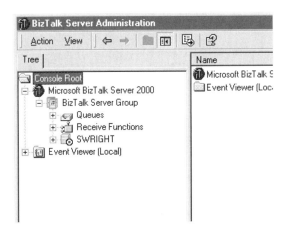

When problems occur in BizTalk Messaging, BizTalk Server Administration is generally the place to start gathering information. As we will see shortly, the Windows 2000 Application Event Log is usually stop 2 on our troubleshooting trip.

Event Logs

Windows 2000 contains event logs that capture system events. These logs are broken out by the type of event. BizTalk Server's events are captured in the Application Log. The Event Viewer is used to examine these logs. This is an MMC snap-in like BizTalk Server Administration. In fact, the BizTalk Server Administration console contains the Event Viewer by default, as shown in Figure 11-3.

Initially, the Application Log is shown in its entirety with the most recent entry first. By selecting View | Filter, you can filter the displayed list of events without affecting the log itself. Figure 11-4 illustrates how to filter for only BizTalk Server–related events. This is useful on production systems where the Application Log may become quite long.

Once the event of interest has been located in the log, detailed information is available by right-clicking the event and selecting Properties. The resulting dialog box, shown in Figure 11-5, gives more detail about the cause of the problem. The Event Log is a much better source of detailed diagnostic information than BizTalk Server Administration in most cases.

Document Tracking

In Chapter 10, we examined the document tracking capabilities of BizTalk Server. The Document Tracking application included in BizTalk Server is also useful for troubleshooting. This tool is the only place where documents can be viewed in all of the forms they take as BizTalk Server transforms them. Before attempting to use Document Tracking for

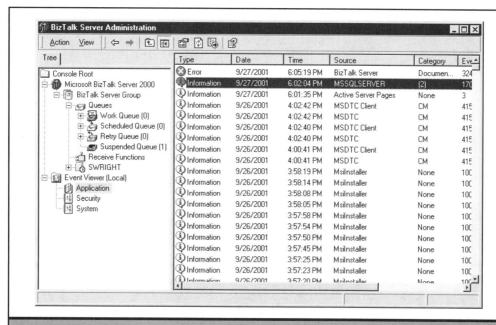

Figure 11-3.   *Event Viewer—Application Log*

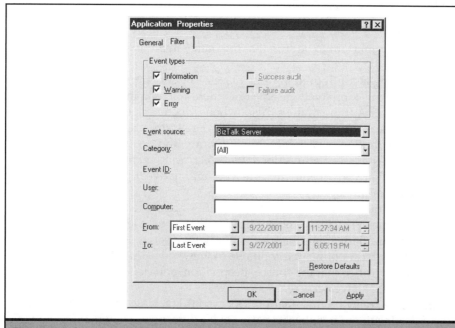

Figure 11-4.   *Event Viewer—Filter tab*

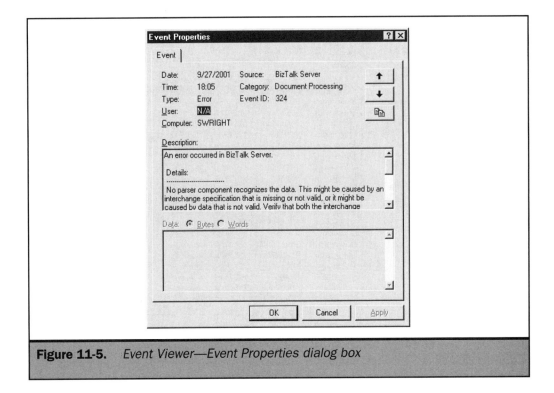

Figure 11-5. *Event Viewer—Event Properties dialog box*

troubleshooting, it is important to be sure that the data you are interested in is going to be logged to the database.

Document Tracking is configured in three places. The server group configuration contains settings that can completely disable document tracking in the group. These are set in BizTalk Server Administration. Also, when a document definition is created, individual fields can be marked for tracking. Last, and most important, each channel definition allows the tracking of each inbound and outbound document in its native form, its XML form, neither, or both. A document's *native form* refers to its appearance in its unparsed state. For XML documents, the XML and native forms are the same, so there is no reason to capture both.

Once Document Tracking captures documents, they are made available through the BizTalk Server Document Tracking web application that is installed as part of BizTalk Server. This web application allows the user to query for a set of documents and view their contents. For troubleshooting, it is valuable to view the listing of documents, as shown in Figure 11-6. Notice that the source, destination, and document type are listed, as well as any errors that have occurred.

Having located the relevant document in Document Tracking, we can now view the contents of the document in either its native or XML form, as shown in Figure 11-7.

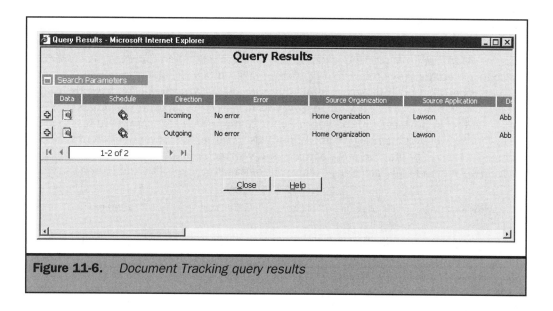

Figure 11-6. *Document Tracking query results*

Most of the formatting problems associated with EDI and flat-file documents will be apparent at this point. Also, mapping errors are easily diagnosed using this technique because you can retrieve the precise XML that was output from the map.

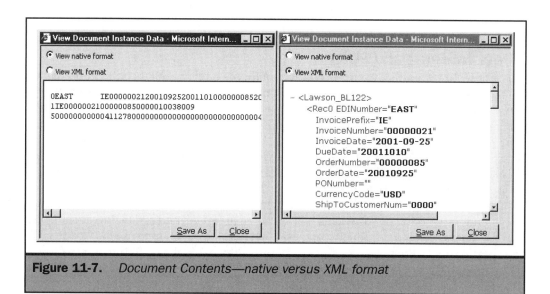

Figure 11-7. *Document Contents—native versus XML format*

Map Test (SDK)

The SDK contains a useful tool for testing maps. This tool is in the SDK\Messaging Samples\MapTest directory under the BizTalk Server installation directory. The program is a script called MapDocument.vbs. This script takes an XML instance document, maps it using a compiled BizTalk Server map, and outputs the XML resulting from the map. There are advantages to using Map Test over using the Test Map option from the BizTalk Mapper. Most important, you can specify a much more realistic example to test than the instance generated internally by the Editor. Also, you can test several different varieties of instances to verify that the map is functioning correctly in all cases.

Map Test is a Visual Basic script that is invoked using the following command line:

```
cscript /nologo MapDocument.vbs Instance.xml Map.xsl Schema.xml
```

MapDocument.vbs contains the logic for Test Map. Instance.xml contains an XML instance to be transformed. Map.xsl is an XSL stylesheet created by the BizTalk Mapper. To get the XSL from a compiled BizTalk map, select File | Save Compiled Map As in the BizTalk Mapper. The Schema.xml file is an optional parameter that is used to allow Map Test to validate the input file prior to transforming it.

The Map Test utility has advantages over setting up a test channel in BizTalk Server to test realistic input documents. One obvious advantage is that it does not require a BizTalk Server. Map Test only depends on the presence of the Microsoft XML Parser library. Note that any documents processed in this way do not appear in the Document Tracking database because they did not pass through BizTalk Server. The disadvantage is that Map Test can only transform XML instances, not EDI or flat files. To use Map Test for these schema types, use the Validate Instance option of the BizTalk Editor, described later, to convert the data into its XML form.

Direct Integration (SDK)

The SDK includes another troubleshooting tool for messaging with the rather odd name, Direct Integration. This tool provides a graphical front-end on the Interchange.Submit( ) call, as shown in Figure 11-8. It allows the user to specify all of the parameters for the call and then submit a document synchronously or asynchronously. Direct Integration is provided in the SDK\Messaging Samples\DirectIntegration\EXE directory under the BizTalk Server installation directory. As with almost all SDK tools, the source code (Visual Basic, in this case) is provided. This can be helpful in understanding how to properly use the Submit call.

Direct Integration is excellent for testing completed channels. During testing, it is also useful for working out problems with parsing, mapping, and serializing documents. When a channel sends a document to a messaging port that is set up to use the "loopback" transport protocol, the output document is immediately displayed to the user. Note that you should use the Submit Sync button to submit the document synchronously in this case. In cases where loopback ports are not used, the document is still available in the Document Tracking database.

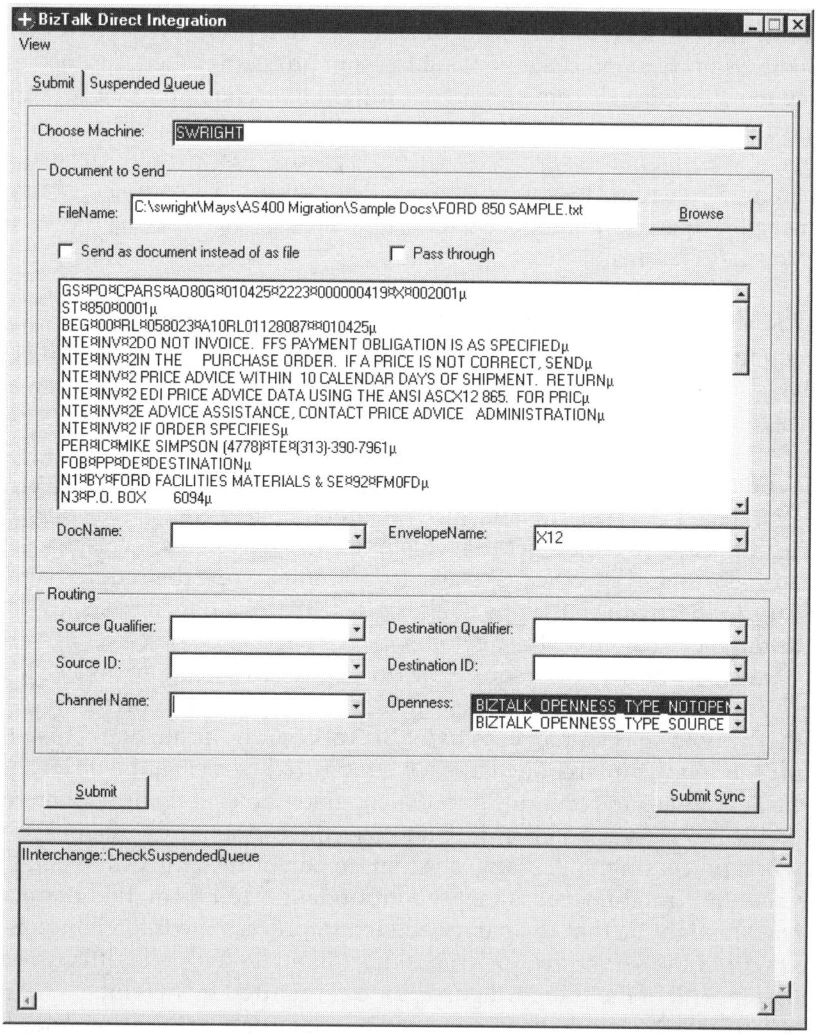

Figure 11-8. *Direct Integration SDK tool*

Document Submission

Submitting a document to BizTalk Server is not a trivial endeavor. Fortunately, there is only one interface to understand. This is the Interchange.Submit call, which we have seen before, and its synchronous version, SubmitSync. All documents are submitted to BizTalk Server using one of these two calls. Even BizTalk Server receive functions use the Submit call under the covers to submit documents to BizTalk Server. We will now examine how BizTalk Server accepts documents and determines what to do with them. This will help us understand document submission problems when they occur.

The key to submitting documents successfully is to understand that BizTalk Server needs to be able to select a set of channels that will process the submitted interchange. Notice that while we submit an *interchange*, channels process *documents*. A single interchange may contain many documents of various types. The process of selecting channels consists of selecting a parser, extracting individual documents, and then routing those documents to the appropriate channel(s).

Parser Selection and Envelopes

The first step in processing an interchange is to determine which parser will be used to convert the inbound interchange into a sequence of documents in XML form. There are two options for making this selection.

The simplest way to select a parser is to specify an envelope in the Submit call. The envelope type indicates which parser will be used. If the parser specified does not recognize the data, then parsing fails and the interchange goes into the Suspended Queue. It is important to remember that Custom XML, flat-file, and Custom parser envelopes use document specifications as part of the envelope definition. For flat files, it is necessary to specify the envelope at all times so that the flat-file parser knows how to parse the flat file. Custom XML envelopes do not need to be specified in most cases. Custom parsers may or may not require the document specification, depending on the implementation of the parser. Envelopes are also discussed in Chapter 6.

The other way to select a parser is to let BizTalk Server locate one. This process involves presenting the interchange to each configured parser in the order they are listed in the Server Group configuration. Each parser looks at the interchange and indicates to BizTalk Server whether it recognizes the format of the data. A common problem when processing interchanges is that no parser recognizes the data. An obvious reason this might occur is that the input data is not formatted correctly. Another reason might be that the parser needed to process the interchange is not configured within the server group. This is most likely to happen with custom parser components since all of the standard parsers are configured by default.

It is also possible that more than one parser might recognize the same data. The parser is not required to parse the entire interchange before accepting it. Typically, the parser looks for key elements such as the ISA header in an X12 interchange or the root element in an XML document. Once the key elements are found, the parser informs BizTalk Server that it recognizes the interchange. Parsing may fail later if the interchange was incorrectly identified. For example, the format of an interchange used with a custom parser might resemble a standard EDI format enough to confuse the EDI parser. In this case, whichever parser is listed first would accept the interchange. If this is a possibility, be sure to list the correct parser first, remove unused parsers, or specify an envelope to select the correct parser.

Because parsers are scanned in order, there is a slight performance gain to be had by arranging parsers according to their frequency of use in your environment and by removing unused parsers.

Routing Documents

Once an interchange has been parsed, it is decomposed, by the parser, into one or more individual XML documents. When the document is processed, it is presented to one or more channels. The routing of documents to a channel is based on several factors. These factors are the openness, source, destination, and document definition associated with the channel and the document.

The openness of a channel or messaging port refers to its ability to receive from multiple source organizations or to send to multiple destinations. An Open Source channel can accept documents of a certain type from any valid source organization. An Open Destination port can deliver documents to any valid destination organization. Note that Open Source and Destination submissions must contain enough information in the document or the Submit( ) call to identify the missing information, or the document will fail to process. In the case of Open Destination documents, the destination transport protocol and address must also be specified. The final option for openness is Not Open. In this case, the channel must contain a source organization, and the messaging port must contain the destination information.

To select the correct source and destination organization, BizTalk Server gathers information from both the Submit call and the interchange envelope. The most common cause of problems in this area is specifying an incorrect qualifier. Each organization may be identified by different identifiers depending on the trading partner being accessed. These identifiers consist of an identifier qualifier and an identifier value. In EDI documents, identifier qualifiers are generally 2-character values. Figure 11-9 illustrates the fields in these envelopes that must match the source and destination in order for a document to be routed properly.

The final step in routing a document to the proper channels is to identify the document definition associated with the inbound document. Don't confuse "document definition" with "document specification." Remember, a document *specification* is an XDR schema that defines the structure of a document. A document *definition* identifies a class of documents within BizTalk Messaging. The document definition may reference a document specification, but it also includes other information. Specifically, it may contain custom document tracking instructions and additional selection criteria. For XML documents, the document specification can be used to identify a document based on its root tag. For EDI documents, the selection criteria are required to identify an incoming document's correct document definition, as shown in Figure 11-10 and Figure 11-11.

Setting the selection criteria on EDI document definitions serves two purposes. For routing, the select criteria allow BizTalk Server to select the proper channels for document processing based on the values in the envelope. When outputting EDI documents, the selection criteria become part of the envelope, as shown in Figure 11-12.

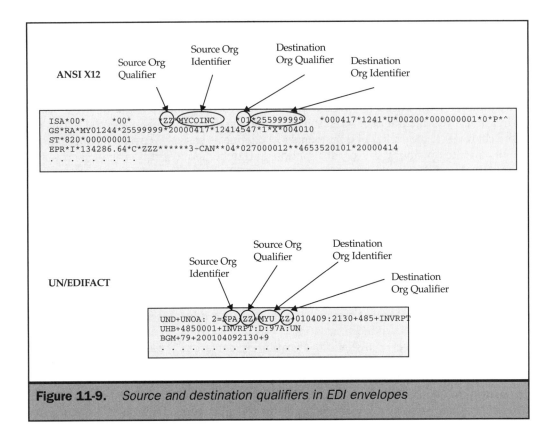

Figure 11-9. *Source and destination qualifiers in EDI envelopes*

Receive Functions

BizTalk Server receive functions serve as an automated interchange-submission mechanism. This allows the mundane task of waiting for documents to appear in a file directory or on a Messaging Queue to be handled in a reliable manner. A receive function is simply a wrapper on the Interchange.Submit( ) method call that is used when submitting any document to BizTalk Server.

Receive functions are configured using the Windows Management Instrumentation (WMI) interface or BizTalk Server Administration console. Setting up receive functions is fairly straightforward, except when using a custom preprocessor component. Custom preprocessors are implemented using the IBTSCustomProcess interface. A preprocessor component allows the developer to transform the inbound interchange prior to its submission to BizTalk Server. The most common reason for doing this is when incoming interchanges contain embedded characters, headers, or footers that are not recognized by BizTalk Server and, therefore, need to be removed. In BizTalk Server Administration, when configuring the receive function, the administrator can select a preprocessor

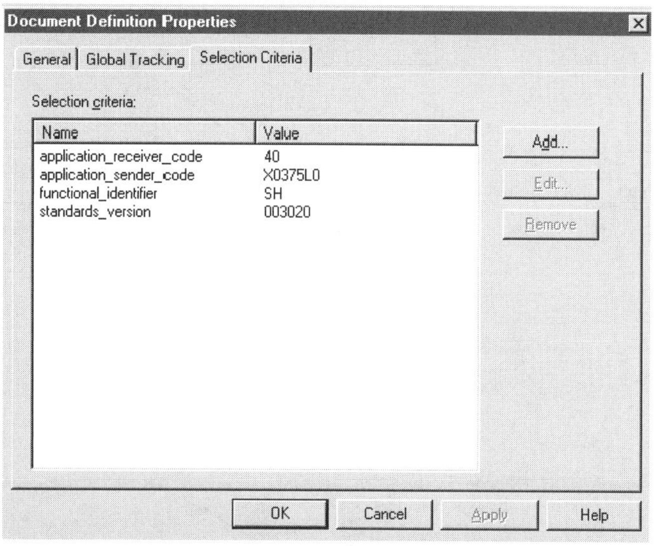

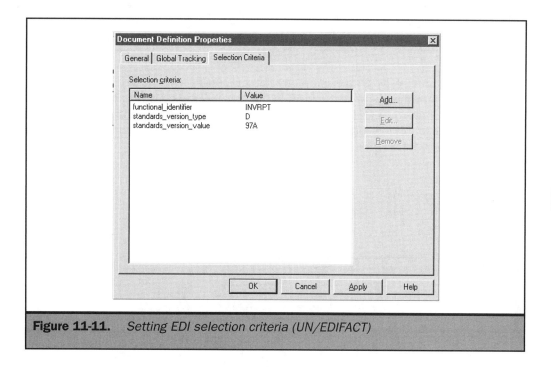

Figure 11-10.   *Setting EDI selection criteria (ANSI X12)*

Figure 11-11.   *Setting EDI selection criteria (UN/EDIFACT)*

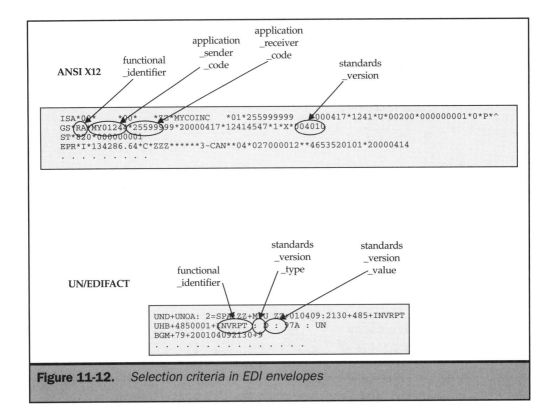

Figure 11-12. *Selection criteria in EDI envelopes*

component. Unfortunately, simply compiling the component with the IBTSCustomProcess interface is not sufficient to make it appear in this list. You must also register the affinity of the DLL as a preprocessor component by making extra registry entries for the component. The following code will perform this registration for a preprocessor given its Program ID (ProgID).

```
' This routine looks up the Class ID of the component
' and then registers its affinity as a pre-processor.
function RegisterPreProcessor(byval ProgID)
    Dim WshShell, clsCatID, ClassID

    Set WshShell = WScript.CreateObject("WScript.Shell")

    ' Category ID for pre-processors
    clsCatID = "{20E8080F-F624-4401-A203-9D99CF18A6D9}"

    ' Look up the Class ID of the component
    ClassID = WshShell.RegRead("HKCR\" & ProgID & "\Clsid\")
```

```
    ' Register the new affinity
    call wshShell.RegWrite("HKCR\CLSID\" & ClassID _
        & "\Implemented Categories\" & clsCatID & "\","")

    ' Return the Class ID to the caller
    RegisterPreProcessor = ClassID
    set wshShell = nothing
end function

OrderPreProcID = RegisterPreProcessor("MyComps.COrderPreProcessor")
```

After registering the component and setting its affinity, the component will appear in the BizTalk Server Administration user interface.

The most common problems associated with receive functions are permission problems and out-of-date configurations. When a receive function encounters an error that prevents it from processing a file, it does not simply record an error and ignore the file, as you might expect. Instead, BizTalk Server completely disables the receive function. When this happens, the Event Log will contain the reason. The receive function must be manually reenabled at a later time—presumably, after the problem has been corrected.

Another common mistake is forgetting that a receive function only runs on a single server within the server group. All paths and security information must be configured properly for a process running on that server.

A File receive function must have the authority to read and delete the file being received. Permitting the receive function to read the files but not giving it write access to the directory is a common mistake. The receive function will not attempt to process a file if it cannot remove it afterward.

By default, receive functions use the security context of the configured account for the BizTalk Messaging Service. In some cases, this may not provide the necessary authority to allow the receive function to access the files. In this case, the User ID and Password should be set in the receive function configuration. These credentials will then be used. This is necessary when accessing a network file share outside of the local domain. Also, the User ID used to access the files must have the Log On Locally user right within Windows 2000 in order to connect across the network. This can be configured in Group Policy.

MSMQ receive functions must also have authority to manage the documents on the queue. The same rules apply for reading and deleting messages in MSMQ that applied when accessing files.

Another common problem encountered with receive functions, especially during development, is that the selections made for channels, envelopes, source and destination qualifiers, and IDs may become outdated. The configuration of a receive function is stored in the Windows Management Instrumentation (WMI) system, which will be covered in Chapter 19. The configuration of these other objects is stored in the BizTalk Management Database. This division means that when an object such as a channel is reconfigured or deleted, no check is made to determine whether any receive functions depend on this object. Since the receive function is just a wrapper around the Submit( ) call, only the name of these objects is stored in the receive function configuration. Therefore, if a referenced object is renamed or deleted, the receive function will quietly fail.

For example, if a receive function were configured to submit documents to a channel named "Great Big Order Channel" and that channel were renamed to "Not So Big Order Channel," then the receive function would automatically be disabled and an error message would be written to the Event Log. The BizTalk Messaging Manager will not generate an error or a warning in this case, because it does not know about receive functions.

Troubleshooting BizTalk Message Processing

Once a document has been submitted to BizTalk Server and a channel has been selected, the inbound document undergoes a series of transformations. This sequence is implemented as a *pipeline*. Readers familiar with Microsoft's Commerce Server product will recognize this architecture. In fact, BizTalk Server and Commerce Server share the same technology for implementing pipelines. This is the reason that many of BizTalk Server's interfaces for implementing its internal components and external custom components, except custom parsers and serializers, use the IPiplineComponent interface from Commerce Server.

Terminology regarding pipelines is a bit confusing. In the Technical Preview edition of BizTalk Server was a concept of a pipeline that was later renamed *channel*. That is not the type of pipeline being referred to in this section.

We will examine those steps in the pipeline that most frequently cause problems. In order of occurrence, these steps are inbound document validation, document mapping, outbound document validation, and serialization. Each step will be examined for its unique problem areas.

Schemas and Inbound Document Validation

When a document is received by BizTalk Server and read from the Work Queue for processing, the first action BizTalk Server takes is to validate that document against the document specification associated with its document definition. If any part of the document fails validation, detailed error messages are added to the Event Log, and the entire document is placed into the Suspended Queue.

Strict validation of inbound documents can be viewed as good or bad. There are two schools of thought on the design of BizTalk Server Schemas. Schemas can be either exacting or tolerant. While there are valid reasons for choosing either approach, the most important thing is to be consistent.

A *tolerant* schema is one that allows data to validate as long as it is in the right general form. This might include the correct tags and attributes. Such schemas generally don't restrict data types and field lengths. They may also allow all fields to be optional and allow all tags to occur zero or more times. The advantage of this type of schema is that it only fails to validate an inbound document in the most extreme of cases. In all other cases, the document passes on to the next stage in the pipeline. When using this type of schema, it is vital that these later stages be "bullet-proofed" to handle any variations or errors that are not being checked during validation.

An *exact* schema is one that allows only completely valid documents to pass validation. All data types and field lengths are specified. All fields and tags are set to appear the correct number of times. Also, when using EDI standard documents, it is important to remove any unused fields or segments. This will guarantee they do not suddenly appear in inbound documents without being noticed. In cases where only a certain set of values is acceptable in a field, the enumeration data type should be used to guarantee that only those values are passed. This type of schema will validate every field in the document and fail if there are any nonstandard entries. The advantage with exact schemas is that you can be certain any document making it past the document validation phase conforms to a rigid set of standards. This reduces the need for error checking code later on.

The debate as to whether exact or tolerant schemas are best really comes down to deciding how document errors will be managed in your BizTalk Server deployment. If errors are to be handled programmatically as a normal part of processing a document, tolerant schemas are a better choice. If BizTalk Server's facilities, such as the Suspended Queue, will be used to isolate document errors for correction outside of the normal flow of documents, then exact schemas are more appropriate. There is one key disadvantage of tolerant schemas to consider. If in the future your trading partner suddenly were to begin sending data in a slightly different manner, a tolerant schema might not catch the change and alert you that it had occurred. The risk of this occurring when transferring documents within an enterprise is lessened but not nil. Because of this, it is generally a good idea to use exact schemas whenever exchanging documents with a trading partner, especially when using EDI.

The following sections contain discussions of specific areas to be aware of when creating schemas or attempting to troubleshoot document validation problems.

Beware of Tags with the Same Name in the BizTalk Editor   The BizTalk Editor is designed to create enhanced XML schemas. In XML, if two tags have the same name in the same namespace, then they are the same tag, by definition. If you define an <ADDRESS> tag in one area of your schema and then attempt to define another tag by the same name, you will notice that all of the properties of the original tag suddenly appear in the Editor window. This is because both instances of this tag refer to the same definition. Altering either definition will automatically alter the other as well. If this is not your intent, you will need to change one of the tag's names. This is the reason that the EDI document schemas that come with BizTalk Server contain tag names like <REF>, <REF_2>, and <REF_3>. This allows each of these segments to be individually configured.

Beware of Copy/Paste in the BizTalk Editor   Using the Edit menu, you can copy and paste entire records within a schema or even between schemas. This is extremely useful when the same structures occur frequently, as is the case with X12 and EDIFACT document schemas. It is important to note, however, that not all properties of the records and fields are copied to the new location. All properties should be checked after the paste is complete to verify that the new record behaves as desired.

A very common problem occurs in flat-file and EDI schemas when copying records. By default, the Source Tag Identifier on the Parse tab is the same as the Tag name. For example, a date time segment would have both a tag name of <DTM> and a source tag identifier of "DTM." However, if you copy and paste this record in the editor, the tag name will be changed to <DTM1> in its new location. This is necessary to allow it to be separately configured, as we saw earlier. However, the source tag identifier has also been quietly changed without any warning or error messages being displayed. This is probably not the desired result in most cases, so you will have to manually correct the value. The same applies to any subrecords of the record that was copied.

Always Specify the Field Order in Non-XML Schemas   The positioning of delimiters in non-XML files is a frequent cause of problems. Specifying the incorrect field order for a record in the schema will generally result in an error message that indicates either a missing or an extra delimiter, or it may cause the document to fail validation altogether.

The Field Order property on the Parse tab of the editor appears for non-XML, nonpositional records. It has three values, as shown in Table 11-1. While these options are simple to understand, things become very complicated when dealing with fields at different levels of the XML schema hierarchy.

At the root level of the schema, the delimiter being configured is the record separator. This may be a carriage return or line feed. It may also be any arbitrary character. At the next level, the delimiter is for separating the fields in the record. The complication here is that the Source Tag Identifier is not considered a field. Therefore, while the segment REF*01*12341 may appear to fit the description of Infix, it is really Prefix because BizTalk Server sees it as *01*12341. At the subfield level, commonly used in EDIFACT documents, the correct field order is Infix because there is no source tag identifier to confuse things. These options are illustrated in Figure 11-13.

Specify Data Types and Cardinality in XML Schemas   When defining an XML schema, BizTalk Server provides powerful additions over traditional Document Type Definitions (DTDs). These additions include the ability to specify maximum and minimum field lengths, enumerated values, and data types for attributes in XML documents.

Set All Options on EDI Schemas   The X12 and EDIFACT document schemas that come with BizTalk Server are a good starting point for most EDI documents. When altering these or defining your own schemas from scratch, it is important not to forget

Field Order	Example	Description
Prefix	*a*b*c	The delimiter appears before each field.
Infix	a*b*c	The delimiter appears between fields.
Postfix	a*b*c*	The delimiter appears after each field.

Table 11-1.   *Field Order Values*

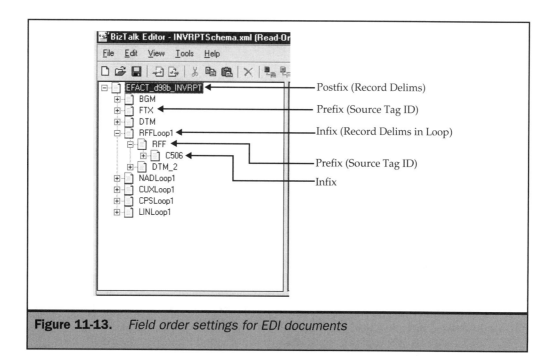

Figure 11-13.   *Field order settings for EDI documents*

that there are four tabs' worth of options for each field and record. These are the Definition, Reference, Parse, and Code List tabs. Failing to set the necessary properties on some of these tabs will cause errors that are extremely difficult to debug at run time. Use the provided schemas as a template when developing custom EDI schemas. Specific settings to be careful of include Standard, Field Order, Source Tag Identifier, and delimiter types.

Validate Schemas and Instances in the BizTalk Editor to Test Schema Definitions

The BizTalk Editor does not prevent the creation of invalid schemas. This seems odd at first, but it makes sense in the context of a schema that is only partially complete. You must have the ability to save your work. When you save a schema, the editor automatically validates the schema and generates errors as necessary. The same check can be made manually without saving by selecting Tools | Validate Specification. This is your first line of defense against invalid schema definitions.

The next line of defense is the Validate Instance option in the Tools menu. This option allows the user to perform a manual document validation in the editor. This is the same check BizTalk Server would perform while processing the document. This tool can validate XML documents or non-XML documents. Note that the document you are validating must be of the same Standard type as the schema you are defining. Only XML documents can validate against XML schemas. Only X12 documents, in their native form, can validate against X12 schemas, and so on. By default, only XML files are listed for validation, so it may be necessary to switch the file type in the open dialog box to show all files. It is also important to note that this tool expects a document, not an interchange. Any envelope information, such as ISA or UNB headers, must be stripped off the document instance, or the document will not validate properly.

This tool is also useful for determining the cause of a document validation error once it has occurred within BizTalk Server. When the document is sitting on the Suspended Queue, you can select the View Document option to retrieve the contents of the document, save this to disk, and validate it against the schema. In some cases, this may yield the XML form of a non-XML document. To run the validation, you will need to change the Standard field on the Reference tab to "XML." This will allow you to perform the validation. Be careful not to save the schema after doing this, or a great many configurations will be lost for your EDI document. Simply switching it back to X12 or EDIFACT will not restore them.

Be Aware of International Requirements When Defining Schemas   BizTalk Server is designed to support the exchange of documents between trading partners anywhere in the world. This is evidenced by its extensive use of Unicode character sets. This doesn't solve all of the problems associated with international document exchange, however. When defining schemas for BizTalk Server, remember that many of the standard ways we do things in our country may not apply elsewhere. Postal codes, phone numbers, addresses, and other such information often are formatted differently in other countries. For example, defining a phone number as a 3-digit area code, 3-digit prefix, and 4-digit suffix will not work outside the United States in most cases. Also, fields containing information such as a U.S. social security number may have no meaning at all outside their country of origin.

Mapping Errors

One of the most powerful features of BizTalk Server is the BizTalk Mapper application. The BizTalk Mapper is used to define transformations from one XML schema to another, graphically. Behind the scenes, the BizTalk Mapper assembles a document called an *XSLT stylesheet*. This stylesheet uses the Extensible Stylesheet Language for Transformation (XSLT) to define the transformations drawn using the BizTalk Mapper application. When you save a map, an XML file is created that contains the XSLT stylesheet, the source and destination schemas, and other information used by the BizTalk Mapper. The only part of the map that is used for performing the mapping is the XSLT stylesheet. XSLT is discussed in Chapter 2.

The XSLT created is like any other machine-generated code. It may or may not carry out your intent. There are many situations in which the maps you create may not behave as expected. Learning how to read the XSLT is an excellent way to debug your maps. It will also give you a better understanding of why the BizTalk Mapper has limitations in dealing with structures such as multiple source loop paths, and certain EDI constructs such as REF and HL segments. To access the compiled XSLT, you can either open the map file in an XML viewer such as Internet Explorer, or you can use the Compile Map option on the Tools menu in the BizTalk Mapper. In the latter case, the compiled XSLT can be viewed by switching to the Output tab, as shown in Figure 11-14.

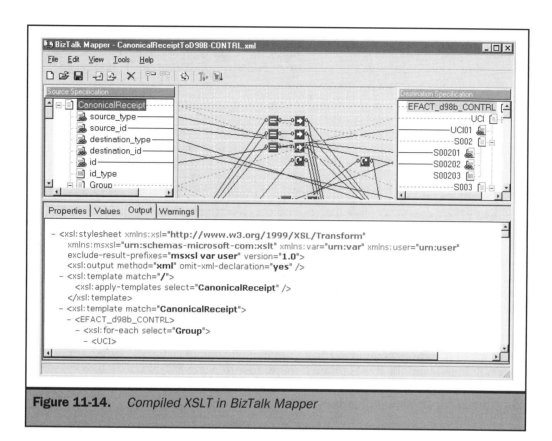

Figure 11-14. *Compiled XSLT in BizTalk Mapper*

Another means of testing a map from within the BizTalk Mapper application is to use the Test Map option on the Tools menu. This option runs a sample XML source document through the map and displays the resulting XML document in the Output tab. You can modify the XML document to some extent using the Values tab. Values entered on the left of this tab are used in the source document that is used for testing. Unfortunately, this ability to test is limited. You can only enter a single value at a time for each field, and there is no way to control the structure of the source XML document.

Once you have compiled and tested your map as much as possible within the BizTalk Mapper, you should continue to test it. Either you can do this by using the Map Test tool from the SDK, or you can install the map in a test channel. The combination of a loopback port and the SDK's Direct Integration tools is very powerful for this. Using the SubmitSync button, the document is sent through the channel and then returned to the application, which immediately displays it.

The following sections describe the most common mapping problems encountered when using BizTalk Server mapping. Some of these suggestions concern the BizTalk Mapper application, and others deal with general debugging procedures.

Check the Option Settings in BizTalk Mapper   The BizTalk Mapper, like most Windows applications, has an Options dialog box (Figure 11-15) that can be accessed by selecting Tools | Options. Unlike most Windows applications, its behavior can be dramatically altered using these options.

The Warnings For Simple Linking Errors option causes warning messages to be displayed when the BizTalk Mapper detects potential problems with a link that you have created. While extremely annoying, these warnings can save you a great deal of time. The types of errors detected are time-consuming to correct later.

The View Compiler Links option causes lightly colored links to appear between record nodes in the source and destination trees. These links show the relationships between source and destination nodes that have been calculated by the map compiler. The links give the user valuable insight into the structure of the output document.

The Allow Record Content Links option allows links between record nodes and functoids. By default, only field nodes can be linked to functoid inputs and outputs.

The Allow Multiple Inputs To Destination Tree Nodes option allows the user to connect more than one input node to a single output node. This is not usually a good idea because it can cause unpredictable results. The Looping functoid can be used to resolve these problems in some cases, but such a map should be rigorously tested.

Heed Data Type Warnings from the BizTalk Mapper   The Warnings For Simple Linking Errors option mentioned in the previous section gives the developer vital information to avoid the most common mapping problems. When one field is connected to another within the BizTalk Mapper, the data types of the two fields are compared. If there is an inconsistency, it is reported immediately.

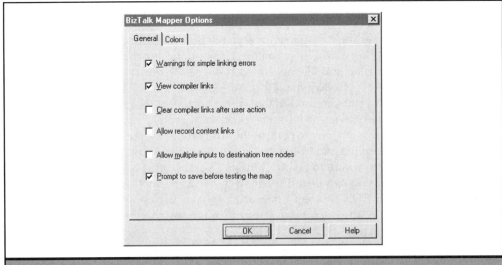

Figure 11-15.   *BizTalk Mapper Options dialog box*

The first step in resolving data type warnings is to verify that the document specifications are correct. If not, the error should be corrected in the BizTalk Editor. The document specification must also be updated in the map. This can be done by opening the Edit menu and selecting either Replace Source Specification or Replace Destination Specification.

If the document specifications are correct, the warning may be resolved in one of two ways: correct the problem in the map or ignore the warning. For example, if a string field is being mapped to a numeric field, a valid input document may result in an invalid output document because the input field may contain nonnumeric data. The developer must decide whether this is acceptable depending on how errors are being handled within their environment. The resulting document will fail and be placed on the Suspended Queue. If this is the desired behavior, the warning may be safely ignored. If, on the other hand, a default value should be substituted or a format conversion performed, the developer should use functoids within the map to carry out these functions.

Keep Document Specs and Maps Up to Date During Development   As you are developing your solution with the BizTalk Editor and BizTalk Mapper, you will find that you frequently need to alter your document specs and maps. Eventually, you will find that the changes you have made don't seem to be having any effect on how BizTalk Server is handling documents. This is because the document specs and maps that exist in the WebDAV repository are not the versions being used by BizTalk Server.

When you update a document specification in the BizTalk Editor and save it to the WebDAV repository, you must update all references to the specification. These references include all document definitions within the BizTalk Messaging Manager and all source and destination specs within any maps you have created. The reason for this is that, in both cases, the document specification is copied out of the WebDAV repository and stored elsewhere.

The document specification for a document definition is stored in the BizTalk Management Database. To update the specification used by a document definition, simply edit the document definition within Messaging Manager and select OK to save. Do not reselect the specification file, or the Messaging Manager will inform you that you cannot alter the specification for a document definition that is in use by a channel.

The source and destination specifications used by a map are stored within the XML file containing the map. To update the map's document specifications, open the map in the BizTalk Mapper, and then open the Edit menu and select either Replace Source Specification or Replace Destination Specification. Don't forget to save the map when you have finished.

When you update a map definition, you also need to update any channels that use the map, because the map definition is also copied into the BizTalk Management Database. You perform this update by editing the channel's definition in the BizTalk Messaging Manager and choosing OK to save the channel. This rereads the map from WebDAV.

Test Custom Functoids and Scripts Extensively   The functoids that are delivered with BizTalk Server have been extensively tested to ensure that your map will not fail because of errors in the functoids it uses. BizTalk Server also gives you the ability to extend the BizTalk Mapper's capabilities in two very powerful ways: custom functoids and scripting.

Custom functoids are written using the IFunctoid interface. This interface allows you to write new functoids that behave just like those included with BizTalk Server. This is an extremely powerful way to extend the mapping capability of BizTalk Server. A custom functoid generates XSLT or scripting code to perform its function. This code becomes part of the map. Custom functoids must be tested extensively to ensure that both the generated code and the functoid itself perform exactly as desired. Creating custom functoids is covered in Chapter 17.

A simpler way to access the power of custom programming in a map is to use the Scripting functoid from the Advanced tab of the functoid palette. This functoid allows the developer to write Visual Basic Scripting Edition (VBScript) code directly into the map. This code can create COM components, access databases, or just about anything else you can imagine. As with any powerful weapon, you should be careful not to point it at your foot. Test, test, test.

Manage Database Functoids Carefully   The Database tab of the functoid palette contains three extremely powerful functoids. The first performs a database query to extract a set of data from a database, the second extracts data from that dataset, and the third provides error information. There are some important factors to consider when using these functoids.

The Database Lookup functoid takes a connection string as one of its parameters. This string must be valid on all servers in the server group that may run the map. For ODBC connection strings, the ODBC Data Source Name must be defined on all servers. Any server names that need to be resolved to IP addresses must resolve correctly. Also, when using Windows integrated security to connect to SQL Server, all servers must be running using a service account that gives them the necessary access to query the database.

Error handling is a bit unusual when using the database functoids. If an error occurs accessing the database, the map will *not* fail. All values extracted from the database will simply appear blank. To determine that an error has occurred, you must access the Error Return functoid. If an error occurred, this functoid will return the error string.

Outbound Document Validation

Outbound document validation is no different from inbound document validation. Once any mapping has been performed, the resulting document is compared to the outbound document specification associated with the channel. If the document is not valid for some reason, an error is logged in the Event Log, and the document is placed on the Suspended Queue.

In most cases, outbound validation errors are caused by mapping errors. The easiest way to determine what went wrong is to extract the document from the Suspended Queue using the View Document option. Next, save it to a file, and then view it in Internet Explorer. Since the document is always in XML at this stage, it is easy to see whether there are structural problems or mismapped fields. If necessary, you can use the BizTalk

Editor to validate the document instance. This will give you a precise description of the problem. Remember, it may be necessary to temporarily change the standard of the document specification to "XML" because you are working with an XML instance.

Serializing Documents

Once the document has been mapped and validated, BizTalk Server must generate the outbound document. This is called *serializing* the document. Serializing is the opposite of *parsing*, which we looked at earlier. As such, many of the problems that cause parsing errors can also cause serialization errors. Each parser component in BizTalk Server has a corresponding serializer component. The serializer converts the XML document used internally within BizTalk Server into a document in a native format such as X12, EDIFACT, or Flat-File.

The most common problem encountered during serialization is also the most confusing. Documents often get generated as XML documents when that is not the intent. By default, if no envelope is specified in the messaging port configuration, all documents are serialized as XML documents. If the envelope specifies a different format, that serializer will be used instead. However, in many cases, if envelope information is missing or some other error occurs, BizTalk Server will frequently fall back to XML automatically instead of generating an error. This can be very confusing. The first step is to be sure that the envelope is defined and used correctly.

The following sections contain specific scenarios that cause problems with serializing documents.

Select the Correct Identifier Qualifier and Identifier Value for the Serializer

Each serializer formats a different type of envelope. The X12 and EDIFACT serializers include the identifier qualifier and identifier value in the ISA or UNB headers, respectively. There are specific restrictions on these values. X12 qualifiers are two characters, and values are up to ten characters. EDIFACT qualifiers are up to 4 characters, and values are up to 35 characters. Always select a valid EDI identifier qualifier when setting up a messaging port that will generate EDI documents.

Always Set Selection Criteria for EDI Documents   Both X12 and EDIFACT

serializers use the Selection Criteria tab of the document definition to set certain fields in their headers. Failing to set these values will always cause errors. In many cases, BizTalk Server will simply output the document as XML. See Figures 11-10 and 11-11 for examples of selection criteria.

Set Additional EDI Envelope Options as Necessary   EDI document headers contain

many fields that are not covered by the identifier qualifier and identifier value, or the selection criteria. BizTalk Server gives access to these parameters through the Advanced button on the final page of the Channel wizard, as shown in Figure 11-16. A full discussion of these options is included in Chapter 6.

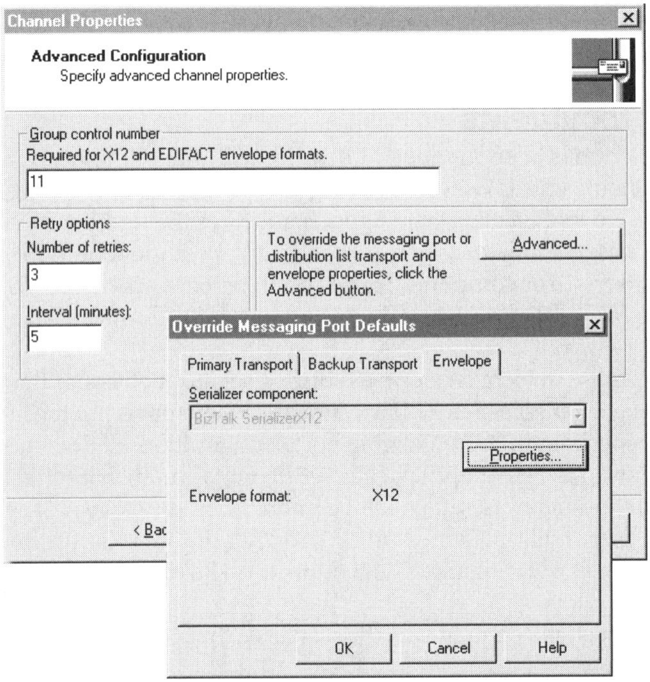

Figure 11-16. Channel wizard—advanced options

Selecting the Envelope tab and clicking the Properties button gives the user access to the rest of the envelope parameters, as shown in Figure 11-17. The parameters available vary from one envelope type to another.

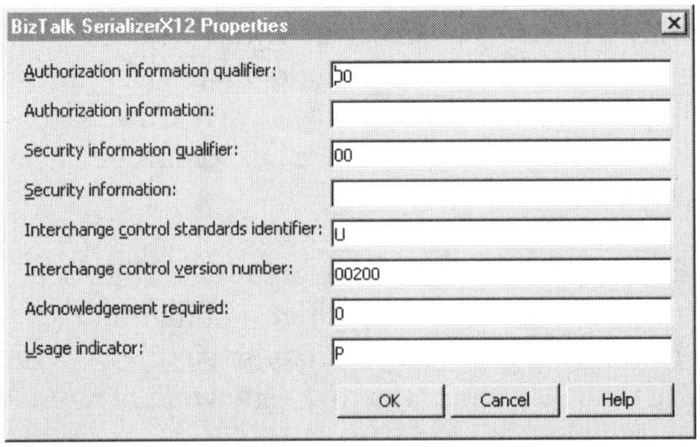

Figure 11-17. Serializer Properties dialog box

Document Delivery

Now that we have transformed the inbound document into an outbound document, we must consider how to deliver it to its correct destination. Many of the most common operational problems occur at this stage because this is where BizTalk Server is frequently dependent on other systems.

Standard Transport Protocols

BizTalk Server comes with several predefined transport protocols. These are HTTP/HTTPS, SMTP, MSMQ, Loopback, and File. Each of these protocols has its own idiosyncrasies, which we will discuss in the following sections.

File Drops   The File protocol is by far the simplest of the transport protocols. The only difficulties generally encountered here are file and directory access permissions. The BizTalk Server service account must have the right to create and write to files in the directory to which you are writing.

If you configure a file as the output of a messaging port, carefully consider the filename used. If a static filename such as C:\temp\MyDoc.xml is used, BizTalk Server will create the file for the first document. Later documents will be appended to that file. For X12 and EDIFACT documents, this is frequently the desired result. In high-volume scenarios, writing to a single file does not work well and may cause other problems because of contention for access to the file. For XML documents, writing to a single file results in a file that does not contain a valid XML document. This is because multiple root elements are in the file. For these documents, you should configure the target filename using the %tracking_id% variable. For example, setting the filename to C:\temp\850_%tracking_id%.xml would result in each XML document being placed in a separate file whose name is derived from its tracking ID.

HTTP and HTTPS   Using the HTTP protocol to transfer data to a web site is extremely convenient in most cases. Of course, the web page at the given URL must be designed to receive data in this manner. Whenever sending data across a public network such as the Internet, be sure to use HTTP with SSL encryption (HTTPS) to protect your data.

If you are sending data to trading partners through a firewall that acts as a proxy server, you will need to configure the proxy settings just as you would for a web browser. This is done using the BizTalk Server Administration console. The proxy server is configured on the General tab of the BizTalk Server Group Properties dialog box, as shown in Figure 11-18. These settings apply to all of the servers in the group. Connectivity issues associated with firewalls and SSL are discussed in Chapter 14.

Simple Mail Transfer Protocol (SMTP)   The SMTP protocol automatically mails the contents of the document to a given e-mail address. BizTalk Server hands the message to the SMTP server configured in the SMTP Host field, as shown in Figure 11-18. This server should be configured to forward e-mail to other mail servers. Many mail servers are configured to prevent forwarding of e-mail. E-mail administrators configure servers

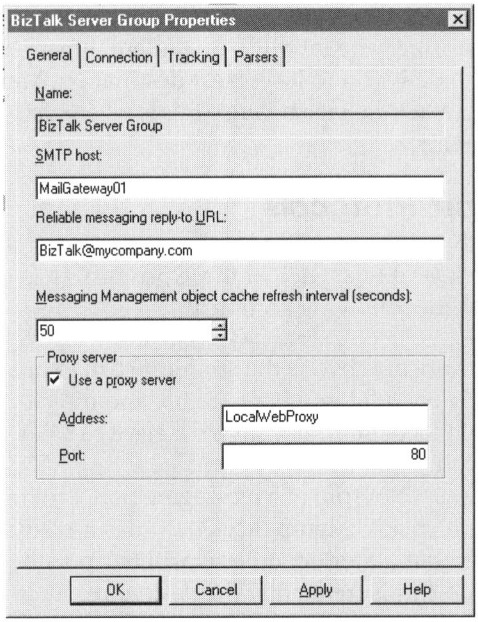

Figure 11-18. *BizTalk Server Group Properties—General tab*

in this way to prevent the server from being used as a conduit for spam. If this is the case, this setting on the e-mail server may need to be changed.

Loopback The Loopback protocol is useful for testing using the Direct Integration SDK tool. It requires no parameters. The outbound document is simply returned to the caller of the SubmitSync method. If the document was submitted using the Submit method, the document is discarded (except for document tracking purposes). Another use of the Loopback protocol is to allow an application to make a call into BizTalk Server as though calling a synchronous function. The document is transformed and returned in a single call.

Message Queuing (MSMQ) The MSMQ protocol is used to place outbound messages on a private or public queue. The most common problems encountered involve security rights on the destination queue. The BizTalk Server service must have the right to add messages to the queue.

Application Integration Components

The Application Integration Component (AIC) transport protocol is designed to allow programmatic extensions to BizTalk Server. The BizTalk Server service must have the authority to execute the AIC and to perform any action taken by the AIC. AICs come in two varieties: lightweight and pipeline.

A *lightweight* AIC implements the IBTSAppIntegration interface in any COM-compatible language. This interface contains only one method, with a single parameter. This parameter is the document to be delivered. Common scenarios for this type of AIC include database update procedures.

A *pipeline* AIC implements the IPipelineComponent interface first introduced in Microsoft's Commerce Server product. Pipeline components are generally implemented in Visual C++ rather than Visual Basic for performance reasons. The advantage of pipeline components is that they allow parameters to be set on the messaging port configuration for the component, whereas lightweight AICs do not. Pipeline AICs also have the ability to exploit different threading models. This can be a significant performance consideration in a large-volume implementation. Typically, pipeline AICs are used to implement to new transport protocols such as FTP.

Like the custom preprocessors we discussed earlier, Application Integration Components must have the AIC category affinity registered, or they will not appear in the BizTalk Messaging Manager interface. The Visual C++ ATL library used to create pipeline components will do this automatically for pipeline AICs. For lightweight AICs developed in Visual Basic, you must add the registry information yourself. This can be done using the following VBScript routine:

```
function RegisterAICClass(byval ProgID)
    dim wshShell, clsCat1ID, clsCat2ID, ClassID

    Set WshShell = WScript.CreateObject("WScript.Shell")

    ' These are the Category ID's for an AIC
    clsCat1ID = "{5C6C30E7-C66D-40E3-889D-08C5C3099E52}"
    clsCat2ID = "{BD193E1D-D7DC-4B7C-B9D2-92AE0344C836}"

    ' Look up the Class ID for the given Prog ID
    ClassID = WshShell.RegRead("HKCR\" & ProgID & "\Clsid\")

    ' Register the category ID's
    call wshShell.RegWrite("HKCR\CLSID\" & ClassID _
        & "\Implemented Categories\" & clsCat1ID & "\","")
    call wshShell.RegWrite("HKCR\CLSID\" & ClassID _
        & "\Implemented Categories\" & clsCat2ID & "\","")

    ' return the Class ID to the caller
    RegisterAICClass = ClassID
    set wshShell = nothing
end function


OrderProcessID = RegisterAICClass("MyAICs.COrderProcess")
```

BIZTALK SERVER
ADMINISTRATION

Document Tracking

We examined BizTalk Server's Document Tracking feature earlier as a debugging tool. Now we will look at how to diagnose problems with the Document Tracking feature itself.

User Interface Problems

The Document Tracking application is a web-based application that is installed on the BizTalk Server. This web site retrieves document information from the Document Tracking Activity database, called InterchangeDTA by default. The connection parameters for this database are the same as those used by the BizTalk Server when recording document-tracking information. These can be configured using the BizTalk Server Administration console.

The Document Tracking web site uses Microsoft's Office Web Components to implement many of its user interface features. When a client web browser first attempts to connect to the web site, the user may be prompted to allow the server to download these components. The components are required in order to use the site, so they should be allowed to install. It is also possible that the security settings within Internet Explorer are set too high to allow the installation of these components. If so, some of the user interface components on the site will appear as empty boxes with a red X in them. You will need to lower the security settings to allow the components to install.

In many cases, an annoying security message will appear that indicates that this page is trying to access data in another domain. This message will appear before every page you access in the site. The best way to eliminate this message is to add the site to your list of trusted sites by selecting Tools | Internet Options in Internet Explorer. Go to the Security tab, select Trusted Sites, and choose the Sites button. Configure the Document Tracking site as a trusted site, as shown in Figure 11-19.

Missing Documents

The most common problem encountered with Document Tracking is that documents may be missing from the database. There are three locations in which document tracking may be configured:

- **BizTalk Server Administration**   The Server Group properties dialog box contains a check box that enables or disables document tracking within the server group. If tracking is disabled, nothing is logged to the DTA database.

- **Document Definition**   The Document Definition dialog box contains a Global Tracking tab that defines data to be collected about a document whenever such documents are processed.

- **Channel Configuration**   The second to last page of the Channel Configuration wizard allows the user to indicate what documents (inbound or outbound) should be tracked and in what form (XML or native).

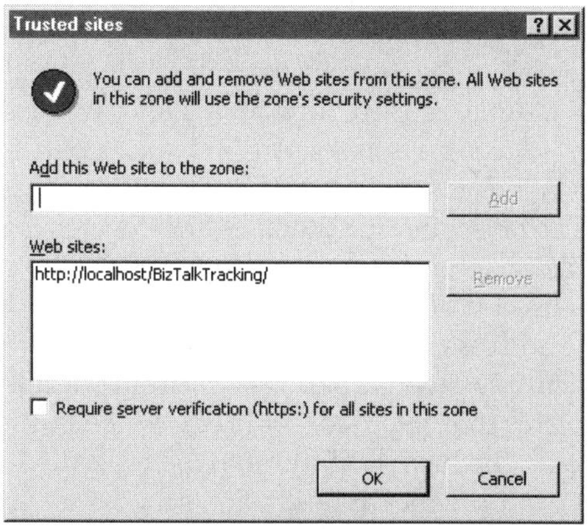

Figure 11-19. *Configure trusted sites in Internet Explorer.*

Troubleshooting Orchestration

BizTalk Orchestration is difficult to troubleshoot because it is difficult to visualize what is happening to a schedule as it is running. It may be sending or receiving data, making calls to COM components, or just waiting for something to happen. This is ironic considering the visual nature of the tool used to create schedules, Microsoft Visio. Understanding and being able recognize this state is critical to debugging problems that arise in Orchestration. Orchestration is covered in detail in Chapters 7 and 8.

BizTalk Server has limited tools for managing Orchestration. In fact, the only real tools for digging into the state of the Orchestration system are included in the SDK, not the main product. We will examine these tools in some detail. We will also explore how BizTalk Orchestration schedules are invoked.

One of the most awkward areas of BizTalk Orchestration is the setup of the COM+ application and persistence database. Troubleshooting these areas will be covered later when we discuss BizTalk Server installation and support.

Invoking Schedules Directly

The natural use of Orchestration within BizTalk Server is to create a schedule that receives a document from BizTalk Messaging, performs some set of processes, and sends a response document through BizTalk Messaging. However, this is only one of many ways in which Orchestration can be used. In fact, Orchestration was designed to function completely independently of BizTalk Messaging. It is useful to understand Orchestration as a stand-alone system. This gives insight into how BizTalk Server manages schedules and allows for testing of schedules in a more controlled environment outside of BizTalk Messaging.

Once you have designed your schedule in the BizTalk Orchestration Designer (a Visio-based application), you compile it into an XLANG document with an .skx extension. This file contains all of the instructions for carrying out the schedule's processes. This file is then used as a template for creating an instance of the schedule to be executed.

All schedules are created using a *moniker*. A Windows moniker is a string that identifies an object or class within Windows. The structure of this string depends on the protocol being accessed. To create an object using a moniker, the developer invokes the GetObject( ) call, passing in the moniker as the object name.

The most commonly used type of moniker is also known as a *Uniform Resource Locator (URL)*. This is the address used to access a page or other resource on the World Wide Web. For example, http://www.microsoft.com/ms.htm is Microsoft's home page. This moniker indicates that the protocol HTTP will be used to access the server www.microsoft.com, from which we will retrieve the file called ms.htm.

The monikers used with BizTalk Orchestration schedules have this form:

sked://{SERVER}{!XLANG Scheduler}/{FilePath}{/PortName}

For Orchestration, the protocol is always *sked*. This represents the BizTalk Orchestration scheduler. All of the sections of the moniker are optional except for the protocol and the File Path.

- **SERVER**   The default server is the local server.
- **XLANG Scheduler**   This refers to the name of the COM+ application that hosts the XLANG application and houses the schedule instance once it is created. The default is XLANG Scheduler.
- **FilePath**   This is the fully qualified path to the compiled XLANG schedule file on the server.
- **PortName**   This is the name of a port within the schedule to which the resulting COM object will refer. Note that this is an Orchestration port, not a Messaging port.

To create an instance of a schedule, the calling application uses the GetObject( ) call as follows:

```
Dim oSchedInstance
set oSchedInstance = GetObject( _
      "sked://swright/c:\temp\mysched.skx/PortA")
```

The oSchedInstance variable now contains a COM reference to an object that acts as a proxy for controlling the schedule.

Workflow Audit Tool

The BizTalk Server SDK contains two tools for monitoring Orchestration. The first is the Workflow Audit Tool. There are actually two directories under the SDK directory for this tool. The first is XLANG Samples\WorkFlowAudit. This directory contains a Visual C++ project that compiles a COM component. The other is XLANG Samples\WorkFlowAuditClient. This directory contains a small VB application that presents a form to start and stop the COM component. Note that the COM component must be manually registered before it can be used. Events are only recorded while the client application is running and the COM component has been started.

Note *When BizTalk Server was originally released, there were problems with the Windows 2000 COM+ event system that prevented the WorkFlow Audit tool from functioning correctly. The fix for this problem was released in a hotfix and is now available as part of Windows 2000 Service Pack 2.*

The idea of the Workflow Audit tool is to monitor COM+ events generated by the XLANG Scheduler as it processes schedules. These events are recorded in the Document Tracking database and are associated with the BizTalk Messaging documents that triggered them, if any. The results of this auditing can be viewed in the Document Tracking web site. Figure 11-20 gives an overview of the architecture of Workflow Audit.

Once event data is collected, it can be viewed using the Document Tracking web application, as shown in Figure 11-21. The user selects a document that triggers an XLANG schedule in the Query Results page. Selecting the icon under the Schedule column results in the display of the Event Log for the XLANG schedule instance associated with the document.

XLANG Event Monitor

The other tool provided in the SDK for monitoring Orchestration is the XLANG Monitor tool. Unlike the other tools in the SDK, there is no source code provided. The XLANG Monitor is located in the SDK\XLANG Tools directory under the BizTalk Server installation directory and is called XLANGMon.exe. This application displays status and event information for all of the schedules running on a system. It also allows this data to be recorded and saved to a file for later analysis.

Note *When BizTalk Server was originally released, there were problems with the Windows 2000 COM+ event system that prevented the XLANG Monitor from functioning correctly. The fix for this problem was released in a hotfix and is now available as part of Windows 2000 Service Pack 2.*

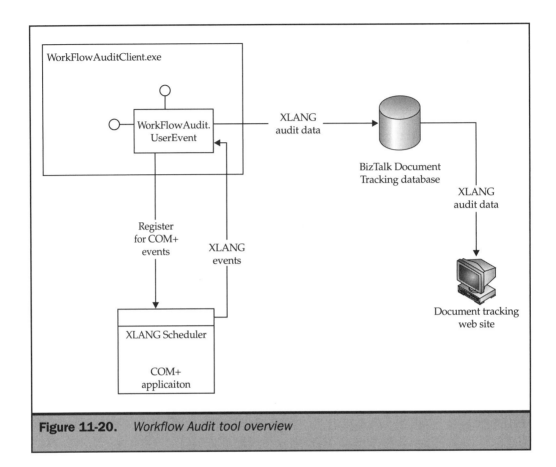

Figure 11-20. *Workflow Audit tool overview*

Event Name	Attribute Name	Attribute Value
OnBTASinkEnter	ActionTag	Action 1
OnBTASinkEnter	ShapeId	015
OnBTASinkEnter	PortId	Port_1
OnBTASinkEnter	MsgType	ElementType_Message_1
OnBTAError	HRESULT	-2147024809
OnBTAScheduleDone	ModuleId	{3300E10D-4C5A-4EA7-962C-2426637B0EF3}
OnBTAScheduleDone	ModuleName	Drawing1
OnBTAScheduleDone	CompletionStatus	-1073455852
OnBTAScheduleDone	ScheduleStartTime	10/2/2001 1:05:10 AM

Figure 11-21. *Workflow audit data in the Document Tracking application*

Troubleshooting Installation and Operational Support

It may seem odd to cover installation at the end of this chapter, when installation is the first thing you do with any piece of software. Unfortunately, to install a piece of software with confidence, you must have some experience with the product. This is a bit of a Catch-22. The same is true for troubleshooting. To troubleshoot the installation process or support production servers, you must understand the basics of troubleshooting the various components of the system. That is why we covered those topics first.

We will look at the installation process and describe common problems that arise. Of course, proper planning is key. By knowing all of the decisions to be made during installation and having thought out all of the options, you will find installation a breeze.

Supporting the BizTalk Server software in a production environment requires the same discipline as any other mission-critical server software. Backups, security, and performance considerations must be addressed before deployment to avoid problems. We will look at ways to avoid problems and minimize their impact when they occur.

Installation Problems

BizTalk Server is a fairly simple product to install in most cases. The installation program is a normal Windows install wizard. We will cover a server installation, but it is also possible to install only the management tools needed to work with a remote BizTalk Server. One excellent feature of the BizTalk Server installer is that if installation fails or is canceled by the user, the installer will go back and uninstall any components it has placed on the system. Installation is covered in Chapter 3.

Database Setup Problems

BizTalk Server installation problems generally arise from the handling of databases. BizTalk Server uses four databases. Three of these support BizTalk Messaging, while the fourth is used to persist schedules in Orchestration. Before installing BizTalk Server, you need to decide where these databases will reside. They need not all exist locally or even on the same remote server.

It is a good idea to verify that you can connect to all of the database servers to be used before beginning to set up BizTalk Server. An important consideration is the network library to be used in connecting to the database servers. In most configurations, the default named-pipes library will work just fine. However, if your SQL Server database is running in a Windows cluster, which is common in production environments, you will need to force the network library to TCP/IP in order to connect.

During installation, the user is given the option to create each database or to connect to an existing, fully installed copy of the database. Obviously, the SQL login used to connect to SQL Server must have the authority to create new databases when necessary. When installing BizTalk Servers in groups, the databases will usually be created during the installation of the first server. Later servers will merely connect to the same databases that already exist.

Each of BizTalk Server's databases has it own purpose and, therefore, different factors need to be considered when deciding how to set them up.

BizTalk Management Database   The Management Database is read frequently by the various servers to refresh their cache. This database should be optimized for read access, and there should be a minimum of networking delay associated with the connection.

BizTalk Shared Queue Database   This database contains the Work, Retry, Scheduled, and Suspended Queues. The Shared Queue database sees a large number of reads and writes, but does not typically grow large because it only contains messages currently in the queue. Backup planning should take this into account. This database will generate large transaction logs if transaction logging is enabled.

BizTalk Document Tracking Database   This database must be optimized for writing. During the processing of a single document, data is written to this database several times. This assumes, of course, that document tracking is enabled in the server group and that the channels are configured to track documents. In a large enterprise, the Document Tracking database should be housed on a separate server, possibly in a cluster, to minimize contention with other BizTalk Server databases. This database will grow very large as more and more documents are added.

Note	*The initial release of BizTalk Server did not contain any means to archive and remove old documents from the Document Tracking database. New stored procedures were introduced in Service Pack 1 for this purpose, but they must be manually installed. See the SP1 Readme file or Chapter 10 for details.*

XLANG Persistence Database   The XLANG database is very different from the other databases used by BizTalk Server. First of all, during installation, you must have a trusted (NT authenticated) connection to the SQL Server. You cannot use a SQL logon and password as you did for the other databases. This means that the database must either be local to the BizTalk Server or be within the same Windows 2000 domain forest. This is a concern in situations where production servers run in workgroups or in a network demilitarized zone (DMZ) configuration. These types of deployments can prevent Orchestration from installing and functioning correctly, and are discussed in Chapter 14.

During the installation procedure, the installer will create a COM+ application that will, by default, host all of your XLANG schedule processes. The installer will also create an ODBC Data Source Name (DSN) with the same name as the COM+ application. These names must remain identical for Orchestration to function properly.

COM+ Applications

During installation, four COM+ applications will be created. Two of these are library applications and need no further configuration. The COM+ applications called BizTalk Server Interchange Application and XLANG Scheduler are server applications that are configured to execute using the Interactive User security context. This means that unless an administrator is logged onto the console, BizTalk Orchestration will not run, and BizTalk Messaging will not accept new documents. This is not acceptable in a production environment where an unexpected server reboot cannot be allowed to disable BizTalk Server until an operator logs on. A service account should be created for BizTalk Server, and the COM+ applications should be reconfigured to use that security context.

By default, the installer creates one COM+ application to host XLANG schedules. BizTalk Server also creates an extension to the COM+ environment that allows any COM+ server application to host XLANG schedules. This configuration is done by opening the Properties dialog box for the COM+ application, as shown in Figure 11-22. Each application now has an XLANG tab that can be used to enable XLANG hosting and configure the necessary database and DSN. Remember, the ODBC DSN must match the COM+ application name exactly in order for Orchestration to function.

XML Parser Versions

There are many components that make up BizTalk Server. One of the most crucial isn't even part of BizTalk Server, although it is installed as part of BizTalk Server installation. This is the Microsoft XML Parser component. This piece of software has undergone a chaotic evolution over the last few years, and it is still undergoing rapid development. Because this component is so critical to BizTalk Server, beware of loading other software packages that might contain versions of this library that have not been fully tested with BizTalk Server. Microsoft recently released a beta of version 4 of the XML library. Many enthusiastic developers eagerly loaded this new software only to find that BizTalk Server no longer functioned. Of course, no one would ever load beta software on a production server, would they? Would they!

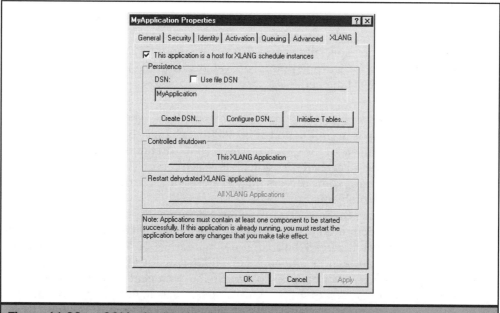

Figure 11-22.   *COM+ Application Properties—XLANG tab*

Support Practices

Now that we have installed BizTalk Server and it is up and running in production, we can go back to our cubicles and forget all about it, right? Wrong! Like any other piece of software, BizTalk Server must be monitored and maintained in order to remain stable in a production environment. Microsoft has long been criticized for unreliability in their products. This is especially true in server applications such as SQL Server and BizTalk Server. The reality is that a production environment is only as stable as the organization supporting it is disciplined. The same companies that have entire departments to support a single mainframe or a few UNIX-based servers, routinely deploy Windows NT or 2000 servers with no permanent staff, no backups, and no change control—and, therefore, no hope of achieving reliability.

Now let's examine the types of tasks that are necessary to minimize the need for troubleshooting and the downtime likely to be experienced as a result of problems. We will cover the areas of change control, security, and monitoring. For more in-depth information, see Microsoft's deployment white paper at http://www.microsoft.com/ BizTalk Server/techinfo/deployment/2000/wp_deploymentConsiderations.asp.

Hardware

The first thing to note is that BizTalk Server is a *server* application, not a run-it-on-an-old-desktop application. BizTalk Server scales down very well for development. I do my development on a laptop running Windows 2000 Server, SQL Server 2000 (Developer), and BizTalk Server 2000 (Developer), but this is not appropriate for production. For a production implementation, BizTalk Server is designed to scale up well on a single system and has built-in features for clustering. Based on the size of your deployment and the volume of data you will be processing, don't skimp on the hardware budget. This is especially true for system memory. 512MB of RAM for each CPU in the server is a good starting point. For systems handling large volumes of documents, the more RAM the better.

Change Control

Once your server group is in production, it is vital that changes be well thought out. Remember that all members of the group use each configuration setting independently. These settings are read and cached occasionally by each server. If you change settings while the group is running, some servers might be using the changed settings before others. This may cause problems.

For example, consider the impact of updating a document specification. Once you update the document definition that uses the document specification, the change is not immediate. Each server will reread the configuration information at a different time. Any documents processed during this time may be validated against the new schema or the old, depending on which server happens to retrieve the document from the Work Queue.

Whenever possible, it is best to shut down all of the servers in the group before making any fundamental changes to the configuration. This will force all servers to refresh their cache with the new settings before processing any documents.

If documents are being received via receive functions, it would be sufficient to simply disable the receive functions until all documents are processed and all servers have updated their in-memory cache. Reenabling the receive functions will restore the flow of documents into the system.

Another useful technique is to avoid changing existing configurations whenever possible. Instead, add a new set of document definitions, channels, and so on. Once all of the servers have had time to read the new configuration, you can divert the incoming flow of documents to the new channel. Once all documents are processed through the old configuration, it can be safely deleted. This requires a great deal of planning, but may be necessary in a system requiring 24 × 7 support.

Most change-control plans consist of at least three tiers of environments to ensure stability: development, test, and production. The development environment is for developing and updating solutions. This environment is typically very flexible and not very stable. The test environment is used to simulate the production environment. Any variation between the test and production environments may lead to problems in production. Only after extensive testing should updates be made to the production environment. Usually, paperwork is generated and meetings take place to be certain that everything has been covered. These are a necessary evil of the trade, and well worth the effort in the long run.

Security

Security in BizTalk Server is handled from two points of view. One is the typical security associated with any Windows server application. Another is the need to protect the documents being exchanged. BizTalk Server covers both of these areas by leveraging mature, existing technologies.

For server security, BizTalk Server utilizes Windows 2000's native security mechanisms of Active Directory, Kerberos, and so on. When BizTalk Server is installed, a user group is created that controls access to BizTalk Server's administration features. Only members of this group, called BizTalk Server Administrators by default, are allowed to administer the server software. There is also a group called BizTalk Server Report Users that controls access to the BizTalk Server Document Tracking web application. In addition to these groups, BizTalk Server's receive functions and service executables should be run using NT service accounts for added safety.

Securing the documents being exchanged is even more important, and a bit more difficult, than securing the server itself. The level of security you need to implement will depend on the nature of the connection between the source and destination systems. In situations in which documents are being passed between internal systems on a company LAN or WAN, encrypting or otherwise hiding the document's contents is not usually necessary. However, most BizTalk Server installations are used to perform some type of EDI exchange with trading partners.

In this case, you need to consider both privacy and authentication. *Privacy* refers to hiding the contents of your documents from unauthorized parties who may be able to intercept the network traffic being used to transport your documents. Encryption is the standard answer to this problem. *Authentication* is the ability to verify that the document being received came from the trading partner it was supposed to come from. This prevents outsiders from sending bogus documents and having them processed as authentic. This is the intellectual equivalent of sending a bunch of pizzas to someone else's house, but it is much more dangerous for a business.

The simplest means of securely transmitting documents from one point to another is to use a secure transmission path. These would include an internal LAN or WAN, a Virtual Private Network (VPN), a value-added network (VAN), or an encrypted Internet connection using SSL. Using a VAN or VPN has the added benefit of handling authentication for you, since they always require a logon sequence of some sort before establishing a connection. SSL can be also used to perform authentication by exchanging client certificates with your trading partner.

When documents must be sent over an unsecured medium such as the Internet, it becomes necessary to utilize BizTalk Server's custom security. BizTalk Server uses Windows 2000's public key infrastructure (PKI) system to manage certificates. Using certificates exchanged with your trading partners, you can digitally sign documents for authentication and encrypt them for privacy. The certificates are configured on the channels and ports used to send and receive these documents. The drawback is that your trading partner must use a system that understands how to encrypt and decrypt documents correctly for BizTalk Server.

Monitoring and Maintenance

Monitoring a BizTalk Server installation is not any more difficult than maintaining any other type of mission-critical server. We will briefly discuss strategies to consider for monitoring your deployment.

The most useful tool for developing custom monitoring applications is the Windows Management Instrumentation (WMI) system. This provides an easy-to-use API for monitoring and manipulating BizTalk Servers remotely. BizTalk Server's WMI implementation is covered in detail in Chapter 19.

A key aspect of maintaining any server deployment is to regularly back up the data necessary to restore the system quickly. For BizTalk Server, almost all of the data needed is stored in the four SQL Server databases discussed earlier. A backup and recovery strategy must be developed for these databases prior to deployment.

In day-to-day operation, the most important items to monitor are the Application Event Log and the Suspended Queue. Any errors registered by BizTalk Server or any documents that fail in processing must be immediately investigated. In high-volume scenarios, a problem that causes one error can often cascade into a massive problem very quickly. Early warning is the best defense to keep your servers running fast and free of errors.

The
Complete
Reference

Part V

Deploying BizTalk Server

Chapter 12

Planning, Deploying, and Optimizing a BizTalk Server Solution

In this chapter, we will discuss deploying and optimizing a BizTalk Server solution. Aside from the actual development of the BizTalk Server application, there are several critical steps in deploying a BizTalk Server solution. First, you must determine the infrastructure demands of the application. Second, you must determine what the application's reliability needs are. Once an application's availability and reliability needs have been calculated, you must design a BizTalk Server deployment that at a minimum meets these projections and, ideally, will be able to scale if necessary. After the application is developed in the development environment, it must be deployed onto the production servers. Because moving an application from the development environment to the test environment and then to the production environment can be complex, it is best to have a procedure in place ahead of time.

BizTalk Server Databases

Before discussing the deployment options available for BizTalk Server 2000, let's take a look at the four databases that BizTalk Server uses. Understanding how BizTalk Server uses these databases is the key to successfully designing and deploying BizTalk Server installations. The four databases are:

- **BizTalk Messaging Management**   The BizTalk Messaging Management database stores all of the configurations of BizTalk Messaging components and receive functions. Of the four databases, this database will have the least activity. The default name for this database is InterchangeBTM.

- **Shared Queue**   The Shared Queue database stores all of the documents and interchanges submitted to BizTalk Server. Because all documents and interchanges submitted asynchronously to a BizTalk server or server group will be written and read from this database, it will be used heavily, relative to the other four databases. The default name for this database is InterchangeSQ.

- **Tracking**   The Tracking database stores all of the documents and interchanges that are being tracked. The activity of this database will vary depending on how much information you are tracking when processing documents. The default name for this database is InterchangeDTA.

- **Orchestration Persistence**   The Orchestration Persistence database stores information about currently running and dehydrated XLANG schedules and messages. The activity of this database will depend on the number of outstanding long-running transactions and the number of concurrently processed documents. The default name for this database is XLANG.

BizTalk Server Fault Tolerance and Load Balancing

When designing your BizTalk Server deployment, you should take into account two things that on the surface are very different, but that are very closely related: fault tolerance and load balancing. Fault tolerance gives your BizTalk Server the capability to withstand a system hardware failure. Load balancing spreads the workload over multiple computers. Often, fault tolerance will also provide load balancing, and load balancing will provide fault tolerance. There are several ways to add fault tolerance and load balancing to your BizTalk Server installation.

BizTalk Server Groups

To better handle applications with large performance needs, multiple BizTalk Servers can be placed into one or more BizTalk Server groups. Once in the BizTalk Server groups, the individual BizTalk Servers can be centrally configured, managed, and monitored. There are four main resources in common among BizTalk Servers in a BizTalk Server group:

- A single Shared Queue database
- A single Tracking database
- All receive functions
- All required components from processing documents and interchanges, such as application integration components (AICs).

Note   *See Chapter 17 for more information on creating AICs*

BizTalk Server Groups and BizTalk Server Databases

One of the primary reasons for creating BizTalk Server groups is to centrally manage and monitor BizTalk Server databases resources. Let's take a look at how BizTalk Server groups affect the placement of the BizTalk databases.

- **BizTalk Messaging Management**   The BizTalk Messaging Management database is not heavily used. In general, one database will suffice for all Server groups, and all BizTalk Servers will be able to use the same messaging components. Unlike with the other databases, it is not a straightforward procedure to move the BizTalk Messaging Management database; thus, when installing BizTalk Servers in your production environment, you should carefully plan which SQL Server computer will host this database.

- **Shared Queue**   One Shared Queue database is shared by each BizTalk Server in a Server group. All documents and interchanges received by the BizTalk Server groups will be written to the Shared Queue database and read by the individual BizTalk Server that will process it. Ideally, because of the high amount of activity this database will handle, this database should be placed on a dedicated SQL Server.

- **Tracking**   There is one tracking database per BizTalk Server group. Because the activity of this database will vary greatly depending on the quantity of information that you track, your placement of this database will change. Here is one thing to keep in mind: while this database will be written to frequently, it will be read from infrequently, and so you should place it on an SQL Server with a disk subsystem optimized for write operations. For more information on optimizing databases, see "Optimizing BizTalk Server Databases" later in this chapter.

- **Orchestration Persistence**   Each BizTalk Server can have its own Orchestration Persistence database. You should place these databases according to the number of long-running transactions that will be dehydrated and rehydrated.

BizTalk Server Groups and Receive Functions

All receive functions are shared in a single BizTalk Server group, but you have the option of selecting which BizTalk Servers participate in receiving documents and which servers participate in processing documents. You could have the document processing workload distributed among the BizTalk Servers. For example, a company has deployed a BizTalk Server group with two BizTalk Servers. The company's web site receives orders and places them into a message queue that is monitored by a message queuing receive function. The message queuing receive function submits the document to the BizTalk Server group, where it is placed in the Shared Queue database work queue. The first available BizTalk Server in the BizTalk Server group picks up the order from the work queue and processes the order. Thus, assuming that on average each order is processed in about the same amount of time, each server will handle half of the incoming orders on a first-come first-serve basis.

You could also have some servers participate in receiving documents and some servers participate in processing documents. This configuration is particularly useful when you have custom preprocessors that complete complex operations, such as decryption, or that have a high volume of incoming documents. For example, a company receives a high volume of encrypted orders from trading partners. The company has installed three BizTalk Servers in a single BizTalk Server group. One BizTalk Server receives, decrypts, and validates incoming orders; it uses a message queuing receive function to place the orders in the Shared Queue database work queue. The other two BizTalk Servers in the Server group monitor the work queue to process the orders. Thus, the burden of CPU-intensive decryption and order processing has been isolated to specific servers by using a BizTalk Server group. To configure a BizTalk Server's role in a BizTalk Server group:

1. Open the BizTalk Server Administration MMC, expand **Microsoft BizTalk Server 2000**, select the server group that contains the server you want to configure, and then click the server.

2. From the Action menu, select Properties.

3. Restart the server.

There will be several options to configure (see Figure 12-1):

■ **Maximum Number Of Receive Function Threads Allowed**   The default value for this setting is 4. If this server is dedicated to receiving documents, you may wish to set this threshold higher.

■ **Participate In Work-Item Processing**   This check box determines whether or not the server participates in processing orders. If the box is not checked, the server will not monitor the work queue.

■ **Maximum Number Of Worker Threads Per Processor Allowed**   The default value for this setting is 4. If this server is dedicated to processing documents,

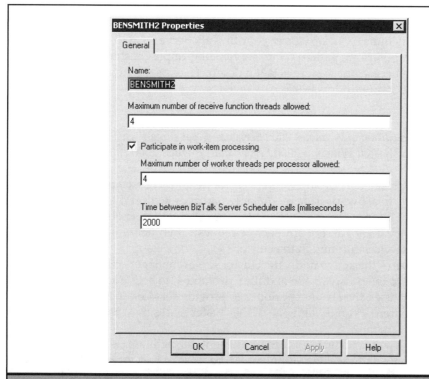

Figure 12-1. *BizTalk Server configuration settings*

you may wish to set this threshold higher. Microsoft recommends setting this between 14 and 16 for optimum performance under normal circumstances.

■ **Time Between BizTalk Server Scheduler Calls** This option controls how often the work queue is polled for new documents. The value is stored in milliseconds.

Clustering BizTalk Server Resources

In a simple BizTalk Server group deployment scenario, each server can provide the same services, such as receive functions, transporting information, and XLANG orchestration processing. In the event that one member server goes out of service, the rest of the servers in the group will pick up the load and continue processing the documents. Ideally, the client will not notice the failure of the BizTalk Server.

However, there are some drawbacks to using a BizTalk Server group alone. In certain situations, interruption of services may occur if one machine goes down in a BizTalk Server group. For example, if some messages remain in the local message queue or file location on the failed server, those messages will not get processed until the failed server is functional. Clients that are sending messages to the local data store of the failed server would not have their documents processed. Depending on the client implementation, this situation may prevent the client from sending any further messages to be processed, even though other BizTalk Servers are still available.

To solve this dilemma, you can *cluster* your BizTalk Servers, so that multiple BizTalk Server computers are gathered into server subgroups. Clustering provides continuous service in case one system is taken down. To use server clusters, you must install BizTalk Server on Windows 2000 Advanced Server or Datacenter Server.

> **Note** *The Standard edition of Windows 2000 Server does not support clustering. There is no upgrade path between Windows 2000 Server and Windows 2000 Advanced Server.*

The Microsoft Cluster Service supports *active-passive* and *active-active* node clustering (more on this later). In active-passive mode, only one node within the cluster provides services to clients. This is called the *active* node. The other nodes, called *passive* nodes, are running, but they do not accept any service requests. In other words, the active node *owns* all the services running in the cluster.

Upon the failure of the active node, the cluster server manager will transfer the clustered resource to the passive node and then promote it to active status (see Figure 12-2). To the user, the cluster continues to provide services and the loss of the first node is transparent, even though one of the cluster nodes may have suffered a catastrophic hardware failure.

Although this type of cluster is easy to implement, the active-passive clustering design gives you only half the computing power, because only one node is running at a time. The other nodes remain idle, even when the first node is under heavy load.

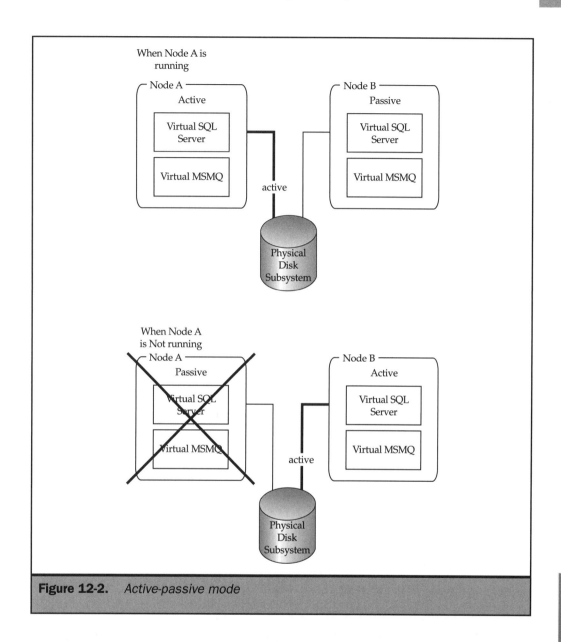

Figure 12-2.   *Active-passive mode*

The second type of cluster is called active-active mode. In this mode, all the nodes (or machines) within a cluster provide services (see Figure 12-3). In *active-active* mode, each node in the cluster provides a particular set of services. For example, suppose an SQL Server instance is running on one node, and you want the second node to help in processing requests to this SQL Server instance. In active-passive mode, this is not

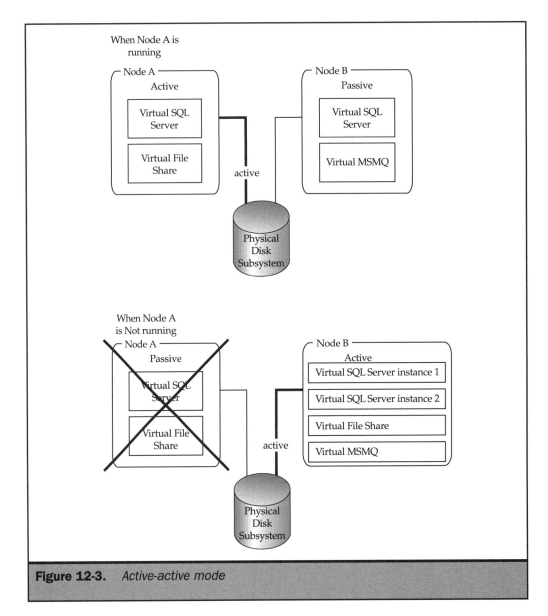

Figure 12-3. *Active-active mode*

possible. However, if a second SQL Server instance is running on the second active machine in the cluster, you can route some processing requests to the second node, so that each node is providing the service to a different SQL Server instance. The active-active mode utilizes all the computing power of several nodes in a cluster.

Active-active mode can take advantage of the processing power of multiple server nodes in the network, but the fact that each node must host different services makes load balancing less than perfect. For example, only one server provides BizTalk messaging or orchestration.

The current implementation of clustering allows a maximum of four nodes in each cluster. But what if, for example, you want to add five more BizTalk Servers to balance a particular load? To solve this problem, you can *combine* the BizTalk Server group and a database cluster to provide both scalability and fault tolerance.

In Figure 12-3, five BizTalk Servers are working together in a server group. In this scenario, the BizTalk Server database is located on a database cluster running in active-active mode between Cluster A and Cluster B. All the document processing will occur on five well-balanced BizTalk Servers, while the database cluster provides a database service with fault tolerance.

There are four BizTalk Server resources that can be clustered:

- **File shares**   BizTalk Server file receive functions can be made fault tolerant by clustering the file shares that the file receive function monitors.

- **Message queues**   BizTalk Server message queuing receive functions can be made fault tolerant by clustering the message queue.

- **BizTalk Server databases**   BizTalk Server databases are stored in SQL 7.0 or SQL 2000 databases, which can be clustered. This is the most compelling resource to cluster.

- **Web Distributed Authoring and Versioning (WebDAV) repository**   Because the WebDAV repository is an IIS resource, it can be clustered for fault tolerance.

Note	*Explaining how to install cluster servers is outside of the scope of this book. For information on installing BizTalk Server Clusters, see the BizTalk Clustering white paper from Microsoft at http://www.microsoft.com/biztalk/techinfo/deployment/wp_clusteringconsiderations.doc.*

COM Component Load Balancing

If your BizTalk Server application relies heavily on functionality provided by COM Components, you should consider using Microsoft Application Center 2000 to cluster or load-balance COM Components. Clustering COM Components will enable XLANG schedules and AICs to be fault tolerant, similar to how the Cluster server enables applications like SQL Server to be fault tolerant. You can also use COM Component load balancing to balance the load on individual COM Components called during the execution of an XLANG schedule or an AIC. Using Application Center Component Load Balancing, you can route the requests to COM or COM+ applications intelligently, depending on the current traffic and the server hardware. Details on how to configure Application Center 2000 are outside the scope of this book, but if you are planning a BizTalk Server deployment that has a heavy reliance on COM applications or will require a high level of performance from COM applications, you should include this in your proof of concept planning.

Deploying BizTalk Server

There are several phases to deploying BizTalk Server, and at the end of each phase you will need to redeploy your BizTalk solution to a new environment. Similarly, you may need to redeploy your BizTalk Servers in a disaster recovery incident. For example, once you have developed your BizTalk solution in the development environment, you will need to deploy this solution to a test environment or proof of concept network. You could install the entire solution manually each time, but this would be time consuming and it could easily lead to errors and inconsistencies. This section will discuss how to automate the deployment of your BizTalk solution.

Deploying BizTalk Messaging Objects

When it comes to the configuration, most of us would prefer an automatic installation script over manual installation. BizTalk Server Messaging was built with easy deployment in mind. BizTalk Messaging objects (messaging ports, channels, document specifications, document maps, and organizations) are created manually with BizTalk Messaging Manager.

Scripting Messaging Object Creation

There are three main options for moving messaging components from the BizTalk Servers where they were created to other BizTalk Servers, such as might be required when making the transition from a development environment to a production environment.

- Use the BizTalk Messaging Manager in the target BizTalk Server to manually recreate the messaging components.

- Back up the SQL Server database used to store messaging components (InterchangeBTM) on the source BizTalk Server, and restore it to the target BizTalk Server.

- Create Visual Basic scripts that use the BizTalk Messaging Configuration application programming interfaces (APIs) and the BizTalk Windows Management Instrumentation (WMI) interfaces to create all the necessary BizTalk messaging components to be executed on the target BizTalk Server.

While the first option is effective, it does not scale well. Often, applications must be installed and reinstalled several times in a test environment; completing this task manually would be very inefficient. While the second option may appear on the surface to be appealing, unless the two BizTalk Servers have the same name, this procedure can quickly become quite cumbersome due to the SQL Server and BizTalk Server dependencies in the computer name.

That leaves us with the third, and last, option, which is the preferred method. While creating a script for all the necessary messaging components may appear to be an enormous task, in the long run it's the best solution. Although you will have to overcome the initial learning curve of scripting for BizTalk Server, once you have mastered it, you will be able to greatly streamline the deployment of messaging objects by fully automating their creation. This will also be helpful in recovering from a disaster, as you will be able to fully recreate the BizTalk messaging components by simply executing a script. The object model used to create BizTalk messaging components is documented in the BizTalk Server Help file. Additionally, examples of how to create BizTalk messaging components using Visual Basic scripts can be found on the BizTalk Server 2000 CD in the \Program Files\Microsoft BizTalk Server\Tutorial\Setup directory.

Here is a Visual Basic script that creates a BizTalk document specification, two organizations, a channel, and a messaging port:

```
Const SERVER_NAME = "BENSMITH2"
Const SOURCE_ORGANIZATION = "Source Org"
Const DESTINATION_ORGANIZATION = "Destination Org"
Const DOCUMENT_DEFINITION_NAME = "CanonicalReceipt"
Const DOCUMENT_DEFINITION_FILE_NAME = "CanonicalReceipt.xml"
Const DOCUMENT_MAP_FILE_NAME = "CanonicalReceiptTo4010-997.xml"
Const DESTINATION_FILE_NAME = "c:\test"
Set objConfig = CreateObject("BizTalk.BizTalkConfig")
'Create the Document Definition
Set objDocDef = objConfig.CreateDocument
objDocDef.Name = DOCUMENT_DEFINITION_NAME
objDocDef.Reference = "http://" & SERVER_NAME &_
  "/biztalkserverrepository/docspecs/microsoft/" & DOCUMENT_DEFINITION_FILE_NAME
objDocDef.Create
'Create the Organizations
Set objSourceOrg = objConfig.CreateOrganization
Set objDestOrg = objConfig.CreateOrganization
objSourceOrg.Name = SOURCE_ORGANIZATION
objSourceOrg.Create
objDestOrg.Name = DESTINATION_ORGANIZATION
objDestOrg.Create
'Create the Port
Set objPort = objConfig.CreatePort
objPort.Name = "Message Port to " & DESTINATION_ORGANIZATION
objPort.DestinationEndpoint.Organization = objDestOrg.Handle
objPort.PrimaryTransport.Type = 256
objPort.PrimaryTransport.Address = "file://" &_
 DESTINATION_FILE_NAME
objPort.Create
'Create the Channel
Set objChannel = objConfig.CreateChannel

objChannel.Name = SOURCE_ORGANIZATION & " to " & DESTINATION_ORGANIZATION
objChannel.Port = objPort.Handle
objChannel.SourceEndpoint.Organization = objSourceOrg.Handle
objChannel.InputDocument = objDocDef.Handle
objChannel.OutputDocument = objDocDef.Handle

objChannel.MapReference = "http://" & SERVER_NAME &_
```

```
"/biztalkserverrepository/maps/microsoft/" &_
DOCUMENT_MAP_FILE_NAME
objChannel.Create
msgbox "Done!"
```

To verify the execution of this script, use BizTalk Messaging Manager to ensure that the following messaging objects have been created:

- A document definition named "CanonicalReceipt"
- An organization named "Source Organization"
- An organization named "Destination Organization"
- A channel named "Source Organization to Destination Organization"
- A port named "To Destination Organization"

You will also need to deploy the XML schemas and document maps stored in the WebDAV repository. This procedure is merely a cut-and-paste operation. By default, BizTalk Server stores XML schemas and document maps to:

\Program Files\Microsoft BizTalk Server\BizTalk Server Repository

Using BTConfigAssistant

BizTalk Server ships with a tool to help automate the deployment of BizTalk Server messaging objects between deployment phases. The tool, called BTConfigAssistant, is located the following directory:

\Program Files\Microsoft BizTalk Server\SDK\Messaging Samples\BTConfigAssistant

BTConfigAssisant enables you to create a single package, in the form of a Visual Basic Script. You can then use this script to deploy the messaging objects on different BizTalk Servers. The following messaging objects can be captured in a script created with BTConfigAssistant:

- Organizations
- Messaging Ports
- Channels
- Document Definitions
- Envelopes
- AICs
- Serializers
- Parsers

To use the BTConfigAssistant tool, go to the directory:

\Program Files\Microsoft BizTalk Server\Messaging Samples\
BTConfigAssistant\EXE

and execute BTConfigAssistant.exe. The BTConfigAssistant tool will locate all messaging
objects installed on the BizTalk Server and list them in the appropriate tables. You can
then select the messaging objects that you wish to redeploy. For example, if you run the
script from the preceding section and open BTConfigAssistant, you can select the
messaging objects created in the script. Once you have chosen the correct messaging
objects, you can view the scripts that BTConfigAssistant created to redeploy the
selected messaging objects by opening the View menu and clicking Selected Items. The
viewing window has two options to view the configuration details, in XML format or
Visual Basic Script. If you would like to save the script, use the Save As button at the
bottom of the window. To use BTConfigAssistant:

1. Run the script from the preceding section.

2. Run the BTConfigAssistant tool.

3. Select the messaging objects created by the script (see Figure 12-4).

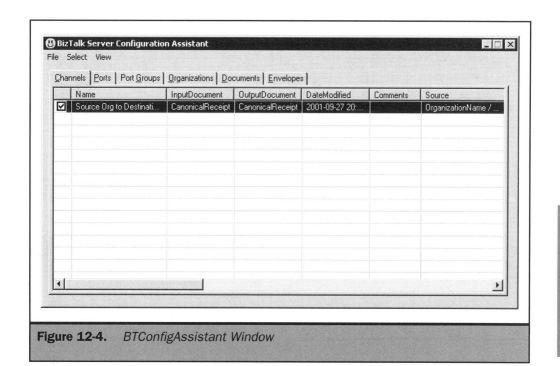

Figure 12-4.   *BTConfigAssistant Window*

4. Open the View menu and click Selected Items.

5. On the VBscript tab, use the Save As button to save the VBscript file (see Figure 12-5).

6. Use the BizTalk Messaging Manager to delete all of the messaging objects created by the script.

7. Run the script created by BTConfigAssistant, and verify the results.

Note When using BTConfigAssistant, you must manually copy all document schemas and maps to the target BizTalk Server.

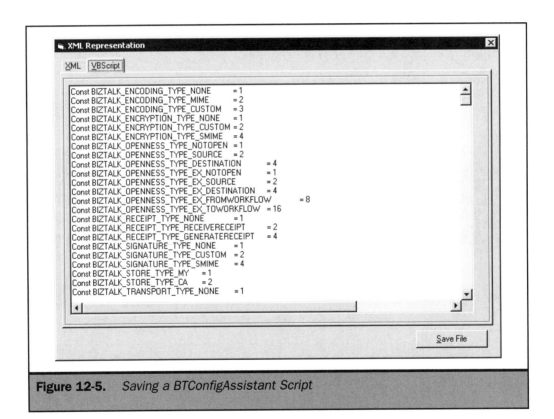

Figure 12-5. Saving a BTConfigAssistant Script

BizTalk Server Performance

Let's take a look at monitoring the performance of BizTalk Server. Monitoring the performance of your BizTalk Server during the test phase of your deployment will help ensure the proper sizing of server hardware and placement of BizTalk Server components, such as the SQL Server databases, that BizTalk uses. Once you are working in the production environment, consistently monitoring the performance of your BizTalk Server enables you to optimize your installation as operating conditions change and also to locate hardware degradation in advance of failure. Monitoring the performance of BizTalk Server is very much like monitoring the performance of any Windows 2000 Server, in terms of the performance monitoring cycle and tools used for performance monitoring.

Performance Monitoring Cycle

The worst time to start performance monitoring is when you think there is a bottleneck. When monitoring the performance of a BizTalk Server, it is helpful to break performance data out into categories. For example, it is common to break hardware performance into four categories or subsystems:

- **Memory**   This includes physical memory or RAM and virtual memory or paging
- **CPU**   Includes CPUs, system bus, system cache
- **Disk**   Includes hard disks and disk controllers
- **Network**   Includes the network interface card

With BizTalk Server, you should also break out the BizTalk-specific systems, such as message queues, work queues, and file receive functions.

For performance monitoring to be effective, you must take several steps:

1. Establish a performance baseline
2. Monitor performance
3. Identify a bottleneck
4. Optimize your configuration

Establishing a Baseline

The performance of every server is tied to the hardware it is installed on, the software that is installed, the configuration of the software, and the processes running on the server at any one given time. Often, you can have servers with the exact same hardware and software configurations, run the same performance tests, and receive different results. This is why, for each BizTalk Server, is it imperative that you first establish a performance baseline for later comparisons. To establish a baseline, select a broad range of performance counters and monitor the server under normal operating parameters. It is important that the baseline is established over time, and over a range of operating conditions. A common mistake that is made in establishing a baseline is to monitor performance only during peak server usage, or during off hours, when servers are the least stressed. You will use this baseline to compare the performance of the server over time when completing routine monitoring.

Monitoring Performance

You should continue to monitor the performance of your BizTalk Servers just as you did when you established the baseline. Ideally, performance monitoring will occur on a regular schedule. You should make sure that all changes to the system— reconfiguration, new hardware, new services—are documented, so that changes in server performance caused by configuration changes are not seen as general changes in performance.

Identifying a Bottleneck

Once you have a history of performance monitoring data to analyze, you can begin to identify the types of bottlenecks that exist. When identifying bottlenecks, you need to be careful to distinguish between performance trends and performance spikes. Without a baseline for comparison and a history of performance data, it is often very difficult to see trends, especially when there is a slow degradation of a particular resource. For instance, on first glance it may not seem odd to see that a BizTalk Server spends 23 percent of its disk activity writing to the hard disks, but if the preceding ten weeks data indicated that this figure had slowly risen from 18 percent, it would be obvious that something is affecting the performance of the disk subsystem. Similarly, it is important to identify performance spikes. For instance, it is normal to see CPU utilization spike at about 80 percent for short periods of time, but it is not normal to see CPU utilization consistently operate at over 80 percent for long periods of time.

Optimizing Your Configuration

Once you have identified a performance bottleneck and have created a list of actions to alleviate the bottleneck, you should prioritize them depending on how likely they are to remove the bottleneck. You should make only a single change to the system at a time, so that you can be certain which change removed the bottleneck. You should also keep in mind that removing one bottleneck often causes another to appear. For instance, you might identify that a BizTalk Server that hosts the Tracking Database is spending too much time writing to the disk subsystem. You have several options to resolve this bottleneck. For example, let's say that you choose to move the tracking database to a different server. While this may remove the bottleneck around disk write time, it may cause a bottleneck in the network subsystem, as all document tracking events are now sent to another server throughout the network.

After you have made a change to optimize the server, you should return to step one, create a new baseline, and continue with the cycle. Performance monitoring is an ongoing task, not a one-time event, and in many ways it is as much an art as it is a technical process.

Tools for Monitoring Performance

Now that we have discussed the process of monitoring the performance of BizTalk Servers, let's take a look at three important tools for this monitoring: the Task Manager, the System Monitor, and the Event Viewer. Each tool has its own role, and none is a substitute for another. It is important to know how to use each tool appropriately. The best way to learn how to use these tools is to monitor the performance of a BizTalk Server, after (or even while) reading this chapter, is to do it! Practice makes perfect!

Task Manager

The Task Manager, a default component of Windows 2000, can be used to get point-in-time and limited historical performance data about applications and processes running on your BizTalk Server. From a performance monitoring standpoint, the Task Manager is a rapid-use tool (see Figure 12-6). You can use it to quickly get the performance of your server, but you would not use it for long term monitoring. There are three ways to open the Task Manager:

- Place the mouse pointer on the taskbar, right-click, and select Task Manager.
- Press CTRL + ALT + DELETE and select Task Manager.
- Press CTRL + SHIFT + ESC.

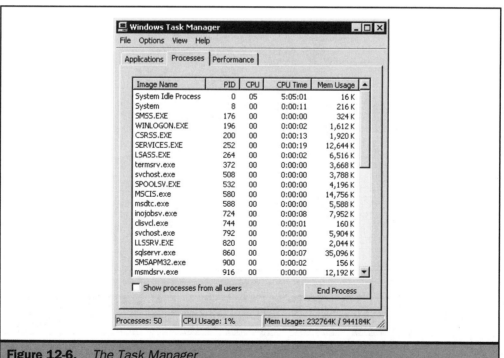

Figure 12-6. *The Task Manager*

The Task Manager displays information about applications and processes currently running on the server, as well as some very basic performance statistics. On the Applications tab in the Task Manager, you can see the status of applications that are currently running and choose to stop an application that cannot be shut down gracefully by right-clicking the application and selecting End Task. The Process and Performance tabs are where the most valuable performance information can be found.

The Process tab in the Task Manager displays all of the current processes running on the server and a handful of performance counters. You can add additional performance metrics by opening the View menu and selecting Select Columns, as shown in Figure 12-7. You can use the performance information on the Process tab in two ways. First, you can record the processes are running on the server during your baseline monitoring and then you can routinely compare the processes running on the server to those that were running during the baseline. This will tell you whether any unusual processes are running or if the server has been altered in anyway. Second, it will allow to you get a quick, real-time view of the amount of system resources being used by a specific process. For instance, you may note that the Message Queue process (mqsvc.exe), which usually uses 10,000KB of memory, is currently using 80,000KB of memory. This quick, informal check would clearly illustrate a potential performance problem with the system.

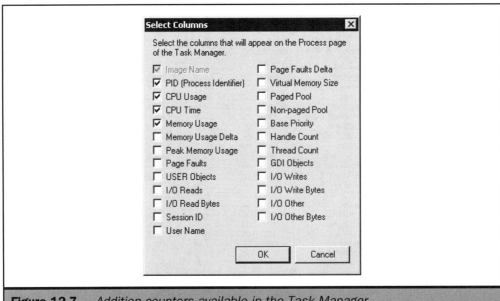

Figure 12-7.   Addition counters available in the Task Manager

Some of the valuable performance counters available in the Task Manager are:

- **Memory Usage**   This counter tracks the current amount of memory being used by the process.
- **CPU**   This counter displays the percentages of time the threads of the current process are using CPU cycles.
- **Thread Count**   This counter displays the number of threads running in the process.
- **Username**   This counter reports the security context the process is running under.

System Monitor

The System Monitor in Windows 2000 is the primary tool for monitoring the performance of your BizTalk Server, including long-term performance (see Figure 12-8). Because the use of the Windows 2000 System Monitor is outside of the scope of this book and is well explained in the Windows 2000 product documentation, our focus will be on the counters that we will need to know to maximize BizTalk Server performance.

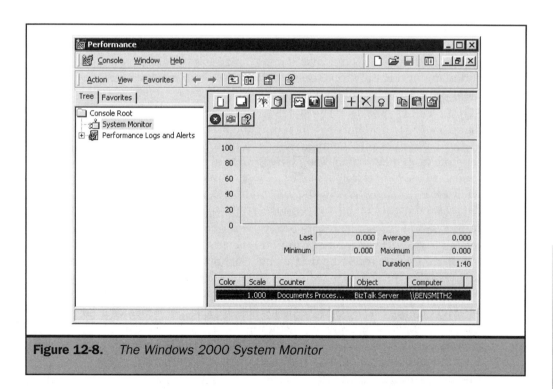

Figure 12-8.   *The Windows 2000 System Monitor*

To open the System Monitor MMC, open the Start menu | Programs | Administrative Tools | Performance.

Once the System Monitor has been started, you need to add objects and counters for instances as shown in Figure 12-9. An *object* is a particular programmatic interface, or collection of interfaces, that you can monitor. *Counters* are measurements of particular aspects of the object. *Instances* are individual units for measurement; for example, if you have two CPUs in your BizTalk Server, there will be three instances of the CPU object—one for each CPU and one for both CPUs. Every object that you add to the System Monitor consumes resources; thus, you must add only the objects on which you are actively collecting data or run the System Monitor on a remote system to monitor your BizTalk Server without using the BizTalk Server's resources for performance monitoring. It is important to recognize that all aspects of an object are measured when an object is added to the System Monitor. For instance, if you add the Documents Mapped/Sec counter of the BizTalk Server object to the performance monitor, even though only the document mappings per second would be shown in the System Monitor, all of the counters for the BizTalk Server object would be tracked. To add counters to the System Monitor, right-click System Monitor and select Add Counters.

There are several important objects and counters specific to the operation of BizTalk Server:

- **BizTalk Server** The BizTalk Server object monitors the performance of BizTalk Server itself. There are 20 counters for the BizTalk Server object; they track such things as document and interchange submission, parsing, processing, and mappings. For obvious reasons, all of these counters are of interest when monitoring your BizTalk Server.

- **SQL Server: Databases** The SQL Server: Databases object tracks performance data about specific databases, including the BizTalk databases. The counters allow you to track the overall activity and performance of the database, separate from other databases. Two counters of particular interest are Active Transactions and Transactions/Sec. These counters will tell you how busy each database is, giving you valuable information as you design the location of databases in your BizTalk Server deployment.

- **Active Server Pages** The Active Server Pages object tracks performance data related to ASP. There are many important counters that you will want to monitor if you are receiving documents via ASP. Of particular interest are the Requests/Sec and Request wait time counters. Your web site should not be the bottleneck in your BizTalk Server deployment under any circumstances.

- **MSMQ Queues** The MSMQ Queues object tracks performance information about specific message queues, including those you have created for your BizTalk Server installation. Using the MSMQ Queues counters, you can track the number of messages in a queue and the size of those messages.

- **MSMQ Service** The MSMQ Service object tracks performance of the MSMQ server, rather than individual queues. You can use this counter to monitor the aggregate performance of MSMQ.

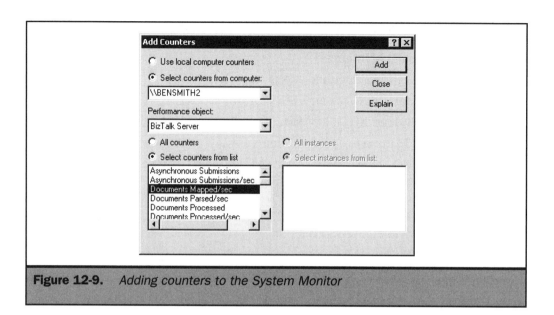

Figure 12-9.   *Adding counters to the System Monitor*

Additionally, you can use the Process object to monitor the performance of specific processes more formally than you can with the Task Manager by adding the Process object and selecting the appropriate instance. There are other performance objects that you should also monitor, although they are more closely related to the general operation of Windows 2000 Server and Advanced Server. These objects include Server, Server Work Queues, Memory, and Physical Disks. In general, use the following guidelines:

- Keep CPU utilization under 80 percent.
- Keep Server work queue length under 2.
- Keep committed memory below the total amount of physical memory.
- Keep Physical Disk performance within manufacturer's guidelines for seek and read times.

The System Monitor itself has several valuable tools. Not only can you use the System Monitor to track the performance of the system, but you can also have the data automatically logged for historical purposes, such as comparing previous and future performance logs. One of the most compelling features of the System Monitor is the capability to have alerts sent when specific counters reach specific thresholds.

For example, using the System Monitor Alerts you could set an alert to occur when there are more than ten messages in a message queue that receives BizTalk messages from trading partners. You can have the System Monitor do any of the follow actions: Write an event to the Event Viewer, send a NETBIOS message using the Messenger Service, start a performance tracking log, or run a command-line program, which you could have send a message to your pager. This would enable you to proactively solve problems related to your BizTalk Server's performance.

To set a System Monitor Alert for BizTalk Server, as shown in Figure 12-10:

1. Open the System Monitor.

2. Expand Performance Logs and Alerts and select Alerts.

3. Right-click Alerts and click New Alert Setting.

4. Name the new alert **BizTalk MSMQ Overflow** and click OK.

5. Click the Add button to add a counter.

6. Add the MSMQ Queue object and the Messages in Queue counter for the servername\private$\order_queue$ message queue (or any message queue that you have created) and click Close.

7. Set the appropriate alert level and check the box on the Action tab to log the alert as shown in Figure 12-11.

Event Viewer

The Event Viewer is a performance monitoring tool that, ideally, you will never want to use. Why? It means that something is wrong. Nonetheless, it is a valuable tool that

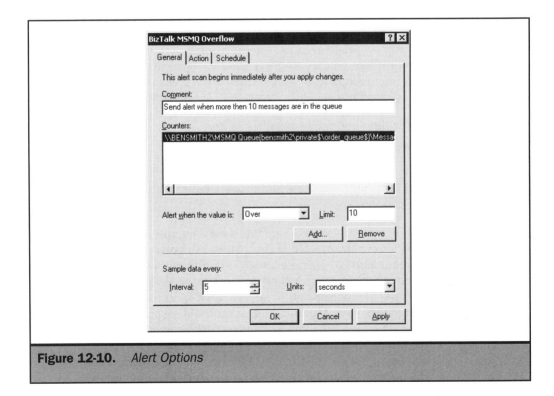

Figure 12-10. *Alert Options*

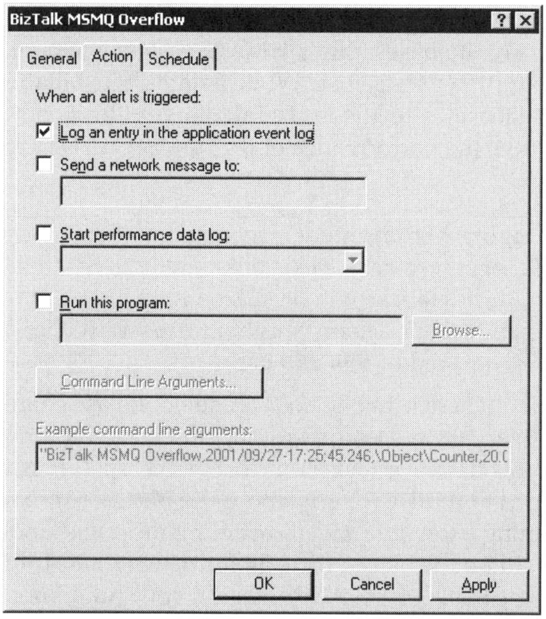

Figure 12-11.   *Adding an Alert*

reports performance warnings about your BizTalk Server. You should monitor the Event Viewer for Warning and Stop events from BizTalk Server. Events from BizTalk Server will have one of two sources: BizTalk Server and BTWSvcMgr. Additionally, you should pay particular attention to services that your BizTalk Server depends on, such as MSMQ. You should immediately address all Stop events and thoroughly investigate all Warning events.

Optimizing Performance

Now that we have discussed monitoring the performance of BizTalk Server, let's take a look at some ways in which you can optimize its performance. Because BizTalk Server relies on both Windows 2000 Server and SQL Server 2000, you will need to optimize these products appropriately. The tuning of Windows 2000 Server and SQL Server are outside of the scope of this book, but you should not discount the need to tune these products. This section will focus on optimizing the databases that BizTalk Server uses and tuning BizTalk Server itself.

Optimizing Databases

BizTalk Server uses four databases: BizTalk Message Management, Shared Queue, Tracking, and Orchestration Persistence. While a default installation of BizTalk Server installs all of these databases directly on BizTalk Server, this is not a requirement. The simplest way to improve the performance of BizTalk Server is to appropriately place these databases.

- ■ **BizTalk Messaging Management**   As noted earlier in the chapter, the BizTalk Messaging Management database is not heavily used. In fact, in many environments, this database will be shared not only by many BizTalk Servers in a server group, but also by many server groups. Little performance-related optimization is required of this database.

- ■ **Shared Queue**   There is one Shared Queue database shared by each BizTalk Server in a server group. Because all documents and interchanges received will be written to this database and then read by the BizTalk Server that will process it, you will need to think carefully about the placement of this database. Unless you are expecting a low volume of incoming messages and interchanges, this database should not be placed directly on an active BizTalk Server, but rather on a stand-alone SQL Server. Additionally, you should not place this database on the same server as the Tracking database, for performance reasons. If you are planning on placing this database on an SQL Server that hosts additional databases, you should determine if the disk access times are acceptable; if not, consider dedicating a disk array to each database.

- ■ **Tracking**   There is one tracking database per BizTalk Server group. Like the Shared Queue database, the Tracking database can experience a high level of activity, depending on the amount of data that is tracked. The Tracking database should not be placed on the same server as the Shared Queue database. A very large quantity of information may be placed into this database; thus, the database should be sized appropriately. Similarly, considering the network traffic that will be generated by having the tracked data sent from the BizTalk Server to the Tracking database, you should have at least 100MB connectivity with layer two switching between your BizTalk Servers and the SQL Server where the Tracking database is placed. Nearly all the activity of this database will consist of write operations; thus, you should tune the physical disk structure where this database is placed for write operations.

- ■ **Orchestration Persistence**   Each BizTalk Server will have its own Orchestration Persistence database. This database has the potential for a high level of activity, depending on the transactions that will be dehydrated and rehydrated. You should avoid placing this database on a SQL Server that is an active BizTalk Server. If your performance monitoring reveals that this database is heavily used, follow the same recommendations as for the Shared Queue database.

Tuning BizTalk Server

There are several things that you can do directly to your BizTalk Server to tune its performance. There are a number of settings for individual BizTalk Servers in the BizTalk Administration MMC, as well as settings that you can make in the Windows 2000 Server Registry to tune BizTalk Server for your deployment.

BizTalk Server Tuning

In the BizTalk Administration MMC, you can change four settings that determine how a BizTalk Server operates, by right-clicking a specific BizTalk Server and selecting the relevant properties as follows:

- **Maximum Number Of Receive Function Threads Allowed**   The default value for this setting is 4. You can increase or decrease this value to any number between 1 and 128 to determine how many threads will be used to gain CPU cycles for receive functions. For example, you would want to raise this value on a server that primarily receives documents.

- **Participate In Work-Item Processing**   This check box determines whether or not the server participates in processing orders. If it is not checked, the server will not monitor the work queue. This will greatly improve the performance of receiving documents.

- **Maximum Number Of Worker Threads Per Processor Allowed**   The default value for this setting is 4. You can increase or decrease the value from between 1 and 128 to determine how many threads will be used to monitor the work queue on the Shared Queue database for processing incoming documents. Microsoft recommends setting this to between 14 and 16 for optimum performance under normal circumstances.

- **Time Between BizTalk Server Scheduler Calls**   The default value is 2,000, stored in milliseconds. This option controls how often the work queue is polled for new documents. Increasing this number will decrease the amount of network and database activity with the Shared Queue database.

BizTalk Messaging Registry Keys

You can make several changes to the Registry to enhance the performance of your BizTalk Server. As always, you should exercise extreme caution in altering the Windows 2000 Registry, and it is strongly recommended that you have tested the system backups before editing the Registry. You should always use the regedt32 utility when editing the Registry. The following keys can be added to HKLM\System\Current Control Set\Services\BTSSVC key as shown in Figure 12-12:

DWORD Value : Name = "NoValidation", Value = "1"

This will disable the validation of specifications. This is roughly the equivalent of setting the Submit with Pass Through flag for all specifications.

DEPLOYING BIZTALK SERVER

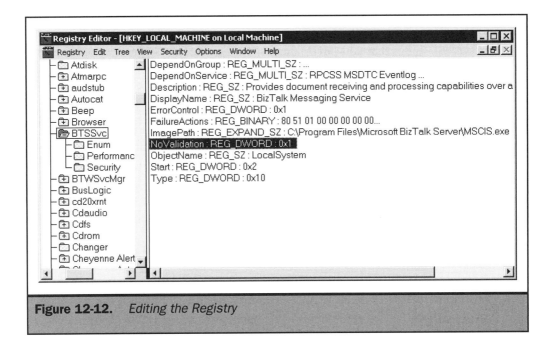

Figure 12-12. *Editing the Registry*

    DWORD Value : Name = "ParserRefreshInterval", Value in millseconds

By default, BizTalk Server checks for newly added parsers every minute. Reducing this interval for stable installations will improve performance.

    DWORD Value : Name = "CacheSize", Value in cached messaging components

By default, BizTalk Server caches 20 messaging components. If your BizTalk Server will regularly be using more than 20 messaging components, you can increase this setting as needed.

    DWORD Value Name = "BatchSize" Value in number of documents to batch

When using a message queuing receive function, BizTalk Server automatically reads up to 20 messages at a time. Increasing this number will decrease database write operations. Note that values greater than 20 have not been tested by Microsoft.

Receive Functions

You can enhance the performance of receiving documents in many ways. In a server group environment, you can create multiple receive functions that all point to the same data source, such as a file location or message queue, by creating a receive function that points to the same target on each BizTalk Server within the server group. This would effectively load-balance the receive function so that every BizTalk Server would participate in retrieving the data from BizTalk Server.

If there is no need to validate the document against a specification, or if you are sure the data being received will always be compliant with its schema, you can select the Submit With Pass-Through Flag check box on the Advanced tab of the receive function's Properties dialog box. By doing this, you arrange that BizTalk Messaging will skip validation, encoding, and encryption of the document and will move the document from the target to BizTalk's share queue much more quickly.

If a channel for a particular receive function is known at design time, you can provide this channel name by selecting it from the Channel Name drop-down list on the receive function Properties dialog box (on the Advanced tab). This will eliminate BizTalk Server's need to search for a channel against its messaging database for the correct path to route this document.

Document Tracking

Document tracking saves the incoming and outgoing documents that pass through BizTalk Server to the tracking database. By doing this, extra time and processing power will be consumed to write the data to the database. You can control tracking in the following ways:

■ You can choose to turn off the tracking by unchecking this check box in the BizTalk Server group Properties dialog box, so that no document passing through the BizTalk Server will be saved to the tracking database. If many large documents are passing through the BizTalk Server, leaving tracking on can significantly degrade performance.

■ You could turn on the data tracking at the channel level. If the majority of documents that pass through BizTalk Server are small, then you can enable data tracking but uncheck the Log Incoming Interchange and Log Outgoing Interchange options in the Properties dialog box for the server group. By doing this, you enable document tracking but disable the default logging for the entire interchange. To log a specific document, determine the channel that this type of document would pass through and enable the logging at the channel level during the channel configuration.

BizTalk Orchestration

There are many things that you can do to optimize BizTalk Server Orchestration. The single biggest thing that you can do is write well-designed and performance-oriented COM Components, a subject that is outside of the scope of this book. There are some other things, however, that will improve the performance of BizTalk Orchestration.

Creating COM Components in Visual Basic for use inside an XLANG schedule will cause performance problems if the server is under a heavy load. Visual Basic COM Components are single-threaded, and thus, CPU time is at a premium. With single-threaded components, new XLANG schedules may have to wait until other XLANG schedules finish. This will degrade the performance of the BizTalk Server Orchestration. Instead, you should consider creating these COM Components in C++.

Visual Basic COM Components used in COM+ server applications can deadlock and cause XLANG schedules to stop responding. To avoid this issue, you must build all COM Components with the Retain In Memory option set from the project properties in the Visual Basic development environment.

The XLANG Scheduler Engine uses ActiveX Date Objects (ADO) to persist the state of the BizTalk XLANG database. ADO, by default, runs as apartment-threaded. To increase the performance of writing data, you can change ADO from *apartment* threading to *both* threading by modifying the Registry; to do so, change the Threading Model value to "Both" for each of the following Registry keys (see Figure 12-13):

- HKLM\SOFTWARE\Classes\CLSID\

{00000507-0000-0010-8000-00AA006D2EA4}\InprocServer32]

- HKLM \SOFTWARE\Classes\CLSID\

{00000514-0000-0010-8000-00AA006D2EA4}\InprocServer32]

- HKLM \SOFTWARE\Classes\CLSID\

{0000050B-0000-0010-8000-00AA006D2EA4}\InprocServer32]

- HKLM \SOFTWARE\Classes\CLSID\

{00000535-0000-0010-8000-00AA006D2EA4}\InprocServer32]

- HKLM \SOFTWARE\Classes\CLSID\

{00000541-0000-0010-8000-00AA006D2EA4}\InprocServer32]

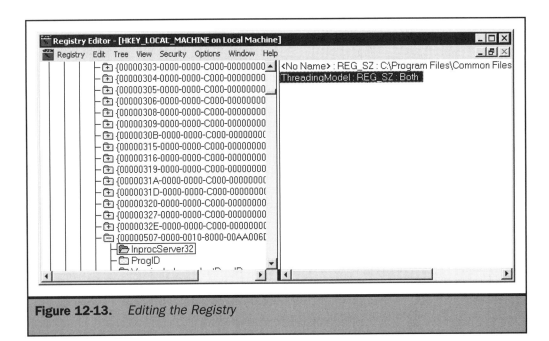

Figure 12-13.   *Editing the Registry*

You also may consider configuring XLANG schedules as transactional COM+ Components. Running an XLANG schedule as a COM+ Component gives you much better performance and control than you have with non-transactional XLANG schedules. However, you will lose the ability to add compensation code for the failure of transactions within the schedule. To change from XLANG-style transactions to COM+-style transactions, open the XLANG schedule in the Orchestration Designer, right-click the Start shape, and select Properties. In the Properties dialog box, select Treat The XLANG Schedule As A COM+ Component under the Transaction Model drop-down list.

The
Complete
Reference

BizTalk
Server

Chapter 13

Securing BizTalk Server

535

BizTalk Server is an enterprise-level product that facilitates the integration of business partners through the processing and transport of commercial data. Obviously, it is vital that you secure the systems on which the software will run, the networks to which they are connected, and the documents that will be exchanged. Failure to do so could compromise confidential data, mission-critical corporate systems, trading partnerships, and, indeed, entire businesses.

Implementing security best-practices requires knowledge of fundamental concepts such as network design, firewall configuration, public key infrastructure (PKI), and server administration. To further secure BizTalk Server deployments, it is crucial to recognize weaknesses that may be exposed by the product and to use the security tools and features provided by BizTalk Server and the underlying operating system. You may also need to protect the actual data that is the currency of electronic business transactions, to avoid legal or ethical repercussions.

Security Concepts

You must grasp certain fundamental security concepts to understand how to protect a BizTalk Server installation. Some of these concepts are specific to Windows 2000 and Microsoft Internet Information Services (IIS), while others are more generic, applying to different platforms and different scenarios. BizTalk Server is able to take advantage of many security features built into Windows 2000, but security is more than just the setting of properties or the installation of software. Security is often an attitude—a good administrator or developer should be always thinking of potential trouble spots that could compromise a network or application, and take steps for prevention rather than cure. If you are already familiar with the basic concepts discussed here, you can skip ahead to the next section, "Enterprise Security".

Note	*Disclaimer! Security is an issue not to be taken lightly, and there is rarely only one way to secure an installation. Although this chapter recommends many courses of action you can take to secure BizTalk Server, you should ensure that you—and your administration team—are completely familiar with security concepts in general before implementing any specific recommendations in a production environment.*

Authentication

One fundamental idea is that of authentication—a user's (or application's) ability to prove its identity to gain access to a computer, program, or document. Windows 2000 does not allow anything to happen unless the appropriate security credentials have been passed to the operating system and they have been verified by the security provider. This authentication may be used to allow a user to open a file on a network share or to allow a piece of software to execute. Even the operating system needs a user account, and many system services impersonate this account to have unfettered access to the computer and its resources.

In a domain-centric network such as that provided by Windows 2000, it can be relatively straightforward to secure those resources, because nobody can gain access without providing a specific user account and password that is checked against a central security accounts management (SAM) database. However, when the network expands to take advantage of the Internet, it is typically impossible to provide unique identities to every user who may attempt to access a host. As a set of Internet services, IIS has a variety of ways to authenticate users who access those services, providing graduated levels of security. These include Basic Authentication, Windows Integrated Authentication, Digest Authentication, and Client Certificates. However, I'll first discuss how Windows handles authentication.

Windows Authentication

Everything that happens on Windows 2000 happens in what is termed a security context. When a user logs on and double-clicks an icon on their desktop, they are doing so in the security context of the user account whose details were provided during that logon. Basically, an encrypted version of the password supplied is compared to a similarly encrypted password stored in the SAM database. If they match, it is reasonable to assume that it is that particular user logging on, as it should not be possible for another user to provide the same password.

Note *Of course, this only holds if the users have been properly educated about strong passwords and security, rather than simply picking their spouse's first name or their date of birth.*

A successful authentication causes an access token to be generated, which the user will proffer whenever they need to perform a task, such as deleting a file or sending a document to a printer. In Windows 2000 with Active Directory installed, the Kerberos protocol can make these exchanges even more secure by incorporating public key infrastructure (PKI) methods such as those discussed later in this chapter.

As mentioned, the same is true for all programs that wish to interact with the operating system. Most applications will run by virtue of the fact that they are instantiated by a logged-on user (the interactive user), so they will run in the security context of that user. However, there are also numerous Windows services that must run in the background even when a user is not logged on. This is true of all Windows 2000 computers, although it is most important for those acting as servers. In such cases, the services must be configured to run in the security context of a particular user account. For obvious reasons, this is called a *service account*.

To illustrate this idea, open a Command Prompt and type the command **set**. This will show a list of environment variables including *username*, which should show the name of the user currently logged on. Now type the following, substituting a time that is about one or two minutes ahead of the current time on your system:

```
at 12:00 /interactive "cmd"
```

This will cause a new Command Prompt window to appear at the designated time. The *interactive* switch means that the window will interact with the desktop. If you type **set** into this new Command Prompt window, you will notice that the environment variables displayed are different, as shown. This is because the new window was instantiated by the "at" command, which means that it was created by the Task Scheduler service. By default, this service runs in the context of the Local System account, which effectively represents the operating system itself. If you're feeling brave, you could try logging on as a user with limited privileges, running the preceding command, and then trying to perform an administrative task in the new window.

```
D:\WINNT\system32\MSTask.exe                                    _ □ ×
NUMBER_OF_PROCESSORS=1
OS=Windows_NT
Os2LibPath=D:\WINNT\system32\os2\dll;
Path=D:\WINNT\system32;D:\WINNT;D:\WINNT\System32\Wbem;D:\Program Files\Microsof
t SQL Server\80\Tools\BINN;D:\WINNT\System32\wbem\;D:\Program Files\Microsoft Bi
zTalk Server\;D:\Program Files\Common Files\Microsoft Shared\Enterprise Servers\
Commerce\
PATHEXT=.COM;.EXE;.BAT;.CMD;.VBS;.VBE;.JS;.JSE;.WSF;.WSH
PROCESSOR_ARCHITECTURE=x86
PROCESSOR_IDENTIFIER=x86 Family 6 Model 8 Stepping 3, GenuineIntel
PROCESSOR_LEVEL=6
PROCESSOR_REVISION=0803
ProgramFiles=D:\Program Files
PROMPT=$P$G
SystemDrive=D:
SystemRoot=D:\WINNT
TEMP=D:\WINNT\TEMP
TMP=D:\WINNT\TEMP
USERPROFILE=D:\Documents and Settings\Default User
windir=D:\WINNT

D:\WINNT\system32>_
```

Service Accounts

The BizTalk Messaging Service and the Microsoft SQL Server service are examples of services that may need to run in the background when no user is logged on. For this reason, during the installation of these products, you will be asked to select a user account under whose security context the services will execute. In many cases, the Local System account is sufficient; but although this account has many powerful administrative privileges, they are all confined to the local machine and have no rights to do anything across a network.

For example, the BizTalk Messaging Service does not need to perform any actions on other computers in the network apart from the SQL Server computers on which the Messaging Management, Shared Queue, and Document Tracking databases reside. However, BizTalk Server is configured to use SQL Server authentication rather than Windows authentication to access those databases, so the fact that the service is running under the Local System account will not cause any problems. Sometimes, however, it is necessary for the Microsoft SQL Server service to communicate with other SQL Server computers. An example was given in Chapter 10 where two SQL

Server computers were linked to allow the archival of data from one system to a database on the other. If the first SQL Server service is configured to log on as the Local System account, it will not have permission to store information in the remote database. This can be circumvented using the sp_addLinkedSrvLogin stored procedure to configure the credentials the first system uses to communicate with the second. In fact, best practices often recommend using a domain user account for the Microsoft SQL Server service instead of the Local System account.

One specific right that the Local System account does have is the right to log on locally. This means that it will log onto Windows as needed to execute certain services. This does not happen interactively, however, so the services appear to run with nobody logged on. Of course, those services will need to interact with Windows at a fundamental level, so another right that's required is the right to act as part of the operating system. However, as mentioned in Chapter 3, if you decide to use a specific account other than Local System for the BizTalk Messaging Service, the account you choose will automatically be given those rights.

Note *Rights and permissions are two different things. Although the account you choose will be assigned certain rights automatically, it will not be assigned access permissions to files, folders, and Registry keys. You will have to configure these permissions manually using Windows Explorer and RegEdt32. Rights may also be configured manually through the local, group, or domain policy in effect.*

Windows services are not the only programs that may need to run with no user logged on interactively. BizTalk Server makes use of numerous COM+ applications, such as the BizTalk Server Interchange application and the XLANG Scheduler application. By default, these are configured to run in the security context of the interactive user. This means that if there is no interactive user—that is, nobody is physically logged on at the computer—the application cannot run. Later in this chapter, we will see how to configure those applications to run in the background using a specially created account, and also how to further secure those applications using roles.

Permissions

Regardless of who or what is logged onto a machine, Windows provides a way to protect files, folders, printers, and Registry keys from unauthorized access. These concepts are so fundamental to all administrators that I will assume you are already familiar with them and only summarize the main points of file and folder permissions here.

First, folders may be shared out to provide access to remote users, and permissions may be set to determine the level of access that individual users, or groups of users, should have on that folder when they connect to it across a network. These are called *share-level permissions*, and we can either grant or deny full control, change, or read access to each account. Second, there are *NT File System (NTFS)* permissions. These operate on a much more granular level, applicable to each individual file within a folder as well as to the folder itself. There are many more options to choose from, including read attributes, delete subfolders and files, take ownership, and so on. These permissions apply to both local and remote users, so they can be used to further restrict access to accounts that have been granted share-level permissions or to restrict users who access files locally. The set of permissions assigned to users or groups for a particular resource gives us something called a *discretionary access control list (DACL)*. Later in this chapter, we will see how these permissions help to secure the web sites created by BizTalk Server.

IIS Authentication

The Internet poses a tremendous security risk if your systems need to be accessible from the outside or if they need to access external resources. Internet Information Services (IIS) provide a number of authentication methods to satisfy different scenarios. For example, if a web site is meant to be available to the general public to provide information or services, it would not be feasible to create an individual user account for every person who might come to the site. However, Windows 2000 will not allow anybody to access resources on a web server unless some kind of security context is available. For this reason, a special user account called IUSR_*Computername* is created by the installation of IIS, where *Computername* is the name of the server. Whenever anonymous users connect to the server, they are actually doing so using the security context of that account, so file and folder permissions should be set to allow or disallow access to that account as appropriate.

In a business environment, however, it would be undesirable to allow anonymous users to access potentially sensitive information or to have access to certain systems. For example, if you have an Active Server Page (ASP) application that will accept purchase orders sent to be submitted to BizTalk Server, you will probably want to ensure that only your business partners can access that page. Therefore, you will probably use NTFS permissions to secure the page and ask users attempting to access it to prove who they are before allowing them to continue. IIS provides a number of methods by which users can authenticate, as shown next, but only two methods are generally available for use in an Internet scenario where different browsers, proxy servers, and firewalls are in use—Basic Authentication and Client Certificates, the latter being configured on the Directory Security tab of the Web Site Properties dialog box under Secure communications.

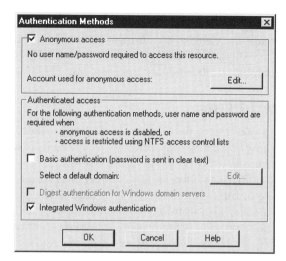

Basic Authentication is a means of querying the requesting user for a valid user name and password to access a particular resource. An HTTP header is sent from the web server to the client specifying that Basic Authentication is required. The client then sends the credentials supplied by the user under Base-64 encoding. This encoding is not secure, however, because an intercepting party can obtain utilities to decode the data and easily determine the user name and password. As a result, Basic Authentication is often combined with Secure Sockets Layer (SSL) technology, which uses a secure version of HTTP called HTTPS in conjunction with a digital certificate to encrypt the data so it cannot be decoded by an intercepting party. The digital certificate also proves the identity of the web server, as certified by a trusted third party. HTTPS, SSL, and digital certificates will be covered in more detail later in this section.

Another feature that SSL provides is the ability for clients to authenticate themselves using a digital certificate. Client Certificate authentication with SSL is even more secure than Basic Authentication with SSL, because it is considerably less likely that unscrupulous users could obtain a legitimate user's Client Certificate, than it is that they could obtain or guess that user's user name and password. IIS also provides the facility for these Client Certificates to be mapped to actual Windows 2000 user accounts in a one-to-one or many-to-one fashion. In the latter case, IIS might be configured such that all users who access the site with a Client Certificate where the e-mail address ends with *@bushwhack.ltd* are authenticated by mapping them to a Windows 2000 user account called *bushwhack*. Later in the chapter, we will see how BizTalk Server can be configured to use a Client Certificate when it transports outbound documents using HTTPS.

Public Key Infrastructure

If you have ever used any of the terms "digital certificate", "digital signature", "private key", or "certificate authority", you may not have realized it, but you were talking about the accepted standard for providing secure communications called the public key infrastructure (PKI). PKI has become widely accepted across multiple platforms and disciplines because of the features it provides—authentication, authorization, confidentiality, integrity, and nonrepudiation.

As we have seen, *authentication* is the process by which an entity such as a user or an application successfully proves its identity to a system. *Authorization* is the process by which that system then provides the entity with permission to perform some task, such as read a file or run a program. *Confidentiality* is the process by which the secure transmission of data is assured such that the data cannot be read by an unauthorized third party. Even without confidentiality there can be *integrity*, such that if a document can be intercepted and read, it cannot be altered without such tampering being detectable. Finally, *nonrepudiation* ensures that the sender of a document cannot later deny that they sent that document.

Digital Certificates

So, you may ask, how does PKI provide all these things? The answer: through digital certificates. A *digital certificate* is an electronic document that acts like its real-world counterpart, in that it proves something within agreed boundaries. For example, if you go into a doctor's office and you see a degree certificate hanging on the wall, you may be unsure whether it's an authentic degree. However, if you examine the official wax seal on the degree and see that it has been awarded by a recognized academic institution, then you will probably put aside your suspicions and get undressed. In the same way, digital certificates are only useful if they are signed by a mutually trusted third party called a *Certificate Authority (CA)*.

So, you inquire further, what are public keys, and where do they come into it? To answer this, I must first explain something about encryption techniques. To encrypt a message, we can apply a mathematical rule—or *algorithm*—to the message to jumble it up. Using the same algorithm, however, there may be multiple ways to encrypt the data. For example, if I were trying to encrypt the message "this is a secret", I could select an algorithm whereby each character was replaced with a letter that is offset from it in the alphabet. So if I decided to offset each letter by three, as shown in the following illustration, I would end up with the encrypted message "wklv lv d vhfuhw". In this case, I would say that the *key* is three. If this message were intercepted in its encrypted form, a human being might take a few minutes to figure it out, even if they knew the algorithm, because they would not know by how many letters each character was offset and would have to try each possibility. It wouldn't take long for them to crack the code, however, because there are only 25 possible values for the key. (If I were to offset each character by 26, the message would be unchanged.) To create a code that even computers find difficult to break, I need a more complicated algorithm and a greater range of possible key values. Because computers deal in binary numbers, the key is described by the number of bits it contains, which gives us the term *key length*.

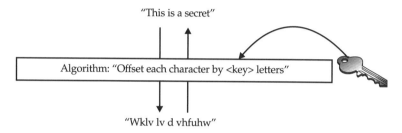

In this fashion, encryption techniques used through the ages typically involved an algorithm and a key. As in the simple example just given, the key to encrypt the data is also used to decrypt the data—the algorithm is simply reversed. Therefore, the process is called *symmetric encryption*. However, the problem arises when I want to let people know what key I'm using to encrypt my data, so that they can readily decrypt it. If I send it to them in an e-mail, the e-mail could be intercepted, and other parties could know my key. Even if I were to try to encrypt the e-mail, I would need another key to do that, and again, I would have to let the recipient of the e-mail know what that key was. This is called the *key distribution problem*, and a solution for the problem was not discovered until the 1960s.

To get around this quandary, a mathematical algorithm is constructed that requires two keys. If the first key encrypts the data, then only the second key can decrypt it, and vice versa. Also, even if you have one of the keys, it would be mathematically impossible (or at least extremely difficult) to determine the value of the second key, as they are not mathematical inverses of each other. So, one key is always kept secret and never divulged—the *private key*—whereas the second key may be freely distributed to all and sundry without fear that it could be used to determine the first. This second key is called the *public key*. The ability to encrypt information with one key and decrypt it with another provides two basic ideas in PKI—digital signatures and digital envelopes.

Digital Signatures

Suppose I want to send a document to a trading partner, and I encrypt it using my private key. If the trading partner has a copy of my public key, they can decrypt the information, as illustrated. However, if you've been paying attention, you'll realize that everyone else in the world could do the same—by definition, my public key is made available to anyone who wants it. That doesn't sound very secure! Well, it's not, but the purpose of such encryption is not to protect the data, but rather to prove who sent it. If the trading partner (and everyone else) is able to decrypt the data using my public key, then that proves that it could only have been encrypted using my private key. And because I never, ever, ever give my private key to anyone else, the document must have come from me. Just as my written signature authenticates my checks for the bank, this digital signature authenticates my documents for any trading partners who receive them.

In actuality, the process is a little more complicated. To digitally sign a document, the body of the document is first passed through a well-known, irreversible encryption algorithm. This creates a fixed-length binary version of the document called a *hash*. This hash is then encrypted using the private key, and the hash and a copy of the public key are added to the end of the original message. When somebody receives this document, they can decrypt the hash using the attached public key and then use the same well-known, irreversible algorithm on the body of the message. If the two hash values match, not only does that prove that the document came from the owner of the public key, but it also proves that the body of the document could not have been tampered with during transmission, because the same hash should never be generated for two different documents.

Digital Envelopes

So what happens when we do want to encrypt data such that only a particular recipient can decrypt it? In this case, we can use the recipient's public key to encrypt the data, as illustrated. Again, although it would be possible for everybody in the world to do the same thing, we all know that only the owner of the corresponding private key will be able to decrypt the data. For this reason, encrypting documents is even easier, because we don't have to have any keys of our own; we simply use the readily available public key of the party to whom we're sending the document. Just as we place confidential letters into sealed envelopes before dropping them in the mail, we can use a digital envelope to seal a document and protect it from unauthorized eyes.

Certificate Authorities

At this stage, you may have recognized one potential flaw in all of this. If I receive a digitally signed document from somebody and it contains a public key that successfully decrypts the hash value, how can I be sure the public key actually belongs to them? Similarly, if I'm about to encrypt my credit card details to send to an e-commerce web site, how can I be sure that the public key I'm using to perform the encryption actually belongs to www.buycoolstuffsecurely.com, rather than www.dodgyblokesinbalaclavas. com? I'd also want to take a close look at that doctor's degree to make sure the name on the certificate was actually the name of the person in front of whom I was about to get naked. Obviously, there needs to be somebody higher up the chain whom everybody trusts and who guarantees the authenticity of these public keys. This is done by a *Certificate Authority (CA)*, who ensures the veracity of public keys by incorporating them into digital certificates. The CA then digitally signs each certificate using their own private key so that we can examine it and see that it was issued by somebody we trust.

Because there are different types of digital certificate that will be used in different scenarios, there are also different types of CA. At the top (or bottom, depending on how you look at it), there is a *root CA*. The root CA has to be explicitly trusted, because when you receive a digital certificate belonging to a root CA, it has also been signed by the root CA. By definition, there is no greater authority, so root CA certificates are self-signed. Root CAs rarely sign certificates for companies or individuals. Instead, they sign certificates for intermediate CAs, who may exist at multiple levels down until you reach a CA to whom you might apply for your own digital certificate. The certificate you receive will be signed by that low-level intermediate CA, and that signature will contain the digital certificate of the CA who in turn authorized the lower CA to grant certificates. This will continue up to the next intermediate CA, and so on, until there is a certificate signed by the root CA, whom we explicitly trust. Therefore, you can always examine the *certificate chain* leading back to the root CA.

One other thing that CAs provide is a Certificate Revocation List (CRL). This is a list of certificates that have been invalidated for some reason—perhaps because the private key was compromised, or because the certificate was being used improperly. This list allows an individual or a system to check digital certificates received for the purposes of authentication or encryption, and to ensure the validity of those certificates.

Secure Sockets Layer

There are many applications of PKI, but perhaps the most common is Secure Sockets Layer (SSL), a technology originally developed by Netscape, and now in global use as the de facto method of securing data transmission with a web server. Contrary to popular belief, SSL is not just a simple matter of encrypting information with a web server's public key and sending it off—there is a little bit more going on in the background. However, I don't want to go into too much detail; I'm discussing it here more as an example of PKI in use.

If a client (such as a browser) wishes to engage in secure data transmission with a web server, the client and server will first have to establish a secure connection. The following steps take place in sequence, as shown in Figure 13-1.

1. The user will initiate a connection by browsing to a URL that uses the *https://* prefix instead of *http://*. This indicates to the server that the client wishes to use SSL. HTTPS uses port 443 for this communication, rather than the standard port 80 used by HTTP.

2. When the server receives a request on this port, it responds by sending its digital certificate. The common name specified on this certificate must be the same as the fully qualified domain name (FQDN) of the web site, for example, www.bushwhack.ltd.

3. The client compares the name on the certificate to the name of the site, examines the date on the certificate to check that it has not expired, and examines the digital signature on the certificate to ensure that it belongs to a trusted CA. If all is in order, the client generates a unique key, which it encrypts using the public key from the server certificate.

4. The server may then request a Client Certificate for authentication purposes, although this is not required.

5. If requested, the client will send an appropriate Client Certificate to provide authentication.

6. The server checks the credentials on the Client Certificate, and if all is in order, sends its response to the original request, encrypting the information with the unique key generated by the client.

7. The client decrypts the response from the server. All subsequent requests and responses will also be encrypted using the session key.

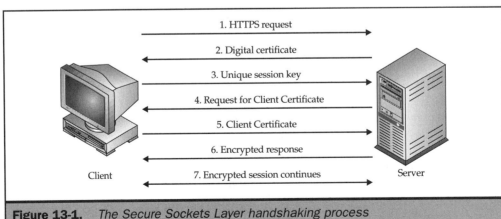

Figure 13-1. *The Secure Sockets Layer handshaking process*

One of the most important things to note here is that the actual information sent by the server is not encrypted using a public key from the client. Likewise, any information sent by the client to the server is not encrypted using the server's public key. Instead, symmetric encryption is used, where the client and server use the same key for encryption and decryption. Earlier, I said that this presented difficulties in terms of key distribution, but using the server's public key to encrypt the session key overcomes that problem. Symmetric encryption is used for two main reasons. First, although it would be possible for the client to encrypt confidential information (such as credit card numbers or passwords) using the server's public key, the server would not be able to encrypt information for the client (such as a bank account balance) unless the client also had a public key. Unfortunately, not all Internet users have a digital certificate of their own, although this might become a reality in the future. Second, using public-private key encryption entails huge overheads in terms of data transfer and processing power, whereas symmetric key encryption is much more efficient, and thus, less demanding on the server and the connection.

Network Security

It is sometimes said that the only surefire way to completely secure a computer system from intrusion is to make sure it's not connected to any other computers and to lock it away in a bank vault. Unfortunately, such a computer system would be little use to anybody unless its job were just to crunch numbers for years on end. In the real world, there are too many advantages afforded by networking computers together to succumb to paranoia. However, when you're considering connecting your corporate network to the Internet, a little paranoia is no bad thing.

Perhaps the most dangerous thing about connecting a network to the Internet is the possibility of intrusion by malicious individuals intent on stealing data, causing damage, denying legitimate service, or simply being mischievous. To avoid such attacks, it is vital to protect the network from intrusion by deploying one or more systems whose job is to detect and prevent unauthorized access. Installing and configuring these *firewall* systems is a mandatory exercise for any enterprise administrator.

However, you will still want some systems on your network to be accessible from the outside world in varying degrees. These could include public web servers, FTP servers, SMTP servers, DNS servers, and Message Queuing servers. You will still want to protect these systems from attack using a firewall, but you will also need to ensure that these systems are not used as a base to launch attacks at the corporate network, so a second firewall is typically placed in between. The area between the external and internal firewalls is protected from the Internet while also kept separate from the corporate network, and is thus called a *demilitarized zone (DMZ)*. Figure 13-2 shows a typical arrangement.

Keeping your network safe is not just about preventing access from outside. For a variety of reasons, you will often want to restrict access to the Internet from inside. For example, you may wish to prevent employees from surfing the web during office hours or from browsing to unsavory sites. Ensuring that all requests to the Internet go through

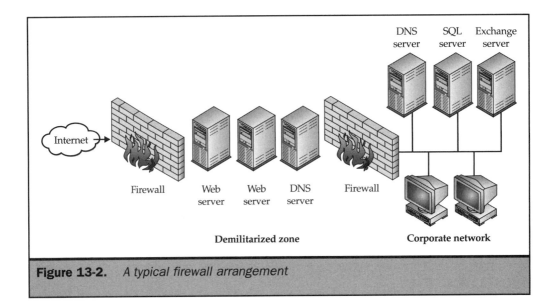

Figure 13-2. *A typical firewall arrangement*

a broker can provide this functionality, so systems that forward requests to the Internet on behalf of the original requestor are called *proxy servers*. Using proxy servers can also have other desirable effects, such as hiding internal network addresses or optimizing the retrieval of frequently requested content.

Firewalls

To protect a network from unauthorized external access, we use firewalls. These may be actual computer systems running firewall software such as Microsoft Internet Security and Acceleration (ISA) Server, or they may be hardware devices such as switches or routers. An external firewall is the first point of defense for all computers within a network, whether they should be accessible to the outside world or not. They provide protection by filtering requests that arrive at the network, examining the Internet Protocol (IP) addresses of the source and destination, the ports being accessed, and even the contents of the network packets.

Firewalls filter requests based on source IP address for a number of reasons. There may be certain IP addresses that are explicitly rejected because they come from undesirable domains, but a more likely scenario is that only certain ranges of addresses might be allowed, because they come from recognized business partners or systems, while all other addresses are rejected. This would be the case for an extranet, where access should only be provided to certain groups rather than to all, or for an intranet, where only recognized addresses belonging to the company are allowed in.

Firewalls also filter requests based on destination IP address. For example, requests to the IP addresses of the outward-facing web servers and the external DNS server might be the only ones allowed by the firewall. This would help to prevent direct access to other systems on the network if a malicious user were able to find out the IP addresses of those systems.

Because there are many different types of requests that can be sent to a network, a firewall has to be able to distinguish between those that should be allowed and those that should be rejected. One way in which a firewall can do this is to look at the source and destination ports of the request and response. For example, when a request is sent to a web server, that request is usually sent over Transmission Control Protocol (TCP) port 80. The HTTP service that runs on the web server is designed to listen for, and respond to, requests that arrive on that port. Therefore, a firewall could reasonably assume that a request from the Internet to the IP address of an outward-facing web server on port 80 is a legitimate request. Similarly, a firewall could assume that a request from the Internet to the IP address of an outward-facing DNS server on port 53 is a legitimate request. However, if the firewall detected a request to the web server on port 23, that would indicate that somebody was trying to use Telnet to gain administrative access to the server, so that request should be blocked. A firewall will typically be configured to disallow access on all ports except those that have been explicitly opened. That way, if for some reason the firewall fails, it will fail closed rather than open.

Finally, the third way that firewalls can protect a network is to actually examine the contents of packets traveling to the network, and to deny malformed or malicious requests. One problem that's becoming increasingly prevalent on the Internet is the so-called *denial of service (DOS)* attack. In a DOS attack, the perpetrator is not trying to gain root access to a server or to sniff confidential data. Instead, he or she is simply trying to kick the system so hard that it falls over, and thus prevents legitimate users from accessing the service. One way in which DOS attacks can be mounted is by sending malformed TCP packets to a server. For example, during the initial handshaking phase between a client and a server, the client sends a packet to which the server must respond. When the server gets an acknowledgement from the client that its response was received, the session can begin in earnest. However, a deliberately engineered packet from the client can hold a false return address such that the server's response is sent to a phantom host, and the server never receives an acknowledgement. The TCP protocol demands that the server should wait a certain amount of time for an acknowledgement to arrive, setting aside resources for the session to follow. If enough such malformed packets are sent to a server in quick succession, all resources are used up and the server crashes. This is a slightly simplistic version of events, but firewalls can detect and trap these types of malformed requests to prevent DOS attacks.

Demilitarized Zones

As discussed, firewalls can protect a network from intrusion, while still allowing legitimate access. However, a single firewall between the Internet and a corporate network sits as a single obstacle to a malicious user and can therefore serve as a single point of failure. With a single firewall, the question arises—where should you place your web servers? Should they exist behind the firewall as part of the corporate network, or in front of the firewall, where they will be more easily accessible, but also more prone to attack? Not only that, but the increasing popularity of dynamic, data-driven web applications for e-commerce and e-business presents another problem. For example, if your e-commerce web site stores product information and customer order details in a database, where should that database be positioned—in the same network as the web servers for ease of access, or on the corporate network where the most protection can be afforded?

A more robust, and more common, scenario is to use two (or even three) firewalls. One firewall sits in front of the entire network, while the second sits in front of the corporate network. In between lies a separate physical subnet—or virtual local area network (VLAN)—called a demilitarized zone (DMZ), where publicly accessible servers should sit. Because the DMZ is neither directly connected to the Internet (the external firewall is in the way) nor directly connected to the corporate network (the internal firewall is in the way), this provides much greater protection and avoids having a single point of failure.

Figure 13-3 shows where different servers might typically be placed in an enterprise scenario. For example, the web server is in the DMZ because it should be accessible to the public. Other servers in the DMZ might include a message queuing server, where applications could drop messages to be retrieved asynchronously; an SMTP server, where incoming mail could be delivered; and a DNS server, so that external clients can discover the IP addresses of the outbound-facing servers.

Behind the second firewall, either on the corporate network or separated from it by a third firewall, lie the infrastructure servers. For example, a Microsoft Exchange Server could retrieve e-mails relayed by the SMTP server in the DMZ, without the Exchange server having to be externally visible. Similarly, the web server in the DMZ could submit documents to an internal BizTalk Server or store data in an internal SQL Server. In

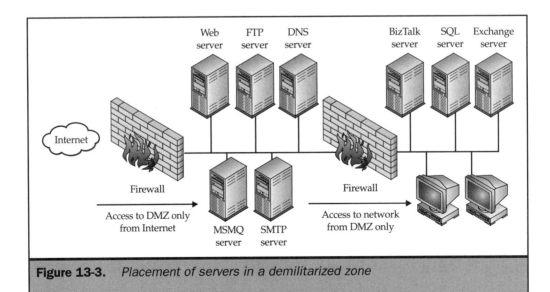

Figure 13-3.   *Placement of servers in a demilitarized zone*

general, as Figure 13-3 shows, the external firewall only allows Internet clients to have access to servers in the DMZ, and the internal firewall only allows access to the servers on the corporate network if the request is coming from one of the computers in the DMZ. There is never a direct route from the Internet to the corporate network. Later in this chapter, we will discuss the placement of BizTalk Server and related servers in a network that uses a DMZ.

Proxy Servers

Another type of host that can provide protection between the Internet and a corporate network is a proxy server. As the name suggests, this server makes requests to the Internet on behalf of clients on the corporate network. As a result, its main goal is to provide outbound security rather than inbound security, although some products, such as Microsoft ISA Server, combine firewall and proxy server features. There are a number of reasons to use a proxy server in an enterprise—to restrict Internet access, to provide *network address translation (NAT)*, and to provide content caching. Figure 13-4 shows the typical placement of a proxy server within a network. Later in this chapter, we will see how the presence of a proxy server on a network requires some extra configuration for BizTalk Server.

First, the proxy server can act as a filter for outbound requests for Internet content. For example, the proxy server may be configured to only allow access to the Internet outside of office hours or during lunch hour. Similarly, individual computers or groups of computers can be allowed or denied access. In Figure 13-3, the computer with IP address 10.0.0.102 can access the Internet, but the others can't. Another restriction might be to prevent clients from accessing dubious content, so that users attempting to browse to www.dodgyandprobablyillegal.com are presented with a friendly warning about conscientious Internet use.

Second, the proxy server can hide the internal network addresses from the outside world, by virtue of the fact that it is the only host that ever makes a direct connection to

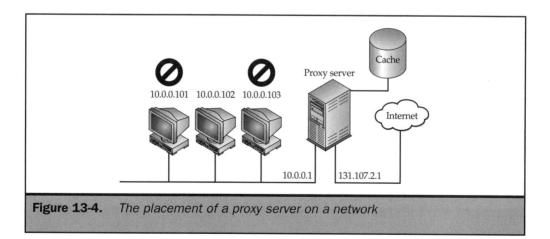

Figure 13-4. *The placement of a proxy server on a network*

the Internet. In Figure 13-4, for example, the internal hosts are configured with specially reserved IP addresses that are only supposed to be used on an internal network. However, whenever any of those clients makes a request to the Internet, the only IP address that the destination web server will see is that of the proxy server—131.107.2.1. Strictly speaking, this is a type of network address translation (NAT), and it is a way to provide Internet access to many internal clients without having to buy many expensive IP addresses.

The third feature that proxy servers provide is content caching. Because the proxy server is the only computer actually connected to the Internet, it makes sense for the server to cache frequently requested content. Thus, when a client makes a request for something that's already in the cache, it can be returned across the local area network in a fraction of the time it would take to retrieve it from the Internet. Of course, content on the Web changes all the time, so some proxy servers automatically update their cache on an ongoing basis so that they will have the most up-to-date content.

Enterprise Security

As discussed earlier in this part of the book, deploying BizTalk Server in the enterprise requires more than simply installing the product on a single machine. There may be multiple computers running BizTalk Server in a server group, at least one SQL Server installation hosting the databases used by BizTalk Server, and possibly web servers, message queuing servers, FTP servers, SMTP relay servers, and Microsoft Exchange servers. Although these systems will all need to communicate with each other to a certain extent, it is highly unlikely that all of them should be directly accessible from the Internet. The placement of each server in relation to existing firewalls and proxy servers is extremely important, and depending on the services that BizTalk Server will require, each firewall may need particular port or IP address-filtering configurations.

Network Considerations

Best practices dictate that you place outward-facing web servers, SMTP servers, and so on, in a demilitarized zone (DMZ) between two firewalls. The external firewall will allow Internet traffic to reach these servers, but the internal firewall will only allow requests that originate within the DMZ to pass through. Therefore, we will usually place infrastructure servers such as those running Microsoft SQL Server and Microsoft Exchange Server on the corporate network behind the internal firewall for their protection. However, we also know that BizTalk Server will usually need to communicate with both Internet clients and back-end systems, so where should it go—behind the external or internal firewall?

Server Placement

BizTalk Server will undoubtedly serve as an invaluable part of your e-business infrastructure, and the last thing you would want is a denial of service (DOS) attack to bring it down, or a cracked password to compromise your business data. For this primary reason, you usually will not place BizTalk Server in the DMZ—you will instead position it behind the internal firewall. There are also plenty of practical and logistical reasons why you would not want to locate BizTalk Server in the DMZ. For example, if your BizTalk servers are used for EAI, it would be desirable to keep them close to the internal application systems with which they will communicate. Similarly, performance will be degraded if BizTalk Server has to communicate with SQL Server through an internal firewall.

You may not be completely convinced, however. Although we've mentioned it already in passing, Chapter 16 will fully discuss how BizTalk Server can accept submitted documents using DCOM, through the Submit and SubmitSync methods of the Interchange object. This may lead you to think that having your trading partners submit their purchase orders through a COM interface is a good thing, and hence you should position your BizTalk servers behind the outer firewall. However, it is inadvisable to allow external trading partners to submit documents directly to BizTalk Server in this way—not just because of the security implications, but also because of the tight coupling of applications it implies. If your BizTalk Server were not available for any reason, the submission attempt would fail.

Another potential security risk of locating BizTalk Server in the DMZ is that the BizTalk Server WebDAV Repository and Document Tracking web sites would be directly accessible from the Internet. Although the NTFS permissions on the WebDAV Repository do not admit the Internet Guest account, all recognized local users have access to the physical directory, and directory browsing is enabled for the virtual directory. Similarly, although the Document Tracking web site is only accessible to members of the BizTalk Server Report Users group, one captured user account would lay all of your business data bare.

Note *Another potential security problem with the Document Tracking database is that the user account—dta_ui_login—created to provide access for the client interface has a blank password. You should rectify this through SQL Server Enterprise Manager and reflect the change in the file connection.vb located in the \Program Files\Microsoft BizTalk Server\BizTalk Tracking\VBScripts directory.*

There can be exceptions. If you have a small enterprise, and BizTalk Server will only be used in B2B scenarios rather than for EAI, you may decide to place BizTalk Server in the DMZ. This will ease restrictions on trading partners to submit documents to BizTalk Server, although this should still be done asynchronously using HTTP, FTP, SMTP, or a message queue, rather than using the COM interface. Also, you will need to configure the internal firewall to allow BizTalk Server to communicate with certain internal systems such as SQL Server, as discussed later in this section. Even for small enterprises, though, I would not recommend placing BizTalk Server in the DMZ.

HTTP Submission

To allow trading partners to submit documents to BizTalk Server using HTTP, it is recommended to use an Active Server Page (ASP) running on IIS within the DMZ. This ASP should then post the document to a Message Queuing server either in the DMZ or behind the second firewall, as shown next. This is preferable to having an ASP submit the document programmatically using the Interchange object, because this would fail if the BizTalk server were unavailable. Once dropped into a private message queue, BizTalk Messaging can then retrieve the document asynchronously using a Message Queuing receive function, and BizTalk Orchestration can retrieve the document using a Message Queuing implementation shape.

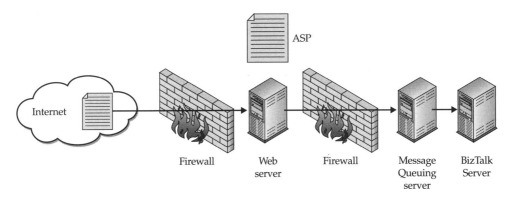

		Firewall	Web server	Firewall

Note   *To enable clustered BizTalk servers to perform transactional reads from a single private message queue, BizTalk Server Service Pack 1 must be installed. Otherwise, the private message queue must exist on the BizTalk server itself, and only that server will be able to host the receive function. For load balancing without Service Pack 1, a custom "fan-out" component can be used to distribute messages to local private message queues, with Windows Management Instrumentation (WMI) determining the load on each BizTalk server.*

SMTP Submission

To allow trading partners to submit documents to BizTalk Server using SMTP, you should place an SMTP relay server (such as that provided by IIS) in the DMZ. This relay server can then be configured to forward e-mails to a computer running Microsoft Exchange Server on the corporate network. This provides greater security than placing the Exchange server itself in the DMZ. As documents arrive to a specially configured inbox on the Exchange server, a script can submit them programmatically, or else to a message queue as with HTTP.

FTP Submission

To allow trading partners to submit documents to BizTalk Server using FTP, it will be necessary to deploy one or more FTP servers (for example, using IIS) in the DMZ. These servers should host virtual directories that map to a physical location such as a shared network folder, as illustrated next. Because it is a security risk to have shared network folders in the DMZ, Internet Protocol Security (IPSec) can be used to encrypt data traveling from the FTP servers to a shared folder behind the internal firewall. A File receive function can then be configured to retrieve posted documents and submit them to BizTalk Server.

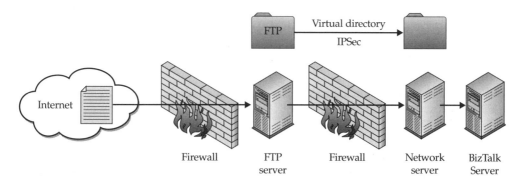

Note   *For more information on IPSec, add the IP Security Policy Management snap-in to a Microsoft Management Console and consult the help file.*

Firewall Considerations

Depending on where you choose to locate BizTalk Server, you will need to configure one or both of the internal and external firewalls in your enterprise to enable communication between the various systems. Your BizTalk Server installation will need to interact with Microsoft SQL Server, and your deployment may also require communication between BizTalk Server, IIS, Exchange Server, and others. Configuring the firewalls that comprise the DMZ will involve setting up port filters and potentially IP filters.

IP Address Restrictions

If you choose to place BizTalk Server behind the internal firewall as recommended, the standard IP address filters created for your external and internal firewalls should suffice. As mentioned, hosts on the Internet should only be able to access hosts within the DMZ, and only those systems in the DMZ should have access to the internal infrastructure servers such as Exchange Server, SQL Server, and BizTalk Server. For outbound communication, you will also need to determine whether BizTalk Server needs to access the Internet directly. For example, in a B2B scenario, messaging ports may be configured to send documents to trading partners using HTTP or SMTP. In such cases, the internal and external firewalls should be chained and configured to allow the BizTalk Server external access by IP address. A cluster of BizTalk servers in a server group will obviously mean that each IP address should be allowed out through the firewalls.

Port Restrictions

As discussed, firewalls are generally configured so that all ports are closed except those that explicitly need to be opened. Because there are various ways in which BizTalk Server can accept and transmit documents, it is important to consider which ports your particular scenario requires. BizTalk Server will always need to communicate with SQL Server, however, so TCP inbound port 1433 will need to be opened on the internal firewall if BizTalk Server is located in the DMZ. If BizTalk Server is behind the internal firewall (as recommended), this configuration will not be necessary.

Note *In a high-security enterprise environment, it is common for administrators to change the default port used by SQL Server. If this is the case, you will need to ensure that the correct port is open.*

Inbound/Outbound HTTP If your trading partners will be submitting documents to a web server in your DMZ, then port 80 inbound will need to be open on the external firewall. If you have a digital certificate installed on your web servers, you can use HTTPS instead, which will require port 443 inbound open on the external firewall. If your BizTalk servers are located behind the internal firewall, then the ports you open on that firewall will depend on how the web servers submit the documents to BizTalk Server. If an ASP will drop the documents into a private message queue, then port 1801 inbound will need to be opened on the internal firewall. If DCOM will be used, then you should use DCOMCNFG to select the port range that will be used and open those ports on the internal firewall, although again, this is not recommended. As discussed, BizTalk Server can also send documents out using HTTP or HTTPS, so ports 80 or 443 outbound would also need to be opened on both firewalls to allow this.

Note *To use DCOM through a firewall, you must open TCP port 135 inbound, as well as the range of ports configured for the component. Port 135 is required by the DCOM Service Control Manager to determine the port through which the remote procedure call (RPC) should pass.*

Inbound/Outbound SMTP If your trading partners will be sending documents using SMTP, they should arrive at an SMTP relay server in your DMZ, which will then forward the e-mails to an Exchange server on the corporate network. In this case, port 25 inbound should be opened on both firewalls. Because the Exchange server is located on the same network as BizTalk Server, there will be no need to open any further ports on the internal firewall, regardless of whether the Exchange server submits documents to BizTalk Server directly, or it drops them into a message queue. Similarly, port 25 outbound will need to be opened on both firewalls if BizTalk Messaging has been configured to transport documents to trading partners using SMTP.

Inbound FTP   To enable FTP access to your trading partners, you will need to open ports 20 and 21 on the external firewall. Because the FTP servers should be configured with virtual directories that point to a shared folder within the corporate network, you will need to configure an IPSec policy for the FTP server, opening TCP ports 50 and 51 inbound on the internal firewall, and UDP port 500 inbound. You will also need to open port 445 inbound on the internal firewall so that the FTP servers can see the network share. Once the documents have arrived at the network share, they are on the same network as any BizTalk Servers, so no further ports will need to be opened. BizTalk Server does not natively support transmitting documents outward using FTP.

It is not usually recommended to open port 445 on a firewall—internal or external—so if you can provide similar functionality using another means, I advise you to do so. However, if you must implement FTP in this way, on no account should you open port 445 in the external firewall!

Inbound/Outbound Message Queuing   It is also possible to enable public message queues in your DMZ that trading partners can submit documents to, and that BizTalk Server can poll using a Message Queuing receive function. Again, port 1801 inbound will have to be opened on both firewalls to allow this. Similarly, open port 1801 outbound on both firewalls to allow BizTalk Messaging or Orchestration to send a document to an external public message queue.

Inbound/Outbound COM Access   There are a number of situations where access to COM components might be required through one or both firewalls. For example, if your BizTalk Server is located in the DMZ, but needs to access a COM component (such as a SAP DCOM connector) on the corporate network, it is possible to open up the internal firewall to do this. However, every extra port opened on a firewall presents a possible security risk, so this is another reason not to place BizTalk Server in the DMZ.

BizTalk Orchestration, on the other hand, may need to access external sites in certain circumstances. If an XLANG schedule will use a COM component implementation, and that COM component is either in the DMZ or out on the Internet (such as a COM proxy for a web service), it will again be necessary to use DCOMCNFG to configure a suitable range of ports. This time, however, these will be outbound ports that need to be opened on the firewall. Again, port 135 outbound should be opened as well to allow the internal server to determine the port required by the object. More interestingly, and also more securely, it is possible for XLANG schedules to use local COM proxies to access external web services, such that only HTTP port 80 or HTTPS port 443 needs to be open on both firewalls. This is a much safer arrangement, because these ports will usually be open for normal HTTP/S traffic.

Using web services with BizTalk Server is covered in Chapter 17.

Server Security

Once you've established where you will place BizTalk Server in your enterprise, the next thing to do is ensure that each individual server is properly secured. For administrative purposes, you will need to make sure that certain users have the necessary privileges to perform certain tasks, but these accounts may only need to be a member of the BizTalk Administrators group rather than the Windows 2000 Administrators group.

Securing each server will involve the application of accepted best practices such as removing unnecessary subsystems and services, but certain services and applications that remain can also be further secured with relatively straightforward configuration. Also, it will be necessary to use Windows 2000 and SQL Server permissions to ensure that web sites and databases used by BizTalk Server cannot be easily compromised.

Administrative Accounts

To perform administrative tasks on BizTalk Server or a BizTalk Server group, certain rights and privileges are required. Depending on the task, it may be necessary for an individual to be a member of the Windows 2000 Administrators group, or it may be sufficient to be a member of the BizTalk Server Administrators group, which is created during the installation of the product. Best practices require that user accounts are given the most limited permissions that still allow their tasks to be performed, so it is important to know which tasks can be carried out by members of each group.

BizTalk Administrator Privileges

During the installation of BizTalk Server, a group is created that is given the name BizTalk Server Administrators by default. Membership in this group is vital to be able to perform most tasks related to the upkeep of a BizTalk Server group. It is recommended that users who need to be able to carry out these functions should be added to the BizTalk Server Administrators group, rather than the Windows 2000 local Administrators group, unless there are specific tasks that require the privileges afforded by membership of the Windows 2000 Administrators group.

The actions that can be performed by users who are members of the BizTalk Server Administrators group but who are not members of the Windows 2000 Administrators group on any server are as follows:

- Add new BizTalk Server groups.
- View and modify BizTalk Server group properties.
- Add new receive functions.

- View and modify receive function properties.
- Remove existing receive functions.

Windows Administrator Privileges

To put it bluntly, the Windows 2000 Administrator is all-knowing and all-powerful. If you are a member of the local Administrators group on a computer running BizTalk Server, you can do just about anything. Even if you cannot explicitly do certain things, you can always give yourself the appropriate permissions to rectify that. Membership of both the BizTalk Server Administrators and Windows 2000 Administrators groups is required on each system if you wish to perform certain additional BizTalk Server-related tasks, as follows:

- Add new servers to a BizTalk Server group.
- View and modify individual server properties including server status.
- Free interchanges on an individual server.
- Remove existing servers from a BizTalk Server group.
- Remove existing BizTalk Server groups.

For example, if you wish to add a computer running BizTalk Server to an existing server group, you must be a member of the BizTalk Server Administrators group, *and* you must be a member of the local Administrators group on that server. Similarly, if you wish to remove an existing BizTalk Server group, you must be a member of the BizTalk Server Administrators group, *and* you must be a member of the local Administrators group on *each* server in the group, or else you will receive an error, as shown. If you click on the node for a BizTalk Server group in the BizTalk Server Administration console, and you do not have the appropriate privileges on one or more of the servers in that group, the status of those servers will appear as "Access Denied".

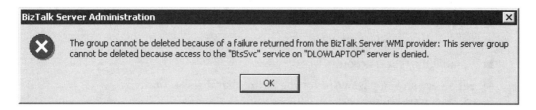

BizTalk Server Administration   ⊠

❌ The group cannot be deleted because of a failure returned from the BizTalk Server WMI provider: This server group cannot be deleted because access to the "BtsSvc" service on "DLOWLAPTOP" server is denied.

OK

If you are a member of the local Administrators group, but you are not a member of the BizTalk Server Administrators group, you will not be able to expand the Microsoft BizTalk Server node in the BizTalk Server Administration console. However, as an administrator, you can always add yourself to that group!

DEPLOYING BIZTALK SERVER

Securing Services

As discussed earlier in the chapter, every service in Windows 2000 requires a security context in which to run. The same is true of COM+ applications used by both the operating system and installed software such as BizTalk Server. It is important to assign the appropriate security contexts to each service for their protection and the security of the installation in general. Also, because each service and subsystem present on Windows 2000 provides another potential means by which an intruder could attack, you should always ensure that only those services actually required for a functional server are running.

Server Hardening

Although Windows 2000 is itself a secure operating system certified by the NSA to C2 level, there are all sorts of extra systems and services running by default on a server to compromise that status. Best practices for servers in general demand that these systems are removed or locked down, and this is no different for BizTalk Server. Also, because security often involves the subtle as well as the obvious, there are certain default settings in the operating system that should be changed.

The following are some recommended steps for securing all Windows 2000 servers—not just those running BizTalk Server. These are as specified in the product documentation, so no further discussion of them will be presented here:

- Turn off NTFS 8.3 name generation.
- Set the system start time to zero seconds.
- Remove the OS/2 subsystem.
- Remove the Portable Operating System Interface for UNIX (POSIX) subsystem.
- Format the hard disk(s) to NTFS.
- Set appropriate NTFS Discretionary Access Control Lists (DACLs).
- Remove all network shares.
- Unbind NetBIOS from TCP/IP unless it is absolutely required.
- Disable IP routing.
- Disable the Guest account.
- Set a very strong password for the Administrators account (at least nine characters).

In addition, Table 13-1 lists a subset of those services that are usually present on a Windows 2000 server, but that are not necessarily required for BizTalk Server to function correctly. If indicated, these services should be disabled.

Service	Required	Comments
Alerter	Yes	Required for performance or security-related administrative alerts if configured.
Certificate Authority	No	Certificate Services, if required, should be installed on a domain controller separate from BizTalk Server.
Computer Browser	No	Only used by NetBIOS for maintaining network lists.
Content Index	No	BizTalk Server does not use Index Server.
DHCP Client	No	BizTalk Server will normally be configured with a static IP address.
FTP Publishing	No	FTP services, if required, should be installed on a separate server in the DMZ.
Messenger	Optional	Required if Alerter service is used.
NetBIOS Interface	Yes	Required for access to UNC paths and other network computers.
Netlogon	Yes	Required for pass-through domain authentication of users and computers.
NNTP	No	NNTP should never be required by BizTalk Server.
Plug and Play	Yes	Required for hardware detection.
Print Spooler	No	BizTalk Server should not be configured as a print server.
Protected Storage	Yes	Required for protection of digital certificate private keys.
Remote Access Services	No	RAS, if required, should be installed on a separate server.
RPC Locator	Yes	Required for BizTalk Server to communicate with other systems.

Table 13-1. *Services Present on Windows 2000 That May Not Be Required*

DEPLOYING BIZTALK SERVER

Service	Required	Comments
RunAs Service	No	Provides a potential security risk by impersonation of administrator credentials.
Server	No	BizTalk Server should not be used for the administration of users and groups.
SMTP	No	SMTP, if required, should be installed on a separate server in the DMZ.
Telephony	No	Should not be needed for BizTalk Server.
Telnet	No	Provides an unacceptable security risk of remote administration and the exchange of clear text passwords.
Terminal Services	Optional	Only required if remote administration will be performed.
Uninterruptible Power Supply (UPS)	Optional	Required if a UPS provides backup power.
Workstation	Yes	Required if file receive functions or BizTalk Messaging ports access UNC paths.

Table 13-1. *Services Present on Windows 2000 That May Not Be Required* (continued)

Securing BizTalk Messaging

BizTalk Messaging is one of the core services in BizTalk Server. As a system service, it is an executable program (MSCIS.exe) that runs in the background on Windows 2000. The service is created during the installation of BizTalk Server, and you must configure it to run under the security context of a particular user account. During installation, you select the user account to use, and this account is automatically given the rights to log on locally and to act as part of the operating system. You can use either the built-in Local System account or a service account created for that purpose. It is usually recommended to create a service account rather than to use Local System, because it is easier to control what that account can and cannot do. However, you must ensure that the service account has the appropriate permissions on any file locations or message queues that will be the target of a receive function.

Securing the BizTalk Server Interchange Application

In addition to the BizTalk Messaging service, a COM+ application called the BizTalk Server Interchange Application provides the IInterchange interface through which documents are submitted for processing by BizTalk Messaging. Because documents have to be submitted to BizTalk Server before any processing can occur, this application is just as important as the service itself. However, whereas the BizTalk Messaging service runs under the security context of an account that has the right to log on locally and act as part of the operating system, the BizTalk Server Interchange Application is configured to run in the security context of the interactive user. In other words, if there is nobody logged onto the server, no documents can be submitted! Obviously, this presents a serious security risk for your BizTalk Server installation, as you would have to leave somebody logged on the server all the time. Also, the application would be running in the security context of that user, who might potentially have administrative privileges.

Therefore, it is crucially important to modify the properties of this application so that it runs in the context of a service account created specifically for that purpose. The service account you create must have the right to log on as a batch job, and this right can be given using the Local Security Policy Microsoft Management Console (MMC). After you've done this, you can associate the service account with the BizTalk Server Interchange Application using the Component Services MMC. Perform the following steps to complete this configuration:

1. Open the Component Services MMC from Start | Programs | Administrative Tools | Component Services.

2. Expand the Component Services, Computers, My Computer, and COM+ Applications nodes.

3. Right-click the BizTalk Server Interchange Application node, and select Properties from the Context menu.

4. In the BizTalk Server Interchange Application Properties dialog box, select the Advanced tab.

5. Clear the Disable Changes check box and click OK.

6. Click Yes in the Warning dialog box that appears.

7. Right-click the BizTalk Server Interchange Application node again, and select Properties from the Context menu. All properties are now editable, as shown in Figure 13-5.

8. In the BizTalk Server Interchange Application Properties dialog box, select the Identity tab.

9. Select the This User option.

10. Enter the details of the user account to be used, or click Browse to select an existing user, and complete the Password and Confirm Password fields.

11. Click OK, and click Yes in the Warning dialog box that appears.

Installing BizTalk Server Service Pack 1 resets the account used by BizTalk Server COM+ applications to their default settings, so you will need to perform these steps again after adding the service pack.

Creating Roles for the BizTalk Server Interchange Application

After you have configured the COM+ application to run in the security context of the service account, you can also modify the application to control who is able to submit documents to BizTalk Messaging. This is again done through the Component Services MMC and requires the creation of a new user role. Perform the following steps to complete this configuration:

1. Open the Component Services MMC from Start | Programs | Administrative Tools | Component Services, and ensure that changes can be made to the BizTalk Server Interchange Application using steps 2 through 6 of the previous procedure.

2. Right-click the BizTalk Server Interchange Application node, and select Properties from the Context menu.

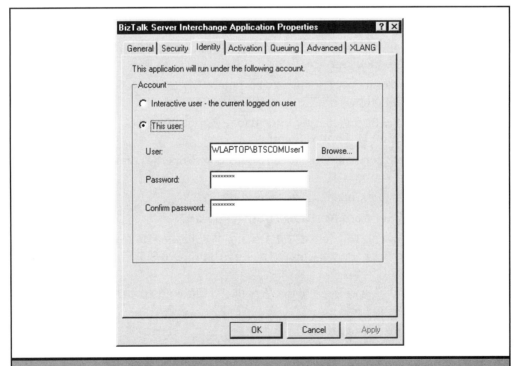

Figure 13-5.   *The BizTalk Server Interchange Application Properties dialog box*

3. In the BizTalk Server Interchange Application Properties dialog box, select the Security tab.

4. Select the check box to Enforce Access Checks For This Application, and choose the option to Perform Access Checks At The Process And Component Level.

5. Click OK and click Yes in the Warning dialog box that appears.

6. Expand the BizTalk Server Interchange Application node, right-click Roles, and choose New | Role from the context menu.

7. In the Role dialog box, enter an appropriate name for the role, such as Submit Documents.

8. Click OK and click Yes in the Warning dialog box that appears.

9. Expand the Roles node, and expand the node for the role you just created.

10. Right-click the Users node, and select New | User from the context menu.

11. In the Select Users Or Groups dialog box, add users and/or groups that should be allowed to submit documents to BizTalk Messaging.

Once you have created the role, you can then associate it with the Submit and SubmitSync methods of the IInterchange interface to permit the users that have been added to the role to submit documents. Perform the following steps to complete this configuration:

1. Expand the BizTalk Server Interchange Application, Components, BizTalk.Interchange.1, Interfaces, IInterchange, and Methods nodes.

2. Right-click the Submit node, and select Properties from the context menu.

3. In the Submit Properties dialog box, select the Security tab.

4. Select the check box for the role you created in the previous procedure, as shown in Figure 13-6, and click OK. This enables users and groups associated with that role to use this method.

5. Repeat the procedure for the SubmitSync method.

Securing BizTalk Orchestration

BizTalk Orchestration is the other core service running on BizTalk Server, although strictly speaking, it's not a system service like BizTalk Messaging; instead it is a collection of services and COM+ applications. In particular, a COM+ application called the XLANG Scheduler acts as a host for running XLANG schedules, and this also persists state information to an Orchestration Persistence database when a schedule will be dormant for a prolonged period. The removal of a dormant schedule from memory and the persistence of the associated state information is called *dehydration*. It is necessary to secure this default application, any other COM+ applications that will also host XLANG schedules, and also the Orchestration Persistence database. Further, you can

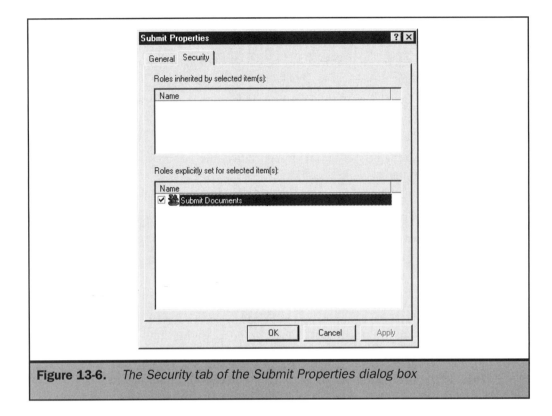

Figure 13-6. *The Security tab of the Submit Properties dialog box*

secure individual XLANG schedules on a more granular level by requiring authentication of the identity of the sender of a message to an implementation technology.

Note *XLANG schedules and BizTalk Orchestration Designer were covered in Chapter 7.*

Securing the XLANG Scheduler Application

As with BizTalk Messaging, there is a default COM+ application created to host running XLANG schedules. This application is also configured to run in the security context of the interactive user, so you should again create a service account for it. One extra important reason for doing this is that COM+ applications that host XLANG schedules require access to the Orchestration Persistence database to store state information for dehydrated schedules. When this database is created, a data source name (DSN) is also configured to hold the connection parameters. These connection parameters specify that the user account under which the application is running should be used to access the database. So if the host application is configured to use the interactive user account, and that logged-on user is not the same user who created the database, it probably won't have the appropriate permissions to store state information in the database.

Therefore, you should first assign a service account for any COM+ applications that will host XLANG schedules. The procedure is exactly the same as that for the BizTalk Server Interchange Application, so I won't repeat it. After that, you should either modify the XLANG Scheduler DSN to use an appropriate SQL Server user account for authentication, or else use SQL Server Enterprise Manager to ensure that the service account has the appropriate permissions on the Orchestration Persistence database. The account should be able to create tables and create procedures on the database.

Using the XLANG Scheduler Application Roles

A number of roles are preconfigured for the XLANG Scheduler COM+ application. These roles provide a default mechanism to secure the application so that only certain users can create, use, or administer XLANG schedules. You will usually need to modify the membership of these roles to properly secure your applications.

XLANG Schedule Creator   This role is used to determine who should be allowed to create instances of XLANG schedules that will be hosted by this application. The membership of this role defaults to the Everyone group when the application is installed. Because it is possible to create interactive applications that instantiate XLANG schedules, it is important that you limit the ability of users to arbitrarily run schedules. The user and group accounts you add to this role will depend on your particular requirements. One thing that you will almost definitely need to do, however, is ensure that the service account used by the BizTalk Messaging service is a member of this role. Otherwise, it would not be possible for a messaging port to instantiate an XLANG schedule directly. The Windows 2000 event log will show an entry for each unsuccessful attempt to create an XLANG schedule instance.

XLANG Schedule User   This role is used to determine the users who should be allowed to interact with running XLANG schedules. By default, the Everyone group is a member of this role. Most of the time, you will configure your business processes to execute automatically, but it is possible to configure a schedule to wait for input in certain circumstances. Only users who have been added to this role will be able to provide such input. The Windows 2000 event log will show an entry for each unsuccessful attempt to interact with a running XLANG schedule instance.

XLANG Schedule Administration   This role is used to determine who should be allowed to modify the properties of the XLANG Scheduler COM+ application. For example, only certain users should be allowed to suspend or shut down XLANG schedule instances, reconfigure the DSN for the application, or modify the identity under which the application runs. By default, only the Windows 2000 Administrators group is a member of this role, and this should be appropriate in most instances. The Windows 2000 event log will show an entry for each time a user who is not a member of the role attempts to administer the XLANG Scheduler application.

XLANG Scheduler Application This role is used to interact with other COM+ applications associated with an XLANG schedule. It therefore represents the XLANG Scheduler application itself, so the service account used for the identity of the application should be a member of this role. In fact, it will probably suffice for this account to be the only member of the role. It defaults to the Everyone group, however, when the application is installed.

Confirming Sender Identity

In Chapter 7, I discussed the implementation of various technologies by which messages could be sent or received by an XLANG schedule. BizTalk Orchestration Designer is the tool used to create XLANG schedules, and for each implementation technology available, there is a binding wizard through which its various properties can be set. In the case of COM Component, Windows Script Component, and Message Queuing implementations, it is possible to specify that the identity of the sender of a message received by one of these technologies should be verified. The details of this configuration were covered in Chapter 7, but I will summarize them here.

The Advanced Port properties page of each binding wizard has an area in which you can specify security information, as shown in Figure 13-7. Under Sender Identity Confirmation, select either Not Required, Optional, or Required. If you choose Not Required, no attempt is made to confirm the identity of the sender. If you choose Optional, the _Sender_ field in the message will be populated with the sender's identity if present. If the sender's identity cannot be confirmed, the message will be accepted, and the schedule will continue regardless. If you choose Required, the sender's identity must be available. Again, it will be placed in the _Sender_ field if present, but if it cannot be confirmed, the message will be rejected, and an error will be written to the Application event log.

Note	*For a message queuing implementation, you may also specify a Windows 2000 user account with permission to write to a particular queue, if required. This option is only available for static queues.*

Document Security

Securing BizTalk Server is not just about installing firewalls and assigning permissions. The day-to-day use of the product involves the receipt and transmission of business documents, and you probably do not want this information falling into the wrong hands or being misrepresented. So far in this chapter, we have addressed a number of key security concepts, such as authentication, authorization, and protection. When exchanging business documents, other issues come into play, such as confidentiality, integrity, and nonrepudiation. Through the use of public key infrastructure (PKI) technology and features already mentioned, such as discretionary access control lists and transport security, we can be confident that our documents are transmitted securely.

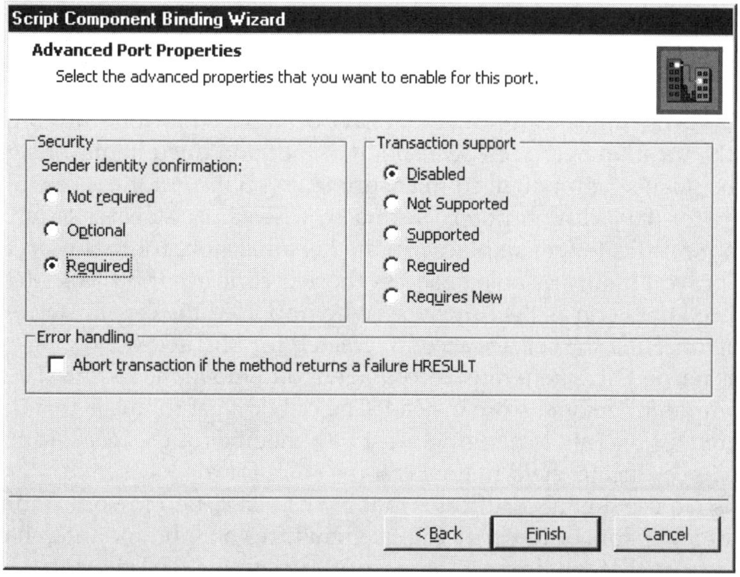

Figure 13-7.   *Advanced Properties page of the binding wizard*

Digital Certificates

As discussed earlier in the chapter, digital certificates provide many important elements of security—authentication, authorization, confidentiality, integrity, and nonrepudiation. By installing, importing, and verifying digital certificates, we can ensure that our business partners are who they claim to be, protect our documents from illegitimate access, read documents encrypted by our trading partners, and ensure the veracity of data. Digital certificates will need to be stored in the appropriate locations for automatic retrieval, and they will also need to be secured themselves. The application of these digital certificates can then be configured through BizTalk Messaging Manager.

Storing Digital Certificates

Windows 2000 provides a number of certificate stores in which to place digital certificates. First of all, certificates may be associated with a computer, user, or service. For each of these locations, there will be a number of stores available, and the list of stores will depend on the software installed. For example, once BizTalk Server is installed, a BizTalk store is created to hold certain certificates.

To view the available locations, and the stores in each location, we can use the Certificates MMC snap-in. This is not available in the Administrative Tools folder by default, but it is a simple matter to create a new MMC and add the appropriate snap-ins to it. In particular, we will be interested in adding a snap-in for the local computer, as shown in Figure 13-8. Here, we can access different stores for certificates, but we are primarily concerned with the Personal store and the BizTalk store.

If you wish to use digital certificates that have been issued to your own organization for client authentication over SSL, decryption of inbound documents, or signing of outbound documents, you will need to ensure that you import these certificates to the Personal store for the local computer. Normally, when a user creates or imports a certificate, that certificate will be placed in the Personal store for that user. However, BizTalk Server would only be able to access those certificates if BizTalk Messaging were configured to log on as the same user who imported the certificates. Although you could log on using the service account created for BizTalk Messaging and import certificates as needed, it is generally recommended to move the required certificates to the Local Computer Personal store instead. The only caveat to this is that the service account created for BizTalk Messaging must be a member of the local Administrators group to access certificates held in the Personal store for the local computer.

If you wish to use digital certificates that have been issued to your trading partners to encrypt outgoing data or to verify digital signatures on inbound interchanges, you will need to ensure that you import these certificates to the BizTalk store for the local computer. This is where BizTalk Messaging looks to find trading partner certificates for these purposes. Similarly, if your trading partners will be sending S/MIME encrypted documents to you via SMTP, you will also need to store a copy of the appropriate digital certificate in the Exchange store if you have an Exchange script that performs any preprocessing before submitting documents to BizTalk Messaging.

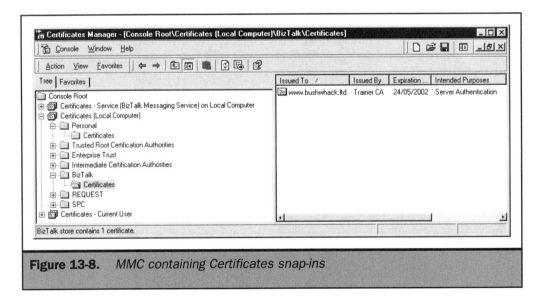

Figure 13-8. *MMC containing Certificates snap-ins*

If you'll pardon the pun, there are two "key" considerations when importing your own organization's certificates using the Certificates MMC snap-in. During the importation process, you will be asked whether you wish to allow the private key for the certificate to be exported, as shown next. You should *not* select this option. If your server were to become compromised (which of course wouldn't happen because you'd taken all the advice in this chapter), a malicious user would have access to your private key. As I said at the beginning of the chapter, you never, ever, ever let anybody have your private key. You may also have the option to enable strong private key protection for the certificate. Although this seems like the kind of thing you would want to do, you should not select this option for certificates that will be used by BizTalk Server. If you were to do so, a prompt would appear every time BizTalk Server attempted to use the certificate. Unfortunately, BizTalk Server has no fingers to click buttons in dialog boxes, so it would fail to access the certificate.

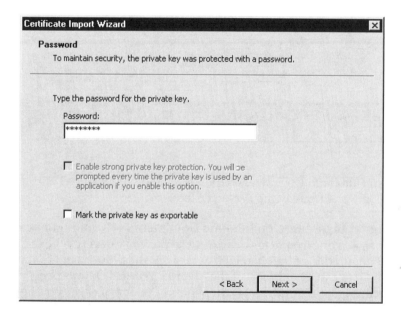

Using Digital Certificates

The selection of digital certificates for encryption, signing, and client authentication is done through BizTalk Messaging Manager. Although this was discussed in detail in Chapter 6, I will present a summary of the necessary configurations here.

Signing Outbound Documents   Figure 13-9 shows the Security Information page of the Messaging Port Wizard. On this page you should select S/MIME from the Signature drop-down menu if you wish to digitally sign outgoing documents. During the configuration of any channels that feed into this messaging port, you will need to

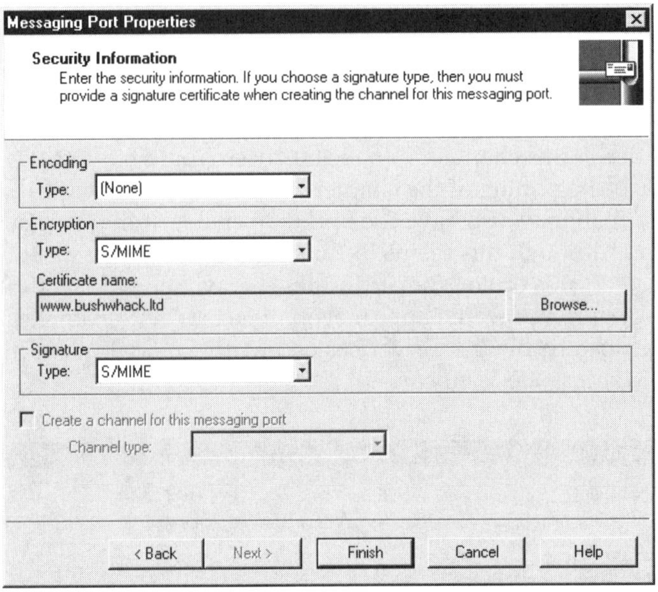

Figure 13-9. *Security Information page of the Messaging Port Wizard*

select the Sign Outbound Document check box, as shown in Figure 13-10, and browse to an appropriate certificate in the Personal store.

Verifying Digital Signatures on Inbound Documents   If your trading partner has sent digitally signed documents to your organization, you can verify the digital signature during the configuration of the channel that receives those documents. Figure 13-11 shows the Inbound Document page of the Channel Wizard. On this page, you should select the Verify Signature Certificate On Inbound Document check box, and browse to an appropriate certificate in the BizTalk store.

Encrypting Outbound Documents   On the Security Information page of the Messaging Port Wizard, shown in Figure 13-9, you can also choose to encrypt the outbound document. This will involve your trading partner's certificate, so you should choose S/MIME from the Encryption drop-down menu, and browse to the appropriate certificate in the BizTalk store.

Decrypting Inbound Documents   If your trading partner sends encrypted documents to your organization, they will do so using your organization's digital certificate. To decrypt the documents, you will need to select the Verify Decryption

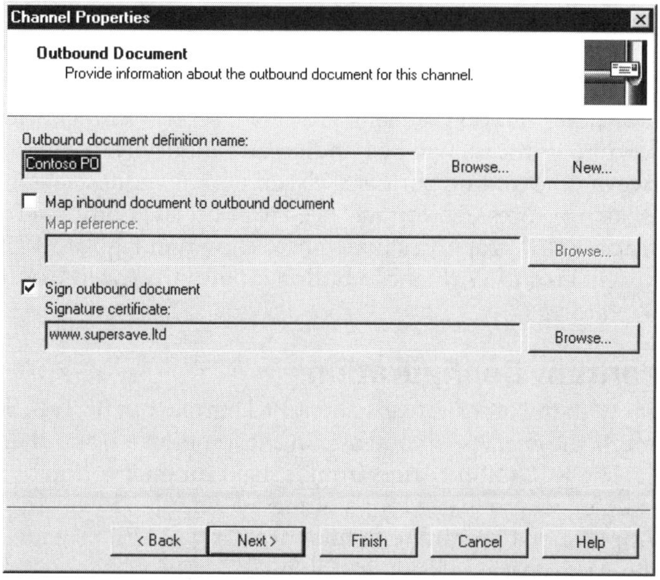

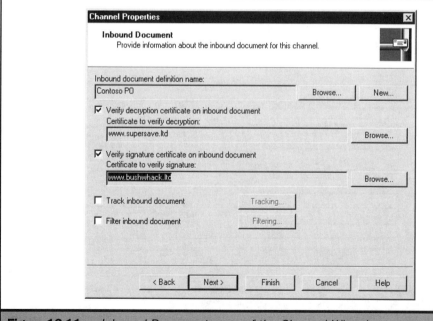

Figure 13-10. *Outbound Document page of the Channel Wizard*

Figure 13-11. *Inbound Document page of the Channel Wizard*

Certificate On Inbound Document check box on the Inbound Document page of the Channel Wizard, shown in Figure 13-11. You can then browse to the appropriate certificate in the Personal store.

Client Authentication   If you are using HTTPS to send documents to your trading partners, the encryption process will be handled automatically, as described earlier in this chapter. However, the trading partner web server may request client authentication during the handshaking process, so you will need to select an appropriate client certificate in the BizTalk SendHTTPX Properties dialog box, shown in Figure 13-12. This dialog box is accessed by clicking the Advanced button on the Advanced Configuration page of the Channel Wizard.

Custom Algorithm Configuration

The only problem with the otherwise excellent PKI support in BizTalk Server is that it automatically selects the encryption and signing schemes used, and there is no easy way to change it. The RC2 (40-bit) algorithm is used for encryption by default, and the SHA-1 (160-bit) algorithm is used for signing by default. However, the Microsoft Cryptographic Application Programming Interface (CryptoAPI) provides many different algorithms for these purposes, as listed in Table 13-2.

The 128-bit-strength encryption algorithms require the Microsoft Enhanced Cryptographic Provider version 1.0. This provider is available with the Microsoft Windows 2000 High Encryption Pack.

To use these alternative algorithms, the BizTalk Messaging Configuration Object Model must be used. In the following code, a channel called *Channel* has already been

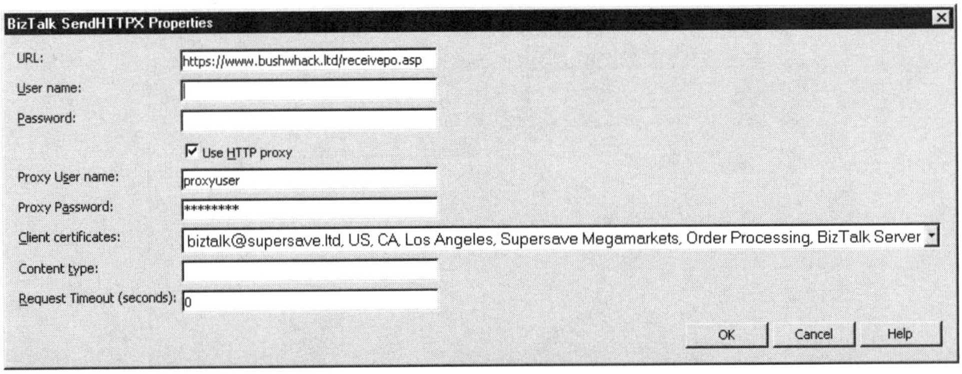

Figure 13-12.   *BizTalk SendHTTPX Properties dialog box*

	Algorithm Constant	**Algorithm Name**
Encryption Algorithms	ENCRYPT_DES_56	DES (56-bit)
	ENCRYPT_RC2_40	RC2 (40-bit)
	ENCRYPT_RC4_40	RC4 (40-bit)
	ENCRYPT_RC4_128	RC4 (128-bit)
	ENCRYPT_RC2_128	RC2 (128-bit)
	ENCRYPT_3DES_112	3DES (112-bit)
	ENCRYPT_3DES_168	3DES (168-bit)
Signature Algorithms	SIGNATURE_SHA	SHA-1 (160-bit)
	SIGNATURE_MD5	MD5 (128-bit)

Table 13-2. *Available Algorithms Provided by the Windows CryptoAPI*

created. The *CurrentSignAlg* and *CurrentEncryptAlg* properties are used to change the default signing and encryption algorithms to MD5 (128-bit) and RC4 (128-bit), respectively.

```
' The organizations, document definitions, messaging port and channel
' have already been created. PortHandle is a variable holding the value
' of the Handle property of the associated messaging port

Channel.SignatureCertificateInfo.Reference = cSignCertRef
Channel.SignatureCertificateInfo.Store = BIZTALK_STORE_TYPE_MY
Channel.Create
ChannelHandle = Channel.Handle
Channel.Clear
Channel.Load ChannelHandle
Set ConfigData =
Channel.GetConfigData(BIZTALK_CONFIGDATA_TYPE_ENCRYPTION, _
     PortHandle, BIZTALK_TRANSPORT_TYPE_SMTP)
ConfigData.CurrentSignAlg = SIGNATURE_MD5
ConfigData.CurrentEncryptAlg = ENCRYPT_RC4_128
Channel.SetConfigData BIZTALK_CONFIGDATA_TYPE_ENCRYPTION, _
     PortHandle, ConfigData
Channel.Save
```

The BizTalk Messaging Configuration Object Model is covered in Chapter 16.

Securing Transports

The final thing to discuss in relation to securing documents exchanged using BizTalk Server is how each transport method can be secured. Again, this was covered in detail in Chapter 6, so I will only summarize the configuration properties here.

HTTP/S Transports   If you use HTTP to transmit documents, you can specify a user name and password to access the URL specified during the configuration of the messaging port. This is done through the BizTalk SendHTTPX Properties dialog box, shown earlier in Figure 13-12. The user name and password provided will be sent as a response to a Basic Authentication request by the web server. BizTalk Server does not support other authentication methods, so it would be advisable to use this in conjunction with HTTPS rather than HTTP. With BizTalk Server Service Pack 1 installed, you also have the option to provide Basic Authentication credentials to a proxy server if you must go through a proxy server to access the Internet. Again, this is visible in Figure 13-12. Similarly, if your trading partners will be sending documents to your organization via HTTP, you should enable HTTPS by installing a web server certificate, and use NTFS permissions to restrict access to the web page to which the documents will be submitted.

SMTP Transport   If you use SMTP to transmit documents, you can encrypt the documents using S/MIME, as discussed earlier in the chapter. It is also possible that the SMTP server configured for use by BizTalk Server requires authentication. Because this server will exist in your own network, BizTalk Server allows both Basic Authentication and NTLM Authentication. However, NTLM authentication will only work if BizTalk Server and the SMTP server are not separated by a firewall or proxy server. In most cases, your SMTP server will be in the DMZ, and BizTalk Server will be behind the internal firewall, so Basic Authentication will have to be used. The exception to this is if you use Microsoft Exchange Server as your SMTP server and have it relay messages to the outer SMTP server. You can specify a user name and password in the BizTalk SendSMTP Properties dialog box, shown in Figure 13-13. The dialog box is accessible through the Advanced button on the Advanced Configuration page of the Channel Wizard.

File Transport   Using the File transport to transmit documents will usually be done in EAI scenarios, as you will not be able to reach across the Internet and access the file systems of your trading partners. However, it is good practice to use NTFS permissions wherever possible to secure your file folders, so it may be necessary to supply a user name and password to access the directory to which you will send your documents. As before, this is accomplished through the BizTalk SendFile Properties dialog box, as

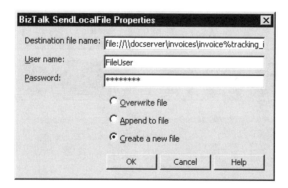

Figure 13-13.   *BizTalk SendSMTP Properties dialog box*

shown next. The dialog box is accessible through the Advanced button on the Advanced Configuration page of the Channel Wizard.

Message Queuing   If you will be using the Message Queuing transport in the messaging ports you configure, you will again need to provide authentication. If the service account being used by BizTalk Messaging does not have the appropriate permissions on a public or private queue, you can specify an explicit user name and password that does have write access to the queue, as shown in Figure 13-14. Also, because Message Queuing servers can also authenticate themselves to clients using digital certificates, you have the option that BizTalk Server should request authentication credentials from the server. In the case of MSMQ 1.0 running on a trading partner's Windows NT 4.0 server, you can ask for a digital certificate to be supplied, or in the case of MSMQ 2.0 running on Windows 2000, you can query Active Directory for the appropriate credentials.

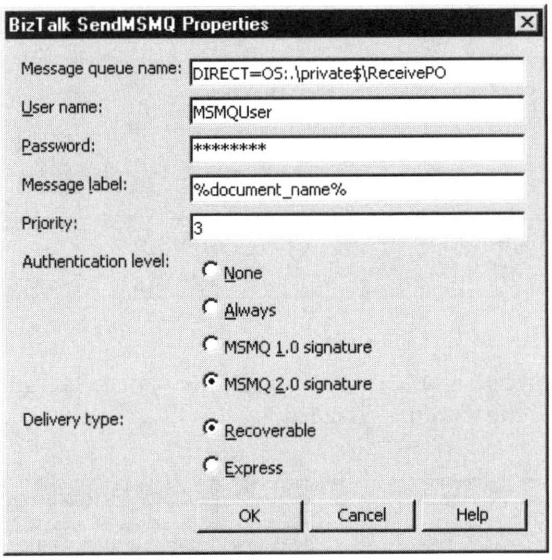

Figure 13-14. *BizTalk SendMSMQ Properties dialog box*

Chapter 14

Integrating BizTalk Server 2000 with Commerce Server 2000

In Chapter 6 we saw how to configure BizTalk Messaging to receive, transform, package, deliver, and track documents by creating virtual objects that represent each step in an automated process. In this chapter we will show how to configure Commerce Server to communicate with these BizTalk Messaging objects. We will also cover how BizTalk Messaging can communicate with Commerce Server. You do not need to be an expert in Commerce Server to understand this integration. You do, however, need to understand how to use the BizTalk Messaging Manager, BizTalk Editor, and BizTalk Document Tracking. Also, you will need to be familiar with the Commerce Server Manager and the Commerce Business Desk. (I highly recommend reviewing Chapter 6 before reading this chapter.) The more you understand what is happening behind the scenes, the better off you will be in solving any problems that may come up. This chapter is not designed to dive deeply into BizTalk Server or Commerce Server's full functionality. We are only going to cover the out-of-the-box settings that need to be made to integrate the two and show some samples of this integration. You should also review the Microsoft Knowledge Base article Q294275 titled "Issues with Interoperability Between Commerce Server and BizTalk Server" and the Commerce Server Resource Kit.

This chapter also includes two step-by-step walk-throughs that should take you past the initial configuration confusions. (For enhanced supplier-enablement functionality, such as the exporting of catalogs to trading partners or the automatic processing of purchase orders from BizTalk Server to Commerce Server, you can refer to Chapter 19, which includes a discussion on the BizTalk Server Accelerator for Suppliers.) We will finish with some tips, and I will point you in the right direction for more information.

Why Integrate?

Why do these products need to integrate? Let's say a business called Retail (I choose this scenario to go along with the step-by-step example later), has as its primary business selling computer books over the Internet. One day, the Retail executives notice that a large number of users were asking where to buy flowers to go along with their books. (Yeah, I know it sounds kind of far-fetched, but again it goes along with the example later.) After analyzing web logs, Retail's technology team noticed that a hot exit point from their site was this web site called Sweet Forgiveness, which just so happens to be in the flower business.

Seeing this, Retail decides to offer their users a better way to access all these products. The quick option is to just redirect their users to the other site. Doing this has many disadvantages to Retail, including the following:

- Users leave their site.
- They lose control of what the users see on the other site. (For example, there may possibly be links to competing book retailers on the other site.)
- They are not directly compensated for what the user may purchase from the site.

Retail does not want to send users off to some other site. What to do?

Retail's final decision is to partner with Sweet Forgiveness and import their catalog of flowers periodically to their site. Sweet Forgiveness is excited about the possibility of more revenue and believes it will be a win-win business decision. They are both currently running Commerce Server and have just learned that when an item is purchased, Commerce Server 2000 can split the order, creating a separate order form with only the Sweet Forgiveness products, and send it on to BizTalk Server. Once the purchase order is received in BizTalk Server, Retail can send it to Sweet Forgiveness. (It is important to note that this is a separate order form being sent from Commerce Server and that all of the original order information is still available using the Commerce Business Desk.) The good thing about this solution is that the user will not need multiple shopping baskets, and they are not forced to leave Retail's site. So everyone is happy.

Commerce Server 2000 has the built-in capability to have multiple catalogs that support multiple partners. Your partners can send you a catalog of their products, and they can fill orders for products that you sell.

So you see, the Commerce Server–BizTalk Server partnership provides basically everything you need to build an effective online business. Commerce Server also includes user profiling and management, product and service management, transaction processing, and targeted marketing. BizTalk Server adds a secure catalog exchange, order management, workflow, and reliable document delivery. Combined, they create a comprehensive system customizable for your specific business-to-business needs.

Out-of-the-Box Integration

We will now cover the steps needed to successfully process a Commerce Server purchase order (PO) coming from Retail through BizTalk Server and then on to a file share (Sweet Forgiveness). This process is shown in Figure 14-1. Although this is a sample solution, I will try to make it as realistic as possible. We will use two of the box sites that can be easily downloaded from the Microsoft Commerce Site. Shoppers will shop on the Retail site, which will not only offer its own products, but will also offer products from the other site (Sweet Forgiveness). Once the shopper finalizes his purchase on the Retail site, Retail's Commerce Server will split the order and send a purchase order to Sweet Forgiveness via BizTalk Server.

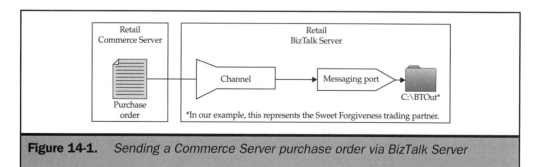

Figure 14-1. *Sending a Commerce Server purchase order via BizTalk Server*

DEPLOYING BIZTALK SERVER

We will use the Retail Solutions Site (Retail.pup) as our retail site. Our partner site will use the Sweet Forgiveness Solution Site (Sweet.pup). Both sites can be downloaded from http://www.microsoft.com/commerceserver/.

System Setup

We will start from a new installation of Windows 2000 Advanced Server as a stand-alone member server with the latest service packs. Next, we install SQL Server 2000, Commerce Server 2000, and Commerce Server Service Pack 1. We will also need to install BizTalk Server 2000 and BizTalk Server Service Pack 1A. For guidance on installing BizTalk Server, refer to Chapter 3. Also note that for this example we are installing everything on a single server.

Initial Site Setup

Now that we have the servers' products installed, we can now do the following.

- Install both solution sites using the default settings.
- Export the product catalog from the partner site. Accomplish this by using the Sweet Business Desk. If you visit http://server/sweetbizdesk, you will be asked to install the Business Desk client HTML application. After it's been installed, open the Business Desk from the desktop or the Start menu. Then select Catalog | Catalog Editor | SweetProducts | Export Catalog | Export XML. Remember where you put this file, because you will be importing it later.
- Open the Retail Business Desk by typing the URL **http://<servername>/retailbizdesk**, in your browser. Again, you will be asked to install the Business Desk client HTML application. After it's been installed, open the Retail Business Desk from the desktop or the Start menu. On the main page under "Getting Started", you will see the Business-to-Consumer Tutorial. Complete this tutorial, which shows you how to populate the Retail site with products, shipping, and tax info. See Figure 14-2.
- Next, we will need to import the Catalog file you exported earlier into the retail site using the Retail Business Desk. Select Catalog | Catalog Editor | Import Catalog | Import XML.

I will explain how to automate the catalog export and import via BizTalk Server later in this chapter.

Configuring BizTalk Server

Since BizTalk Server will need to know who is sending the purchase order, we will rename the Home Organization to "Retail" to represent our own company. (This is the company that's going to send the purchase order based on a customer's purchases.) We will configure an application here called "Commerce Server" to represent the fact that Commerce Server is an internal application to the Home Organization. We will also need to create a directory on the local machine to hold the transmitted purchase orders. We will call this directory "c:\btout".

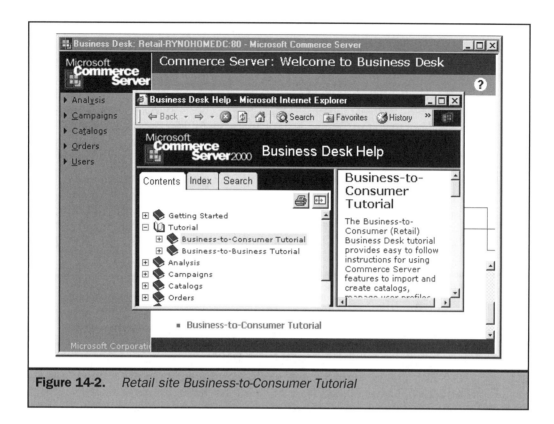

Figure 14-2.   *Retail site Business-to-Consumer Tutorial*

Rather than stepping you through each wizard in the Messaging Manager, I have created tables with the values to enter. If you want more information on the different fields in the BizTalk Messaging Manager, please refer to Chapter 6.

1. Using the BizTalk Messaging Manager, rename the Home Organization to **Retail**, and create an application in this organization called **Commerce Server**. Use Table 14-1 as a reference for Retail (Home) Organization Properties.

Tab	Field Name	Value
General	Organization Name	Retail
Applications	Application Name	Commerce Server

Table 14-1.   *Retail (Home) Organization Settings*

DEPLOYING BIZTALK SERVER

2. Commerce Server requires that the source and the destination servers contain the same POSchema.xml and CatalogXMLSchema.xml files, which it includes with the sample sites. Since we are only concerned with the Purchase Order for now, we will just import POSchema.xml. Copy the POSchema.xml file located in the Retail site root (c:\inetpub\wwwroot\retail) to the Program Files\Microsoft BizTalk Server\BizTalkServer Repository\DocSpecs\Microsoft. This is a WebDAV store, which is basically a file folder accessible via HTTP. You can also open this file in the BizTalk Editor and use the menu option Store To WebDAV.

3. Now we go back to the BizTalk Messaging Manager and create a document definition called **Purchase Order** and link it to the poschema.xml file in the BizTalk Repository. Remember, to create a document definition, select BizTalk Messaging Manager | File | New | Document Definition. Also, be sure to click the Document Specification tab to link your document. We do this so BizTalk Server will know how to work with the Purchase Order document.

4. The folder you created earlier (c:\btout) will be used as the destination folder where BizTalk Server will place the Sweet Forgiveness Products purchase order. Now we are ready to set up a messaging port to organization, calling it **Port to send PO to Sweet Forgiveness**. (Refer to Chapter 6 to see how to create channels and messaging ports.) The organization identifier should be set to **Organization / Sweet Forgiveness**. Also set the Primary Transport Type to File, and configure the messaging port to point to **file://c:\btout\ PO%tracking_id%.xml**. (See Table 14-2 for the settings.) We will have BizTalk Server deposit the purchase orders belonging to Sweet Forgiveness here.

Window	Field Name	Value
General	Port Name	Port to send PO to Sweet Forgiveness
Destination	Organization Name	Sweet Forgiveness
	Transport	File://c:\\btout\PO%tracking_id%.xml
Envelope	Envelope	None
	Org Identifier	Organization / Sweet Forgiveness
Security Info	Encoding	None
	Encryption	None
	Signature	None

Table 14-2. *"Port to send PO to Sweet Forgiveness" Port Settings*

When you create a messaging port, you are also prompted to create a channel to the port. We will create the channel from an application called **Channel to receive PO from Commerce Server** using the application "Commerce Server" and organization identifier **Organization / Retail** and assigning it the inbound and outbound document definition that we created earlier called PurchaseOrder. (See Table 14-3 for settings.)

5. The default SendLocalFile settings are set to overwrite the file. This will not matter in our case, because we configured BizTalk Server to name the file with a Tracking ID. If you want, you can reopen the RetailPO channel and step through to the last dialog box called Advanced Configuration, click the Advanced button, and you will see the SendLocalFile settings.

Now we are done with the BizTalk Messenger configuration. Next, we will look at the Commerce Server configurations.

Configuring Commerce Server to Work with BizTalk Server

To configure the Retail site to work with BizTalk Server, do the following.

Open the Commerce Server Manager MMC, and expand Commerce Server Manager, expand Commerce Sites, expand the Retail Site, and then expand Site Resources. In the left pane, right-click App Default Config and select Properties. Follow Table 14-4 and enter the values for each option. The options are explained in the right column. When you've finished, compare your values with Figure 14-3. Note: After you change these properties, you must unload the application from memory on the web server for the changes to take effect. It is not necessary to use either IISReset or to reboot the server. Simply go into Internet Services Manager and click the Unload button on the Home Directory tab to unload the application.

Window	Field Name	Value
General	Channel Name	Channel to receive PO from Commerce Server
Source Application	Application Name	Commerce Server
	Organization Identifier	Organization / Retail
Inbound Document	Name	Purchase Order
Outbound Document	Name	Purchase Order

Table 14-3. *"Channel to receive PO from Commerce Server" Channel Settings*

Option	Value	Explanation
BizTalk Catalog Doc Type	N/A	Document definition in BizTalk Server that relates to this site's catalog; blank for this example
BizTalk Options	1	1—Enables integration with BizTalk Server for document exchange 0—Disable integration
BizTalk PO Doc Type	Purchase Order	Document definition in BizTalk Server that relates to this site's purchase order
BizTalk Source Org Qualifier	OrganizationName	Alias qualifier for this site in BizTalk Server
BizTalk Source Org Qualifier Value	Retail	Alias value for this site in BizTalk Server
BizTalk Submit Type	1	1—Submits documents asynchronously

Table 14-4. *Retail Site Commerce Server Settings to Enable BizTalk Server*

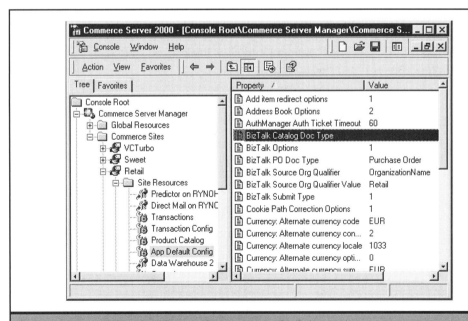

Figure 14-3. *Retail Commerce Server site's BizTalk settings*

Now we need to configure the Retail Commerce Server so it knows that the products in the imported catalog are for the specific vendor (which we called Sweet Forgiveness in BizTalk Server). To do this, we need to open the Retail Site Business Desk and go to Catalogs | Catalog Editor, select SweetProducts, and then click the Open File icon. This will bring up the Catalog Properties. Here, we can click the Select Vendor button to the right of Vendor ID and should see Sweet Forgiveness listed. Highlight and select this vendor. (If you want multiple partners for each catalog, you will need to change the _additem.asp file located in the root of the Retail site.)

Testing Our Solution

To test our solution, we will need to make a purchase on the Retail site. We will want to make sure that we purchase at least one product from each catalog in the same shopping basket. Once you have an order number, take a look at the contents of the directory that you specified in the Transport field of your Wholesale Messenger Port (c:\btout). You should find an XML document with a GUID as part of the name. (This represents the tracking number.) Each purchase you make will result in another file. Let's take a look now and verify the information in the file by clicking it and opening it in Internet Explorer. Notice there is no name or contact info, just what was ordered and where it needs to be shipped. See Figure 14-4.

You can also track your order by using BizTalk Document Tracking. (See Chapter 10.)

Figure 14-4. *Purchase order sent to Sweet Forgiveness*

Commerce Server 2000 Order Management

We have walked through how to send an order automatically. Commerce Server also has the capability to receive orders sent from BizTalk Server. To do this, we use the _recvpo.asp page. Instead of sending the document to a file folder, we send it HTTP/HTTPS to _recvpo.asp (also located in the root of your site), where the DictionaryXMLTransforms component converts the XML back to an order form object. Commerce Server then runs a pipeline on the order form and saves it to the Commerce Server database.

Another way to process and send an order form is to send it to a queue with either your BizTalk Server or the BizTalk Server at the vendor installation polling the queue. Using this configuration, you can install BizTalk Server and Commerce Server on separate servers.

Commerce Server Catalog

We have seen how to use BizTalk Server to send purchase orders generated by Commerce Server. Now we will cover the product catalog itself. To get more familiar with the Catalog schema, open up the XML file that you imported earlier. The XML elements in this file are divided into three groups:

- **MSCommerceCatalogCollection**   The root node for a Catalog file.
- **Catalog Schema Elements**   These elements can be used to extend the catalog.
  - **AttributeDefinition**   Describes an aspect of a property.
  - **PropertiesDefinition**   Holds the property definitions.
  - **Definition**   Describes a type of product or category.

It is also possible to export or import a catalog as a comma-delimited CSV file, but you will lose all the hierarchy information. Even if you do not use Commerce Server as the source of your catalog, you can still benefit from using BizTalk Server to deliver your product catalog to Commerce Server. Refer to Microsoft Knowledge Base article Q296210. It explains that version 1.0 of the catalog schema that comes with Commerce Server cannot be easily mapped using BizTalk Mapper. You will have to upgrade to Commerce Server Service Pack 1 to use the new catalog schema (version 1.5) that can be mapped. Also, there is an example of using the looping functoid with a Commerce Server schema given in Chapter 5.

Custom Integration

Now we will see what can be done if we customize. One of the best examples of customization I have seen to date is the following. There is also a Microsoft Knowledge Base article coming out on this soon. (Thanks to Michael Shea and Trace Young of Microsoft for letting me reuse their code for this walk-through.)

In this example, we will automate the process of exporting and importing the product catalog used earlier. We will be configuring Microsoft Commerce Server 2000 to send and receive catalogs via Microsoft BizTalk Server 2000. As you see in the diagram in Figure 14-5, we will be sending the product catalog from Sweet Forgiveness to BizTalk Server, triggering an ASP page to invoke another process running code in a scriptor that will import the product catalog into the Retail site.

1. We must first modify the site options for the Sweet (Wholesaler) site. We do this by editing the App Default Config properties in Commerce Server Manager. Configure the site options as shown in Table 14-5.

2. Next copy catalogxmlschema.xml to the BizTalk Server WebDAV Repository using the following steps:

   a. Launch the BizTalk Editor.

   b. Select Tools | Import, select XDR Schema, and click OK.

   c. Open Program Files | Microsoft Commerce Server | CatalogXMLSchema.xml.

   d. In the top-left pane of the Editor, navigate down to MSCommerceCatalog Collection | CatalogSchema | AttributeDefinition, and create a new field (Edit | New Field) named **MaxLength** with a data type of **Number**.

   e. From the File menu, select Store To WebDAV. The BizTalk Editor will display a dialog box asking "Are sure that you want to save this specification?" Click the Yes button, navigate to the Microsoft folder, and save the schema with the name **catalogxmlschema.xml**.

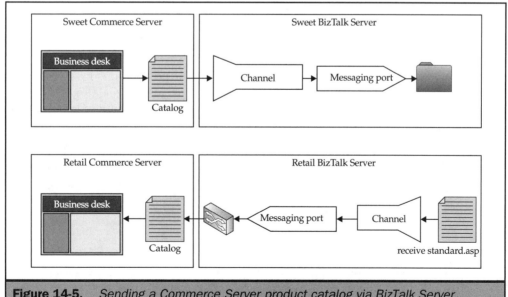

Figure 14-5. *Sending a Commerce Server product catalog via BizTalk Server*

Option	Value	Explanation
BizTalk Catalog Doc Type	Catalog	Document definition in BizTalk Server that relates to this site's catalog
BizTalk Options	1	1—Enables integration with BizTalk Server for document exchange 0—Disables integration
BizTalk PO Doc Type		Document definition in BizTalk Server that relates to this site's purchase order (not used in this example)
BizTalk Source Org Qualifier	OrganizationName	Alias qualifier for this site in BizTalk Server
BizTalk Source Org Qualifier Value	Sweet Forgiveness	Alias value for this site in BizTalk Server
BizTalk Submit Type	1	1—submits documents asynchronously

Table 14-5.   *Sweet Site Commerce Server to Enable BizTalk Server*

3. Create the Catalog document definition in the BizTalk Messaging Manager by using **Catalog** as the Document Definition name. Then select the check box for document specification, browse to the catalogxmlschema.xml file in the WebDAV repository that was imported earlier, and click OK.

4. Now, we will create the first of our two channel/port pairs needed for this solution. Create a Messenger Port To Application called **Port to send Catalog to BizTalk** with the settings in Table 14-6 and a Channel From Organization called **Channel to receive Catalog from Sweet Forgiveness** with the settings in Table 14-7.

5. Next we need to create the port to an organization called **Port to send Catalog to Retail** with the settings in Table 14-8. In the Security Information dialog box, select the option to Create A Channel For This Messaging Port, and choose a Channel type of From An Organization to create a channel called **Channel to receive Catalog from BizTalk** with the settings in Table 14-9.

Window	Field Name	Value
General	Port Name	Port to send Catalog to BizTalk
Destination	Application Name	Commerce Server
	Transport	http://<*yourServer*>/retail/receivestandard.asp
Envelope	Envelope	None
	Org Identifier	Organization / Retail
Security Info	Encoding	None
	Encryption	None
	Signature	None

Table 14-6.   *Settings for "Port to send Catalog to BizTalk" Port*

Window	Field Name	Value
General	Channel Name	Channel to receive Catalog from Sweet Forgiveness
Source Organization	Organization Name	Sweet Forgiveness
	Application Identifier	Organization / Sweet Forgiveness
Inbound Document	Name	Catalog
Outbound Document	Name	Catalog

Table 14-7.   *Settings for "Channel to receive Catalog from Sweet Forgiveness" Channel*

DEPLOYING BIZTALK SERVER

Window	Field Name	Value
General	Port Name	Port to send Catalog to Retail
Destination	Organization Name	Sweet Forgiveness
	Transport	BizTalk Scriptor
Envelope	Envelope	None
	Org Identifier	Organization / Sweet Forgiveness
Security Info	Encoding	None
	Encryption	None
	Signature	None

Table 14-8. *Settings for "Port to send Catalog to Retail" Port*

Window	Field Name	Value
General	Channel Name	Channel to receive Catalog from BizTalk
Source Organization	Organizational Name	Sweet Forgiveness
	Organization Identifier	Organization / Sweet Forgiveness
Inbound Document	Name	Catalog
Outbound Document	Name	Catalog

Table 14-9. *Settings for "Channel to receive Catalog from BizTalk" Channel*

6. Next, go back to the last dialog box of the Catalog Import Channel. In the Advanced Configuration dialog box, click the Advanced button. On the Primary Transport tab, click the Properties button. Replace the existing default script with the following script block.

```
function MSCSExecute(config, orderform, context, flags)
soutput = orderform.Value("working_data")

Dim fso, MyFile
Set fso = CreateObject("Scripting.FileSystemObject")
Mydrive = "c:\btout\"
MyDate = cstr(Date)
MyTime = cstr(Time)
Filename = MyDate & MyTime & ".xml"
FileName = Replace(FileName, "/", "")
FileName = Replace(FileName, ":", "")
Filename = Mydrive & FileName
Filename = Replace(Filename, " ", "")
Set MyFile = fso.CreateTextFile(Filename, True, true)
MyFile.WriteLine(soutput)
MyFile.Close
set appcfg = createobject("commerce.appconfig")
set catalogmanager = createobject("commerce.catalogmanager")
appcfg.initialize("retail")
set optdict = appcfg.getoptionsdictionary("")
connstr = optdict.s_CatalogConnectionString
catalogmanager.initialize connstr, true
catalogmanager.importxml Filename, TRUE, FALSE
    MSCSExecute = 1   'set function return value to 1
end function

sub MSCSOpen(config)
    'optional open routine
end sub

sub MSCSClose()
    'optional close routine
end sub
```

In the preceding BizTalk Server scriptor, the order form is used to pass in the contents of the XML document. When you grab the working data node, you have the XML document. In this case, we grab the XML document and use the scripting.filesystemobject to write out the XML document to a file.

7. Now we must configure the Receivestandard.asp file to receive the catalog. Receivestandard.asp is a file that receives XML documents and calls the BizTalk Server interchange.submit method. We will modify this file to call a specific channel. We do this in the Retail site since this is the site that is receiving the catalog. We will be calling the channel "Channel to receive Catalog from BizTalk". Change line 89 of Receivestandard.asp in the Retail Virtual Root as follows:

Before:

```
SubmissionHandle = interchange.submit( 1, PostedDocument )
```

After:

```
SubmissionHandle = interchange.submit(1, PostedDocument,,,,,,"
Channel to receive Catalog from BizTalk")
```

This will take the PostedDocument, which is the exported catalog, and submit it to the "Channel to receive Catalog from BizTalk".

8. Finally, let's verify that you have a c:\btout directory on your BizTalk Server.

Testing Our Solution

Test to ensure that catalogs sent from the Sweet Forgiveness (Wholesaler) site are automatically imported into the Retail site. From the Sweet Forgiveness Site Business Desk, go to Catalogs | Catalog Editor and highlight the catalog that you want to send. Next, press the Send Catalog key combination (ALT-S) or click the envelope icon, select Retail in the Select Vendor dialog box, and click the OK button.

What Happens When We Press the Button?

1. The Process_Send( ) subroutine in Sweet\Catalogs\Editor\list_Catalogs.asp runs and performs the following tasks:

■ Calls the ExportXML method of the Commerce Server 2000 CatalogManager object and exports the catalog you selected to the root of the Sweetbizdesk virtual directory.

■ Loads an instance of the Microsoft XML DOM Object and loads the exported file into the XML DOM.

- Calls the BizTalk Server Interchange.Submit method, which submits the XML contained in the DOM to the BizTalk "Channel to receive Catalog from Sweet Forgiveness".

- Deletes the catalog from the root of the sweetbizdesk virtual directory.

2. The BizTalk Server "Channel to receive Catalog from Sweet Forgiveness" validates the submitted catalog against the Catalog schema and passes the catalog to the "Port to send Catalog to BizTalk".

3. The BizTalk Server "Port to send Catalog to BizTalk" hands the catalog off to the specified transport address http://localhost/retail/receivestandard.asp.

4. Receivestandard.asp performs another BizTalk Server Interchange.Submit of the catalog to the "Channel to receive Catalog from BizTalk".

5. The "Channel to receive Catalog from BizTalk" validates the submitted catalog against the Catalog schema (again) and passes the catalog to the "Port to send Catalog to Retail".

6. The "Port to send Catalog to Retail" hands the catalog off to the specified transport address of BizTalk Server Scriptor.

7. The BizTalk Server Scriptor then writes a copy of the catalog to the C:\btout directory on the BizTalk Server and calls the ImportXML method of the Commerce Server 2000 CatalogManager object to import the catalog into the Retail site.

Note   *You will need to add the Sweet Forgiveness vendor to your new catalog and select Update Catalog in the Retail Site Business Desk to make the previous purchase order example continue to operate.*

Summary

In review, we have seen how to communicate between Commerce Servers via BizTalk Server. We now know how to successfully export a catalog and import that catalog via BizTalk Server. Also, we have seen how to configure Commerce Server to send purchase orders from a catalog to a particular site using BizTalk Server.

It is important to note that there are size restrictions when sending documents via BizTalk Server. For example, pushing a 75MB product catalog through BizTalk Server is not very smart (or doable unless certain options like Turn Off Document Tracking are selected. There also are some issues faced when installing BizTalk Server, Commerce Server, and SQL Server on different machines—for example, if you are trying to export

DEPLOYING BIZTALK SERVER

a catalog to BizTalk Server via a message queue, because they have a 4MB limit. Look at that KB article I referenced at the beginning of this chapter for more info.

We have also seen how _recvpo.asp, receivestandard.asp, and list_Catalogs.asp do a lot of the work for this integration, and there are multiple schemas out of the box like POSchema.xml and CatalogXMLSchema.xml to make it easier.

All of this seems complicated at first, but after you do it a couple of times, it becomes second nature. I'm sure that since these are both fairly new products, there will be some minor problems. But from my experience, the Microsoft Support teams and the product help files are quite good.

I would like to end this chapter with some good news for .NET fans. While I was at Tech Ed 2001, the Commerce Server team announced that they would be releasing a CS2K.NET Interoperability SDK. Among other things, it will include wrappers for the CS2K COM components so that they can be called from ASP.NET. There will also be sample code.

Chapter 15

Implementation
Case Studies

Though walking through the BizTalk Server tutorial gives you a good start to understanding the product, applying your knowledge to real-world projects is the next key step. Message processing and application integration are two of the most important features of BizTalk. Thus, the following case studies will focus on how to model complicated document structures with BizTalk Editor, how to submit messages from legacy applications to BizTalk Server, how to build a universal interface for your legacy system by developing Application Integration Components (AICs), and how to leverage XML named tags to match parameters in your integration.

For application-specific accelerators such as RosettaNet Accelerator, please refer to Chapter 19.

The two real-world case studies this chapter will discuss are as follows:

- Implementing SAP R/3 EDIFACT outbound messages using BizTalk Server 2000 for EDIFACT 93A ORDERS messages. The SAP object in the sample is a Purchase Order. We will discuss several ways of transferring data from SAP to BizTalk Server; none uses IDOC. This significantly simplifies the EDI implementing process.

- Inbound order processing with SAP R/3 using BizTalk Server 2000.

The purpose of these two case studies is to show you the normal process for implementing BizTalk Server 2000 in an EDI environment and to overcome some shortcomings in the product. In addition, they will show you how to integrate BizTalk Server 2000 with your back-end system and Outlook/Exchange Server 2000.

The reason I chose SAP R/3 is that it is the most widely used ERP package, and you are likely to deal with it in the future. Even if you never encounter it, the case studies presented here will give you a good idea of how to deal with your situation. After finishing the chapter, you may wonder why I did not use Orchestration in the case studies. It's because I've tried to keep the whole process simple. It will not take you long to convert these case studies into a working Orchestration flowchart.

Before you dive into this chapter, make sure you are familiar with the following topics:

- Creating a specification for a delimited flat file in BizTalk Editor.
- Creating specification map in BizTalk Mapper.
- Creating a simple Application Integration Component (AIC). (The AIC is not for production purposes. For production, you need to convert your code into Visual C++ for better performance and stability. See related MS Knowledge Base Article Q291670 on this topic.)
- Creating receive functions for MSMQ and files.
- Configuring various objects in the Messaging Manager.

Some experience with Exchange Server client-side scripting and R/3 BAPI (Object Oriented Programming Interface of R/3) is helpful but not essential. I will explain these concepts during the demonstration.

Case Study 1: Implementation of SAP R/3 EDIFACT by Using BizTalk Server 2000

Implementing EDI for SAP R/3 has never been simple. It requires an IDOC file, shared directory, IDOC to EDI message mapping, and a value-added network (VAN). Companies spend tons of money on implementing this required business process, but only large companies can afford such a huge investment. It poses a threat to the survival of the small companies because the big companies may stop doing business with them if they do not have EDI/e-business ability in the future. While XML-EDI is coming, it's still a long way from widespread adoption. The mainstream of EDI uses EDIFACT and X12. Of course, with the introduction of several XML exchange frameworks, like BizTalk, RosettaNet, and cXML, EDIFACT and X12 may eventually be replaced.

BizTalk Server 2000 provides a low-cost EDI solution by using the infrastructure built inside the Windows 2000 and Internet standard protocol: SMTP, HTTP/HTTPS. Though it is not a true EDI solution, in the sense of EDIFACT/X12 (especially because BizTalk Server does not support VAN), it is still an affordable solution for small or medium companies. You need to consider two important facts when you decide whether to use EDI with BizTalk Server: many big companies are moving to accept EDI messages by SMTP/HTTP—for example, Hewlett-Packard and Compaq. Most of the missing functionalities can be supplied by custom development. See the EDI implementation white paper on http://www.microsoft.com/biztalk. The bottom line is, if you are required to use VAN, then BizTalk Server is not up to your job. Now we will more closely examine the whole process of implementing EDIFACT messages outbound for SAP R/3.

Phase 1: Prepare XML Message Inside SAP R/3

Because it is R/3, you will need to write some ABAP, SAP R/3's proprietary development language. You can use the template provided by BizTalk Server (for example, Purchase Order specification) or create you own specification for the output XML message. To construct your XML messages, you have the following options:

- You can use string operation in ABAP to construct XML messages.
- You can invoke MSXML DOM COM objects to create XML messages, but for this option, you need to configure SAP com4abap (a SAP program enabling ABAP to invoke a COM automation object on a remote Windows NT/2000 Server) service for your SAP R/3 server.

To keep the sample simple, we will use the ABAP string operation to construct our XML message. This is always the fastest way to construct an XML message, though you need to take care of the escape characters in XML, for example, &.

Phase 2: Submit the Message to BizTalk Server

This is the most critical step in the whole process. It is also the most problematic step in the traditional EDI, because the communication between R/3 and external applications has never been simple. You have several options:

- Create a file receive function for a directory, and then use the SAPFTP (SAP's implementation of an FTP client) function to send the message as a file to that directory.

- Create an MSMQ receive function. You write a COM object receiving messages from SAP R/3 and then put the message into the MSMQ.

- Directly invoke the Interchange.Submit( ) or Interchange.SubmitSync( ) method inside ABAP.

The rest of the options will require you to install com4abap server for a specific server. In our case study, I will use the first option because configuring and programming com4abap needs some expertise on R/3 Basis knowledge and ABAP programming knowledge.

Phase 3: Configure the BizTalk Messaging Manager

In this step, you will create several objects: document specifications, organizations, messaging ports, and channels.

Putting the entire piece together, we will have the following flowchart for a SAP R/3 EDI outbound implementation:

Now that we have a clear picture of how the process works, we will go through the process step by step and deliver a working EDI sample. Those who do not have an R/3 system can manually construct a piece of XML message and then continue with the rest of the process.

Before we start, let's look at the checklist for this case study:

1. Create a specification for R/3 XML messages.

2. Modify the EDIFACT specification template to meet your partner's requirements.

3. Create a map for the specifications in steps 1 and 2.

4. Create a document specification in BizTalk Messaging Manager.

5. Maintain an organization in BizTalk Messaging Manager.

6. Maintain messaging ports in Messaging Manager.

7. Create a channel in Messaging Manager.

8. Create a file receive function in BizTalk Administration.

9. Manually create a test message to make sure the configuration works correctly.

10. Write an ABAP program to put all the pieces together.

It is quite a long list. At the end of the case study, your implementation may require more steps, which I will describe in the "Production Concerns for Case Study 1" section.

Step 1: Create a Specification for R/3 XML Messages

Open your BizTalk Editor to construct a Blank XML Specification with the name **SAPPO**. Rename the root record **SAPPO**. Select the root record, and create six records, assuming the root record SAPPO is at level 0.

- Header (level 1, occurrences = 1)
- PartnerLoop (level 1, occurrences > 0)
- Partner (level 2, occurrences = 1)
- ItemLoop (level 1, occurrences > 0)
- Item (level 2, occurrences = 1)
- Total (level 1, occurrences = 1)

Create the fields for the corresponding nodes as listed in the following table. (All the fields are created as attributes of the nodes.)

Node	Field Name	Data Type	Length
Header	PONum	Number	10
Header	Currency	String	3
Partner	PartyQualifier	String	2
Partner	IdDentification	String	17
Partner	PartyID	Number	2
Partner	PartyName	String	35
Item	ItemNO	Number	6
Item	AdditionalNO	String	35
Item	Quantity	Nurrmber	15
Item	Measure	String	4
Item	Date	Number	8
Item	Price	Number	15
Total	TotalAmount	Number	17

The final version of the SAPPO specification should look like Figure 15-1.

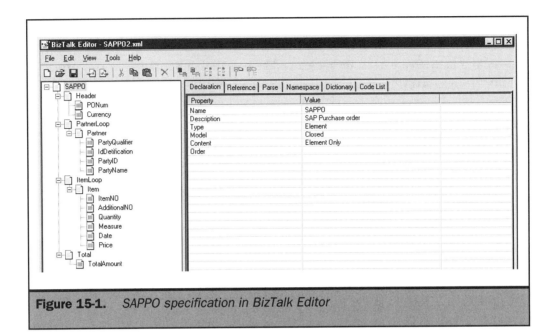

Figure 15-1. *SAPPO specification in BizTalk Editor*

Then save the specification to the WebDAV directory for later use.

An instance of our newly created schema should look similar to this:

```
<SAPPO>
<Header PONum="4500089150" Currency="USD"/>
<Partner PartyQualifier="BY" IdDetification="850004721"
PartyID="91" PartyName="XXX Enterprise"/>
<Partner PartyQualifier="DP" IdDetification="850004722"
PartyID="92" PartyName="XXX Enterprise"/>
<Item ItemNO="000010" AdditionalNO="AdditionalNO_1" Quantity="4"
Measure="PC" Date="20000909" Price="200"/>
<Item ItemNO="000020" AdditionalNO="AdditionalNO_2" Quantity="5"
Measure="PC" Date="20000909" Price="500"/>
<Total TotalAmount="3300"/>
</SAPPO>
```

Step 2: Modify EDIFACT Specification
Template to Meet Partner Requirement

In our case study, we will use EDIFACT Version D93A ORDERSSchema.xml as our
EDI message template. Open your BizTalk Editor and select | New | EDIFACT |

D93A | ORDERSSchema.xml. You must customize the EDIFACT specification before you use it. Add the fields you need, and remove the unnecessary fields.

Rename the root record **EDIORDER**. Figure 15-2 and Figure 15-3 show the modified layout of the ORDERS schema. Due to the length of the EDIFACT message, I will not list all the fields shown in the illustration; by using the EDIFACT schema template in BizTalk Editor, you should be able to reproduce the message.

Notice the following points regarding the EDIFACT message:

- Segments UNA, UNB, UNH, UNT, and UNZ will be created automatically by BizTalk Server 2000. They contain control information of the EDI message. In EDI terminology, UNA, UNB, and UNH are EDIFACT interchange headers, while UNT and UNZ are EDIFACT interchange footers.

- You need to coordinate the data type between your source message and EDI message. For example, in SAP R/3 the customer name can be 40 characters, but some EDI messages only allow 35 characters. Save test time by taking care of these small details.

- Whenever you want to add new segments/fields, always try to copy from the template specification. You can open two copies of BizTalk Editor. Select the segment/field you want to copy, choose the Copy button, switch to the other BizTalk Editor, place the cursor at the parent record, and select the Paste button. Following this practice will ensure you always use the correct data type in the specification.

Then save the EDI specification to the WebDAV directory for later use. Please refer to Chapter 4 for more details on BizTalk Editor.

Step 3: Create a Map for the Specifications in Steps 1 and 2

Now we move on to create a map for the specification we just created in steps 1 and 2. Start your BizTalk Mapper from the Start menu. Choose Tools | Options, and you will see the screen shown in Figure 15-4. Select the option Allow Record Content Links.

The reason we need to activate this option is that we need to map the recursive items in both specifications. Field-level mapping cannot produce the recursive entries properly. We need to map both field and record levels to make sure the map produces the desired result. Your mapping result should resemble Figure 15-5.

Here are some tricky things you need to keep an eye on when you create mapping for this case study:

- For recursive segments such as PartnerLoop, mapping just at the field level will not produce the correct result. In addition to field-level mapping, you also need to map the corresponding segment. In our sample, we need to map PartnerLoop to NAD-SG3-SG5.

- For some items, the appearance of the EDIFACT segment depends on the content of the source fields. In some cases, if the source field is empty, the EDI segment should not appear at all in the message because there is no content. For doing this, you need the help of a logical functoid.

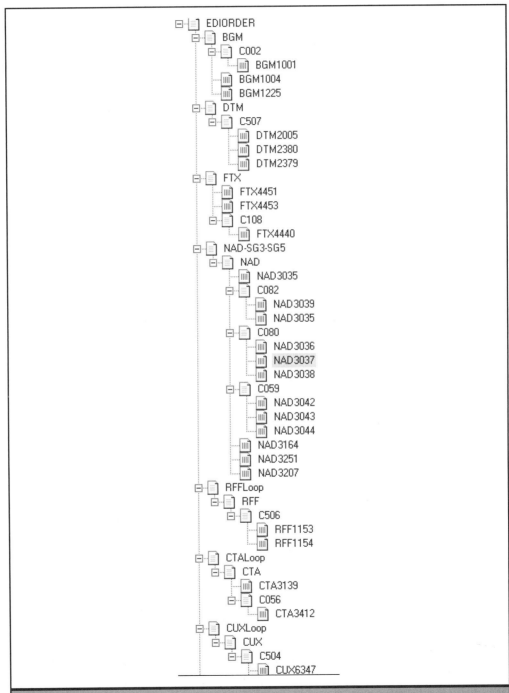

Figure 15-2. *Edit EDIFACT D93A ORDERS message in BizTalk Editor*

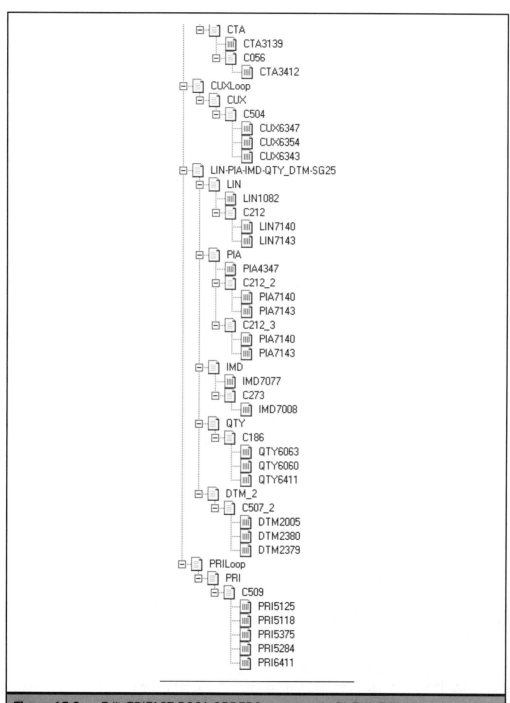

Figure 15-3.   *Edit EDIFACT D93A ORDERS message in BizTalk Editor*

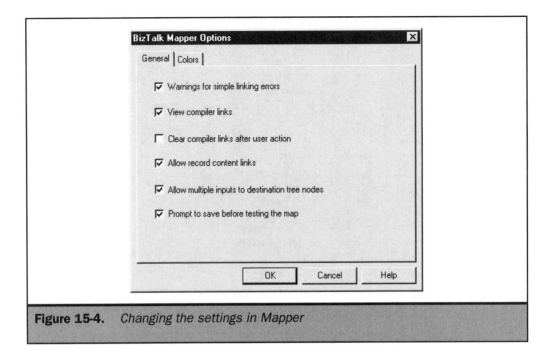

Figure 15-4. *Changing the settings in Mapper*

For example, not every PO will have content in the Additional NO field, so if the Additional NO field is empty, segment C212 should not appear at all. You not only need to map the Additional NO to LIN7140, but you also need to link Additional NO with C212 through the logical functoid. You do a comparison in the functoid; if Additional NO is empty, it returns false; otherwise it returns true. By following this rule, you will conditionally control the appearance of the EDI segment. The functoid you need to use looks like this:

Save the map to the WebDAV directory for later use.

Step 4: Create Document Specification in BizTalk Messaging Manager

Now we change to BizTalk Messaging Manager to configure for our case study. Open the BizTalk Messaging Manager from your Start menu. Choose File | New | Document Definition.

First, create a document specification for the specification in step 1, and give it the name **SAPPO**. Then select the corresponding XML file from the WebDAV repository.

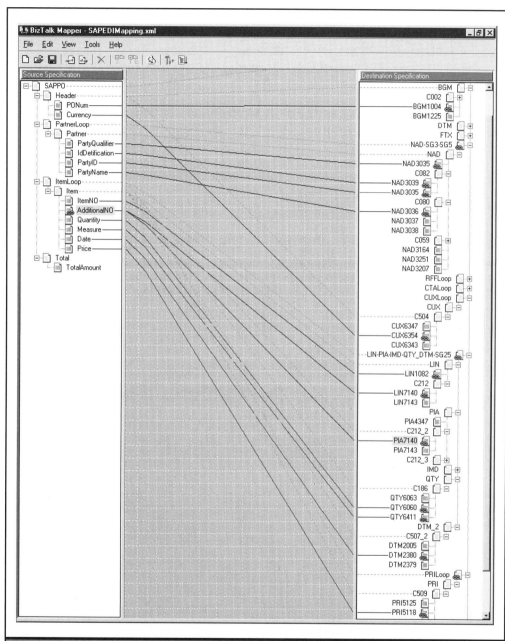

Figure 15-5. *Mapper result*

Create the document specification for the EDI specification in step 2, giving it the name **EDIORDER**. After filling out the General tab, you will also need to fill out the Selection Criteria tab, as shown in Figure 15-6.

These entries are required for the EDIFACT message. Otherwise, you will receive an error message when you submit the document to BizTalk Server 2000.

Step 5: Maintain Organization in BizTalk Messaging Manager

Now we need to create an organization for our trading partner. In our sample, we will create an organization with the name **BookBiz**, as shown in Figure 15-7.

Qualifier fields are limited to four digits. If your entry is longer than four digits, you will receive an error from BizTalk Server when it processes the document. The limitation comes from EDIFACT, not BizTalk Server.

You also need to change your home organization's qualifier to conform to this limitation.

Step 6: Maintain Messaging Port in Messaging Manager

Before we continue in Messaging Manager, we need to configure our SMTP setting in the Server Group. Start your BizTalk Administration from the Start menu. Right-click on the Server Group your server is in, choose Properties, and then specify the SMTP Host as shown in Figure 15-8. Make sure that you have already configured Smart Host on your SMTP host if you want to send external Internet mail.

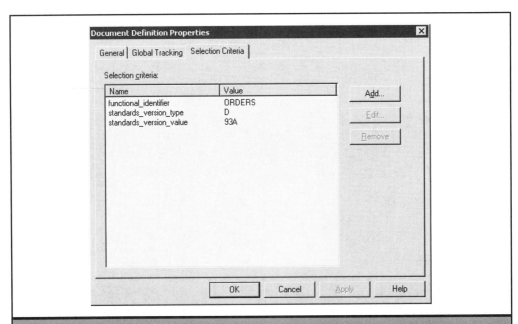

Figure 15-6. *Selection criteria for EDI document definition*

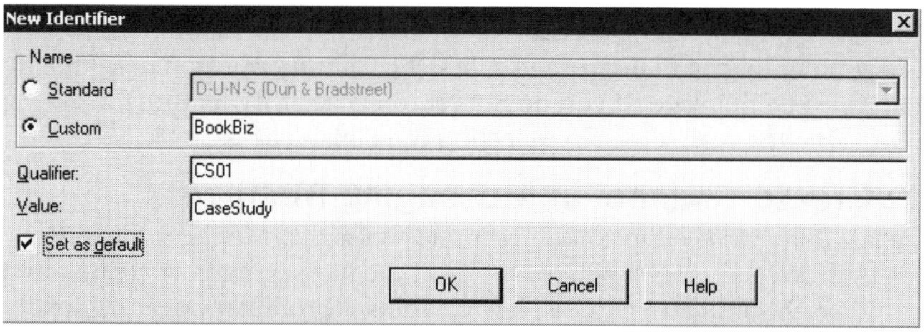

Figure 15-7.   *Organization qualifier*

Go back to the Messaging Manager, and choose File | New | Messaging Port | To An Organization. Give a name to your Messaging Port. We use **BizBook** for our case study. On the second screen, select the organization we created in the previous step, and choose SMTP as your primary transport. Enter your e-mail address as the destination. The reason we choose SMTP is that in most of the EDI implementation, you will likely

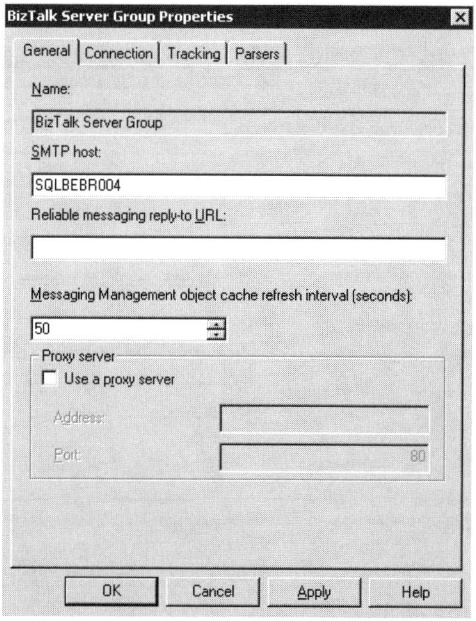

Figure 15-8.   *Setting up the SMTP host*

send SMTP mail to your partner. On the next screen, select the EDI document definition as your envelope information, and enter an interchange control number. The number serves as a counter for the EDI message. Click the Delimiter button to set the desired limiter for your EDI message. If you do not require a security feature for the moment, you can complete the next screen by selecting the Finish button.

Step 7: Create Channel in Messaging Manager

This is the last thing we need to configure in the Messaging Manager. Channel is always associated with a certain messaging port. Select the messaging port created in the last step, and then right-click and choose New Channel | From An Organization. Name the channel; we still use **BookBiz** as the name. In the next screen, select the source organization for our case study; here, it is our home organization. The information in the next few screens is inbound and outbound document definition and related mapping information. Choose from the document definition and WebDAV repository. In the Advanced Configuration screen, select the Advanced button. You can overwrite some settings in the related messaging port. The most important tab is the Envelope tab. By choosing the Properties button, you will see the screen shown in Figure 15-9.

On this screen, you will find information related to the segments UNB and UNH. For example, the partner will require you to set the Test Indicator to 1 for any EDI test message. By now you have finished all the settings in Messaging Manager for your first EDI implementation. Please refer to Chapter 6 for a thorough discussion of Messaging Manager.

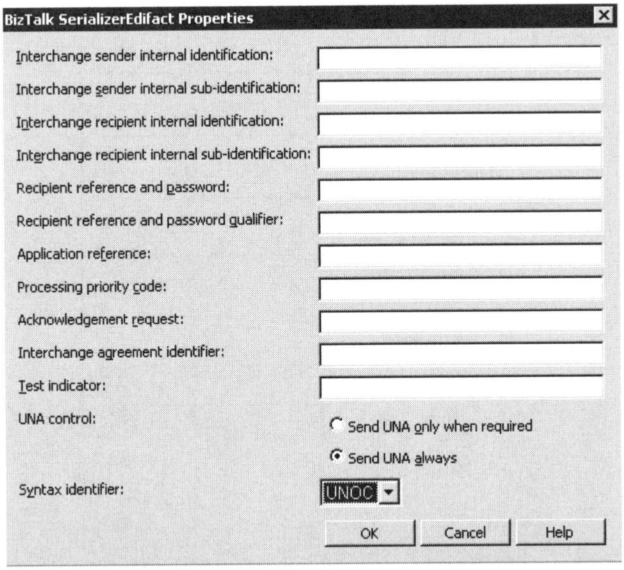

Figure 15-9.   *EDI control header detail*

Step 8: Create a File Receive Function in BizTalk Administration

First, create a directory somewhere on your hard disk. Then create a file receive function for this directory in BizTalk Administration. Do not forget to specify your channel in the receive function. If you are not familiar with this step, please refer to Chapter 9.

Step 9: Manually Create a Test Message to Make Sure the Configuration Works

Before we put the SAP R/3 system into the whole picture, we can test the entire process. If you do not have an R/3 system on hand, you still can finish the process. The next step is only for those who have R/3 in-house and who have ABAP knowledge. You can use the message instance for the SAPPO specification as a source message. Save the message as a text file, and put it into the directory associated with the receive function you created. If everything goes well, you will receive an e-mail with content similar to the following:

```
UNA:+.? 'UNB+UNOA:2+1:1+2:2+010226:1153+24'UNG+ORDERS+BIZTALK
2000+HP+010226:1153+24+UN+1:1'UNH+1+ORDERS:1:1:UN''BGM:105+4500089150+9'DTM+
:4:20001205:101'FTX+TXT++:TXT'NAD+BY+850004721:91+:GETRONICS ENTERPRISE+:1
PLACE MADOU'NAD+DP+850004722:92+:GETRONICS ENTERPRISE+:1 PLACE
MADOU'RFF+:KK'CTA:DD::TOM.XU@GETRONICS.COM'CUX+:2:NLG'LIN+000010+:ADDITIONAL
NO_1'PIA+1+:ADDTIONALNO_1'QTY+:21:4:PC'DTM+:2:000909:101'LIN+000020+:ADDITIONAL
NO_2'PIA+1+:ADDTIONALNO_2'QTY+:21:5:PC'DTM+:2:000909:101'PRI+:AAA:200:CT::PC
E'PRI+:AAA:500:CT::PCEUNT+20+1'UNE+1+24'UNZ+1+24'
```

If something goes wrong, check the Suspend Queue in the BizTalk Administration and Windows Event View application log for error information and make corrections as needed. Direct Integration is a very useful tool in the BizTalk Server SDK. It sits at \Program Files\Microsoft BizTalk Server\SDK\Messaging Samples\Direct Integration\ EXE. All the source code is available at the same directory. By using Direct Integration, you can directly submit your message to BizTalk Server without creating any receiving mechanism for BizTalk Server. Figure 15-10 shows Direct Integration in action. After you submit the document, you can even check the Suspended Queue to see whether your document went through.

Step 10: Write ABAP Program to Put All the Pieces Together

For those who are implementing EDI for a SAP R/3 system, the good news is that you are just one step away from success. Sending messages out of SAP is the key to the whole process. In this case study, we choose to use the SAP standard tool: SAPFTP.

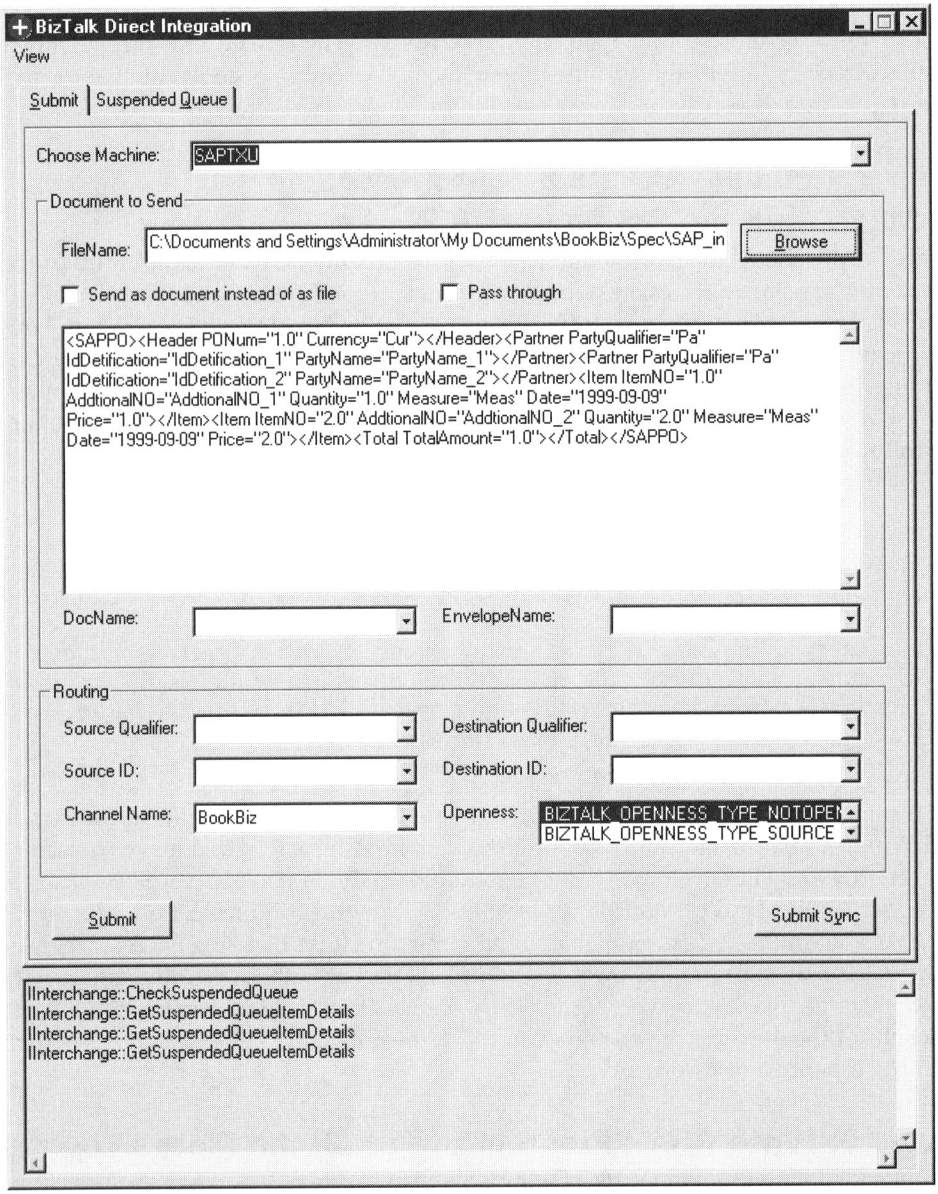

Figure 15-10. *Direct Integration test program*

There are three things you need to do with your ABAP:

1. Collect the information you need, and construct it into an XML string.

2. Download the string as a text file to one of your application servers.

3. Start the SAPFTP on the application server having your download file, and send it to the directory associated with the BizTalk Server file receive function.

You or your development department should have no problem finishing the first two steps. For the third step, I used the latest ABAP object to capsulize all the SAPFTP API into a class, so you can easily adopt it into your code.

```
constants:    pass(15) type c value 'pass'.
interface  FTPCOMMAND.
    types:    FileName(128) type c.
    methods:  setDestFile importing value(file) type FileName,
              getDestFile returning value(file) type FileName,
              setDestination importing value(rfc) type c,
              setPassword importing value(pass) type c,
              setHost     importing value(host) type c,
              commQueueAdd importing value(command) type c,
              ftpConnect,
              ftpSend,
              ftpClose.
endinterface.
class sapFTP definition.
  public section.
      methods: constructor importing pass type c.
      interfaces: FTPCOMMAND.
  private section.
      types:    commLine(128) type c,
                rfcD(32) type c,
                password(64) type c,
                begin of tResult,
                    line(100) type c,
                end of tResult,
                commQueue type standard table of commLine.
      data: DesFile type FileName,
            rfcDest    type rfcD,
            pwd        type password,
            ftpQueue   type commQueue,
            handle     type i,
            host(15)   type c.
```

```
        constants: key type i value 26101957,
                   user(15) type c value 'ftp_user'.
endclass.
class sapFTP implementation.
method FTPCOMMAND~setHost.
  me->host = host.
endmethod.
method constructor.
  call method me->FTPCOMMAND~setPassword exporting pass = pass.
endmethod.
method FTPCOMMAND~setDestFile.
  DesFile = file.
endmethod.
method FTPCOMMAND~getDestFile.
  file = DesFile.
endmethod.
method FTPCOMMAND~setDestination.
  rfcDest = rfc.
endmethod.
method FTPCOMMAND~setPassword.
  data: len type i.
  describe field pass length len.
  CALL 'AB_RFC_X_SCRAMBLE_STRING'
  ID 'SOURCE'      FIELD pass   ID 'KEY'         FIELD KEY
  ID 'SCR'         FIELD 'X'    ID 'DESTINATION' FIELD pwd
  ID 'DSTLEN'      FIELD len.
endmethod.
method FTPCOMMAND~commQueueAdd.
  data: comm type commLine.
  comm = command.
  append comm to ftpQueue.
endmethod.
method FTPCOMMAND~ftpConnect.
  CALL FUNCTION 'FTP_CONNECT'
     EXPORTING USER = USER PASSWORD = PWD HOST = host
     RFC_DESTINATION = rfcDest
     IMPORTING HANDLE = handle.
endmethod.
method FTPCOMMAND~ftpSend.
 data: result type standard table of tResult.
 field-symbols: <comm> type commLine,
                <log>  type tResult.
 loop at ftpQueue assigning <comm>.
```

```
   CALL FUNCTION 'FTP_COMMAND'
       EXPORTING HANDLE = handle COMMAND = <comm> COMPRESS = 'N'
       TABLES DATA = RESULT
       EXCEPTIONS COMMAND_ERROR = 1 TCPIP_ERROR = 2.
  LOOP AT RESULT assigning <log>.
   WRITE AT / <log>-LINE.
  ENDLOOP.
  REFRESH RESULT.
 endloop.
endmethod.
method FTPCOMMAND~ftpClose.
  CALL FUNCTION 'FTP_DISCONNECT'
     EXPORTING HANDLE = handle.
endmethod.
endclass.
*Below is a sample program demonstrating how to use this class in your code.
    data: ftpObj type ref to ftpcommand,
          localdir(80) type c,   "directory where your file sits
          command(128) type c,
          Filename(128) type c.
    create object ftpObj type sapFTP exporting pass = pass.
    call method ftpObj->setDestination exporting rfc = 'SAPFTPA'.
    call method ftpObj->setDestFile exporting file = yourfilename.
    call method ftpObj->setHost exporting host = 'your server'.
    concatenate 'lcd' localdir into command separated by space.
    call method ftpObj->commQueueAdd exporting command = command.
    clear: command.
    concatenate 'cd' 'targetdirectory' into command separated by space.
    call method ftpObj->commQueueAdd exporting command = command.
    clear: command.
    FileName = ftpObj->getDestFile( ).
    concatenate 'delete' FileName into command separated by space.
    call method ftpObj->commQueueAdd exporting command = command.
    clear: command.
    concatenate 'put' FileName into command separated by space.
    call method ftpObj->commQueueAdd exporting command = command.
    clear: command.
    call method ftpObj->ftpConnect.
    call method ftpObj->ftpSend.
    call method ftpObj->ftpClose.
```

The code is straightforward, so you or your development team shouldn't have any problems reading it.

Production Concerns for Case Study 1

Case study 1 illustrates the necessary steps you need to undertake to implement a SAP R/3 EDIFACT outbound scenario. In order to turn it into an industry-strength production solution, you need to pay attention to the following considerations.

To date, SAP R/3 still does not have native support for XML. The quality of the XML string is a big issue. For example, you need to take care of all the escape characters by yourself. In this situation, a better solution would be to use XML DOM through com4abap, if this is possible from your side. The direct benefit is that the XML message you pass to BizTalk is at least a valid XML message. But, according to SAP, the next version R/3 Basis system, with the new name SAP Web Application Server, will have native support for XML, HTTP, SOAP, and other Internet standards. By then, sending/receiving XML will be a piece of cake for R/3. A preferred way will be to have the SAP Web Application Server directly send the XML message through HTTP to the BizTalk receiving ASP page, and vice versa.

The whole process for inbound EDI messages is quite similar to the outbound process. After BizTalk Server receives the EDI message, it will translate the message into the XML format you specified, or you can use the delivered SAP AIC to generate SAP IDOC and then send it to R/3. A better way to do this is to develop a DCOM connector–based AIC for your R/3 system. The communication through SAP's Business Application Programming Interfaces (BAPIs) is what SAP recommends. You can achieve near real-time integration with SAP without losing the advantage of message broker architecture. As usual, use Visual C++ as your final implementation language. A few samples come with SAP R/3 SDK. Programming R/3 DCOM connector with Visual C++ is quite straightforward.

One of the limitations of BizTalk EDI functionality is that it cannot send a batch EDI file (that is, one EDI document with multiple messages inside). This is because XML specification dictates that one document can have only one root node. Also, there is a limitation for the current serializer implementation. (Refer to Chapter 16 for details.) In some cases, your partner will require you to send a batch EDI file. A quick solution for this is to first let BizTalk output all the daily files to a directory. At the end of the day, you run a Windows script (likely, VBScript or JScript) to concatenate all the EDI files into one file. Then submit the document to a pass-through channel sending to your partner. If you plan carefully, you will easily create an automated process.

Error handling is another important issue in a production environment. A possible method is as follows:

- Write a VBScript using the Interchange interface to check the Suspended Queue of BizTalk Server. If it finds any new suspended document, have it send an SMTP mail to the responsible person.
- Use Windows Scheduler to schedule this script as a regular task.

BizTalk Server offers the ability for signed documents. So, if security is a major concern in your project, you should use a certificate to sign your documents. Another option is to use the HTTPS protocol instead of HTTP. See Chapter 13 for details on securing BizTalk Server.

There is no way to fill field 0057 (Association-assigned code) in data element S009 of Segment UNH in the standard BizTalk EDI process. The work-around is illustrated in Figure 15-11. The process is significantly more complicated than the standard EDI process. The key points are as follows:

- The message needs to be processed in BizTalk Server 2000 twice—once in EDIFACT format, and once in Flat-File format. The logic is quite simple: an EDI message is just a kind of complicated flat file with some built-in hierarchy, as shown in Figure 15-12.

- As shown in the Figure 15-12, you need to tell BizTalk Server what kind of file structure it is; you need to specify all the delimiter information. On the Parse tab for the root node, enter the following settings:

  - Field Order: Postfix
  - Delimiter Type: Default Recorder Delimiter
  - Escape Type: Default Escape Character

- On the Parse tab for the level 2 segments (for example, UNA), enter the following settings:

  - Field Order: Prefix
  - Delimiter Type: Default Field Delimiter
  - Escape Type: Default Escape Character

- On the Parse tab for the level 3 segment (for example, C504 in CUX), enter the following settings:

  - Field Order: Infix
  - Delimiter Type: Default Subfield Delimiter
  - Escape Type: Default Escape Character

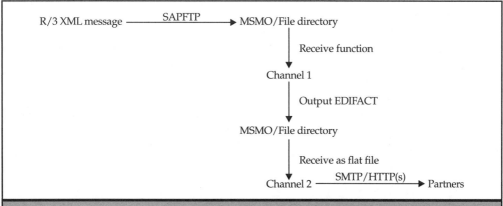

Figure 15-11.   *EDI data flow to overcome the BizTalk EDI defects*

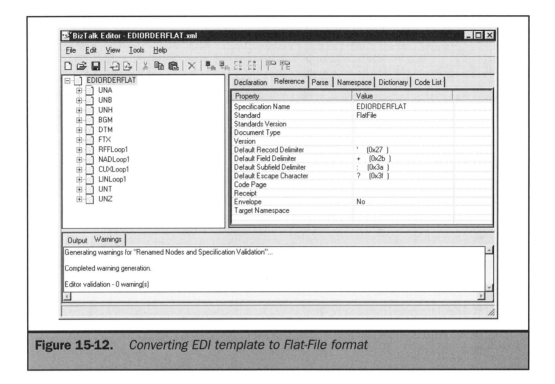

Figure 15-12. Converting EDI template to Flat-File format

The First Channel is the same as the one we used in the case study, except that you should output the result file to MSMQ or another directory. For that MSMQ or directory, you need to create another receive function.

The Second Channel is quite different from the one we used, in that it only processes flat files. The inbound and outbound document will be the same flat-file specification we created for the EDI message. You will put the missing information in the map and simply copy all the remaining information. For the output of this channel, you can directly send it to the partner without any compromise.

To let the second channel work correctly, adjust the parser sequence in BizTalk Server Administration. The Flat-File parser must appear before the EDIFACT parser, as shown in Figure 15-13. Otherwise, BizTalk Server will say that the format of the EDIFACT message is not valid.

We have covered everything you need to know to implement a fully functional EDIFACT solution for your R/3 or other system.

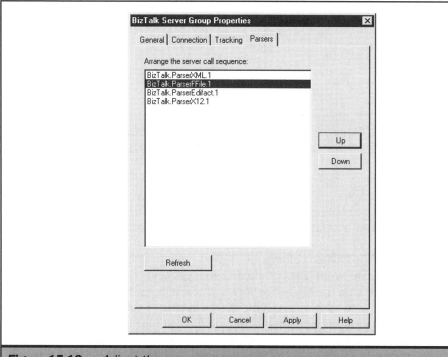

Figure 15-13.   *Adjust the parser sequence*

Case Study 2: Inbound Order Processing with SAP R/3 Using BizTalk Server 2000

In this case study, we will build an inbound process flow for SAP R/3. The scenario is this: Your colleague sends you order information by e-mail attachment to your mailbox, a Visual Basic macro in Outlook extracts the information from the attachment and forwards it to BizTalk Server for processing, and BizTalk Server translates and validates the messages into XML format. After processing, BizTalk invokes an AIC, posting the order directly to the SAP R/3 system and waiting for the order number/error message from R/3. BizTalk Server passes back the information to Outlook. Outlook will mail a notification to the responsible person for the order processing failure. The whole process is illustrated in Figure 15-14.

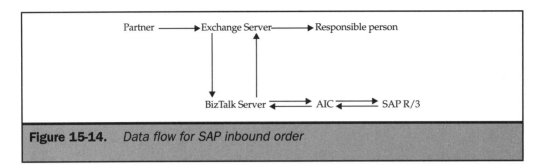

Figure 15-14. *Data flow for SAP inbound order*

Note *To follow and complete this case study, you must have the SAP R/3 system. It is highly recommended that you use the TEST R/3 system in the sample. Any action on your production system is absolutely discouraged because the code illustrated here is not for production purposes. You are at your own risk to follow and complete this case study.*

The reason I chose the Outlook client-side Visual Basic program is that not every company allows setting up event sinks on their Exchange Server because it will require you to install a COM DLL on the Exchange Server. The Exchange Server administrator will worry that the component may crash the server in case of code failure.With the emergence of a message broker like BizTalk Server 2000, you can set up a universal interface for your back-end system. For example, we can reuse the order-processing AIC for all the inbound-order scenarios. BizTalk Server 2000 will always translate the incoming message to the message we want for the AIC. But universal interface is not trivial because you never know what information an incoming message will contain. Although it is difficult to forecast the future message content, the parameters for your interface are always fixed. (Otherwise, we couldn't call it an interface.)

Named parameters enable a good solution to this situation: using the parameter name as the tag name. Then, in our AIC we can enumerate all the parameters and programmatically match them to the interface parameters by name. XML is very suitable for this task because named parameters (tags) are natively supported in XML. For example, given a Visual Basic function prototype like

```
Function Multiple (Para1 as integer, Para2 as integer) as integer
```

we can model this function in an XML instance as

```
<Function name = "Multiple">
        <Para1 Value = "a">
        <Para2 Value = "b">
        <Multiple value = "c">
</Function>
```

This is quite straightforward. So whenever we perform integration between BizTalk and our back-end system, we will model the back-end API's interface into an XML specification in BizTalk Editor and translate the incoming message into the interface XML specification in the BizTalk Mapper. If you build an AIC for every similar process, this obviously defeats the advantage of adopting a message broker like BizTalk Server 2000 in the integration landscape.

Now let's have a look at the checklist for our second case study:

1. Model the inbound message in BizTalk Editor.

2. Model the order creation interface for the SAP R/3 system in BizTalk Editor.

3. Create a map for the specifications created in steps 1 and 2 in BizTalk Mapper.

4. Develop a sample AIC for the SAP R/3 system.

5. Create various objects in Messaging Manager.

6. Develop an Outlook Client macro to put all the pieces together.

There are several ways you can communicate with R/3: via the raw RFC library, DCOM Connector, Java Connector, SAP Business Connector, and SAP Automation ActiveX control. On the Windows platform, the easiest way to integrate with SAP R/3 is through DCOM Connector. This is a wrapper tool developed by SAP. It wraps all the necessary RFC calls into a COM object for easy programming. I will explain in more detail when we get to step 2. Currently the R/3 kernel is still TCP/IP based. According to SAP, the next version of the R/3 kernel will be HTTP based, so by then, you will be able to directly post messages from BizTalk to R/3 using HTTP/HTTPs. There will be no need to write an AIC for this case study. All you need to do is build some logic inside R/3 to finish the transaction by using ABAP Object (the OO extension of the ABAP development language). Microsoft will soon release SAP Accelerator for easy integration with SAP. It will significantly shorten the project time, and many of the functionalities we discussed here will be available out-of-the-box. If you are dedicated to SAP integration, spend some time evaluating SAP Accelerator carefully.

Step 1: Model the Inbound Message in BizTalk Editor

Open your BizTalk Editor and create an XML specification for the partner's inbound order message, as shown in Figure 15-15.

Create a blank specification and name the root record **InBoundOrder**. Create three records for the root node:

- Header (occurrences = 1)
- Partner (occurrences > 0)
- Item (occurrences > 0)

Create the fields for the corresponding nodes as listed in the following table. (All the fields are created as attributes of the nodes.)

Node	Field Name	Data Type	Length
Header	Purch_No	String	12
Header	Doc_Type	String	4
Header	Sales_Org	String	3
Header	Distr_Chan	Number	2
Header	Division	Number	2
Partner	Partn_Role	String	3
Partner	Partn_Numb	Number	12
Partner	ITM_NUMBER	Number	6
Item	ITM_NUMBER	Number	6
Item	Material	String	40
Item	TARGET_QTY	String	17

Note that the field name is exactly the same as the parameter name of the BAPI. Save the file to WebDAV for later use.

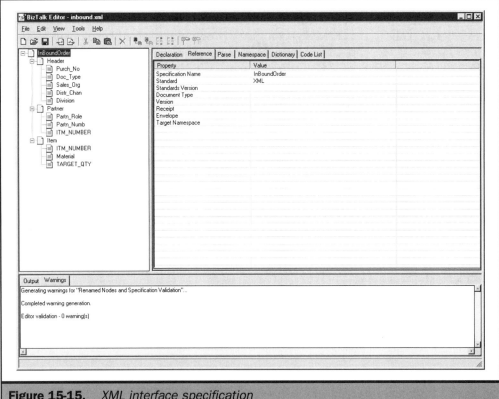

Figure 15-15. *XML interface specification*

Step 2: Model the Order Creation Interface for the SAP R/3 System in BizTalk Editor

There is only one way to communicate with SAP R/3: by Remote Function Call (RFC). RFC is a SAP proprietary protocol used by R/3 to communicate with external systems. Inside SAP R/3, all the application programming interfaces (APIs) are created as ABAP function modules. If you are familiar with other programming languages, a function is a good analogy to an ABAP function module. By using RFC, you can call ABAP function modules in external programs written in C/C++, Visual Basic, and Java; vice versa is also true.

You need considerable expertise in C/C++ language to program against the raw RFC interface. To simplify the RFC programming, SAP provides several wrapper tools:

- **Various connectors** These include DCOM and Java connectors. These are intelligent code generators wrapping the raw RFC calls into COM/Java objects.

- **Business Connector** This enables you to communicate with R/3 by using XML. Business Connector translates all the XML into the corresponding RFC calls for you.

SAP provides two views of the system:

- **Traditional API view** You can access the R/3 system with single-function module calls.

- **Object-oriented view** SAP uses the Business Object Repository (BOR) to organize related function modules and other attributes into Business Objects (for example, Customer, Order). The methods of these Business Objects are called BAPIs.

In this exercise, we will use the Business Object SalesOrder to create our order. You can refer to the SAP RFC SDK for details on using Business Object.

Now let's have a look at the BAPI (method createfromdata2 of Business Object SalesOrder) we will use in this case study: BAPI_SALESORDER_CREATEFROMDAT2. The parameter layout of this function module is as follows:

```
FUNCTION BAPI_SALESORDER_CREATEFROMDAT2.
------------------------------------------------------------------
  IMPORTING
      VALUE(SALESDOCUMENT) LIKE  BAPIVBELN-VBELN OPTIONAL
      VALUE(ORDER_HEADER_IN) LIKE  BAPISDHD1 STRUCTURE  BAPISDHD1
      VALUE(ORDER_HEADER_INX) LIKE  BAPISDHD1X STRUCTURE  BAPISDHD1X
         OPTIONAL
      VALUE(SENDER) LIKE  BAPI_SENDER STRUCTURE  BAPI_SENDER OPTIONAL
      VALUE(BINARY_RELATIONSHIPTYPE) LIKE  BAPIRELTYPE-RELTYPE
         OPTIONAL
      VALUE(INT_NUMBER_ASSIGNMENT) LIKE  BAPIFLAG-BAPIFLAG OPTIONAL
      VALUE(BEHAVE_WHEN_ERROR) LIKE  BAPIFLAG-BAPIFLAG OPTIONAL
```

```
        VALUE(LOGIC_SWITCH) LIKE  BAPISDLS STRUCTURE  BAPISDLS OPTIONAL
        VALUE(TESTRUN) LIKE  BAPIFLAG-BAPIFLAG OPTIONAL
        VALUE(CONVERT_PARVW_AUART) LIKE  BAPIFLAG-BAPIFLAG DEFAULT SPACE
    EXPORTING
        VALUE(SALESDOCUMENT_EX) LIKE  BAPIVBELN-VBELN
    TABLES
        RETURN STRUCTURE  BAPIRET2 OPTIONAL
        ORDER_ITEMS_IN STRUCTURE  BAPISDITM OPTIONAL
        ORDER_ITEMS_INX STRUCTURE  BAPISDITMX OPTIONAL
        ORDER_PARTNERS STRUCTURE  BAPIPARNR
        ORDER_SCHEDULES_IN STRUCTURE  BAPISCHDL OPTIONAL
        ORDER_SCHEDULES_INX STRUCTURE  BAPISCHDLX OPTIONAL
        ORDER_CONDITIONS_IN STRUCTURE  BAPICOND OPTIONAL
        ORDER_CFGS_REF STRUCTURE  BAPICUCFG OPTIONAL
        ORDER_CFGS_INST STRUCTURE  BAPICUINS OPTIONAL
        ORDER_CFGS_PART_OF STRUCTURE  BAPICUPRT OPTIONAL
        ORDER_CFGS_VALUE STRUCTURE  BAPICUVAL OPTIONAL
        ORDER_CFGS_BLOB STRUCTURE  BAPICUBLB OPTIONAL
        ORDER_CFGS_VK STRUCTURE  BAPICUVK OPTIONAL
        ORDER_CFGS_REFINST STRUCTURE  BAPICUREF OPTIONAL
        ORDER_CCARD STRUCTURE  BAPICCARD OPTIONAL
        ORDER_TEXT STRUCTURE  BAPISDTEXT OPTIONAL
        ORDER_KEYS STRUCTURE  BAPISDKEY OPTIONAL
        EXTENSIONIN STRUCTURE  BAPIPAREX OPTIONAL
        PARTNERADDRESSES STRUCTURE  BAPIADDR1 OPTIONAL
```

Keyword importing, exporting, and tables correspond to the normal programming keyword input, output, and arrays. From the Parameters list you can see that not all the parameters are required. In our case study, we will only deal with the following parameters:

- ORDER_HEADER_IN in the importing parameter containing order header information
- SALESDOCUMENT_EX in the exporting parameter containing the created order number
- RETURN in the tables parameter containing system message for any information/error
- ORDER_ITEMS_IN in the tables parameter containing item detail information
- ORDER_PARTNERS in the tables parameter containing partner detail information

In this case study, we will use the same XML specification as in step 1 for this function module. In real-world production, you have to build a more delicate interface XML specification if you want to make it a universal interface. However, I still will show you how to use name-based methods to programmatically match parameters. The code we will see shortly is totally independent of the XML specification you created here.

Step 3: Create a Map for the Specifications Created in Step 1 and Step 2 in BizTalk Mapper

You will not need a map in this case study, because we use the same specification for both inbound and outbound in the channel.

Step 4: Develop a Sample AIC for SAP R/3 System

There are two substeps in this step:

1. Generate the COM object wrap for Business Object SalesOrder in DCOM Object Builder.

2. Create an AIC in Visual Basic for R/3 Integration.

3. First, you need to start DCOM Connector. Then set up the destination for your test R/3 system, as illustrated in Figure 15-16.

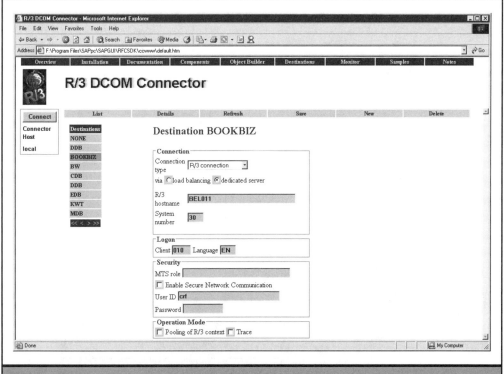

Figure 15-16.   *Set up destination in SAP DCOM Connector*

After creating the destination, you should check the Details tab to see whether you can successfully connect to your system by supplying a temporary user ID and password. Remember, for security reasons, you should not store the user name and password in the destination definition.

In the next step, we go to the Object Builder to build a COM Object wrapping all the necessary RFC calls for the SalesOrder Business Object, as shown in Figure 15-17.

In the R/3 DCOM Connector Object Builder screen, you will first need to log onto the destination we created. Then you will need to add the Business Object you want to the right list box. You need to select two objects: SalesOrder and BapiService. You need to add BapiService because you need to commit the transaction and get some detailed error messages in case of a problem. Separating transaction function module and commit will give you better control on the overall transaction you will perform in your program. You also need to select the Session check box, because we will use Session in our code. Session is used to maintain the same RFC context for all the objects within the session.

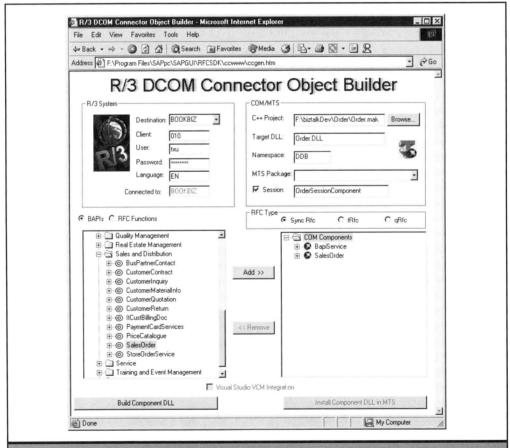

Figure 15-17. Generate COM wrapper object for Business Object

For example, you only need to supply the user/password to Session, and all the objects in the session will inherit the information from Session. For more detailed information, please check the DCOM Connector documentation. In the upper-right frame, you specify the build information for the generated C++ code. You must have MS Visual C++ 5.0 or above on your machine. Refer to the DCOM Connector documentation for all the other settings. After you build and register the component, we can move on to build the AIC for order creation in R/3.

The AIC we will create will implement interface IBTSAppIntegration. See Chapter 17 for information on how to create an AIC implementing this interface. Make sure you add the Order COM object to your project reference.

Our sample inbound order will look like the following. (Make sure to replace all the values that apply to your R/3 system.)

```
<InBoundOrder>
<Header Purch_No="CustomerPO_1" Doc_Type="Orde" Sales_Org="Sal" Distr_Chan="10" Division="10"/>
<Partner Partn_Role="Par" Partn_Numb="10" ITM_NUMBER="10"/>
<Partner Partn_Role="Par" Partn_Numb ="20" ITM_NUMBER="20"/>
<Item ITM_NUMBER ="10" Material="MaterialNO_1" TARGET_QTY="10"/>
<Item ITM_NUMBER ="20" Material="MaterialNO_2" TARGET_QTY="20"/>
</InBoundOrder>
```

Inside the AIC, we parse the document using XML DOM, and then pass the parameters to our BAPI and return the result. For a detailed code explanation, please refer to the DCOM Connector samples installed with your standard SAP front-end.

Following is the code we will put in our AIC:

```
Implements IBTSAppIntegration
Private sapSession As DDBOrderLib.OrderSessionComponent
Private sapOrder As DDBOrderLib.SalesOrder
Private sapService As DDBOrderLib.BapiService

Private Sub Class_Initialize()
' we initialize all the sap related parameters in the class event
    Set sapSession = CreateObject("DDBOrderLib.OrderSessionComponent.1")
    sapSession.PutSessionInfo "BookBiz", "User", "Password", "E", "010"
    sapSession.KeepSAPContext = True
    Set sapOrder = sapSession.CreateInstance("DDBOrderLib.SalesOrder.1")
    Set sapService = sapSession.CreateInstance("DDBOrderLib.BapiService.1")
End Sub

Private Function IBTSAppIntegration_ProcessMessage(ByVal bstrDocument As String) As String
On Error GoTo errorlabel
    Dim oDOM As New DOMDocument
    Dim oNodeList As IXMLDOMNodeList
    Dim oNode As IXMLDOMNode
    Dim oAttr As IXMLDOMAttribute
```

```
Dim orderHead As ADODB.Recordset
Dim orderItem As ADODB.Recordset
Dim orderPartner As ADODB.Recordset
Dim orderReturn As ADODB.Recordset
Dim orderNumber As Variant
'we use the SAP standard method DimAs to initialize all the table 'parameters
sapOrder.DimAs "BapiCreateFromDat2", "Order_Header_In", orderHead
sapOrder.DimAs "BapiCreateFromDat2", "Order_Items_In", orderItem
sapOrder.DimAs "BapiCreateFromDat2", "Order_Partners", orderPartner
sapOrder.DimAs "BapiCreateFromDat2", "Return", orderReturn

oDOM.loadXML bstrDocument
Set oNodeList = oDOM.getElementsByTagName("Header")
'if there is no nodelist the nodelist.length = 0
Set oNode = oNodeList.Item(0)
With orderHead
    .AddNew
    For Each oAttr In oNode.Attributes
    'the reason we use the same name for our message tag as the
'parameter is that we can dynamically fill the contents, this makes our AIC
'a universal interface for SAP
        .Fields(oAttr.baseName) = oAttr.nodeValue
    Next
    .Update
End With

Set oNodeList = oDOM.getElementsByTagName("Partner")
With orderPartner
 For Each oNode In oNodeList
    .AddNew
  For Each oAttr In oNode.Attributes
      .Fields(oAttr.baseName) = oAttr.nodeValue
  Next
    .Update
 Next
End With

Set oNodeList = oDOM.getElementsByTagName("Item")
With orderItem
    For Each oNode In oNodeList
        .AddNew
      For Each oAttr In oNode.Attributes
          .Fields(oAttr.baseName) = oAttr.nodeValue
      Next
        .Update
    Next
```

```
    End With
    'we use named parameters
    sapOrder.BapiCreateFromDat2 SalesDocument:=orderNumber,
order_header_in:=orderHead, order_items_in:=orderItem,
order_partners:=orderPartner, return:=orderReturn
    If CStr(orderNumber) <> "" Then
        'if succeed we commit the transaction
        sapService.CommitWorkAndWait
        IBTSAppIntegration_ProcessMessage = orderNumber
    Else
    ' if fail, we return the fail reason
    orderReturn.MoveFirst
        While Not orderReturn.EOF
            ' concatenate the string as you wish here
            orderReturn.MoveNext
        Wend
    End If
    Exit Function
errorlabel:
    ' report any unexpected errors
    IBTSAppIntegration_ProcessMessage = Err.Description
End Function
```

Be sure to replace appropriate variables with the values valid in your R/3 system. Then refer to the SDK chapter on how to register and compile the component. Now we can move to the next step: setting up the entire process in Messaging Manager.

Step 5: Create Various Objects in Messaging Manager

Now set up the document definition, messaging port (using our SAP AIC), and channel. Use the test program we used in Chapter 16 to test all the things you set up. Use SubmitSync to see the result.

Step 6: Develop Outlook Client Macro to Put All the Pieces Together

Congratulations! You are just one step from success. We will write a simple script in Outlook that, whenever an item arrives, will extract the attachment content and submit it to BizTalk Server. If something goes wrong, it will mail a message to the responsible person. Here is the code for the final touch on our case study. The code is developed in the Outlook 2000 Visual Basic Editor.

```
Private Sub Application_NewMail()
Dim oNS As Outlook.NameSpace
Dim oFolder As Outlook.MAPIFolder
```

```
    Dim oItem As Object
    Dim oAttachment As Attachment
    Dim strTemp
    Dim oMessage As Outlook.MailItem

    Dim oInterchange As New Interchange
    Dim vResponse As Variant
    Dim strChannel As String
    Dim RouteType As BIZTALK_OPENNESS_TYPE
    RouteType = BIZTALK_OPENNESS_TYPE_NOTOPEN
    strChannel = "BTSSAPIntegration"

     Set oNS = Application.GetNamespace("MAPI")
     Set oFolder = oNS.GetDefaultFolder(olFolderInbox)
     strTemp = oFileObject.GetSpecialFolder(2)
'we need to download the attachment in order to read the content
     FileName = strTemp & "\" & "ABN.txt"
     For Each oItem In oFolder.Items
         If oItem.Class = olMail And oItem.UnRead Then
             For Each oAttachment In oTest.Attachments
                 oAttachment.SaveAsFile FileName
                 Set oContent = oFileObject.OpenTextFile(FileName)
                 result = oContent.ReadAll
'submit the attachment to BizTalk and wait for the answer
                 oInterchange.SubmitSync RouteType, result,,,,,,strChannel,,,,,vResponse
                 'you judge the result here, if error send a mail to responsible person
                 'if error occurs
                     Set oMessage = myolApp.CreateItem(olMailItem)
                     oMessage.To = "responsible person"
                     oMessage.Body = CStr(vResponse)
                     oMessage.Subject = "Error in SAP order creation"
                     oMessage.Send
                 'End If
                 oContent.Close
                 MsgBox result
                 oFileObject.DeleteFile FileName
             Next
'in order to keep the inbox small, we move the item to a local folder
         oItem.UnRead = False
         oItem.Move oNS.Folders("mailtest")
     End If
    Next
End Sub
```

The Complete Reference

Part VI

Extending BizTalk Server

Chapter 16

Using the BizTalk Server SDK

L ike other Microsoft products, BizTalk Server is released with a complete Software Development Kit (SDK) to help customers efficiently extend the system. The SDK is COM based and requires the knowledge of at least one of the COM-aware programming languages, such as Visual Basic (VB), Visual C++, or Borland C++. The SDK includes

- A set of Microsoft Interface Definition Language files for interface prototypes
- Message processing samples
- XLANG samples and an XLANG monitor tool

You can extend two groups of COM (Component Object Model) interfaces: message processing and application integration, as shown in Figure 16-1.

This chapter shows you how to implement these interfaces to extend the BizTalk Server. VB is an excellent choice for rapidly creating prototypes and for testing. When everything is working correctly, implement the same functionality in Visual C++ for production use to achieve greater performance and stability—especially for Application Integration Components (AICs). There are several Microsoft Knowledge Base articles dealing with the language choice for custom components. Visit the web site http://support.microsoft.com and search on BizTalk Server with the key words "custom component".

Configuring BizTalk Messaging Programmatically

This section gives you a structural view of the BizTalk Server configuration object model. It is not intended to replace the BizTalk Server online documentation. For detailed parameter information for methods, refer to the online documentation.

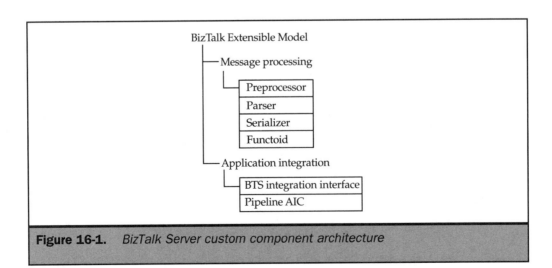

Figure 16-1. *BizTalk Server custom component architecture*

Normally, you can configure all the messaging settings in BizTalk Messaging Manager manually. When you work on a large project, the settings in BizTalk Messaging Manager may become very complicated on your development BizTalk Server group. Manually duplicating everything to your production server group is both time-consuming and error-prone. Because BizTalk Server is implemented as a set of COM components, it gives us the chance to programmatically configure the messaging settings by using a set of COM interfaces. With these COM programming interfaces, you can write a program to export settings from your development BizTalk Server group to your production server group. The BTConfigAssistant sample in the SDK permits you to easily transport configuration between BizTalk Server groups.

IBizTalkConfig Interface

Figure 16-2 shows how the interface IBizTalkConfig is the entry point of the BizTalk Server configuration object model. From IBizTalkConfig, you can enumerate all the objects in BizTalk messaging, as well as create new ones. If you want to have typed access to the object model in Visual Basic, you have to add the following reference to your project: **Microsoft BizTalk Server Configuration Object 1.0 Type Library**. The access from VBScript will be as follows:

```
ObjBizConfig = CreateObject("BizTalk.BizTalkConfig")
```

IBizTalkConfig

Properties (all are read-only ADO recordset)

Certificates	All specified certificates
Channels	All BizTalkChannel objects
Documents	All BizTalkDocument objects
Envelopes	All BizTalkEnvelope objects
Organizations	All BizTalkOrganization objects
PortGroups	All BizTalkPortGroup objects
Ports	All BizTalkPort objects

Methods

CreateChannel	Return an interface to a new BizTalkChannel object (IBizTalkChannel)
CreateDocument	Return an interface to a new BizTalkDocument object (IBizTalkDocument)
CreateEnvelope	Return an interface to a new BizTalkEnvelope object (IBizTalkEnvelope)
CreateOrganization	Return an interface to a new BizTalkOrganization object (IBizTalkOrganization)
CreatePortGroup	Return an interface to a new BizTalkPortGroup object (IBizTalkPortGroup)
CreatePort	Return an interface to a new BizTalkPort object (IBizTalkPort)

Figure 16-2. *BizTalk Server configuration object model*

IBizTalkBase Interface

In the BizTalk Server configuration object model, methods common to most of the objects are defined in the IBizTalkBase interface, and the following objects/interfaces implement the IBizTalkBase interface:

- BizTalkChannel
- BizTalkDocument
- BizTalkEnvelope
- BizTalkOrganization
- BizTalkPort
- BizTalkPortGroup

You will never initiate or see this interface. The methods and properties of this interface are always invoked on the corresponding objects, rather than by creating an actual IBizTalkBase interface. See Figure 16-3.

Other Interfaces

The rest of the interfaces are related to the detail objects. You can programmatically manipulate these objects through corresponding interfaces. If you are familiar with

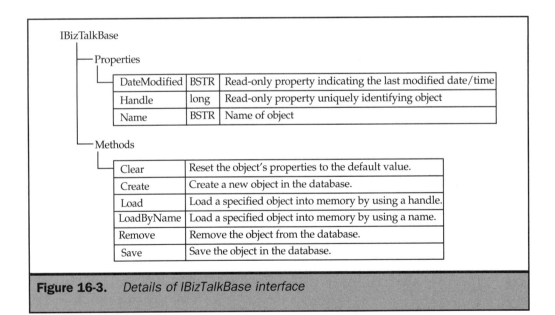

IBizTalkBase

— Properties

DateModified	BSTR	Read-only property indicating the last modified date/time
Handle	long	Read-only property uniquely identifying object
Name	BSTR	Name of object

— Methods

Clear	Reset the object's properties to the default value.
Create	Create a new object in the database.
Load	Load a specified object into memory by using a handle.
LoadByName	Load a specified object into memory by using a name.
Remove	Remove the object from the database.
Save	Save the object in the database.

Figure 16-3. *Details of IBizTalkBase interface*

Messaging Manager, you can easily understand the properties/methods of these objects/interfaces. These interfaces are

- IBizTalkChannel
- IBizTalkDocument
- IBizTalkEnvelope
- IBizTalkOrganization
- IBizTalkPort
- IBizTalkPortGroup
- IBizTalkEndPoint
- IBizTalkServiceWindowInfo
- IBizTalkTransportInfo
- IBizTalkCertificateInfo
- IBizTalkLoggingInfo

When BizTalkPort and BizTalkChannel objects are created, BizTalk Server automatically creates some associated subobjects. You can access these subobjects by using properties of BizTalkPort and BizTalkChannel objects.

Subobject	Associated	Object Property to Set
BizTalkEndPoint	BizTalkPort	DestinationEndpoint
BizTalkEndPoint	BizTalkChannel	SourceEndpoint
BizTalkLoggingInfo	BizTalkChannel	LoggingInfo
BizTalkTransportInfo	BizTalkPort	PrimaryTransport, SecondaryTransport
BizTalkServiceWindowInfo	BizTalkPort	ServiceWindowInfo
BizTalkCertificateInfo	BizTalkPort	EncryptionCertificateInfo
BizTalkCertificateInfo	BizTalkChannel	SignatureCertificateInfo, VerifySignatureCertificateInfo, or DecryptionCertificateInfo

A Configuration Example

Here is an example of how to programmatically set up the document definition, messaging port, and organization. The sample is written in VBScript.

```
Dim BTConf, doc, org, port
Set BTConf = CreateObject("BizTalk.BizTalkConfig")
Set doc = BTConf.CreateDocument
Set org = BTConf.CreateOrganization
Set port = BTConf.CreatePort
dim lOrg
org.clear
org.name = "ConfigureTest"
org.comments = "BTS configuration test"
lOrg = org.Create
doc.clear
doc.name = "ConfigureTest"
doc.reference = "http://SAPTXU/BizTalkServerRepository" _ & _
"/DocSpecs/BookBiz/parserdoc.xml"
doc.create
port.clear
port.name = "ConfigureTest"
port.DestinationEndPoint.Organization = lOrg
port.PrimaryTransport.Address = "mailto:tom_xu@msn.com"
port.PrimaryTransport.Type = 8    'BIZTALK_TRANSPORT_TYPE_SMTP
port.PrimaryTransport.Parameter = "mailto:tom_xu@msn.com"
port.Create

msgbox "finish"
```

If you go to BizTalk Messaging Manager, you can check the results of this script.

Submitting Documents Programmatically

Besides submitting documents to BizTalk Server by using receive functions, you can also programmatically submit documents to BizTalk Server by using the IInterchange interface. The most important methods in this interface are Submit( ) and SubmitSync( ) (synchronous version of Submit). These methods allow you to submit documents to a run-time messaging service within your program. The remainder of the interface consists of three methods for dealing with failure messages.

The Submit method has the parameters shown in the next table.

Parameter	Type	Description
lOpenness	BIZTALK_OPENNESS _TYPE enumeration	Specifies whether associated BizTalkPort can be open.
Document	String	Document instance in string; if this parameter is not passed, FilePath must be provided.
DocName	String	Name of the document definition in the submitted document. It must not be passed if PassThrough is set to True.
SourceQualifier	String	Qualifier of the source organization. It must be used with the SourceID parameter and cannot be passed if PassThrough is set to True.
SourceID	String	Value of the qualifier of the source organization. It must be used with a SourceQualifier parameter.
DestQualifier	String	Qualifier of the source organization. It must be used with the SourceID parameter and cannot be passed if PassThrough is set to True.
DestID	String	Value of the qualifier of the source organization. It must be used with a SourceQualifier parameter.
ChannelName	String	Name of the BizTalk Channel. Optional parameter unless PassThrough is set to True.
FilePath	String	A full qualified path that contains the document to be submitted exclusively with the Document parameter.
EnvelopeName	String	Name of the envelope will be used to break the interchange into documents, e.g., Flat-File envelope.

Parameter	Type	Description
PassThrough	Long	When this parameter is set to True, no decryption, decoding, or signature verification is performed on the document, and the ChannelName parameter must be provided. This parameter is very important if you are passing binary data.
Return value	String	A unique identifier for the submitted document (GUID). It can be used to query the status of the submitted document.

SubmitSync( ) has one more parameter (ResponseDocument) than Submit( ). ResponseDocument is a variant parameter containing an option response document. Response documents may be returned from synchronous protocols such as AICs. This is very useful in real-time integration with your back-end system, as we will see in the section "Case Study 2: Inbound Order Processing with SAP R/3 Using BizTalk Server 2000" in Chapter 15. Use of this method adversely affects the scalability of the BizTalk Server group, but it will save you from checking the Suspended Queue for possible failures. The interchange is complete by the time the method returns.

The BIZTALK_OPENNESS_TYPE enumeration has one of the values in the table that follows:

Name	Value	Description
BIZTALK_OPENNESS_TYPE_ NOTOPEN	1	Specifies that this instance of the object is not open
BIZTALK_OPENNESS_TYPE_ SOURCE	2	Specifies that the source organization of this instance of the object is open and must be determined
BIZTALK_OPENNESS_TYPE_ DESTINATION	4	Specifies that the destination organization of this instance of the object is open and must be determined

When you are going to submit documents to BizTalk Server in your program, be sure that you add the reference **Microsoft BizTalk Server Interchange 1.0 Type Library** to your project. There is nothing special in using Submit ( )/SubmitSync( ), except that the configuration of the IInterchange COM+ application is something you need to pay attention to. The IInterchange interface runs as a COM+ application under

Windows Component Service. It runs under the interactive user account by default. This causes problems when you log off the machine and submit the document from the background. It will simply fail because there is no interactive user. The same problem exists for the BizTalk Messaging Service in Windows Service Manager. You must create a Windows service account for both of them. If you plan to submit documents from a remote client, you have to create the same service account (with the same password) on the remote client. Otherwise, the submission will fail. Refer to the online documentation for details on how to submit a document from a remote client.

The other three methods in the IInterchange interface are

- CheckSuspendedQueue
- GetSuspendedQueueItemDetail
- DeleteFromSuspendedQueue

You can use them to write some utility programs for daily operation monitoring in a production environment. For example, you can schedule a program to check the Suspended Queue twice a day and to send a notification if there are suspended items in the queue.

Sample program DirectIntegration in the SDK well illustrates all the methods in the IInterchange interface. You should spend some time examining this sample. Except for the user account settings for BizTalk Messaging service and the IInterchange COM+ application, there is nothing tricky about submitting the document programmatically. "Case Study 2: Inbound Order Processing with SAP R/3 Using BizTalk Server 2000," in Chapter 15, demonstrates how to use the SubmitSync( ) interface in a real-time integration.

Message Processing

BizTalk is well known to be XML-centric. Unfortunately, some legacy systems and proprietary systems do not have any knowledge of XML. Modifying all these systems is impractical. Fortunately, the BizTalk Server development team anticipated this unique challenge and provides us with a set of well-documented interfaces for proprietary message format, covered in the following sections.

Custom Preprocessor

Custom Preprocessor is the simplest interface to implement. It must be used in association with receive functions in BizTalk Server. You only need to implement the IBTSCustomProcess interface, which contains two methods:

- **Execute**   Transforms the data prior to submitting the data to the BizTalk Server for processing.
- **SetContext**   Retrieves the IBTSCustomProcessContext interface pointing to the BTSCustomProcessContext object, which contains the context information associated with the data being processed. All the properties are read-only.

The scenario we use for Custom Preprocessor is as follows: We use the receive function to send an MS Access Northwind sample database file to BizTalk Server. The receive function will invoke our Custom Preprocessor component to transform the information into an XML string. The output of this sample will be a well-formed and valid XML presentation of the Northwind order information. (Only one order is retrieved.)

I will try to keep the sample as simple as possible. My aim is to show you the whole process for implementing the IBTSCustomProcess interface, but not the special logic inside the Preprocessor itself.

Step 1: Create a Specification of Our Sample

1. Open the BizTalk Editor to create a new XML document specification.

2. Rename the root record **NorthwindOrder**.

3. Select the root record and create three subrecords: **OrderInfo**, **DateInfo**, and **ShippingInfo**.

4. Create the fields for the corresponding nodes as listed in the following table. (All the fields are created as attributes of the nodes.)

Record	Field Name	Data Type	Length
OrderInfo	OrderID	Integer	N/A
OrderInfo	CustomerID	String	5
OrderInfo	EmployeeID	Integer	N/A
DateInfo	OrderDate	String	10
DateInfo	RequiredDate	String	10
DateInfo	ShippedDate	String	10
ShippingInfo	ShipName	String	40
ShippingInfo	ShipAddress	String	60
ShippingInfo	ShipCity	String	15
ShippingInfo	ShipRegion	String	15
ShippingInfo	ShipPostalCode	String	10
ShippingInfo	ShipCountry	String	15

Step 2: Create a VB Project to Implement the IBTSCustomProcess

1. Open Visual Basic 6 (with SP4) to create an ActiveX DLL project with the name **FirstPreprocessor**. Then rename the class module **Process**.

2. Choose Project | References, and add the following references to the project:

- Microsoft ActiveX Data Objects 2.6 Library
- Microsoft BizTalk Server Application Interface Component
- In the class module, we first put the following:

```
Implements IBTSCustomProcess
Private Sub IBTSCustomProcess_Execute( _
ByVal vDataIn As Variant, _
ByVal nCodePageIn As Long, _
ByVal bIsFilePath As Boolean, _
nCodePageOut As Variant, _
vDataOut As Variant)
End Sub
Private Sub IBTSCustomProcess_SetContext( _
ByVal pCtx As BTSComponentsLib.IBTSCustomProcessContext)
End Sub
```

The method we need to implement is IBTSCustomProcess_Execute. Method IBTSCustomProcess is required in the interface, but you do not need to do anything there. Here is a list of all the parameters for method IBTSCustomProcess_Execute:

Parameter	Description
vDataIn	The content depends on the type of receive function. For a message-queue receive function, the content is either an array or a BSTR. For a file receive function, it contains the path of the file.
nCodePageIn	Code page for the vDataIn parameter.
bisFilePath	If it is invoked through a file receive function, this value is True; otherwise, it is False.
nCodePageOut	Code page for the vDataOut parameter.
vDataOut	This is a BSTR sent to BizTalk Server for processing. The content must match the input document specification.

You should also adjust the project settings by choosing Project | FirstPreprocessor Properties | General tab, and then selecting the Unattend Execution and Retain In Memory options.

The core part of the implementation is to retrieve the info from an MS Access file and to construct it into an XML string. To keep the program simple, I use string concatenation to construct the XML string. In real production coding, you should use the DOM to construct the XML stream.

Here is the implementation of the Execute method:

```
Dim strXML As String   'The result XML string
Dim strFile As String  'the received filename
        'Retrieve filename including the full path
'I assume that BizTalk always receives this file through file
'receive function. In your production project, you need to check the value 'of bIsFilePath
    strFile = CStr(vDataIn)

    'Open the file with the Jet OLEDB provider
    Dim dbConn As New ADODB.Connection
    dbConn.ConnectionString = "Provider=Microsoft.Jet.OLEDB.4.0;Data Source=" & strFile
    dbConn.Open
    Dim rsOrder As New ADODB.Recordset
    Dim strSQL As String
'we only need one record for our test purpose
    strSQL = "select top 1 * from Orders"
    rsOrder.Open strSQL, dbConn, adOpenForwardOnly, adLockReadOnly
    rsOrder.MoveFirst
    'begin to construct the result XML string
    strXML = "<NorthwindOrder><OrderInfo OrderID="""
    While Not rsOrder.EOF
        strXML = strXML & rsOrder.Fields("OrderID") & """ CustomerID=""" _
        & rsOrder.Fields("CustomerID") & """ EmployeeID=""" _
        & rsOrder.Fields("EmployeeID") & """ />"
        strXML = strXML & "<DateInfo OrderDate=""" & rsOrder.Fields("OrderDate") & """ RequiredDate=""" _
        & rsOrder.Fields("RequiredDate") & """ ShippedDate=""" _
        & rsOrder.Fields("ShippedDate") & """ />"
        strXML = strXML & "<ShippingInfo ShipName=""" & rsOrder.Fields("ShipName") & """ ShipAddress=""" _
        & rsOrder.Fields("ShipAddress") & """ ShipCity=""" _
        & rsOrder.Fields("ShipCity") & """ ShipRegion=""" _
        & rsOrder.Fields("ShipRegion") & """ ShipPostalCode=""" _
        & rsOrder.Fields("ShipPostalCode") & """ ShipCountry=""" _
        & rsOrder.Fields("ShipCountry") & """ />"
        rsOrder.MoveNext
    Wend
    rsOrder.Close
    strXML = strXML & "</NorthwindOrder>"
    'Set the transformed XML String
    vDataOut = strXML
     dbConn.Close
```

Be sure to always return the vDataOut, or you will raise exceptions. As you can see from the C++ interface description from the documentation, vDataOut is an [out] parameter. Never remove the file explicitly in your program, because BizTalk Server will do it for you.

The code is quite straightforward, and you should be able to understand it without any problem. Now let's look at the steps for putting our first preprocessor in action:

1. Compile the project into DLL: FirstPreprocessor.dll.

2. Register the DLL with regsvr32 utility.

3. Create a REG file as follows:

```
Windows Registry Editor Version 5.00
[HKEY_CLASSES_ROOT\CLSID\{79426E94-15BC-479C-8FC7-8ED3BE66EE8C}\
Implemented Categories\{20e8080f-f624-4401-a203-9d99cf18a6d9}]
```

Here, 79426E94-15BC-479C-8FC7-8ED3BE66EE8C is the Class ID of our preprocessor, and 20e8080f-f624-4401-a203-9d99cf18a6d9 is the custom preprocessor implementation category. We need to add the implemented categories key to let the system know that the component is a custom preprocessor.

1. Start the BizTalk Messaging Manager.

2. Create an organization with the name **Preprocessor**.

3. Create the document definition pointing to the XML specification we created in the beginning of this chapter.

4. Create a messaging port to organization "Preprocessor". The primary transport is file transport. Enter the directory name we created for receiving the result and the filename.

5. Create a channel for the preceding messaging port. The channel source is from the default home organization; the inbound and outbound specifications are the same as we created in the previous step.

6. Start the BizTalk Administration program, and create a file receive function pointing to the directory you created in step 1. In the Preprocessor drop-down list, you will see our component. In the Advanced tab, put our newly created channel.

7. Put the sample Northwind.mdb file into the source directory to which the file receive function points. After a few seconds, you should see an output file sitting in the output directory you created before.

Custom Parser

One of the limitations of Custom Preprocessor is that it can only be used in conjunction with receive functions. Another limitation is that Custom Preprocessor can do nothing more than wrap the documents in a parent structure or totally reorganize the file. We need a more generic solution to deal with the special message format.

There are quite a few scenarios requiring you to implement a custom parser. For example, EDI batch messages contain multiple groups and multiple EDI messages. With XML, EDI batches are illegal because XML specifications dictate that each XML document only has one root node. So it is necessary to create a custom parser to handle this situation. The parser will break the batch message into documents and submit them to BizTalk for processing one after another.

To create our own custom parser, we need to implement the IBizTalkParserComponent. Unfortunately, the parameter type used in this interface makes it impossible to implement this interface in Visual Basic. The only choice for the moment is C++. I will implement this interface with Visual C++ 6.0 SP5.

To correctly process the inbound messages, BizTalk Server has various parser components for different message formats—for example, XML, Flat-File, EDIFACT, and X12. The sequence of the parser components is very important; it determines the order in which the message will be processed by each parser component. A wrong parser component order will lead to parsing errors. You can adjust the *parser* component order in BizTalk Administration.

Following is a list of all the methods in this interface:

Method	Description
GetGroupDetails	Gets details of the group for the Tracking database. This method is called only if there are groups in the interchange.
GetGroupSize	Gets the size of the group after all documents in the group are parsed. This method is called only if there are groups in the interchange. If this is not the last group, then GetGroupDetails will be the subsequent call.
GetInterchangeDetails	Gets information about the organization identifiers of the source and destination BizTalk Organization objects, if any, and also gets the envelope information.
GetNativeDocumentOffsets	Identifies offsets from the beginning of the stream for final details about the group in the Tracking database for final logging.
GetNextDocument	Examines the data in a document and determines when to get the next document if this is not the last document.
GroupsExist	Determines whether the interchange contains groups.
ProbeInterchangeFormat	Determines whether the parser can handle the interchange.

BizTalk will call these methods when it receives a candidate interchange. See Figure 16-4. Though the sequence of these calls depends on the content of the interchange, the first three calls are always the same:

- ProbeInterchangeFormat
- GetInterchangeDetails
- GroupsExist

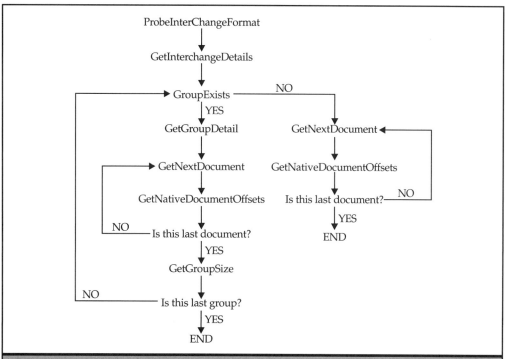

Figure 16-4.   *Calling sequence of the methods in IBizTalkParserComponent Interface*

Depending on the return value from GroupsExist, the subsequent calls will vary with the situations, as described next.

If groups do not exist, the steps are as follows:

1. GetNextDocument
2. GetNativeDocumentOffsets

There will be a loop for items 1 and 2 until the last document is reached.

If groups exist, the steps are as follows:

1. GetGroupDetails
2. GetNextDocument
3. GetNativeDocumentOffsets
4. GetGroupSize

There will be a loop for items 1 through 4 until the last document in the last group is reached.

The following tables show a possible sequence for calling the methods.

Just imagine you need to produce an inventory report for your company according to location. The whole inventory report is an interchange, each location is a group, and each material status/quantity inside the specific location is a document. You create the specification for each material status/quantity detail. It is the parser's job to break down the whole interchange into a single document.

If you have an interchange with two groups, with two documents in the first group and one in the second, the methods are called in the following sequence:

Method	Return
ProbeInterchangeFormat	Non-empty format string.
GetInterchangeDetails	N/A
GroupsExist	True.
GetGroupDetails	N/A
GetNextDocument	The LastDoc parameter is set to False.
GetNativeDocumentOffsets	N/A
GetNextDocument	The LastDoc parameter is set to True.
GetNativeDocumentOffsets	N/A
GetGroupSize	The LastGroup parameter is set to False.
GetGroupDetails	N/A
GetNextDocument	The LastDoc parameter is set to True.
GetNativeDocumentOffsets	N/A
GetGroupSize	The LastGroup parameter is set to True.

If you have an interchange with two documents, the methods are called in the following sequence:

Method	Return
ProbeInterchangeFormat	Non-empty format string.
GetInterchangeDetails	N/A
GroupsExist	False.
GetNextDocument	The LastDoc parameter is set to False.
GetNativeDocumentOffsets	N/A
GetNextDocument	The LastDoc parameter is set to True.
GetNativeDocumentOffsets	N/A

Step 1: Create Specification and Map for Our Test Document   The document we will use in the first custom parser will be extremely simple. Actually, it can be parsed using the standard BizTalk Server XML parser. I chose this sample to show you how the parser works. With the extraordinary modeling ability of BizTalk Editor, it is difficult to find a real-world sample for the parser. However, which format we use is unimportant; what we need to master is how the parser works. Following is the schema generated by BizTalk Editor for the test document:

```
<?xml version="1.0"?>
<!-- Generated by using BizTalk Editor on Sun, Jul 15 2001 10:59:10 PM -->
<!-- Microsoft Corporation (c) 2000 (http://www.microsoft.com) -->
<Schema name="ParserDoc" b:BizTalkServerEditorTool_Version="1.0"
b:root_reference="ParserDoc" b:standard="XML" xmlns="urn:schemas-microsoft
com:xml-data" xmlns:b="urn:schemas-microsoft-com:BizTalkServer"
xmlns:d="urn:schemas-microsoft-com:datatypes">
<b:SelectionFields/>

<ElementType name="ProcessStatus" content="empty" model="closed">
<b:RecordInfo/>
<AttributeType name="Value" d:type="string" d:maxLength="10"d:minLength="1">
<b:FieldInfo/></AttributeType>
<attribute type="Value" required="no"/>
</ElementType><ElementType name="ParserDoc" content="eltOnly" model="closed">
<description>Used for parser test</description><b:RecordInfo/>
<element type="ProcessStatus" maxOccurs="1" minOccurs="0"/>
</ElementType></Schema>
```

The input of the document will be

```
<ParserDoc>
    <ProcessStatus Value="Inbound"/>
</ParserDoc>
```

The output of the document will be

```
<ParserDoc>
     <ProcessStatus value="Parsed"/>
</ParserDoc>
```

Now you go to the BizTalk Mapper to create a map for the preceding specification according to the input and output.

The sample interchange we will use is as follows:

```
<ParserDocGroups>
 <Group name="Group1">
```

```
<ParserDoc>
 <ProcessStatus Value="Inbound"/>
</ParserDoc>
<ParserDoc>
 <ProcessStatus Value="Inbound"/>
</ParserDoc>
</Group>
<Group name="Group2">
 <ParserDoc>
  <ProcessStatus Value="Inbound"/>
 </ParserDoc>
</Group>
</ParserDocGroups>
```

At the end of the processing, we should be able to receive three documents with the ProcessStatus changed to "Parsed".

Step 2: Configure Message Manager and BizTalk Administration

1. Create two folders for our sample (for example, **c:\parserinput** and **c:\parseroutput**).

2. Create an organization with the name **ParserOrg**.

3. Create a messaging port for this Organization, and output the document to c:\parseroutput.

4. Create a channel with the name **ParserChannel** for the messaging port we just created.

5. Create a file receive function for directory c:\parserinput with reference to the channel ParserChannel.

Now, create a document with one instance of ParserDoc inside and put it into C:\parserinput. You should shortly see an output document in c:\parseroutput with the status changed. If something goes wrong, check all the settings until it works.

Step 3: Program the IBizTalkParserComponent in Visual C++ 6.0

1. Start the Visual C++ program from your Start menu, and create a new project with the name **FirstParser** using the ATL COM APP Wizard. The parser will be implemented as a dynamic link library.

2. Add a new ATL Simple Object with the name **MyParser**. This is the component that will implement the IBizTalkParserComponent interface.

3. In the MyParser.h header file, you need to add the following header files from the BizTalk Server SDK:

```
#include "bts_sdk_guids.h"
#include "BTSParserComps.h"
```

Make sure that you add the BizTalk Server SDK include directory to your Visual C++ build environment through Tools | Options.

4. Still inside the MyParser.h header file, add **Public IBizTalkParserComponent** to the class inheritance list. Copy the member function list from BTSparserComps.h into the CMyParser class definition, and remove the virtual key word and "=0" pure virtual function symbol as follows:

```
HRESULT STDMETHODCALLTYPE ProbeInterchangeFormat(
          /* [in] */ IStream __RPC_FAR *pData,
          /* [in] */ BOOL FromFile,
          /* [in] */ BSTR EnvName,
          /* [in] */ IStream __RPC_FAR *pReceiptData,
          /* [retval][out] */ BSTR __RPC_FAR *Format);
HRESULT STDMETHODCALLTYPE GetInterchangeDetails(
          /* [in] */ IDictionary __RPC_FAR *Dict);
HRESULT STDMETHODCALLTYPE GroupsExist(
          /* [retval][out] */ BOOL __RPC_FAR *GrpsExist);
HRESULT STDMETHODCALLTYPE GetGroupDetails(
          /* [in] */ IDictionary __RPC_FAR *Dict);
HRESULT STDMETHODCALLTYPE GetGroupSize(
          /* [out] */ long __RPC_FAR *GroupSize,
          /* [out] */ BOOL __RPC_FAR *LastGroup);
HRESULT STDMETHODCALLTYPE GetNextDocument(
          /* [in] */ IDictionary __RPC_FAR *Dict,
          /* [in] */ BSTR DocName,
          /* [out] */ BOOL __RPC_FAR *DocIsValid,
          /* [out] */ BOOL __RPC_FAR *LastDocument,
          /* [out] */ enum GeneratedReceiptLevel __RPC_FAR *ReceiptGenerated,
          /* [out] */ BOOL __RPC_FAR *DocIsReceipt,
          /* [out] */ BSTR __RPC_FAR *CorrelationCompProgID);
HRESULT STDMETHODCALLTYPE GetNativeDocumentOffsets(
          /* [out] */ BOOL __RPC_FAR *SizeFromXMLDoc,
          /* [out] */ LARGE_INTEGER __RPC_FAR *StartOffset,
          /* [out] */ long __RPC_FAR *DocLength);
```

5. Still inside MyParser.h, add the line **COM_INTERFACE_ENTRY (IBizTalkParserComponent)** to the COM_MAP and the implement category so that BizTalk will know that this is a custom parser component. This step is very important, so don't forget it.

```
BEGIN_CATEGORY_MAP(CParser1)
     IMPLEMENTED_CATEGORY(CATID_BIZTALK_PARSER)
END_CATEGORY_MAP()
```

6. You also need to add some private data members and help functions and to initialize all the data members in the constructor.

```
IStream*    m_pData;
Long     m_TotalNumDocs;
Long     m_TotalGroups;
Long     m_LastDocEndIndex;
Long     m_LastDocLength;
Long     m_CurrentDocument;
Long     m_CurrentGroup;
Long     m_TotalDoc;
long     m_DocLen;
long     m_LastLen;
long     m_DocBegin;
     BOOL     IsValidDocType(IStream* pStream);
     BOOL     GetDoc(BSTR* Doc);
     BOOL     CountGroups();
     BOOL     GroupDocs(long * GroupIndex);
```

7. Override the FinalRelease method so that we can release our Istream interface:

```
void FinalRelease()
{
     if(m_pData != NULL){m_pData->Release();}
}
```

8. Declare these constants at the beginning of MyParser.cpp:

```
const int  TEST_BYTES = 20;
const char* END_OF_DOC = "</ParserDoc>";
const char* BEGIN_OF_DOC = "<ParserDoc>";
const char* END_OF_GROUP = "</Group>";
const char* BEGIN_OF_GROUP = "<Group";
const char* END_INTERCHANGE = "</ParserDocGroups>";
const char* TEST_DOC_IDENTIFIER = "ParserDoc";
```

9. Implement a skeleton for all the IBizTalkParserComponent methods. Then compile the project, ensuring there are no errors.

10. The first method we will look at is ProbeInterchangeFormat. In this method, we need to check whether the parser can handle the document. If it can, we must insert a Format parameter. Here is the implementation of this function:

```
HRESULT STDMETHODCALLTYPE CMyParser::ProbeInterchangeFormat(
     IStream __RPC_FAR *pData,
     BOOL FromFile,
     BSTR EnvName,
     IStream __RPC_FAR *pReceiptData,
     BSTR __RPC_FAR *Format)
```

```
{
HRESULT hr;
//data type used by IStream method
STATSTG stats;
LARGE_INTEGER dLibMove;
hr = pData->Stat(&stats, 0);
//move the point to the beginning of the stream
if ( SUCCEEDED(hr))
{
    dLibMove.QuadPart=0;
    hr = pData->Seek(dLibMove, STREAM_SEEK_SET,NULL);
}
// now check if my parser can handle this document, if can't, give it
//back to BizTalk
if(!IsValidDocType(pData))
{
    hr = pData->Seek(dLibMove, STREAM_SEEK_SET,NULL);
    return S_FALSE;
}
//now we need to fill Format parameter to tell BizTalk that
//we can handle this document
if ( SUCCEEDED(hr))
{
// this is necessary because Pointer to a BSTR that contains the format.
//If the server recognizes the format, it must fill in Format
//with a nonempty string and hold on to (add a reference count to)
//the IStream interface because it is not given back to the component.
m_pData = pData;
pData->AddRef();
CComBSTR bstrFormat;
bstrFormat = *Format;
bstrFormat = "Customer XML";
*Format = bstrFormat.Detach();
ULONG bytesread;
BYTE* pbData = new BYTE[stats.cbSize.LowPart+1];
hr= pData->Read((void*)pbData, stats.cbSize.LowPart, &bytesread);
delete [] pbData;
}
return hr;
}
```

In this function implementation, we use a help function—IsValidDocType—to detect the document format.

```
BOOL CMyParser::IsValidDocType(IStream * pStream)
{
HRESULT hr;
ULONG bytesread ;
BOOL retval = FALSE;
    //we just check the first 20 bytes to see if it contains ParserDoc
BYTE * pbData = new BYTE[TEST_BYTES + 1];
```

```
//now we read the first 20 bytes of the interchange and check the contents
hr = pStream->Read((void*)pbData, TEST_BYTES, &bytesread);
if (SUCCEEDED(hr))
{
//make sure the last byte is null
memset(pbData+bytesread,0,1);
//do the string test
char * result = NULL;
result = strstr((char*)pbData, TEST_DOC_IDENTIFIER);
retval = ( result==NULL) ? (FALSE) : (TRUE);
}
delete [] pbData;
return retval;
}
```

11. Now we move on to the next function in the call sequence, GetInterchangeDetails. In this function, you can retrieve some useful information from BizTalk Server (for example, the envelope used and the source and destination organization identifiers). Normally, you will not need to do anything here. So we only return S_OK to BizTalk Server.

```
HRESULT STDMETHODCALLTYPE CMyParser::GetInterchangeDetails(
     IDictionary __RPC_FAR *Dict)
{
//No action needed in our case study, but you can get envelope information //here
     return S_OK;
}
```

12. After getting the related information and pointer to the data stream, it is time for us to tell BizTalk Server if there are groups in our interchange. This is the responsibility of function GroupsExist. Following is the implementation of this function:

```
HRESULT STDMETHODCALLTYPE CMyParser::GroupsExist(
     /* [retval][out] */ BOOL __RPC_FAR *GrpsExist)
{
    *GrpsExist = CountGroups();
     return S_OK;
}
```

I developed the help function CountGroups( ) to tell BizTalk Server if there are groups:

```
BOOL CMyParser::CountGroups()
{
HRESULT hr;
BOOL retval = FALSE;
STATSTG stats = {0};
LARGE_INTEGER Move = {0};
BYTE*pbData= 0; //store the data
ULONG bytesread;
char * result = NULL;
```

```
long GroupCount =0;
m_TotalGroups = 0;
hr=m_pData->Stat(&stats, 0);
if(SUCCEEDED(hr))
{
//make sure we are at the beginning of the stream
Move.QuadPart=0;
hr = m_pData->Seek(Move,STREAM_SEEK_SET,NULL);
}
//we load the whole document
pbData = new BYTE[stats.cbSize.LowPart + 1];
hr = m_pData->Read((void*)pbData, stats.cbSize.LowPart, &bytesread);
//make sure the last byte is null
memset(pbData+bytesread,0,1);
//in strstr, if second parameter points to a string of zero length, the
function returns string.
result = strstr((char*)pbData, "");
while(result != NULL)
{
result = strstr(result, END_OF_GROUP);
if (result != NULL)
{
    GroupCount++;
    result++;
}
}
m_TotalGroups = GroupCount;
retval = (GroupCount > 1) ? (TRUE): (FALSE);
delete [] pbData;
return retval; }
```

The logic for this piece of code is quite simple: We check the data stream to see if any group trailers exist. If so, we count them. In the code samples, you will see similar code appear repeatedly. I did this to simplify illustration and readability. In the real production code, you need to optimize related code.

13. After determining whether there are groups, BizTalk needs group details. It calls GetGroupDetails. In this function, set the group counter and number of documents for the group. You will need this information to tell BizTalk Server if the processing has reached the last document/group. Following is the implementation of this function:

```
HRESULT STDMETHODCALLTYPE CMyParser::GetGroupDetails(
    IDictionary __RPC_FAR *Dict)
{
    m_CurrentDocument = 0; //group document counter
    m_CurrentGroup++;    //group counter
    GroupDocs(&m_CurrentGroup); //calculate how many documents in the current group
    return S_OK;
}
```

The help function GroupDocs sets the number of the documents in the current group. Let's look at its implementation:

```
BOOL CMyParser::GroupDocs(long * GroupIndex)
{
HRESULT hr;
BOOL retval = FALSE;
STATSTG stats = {0};
LARGE_INTEGER Move = {0};
BYTE*pbData= 0;
ULONG bytesread;
char * result = NULL;
long DocCount =0;

hr=m_pData->Stat(&stats, 0);
if(SUCCEEDED(hr))
{
//make sure we are at the beginning of the stream
Move.QuadPart=0;
hr = m_pData->Seek(Move,STREAM_SEEK_SET,NULL);
}
//we load the whole document
pbData = new BYTE[stats.cbSize.LowPart + 1];
hr = m_pData->Read((void*)pbData, stats.cbSize.LowPart, &bytesread);
//make sure the last byte is null
memset(pbData+bytesread,0,1);

//we get the end position for the current group
result = strstr((char*)pbData, "");
char* END_POS;
for (int i=0; i<(*GroupIndex);i++)
{
result = strstr(result, END_OF_GROUP);
result++;
}
END_POS = result;
result = NULL;
result = strstr((char*)pbData, "");
    //move to the beginning of the current group
for (i=0; i<(*GroupIndex);i++)
{
result = strstr(result, BEGIN_OF_GROUP);
result++;
}
```

```
for(;; )
{
result = strstr(result, END_OF_DOC);
//check if we exceed the end of group or end of the whole stream
if ( (result > END_POS) || (result==NULL))
break;
else
{
DocCount++;
result++;
}
}
m_TotalNumDocs = DocCount;  // set the number of docs for the group
retval = (DocCount > 1) ? (TRUE): (FALSE);
delete [] pbData;
return retval; }
```

Member method CMyParser::GroupDocs only has one parameter—
GroupIndex, which identifies the current group being processed. So the
function sets a start and end position for searching for and counting the
documents.

14. Now that BizTalk knows the group it will deal with, it will move to the
most important function in the whole process: GetNextDocument. In this
function, you need to extract the single document and put it into the dictionary
WORKING_DATA entry. I included the utility include file—computil.cpp—for
easy dictionary operation. This is the utility file that comes from Commerce
Server SDK. You can download this file from the Microsoft web site—http://
www.microsoft.com/biztalk/techinfo/development/2000/wp_parsersAnd
Serializers. Now let's have a look at how we can get the document for BizTalk.

```
HRESULT STDMETHODCALLTYPE CMyParser::GetNextDocument(
    IDictionary __RPC_FAR *Dict,
    BSTR DocName,
    BOOL __RPC_FAR *DocIsValid,
    BOOL __RPC_FAR *LastDocument,
    enum GeneratedReceiptLevel __RPC_FAR *ReceiptGenerated,
    BOOL __RPC_FAR *DocIsReceipt,
    BSTR __RPC_FAR *CorrelationCompProgID)
{
HRESULT hr;
// we do not deal with receipt in this case study
*DocIsReceipt = FALSE;
*ReceiptGenerated = NoReceiptGenerated;
m_CurrentDocument++;  //current group document counter
m_TotalDoc++;     //total document counter
```

```
//ok we need to put the next document into the WORKING_DATA fields of *Dict
CComBSTR BSTRDoc;
*DocIsValid = GetDoc(&BSTRDoc);   //get the document stream
hr = PutDictValue(Dict, L"WORKING_DATA", BSTRDoc);
*LastDocument=(m_CurrentDocument==m_TotalNumDocs) ? (TRUE):(FALSE); //if
this is the last document
return hr;
}
/*
```

Please notice that we need to tell BizTalk whether this is the
last document we deal with in parameter *LastDocument. The real
work is all in the help function GetDoc().

```
*/

BOOL CMyParser::GetDoc(BSTR*Doc)
{
HRESULT hr;
BOOL retval = FALSE;
CComBSTR bstrData;
STATSTG stats = {0};
LARGE_INTEGER Move = {0};
BYTE*pbData= 0;
ULONG bytesread;
char * result = NULL;

hr=m_pData->Stat(&stats, 0);
if(SUCCEEDED(hr))
{
//make sure we are at the beginning of the stream
Move.QuadPart=0;
hr = m_pData->Seek(Move,STREAM_SEEK_SET,NULL);
}
//we load the whole document here
pbData = new BYTE[stats.cbSize.LowPart + 1];
hr = m_pData->Read((void*)pbData, stats.cbSize.LowPart, &bytesread);
//make sure the last byte is null
memset(pbData+bytesread,0,1);

//we get the end position for the current doc
result = strstr((char*)pbData, "");
char *BEGIN_POS, *END_POS;
    long DocLength;
for (int i=0; i<(m_TotalDoc);i++)
```

```
{
result = strstr(result, END_OF_DOC);
result++;
}
END_POS = result + strlen(END_OF_DOC) - 2;

//now we search from the begin of the current document
result = NULL;
result = strstr((char*)pbData, "");
for ( i=0; i<m_TotalDoc;i++)
{
result = strstr(result, BEGIN_OF_DOC);
result++;
}
BEGIN_POS = result - 1;
m_DocBegin = BEGIN_POS;
//the length for the current document
DocLength = END_POS - BEGIN_POS + 1;
m_DocLen = DocLength;
//we store the total length of the document till now
m_LastLen = m_LastLen + DocLength;
    //we copy the document we want into a string
char * pCurrentDocument;
pCurrentDocument = new char[DocLength+1];
memset((void*)pCurrentDocument,0, DocLength+ 1);
strncpy(pCurrentDocument, (char*)BEGIN_POS, DocLength);
bstrData = pCurrentDocument;
*Doc = bstrData.Detach();
    retval = TRUE;
delete [] pCurrentDocument;
delete [] pbData;
return retval;
}
```

Our plan was to find the end and beginning of the document and then to copy the bytes into a string. The whole logic of the program should be very clear to you, but counting the position may be a bit tricky.

15. Now BizTalk needs to log the original document into the tracking database, so you need information from the function GetNativeDocumentOffsets:

```
HRESULT STDMETHODCALLTYPE CMyParser::GetNativeDocumentOffsets(
     BOOL __RPC_FAR *SizeFromXMLDoc,
     LARGE_INTEGER __RPC_FAR *StartOffset,
     long __RPC_FAR *DocLength)
```

```
{
//we tell BizTalk that we will set the information by ourselves.
*SizeFromXMLDoc = FALSE;
StartOffset->QuadPart= m_DocBegin;*DocLength = m_DocLen;
return S_OK;
}
```

The purpose of this method is to inform BizTalk Server how to extract the last parsed document in the stream. This will enable BizTalk Server to log the incoming document in its native format. We must set the parameter *SizeFromXMLDoc to False; otherwise, BizTalk will have no idea how to read the native document. The information we need to provide here is the start position and length of the last parsed document.

16. If the document BizTalk processed is not the last document, it will continue to call GetNextDocument and GetNativeDocumentOffsets. After BizTalk finishes parsing all the documents in the group, the next method it will call is GetGroupSize. This function will inform BizTalk Server if this is the last group. If it is, the process ends here; if it isn't, a new loop begins: GetGroupDetails to GetNextDocument to GetNativeDocumentOffsets to GetGroupSize.

```
HRESULT STDMETHODCALLTYPE CMyParser::GetGroupSize(
      long __RPC_FAR *GroupSize,
      BOOL __RPC_FAR *LastGroup)
{
*LastGroup = (m_CurrentGroup==m_TotalGroups) ? (TRUE) : (FALSE);
return S_OK;
}
```

Keep one thing in mind: After BizTalk leaves your parser, the seek point of the stream should not stay at the beginning of the stream. Otherwise, BizTalk will complain that nothing is read in the event log. You can test this by adding code to move the stream to its beginning position at the end of the GetGroupSize function.

17. Compile the project. Start up BizTalk Administration. Open the Server Group Properties dialog box Parsers tab, and click the Refresh button. Move your parser to the first item, as illustrated in Figure 16-5. Save your settings. Now you are ready to see the results of your hard work.

18. Drop the test message into C:\ParserIn directory. After a few seconds, you should see three parsed documents in the C:\ParserOut directory.

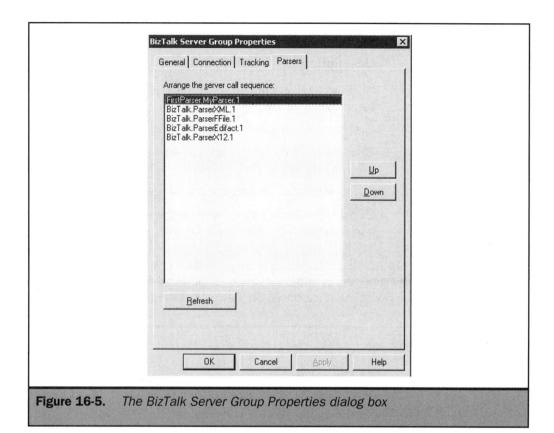

Figure 16-5.   *The BizTalk Server Group Properties dialog box*

Production Concerns for the Sample Parser

The code presented here can only handle messages from file (ASCII text), not Unicode messages (for example, from MSMQ).

Also, the code is not optimized. In a production environment, you need to code more efficiently and add an error-handling mechanism.

As you have seen, "implementing a parser" means to parse the incoming message into pieces BizTalk Server can understand.

Custom Serializer

Serializer does exactly the opposite of the parser; it writes the document to a particular format from the internal XML presentation. Instead of having the seven methods of a parser interface, serializer's IBizTalkSerializerComponent interface only has five methods.

The following table lists the five methods of the interface IBizTalkSerializerComponent:

Method	Description
AddDocument	Adds an XML document for storage by the serializer component.
GetDocInfo	Gets details of the document.
GetGroupInfo	Gets details of the group, such as size and offset, for the Tracking database. Only called when there are groups.
GetInterchangeInfo	Gets information about the interchange created.
Init	Outputs the document instance to the serializer component and indicates where it should be sent.

Now let's have a look at the call sequence of these methods. See Figure 16-6.

The following tables show the possible sequences of calling the methods of the IBizTalkSerializerComponent interface, based on the various sample interchanges.

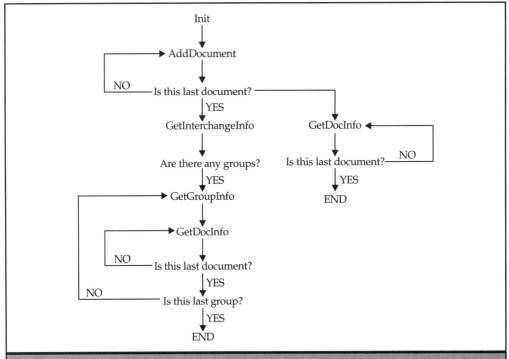

Figure 16-6. *Calling sequence of methods in IBizTalkSerializerComponent interface*

If you have an interchange with one document, the methods are called in the following sequence:

Method	Return
Init	The NumDocs parameter is set to 1.
AddDocument	The DocHandle parameter is set to 0.
GetInterchangeInfo	The numGroups parameter is set to 0.
GetDocInfo	The DocHandle parameter is set to 0.

If you have an interchange with one group, with one document in the group, the methods are called in the following sequence:

Method	Return
Init	The NumDocs parameter is set to 1.
AddDocument	The DocHandle parameter is set to 0.
GetInterchangeInfo	The numGroups parameter is set to 1.
GetGroupInfo	The NumDocs parameter is set to 1.
GetDocInfo	The DocHandle parameter is set to 0.

If you have an interchange with two groups, with two documents in the first group and one in the second, the methods are called in the following sequence (assuming support of batching):

Method	Return
Init	The NumDocs parameter is set to 3.
AddDocument	The handle parameter is set to 0.
AddDocument	The handle parameter is set to 1.
AddDocument	The handle parameter is set to 2.
GetInterchangeInfo	The numGroups parameter is set to 2.
GetGroupInfo	The NumDocs parameter is set to 2.
GetDocInfo	The handle parameter is set to 1.
GetDocInfo	The handle parameter is set to 0.
GetGroupInfo	The NumDocs parameter is set to 1.
GetDocInfo	The handle parameter is set to 2.

Notice that for the current release of this interface, the third scenario will never happen, because the interface can only process one document at a time. In other words, it does not support batches. That's the reason why the EDI serializer cannot output compressed EDI messages. For this reason, it is impossible for us to implement a serializer that can produce the same document as our input test file.

The implementation of the serializer is quite similar to the parser. Just remember several things:

- You need to create a specification for the output format as envelope. The envelope format must be "CUSTOM".

- In the Channel advanced settings, you need to choose your serializer explicitly.

Let's have a look here at the most important methods: Init and AddDocument. A possible implementation for Init( ) will be

```
HRESULT STDMETHODCALLTYPE CMySerializer::Init(BSTR srcQual, BSTR srcID,
BSTR destQual, BSTR destID,
long EnvID, IDictionary __RPC_FAR *pDelimiters,
IStream __RPC_FAR *OutputStream, long NumDocs, long PortID)
{
HRESULT hr;
//grab the stream pointer, you won't get another chance, BizTalk will not
return the Stream to the component again
hr = OutputStream->AddRef ();
m_DataStream = OutputStream;
//make sure the stream is at the beginning.
Move.QuadPart = 0;
hr = m_DataStream->Seek (Move, STREAM_SEEK_SET, NULL);
return hr;
}
```

The parameter NumDocs will always be 1 in this release. So it can only process one document for the moment.

AddDocument is the place you do your work to reformat the message. The internal XML representation of the data is in the WORKING_DATA entry in the dictionary. You transform it and then store it into the stream.

A possible implementation for AddDocument will be

```
HRESULT STDMETHODCALLTYPE CMySerializer::AddDocument(long DocHandle,
IDictionary __RPC_FAR *Transport,
BSTR TrackID, long ChannelID)
{
```

```
HRESULT  hr;
CcomVariant  IncomingXML;
CComBSTR  OutgoingXML;
ULONG  byteswritten;
m_LastDocHandle = DocHandle; //you need to store this number for GetDocInfo
hr = GetDictValue(Transport, L"working_data", &IncomingXML);
//just ensuring proper type
if(SUCCEEDED(hr)){hr = IncomingXML.ChangeType (VT_BSTR);}
OutgoingXML+="<ParserDocGroups><Group name=\"Group1\">";
OutgoingXML+=IncomingXML.bstrVal ;
OutgoingXML+="</Group></ParserDocGroups>";
if(SUCCEEDED(hr))
{
m_LastDocLength = OutgoingXML.Length () * 2;
hr = m_DataStream->Write((void*)OutgoingXML.m_str , m_LastDocLength,
&byteswritten);
m_CurrentStreamPos +=byteswritten;
}
return hr;
}
```

Writing the remaining part of the program will be an exercise for you. With the knowledge from the parser implementation, you should not have problems.

Custom Functoid

While BizTalk Mapper comes with a lot of standard functoids, from time to time you will have specific requirements in data transformation—for example, a value lookup functoid for an R/3 system. The separation of data transformation from application integration is very important; otherwise, you will never have a universal interface that can handle a bunch of similar integration scenarios. For example, if you build a customer-number lookup function into your integration code, you might not be able to reuse this integration interface, because the lookup procedure might change in another scenario.

There are two ways, covered next, that you can implement specific transformation logic.

Using the Scripting Functoid

On the Advanced tab of the Functoid Palette, the first functoid is the Scripting functoid. This functoid accepts a variable number of parameters, and you have to code the logic in VBScript.

Developing Your Own Functoid

In terms of data transformation, there is no difference between using the Scripting functoid and developing a custom functoid. The difference lies in reusability. If the transformation logic is generic, you should implement it as a custom functoid in order to reuse it in different scenarios. If the transformation logic is project dependent, you may want to use the Scripting functoid.

A functoid component is an in-process COM DLL implementing the IFunctoid interface. The code layout of the IFunctoid implementation is fixed. You can just copy the functoid sample in the BizTalk Server 2000 SDK as a template for your own implementation.

The IFunctoid interface has two properties and three methods, shown in the two tables that follow.

Property Name	Description
FunctionsCount	A read-only long value indicating how many functoids are implemented by the DLL
Version	A read-only long value indicating the version of the DLL

Method Name	Description
GetFunctionParameter	Returns the connection-type bit flags for the specified parameter, which is identified by an index number
GetScriptBuffer	Returns the script code used to implement the functoid
GetFunctionDescripter	Returns information about a specific functoid, which is identified by an index number

The GetFunctionParameter method has the following signature:

```
object.GetFunctionParameter( _
    funcId As FUNCID, _
    lParameter As Long _
)
```

Input parameter funcId is a zero-based long value identifying the functoid inside the component; it is only unique inside the DLL. Input parameter lParameter is a zero-based long value identifying the parameters of the functoid; a value of –1 indicates the parameter is an output parameter. The return value is one of the values of CONNECTION_TYPE enumeration. The CONNECTION_TYPE is used by the Mapper to control the type of links allowed for both input and output parameters.

The CONNECTION_TYPE enumeration defines the following values:

Name	Value	Description
CONNECT_TYPE_NONE	0	The connection type is none.
CONNECT_TYPE_FIELD	1	The connection type is field.
CONNECT_TYPE_RECORD	2	The connection type is record.
CONNECT_TYPE_RECORD_CONTENT	4	The connection type is record content.
CONNECT_TYPE_FUNC_STRING	8	The connection type function is string.
CONNECT_TYPE_FUNC_MATH	16	The connection type function is mathematical.
CONNECT_TYPE_FUNC_DATACONV	32	The connection type function is data conversion.
CONNECT_TYPE_FUNC_DATETIME_FMT	64	The connection type function is date/time format.
CONNECT_TYPE_FUNC_SCIENTIFIC	128	The connection type function is scientific.
CONNECT_TYPE_FUNC_BOOLEAN	256	The connection type function is Boolean.
CONNECT_TYPE_FUNC_SCRIPTER	512	The connection type function is script.
CONNECT_TYPE_FUNC_COUNT	1024	The connection type function is count.
CONNECT_TYPE_FUNC_INDEX	2048	The connection type function is index.
CONNECT_TYPE_FUNC_CUMULATIVE	4096	The connection type function is cumulative.
CONNECT_TYPE_FUNC_VALUE_MAPPING	8192	The connection type function is value mapping.
CONNECT_TYPE_FUNC_LOOPING	16384	The connection type function is looping.
CONNECT_TYPE_FUNC_ITERATION	32768	The connection type function is iteration.

Name	Value	Description
CONNECT_TYPE_FUNC_DBLOOKUP	65536	The connection type function is database lookup.
CONNECT_TYPE_FUNC_DBEXTRACT	131072	The connection type function is database extraction.
CONNECT_TYPE_ALL	−1	The connection type includes all connection types.
CONNECT_TYPE_ALL_EXCEPT_ RECORD	−3	The connection type includes all connection types except records.

The GetScriptBuffer method has the following signature:

```
object.GetScriptBuffer( _
    cFuncId As FUNCID, _
    lInputParameters As Long _
)
```

Parameter cFuncId is the unique zero-based functoid identifier inside the DLL. Parameter lInputParameters is the number of the connected input parameters of the functoid. The return value is a string of the implementation code of the functoid. As you are aware, it is the script code returned here that controls the behavior of the functoid, and the script code is the only way you can perform your transformation logic. Implementation of a functoid will not allow you to do any operation beyond the reach of the VBScript code (in this release).

The GetFunctionDescripter method has the following signature:

```
object.GetFunctionDescripter( _
    lIndex As Long, _
pFuncCategory As, _
pScriptCategory As SCRIPT_CATEGORY, _
pFuncType As FUNC_TYPE, _
pbstrName As String, _
pbstrToolTip As String, _
plBitmapID As Long, _
plParmCount As Long _
)
```

The following table lists descriptions of parameters.

Parameter Name	Description
lIndex	Index of the functoid.
pFuncCategory	A value of FUNC_CATEGORY enumeration.
pScriptCategory	A value of SCRIPT_CATEGORY. This value must be set to SCRIPT_CATEGORY_VBSCRIPT for this release.
pFuncType	A value of FUNC_TYPE.
pbstrName	Name of the functoid.
pbstrToolTip	ToolTip text for the functoid.
plBitmapID	Icon ID for the functoid. You need to use the VB Resource Editor to add the icon and give it a unique ID number.
plParmCount	Number of the parameters implemented by the functoid.
Return value	Unique identifier of the functoid.

The FUNC_CATEGORY enumeration defines the following values:

Name	Value	Description
FUNC_CATEGORY_STRING	3	The function category is string.
FUNC_CATEGORY_MATH	4	The function category is mathematical.
FUNC_CATEGORY_DATACONV	5	The function category is data conversion.
FUNC_CATEGORY_DATETIME_FMT	6	The function category is date/time format.
FUNC_CATEGORY_SCIENTIFIC	7	The function category is scientific.
FUNC_CATEGORY_BOOLEAN	8	The function category is Boolean.
FUNC_CATEGORY_SCRIPTER	9	The function category is script.
FUNC_CATEGORY_COUNT	10	The function category is count. This value is not supported for this release.

Name	Value	Description
FUNC_CATEGORY_INDEX	11	The function category is index.
FUNC_CATEGORY_CUMULATIVE	12	The function category is cumulative.
FUNC_CATEGORY_VALUE_MAPPING	13	The function category is value mapping. This value is not supported for this release.
FUNC_CATEGORY_LOOPING	14	The function category is looping. This value is not supported for this release.
FUNC_CATEGORY_ITERATION	15	The function category is iteration. This value is not supported for this release.
FUNC_CATEGORY_DBLOOKUP	16	The function category is database lookup.
FUNC_CATEGORY_DBEXTRACT	17	The function category is database extraction.
FUNC_CATEGORY_UNKNOWN	31	The function category is unknown.

The SCRIPT_CATEGORY enumeration defines the following values:

Name	Value	Description
SCRIPT_CATEGORY_VBSCRIPT	0	The custom functoid function is written in the Microsoft Visual Basic Scripting Edition (VBScript) language.
SCRIPT_CATEGORY_JSCRIPT	1	The custom functoid function is written in the Microsoft JScript language. This value is not supported for this release.
SCRIPT_CATEGORY_XSLSCRIPT	2	The custom functoid function is written in the Extensible Stylesheet Language (XSL). This value is not supported for this release.

The FUNC_TYPE enumeration defines the following values:

Name	Value	Description
FUNC_TYPE_STD	1	The functoid accepts a fixed number of inputs.
FUNC_TYPE_VARIABLEINPUT	2	The functoid accepts a variable number of inputs.
FUNC_TYPE_SCRIPTOR	3	The functoid's script code can be modified by the user.

The best way to understand this interface is to walk through a concrete implementation. Please refer to the SDK SampleFunctoid sample. It is well commented and easy to understand. There is really nothing complicated in implementing a functoid. When you implement your own functoid, the following steps are required:

1. Create an ActiveX DLL project in Visual Basic.

2. Rename the project.

3. Rename the default class module. (The progID for this component will be projectname.classmodulename.)

4. Choose Project | References, and add the following reference to your project: **Microsoft BizTalk Server Canned Functoids 1.0 Type Library**.

5. After you create the DLL, remember to register your component with the following script:

```
Windows Registry Editor Version 5.00

[HKEY_CLASSES_ROOT\CLSID\{DE549168-65D8-48D7-A2C3-
8B66F71F0E57}\Implemented Categories\{2560F3BF-DB47-11d2-B3AE-
00C04F72D6C1}]
```

6. Replace the CLSID with your component CLSID. The number 2560F3BF-DB47-11d2-B3AE-00C04F72D6C1 represents the implementation category canned function. It tells BizTalk Server that this component implements the IFunctoid interface.

XLANG Schedule Interfaces

You can programmatically administrate and load the XLANG schedule through a group of interfaces provided by the XLANG run time. We can divide interfaces into two groups: administration interfaces and schedule instance interfaces.

Administration Interfaces

The interfaces in this section provide access to XLANG Scheduler System Managers and XLANG group managers. (A *group manager* is the COM+ application that has been designated as an XLANG schedule host.) Each computer can have only one XLANG Scheduler System Manager running. An XLANG Scheduler System Manager provides moniker resolution and maintains a collection of group managers.

IWFSystemAdmin

This interface gives you control over all the XLANG Scheduler Engines, or XLANG Group Manager. The XLANG Scheduler Engine is the COM+ application designated as an XLANG scheduler engine. By default, your system will have the BizTalk Standard XLANG scheduler engine (sked://!XLANG Scheduler). In VB, the name of this interface is SysMgr.

The IWFSystemAdmin interface defines the following properties:

Property	Type	Description
Count	long	Contains the number of group managers associated with this XLANG Scheduler System Manager
FullyQualifiedName	BSTR	Contains the fully qualified DNS-style name of the XLANG Scheduler System Manager
IsWorkflowHost	VARIANT_BOOL	Checks whether the COM+ server application is an XLANG Scheduler Engine host
Item	BSTR	Returns a reference to the named schedule group
UseFileDSN	VARIANT_BOOL	Indicates whether a file Data Source Name (DSN) is used for dehydrating the XLANG schedule instances

The IWFSystemAdmin interface defines the following methods:

Method	Description
ShutdownAll	Shuts down all group managers
ShutdownApp	Shuts down a specific group manager
Startup	Starts all group managers
TestAdminStatus	Checks a caller for XLANG Scheduler Engine administrator access

The following VB code can enumerate all the XLANG Scheduler Engines in your system. (By default, you will only get one—the one installed by BizTalk Server.)

You need to add XLANG Scheduler–System Manager and XLANG Scheduler Runtime Type Library to your VB project references.

```
Dim SchedulerEngines As SysMgr
Dim DetailEngine As IWFGroupAdmin
Set SchedulerEngines = GetObject("sked://")
For Each DetailEngine In SchedulerEngines
    MsgBox ("Scheduler Engine: " + DetailEngine.FullyQualifiedName)
Next
```

GroupAdmin

Inside the IWFSystemAdmin are IWFGroupAdmin objects. For example, one of them will be the interface pointing to the default XLANG Scheduler Engine (sked://!XLANG Scheduler).

The IWFGroupAdmin interface defines the following properties:

Property	Type	Description
Count	long	The number of running schedule instances associated with this group manager.
FullyQualifiedName	BSTR	The moniker of this group manager.

Property	Type	Description
InstanceIsResident	VARIANT_BOOL	A value that indicates whether the specified schedule instance currently resides in memory.
InstanceIsSuspended	VARIANT_BOOL	A value that indicates whether the specified schedule instance is currently in a suspended state.
Name	BSTR	The name of this group manager.
UseFileDSN	VARIANT_BOOL	A value that indicates whether a file Data Source Name (DSN) is used for dehydrating the schedule instances.

The IWFGroupAdmin interface defines the following methods:

Method	Description
ResumeInstance	Resumes the execution of a schedule in a suspended state
Shutdown	Dehydrates all running schedule instances and stops the group manager
Startup	Starts all the dehydrated schedule instances for the current group manager
SuspendInstance	Pauses execution of the schedule instance
TerminateInstance	Stops execution of the schedule instance

Through this interface, you will be able to get to the detail XLANG schedule instance. The next step is how to manipulate detail instances, and this is the task of the next two interfaces.

The following VB code enumerates the names of all the running XLANG schedule instances:

```
Dim SchedulerEngines As SysMgr
Dim DetailEngine As IWFGroupAdmin
Dim ScheduleInstance As IWFWorkflowInstance
Set SchedulerEngines = GetObject("sked://")
For Each DetailEngine In SchedulerEngines
    MsgBox ("Scheduler Engine: " + DetailEngine.FullyQualifiedName)
    For Each ScheduleInstance In DetailEngine
```

```
        MsgBox ("XLANG Schedule: " + ScheduleInstance.FullyQualifiedName)
    Next
Next
```

Schedule Instance Interface

The interfaces in this section provide access to XLANG schedule instances and XLANG ports. An XLANG *schedule instance* is a running XLANG schedule that can return status and other information. A proxy interface can be used to access the COM-bound port in the XLANG schedule.

WFWorkflowInstance

After you get the schedule instance from the IWFGroupAdmin interface, you can use the IWFWorkflowInstance interface to navigate the ports of an XLANG schedule instance, check the completion status, and determine whether the schedule instance completed successfully. Use this interface to gather information about a specific, running schedule instance. Following is the detail of this interface.

The IWFWorkflowInstance interface defines the following properties:

Property	Type	Description
CompletionStatus	Long	A value that indicates the success or failure of the schedule instance.
FullPortName	BSTR	The full name of a port in a form usable by the associated technology.
FullyQualifiedName	BSTR	The fully qualified name of this schedule instance.
InstanceId	BSTR	The unique identifier associated with this schedule instance.
IsCompleted	VARIANT_BOOL	A value that indicates whether the schedule instance completed.
ModuleId	BSTR	The unique identifier of the XML module that contains the schedule and binding information.

Property	Type	Description
ModuleName	BSTR	The name of the XML module that contains the schedule and binding information.
ParentInstanceID	BSTR	The unique identifier of the parent schedule instance.
Port	IUnknown	A reference to the named port. This is applicable only to COM-based port bindings.

The IWFWorkflowInstance interface defines the following method:

Method	Description
WaitForCompletion	Blocks until the schedule instance completes

After you get the detail schedule instance, you might want to execute a method on the port bound to a COM object. You can do this by using the last interface in the group.

FProxy

By using this interface, you can execute a port's COM object method. The IWFProxy interface defines the following properties:

Property	Type	Description
FullyQualifiedName	BSTR	The fully qualified name of a COM-bound port
WorkflowInstance	IWFWorkflowInstance	The current schedule instance

The following code shows that you can execute a COM method on a specific port:

```
Dim SchedulerEngines As SysMgr
Dim DetailEngine As IWFGroupAdmin
Dim ScheduleInstance As IWFWorkflowInstance
Dim MyPort As IWFProxy
```

```
Set SchedulerEngines = GetObject("sked://")
For Each DetailEngine In SchedulerEngines
    MsgBox ("Scheduler Engine: " + DetailEngine.FullyQualifiedName)
    For Each ScheduleInstance In DetailEngine
        MsgBox ("XLANG Schedule: " + ScheduleInstance.FullyQualifiedName)
        Set MyPort = ScheduleInstance.Port("MyPort")
        MyPort.ExecuteMyCOMMethod
    Next
Next
```

Though the interfaces discussed in this section are organized in a hierarchy, when you do real programming, it is unnecessary to navigate from top interfaces to get to a certain object. For all the interfaces, you can also get objects by using monikers. (The top-down navigation method is useful when you develop some utility programs for handling XLANG Scheduler and XLANG schedule instances.)

For the IWFGroupAdmin interface:

```
Dim DetailEngine As IWFGroupAdmin
Set DetailEngine = GetObject("sked://!XLANG Scheduler")
```

For the IWFWorkflowInstance:

```
Dim ScheduleInstance As IWFWorkflowInstance
Set ScheduleInstance = GetObject("sked:///C:\myschedules.skx")
```

For the IWFProxy:

```
Dim MyPort As Object
Set MyPort = GetObject("sked:///C:\ myschedules.skx/myport")
```

In this chapter, we covered some major interfaces offered by the BizTalk Server SDK. You can see that BizTalk Server is not just a prepackaged solution, but also a powerful development platform. By using the SDK, you can reach nearly every corner of BizTalk Server and customize it to meet your business requirements. As the .NET platform emerges, I hope that we can use the .NET programming languages to program these interfaces.

Chapter 17

Application Integration
and Web Services

679

The true power of BizTalk Server is shown by its open, easy, and flexible integration with existing applications and environments. Integration is provided by BizTalk Server Messaging, which connects directly to an application or proprietary protocol. If BizTalk Server doesn't already provide the appropriate connection needs for your applications or architecture—for example, HTTP (HyperText Transfer Protocol), MSQueue, or SMTP (Simple Mail Transfer Protocol)—you can easily add it. The flexibility and power of BizTalk's integration come from normal Component Object Model (COM) components that implement a special BizTalk interface. The type of application integration or connection used determines which type of BizTalk interface is needed, from simple to complex configurations. These COM components in BizTalk's world are called *Application Integration Components*, or *AICs*.

Introducing Application Integration Components

AICs are normal COM components that implement a specific BizTalk Server application integration interface. These interfaces are used internally by BizTalk Messaging Services for all document transport methods. The two types of interfaces to AICs are called *lightweight* and *pipeline*. These interfaces are discussed in detail in the sections "Lightweight AICs" and "Pipeline AICs", later in this chapter.

Lightweight AICs implement the IBTSAppIntegration interface, which is the simplest interface to implement because it does not provide custom BizTalk Server Channel–specific configurations or properties. BizTalk Server Channel configuration options are provided by the pipeline interfaces, IPipelineComponent and IPipelineComponentAdmin, which let you configure the component at design time.

Building AICs

AICs can be used to connect channeled BizTalk outbound documents to your applications or protocols. You can customize how BizTalk communicates with your application architecture. For example, you can use an AIC to extend BizTalk to channel or route documents through a proprietary protocol. Another frequently requested AIC sends BizTalk documents directly to a database. A less obvious need for an AIC might be to provide extra modifications of outbound documents. Such modifications could range from document encryption, compression, or even (Extensible Markup Language) XML namespace support. Depending on your needs, AICs can provide the ultimate flexibility to modify documents, connect, or integrate BizTalk into an application architecture. Figure 17-1 depicts the openness provided by the BizTalk Messaging Port transports supplied via AICs.

How AICs Work

When an application submits a document to BizTalk Interchange interfaces, BizTalk will begin to process the document in the BizTalk Messaging Channel. In the channel, the document is parsed, mapped, serialized, and then transmitted to a messaging port that

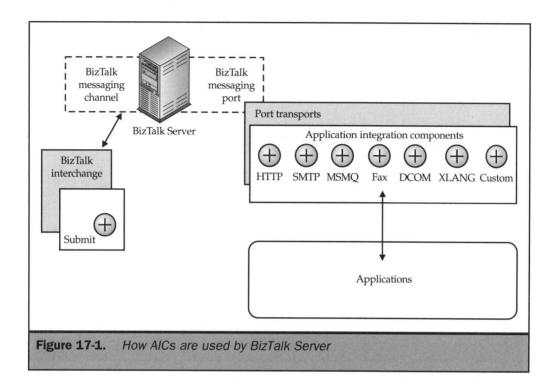

Figure 17-1.   *How AICs are used by BizTalk Server*

defines which AIC should be instantiated by BizTalk. After instantiating the AIC, BizTalk loads the appropriate AIC run-time configurations and passes the document into it. If the document was submitted to the channel synchronously, the AIC returns the resulting document on the same thread. Figure 17-2 shows how document transportation works.

Native BizTalk Server AICs

BizTalk ships with numerous AICs that should represent the starting point before you build custom AICs. Microsoft, from the early beta releases of BizTalk, has added and removed a couple of AICs. Table 17-1 shows a summary of the AICs that currently exist in BizTalk.

Alternative Methods of Integration

One of the downfalls of AICs is that they interact directly with BizTalk Messaging Services, and thus require that you build a specific component for specific interaction with BizTalk. Unfortunately, you may find yourself in a predicament in which you do not have the option of building AICs, such as when your application is dependent on several documents or a particular business logic. Thus, an alternative solution to AICs, BizTalk Orchestration, lets you call COM components or script components to handle the necessary application integration directly, without the need to implement any specific BizTalk interfaces. This is extremely handy, for example, when you're using a third-party application and do not have control of the application interfaces.

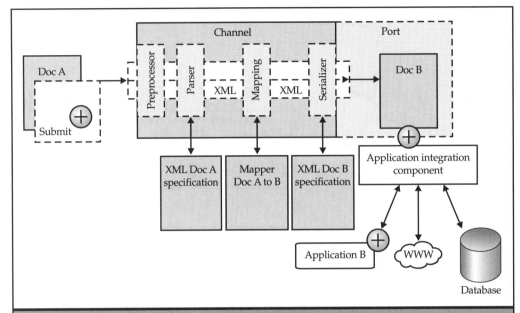

Figure 17-2. *The actions of a document submitted into an AIC*

AIC Name	Description	ProgID	BizTalk Version
Microsoft BizTalk Scriptor Pipeline Component (ScriptorAIC)	A pipeline AIC that lets you run a script as your AIC; helpful for debugging	BizTalk.Scriptor.1	BizTalk Server 2000 final release
Microsoft BizTalk Orchestration Activation Component	A pipeline AIC activated when you set the port to run an XLANG schedule; configured directly in the Messaging Port Properties Wizard, it has no corresponding pipeline ASP pages	BizTalk.BPOActivation.1	BizTalk Server 2000 final release
Microsoft BizTalk BinaryFromText Pipeline Component	A pipeline AIC that decodes encode64 text to binary format	BizTalk.BinaryFromText.1	BizTalk Server 2000 final release

Table 17-1. *AICs That Ship with BizTalk Server in ShareComp.dll*

AIC Name	Description	ProgID	BizTalk Version
Microsoft BizTalk BinaryToText Pipeline Component	A pipeline AIC that encodes binary to encode64 text format	BizTalk.BinaryToText.1	BizTalk Server 2000 final release
Microsoft BizTalk DecodeMIME Pipeline Component	A pipeline AIC that decodes MIME messages; used when you specify the Ports Encoding Type in the Port Wizard	BizTalk.DecodeMIME.1	BizTalk Server 2000 final release
Microsoft BizTalk DecodeSMIME Pipeline Component	A pipeline AIC that decodes S/MIME messages; used when you specify the Ports Encoding Type as MIME and Encryption type as SMIME in the Port Wizard	BizTalk.DecodeSMIME.1	BizTalk final release
Microsoft BizTalk DecryptPKCS Pipeline Component	A pipeline AIC that decodes Digital Certificate when using SMIME messages; used when you specify the Ports Encoding Type as MIME and Encryption type as SMIME, and select a Digital Certificate in the Port Wizard	BizTalk.DecryptPKCS.1	BizTalk Server 2000 final release
Microsoft BizTalk DigitalSig Pipeline Component	A pipeline AIC that adds an S/MIME digital signature to messages; used when you specify the ports to use a Signature in the Port Wizard	BizTalk.DigitalSig.1	BizTalk Server 2000 final release

Table 17-1. *AICs That Ship with BizTalk Server in ShareComp.dll* (continued)

AIC Name	Description	ProgID	BizTalk Version
Microsoft BizTalk EncodeMIME Pipeline Component	A pipeline AIC that encodes MIME messages; used when you specify the Ports Encoding Type in the Port Wizard	BizTalk.EncodeMIME.1	BizTalk Server 2000 final release
Microsoft BizTalk EncodeSMIME Pipeline Component	A pipeline AIC that encodes S/MIME messages; used when you specify the Ports Encoding Type as MIME and Encryption type as SMIME in the Port Wizard	BizTalk.EncodeSMIME.1	BizTalk Server 2000 final release
Microsoft BizTalk EncryptPKCS Pipeline Component	A pipeline AIC that encrypts Digital Certificate when using SMIME messages; used when you specify the Ports Encoding Type as MIME and Encryption Type as SMIME, and select a Digital Certificate in the Port Wizard	BizTalk.EncryptPKCS.1	BizTalk Server 2000 final release
Microsoft BizTalk SendFax Pipeline Component	A pipeline AIC used to send a document fax from a port; interface exists in the released version of BizTalk component but is not registered nor are the supporting pipeline configuration files shipped with the final release	BizTalk.SendFax.1	BizTalk Server Preview

Table 17-1.   *AICs That Ship with BizTalk Server in ShareComp.dll* (continued)

AIC Name	Description	ProgID	BizTalk Version
Microsoft BizTalk SendFTP Pipeline Component	A pipeline AIC used to send a document via FTP from a port; interface exists in the released version of BizTalk component but is not registered nor are the supporting pipeline configuration files shipped with the final release	BizTalk.SendFTP.1	Pre-BizTalk release
Microsoft BizTalk SendHTTPX Component	A pipeline AIC used when setting the Port Transport Type to HTTP or HTTPS; extra HTTP configuration information is provided by the corresponding pipeline ASP pages	BizTalk.SendHTTPX,1	BizTalk Server 2000 final release
Microsoft BizTalk SendLocalFile Pipeline Component	A pipeline AIC used when setting the Port Transport Type to File; configuration info is provided by the corresponding pipeline ASP pages	BizTalk.SendLocalFile.1	BizTalk Server 2000 final release
Microsoft BizTalk SendMSMQ Pipeline Component	A pipeline AIC used when setting the Port Transport Type to Message Queue; extra configuration info is provided by the corresponding pipeline ASP pages	BizTalk.SendMSMQ.1	BizTalk Server 2000 final release

Table 17-1. *AICs That Ship with BizTalk Server in ShareComp.dll* (continued)

AIC Name	Description	ProgID	BizTalk Version
Microsoft BizTalk SendSMTP Pipeline Component	A pipeline AIC used when setting the Port Transport Type to SMTP; extra configuration info is provided by the corresponding pipeline ASP pages	BizTalk.SendSMTP.1	BizTalk Server 2000 final release
Microsoft BizTalk VerifyDigitalSig Pipeline Component	A pipeline AIC that validates an S/MIME digital signature	BizTalk.VerifyDigitalSig.1	BizTalk Server 2000 final release
Microsoft BizTalk Server Application Integration Component Library	AIC that connects to SAP; found in AICComp.dll	BizTalk.App IntegrationSAP.1	BizTalk Server 2000 final release

Table 17-1. *AICs That Ship with BizTalk Server in ShareComp.dll* (continued)

Lightweight AICs

The simplest integration interface supported by BizTalk is *IBTSAppIntegration*. AICs that implement this interface are known as *lightweight* AICs. These interfaces are considered lightweight because they have no design-time configuration support and expose only a single method, *ProcessMessage*, as shown in Figure 17-3. Because no configuration is assumed with lightweight AICs, only the standard COM component–specific configuration information is used and must be configured on an AIC object basis rather than per BizTalk Messaging Channel. The normal COM component configurations apply: hard-coding configuration values in the COM component code, setting up a COM+ constructor string to be used when setting up the COM+ application, reading a specific registry key, and so on. The true benefits of the lightweight AICs are that they are fast and quick to build.

IBTSAppIntegration Interface

The simple IBTSAppIntegration interface can be used to receive a BizTalk document from a BizTalk Messaging Port and return a response document if supplied. The interface defines only one method, called ProcessMessage. Because this interface supports no design-time configuration, the AIC component is instantiated only when the server sends a document to it at run time.

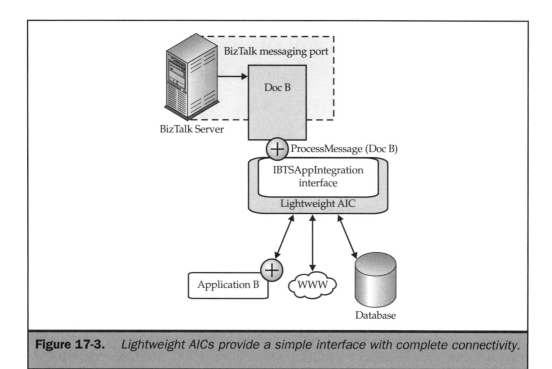

Figure 17-3.   *Lightweight AICs provide a simple interface with complete connectivity.*

ProcessMessage Method   BizTalk Server will execute the ProcessMessage method by passing and returning a document as a string from a BizTalk Messaging Channel. The return document is needed only if the document was submitted via the IInterchange. SubmitSync method. Within the ProcessMessage method, you can add custom code to manipulate, send, and transmit the document. (You must raise errors by equating the Err.number to the appropriate number; see the section "Errors", later in this chapter.)

Following is information needed to add custom code.

- **Windows NT/2000**   Requires Windows 2000 Server Pack1 (SP1) or later
- **Header**   Include btsaic.h
- **Library**   Use Microsoft BizTalk Server Application Interface Components 1.0 Type Library (btscomplib.tlb)

The syntax for ProcessMessage in C++ is

```
HRESULT ProcessMessage(
    BSTR bstrDocument,
    BSTR* pbstrResponseDocument
);
```

where parameter bstrDocument [in] is a BSTR that contains the document, and pbstrResponseDocument [retval, out] is a pointer to a BSTR that contains the response document.

The code returns an error that can be defined by BizTalk Server (see the "Errors" section, later in the chapter).

The syntax for ProcessMessage in Visual Basic is

```
object.ProcessMessage( _
bstrDocument As String _
)
```

where the parameter **bstrDocument** is a string that contains the document. The script returns a string that contains the response document. The Err.Number is equal to the appropriate BizTalk Server-defined error in the section "Errors", later in the chapter. In this case, no error is raised, and BizTalk Server assumes the AIC completed and processed the data.

Creating a Lightweight AIC

The following procedure creates a simple example of a lightweight AIC that makes it possible to connect to a database and update the database with data derived from a string submitted to BizTalk Server. The string could be an XML string that is loaded into an MSXML2.XMLDocument object to ease the extraction of the data for updating. This is accomplished in the following way:

1. Select File | New Project from the menu. In the New Project window, create a Visual Basic ActiveX DLL project by selecting ActiveX DLL.

2. Select Project | Project Properties and rename the project as you wish in the Project Properties window. Rename the class by selecting the default Class1 under Class Modules in the Project Explorer. In the Properties window, rename the Class1. Set the MTSTransactionmode Properties of the Class Properties to a value of 1 – NoTransactions If Debugging Only.

3. Now add the following references to the needed Components via the menu option Project\References:

   - Microsoft BizTalk Server Application Interface Components 1.0 Type Library

   - Microsoft ActiveX Data Objects 2.6 Library

   - Microsoft XML 3.0

   - Custom DataLib4AICs.SaveDB   Data object which encapsulates the NorthWind database update. See sample code setup.

4. Add this code in the Code window:

```
Implements IBTSAppIntegration
```

Add this code:

```
Private Function IBTSAppIntegration_ProcessMessage(ByVal
bstrDocument As String) As String
```

5. Add your business logic in the IBTSAppIntegration_ProcessMessage function. In this example, you'd do the following:

   a. Write code to connect to the database.

   b. Extract XML data to build a SQL Update statement and execute the statement with the connection.

   c. Raise an error value of 2 if an error occurs for BizTalk.

6. Compile the DLL.

7. Add the DLL to your new COM+ application or register the component *with affinity* (see the section "Registering AICs", later in this chapter).

8. In the BizTalk Messaging Manager, create a port with the transport type set to Application Integration Component; then select Previously Compiled DLL AIC Name.

Example Code: DB_LightweightAIC   Notice that the following example code has minimal error handling (if any) to minimize text and aid in readability:

```
Option Explicit
Implements IBTSAppIntegration

Const c_strConnString = "Provider=sqloledb;Data Source=(local);Initial
Catalog=Northwind;"
Const c_strTableName = "Orders"
Const c_strUID = "sa"
Const c_strPassword = "password"


Private m_strLogFullPath As String

Private Function IBTSAppIntegration_ProcessMessage(ByVal bstrDocument As String)
As String
    Dim iReturn As Integer
    On Error GoTo ExecuteError
```

```
    ' call business logic
    Call AddToDB(ByVal bstrDocument)

    IBTSAppIntegration_ProcessMessage = 0

    Exit Function
ExecuteError:
    Err.Raise 2, , "Custom Error Message"
End Function

Private Sub AddToDB(ByVal bstrDocument)
 On Error GoTo ExecuteError

  ' Set normal COM component for inserting in DB
 Dim objSaveDb As DataLib4AICs.SaveDB
 Set objSaveDb = New DataLib4AICs.SaveDB

  ' call normal component to add to db
 Call objSaveDb.AddToDB (bstrDocument, c_strConnString, c_strTableName,
c_strUID, c_strPassword)

  Exit Sub
ExecuteError:
    Err.Raise 2, , "Custom Error Message"
End Sub
```

Pipeline AICs

The simple design of the lightweight AIC does not work well if the AIC needs channel-specific configurations; a pipeline AIC should be used instead. A pipeline AIC is a COM component that implements the IPipelineComponent and IPipelineComponentAdmin interfaces borrowed from Site Server Commerce Edition 3.0 and Microsoft Commerce Server 2000. BizTalk Server uses the pipeline technology to provide a simple, flexible, and easy-to-develop framework for binding design-time configurations to COM components.

The design-time configuration is provided by building specific form-based Active Server Pages (ASP) that correspond to a specific pipeline AIC. The information entered in the ASP is then automatically loaded at run time into the pipeline AIC. At design time, the SetConfigData method saves the configuration data to your pipeline AIC and sends it to a database. At design time, GetConfigData loads the configuration entered from your AIC to the design-time graphical user interface (GUI). The core AIC processing or manipulation of the document that was initially done with the lightweight AIC's IBTSAppIntegration.ProcessMessage method is now done with the IPipelineComponent.Execute method instead. The configuration information and document for processing are passed into the Execute method by BizTalk Server as a Dictionary object. A pipeline AIC must implement the IPipelineComponent interface at a minimum.

IPipelineComponent Interface

The pipeline AIC implements the IPipelineComponent interface. The passing of the document from the BizTalk Messaging Port by BizTalk Server is done via an Execute method. The other method of the IPipelineComponent, the EnableDesign method, easily switches your pipeline AIC from a default run-time component to a design-time component. If your pipeline AIC is in run-time mode and no other pipeline configuration information is required, the IPipelineComponent interface is the only interface required by BizTalk Server. If configuration information is required, before calling the Execute method, BizTalk Server will attempt to load the pipeline configuration information into a transport Dictionary object via another interface called IPipelineComponentAdmin which interfaces methods SetConfigData. BizTalk Server sets the document as a string called "working_data" in the transport dictionary's named entry value. The transport dictionary is then passed via the Execute method, as shown in Figure 17-4.

The EnableDesign Method   The EnableDesign method lets you switch the pipeline AIC from design-time mode to the default run-time or execution mode. BizTalk Server calls the EnableDesign method when the pipeline AIC Property page is displayed. To

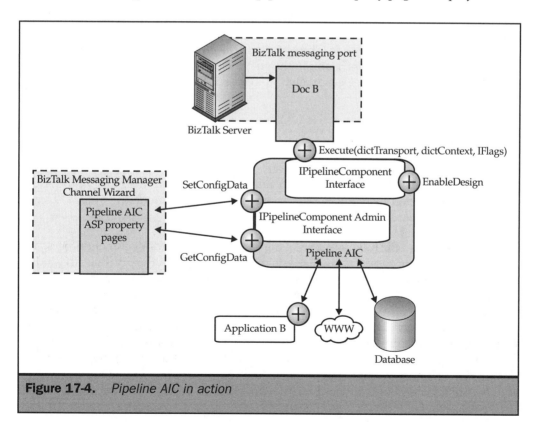

Figure 17-4.   *Pipeline AIC in action*

set this up, click the Channel Properties Wizard's Advanced Configurations button to display the Override Messaging Port Defaults page. In this page, click the AIC Properties button. This sets the **fEnable** parameter to a Boolean "true", enabling the design-time mode of the pipeline AIC.

Here are the EnableDesign method scripting requirements:

- **Windows NT/2000**   Requires Windows 2000 SP1 or later
- **Header**   Include pipecomp.h
- **Library**   Use Microsoft Commerce 2000 Default Pipeline Components Type Library (pipecomplib.tlb)

The syntax for the EnableDesign method in C++ is shown here:

```
HRESULT EnableDesign(
    BOOL fEnable
);
```

where the parameter **fEnable** is a Boolean value that determines the mode of the AIC component. The default value is "false", indicating execution mode. A value of "true" sets the AIC to design-time mode. The script returns an error, as defined by BizTalk Server (see the section "Errors", later in the chapter).

The syntax for the EnableDesign method in Visual Basic is shown here:

```
object.EnableDesign( _
    fEnable As Boolean _
)
```

where the parameter **fEnable** is a Boolean value that determines the mode of the AIC component. The default value is "false", indicating execution mode. A value of "true" sets the AIC to design-time mode. No return is implemented.

Execute Method   BizTalk Server calls the Execute method for document processing. A document string is passed to the Execute method along with the pipeline AIC and channel configurations information in the form of a transport dictionary object. The named entry, working_data, of the transport dictionary contains the value of the document string. For IInterchange.SubmitSync support, the named entry ResponseField in the transport dictionary should be set to the response document string. Other transport dictionary–named entry values can be created and returned for further processing.

The transport dictionary object submitted to pipeline AICs includes the named entry string values shown in Table 17-2.

Transport Dictionary Named Entry Value	Description
Working_Data	Document for processing submitted into the AIC by BizTalk Server from the channel.
ResponseField	Return document value required for SubmitSync support.
Src_ID_Type	Qualifier for the source organization; value can come from a parameter supplied in a Submit call or from a receive function in the BizTalk Server Administration user interface. A parser can overwrite this value to manipulate the routing info used for channel selection.
Src_ID_Value	Contains the value of the qualifier of the source organization. This value can come from a parameter supplied in a Submit call or from a receive function in the BizTalk Server Administration user interface. A parser can overwrite this value to manipulate the routing info used for channel selection.
Dest_ID_Type	Qualifier for the destination organization. This value can come from a parameter supplied in a Submit call or from a receive function in the BizTalk Server Administration user interface. A parser can overwrite this value to manipulate the routing info used for channel selection.
Dest_ID_Value	Contains the value of the qualifier of the destination organization. This value can come from a parameter supplied in a Submit call or from a receive function in the BizTalk Server Administration user interface. A parser can overwrite this value to manipulate the routing info used for channel selection.
Document_Name	Name of the input document definition.
Tracking_ID	Key value based on the globally unique identifier (GUID) and used for tracking.
src_filename	Available in BizTalk Server SP1; contains the incoming source filename when used with file receive function, or Submit specifies the filename.
src_filepath	Available in BizTalk Server SP1; contains the incoming source file path (example: C:\Temp) when the file was submitted with a file receive function or Submit.

Table 17-2.   *Some Transport Dictionary Name Entries Passed to the Execute Method by BizTalk Server*

The Execute method requires the following:

- **Windows NT/2000** Requires Windows 2000 SP1 or later
- **Header** Include pipecomp.h
- **Library** Use Microsoft Commerce 2000 Default Pipeline Components Type Library (pipecomplib.tlb)

The syntax for the Execute method in C++ is

```
HRESULT Execute(
  IDispatch* pDispOrder,
  IDispatch* pDispContext,
  long lFlags,
  long* plErrorLevel
);
```

and the parameters are

- **pDispOrder** [in] is a pointer to the transport Dictionary object.
- **pDispContext** [in] is not currently supported.
- **lFlags** [in] is reserved.
- **PlErrorLevel** [out, retval] is reserved.

The script returns an error that occurred, defined by BizTalk Server (see "Errors", later in the chapter).

The syntax for the Execute method in Visual Basic is

```
object.Execute( _
  pDispOrder As Object, _
  pDispContext As Object, _
  lFlags As Long _
)
```

and the parameters are

- **pDispOrder** is sent in as the transport CDictionary Object.
- **pDispContext** is not supported.
- **lFlags** is reserved.

The script returns the error level defined as a Long. The AIC must return the proper error level and raise the correct error in Err.Number. (See "Errors", later in the chapter.)

IPipelineComponentAdmin Interface

The IPipelineComponentAdmin interface is used to pass the setup configuration information for a messaging port to a pipeline AIC. Binding is provided via the

IPipelineComponentAdmin interface's two methods, GetConfigData and SetConfigData. GetConfigData is used to load, or *get,* the configuration data into the CDictionary object, whereas the SetConfigData method lets you remove information from the CDictionary object and *sets* the configuration data for the AIC.

GetConfigData Method   The GetConfigData method is used to get the configuration data of the pipeline AIC into a returning dictionary object. When a BizTalk Server Messaging Port is created, BizTalk Server will call the GetConfigData method to load the configuration data and variables for the messaging port(s) autoconfiguration. This method is also used when BizTalk Server loads the Channel Wizard's Advanced Configuration property page with the dictionary object's values at design time.

The GetConfigData method requires the following:

- ■ **Windows NT/2000**   Requires Windows 2000 SP1 or later.
- ■ **Header**   Include pipecomp.h.
- ■ **Library**   Use Microsoft Commerce 2000 Default Pipeline Components Type Library (pipecomplib.tlb).

The syntax of the GetConfigData method in C++ is shown here:

```
HRESULT GetConfigData(
  IDispatch** ppConfigDictionary
);
```

where the parameter **ppConfigDictionary** [out, retval] is the address of a pointer to a dictionary object from which the user interface can read the configuration data. An error occurs, as defined by BizTalk Server (see "Errors", later in the chapter).

The syntax of the GetConfigData method in Visual Basic is

```
object.GetConfigData()
```

where no parameters are set, but the code returns a CDictionary object from which the user interface can read the configuration data.

SetConfigData Method   The SetConfigData method sets or gives the pipeline AIC a chance to set and validate the configuration information from a dictionary object sent in by BizTalk Server. At design time, the SetConfigData method updates the changes from the Channel Wizard Advanced property page to the pipeline AIC and sends the dictionary data to a database. During run time, the SetConfigData method is also called by BizTalk Server to configure the necessary variables in the pipeline AIC, before the processing of a document is sent into the port with the IPipelineComponent's Execute method. As with most implemented pipeline AIC methods, any errors should be raised and set manually according to the "Errors" section, later in this chapter.

The SetConfigData method requirements are shown here:

- **Windows NT/2000**   Windows 2000 SP1 or later.
- **Header**   Include pipecomp.h.
- **Library**   Use Microsoft Commerce 2000 Default Pipeline Components Type Library (pipecomplib.tlb).

The syntax of the SetConfigData method in C++ is

```
HRESULT SetConfigData(
  IDispatch* pConfigDictionary
);
```

where the parameter pConfigDictionary [in] is a pointer to a dictionary object that contains the configuration information. The code returns an error that occurred, as defined by BizTalk Server (see the "Errors" section, later in the chapter).

The syntax of the SetConfigData method in Visual Basic is

```
object.SetConfigData( _
  pConfigDictionary As Object _
)
```

where the parameter **pConfigDictionary** is a *CDictionary* object that contains the configuration information and has no return value.

IDictionary Interface (C++) or CDictionary Object (Visual Basic)

The IDictionary interface for C++ or the CDictionary object for Visual Basic is merely a general-purpose collection. It uses a name paired with a value stored in an enumerable collection. The Value type is defined as a VARIANT providing storage for all types of values, including other objects.

The IDictionary interface object requires

- **Windows NT/2000**   Requires Windows 2000 SP1 or later.
- **Header**   Include commerce.h.
- **Library**   Use Microsoft Commerce 2000 Core Components Type Library (MscsCore.dll).

The properties of the CDictionary object are shown in the following sections.

Value Property   The Value property gets or sets the value of the associate entry name. You can call the property by treating the entry name as a property. For example, both lines of this Visual Basic code work in the same way:

```
CDictionary.Value("working_data")
CDictionary("working_data")
```

The syntax for the Value property get property method in C++ is shown here,

```
HRESULT get_Value(
  BSTR bstrName,
  VARIANT* Value
);
```

where the parameter bstrName [in] is a BSTR that contains the name. [Out, retval] is a pointer to a VARIANT used to return the value.

The syntax for the Value property set property method in C++ is shown here,

```
HRESULT put_Value(
  BSTR bstrName,
   VARIANT Value
);
```

where the parameter bstrName [in] BSTR contains the name. The value is [in] a VARIANT that contains the value.

The syntax for the Value property in Visual Basic is shown here:

```
object.Value( _
 bstrName As String _
 )
```

where the parameter **bstrName** is a String that contains the name. The return value is a VARIANT that contains the value.

Count Property   The read-only property Count returns the number of elements in the CDictionary object. The requirements for the Count property are

- **Windows NT/2000**   Requires Windows 2000 SP1 or later
- **Header**   Include commerce.h
- **Library**   Use Microsoft Commerce 2000 Core Components Type Library (MscsCore.dll)

The syntax of the Count property in C++ is

```
HRESULT get_Count(
 long* Count
);
```

The parameter Count [out, retval] is a Long used to return the number of dictionary elements. It returns an error that occurred, as defined by BizTalk Server (see the "Errors" section).

The syntax of the Count property in Visual Basic is

```
objCDictionary.Count
```

where there are no parameters. This property returns a Long that contains the count.

NewEnum Property   This property is available only for C++ code. The NewEnum property is the Enumerator object for the CDictionary object, which is an IUnknown interface pointer. The Enumerator object implements the IEnumVariant interface. For enumerations, the call is made to the QueryInterface of this object.

The requirements for the NewEnum property for C++ are

■ **Windows NT/2000**   Requires Windows 2000 SP1 or later.

■ **Header**   Include commerce.h.

The syntax of the NewEnum property for the get method is

```
HRESULT get_NewEnum(
  IUnknown** _NewEnum
);
```

where the parameter is _NewEnum [out, retval], the address of a pointer to an IUnknown interface. The returned object implements the IEnumVariant interface by calling the QueryInterface through the returned pointer. QueryInterface will return another pointer to the IEnumVariant for this object. The Next method of the IEnumVariant is used to enumerate through the elements. The Value method can be called to return the elements' values. It returns an error defined by BizTalk Server (see the "Errors" section).

Prefix Property   The Prefix property sets a filter to exclude entries by the defined prefix parameters. The resulting filtered contents stored in the CDictionary object are the only entries saved. All entries filtered out by the defined Prefix property are not saved. The default Prefix filter is an underscore (_). Thus, if you create a named entry starting with an underscore, it will not be saved in the CDictionary object.

The requirements for the Prefix property are

■ **Windows NT/2000**   Requires Windows 2000 SP1 or later.

■ **Header**   Include commerce.h.

■ **Library**   Use Microsoft Commerce 2000 Core Components Type Library (MscsCore.dll).

The syntax of the Prefix property get method in C++ is

```
HRESULT get_Prefix(
  BSTR* Prefix
);
```

where the parameter is Prefix [out, retval], a pointer to a BSTR that contains the prefix. It returns an error that is defined by BizTalk Server (see the "Errors" section).

The syntax of the Prefix property put method in C++ is

```
HRESULT put_Prefix(
 BSTR Prefix
);
```

where the parameter is **Prefix** [in], a BSTR that contains the prefix. It returns an error that occurred defined by BizTalk Server (see the "Errors" section).

The syntax of the Prefix property in Visual Basic is

```
object.Prefix
```

where no parameters are set. It returns a string that contains the prefix.

GetMultiple Method   The GetMultiple method returns the specified entries from a CDictionary object. The GetMultiple method will fail if called from VBScript because the parameters used by this method are not supported in VBScript.

The requirements for the GetMultiple method are

- **Windows NT/2000**   Requires Windows 2000 SP1 or later.
- **Header**   Include commerce.h.
- **Library**   Use Microsoft Commerce 2000 Core Components Type Library (MscsCore.dll).

The syntax for the GetMultiple method in C++ is

```
HRESULT GetMultiple(
 long cb,
 const LPOLESTR rgolestr[ ],
 VARIANT rgvar[ ]
);
```

where the parameters are

- **cb** [in] is a Long that specifies the number of values to retrieve.
- **rgolestr** [in, size_is(cb)] is an array of strings that identifies the dictionary object named entries for which the values should be retrieved.
- **rgvar** [out, size_is(cb)] is an array of variants. This parameter is marked as an [out]. Thus, it will return with an array containing the values associated with the dictionary object entries identified by the **rgolestr** array.

It returns an error that occurred as defined by BizTalk Server (see the "Errors" section). The syntax for the GetMultiple method in Visual Basic is

```
object.GetMultiple( _
  cb As Long, _
  rgolestr As String, _
  rgvar As Variant _
)
```

where the parameters are

- cb is a Long defining the number of values to retrieve.
- rgolestr is an array of string values identifying the CDictionary object entries to retrieve.
- rgvar is an array of variants. rgvar is ByRef and thus it will contain an array with the corresponding values associated with the CDictionary object entries defined by the rgolestr array.

It has no return values.

PutMultiple Method   The PutMultiple method adds entries to the CDictionary object. If named entries exist, they are rewritten and their respective values are changed. The two parameters, the rgolestr and rgvar arrays, have a one-to-one mapping between the elements. This means the array element specified at rgolestr[1] is mapped to the value rgvar[1]. If rgolestr[1] already exists, the old value will be overwritten in rgvar[1]. The PutMultiple method will not work with VBScript because the specific data types used by the parameters are not supported.

The requirements for PutMultiple method are

- **Windows NT/2000**   Requires Windows 2000 SP1 or later.
- **Header**   Include commerce.h.
- **Library**   Use Microsoft Commerce 2000 Core Components Type Library (MscsCore.dll).

The syntax for the PutMultiple method in C++ is

```
HRESULT PutMultiple(
  long cb,
  const LPOLESTR rgolestr[ ],
  const VARIANT rgvar[ ]
);
```

where the parameters are as follows:

- cb [in] is a Long that identifies the number of elements in the rgolestr and rgvar arrays.

- rgolestr [in, size_is(cb)] is an array of strings that contains the named entry to add to the CDictionary object.

- rgvar [in, size_is(cb)] is an array of VARIANTs with the corresponding values of the named entry defined in the rgolestr array to add to the dictionary object.

The script returns an error that occurred, defined by BizTalk Server (see the "Errors" section).

The syntax for the PutMultiple method in Visual Basic is

```
object.PutMultiple( _
 cb As Long, _
 rgolestr As String, _
 rgvar As Variant _
)
```

The parameters are as follows:

- cb is a Long that identifies the number of elements in the rgolestr and rgvar arrays.

- rgolestr is an array of strings that contains the names to add to the CDictionary object.

- rgvar is an array of VARIANTs that contains the values to add to the CDictionary object.

The script has no return value.

Pipeline AIC Property Pages

The pipeline AIC property configurations made by the BizTalk Messaging Manager are controlled with two ASP property pages. The ASP property pages bind the AIC configuration information provided by the CDictionary object from the IPipelineComponent. GetConfigData method. One ASP page is used for posting the data and the other one is used for reading the data. The filenames of the ASP pages must match the AIC's ProgID and all dots must be removed and replaced with underscores. For example, if the pipeline AIC ProgID is DB_PipelineAIC.Pipeline, the ASP file would be named DB_PipelineAIC_Pipeline.asp. The posting file must also have _post appended to the ProgID: DB_PipelineAIC_Pipeline_post.asp. The file must be placed in the BizTalk install directory under the MessagingManager\Pipeline folder.

In the file script, all the work is done behind the scenes in the included header and footer files, pe_edit_header.asp and pe_edit_footer.asp. The functions in the include files write properties to the AIC and return these values from the AIC. For example, the function used to display the value of the property from an AIC is the InputText subroutine in an HTML input text box element along with a label. Table 17-3 shows the subroutines provided for displaying the AIC properties in different forms of HTML elements.

Pipeline ASP Property Configuration Control Subroutines	Description
InputText(*field*)	Displays a label and an HTML input text box with the AIC property's value defined as *field*.
InputTextArea(*field*)	Displays a label and an HTML text area box with the AIC property's value defined as *field*.
InputTextAccel(*field*, *accel*)	Displays a label and an HTML input text box with the AIC property's value defined as *field* and also an accelerator key, *accel*, to access it.
InputPassword(*field*)	Displays a label and an HTML input password with the AIC property's value defined as *field*.
InputPasswordAccel(*field*, *accel*)	Displays a label and an HTML password text box with the AIC property's value defined as *field* and an accelerator key, *accel*, to access it.
DisplayReadonlyText(*field*)	Displays a label and an HTML disabled input text box with the AIC property's value defined as *field*.
InputSelection(*field*, *list*, *accel*)	Displays a label and an HTML drop-down list with the AIC property's value defined as *field* and an accelerator key, *accel*, to access it. *list* represents the items in the drop-down list.
InputArray(*field*, *arr*)	Displays a label and an HTML drop-down list with the AIC property's value defined as *field*. *arr* represents the items in the drop-down list.
InputArrayAccel(*field*, *arr*, *accel*)	Displays a label and an HTML drop-down list with the AIC property's value defined as *field* and an accelerator key, *accel*, to access it. *arr* represents the items in the drop-down list.
InputSimpleListAccel(*field*, *listname*, *accel*)	Displays a label and an HTML drop-down combo-box list with the AIC property's value defined as *field* and also an accelerator key, *accel* (for example, CTRL-T), to access it. *listname* represents a dictionary object used to display the items in the drop-down list.

Table 17-3. *Pipeline AIC ASP Property HTML Configuration Subroutines*

Pipeline ASP Property Configuration Control Subroutines	Description
InputSimpleList(*field, listname*)	Displays a label and an HTML drop-down combo-box list with the AIC property's value defined as *field*. *listname* represents a dictionary object used to display the items in the drop-down list.
InputOption(*name, value*)	Adds an HTML option with the specified *name* and *value* to an existing drop-down combo box.
InputRadioAccel(*name, value, custom_title, table_entry, accel*)	Displays an HTML input radio with the AIC property's value defined as *value*. *custom_title* represents the label, and *table_entry* represents an optional descriptive text.
InputRadio(*name, value, custom_title, table_entry*)	Displays an HTML input radio with the AIC property's value defined as *value* and also an *accel* accelerator key to access it. *custom_title* represents the label, and *table_entry* represents an optional descriptive text.
InputCheckboxAccel(*name, accel*)	Displays a label and an HTML input check box with the AIC property's value defined as *field* and an *accel* accelerator key to access it.
InputCheckbox(*name*)	Displays a label and an HTML input check box with the AIC property's value defined as field.
InputNumberAccel(*field, accel*)	Displays a label and an HTML input text box with the AIC property's value defined as *field* and an *accel* accelerator key to access it. *field* represents a numeric variable.
InputNumber(*field*)	Displays a label and an HTML input text box with the AIC property's value defined as *field*. *field* represents a numeric variable.
InputFloatAccel(*field, accel*)	Displays a label and an HTML input text box with the AIC property's value defined as *field* and an *accel* accelerator key to access it. *field* is treated as a float.
InputFloat(*field*)	Displays a label and an HTML input text box with the AIC property's value defined as *field*. *field* is treated as a float.

Table 17-3.   *Pipeline AIC ASP Property HTML Configuration Subroutines* (continued)

The AIC ProgID _post.asp page has another set of functions and subroutines to help save the posted data from the initial property page. For each of the HTML element types–based methods used in the initial property ASP page, a corresponding *save* appears in the post ASP page. For example, the InputText subroutine used has a corresponding GetInputText function to capture the data posted by the HTML input text box defined. The same is true with the other HTML elements. Table 17-4 shows the functions available in the _post.asp page.

All the functions shown in Table 17-4 store the results to a CDictionary object that is then sent into the pipeline AIC from BizTalk with IPipelineComponent.SetConfigData and sent to a database via a subroutine called ProcessInput in the included file, pe_global_ edit.asp. ProcessInput stores the values retrieved as named entry/value pairs, in a global variable CDictionary object called *Dict*. The MS Commerce Server 2000 pipeline is a COM component called Commerce.Page, which is responsible for building and storing the global CDictionary object *Dict*. The *Dict* object is then stored back to the pipeline AIC with the VerifyConfigData method from the ASP included file pe_config_ utils.asp. VerfiyConfigData actually calls the SetConfigData method of the pipeline AIC via the BizTalk.BizTalkDBInternal object.

Pipeline ASP Post Property Configuration Control Functions	Corresponding Pipeline ASP Property Configuration Control Subroutine	Description
GetInputText(*field, min, max*)	InputText, InputTextAccel, InputTextArea, DisplayReadonlyText	Processes posts made from HTML input element named *field* that has a value with a minimum (*min*) and a maximum (*max*) length.
GetInputPassword(*field, min, max*)	InputPassword	Processes posts made from HTML input password element named *field* that has a value with a minimum (*min*) and a maximum (*max*) length.
GetSelection(*field, min, max*)	InputSelection, InputArray, InputArrayAccel, InputSimpleListAccel, InputSimpleList	Processes posts made from an HTML select element named *field* that has a value with a minimum (*min*) and a maximum (*max*) length.

Table 17-4. *Pipeline AIC POST ASP Property HTML Configuration Subroutines*

Pipeline ASP Post Property Configuration Control Functions	Corresponding Pipeline ASP Property Configuration Control Subroutine	Description
GetInputNumber(*field*, *min*, *max*)	InputNumber, InputNumberAccel	Processes posts made from an HTML input element named *field* that has a value with a minimum (*min*) and a maximum (*max*) length. Convert the value to a numeric value.
GetInputFloat(*field*, *min*, *max*)	InputFloat, InputFloatAccel	Processes posts made from an HTML input element named *field* that has a value with a minimum (*min*) and a maximum (*max*) length. Convert the value to a float.
GetCheckBox(*field*)	InputCheckbox, InputCheckboxAccel	Processes posts made from an HTML input check box element named *field*.

Table 17-4. *Pipeline AIC POST ASP Property HTML Configuration Subroutines* (continued)

Creating a Pipeline AIC

The lightweight AIC example can be made more generic by use of pipeline AIC. The lightweight AIC in our example hard-codes the configuration values in the component itself. This is sometimes not advisable. The pipeline AIC provides the framework for setting these configuration values equal to global variables defined for run time but passed in by design time via the Channel Wizard's Advanced Configuration property page. The global variables can now be configured to connect to a database on a per-channel basis, reusing the pipeline AIC code. The same example code can be used from the lightweight AIC example, as the AIC will update a database with some data based on a string, except this time it's submitted as a CDictionary object by BizTalk. The CDictionary "working_data" named entry is an XML string document that can be loaded into an MSXML2.XMLDocument object to ease the extraction of the data for updating. This is accomplished in the following manner:

1. Create a Visual Basic ActiveX DLL project by selecting ActiveX DLL in the New Project window.

2. Rename the project in the Project Properties window by selecting
   Project | Project Properties. Rename the class by selecting the default
   Class1 under Class Modules in the Project Explorer. In the Properties
   window, rename the (Name) Class1.

3. Set the MTSTransactionMode properties under Class Properties to a
   value of 1 – NoTransactions If Debugging Only.

4. Add the following references to the needed components by choosing
   Project | References:

   ■ **Microsoft Commerce 2000 Core Components Type Library**
   C:\Program Files\Common Files\Microsoft Shared\Enterprise
   Servers\Commerce\MscsCore.dll

   ■ **Microsoft Commerce 2000 Default Pipeline Component Type
   Library**   C:\Program Files\Common Files\Microsoft Shared\
   Enterprise Servers\Commerce\pipecomplib.tlb

   ■ **Microsoft ActiveX Data Objects 2.6 Library**

   ■ **Microsoft XML 3.0**

   ■ **Custom DataLib4AICs.SaveDB**   Data object that encapsulates
   the NorthWind database update.

5. Add the Implements IPipelineComponentAdmin in the Code window.

6. Add the Implements IPipelineComponent in the Code window.

7. Add the Private Sub IPipelineComponent_EnableDesign(ByVal fEnable As Long)
   to support switching between design-time and run-time configurations by
   BizTalk.

8. Add the private function:

```
IPipelineComponent_Execute(ByVal dictTransport As Object, ByVal
pdispContext As Object, ByVal lFlags As Long) As Long
```

   Add the business logic in the IPipelineComponent_Execute function. In this example,
   load the XML document passed in by BizTalk via the CDictionary object:

```
bstrDocument = dictTransport("working_data")
```

9. Call business logic passing in the XML document via the AddToDB subroutine.
   AddToDB extracts XML data to build a SQL update statement and Executes the
   statement with the connection.

10. Set the ResponseField of the global CDictionary object for BizTalk to something
    for synchronous requests to the AIC:

```
dictTransport.Value("ResponseField") = 0
```

11. Return successfully by returning the function Set IPipelineComponent_Execute equal to 0 or by raising an error value of 2 if an error occurs for BizTalk.

12. Add the private function:

```
IPipelineComponentAdmin_GetConfigData() As Object
```

Insert any global variables that need to be loaded into a CDictionary object for design-time configuration used by the pipeline AIC's ASP configuration property pages, as in this example code:

```
objectConfig.Value("DB_Name") = m_strDBName
```

13. Add Private Sub:

```
IPipelineComponentAdmin_SetConfigData(ByVal pDict As Object)
```

14. Set any global variables from a CDictionary object at run time and design time in the IPipelineComponentAdmin_SetConfigData, as in the example code that follows:

```
m_strDBName = CStr(pDict("DB_Name"))
```

15. Compile the DLL.

16. Add the DLL to a new COM+ application or add the BizTalk affinity (see the upcoming section "Registering AICs").

17. Create two ASP pages that implement the pipeline AIC template: one is for posting, and the other, for reading. Configure the input values appropriately to match the named entries that are retrieved and set via GetConfigData and *SetConfigData* in the newly compiled DLL. For example, DB_PipelineAIC_Pipeline.asp would have the input call InputText("DB_Name"). DB_PipelineAIC_Pipeline_Post.asp would have the input call GetInputText("DB_Name", 0, bufsize_medium).

18. Move these two ASP pages to the BizTalk install directory's subfolders that are installed by BizTalk: C:\Program Files\Microsoft BizTalk Server\MessagingManager\Pipeline.

19. In the BizTalk Messaging Manager, create a port with the transport type set to Application Integration Component and select Previously Compiled DLL AIC Name.

20. Create a channel that uses the previously created port. On the Advanced Configurations page of the Channel Wizard, click the Advanced button to bring up the override options. The Properties page of the Primary Transport Component of the Override Messaging Port Defaults page displays another pipeline AIC's property page, where configuration information such as "DB_Name" can be specified on a per-channel basis.

Example Code: DB_PipelineAIC Note that the following example code has minimal error handling (if any) to minimize text and maximize readability:

```
Option Explicit

Implements IPipelineComponentAdmin
Implements IPipelineComponent

' Declare string values used by component
Private m_strServerName, m_strDBName, m_strTableName, m_strUID, m_strPassword, _
m_strLogFullPath As String

Private Sub IPipelineComponent_EnableDesign(ByVal fEnable As Long) 'Do Nothing
End Sub

Private Function IPipelineComponent_Execute(ByVal dictTransport As Object, _
    ByVal pdispContext As Object, _
    ByVal lFlags As Long) As Long

 Dim bstrDocument As String
 bstrDocument = dictTransport("working_data")

  ' call business logic
 Call AddToDB(ByVal bstrDocument)

  'return something for submitsync
 dictTransport.Value("ResponseField") = 0

  'return success
 IPipelineComponent_Execute = 0

 Exit Function
ExecuteError:
    IPipelineComponent_Execute = 2 'Serious Error Occurred
    LogFail ("The following Error was encountered: " + Err.Description)
End Function

Private Function IPipelineComponentAdmin_GetConfigData() As Object
    Dim objectConfig As New CDictionary
    objectConfig.Value("Server_Name") = m_strServerName
    objectConfig.Value("DB_Name") = m_strDBName
    objectConfig.Value("Table_Name") = m_strTableName
    objectConfig.Value("UID") = m_strUID
    objectConfig.Value("Password") = m_strPassword
```

```
      Set IPipelineComponentAdmin_GetConfigData = objectConfig
End Function

Private Sub IPipelineComponentAdmin_SetConfigData(ByVal pDict As Object)
    ' set parameters based on dictionary values
    If Not IsNull(pDict("Server_Name")) Then
        m_strServerName = CStr(pDict("Server_Name"))
    End If
    If Not IsNull(pDict("DB_Name")) Then
        m_strDBName = CStr(pDict("DB_Name"))
    End If
    If Not IsNull(pDict("Table_Name")) Then
        m_strTableName = CStr(pDict("Table_Name"))
    End If
    If Not IsNull(pDict("UID")) Then
        m_strUID = CStr(pDict("UID"))
    End If
    If Not IsNull(pDict("Password")) Then
        m_strPassword = CStr(pDict("Password"))
    End If
End Sub

Private Sub AddToDB(ByVal bstrDocument)
 On Error GoTo ExecuteError

 ' Set normal COM component for inserting in DB
 Dim objSaveDb As DataLib4AICs.SaveDB
 Set objSaveDb = New DataLib4AICs.SaveDB

 Dim strConnString As String
 strConnString = "Provider=sqloledb;Data Source=(local);Initial Catalog=" &
m_strDBName & ";"

 ' make the call to the normal db component
 Call objSaveDb.AddToDB(bstrDocument, strConnString, m_strTableName, m_strUID,
m_strPassword)

 Exit Sub
ExecuteError:
    Err.Raise 2, , "Custom Error Message"
End Sub

Private Sub LogFail(strFail As String)
    Dim lFileHandle As Long
```

```
    'On Error Resume Next
    lFileHandle = FreeFile()
    If m_strLogFullPath = "" Then
        Open App.Path + "\DB_PipelineAIC.log" For Append As lFileHandle
    Else
        Open m_strLogFullPath For Append As lFileHandle
    End If
    Print #lFileHandle, "[FAIL] " & strFail
    Close #lFileHandle
End Sub
```

Errors

All BizTalk AIC interfaces use the standard COM method for determining whether or not methods or properties operated successfully. For C++, the errors are the return values or COM HRESULTs of the methods and properties (get_ and put_). As in all normal C++ COM components, all applications must explicitly check for errors by examining the return values. Visual Basic uses its normal method for checking for errors by placing the error in the global Err object. Err events are executed appropriately.

Two types of error messages can be raised:

- **Standard COM**   Most of the error messages are related to component interface, argument, and marshalling errors. Refer to Microsoft SDK COM documentation for the latest list of errors.

- **BizTalk Server 2000**   For C++ developers, error messages are included in the BizTalk error configuration file: bts_config_errors.h. Errors listed contain both design-time and run-time error messages. It is impractical to include all the errors here; refer to the BizTalk Server 2000 error messages in the BizTalk Server SDK documentation.

Registering AICs

For BizTalk to recognize a COM component as an AIC, it must identify itself as a valid BizTalk Server component and then as a BizTalk AIC. BizTalk will search through two locations for identifiable AICs:

- COM+ catalog
- Registry

COM+ Catalog

If the AIC is placed in COM+, BizTalk will find the components that implement the correct interface (IBTSAppIntegration or IPipelineComponent) in the COM+ catalog and automatically recognize them as valid BizTalk components and BizTalk AICs. The AIC will then be granted all the COM+ benefits: pooling, transactions, just-in-time (JIT) object creation, enhanced memory management, easier debugging (see the upcoming section "Debugging") and extended security. These features make COM+ the preferred way of registering BizTalk AICs. The procedure for registering the AIC as a COM+ application is easy: you simply drag and drop the component into a new or existing COM+ application in the Component Service Management snap-in.

Registry

AICs not placed in COM+ are required to be manually entered into the normal COM components CLSID registration location in the Registry. The entries are placed into the Implement Categories subkey location: HKEY_LOCAL_MACHINE\SOFTWARE\Classes\CLSID\{AIC_CLSID}\Implemented Categories. The two keys to add to the Implemented Categories key are

- *{5C6C30E7-C66D-40e3-889D-08C5C3099E52}*
- *{BD193E1D-D7DC-4b7c-B9D2-92AE0344C836}*

The first key added, *{5C6C30E7-C66D-40e3-889D-08C5C3099E52}* or the category *CATID_BIZTALK_COMPONENT*, tells BizTalk Server that this COM class is a valid BizTalk Server component and is used by customer components such as BizTalk Server Messaging preprocessors. (Refer to Chapter 16 for more details on custom components for BizTalk.) The second category, dubbed "affinity", *CATID_BIZTALK_AIC* or *{BD193E1D-D7DC-4b7c-B9D2-92AE0344C836}*, registers the class as an AIC. Only components that have affinity will show up in the Primary Transport AIC list available via BizTalk Server Messaging Managers Port Wizard.

Debugging

The choice of adding the AIC to COM+ makes debugging easier. For example, adding the AIC into COM+ will automatically allow integrated debugging in Visual Basic to work as long as the AIC DLL is compiled with the Transaction mode property set to NoTransactions instead of the default NotanMTSObject. Also, make sure you build the component and then set the project properties for binary compatibility for the DLL.

Binary compatibility ensures that each time you compile the DLL, you do not generate a new globally unique identifier (GUID) for the object. This allows for complete debugging integration, such as setting breakpoints and stepping through the AIC code.

Configuring BizTalk Message Ports to Use AICs

After creating and registering AICs of your choice, setting up a BizTalk Messaging Port should be a simple matter of selecting it as the transport in the Primary Transport dialog, as shown in Figure 17-5. A list of all the AICs on the system is displayed by the New Messaging Port Wizard in the BizTalk Messaging Manager.

After creating the channel that sends the configured port information and uses the desired AIC for transport, the design-time configuration of the pipeline AIC is available in the New Channel Wizard on the Advanced Configuration page, shown in Figure 17-6. If the AIC is not a pipeline AIC, no configuration data is available. (Refer to Chapter 6 for a complete discussion on BizTalk Messaging, including selection and configuration of AICs.)

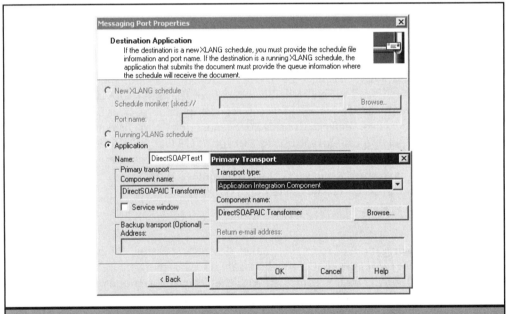

Figure 17-5. *AIC configuration begins when you select the primary transport type as an Application Integration Component.*

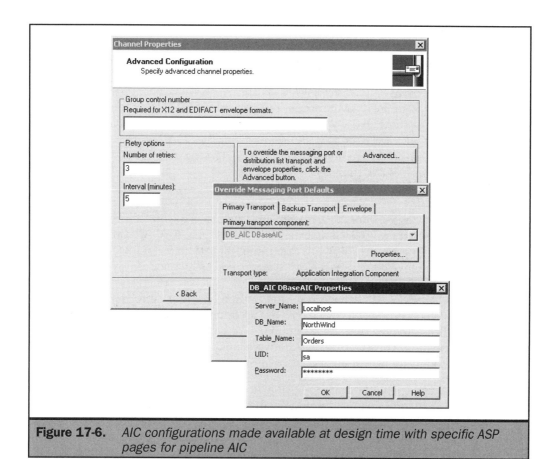

Figure 17-6. *AIC configurations made available at design time with specific ASP pages for pipeline AIC*

Implementing SOAP

The rise of XML for data markup has sparked an interest in using XML to mark up elements such as objects and protocols. One such markup protocol is the Simple Object Access Protocol (SOAP). SOAP is an effective means of executing methods through firewalls to replace remote procedure calls across dissimilar operating systems, which is why Web Services uses SOAP as its protocol format. The true power of SOAP is its simplicity and ease of implementation—any application can use it today.

Introducing SOAP

SOAP is an XML-based specification for invoking methods, such as components, objects, servers, and/or anything that can accept and then respond to a method request. The invocation of methods, as defined in the W3C (World Wide Web Consortium) submission, uses a standard, well-defined XML format transported via HTTP. Although the W3C specification confines SOAP to use with HTTP, SOAP can be used on any type of protocol that can transport XML: SMTP, DCOM, IIOP, and so on. The SOAP specification provides a standard syntax for describing the method, parameters, return values, and exceptions in an XML format as a SOAP message.

SOAP Message

The SOAP message has the same XML document structure as the BizTalk Framework 2.0. In fact, the BizTalk Framework 2.0 is an extension of SOAP 1.1. A SOAP XML document limits itself to requiring <SOAP-ENV:Envelope xmlns:SOAP-ENV="http://schemas .xmlsoap.org/soap/envelope/"> as the root element and a child node body < SOAP-ENV:Body>, as shown in Figure 17-7.

Note the SOAP-ENV namespace; refer to Chapter 2 for more information on XML and uses of namespaces. The envelope also has an optional < SOAP-ENV:Header> child node, which is the BizTalk specification used to provide routing and other necessary information. The < SOAP-ENV:Body> element will always contain the requested method, response, or errors.

Request To invoke a method with SOAP in accordance with the W3C specification, an HTTP POST (or M-POST) must be made to the web server from a client. The POSTed data is the XML script representing the SOAP request to execute a method. A web server that understands a SOAP request and is capable of responding appropriately is called a SOAP server, SOAP listener, or web service. A simple example will help clarify the SOAP XML request syntax.

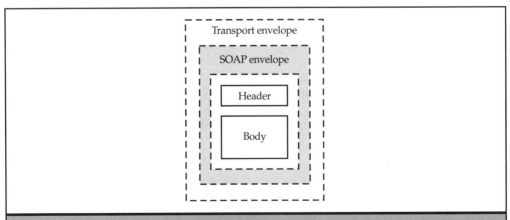

Figure 17-7. *A SOAP envelope consists of an optional header and required body elements.*

Here is an example VB method request:

```
Set objSDb = CreateObject("SoapAICServer.SaveDB")
bstrDocument = "hello"
iReturn = objSDb.AddToDB(bstrDocument)
```

Here is the equivalent HTTP SOAP message request for the method:

```
POST /soapaic/server/SoapAIC.ASP HTTP/1.1
Host: localhost
Content-Type: text/xml, charset="utf-8"
Content-Length: nnnn
SOAPAction: "http://tempuri.org/action/SaveDB.AddToDB"
<SOAP-ENV:Envelope
SOAP-ENV:encodingStyle="http://schemas.xmlsoap.org/soap/encoding/" xmlns:SOAP-
ENV="http://schemas.xmlsoap.org/soap/envelope/">
    <SOAP-ENV:Body>
        <AddToDB>
            <bstrDocument>
            hello
            </bstrDocument>
        </AddToDB>
    </SOAP-ENV:Body>
</SOAP-ENV:Envelope>
```

Notice that the <AddToDB> element or requested method is added directly under the <SOAP-ENV:Body>, or Body, element. All of a method's parameters are added directly to the *method* element: <bstrDocument> is added as a child element to the <AddToDB>. The parameter value is then added as a value of <bstrDocument>. The only part missing in the SOAP document from the equivalent VB example is objSDb, from which the method is executed.

The objSDb in SOAP has no existence in the SOAP request because the SOAP syntax provides the vocabulary on how to request method(s), not objects. So where does the objSDb come from? In most cases, the web page or web server that receives the POSTed SOAP request will know what the objSDb is. The AddToDB example, which was built with Microsoft's implementation of SOAP, uses both the web page POSTed to and the SOAPAction HTTP header. The SOAPAction HTTP header is a defined SOAP property; in the Microsoft SOAP Toolkit, it is used to describe which objSDb is requested: http://tempuri.org/action/SaveDB.AddToDb. The URL http://tempuri.org is the default NAMESPACE for this SOAP request. SaveDB is the objSDb. The ASP page posted to a SOAP listener or SOAP server)—for example, /soapaic/server/SoapAIC.ASP knows which COM component SaveDB is, and should invoke the method AddToDB. The SoapAIC.ASP is responsible for returning the SOAP response with the results of the objSDb.AddToDB method.

Response SOAP defines that for every request, a response must be received. The response from the SOAP server can be the results of the method requested or any errors generated during the request. The simple example of the SOAP response of the preceding SOAP request example helps explain the syntax of the SOAP Response message.

Here is an example of a VB method request:

```
iReturn = objSDb.AddToDB(bstrDocument)
```

Here is the equivalent HTTP SOAP message request for the method:

```
HTTP/1.1 200 OK
Server: Microsoft-IIS/5.0
Content-Length: nnnn
Content-Type: text/xml; charset="UTF-8"

<?xml version="1.0" encoding="UTF-8" standalone="no"?>
<SOAP-ENV:Envelope
SOAP-ENV:encodingStyle="http://schemas.xmlsoap.org/soap/encoding/"
xmlns:SOAP-ENV="http://schemas.xmlsoap.org/soap/envelope/">
    <SOAP-ENV:Body>
        <AddToDBResponse>
            <Result>0</Result>
        </AddToDBResponse>
    </SOAP-ENV:Body>
</SOAP-ENV:Envelope>
```

This SOAP response shows that the requested method, AddToDB, returned correctly. Notice that the <AddToDB> child does not exist in the <SOAP-ENV:Body>, as per our request; instead, the element <AddToDBResponse> appears. The Response suffix is added to the requested method. The actual method result is the value in the <Result>: 0. At this point, SOAP has completed its desired task—to provide the syntax to invoke the method AddToDB and to understand the results. In accordance to the VB example, the client application would need to map the <Results> value to the long typed variable iReturn. Luckily, SOAP toolkits are available to do this mapping automatically.

SOAP Toolkits

The automation of the SOAP syntax to and from COM components or Java objects is provided by SOAP toolkits. Toolkits are available for specific programming languages. For example, MS Visual Studio programmers can take advantage of the Microsoft SOAP Toolkit. Java programmers can use the Apache SOAP Toolkit, originally produced by

IBM. These toolkits provide a broad range of functionality, from automatically generating SOAP servers and clients based on an existing COM component or Java classes, respectively. The toolkits even provide a high-level abstraction by mapping SOAP client returns to the normal programming language, including automatic type conversion. These toolkits simplify the development process and speed up the introduction of SOAP to applications today.

The previous SOAP Requests/Reponses and VB example AddToDB can be exemplified with the Microsoft Toolkit in VB as follows:

```
Set objSDb = CreateObject("MSSOAP.SoapClient")
Call objSDb.mssoapinit(wsdlUrl, "", "", wsmlUrl)
iReturn = objSDb.AddToDB(strDocIn)
```

The Microsoft SOAP Toolkit 2.0 requires only minor changes from the initial VB example to use and implement SOAP fully. Behind the scenes, the Microsoft SOAP Toolkit 2.0 provides complete SOAP message request and response processing, automatic mapping of returns, and data type conversions. The changes are the creation of the MSSOAP.SoapClient object and initialization to load the SOAP XML interfaces into the objSDb with the mssoapinit method. The mssoapinit method loads an XML schema-based description of the SoapAICServer.SaveDB components: wsdlUrl and wsmlUrl. The wsdlUrl and wsmlUrl components are also generated by the MS SOAP Toolkit and represent the SoapAICServer.SaveDB component in an XML format called *Web Service Definitions Language* (*WSDL*). A corresponding SOAP Server ASP file is also generated.

Note *For more information on these toolkits, refer to http://msdn.microsoft.com/soap/ or http://xml.apache.org/soap/.*

SOAP AICs

SOAP-based AICs are normal lightweight AICs or pipeline AICs, except that they implement SOAP as the transport for connectivity—in other words, they become a SOAP client. Since SOAP connectivity is extremely vast, flexible, and relatively standardized, AICs that use SOAP as the syntax greatly open BizTalk integration into all types of operating systems and applications that understand the SOAP syntax or can produce an XML response.

SOAP flexibility also provides a couple of ways to produce SOAP AICs: raw SOAP XML AIC, direct SOAP AIC, and Microsoft SOAPClient AIC. Figure 17-8 represents the MS SOAPClient AIC. Microsoft SOAPClient AIC uses the simplest method of invoking a SOAP method via Microsoft SOAPClient. The raw SOAP AIC avoids using SOAPClient and builds the SOAP XML method payload manually for submission. Finally, the direct SOAP AIC attempts to move the SOAP XML format directly into BizTalk Messaging for full use of all normal BizTalk Server tools, such as mapping from XML format to SOAP.

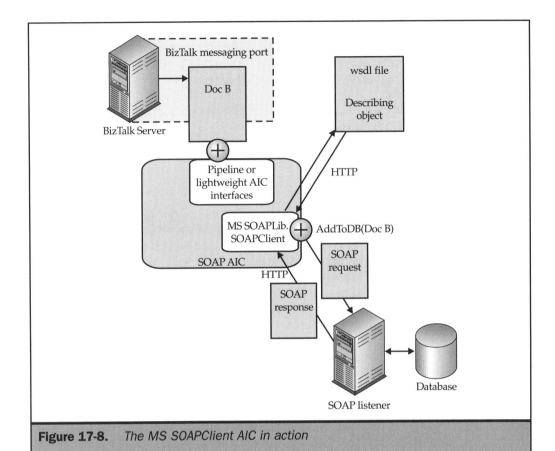

Figure 17-8. *The MS SOAPClient AIC in action*

MS SOAPClient AIC

The high level of abstraction of the MS SOAP Toolkit makes the creation of an AIC virtually the same process as creating a normal lightweight AIC or pipeline AIC. This makes it the easiest SOAP-based AIC to produce. Only a few additional steps are required to create an MS SOAPClient AIC instead of a typical AIC:

1. Get the URL of the Web Services Description Language (WSDL) and Web Services Meta Language (WSML) file or generate a SOAP server corresponding to the schema based on the MS SOAP Toolkit WDSL Wizard. Ensure that the SOAP server is set up as necessary. WSDL provides the schema structure of the SOAP message XML format for each method, along with many other details such as where to find the corresponding SOAP listener. WSML files provide references to other components and custom data types.

2. Create the MSSOAP.SoapClient object.

3. Call the SoapClient object's mssoapinit method, providing access to the URL of WDSL and WMSL files as necessary.

4. Proceed with the normal AIC development processes.

A pipeline AIC implementation will work well for a SOAPClient AIC because the URLs for the WSDL and WSML can be passed in via a dictionary object. Note that a possible performance issue arises with the MS SOAPClient; this issue is related to the loading and parsing of the WSDL and WSML files. The high abstraction of the MS SOAPClient base comes at a price—performance. In some cases, it might be better to deal directly with the SOAP response and request message. After all, it's only XML.

Creating an MS SOAPClient AIC   Our example of updating a database can now be expanded one step further by moving the AddToDB function as a method to a SOAP listener or SOAP server. This SOAP listener provides a simple test of the flexibility and ease of use of the SOAP syntax. Later, the MS SOAPClient AIC can be moved behind firewalls or tested against some other operating system that runs as a SOAP listener. The following procedure shows how to move the AddToDB function to a SOAP listener or server:

1. Install MS SOAP Toolkit 2.0 SP2 or later from http://msdn.microsoft.com/soap/.

2. Create a SOAP listener. To do this,

    a. Create a VB ActiveX DLL and rename it appropriately.

    b. Add a function such as AddToDB from the lightweight AIC code example.

    c. Compile the code.

    d. Create an IIS virtual directory from which to run the SOAP listener.

    e. Using the MS SOAP WSDL Wizard, point to the newly created DLL and select the methods to expose, such as AddToDB, to generate a corresponding WSDL file, WSML file, and SOAP listener ASP page. Set the listener URI to the URL of the IIS virtual directory created in the previous step. Set the listener type to ASP, and store the files in the same folder path of the IIS virtual directory from the preceding step.

3. Create the MS SOAPClient AIC. Start by creating an empty standard VB ActiveX DLL implementing the necessary pipeline interfaces and methods. See the "Pipeline AICs" section, earlier in the chapter.

4. Add the following references to the needed components by choosing Project | References:

    ■ **Microsoft SOAP Type Library**   (C:\Program Files\Common Files\ MSSoap\Binaries\MSSOAP1.dll)

- **Microsoft Commerce 2000 Core Components Type Library** C:\Program Files\Common Files\Microsoft Shared\Enterprise Servers\Commerce\ MscsCore.dll

- **Microsoft Commerce 2000 Default Pipeline Component Type Library** C:\Program Files\Common Files\Microsoft Shared\Enterprise Servers\ Commerce\pipecomplib.tlb

5. Define wsdlUrl and wsmlUrl as global variables to hold the URI of the SOAP listener.

6. Configure SetConfigData and GetConfigData to set or load the global variables or the CDictionary object, respectively.

7. Set up the two corresponding pipeline ASP pages to get and set the CDictionary values: wsdlUrl and wmdlUrl.

8. Move these two ASP pages to the BizTalk install directory under the MessagingManager\Pipeline subfolders created during BizTalk installation: C:\Program Files\Microsoft BizTalk Server\MessagingManager\pipeline.

9. In the IPipelineComponent_Execute function, create the MSSOAP.SoapClient object and initialize the SOAP listener's interface into the object by calling the mssoapinit(wsdlUrl, "", "", wsmlUrl) method.

10. Now call the method exposed by the SOAP listener as if the object were a normal local COM component—for example, objSDb.AddToDB(dictTransport .working_data), where AddToDB is the SOAP listener's methods and objSDb is the initialized MS SOAPClient.

Example Code: PipelineMSSOAPClientAIC Note that the following example code has minimal error handling (if any) to aid in minimizing text and maximizing readability:

```
Option Explicit

Implements IPipelineComponentAdmin
Implements IPipelineComponent

' Declare string values used by component
Private wsdlUrl, wsmlUrl, m_strLogFullPath As String

Private Sub IPipelineComponent_EnableDesign(ByVal fEnable As Long)
End Sub

Private Function IPipelineComponent_Execute(ByVal dictTransport As Object, _
    ByVal pdispContext As Object, _
    ByVal lFlags As Long) As Long

 Dim iReturn As Long
 Dim objSDb As MSSOAPLib.SoapClient
```

```
    Set objSDb = CreateObject("MSSOAP.SoapClient")

    Call objSDb.mssoapinit(wsdlUrl, "", "", wsmlUrl)

    ' invoke normal COM method to insert to DB
    iReturn = objSDb.AddToDB(dictTransport.working_data, "", "", "", "")

    'return something for submitsync
    dictTransport.Value("ResponseField") = iReturn

    'return success
    IPipelineComponent_Execute = 0
    Exit Function
ExecuteError:
    IPipelineComponent_Execute = 2 'Serious Error Occurred
    LogFail ("The following Error was encountered: " + Err.Description)
End Function

Private Function IPipelineComponentAdmin_GetConfigData() As Object
    Dim objectConfig As New CDictionary
    objectConfig.Value("wsdlUrl") = wsdlUrl
    objectConfig.Value("wsmlUrl") = wsmlUrl
    Set IPipelineComponentAdmin_GetConfigData = objectConfig
End Function

Private Sub IPipelineComponentAdmin_SetConfigData(ByVal pDict As Object)
    ' set parameters based on dictionary values
    If Not IsNull(pDict("wsdlUrl")) Then
        wsdlUrl = CStr(pDict("wsdlUrl"))
    End If
    If Not IsNull(pDict("wsmlUrl")) Then
        wsmlUrl = CStr(pDict("wsmlUrl"))
    End If
End Sub

Private Sub LogFail(strFail As String)
    Dim lFileHandle As Long
    lFileHandle = FreeFile()
    If m_strLogFullPath = "" Then
        Open App.Path + "\PipelineMSSOAPClintAIC.log" For Append As lFileHandle
    Else
        Open m_strLogFullPath For Append As lFileHandle
    End If
    Print #lFileHandle, "[FAIL] " & strFail
    Close #lFileHandle
End Sub(3)Raw SOAP XML AIC
```

The high-level abstractions of the MS SOAPClient might lead to too much overhead or low-level control. Although it is always better, in the sense of development time, costs, and ease, to work with high-level abstractions, it might be necessary to implement a custom raw SOAP XML client AIC. In essence, the raw SOAP XML AIC will become its own SOAP client.

The process of building a SOAP client is not complex, depending on how generic and flexible the SOAP client needs to be. Because a generic high- and low-level abstraction for a SOAP client already exists, it would not make sense to reproduce these efforts. It is therefore most likely that the raw SOAP XML AIC will be tightly coupled to a specific SOAP request and response—likely, a lightweight AIC; but if the SOAP server's URL is a configuration issue, a pipeline AIC can be used.

The steps to produce a Raw SOAP XML AIC are as follows:

1. Build a string or use the MS XML document model to build a specific SOAP request.

2. Use the ServerXMLHTTP object from the MS XML technology to open a POST to an HTTP URL where the SOAP server is located.

3. Add the SOAPAction header if necessary.

4. Send the SOAP request message.

5. Check (via the Status property) that the POST was successful in the error-handling routine.

6. Check the SOAP response message for any errors using the responseXML property.

The design of the raw SOAP XML AIC eliminates some of the overly high abstraction processing from the MS SOAPClient version, and provides optional and easy customization. Since no level of abstraction is present, this raw SOAP XML AIC can be customized to be as specific as necessary but also requires a greater understanding of the SOAP specification.

Creating Raw SOAP AIC   To create a raw SOAP AIC, the previous setup of the MS SOAP Toolkit will be used. The most difficult task is determining what the raw XML SOAP request message will look like in comparison to the method requested. To make this determination, and for general debugging purposes, the MS SOAP Toolkit 2.0 provides a handy application called the Tracer Utility. This application traces requests sent over a specific HTTP port and redirects them to another port. In doing so, the utility captures incoming SOAP request and response messages.

The following procedure creates a lightweight AIC component template outline that implements the appropriate interfaces and functions:

1. Choose Project | References and add the following references to the needed components:

   - Microsoft BizTalk Server Application Interface Components 1.0 Type Library
   - Microsoft XML 3.0

2. Set a constant variable pointing to the SOAP listeners:

```
Const soapServerURL = "http://localhost/soapaic/server/soapaic.asp"
```

3. In the IBTSAppIntegration_ProcessMessage function, begin to build the XML SOAP request message as a string or with the MSXML document objects.

4. Extract the document string passed from BizTalk and place it as necessary in the XML SOAP request message.

5. Open an HTTP connection to the SOAP listener with a request type set to POST. This can be done with MSXML2.ServerXMLHTTP30 object.

6. Set the ContentType HTTP header to text/xml and encoding format to utf-8.

7. Add the *SOAPAction* HTTP header.

8. Use the ServerXMLHTTP30's Send method to send the SOAP request to the SOAP listener.

9. Capture the return and check for any errors in the ServerXMLHTTP30's Status.

10. Return back for BizTalk Interchange Submitsync requests.

Code Example: RawSOAPLightWeight   Note that the following example code has minimal error handling (if any) to minimize text and enhance readability:

```
Option Explicit

Implements IBTSAppIntegration

Const soapServerURL = "http://localhost/soapaicserver/soapaic.asp"

Private Function IBTSAppIntegration_ProcessMessage(ByVal bstrDocument As String)
As String
    Dim strSOAPRequest As String
    Dim serverHTTPXML As MSXML2.ServerXMLHTTP30
    Dim objReturnDoc As MSXML2.DOMDocument30

    'manually build SOAPRequest
    strSOAPRequest = "<?xml version='1.0' encoding='UTF-8' standalone='no'?>"
    strSOAPRequest = strSOAPRequest & "<SOAP-ENV:Envelope SOAP-
ENV:encodingStyle='http://schemas.xmlsoap.org/soap/encoding/' xmlns:SOAP-
ENV='http://schemas.xmlsoap.org/soap/envelope/'>"
    strSOAPRequest = strSOAPRequest & "<SOAP-ENV:Body>"
    strSOAPRequest = strSOAPRequest & "<SOAPSDK1:AddToDB
xmlns:SOAPSDK1='http://tempuri.org/message/'>"

    strSOAPRequest = strSOAPRequest & "<strXMLRecordIn>"
    'manually add value of parameter
    strSOAPRequest = strSOAPRequest & bstrDocument
```

```
    strSOAPRequest = strSOAPRequest & "</strXMLRecordIn>"
    strSOAPRequest = strSOAPRequest & "<strConStringIn/>"
    strSOAPRequest = strSOAPRequest & "<strSqlIn/>"
    strSOAPRequest = strSOAPRequest & "<strUserIdIn/>"
    strSOAPRequest = strSOAPRequest & "<strPasswordIn/>"
    strSOAPRequest = strSOAPRequest & "</SOAPSDK1:AddToDB>"
    strSOAPRequest = strSOAPRequest & "</SOAP-ENV:Body>"
    strSOAPRequest = strSOAPRequest & "</SOAP-ENV:Envelope>"
    serverHTTPXML.Open "POST", soapServerURL
    serverHTTPXML.setRequestHeader "Content-Type", "text/xml, CharSet=""utf-8"""
    serverHTTPXML.setRequestHeader "SOAPAction",
"http://tempuri.org/action/SaveDB.AddToDB"

    'now send XML string to server
    serverHTTPXML.send strSOAPRequest

    objReturnDoc = serverHTTPXML.responseXML

    IBTSAppIntegration_ProcessMessage = 0

    Set serverHTTPXML = Nothing
    Exit Function
ExecuteError:
    Err.Raise 2, , "Custom Error Message"
End Function
```

Direct SOAP AIC

The best implementation of SOAP would be to move its XML syntax directly into BizTalk, which currently supports XML and HTTP posting. This empowers BizTalk Server's main messaging features: XML mapping. An obvious example might be to use BizTalk Server Messaging Engine to transform a legacy application request into another application that is running a SOAP listener and respond back again without any coding. It would, therefore, seem to make sense to try to create an HTTP transport BizTalk channel with a SOAP document specification for BizTalk and map an existing XML format to the SOAP request. However, two obstacles exist for this scenario:

1. BizTalk Server does not support multiple namespaces in a BizTalk document specification because the XDR format used in the BizTalk document specification assumes each namespace is based on its own schema.

2. The HTTP transport pipeline that ships with BizTalk does not allow for custom HTTP headers such as the needed header SOAPAction.

The SOAP XML syntax usually relies heavily on namespaces, rendering it unsupported directly. Importing a SOAP document into the BizTalk Editor will remove all colons (:) that separate the namespace prefixes and replace them with underscores (_). Also, not all the custom namespaces will be imported, as displayed in Figure 17-9.

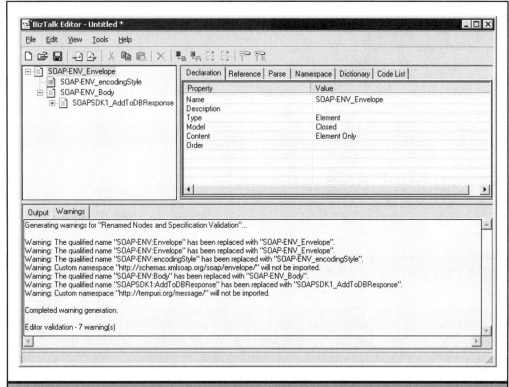

Figure 17-9. *BizTalk Editor generates errors when importing a normal SOAP request.*

Even if the SOAP XML syntax magically worked, the HTTP transport pipeline shipped with BizTalk does not allow for custom HTTP headers to be added. The steps to create a direct SOAP AIC are as follows:

1. Accept and create the BizTalk request SOAP document specification according to the defaults of the BizTalk Editor on importing the SOAP request message.

2. If converting from one document specification to another, create a BizTalk mapper file.

3. Create a normal pipeline AIC that repairs the "working_data" XML document to a normal SOAP request by converting the underscores back to colons. Add the necessary namespaces as necessary.

4. Use the ServerXMLHTTP object from the MS XML technology to open a POST to an HTTP URL where the SOAP server is located.

5. Add the SOAPAction header if necessary.

6. Send the SOAP request message.

7. Check (using the Status property) that the POST was successful in error-handling routing.

8. Check the SOAP response message for any error with the responseXML property.

The obvious benefit to this method is that now the SOAP requests can be handled as normal BizTalk documents, avoiding unnecessary coding in AICs. This technique also represents a possible solution to the known multiple namespace limitation in BizTalk Server today—for example, the default ADO XML format, the WebDAV XML format, and so on.

Registering SOAP AICs

The registration of SOAP AICs is no different than that of normal AICs because they all must use a normal COM AIC that functions as a SOAP client. See the section "Registering AICs", earlier in this chapter.

Configuring BizTalk Messaging Ports to Use SOAP AICs

After creating and registering the SOAP AIC of choice, setting up a BizTalk Messaging port should be a simple matter of selecting it as the transport. A list of all the AICs on the system is displayed by the New Messaging Port Wizard in the BizTalk Messaging Manager. After creating the channel that sends the configured port and uses the desired AIC for transport, the design-time configurations of the pipeline AIC are available in the New Channel Wizard's Advanced Configuration page. If the AIC is not a pipeline AIC, no configuration data is available. For more information, refer to the section "Configuring BizTalk Messaging Ports to Use AICs", earlier in this chapter.

Implementing Web Services

Web Services are an expansion of SOAP. In fact, they utilize SOAP to invoke the service methods. The Web Service provides an application that implements itself as a SOAP listener or SOAP server. The application can decide what methods it wants to expose and how it wants to expose them in the form of a Web Service. The exposure is really a form of publishing of the Web Service interface to a central location for all consumers (clients) to discover using two XML protocol techniques: Discovery Protocol (DISCO) and/or Universal Description, Discovery, and Integration (UDDI).

Web Services are both Web and application components. The power of Web Services is that they are loadable just-in-time, bringing dynamically expanding functionality to applications and architectures. The building blocks of Web Services are based on the XML standard proposed specifications, making Web Services completely platform neutral and self-contained via SOAP; Discovery Protocol (DISCO); and Universal Description, Discovery, and Integration (UDDI).

A URL points to a Web Service's description: a modified XML schema formatted file or a Web Service Definition Language (WSDL) file, as shown in Figure 17-10. The WSDL file defines the available services and their methods. Also included in this file are the method parameters and data types (*in* and *out*). The WSDL file is used by the consumer to invoke a Web Service method. The invoking technique is done via SOAP.

Web Services make SOAP listeners dynamic and available. Any Web Service's methods can be bound to any application by finding the application and invoking its methods just-in-time. This radically changes how a client application implements its features and functionality. Some of the major software manufacturers, such as Microsoft and IBM, believe that just-in-time discovery and binding of Web Services in applications will revolutionize application development and sales. For example, Microsoft introduces Web Services as a cornerstone technology in its .Net Framework, and IBM has also released the Web Service Toolkit.

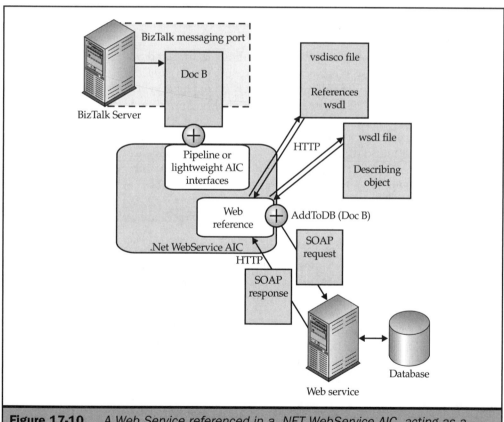

Figure 17-10. *A Web Service referenced in a .NET WebService AIC, acting as a Web Service client or consumer*

For more information on Web Services, refer to the MS Visual Studio.NET SDK, or the URLs http://msdn.microsoft.com/webservices/ and http://www-106.ibm.com/developerworks/webservices/.

Web Service AICs

Web Service AICs are not much different than SOAP AICs, except that the former will take advantage of the dynamic discovery capabilities implemented in Web Services. A Web Services AIC will dynamically expand BizTalk Server's integration capabilities just-in-time and with no extra coding. A perfect example of this would be producing a pipeline AIC that requires two parameters: the URL of the Web Service repository and what Web Service name to call. Notably, such a dynamic and completely generic Web Service AIC will suffer a performance hit for just-in-time lookups. Depending on the level of developer abstraction, Web Service AICs can be built using almost the same techniques used for SOAP AICs. The use of Microsoft's Web Services Toolkit in Visual Studio.NET will provide a powerful, high-level layer of abstraction.

Web Services AIC in C#

The Microsoft .NET Framework provides the ability to turn and build any component into a Web Service. It is even easier with Microsoft Visual Studio.NET. The ease of building a .NET Web Service will unfortunately be overshadowed by a few extra steps needed to make the C# .NET Framework assembly or component—the Web Service consumer or client—compatible with BizTalk Server or COM. In the .NET Framework world this is called *interop*—the interoperability between the old COM and the .NET Framework's new foundation is called the Common Language Runtime (CLR). CLR provides a powerful means of creating a universal language with perfect data typing definitions. .NET Framework with CLR hosts huge amount of power and flexibility.

For more information on .Net, CLR, and C#, refer to the Microsoft Visual Studio SDK.

Interestingly enough, although BizTalk is part of Microsoft's .NET Server arsenal, it does not understand or have a connection to CLR or the .Net Framework. BizTalk Server uses COM as its foundation. The use of the .NET Framework's *COM interop* technique is required to construct a C# class, which implements a BizTalk COM interface function and is available as a true BizTalk AIC.

Following is an outline of the steps needed to produce a Web Service with the necessary functionality exposed and, if necessary, to publish a central Web Service repository. This becomes a published SOAP server or listener: a.k.a. Web Service.

1. Create a class in .NET and add a reference to the normal COM BizTalk AIC interfaces for either a lightweight or a pipeline AIC.

2. Add a Web reference, pointing to the discovery file (vsdisco) or directly to the WSDL file of the Web Service.

3. As with a normal AIC, add implementations to the AIC interface along with the mandatory interface methods—for example, ProcessMessage for a lightweight AIC.

4. Add the business logic code to the ProcessMessage method or the Execute method to call the Web Service's methods.

5. Build the .NET assembly.

6. Register the .NET assembly's type library (TLB) as a normal COM object.

7. Add affinity values to the Registry or add the .NET assembly into COM+ along with MSCOREE.DLL.

Creating a Web Service AIC in C# .NET   The majority of the tricky work is in setting up the .NET assembly or component so that COM and BizTalk recognize it. The code is easier to create with C# in Visual Studio.Net because these languages include the necessary syntax elements. Web Services are integral parts of .NET. This means that they are as easy to use as local components. .NET holds loads of power that can be unleashed easily as Web Services and as BizTalk AICs.

The following steps are used to create a Web Service and a COM interop .NET assembly that implements the lightweight AIC BizTalk interfaces using C#.

1. From the menu, choose to create a new C# project—an ASP.NET Web Service.

2. Change the default name from WebService1 to something of your choosing. Visual Studio .NET will automatically create an IIS virtual directory and create most of the necessary files.

3. Add a reference by using System.Data.SqlClient and System.Xml.

4. Create a new method for the class, as with the other examples, using AddToDB, and taking in a string parameter and returning a long.

5. Add the necessary business logic with the new method. In this example, the AddToDB function loads the string and connects to the database defined using the SQLConnection class. If connecting to a database other than one created in SQL 7.0 or later, use the OleDbConnection class instead.

6. Build and test the Web Service. The Visual Studio.Net debugger automatically loads a browser and points to the Web Services URI—for example, http://localhost/webserviceaicserver/webserviceaicserver.aspx. This displays an HTML page with the SOAP request message, the SOAP response message, and GET, and POST requests.

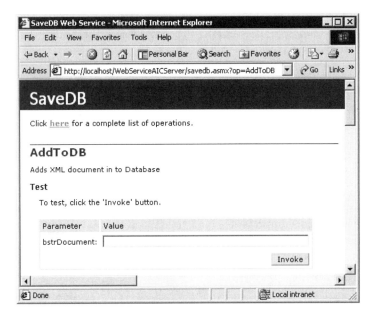

7. Now create a new C# class project. This C# class will call the Web Service and implement the COM BizTalk lightweight AIC interface and its methods.

8. Add a reference to the Web Service created in step 6 by right-clicking References in the Solutions Explorer and selecting Add Web Reference.

9. The Add Web Reference Explorer allows you to discover new Web Services to add to an application. In this case, type the URL into the Web Service by pointing to its URI with vsdisco appended to it: http://localhost/webserviceaicserver/webserviceaicserver.vsdisco. If the Add Web Reference Explorer finds the vsdisco file, it will add the reference defined to the WDSL file. This enables the Add Reference button, which you click.

10. A default Web reference will now be displayed in the Solutions Explorer. Change the default name of the Web reference to something that resembles a Web service interface—for example, WSAic, which will now be the reference class type used in the code.

11. Add the reference to COM BizTalk IBTSAppIntegration by right-clicking the References and selecting Add Reference to choose the Microsoft BizTalk Server Application Interface Components From COM tab. Doing this will likely generate

a warning that there is no primary interop assembly for the COM component. This is normal, because .NET must create a proxy wrapper for the COM component to proxy requests from the .NET-managed object to the .Net-unmanaged object (COM component). This wrapper also maps the COM-type interfaces to .NET CLR types.

12. With the references exposed, set the Projects properties to have the class automatically register itself as a COM component. To do this, right-click the Project name in the Solution Explorer and select Properties. In the Project Properties window, under Configuration Properties\Build, set the Outputs option and the Register for COM interop value equal to "true".

13. At this point, the C# class is completely configured to call the COM BizTalk IBTSAppIntegration interface and to be registered into COM's Registry. Load BTSComponentsLib into the class using BTSComponentsLib.

14. Set the class to implement the IBTSAppIntegration in C# like this:

```
public class Class1 : IBTSAppIntegration
```

15. Add the IBTSAppIntegration.ProcessMessage method and call the class's business logic method.

16. Implement the other necessary business logic functions, such as test(), which calls the Web Service object, and the AddToDB method. This simple client implementation of a Web Service automatically discovers the Web Service class schema (WSDL) and loads it. It even generates all the necessary SOAP requests, reads the SOAP responses from the SOAP listener, and sets the appropriately defined return variables.

17. Build the Web Service AIC C# Class and place the type library (TLB) into a COM+ application. Be sure to add it with the COM+ Install New Component Wizard. For COM+ to accept the .NET component, you must add a reference to %System32%\MSCOREE.DLL (.NET Core Execution Engine) at the same time that you install the C# AIC class. Now BizTalk will find the C# class as it would a normal COM+ AIC that implements its interfaces.

Code Example in C#.NET: WebServiceLightweightAIC   Notice that the following example code has minimal error handling (if any) to minimize text and maximize readability:

```
using System;
using System.Xml;
using BTSComponentsLib;

namespace WebServiceLightWeightAIC
{
```

```
/// <summary>
/// Class1 Calls ProcessMessage making this an Interop with COM
/// BizTalk Lightweigth AIC
/// </summary>
public class Class1 : IBTSAppIntegration
{
    public Class1()
    {
        // TODO: Add constructor logic here
    }

    string IBTSAppIntegration.ProcessMessage(string strDocIn)
    {
        return this.test(strDocIn);
    }

    public string test(string strDocIn)
    {
        WSAic.SaveDB oWSAic = new WSAic.SaveDB();
        long iReturn;
        iReturn = oWSAic.AddToDB(strDocIn);
        return iReturn.ToString();
    }
}
```

Registering Web Services AICs

The normal AIC registration process is still needed for BizTalk to recognize .NET-based AICs. In addition to the Web Service being registered into the central repository (if necessary), the interoperability registration of the AIC class in .NET and COM, called COM interop, must occur. To register the Web Service with .NET and COM, a couple of steps are required. The steps and circumstances are described next.

In VS.Net: Right-click the Project name in the Solution Explorer and select Properties | Configuration Properties | Build.

■ Set the Outputs option, Register For COM Interop, equal to "true".

or

■ Run regasm /t *classname* to add the .NET assembly or component into the Registry.

- In VS.NET: Compiling will automatically add the assembly or component to the .NET global assembly cache (GAC).

or

- Add the .NET assembly to the .NET global assembly cache (GAC) using gacutil.exe.
- Using the COM+ Component Install Wizard, add the .NET assembly to COM+ and the mscoreee.dll file to the same COM+ package at the same time.

Configuring BizTalk Messaging Ports to Use Web Service AICs

After creating and registering the Web Service AIC of choice, setting up a BizTalk Messaging Port should be a simple matter of selecting it as the transport type. A list of all the AICs on the system is displayed by the New Messaging Port Wizard in the BizTalk Messaging Manager. After creating the channel that sends the configured port and uses the desired AIC for transport, the design-time configuration of the pipeline AIC is available in the New Channel Wizard on the Advanced Configuration page. If the AIC is not a pipeline AIC, no configuration data is available. For more information, refer to the section "Configuring BizTalk Messaging Ports to Use AICs", earlier in this chapter.

Chapter 18

WMI Integration

In Chapter 15, we saw how to configure BizTalk Messaging using the BizTalk Configuration Objects. These objects allow us to create, modify, and destroy the logical elements used in processing documents through the messaging system. These logical elements include organizations, document definitions, envelopes, messaging ports, distribution lists, and channels. What we cannot do with the BizTalk Configuration Objects is work with the more concrete resources of the BizTalk Server system. These are resources that make up the actual software and hardware of the system. These resources include BizTalk servers, server groups, databases, shared queues, and receive functions. These BizTalk resources are configured using the Windows Management Instrumentation (WMI) interface.

In this chapter we will explore how to use WMI to query and manage these resources programmatically. We are going to look at what WMI is and how it relates to BizTalk Server. Then we will examine each of these objects in some depth and explore how to manipulate them with administration scripts. This chapter will present all code in VBScript, but the same techniques are applicable from any language that can access the WMI COM interfaces.

WMI Overview

Windows Management Instrumentation is Microsoft's implementation of the Web-Based Enterprise Management (WBEM) system management platform. WMI was introduced with Microsoft's Windows 2000 operating system. WBEM is a standard developed by the Distributed Management Task Force (DMTF) to create a platform-neutral and vendor-neutral means of accessing system state and diagnostic information across various systems within an enterprise. The interface also allows managed components to be configured using a Common Information Model (CIM).

Additional information regarding WMI is available on the Microsoft Developer Network (MSDN) web site at http://msdn.microsoft.com/. The Distributed Management Task Force web site is available at http://www.dtmf.com/. This site contains details about the WBEM Initiative and the Common Information Model.

WMI Architecture

The WMI architecture is designed to be both simple and flexible. The system allows system resources to be abstracted in a consistent way no matter what type of resource you are using. The architecture defines how information about resources is managed, queried, and altered. For a high-level overview of the WMI architecture, see Figure 18-1.

The central concept in WMI is the *Common Information Model (CIM)*. CIM is an object-oriented model developed by the DMTF as part of the WBEM Initiative. This model represents each resource in the system as an instance of a class. The model supports the usual object-oriented concepts of abstraction, encapsulation, and inheritance. For example, "Network Adapter #1" would be an instance of the "Network Adapter" class. By referencing this instance, the properties and configurations of this object can be queried

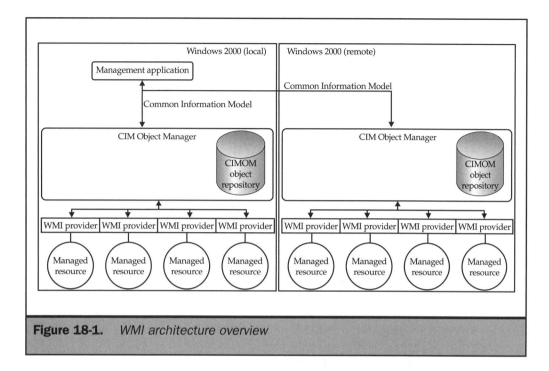

Figure 18-1.   *WMI architecture overview*

and altered. A CIM instance object represents a managed object in the system. By referencing the class, the structure and relationships between objects can be explored. A CIM object that represents a class of objects, as opposed to an instance of that class, is referred to as a *class object*.

The Common Information Model is used by a management application to implement a set of system-configuration or information-retrieval actions. The most common types of WMI management applications are MMC snap-ins, such as BizTalk Server Administration, and scripts executed using the Windows Scripting Host (WSH). The examples in this chapter will be written in Visual Basic Scripting Edition (VBScript).

The main software component of the WMI architecture is the CIM Object Manager (CIMOM). This is the middle layer of the architecture shown in Figure 18-1. CIMOM is responsible for servicing all requests made through WMI and managing the storage of CIM schema information.

CIMOM services configuration and information requests through the use of *WMI providers.* A WMI provider acts as a liaison between the generic Common Information Model and the specific system resources being managed as shown at the bottom of Figure 18-1. BizTalk Server's WMI provider provides interfaces to manage all of the servers, server groups, queues, and receive functions associated with BizTalk Server. Those familiar with Microsoft's Open Database Connectivity (ODBC) technology will recognize a similarity in architectures between WMI and ODBC. The WMI providers offer the same type of functionality to a management application that an ODBC Driver provides to a database application. The CIM Object Manager is analogous to the ODBC Driver Manager.

CIMOM stores information about the object classes and instances in the CIMOM Object Repository. Apparently, the DMTF decided that these acronyms were nested deeply enough and didn't refer to the Object Repository as "CIMOMOR". The Object Repository contains schema information about all managed objects in the system. These include their class names, properties, methods, and so on. Selected instance information is stored as well. While the CIMOM Object Repository isn't a true relational database, it is used similarly. Microsoft even has an ODBC driver that allows database applications to access the Object Repository as though it consisted of relational tables. This driver provides read-only access and is intended for reporting applications.

The schema information stored in the CIMOM Object Repository is represented in a Managed Object Format (MOF) file. This is a text file that is very similar in format to the Interface Definition Language (IDL) used by Microsoft's development tools to define COM interfaces. An MOF file contains the properties, methods, and relationships between a set of classes. BizTalk Server's MOF file can be found in the \Setup subdirectory under the BizTalk Server installation directory and is called InterchangeProvSchema.mof. This file is an excellent source of information about the WMI classes implemented by the BizTalk Server WMI provider. It is also interesting to look through this file and notice the properties and methods that are commented out. Comments start with "//". There appear to be many features that either didn't make it into the final product or were in the product and were removed. For example, there are removed properties for supporting automated purging of the Document Tracking Database and FTP as an outbound Transport Protocol.

BizTalk Messaging Manager vs. BizTalk Server Administration

At first glance, BizTalk Server appears to have two distinct administration tools: BizTalk Messaging Manager and BizTalk Server Administration. These tools actually serve two very different purposes and are designed for use by two different groups of professionals.

In Chapter 6, we looked at how we use the BizTalk Messaging Manager to configure details of how documents are processed. These details include the document definitions, messaging ports, channels, and other configurations that determine how a document is transformed and delivered to a trading partner. This application is actually a thin client wrapper around an Active Server Pages (ASP) web application that can be found in the MessagingManager directory under the BizTalk Server installation directory. This web site is installed in the server's IIS configuration as part of BizTalk Server installation. This application uses the BizTalk Server Configuration Objects discussed in Chapter 15 to administer these objects. The BizTalk Messaging Manager is intended for use by developers and document specialists for managing processes within BizTalk Messaging.

BizTalk Server Administratration, described in Chapter 9, is used to configure the BizTalk Server software components. These components include servers, server groups, shared queues, and receive functions. The BizTalk Server Administratration console is a Microsoft Management Console (MMC) that contains two snap-ins: Microsoft BizTalk Server 2000 and the Windows 2000 Event Log. Because BizTalk Server Administration is an MMC snap, it can be included in any MMC console configuration file. The BizTalk Server MMC snap-in provides an interface to query and manage BizTalk Server through the Windows Management Instrumentation (WMI) provider implemented by BizTalk Server. The BizTalk Server Administration MMC snap-in is intended for use by System Administrators in a production environment.

An easy way to remember which features are configured through WMI and which are configured through the BizTalk Server Configuration Object Model is to consider which administration tool you would use to do the configuration interactively. If you would use the BizTalk Messaging Manager to perform the configuration, then the BizTalk Server Configuration Object Model would be used to perform the function programmatically. If you would use the BizTalk Server Administration to perform the configuration, then the settings required are accessible via the WMI interface.

Generic WMI Code Objects

WBEM and WMI define a set of basic object classes that implement the interface through which a management application queries and modifies managed objects. This object model is generic enough to be applicable to any type of CIM object or class. BizTalk Server's WMI provider works in the background to satisfy the requests made through this interface. The VBScript code in this chapter will manipulate BizTalk Server's settings using the WMI object model.

We will examine only the most common objects and interfaces used when managing BizTalk Server. A more complete reference for the WMI object model is available at Microsoft's MSDN web site. To access these objects through early binding in Visual Basic, it is necessary to set a reference to the Microsoft WMI Scripting v1.1 Library. This library is contained in a type library called wbemdisp.tlb that exists in the system32\wbem directory under your Windows installation directory.

Monikers

While monikers are not really objects, they are used extensively to address them. A Windows *moniker* is a string that identifies an object or class within Windows. The structure of this string depends on the protocol being accessed. To create an object using a moniker, the management application invokes the GetObject( ) call, passing in the moniker as the object name.

The most commonly used type of moniker is also known as a Uniform Resource Locator (URL). This is the address used to access a page or other resource on the World Wide Web. For example, http://www.microsoft.com/ms.htm is Microsoft's home page.

This moniker indicates that the protocol "http" will be used to access the server www.microsoft.com from which we will retrieve the file called ms.htm.

Another use of monikers that you encounter when using BizTalk is to create and manage BizTalk Orchestration schedules. See Chapters 7 and 8 for more details on using BizTalk Orchestration.

Monikers are used within WMI to access specific resources or classes of resources. A moniker in WMI has this form:

```
winmgmts: {SECURITY}!\\{SERVER}\{NAMESPACE}:{CLASS}.{KEY}
```

For WMI, the "protocol" is always winmgmts. This represents the Windows Management Instrumentation system. All of the sections of the moniker are optional except for the protocol and the namespace.

The namespace identifies what WMI provider is going to be accessed, and therefore what type of resources will be managed. The namespace for BizTalk Server is "MicrosoftBizTalkServer". Namespaces in WMI are hierarchical. BizTalk Server's namespace is directly beneath the root namespace. The simplest moniker used to access BizTalk Server is:

```
winmgmts:root\MicrosoftBizTalkServer
```

This moniker returns an object representing the BizTalk WMI Provider on the local server.

The security section of the moniker defines the way in which DCOM authentication levels and user credential impersonation will be handled while accessing the managed object. By default, these parameters are set as "{authenticationLevel=pktPrivacy, impersonationLevel=impersonate}!". These settings protect the network exchanges created by your WMI calls and allow WMI to pass your credentials to other systems. These are the recommended values for these options and should not be changed in most cases. See the MSDN web site for more details.

The server name can be a system name or an IP address. Specifying a "." (dot) for the server means that the local system should be used. If the server section of the moniker is not given, "." is the default. Valid monikers to access BizTalk Server on the local server (BTSDev) would include:

```
winmgmts:root\MicrosoftBizTalkServer
winmgmts:\\.\root\MicrosoftBizTalkServer
winmgmts:\\BTSDev\root\MicrosoftBizTalkServer
```

The class section of the moniker indicates the type of object to be manipulated. BizTalk Server implements several object classes that will be detailed later in this chapter. Specifying a class name will return an object representing that class of object, not a particular instance of the object. It is possible to enumerate the instances of a class from a class object. To retrieve the class object representing all BizTalk Servers, the moniker would be:

```
winmgmts:\\.\root\MicrosoftBizTalkServer:
                MicrosoftBizTalkServer_Server
```

The final section of the moniker allows the retrieval of a specific instance of a managed object by specifying its key fields. The object returned represents one object of the class given. This object can then be used to manage that resource using the properties and methods associated with its class. The moniker for our test server would be:

```
winmgmts:\\.\root\MicrosoftBizTalkServer:
            MicrosoftBizTalkServer_Server.Name='BTSDev'
```

The key field name, "Name", may be omitted if there is only one key field for the class. In this case, the following is equivalent:

```
winmgmts:\\.\root\MicrosoftBizTalkServer:
            MicrosoftBizTalkServer_Server='BTSDev'
```

In cases where there are multiple key fields, the moniker looks like this:

```
winmgmts:\\.\root\MicrosoftBizTalkServer:
            MicrosoftBizTalkServer_Queue
            .QID='51',Group='BizTalk Server Group'
```

Monikers allow easy access to any level of the WMI object hierarchy. It is also possible to traverse from object type to object type using the properties and methods of the WMI object model and those implemented by the WMI providers.

SWbemLocator

The SWbemLocator class is used to establish an initial connection to a WMI provider on a local or remote host. This class allows the programmer to connect using an alternate set of logon credentials for a remote system. If the logon credentials are not supplied, the User ID and Password of the current user running the management application are used. SWbemLocator has only a single method, ConnectServer.

```
Dim objLocator 'As SWbemLocator
Dim BTS 'As SWbemServices
```

```
set objLocator = CreateObject("WbemScripting.SWbemLocator")

set BTS = objLocator.ConnectServer _
            ("BTSDev","root\MicrosoftBizTalkServer", _
            "administrator", "IloveBizTalk!!!")
```

Unlike most WMI objects, SWbemLocator objects are created using CreateObject( ), not through a moniker using GetObject( ). The ConnectServer( ) method is then used to connect to the BizTalk Server namespace on the BizTalk Server. The object returned from ConnectServer is an SWbemServices object.

If the UserID and Password were not supplied, the preceding example would be equivalent to using a GetObject call to retrieve the namespace of the BizTalk WMI provider. The difference in the two techniques is the opportunity to use alternative logon credentials. The User ID and Password can only be used to connect to a remote system. For a local connection, leave them empty.

SWbemServices

The SWbemServices class represents a connection to a WMI provider on a specified local or remote system. Specifically, this object gives the caller access to a WBEM object that can be used to query objects within the namespace. It can also be used to directly manipulate these objects.

The only method of the SWbemServices class that we will deal with for these examples will be the ExecQuery method. This method accepts a query string and returns a collection of objects within the referenced namespace. The query language used is very similar to the Structured Query Language (SQL) used to query relational databases. It is called the WMI Query Language (WQL).

This example creates an object for the BizTalk Server namespace and then queries the servers that are configured for BizTalk Server.

```
Dim BTS 'as SWbemServices
Dim osServers 'as SWbemObjectSet

Set BTS = GetObject("winmgmts:root\MicrosoftBizTalkServer")

Set osServers = BTS.ExecQuery( _
            "select * from MicrosoftBizTalkServer_Server")
```

This example uses GetObject( ) to return a reference to an SWbemServices object representing the BizTalk WMI provider. This object is then used to invoke the ExecQuery( ) method to return a collection of BizTalk server objects. The collection class used, SWbemObjectSet, is described next.

There are several other methods on the SWbemServices object that allow direct access to managed objects and asynchronous functions. These are fully documented in MSDN.

SWbemObjectSet

The SWbemObjectSet class represents a collection of WMI managed objects. This collection can be generated through several means. In our examples, we will obtain our object sets by executing a query against an SWbemServices object.

This object has the usual properties of a fully automated collection class. Its primary method and property are Item and Count. Item is the default method of this class. Unfortunately, the index used for the Item method is the full path of the object's moniker. This limits the usefulness of indexing directly into the collection, since you must know the object's key, not just an index number, to access it. Count is the number of managed objects in the collection.

The usual technique used to retrieve the elements of a WMI object set is to use an enumerator. In VB or VBScript, this is performed using the "for … each …" construct as follows:

```
Dim BTS 'as SWbemServices
Dim osServers 'as SWbemObjectSet
Dim objServer 'as SWbemObject

Set BTS = GetObject("winmgmts:root\MicrosoftBizTalkServer")
Set osServers = BTS.ExecQuery( _
              "select * from MicrosoftBizTalkServer_Server")

for each objServer in osServers
    ' Operate on objServer
next
```

In this example, we query the BizTalk service for a list of the servers configured. We then loop through the objects in the object set. Each object returned represents a single managed object.

SWbemObject

The SWbemObject class is the basic unit within the WBEM Object Model. An instance of this class represents a class or a single managed object within WMI. All of the properties and methods of the object are exposed through this object. The managed object can also be added and removed from the configuration.

The SWbemObject class may also be used to represent an entire class of WMI objects. This is called a *class object*. For example, it may represent a single BizTalk Server receive function, or it may represent the Receive Function class of objects. This distinction is important when using the properties and methods of the SWbemObject because they are applied to the entire class of object, not just a single instance of the class.

The following table contains the most commonly used properties of the SWbemObject class. Note that the "_" (underscore) characters at the end of the names are required.

Name	Type	Access	Description
Derivation_	string( )	R	This property contains an array of the classes from which this WMI object or class is derived.
Path_	SWbemObjectPath	R	This property represents the full moniker path of the object or class. The SWbemObjectPath is used to represent this information.
Properties_	SWbemPropertySet	R	This property is a collection of properties for the object. While this collection is Read-Only, the properties themselves may or may not be alterable depending on the definition of the property.
Methods_	SWbemMethodSet	R	This property is a collection of objects representing the methods of the object or class.

The next table presents the most commonly used methods of the SWbemObject class. Again, the "_" (underscore) characters are required.

Name	Type of Instance	Description
SpawnInstance_	Object or class instance	This method creates an empty instance object for the class. The object created is empty. This method can be used from either a class instance or an object instance, but the new object is empty in either case.

Name	Type of Instance	Description
Put_(iFlags)	Object instance only	This method is used to create or alter managed objects in WMI. This method writes object information to the WMI provider for permanent storage. When an object is created using SpawnInstance_, it is only resident in the memory space of the management application. To make the object changes permanent, the Put_ method must be invoked. The iFlags parameter is used to indicate whether the object should be created (2) or updated (1). MSDN defines other values for this parameter that are not supported by BizTalk Server's WMI provider.
Delete_	Object instance only	This method is used to destroy a managed object. The object destroyed is the object currently represented by the SWbemObject instance.
ExecMethod_	Object instance only	This method executes one of the public methods on the managed object.
Instances_	Class instance only	This method returns an SWbemObjectSet containing a collection of all objects of a class.

To allow easier scripting, the SWbemObject class fully supports automation of the managed object. This allows the properties and methods of the managed object class to be referenced directly through the SWbemObject interface. For example, consider the following code fragment:

```
Dim objRecFunc

set objRecFunc = _
    GetObject("winmgmts:root\MicrosoftBizTalkServer:" _
      & "MicrosoftBizTalkServer_ReceiveFunction='MyReceiver'")
```

```
msgbox objRecFunc.Comment
objRecFunc.Comment = "Your Comment Here!"
objRecFunc.Put_(1)
```

This script retrieves a Receive Function object from WMI, displays its Comment property, and changes it. Note that the Properties_ collection did not have to be explicitly referenced. The same technique is valid when accessing methods through ExecMethod_( ).

SWbemObjectPath

The SWbemObjectPath class is used to construct or examine a managed object's path. An object's path is the same as its moniker except that it does not include the "winmgmts:" prefix.

```
Dim objServer 'As SWbemObject

set objServer = GetObject _
        ("winmgmts:\\.\root\MicrosoftBizTalkServer:"
         & "_MicrosoftBizTalkServer_Server='BTSDev'")

MsgBox objServer.Path_.Path
```

The Path_ property of the SWbemObject class returns an SWbemObjectPath object that represents the object's path. This sample displays a string like this:

```
\\BTSDev\root\MicrosoftBizTalkServer:
     MicrosoftBizTalkServer_Server.Name='BTSDev'
```

Notice that the server name has been filled in where we originally placed a "."(dot). This happens because the Path_ property represents the path to the managed object and is not dependent on how the SWbemObject instance was created.

The SWbemObjectPath class is useful when constructing object paths piece by piece. The properties and methods listed in Table 18-1 and Table 18-2 can be used with objects of this class.

The SWbemObjectPath class is useful when it is necessary to refresh an object's state. The DisplayName property is a completely formed moniker for the object. Therefore, you can refresh the state of any managed object like this:

```
Set objMyObject = GetObject(objMyObject.Path_.DisplayName)
```

Name	Type	Access	Description
Path	String	RW	Full path of the object without the "winmgmts:" moniker prefix.
RelPath	String	RW	Path of the object relative to its namespace. This does not include the server, namespace, or moniker prefix.
Server	String	RW	Name of the server used to access this object.
Namespace	String	RW	Identifier for the WMI provider that is managing this object.
ParentNamespace	String	R	Namespace that resides above this namespace in the WMI hierarchy. Always "root" for BizTalk Server objects.
DisplayName	String	RW	Complete object moniker including all options.
Class	String	RW	Name of the WMI class this object represents or is an instance of.
IsClass	Boolean	R	True = This object represents a WMI Class. False = This object represents a Managed Object.
IsSingleton	Boolean	R	Indicates that the object is a singleton instance.
Key	Collection	R	Set of name/value pairs defining the key of the current instance object.

Table 18-1. *SWbemObjectPath Properties*

SWbemLastError

The WMI object model contains a special class for error handling. This object is somewhat unusual in that you can only create an instance of the class after an error has occurred.

Name	Description
SetAsClass	Forces the path to address a Class
SetAsSingleton	Forces the path to address a singleton instance

Table 18-2. *SWbemObjectPath Methods*

The BizTalk WMI help file contains a complete example for using this class to extract error information.

BizTalk WMI Provider Object Classes

Now we turn our attention to the specific resources managed by the BizTalk WMI provider. The classes defined in InterchangeProvSchema.mof cover all of the software components associated with BizTalk Server. These include servers, groups, queues, and receive functions. We will examine the purpose of each object class and present sample scripts for manipulating them. We will also describe the properties and methods of each class. For additional information, Microsoft has published a BizTalk WMI help file on its web site. At this writing, it is available at http://www.microsoft.com/biztalk/techinfo/productdoc/2000/WMIdownload.asp. The filename is BTSwmi.chm.

The properties of each class will be presented in a table that includes each property's name and description. Properties of these instance objects may be Read/Write, Read-Only, or Write-Only. These are indicated by "RW", "R", and "W", respectively, in the Access column of the table. The names of key fields will be marked with the word "KEY". WMI supports the basic types for property values in the following table.

Type Name	Description
String(n)	Variable-length character string
Long	32-bit Integer number
Boolean	True/False value. False = 0
Array( )	A SAFEARRAY object
Byte( )	An array of bytes used to return Unicode data; an indication of the code page is always associated with this type of data

Type Name	Description
Datetime	Date/Time values, also called timestamps, are returned from the BizTalk WMI provider as strings with the format: CCYYMMDDHHNNSS... CCYY—Year (4-digit) MM—Month DD—Day HH—Hour (24-hour clock) NN—Minutes SS—Seconds There are additional characters at the tail end of this string that may contain fractional seconds and a GMT offset indicator. These can be safely ignored in most cases.

BizTalk Management Database

The first class we will examine represents the local server's connection to the BizTalk Management Database. This database contains all of the configurations managed via the BizTalk Messaging Manager application. It acts as the central control point for the BizTalk Server group.

class MicrosoftBizTalkServer_MgmtDB   This class represents the local server's connection to the BizTalk Management Database and, thereby, to all other BizTalk Server resources. This configuration is specific to the server on which it is accessed. The following table lists the BizTalk Management Database properties.

Name	Type	Access	Description
LocalServer (KEY)	String(63)	R	Name of the local server
MgmtDbLogon	String(256)	RW	SQL Server User ID used for the Management Database connection
MgmtDbName	String(123)	RW	Database name in SQL Server for the Management Database
MgmtDbPassword	String(63)	W	Password used to connect to the Management Database
MgmtDbServer	String(60)	RW	Server name of the SQL Server containing the Management Database

It is important to note that each BizTalk server has only one instance of this class. That instance is for the local server. This data can be used by management applications to find the Management Database. This is useful for reporting tools or other database applications, as in the following example:

```
Dim objMgmtDB 'As SWbemObject
Dim CONN 'As ADODB.Connection
Dim strConn 'As String
Set objMgmtDB = GetObject( _
   "winmgmts:\\BTSDev\root\MicrosoftBizTalkServer:" _
   & "MicrosoftBizTalkServer_MgmtDB='BTSDev'")

strConn = "Provider=SQLOLEDB.1;Persist Security Info=False" _
          & ";Data Source=" & objMgmtDB.MgmtDBServer _
          & ";User ID=" & objMgmtDB.MgmtDBLogon _
          & ";Initial Catalog=" & objMgmtDB.MgmtDBName & ";"

Set CONN = CreateObject("ADODB.Connection")
CONN.Open strConn
```

Note that the server name used in the moniker is the same as the system name given in the object's key. This will always be true when accessing objects of this class. At this point the ADO connection object is ready for use.

It is possible to alter these connection settings. Because these settings have such global scope, it is easy for BizTalk Server to get confused if its Management Database suddenly changes. The only safe reasons for updating these settings programmatically would be because either the Management Database has been moved or because the User ID and/or Password used to connect have changed. A server should never be set up to point at an unrelated management database. The server will not function correctly. The following script shows how to change the logon parameters used to connect to the Management Database:

```
Dim objMgmtDB 'As SWbemObject

Set objMgmtDB = GetObject( _
   "winmgmts:\\BTSDev\root\MicrosoftBizTalkServer:" _
   & "MicrosoftBizTalkServer_MgmtDB='BTSDev'")

objMgmtDB.MgmtDBLogon = "NewLogon"
objMgmtDB.MgmtDBPassword = "Way$tr0nGpAswrd"
objMgmtDB.Put_ (2) ' Update
```

For safety reasons, it is probably best to change these settings through the BizTalk Server Administration interface. In either case, the servers that use the Management Database should be taken offline before such changes are made.

BizTalk Server Group Settings

The next class we will examine represents the entire BizTalk Server Group. A group of BizTalk servers share databases and, most importantly, a common Work Queue in the Shared Queue database. This allows them to act as both a load-balancing cluster and a redundancy cluster without the use of Windows 2000 Cluster Services. A Windows cluster utilizing Cluster Services requires identical, specialized hardware and OS configuration. These restrictions do not apply to BizTalk Server groups. The Group class defines those properties and methods that have scope across the entire group. Server Groups are dicussed in Chapter 9.

class MicrosoftBizTalkServer_Group   This class represents a group of BizTalk servers joined into a server group. The servers in the group share the same management database, shared queues, and Document Tracking database (see Table 18-3 and Table 18-4).

Name	Type	Access	Description
Name(KEY)	String(256)	RW	Name of the BizTalk server group.
DateModified	datetime	R	Date this instance was last modified. Format: CCYYMMDDHHNNSS…
Configuration CacheRefresh Interval	Long	RW	Each server in the group periodically reads the configuration from the Management Database and caches it in memory. This property sets the number of seconds between refreshes of this cache. Defaults to 50 seconds.
ConnectToDbStatus	Long	R	Status of the Document Tracking and shared queue database connections. Values: 0—Both connections OK 1—DTA connection failed 2—SQ connection failed 3—Both connections failed
DocTrackDbLogon	String(256)	RW	SQL Server User ID to use when connecting to the Document Tracking database.

Table 18-3. *BizTalk Server Group Properties*

Name	Type	Access	Description
DocTrackDbName	String(123)	RW	SQL database name of the Document Tracking database.
DocTrackDbPassword	String(63)	W	Password used to connect to the Document Tracking database.
DocTrackDbServer	String(60)	RW	Machine name of the SQL Server hosting the Document Tracking database.
EnableDocument Tracking	Boolean	RW	This flag indicates whether document tracking is enabled or disabled within the group. Default is 1 (Enabled).
LoggingPointState	Long (Bitmask)	RW	Set of flags indicating which type(s) of events should be logged in the Document Tracking database. Bit Mask Values (ORed): 001—Incoming interchanges 010—MIME BLOBs 100—Outgoing interchanges
ParserOrder	String Array	RW	Contains an array of Class IDs (GUID) for each parser configured in the group. Parsers are listed in the order they are used.
ProxyHost	String(256)	RW	Hostname used to access the Internet via a proxy server.
ProxyPort	Long	RW	IP Port used to access the Internet via a proxy server.
QueueDbLogon	String(256)	RW	SQL Server User ID to use when connecting to the shared queue database.
QueueDbName	String(123)	RW	SQL database name of the shared queue database.
QueueDbPassword	String(63)	W	Password used to connect to the shared queue database.
QueueDbServer	String(60)	RW	Machine name of the SQL Server hosting the shared queue database.
ReliableMessaging ReplyToURL	String(512)	RW	This URL (including protocol name) is used by other servers when returning receipts to this server when using BizTalk Framework Reliable Messaging.

Table 18-3. *BizTalk Server Group Properties* (continued)

Name	Type	Access	Description
RetryQueueCount	Long	R	Current number of documents in the Retry Queue.
ScheduledQueue Count	Long	R	Current number of documents in the Scheduled queue.
SMTPHost	String(256)	RW	When sending interchanges using the SMTP protocol, this SMTP host is used to send messages. In most cases, this server should be set up to forward mail to other systems across the Internet.
SuspendedQueue Count	Long	R	Current number of documents in the Suspended Queue.
UseProxyServer	Boolean	RW	Indicates whether to use a Proxy Server when communicating over IP. Defaults to 0 (no proxy).
WorkQueueCount	Long	R	Current number of documents in the Work Queue.

Table 18-3. *BizTalk Server Group Properties* (continued)

The Document Tracking and Shared Queue database connection settings are accessible through this class just as the Messaging Management Database settings were through the previous class. As before, all servers in the group should be offline before moving either of these databases.

Name	Parameters	Description
RefreshParser ListFromRegistry	None	This method rereads the parser list from the System Registry.
PurgeSuspended Queue	None	This method deletes all messages from the Suspended Queue. No backup is made. This data is lost.

Table 18-4. *BizTalk Server Group Methods*

This class is useful for monitoring the state of the shared queues because it contains a count of the messages in each queue. The messages in the queues cannot be accessed from this class. The Queue class and its subclasses can be used to access individual messages and are described later in this chapter.

```
Dim objGroup 'As SWbemObject

Set objGroup = GetObject( _
  "winmgmts:\\BTSDev\root\MicrosoftBizTalkServer:" _
  & "MicrosoftBizTalkServer_Group='BizTalk Server Group'")

MsgBox "Work Queue = " & objGroup.WorkQueueCount & "," _
  & "Retry Queue = " & objGroup.RetryQueueCount & "," _
  & "Scheduled Queue = " & objGroup.ScheduledQueueCount & "," _
  & "Suspended Queue = " & objGroup.SuspendedQueueCount
```

Another useful aspect of this class is the ability to purge all messages out of the Suspended Queue using the PurgeSuspendedQueue. This method should be used with care. The messages are permanently deleted with no backup. In most cases, it will be more appropriate to access the messages individually using the SuspendedQueue class described later in this chapter. This will allow the messages to be individually processed or archived before being deleted.

Managing BizTalk Servers

The Servers class represents a BizTalk Messaging Server that is part of the group. The server may or may not actively process items from the Work Queue, but it is still a member of the group. The server's state can also be accessed through this class.

class MicrosoftBizTalkServer_Server   This class represents individual BizTalk servers within a server group. Each server is a separate instance (see Table 18-5 and Table 18-6).

Name	Type	Access	Description
Name(KEY)*	String(63)	RW	The BizTalk server's machine name.
DateModified	Datetime	R	Date this instance was last modified. Format: CCYYMMDDHHNNSS…
GroupName	String(256)	R	Name of the BizTalk Server group to which this server belongs.

Table 18-5.   *BizTalk Server Properties*

Name	Type	Access	Description
MaxRecvSvc ThreadsPer Processor	Long	RW	Maximum number of simultaneous receive function threads allowed per CPU. Defaults to 4.
MaxWorker ThreadsPer Processor	Long	RW	Maximum number of Worker threads allowed per CPU. Worker threads read and process documents from the Work Queue. Defaults to 4. Note: A SubmitSync( ) call runs on the thread of the caller and does not use a worker thread.
ParticipateIn WorkItem Processing	Boolean	RW	Indicates whether a server should process items from the Work Queue. A server that does not participate only runs receive functions. Defaults to 1 (participate).
SchedulerWait Time	Long	RW	This property represents the lag time the BizTalk Server scheduler waits between tries. Defaults to 2000 milliseconds.
ServiceState		R	Status of BizTalk Messaging on the server. Values: 0—Stopped 1—Running 2—Error 3—Access Denied 4—Unknown

* The Name property is documented as Read/Write but in practice it is Read-Only. The server group name should be set during installation of the first server in the group.

Table 18-5. *BizTalk Server Properties* (continued)

Name	Parameters	Description
FreeInterchanges	None	This method disassociates all interchanges assigned to this server, thus allowing them to be processed by other servers. Typically, this is done in response to a server failure. The failed server's interchanges should be freed to allow processing by the surviving members of the group.
StartServer	None	Starts BizTalk Messaging on the server.
StopServer	None	Stops BizTalk Messaging on the server.
RegisterServerInAD*	None	Registers this server in the domain's Active Directory service.
UnregisterServerInAD*	None	Removes this server from the domain's Active Directory service.

* These methods were added in BizTalk Service Pack 1.

Table 18-6. *BizTalk Server Methods*

Managing Server States

The Server class gives us the ability to easily monitor the servers in our group. Specifically, the ServiceState property allows us to find any servers that are not running properly.

```
Dim BTS 'As SWbemServices
Dim osFailedServers 'As SwbemObjectSet

Set BTS = GetObject( _
    "winmgmts:\\BTSDev\root\MicrosoftBizTalkServer")
Set osFailedServers = BTS.ExecQuery( _
    "select *" _
    & "  from MicrosoftBizTalkServer_Server" _
    & " where ServiceState <> 1")

If osFailedServers.Count > 0 Then
    ' Perform error handling
End If
```

This code fragment uses the ExecQuery method to search for all servers whose ServiceState is not 1 (Running). Only servers that have potential problems will appear in the resulting Object Set.

The primary methods of the Server class are StopServer and StartServer. These methods are used to bring the BizTalk Messaging Service up and down programmatically. This script stops the server, gets a new copy of the server object, and then restarts it.

```
Dim objServer 'As SWbemObject

Set objServer = GetObject( _
  "winmgmts:root\MicrosoftBizTalkServer:" _
  & "MicrosoftBizTalkServer_Server='BTSDev'")

objServer.StopServer

' This is a simple way to refresh the state of any Managed Object
Set objServer = GetObject(objServer.Path_.DisplayName)

' Manipulate the server while it is offline

objServer.StartServer
```

Adding and Removing BizTalk Servers

Through the WMI system it is possible to add and remove managed objects programmatically in some cases. For BizTalk Servers, it is best to use the administrative tools for these functions. However, if it is necessary to delete a server from the server group programmatically, it is actually very simple to do.

```
Dim objServer 'As SWbemObject

Set objServer = GetObject( _
  "winmgmts:root\MicrosoftBizTalkServer:" _
  & "MicrosoftBizTalkServer_Server='BTSOldServer'")

objServer.Delete_
```

This simple script will remove the server from the group and shut down its BizTalk Messaging Services if it is accessible. Again, this type of large-scale configuration is probably best done interactively using the administration interface provided by BizTalk Server.

Managing Shared Queues

All documents that are processed by BizTalk Server pass through its shared queue system except for those submitted for synchronous processing using the SubmitSync( ) method. Chapter 9 contains more detail on the Shared Queues and their use.

Initially, a message is placed on the Work Queue, where it remains until there is a BizTalk Server available to process it. If a messaging port is configured with a service window, the message may be placed in the Scheduled Queue until the window opens and the message can be sent. If transmission of a document to its destination fails, the message will be placed on the Retry Queue, where the transmission will be retried. If the document produces an error during processing or the configured number of transmission attempts has been exhausted, the message will be placed into the Suspended Queue. This final queue acts as a message graveyard. Messages that end up in the Suspended Queue remain there until some external process removes them. This cleanup can be performed through the BizTalk Server Administration or programmatically, as we will see shortly.

The messages and documents that reside in BizTalk Server's Shared Queue system physically reside in the Shared Queue database. The default name for this database is InterchangeSQ. A brief examination of this database will show that it is not designed for easy querying by traditional database tools. Instead, developers who wish to access the data in these queues should use the classes provided by the BizTalk WMI provider.

The BizTalk WMI classes for shared queues use the Common Information Model's support for inheritance, as shown in Figure 18-2. A common base class represents the

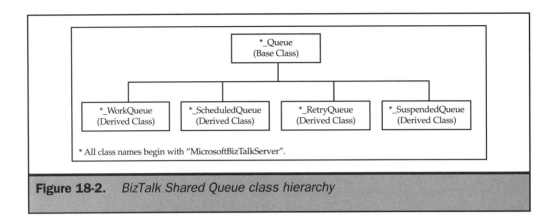

Figure 18-2. *BizTalk Shared Queue class hierarchy*

entire shared queue system and subclasses that represent each of the four queues in the system. One point of frequent confusion is that instances of these classes represent messages within a queue, not the queue itself. Care should be taken when accessing queued messages through these classes. Messages move in and out of queues very rapidly in some cases. These changes are not immediately reflected in the SWbemObject instances created through WMI. This can result in unpredictable behavior. For example, if a Work Queue message were processed by a server and removed from the system just prior to a management application attempting to move it to the Suspended Queue, the attempt to move the message would fail.

The actions allowed on messages vary depending on the queue in which they reside. All of the properties for these classes are read-only. There are no methods on the base Queue class. No alterations are allowed to the messages while they are within the shared queue system. Messages may only be deleted from the Suspended Queue. Any attempt to delete messages residing in another queue will fail. The only action that can be performed on messages in other queues is to move them to the Suspended Queue. From there, they can be removed from the system using the normal SWbemObject "Delete_" method, as described later in this chapter.

class MicrosoftBizTalkServer_Queue   This class represents the contents of BizTalk Server's shared queue system. This is the generic class from which the specific shared queue classes are derived. All of the properties of the Queue class are available in the derived classes (see Table 18-7). Note that the instances returned from this class represent specific messages in a queue, not the queue itself.

Name	Type	Access	Description
QID(KEY)	Long	R	BizTalk Server-assigned ID for the message while in the shared queue system
Group(KEY)	String(256)	R	Name of the BizTalk Server group in which the message resides
Destination	String(512)	R	Description of the organization that is to receive this message
Source	String(64)	R	Description of the organization that sent this message
Timestamp	Datetime	R	Timestamp for when the message was created or last updated Format: CCYYMMDDHHNNSS…

Table 18-7. *Shared Queue Properties (All Queue Types)*

Retrieving Messages

The Queue class can be used to retrieve messages from any of BizTalk Server's shared queues, as shown next. The messages retrieved can be from any, or all, of the shared queues in the system.

```
Dim BTS 'As SWbemServices
Dim osMessages 'As SWbemObjectSet
Dim objMessage 'As SWbemObject

Set BTS = GetObject( _
    "winmgmts:\\.\root\MicrosoftBizTalkServer")

Set osMessages = BTS.ExecQuery( _
    "Select * from MicrosoftBizTalkServer_Queue")
```

```
For Each objMessage In osMessages
    ' Display particulars about the message
    MsgBox "QID=" & objMessage.QID & Chr(13) & Chr(10) _
    & "Timestamp=" & objMessage.TimeStamp & Chr(13) & Chr(10) _
    & "Source=" & objMessage.Source & Chr(13) & Chr(10) _
    & "Destination=" & objMessage.Destination  & Chr(13) & Chr(10) _
    & "Class Name=" & objMessage.Path_.Class

    select case objMessage.Path_.Class
        case "MicrosoftBizTalkServer_WorkQueue":
            ' Process Work Queue Message

        case "MicrosoftBizTalkServer_RetryQueue":
            ' Process Retry Queue Message

        case "MicrosoftBizTalkServer_ScheduledQueue":
            ' Process Scheduled Queue Message

        case "MicrosoftBizTalkServer_SuspendedQueue":
            ' Process Suspended Queue Message
    end select
Next
```

This script uses the SWbemServices object to query the Queue class for all of the messages that are currently in the shared queue system. We then loop through the messages displaying each message's QID, Timestamp, Source, Destination, and Class. The message box will present a summary, such as:

```
QID=51
Timestamp=20010621161805.000000-300
Source=MyOrg
Destination=
Class=MicrosoftBizTalkServer_WorkQueue
```

Using the Class property of the SWbemObjectPath class, we are able to retrieve the "real" class of the object. In this case, the message resides on the Work Queue. Therefore, even though we queried the Queue class, we are able to determine that this object is actually an instance of a subclass of the Queue class. Using this information, we can then use a Select statement in VBScript to perform processing appropriate to each class of message.

Manipulating Queue Contents

We will now examine each subclass within the shared queue system. Each of these classes has its own properties to describe the specifics of each message. However, because they are a subclass of the Queue class, they also expose the properties of the Queue class. There is no need to retrieve the same message using a different class name in order to access the base class properties. The same is true for objects retrieved using the base class name. The queue-specific properties and methods will always be accessible. This is the power of inheritance within the Common Information Model used by WMI.

Work Queue   The Work Queue contains messages that have been submitted but have not yet been fully processed. When a server retrieves a message from the Work Queue for processing, it merely marks the entry as in process. The message is not removed until processing is complete or the message is moved to another queue.

class MicrosoftBizTalkServer_WorkQueue   This class represents the contents of the Work Queue. The messages in this queue have been successfully parsed and submitted for processing. This class is derived from the base Queue class. All of the properties of the Queue class are available in instances of this class. Note that the instances returned from this class represent specific messages in a queue, not the queue itself (see Table 18-8 and Table 18-9).

Name	Type	Access	Description
DocName	String(256)	R	Name of the document definition for this document
EngineState	Long	R	Indicates the state of processing for this document Values: 29—Processing 30—Receipt correlation 31—Transmission (service window) 33—Transmission (no service window)
ProcessingServer	String(63)	R	Name of the last BizTalk Server to handle this document

Table 18-8.   *Work Queue Properties*

Name	Parameters	Description
MoveToSuspendedQueue	None	This method moves a message from the Work Queue to the Suspended Queue. In effect, this cancels the sending of the message.

Table 18-9. *Work Queue Methods*

Messages move in and out of the Work Queue very rapidly unless all servers are stopped. In most cases, querying this queue is not very useful. Reasons for doing so might include the need to monitor how many outstanding documents are awaiting processing. This can be used for determining whether additional servers need to be deployed. A frequent queue length of greater than a few documents may indicate that it is time to scale out your BizTalk Server deployment.

```
Dim BTS 'As SWbemServices
Dim osMessages 'As SwbemObjectSet

Set BTS = GetObject( _
    "winmgmts:\\.\root\MicrosoftBizTalkServer")

Set osMessages = BTS.ExecQuery( _
    "Select * from MicrosoftBizTalkServer_WorkQueue" _
    & " Where DocName='MyDocDef'")

' record the length of the Work Queue
msgbox osMessages.Count
```

This script queries the entries in the Work Queue and then reports the number of messages of the type MyDocDef. This can also be done using the Group class described earlier in this chapter. The Group class allows you to retrieve the length of the queues, but does not retrieve the actual messages or allow you to count only certain types of documents.

The MoveToSuspendedQueue method can be used to transfer a message from the Work Queue to the Suspended Queue. This method exists for all of the Queue subclasses except for the Suspended Queue itself. This method must be used before deleting the message because messages can only be deleted from the Suspended Queue.

Retry Queue   The Retry Queue contains messages that, for whatever reason, need to be transmitted again. These messages could also be waiting for a receipt for reliable messaging. Each message has a maximum number of retries before BizTalk Server will give up and dump it into the Suspended Queue. Messages waiting to be retried must still obey any service windows involved and, therefore, this information is associated with these queue entries as well. The Retry Queue is somewhat more static than the Work Queue in that messages don't typically come and go as quickly.

class MicrosoftBizTalkServer_RetryQueue   This class represents the contents of the Retry Queue. The messages in this queue are awaiting retransmission. This class is derived from the base Queue class. All of the properties of the Queue class are available in instances of this class. Note that the instances returned from this class represent specific messages in a queue, not the queue itself (see Table 18-10 and Table 18-11).

Typically, when a message goes on to the Retry Queue, it should be left there until any retries have been attempted. The following script searches the queue for any

Name	Type	Access	Description
LastRetryTime	Datetime	R	Time of the last attempt to send this message. Format: CCYYMMDDHHNNSS…
ProcessingServer	String(63)	R	Name of the BizTalk server that last attempted to send this message.
RemainingRetryCount	Long	R	The remaining number of times the message will be retransmitted before being moved to the Suspended Queue.
RetryInterval	Long	R	Number of minutes between transmission attempts for this message.
ServiceWindowFromTime	Datetime	R	For messages that are restricted to a service window, this is the time at which the window starts. The date part of this value is "00000000." Only the time part is valid. Format: 00000000HH0000…
ServiceWindowToTime	Datetime	R	For messages that are restricted to a service window, this is the time at which the window ends. The date part of this value is "00000000." Only the time part is valid. Format: 00000000HH0000…

Table 18-10.   *Retry Queue Properties*

Name	Parameters	Description
MoveToSuspendedQueue	None	This method moves a message from the Retry Queue to the Suspended Queue. In effect, this cancels any outstanding retries for the message.

Table 18-11. *Retry Queue Methods*

messages that have not been retried within the last hour. In practice, this would not happen unless there were no servers available to attempt transmission, or the retry interval had been set extremely long.

```
Dim osMessages 'As SWbemObjectSet
Dim objMessage 'As SWbemObject
Dim dtRetryTime 'As Date

Set BTS = GetObject( _
    "winmgmts:\\.\root\MicrosoftBizTalkServer")

Set osMessages = BTS.ExecQuery( _
    "Select * from MicrosoftBizTalkServer_RetryQueue")

For Each objMessage In osMessages
    ' Convert BizTalk Server's odd date format to something we can use
    dtRetryTime = TimestampToDatetime(objMessage.LastRetryTime)

    ' If the message hasn't been retried in the last hour
    ' report it and move it to the Suspended Queue
    If DateAdd("h", 1, dtRetryTime) < Now Then

        MsgBox "QID=" & objMessage.QID & Chr(13) & Chr(10) _
            & "Last Retry=" & dtRetryTime & Chr(13) & Chr(10) _
            & "Server=" & objMessage.ProcessingServer & Chr(13) & Chr(10) _
            & "Source=" & objMessage.Source & Chr(13) & Chr(10) _
```

```
        & "Destination=" & objMessage.Destination

        objMessage.MoveToSuspendedQueue
    End If
Next


' This is a utility function to convert
' timestamps into a date/time value.
Function TimestampToDatetime(strTimestamp)

    ' BTS Timestamp: CCYYMMDDHHMMSS...
  TimestampToDatetime = _
    CDate(Mid(strTimestamp, 5, 2) _
        & "/" & Mid(strTimestamp, 7, 2) _
        & "/" & Mid(strTimestamp, 1, 4) _
        & " " & Mid(strTimestamp, 9, 2) _
        & ":" & Mid(strTimestamp, 11, 2) _
        & ":" & Mid(strTimestamp, 13, 2))


End Function
```

The example shows the use of datetime values within WMI. Unfortunately, the datetime values returned from WMI are not recognized as dates by VB or VBScript. Therefore, you must do some string parsing on them before using them. The TimestampToDatetime utility function shown preceding is an easy way to do this. However, do not use this function for datetime values returned for the service window start and end times. These values have "00000000" for the date and will cause an error if handled in this way.

This example also cancels the remaining retries for these messages by transferring them to the Suspended Queue. They can be resubmitted later, if desired. In that case, they will simply be retransmitted since they have already gone through the BizTalk Messaging Pipeline.

Scheduled Queue   The Scheduled Queue class represents the contents of the Scheduled Queue. The messages in this queue are awaiting the opening of their service window. Unlike the Retry Queue, BizTalk Server has not yet attempted to transmit these messages. The service window defines a period during which the message may be sent. For example, if an interchange were produced at 2:00 P.M. but the service window only allowed transmission between 2:00 A.M. and 5:00 A.M., then this message would remain on the Scheduled Queue from 2:00 P.M. until 2:00 A.M.

class MicrosoftBizTalkServer_ScheduledQueue   This class represents the contents of the Scheduled Queue. The messages in this queue are awaiting the opening of their service window. This class is derived from the base Queue class. All of the properties of the Queue class are available in instances of this class. Note that the instances returned from this class represent specific messages in a queue, not the queue itself (see Table 18-12 and Table 18-13).

Name	Type	Access	Description
ProcessingServer	String(63)	R	Name of the BizTalk server that last worked with this interchange.
ServiceWindowFromTime	Datetime	R	For messages that are restricted to a service window, this is the time at which the window starts. The date part of this value is "00000000." Only the time part is valid. Format: 00000000HH0000…
ServiceWindowToTime	Datetime	R	For messages that are restricted to a service window, this is the time at which the window ends. The date part of this value is "00000000." Only the time part is valid. Format: 00000000HH0000…

Table 18-12.   *Scheduled Queue Properties*

Name	Parameters	Description
MoveToSuspendedQueue	None	This method moves a message from the Scheduled Queue to the Suspended Queue. In effect, this cancels the sending of the message.

Table 18-13.   *Scheduled Queue Methods*

Accessing the Scheduled Queue is no different from accessing any other queue. The following script simply queries the messages in the Scheduled Queue and displays their service windows.

```
Dim BTS 'As SWbemServices
Dim osMessages 'As SWbemObjectSet
Dim objMessage 'As SWbemObject

Set BTS = GetObject( _
    "winmgmts:\\.\root\MicrosoftBizTalkServer")

Set osMessages = BTS.ExecQuery( _
    "Select * from MicrosoftBizTalkServer_ScheduledQueue")

For Each objMessage In osMessages
  MsgBox "QID=" & objMessage.QID & Chr(13) & Chr(10) _
    & "Window Opens at " _
        & objMessage.ServiceWindowFromTime _
        & Chr(13) & Chr(10) _
    & "Window Closes at " _
        & objMessage.ServiceWindowToTime
Next
```

Remember that the service window times are presented using the CCYYMMDDHHMMSS… format that we have seen before. In this case, the date, minutes, and seconds are always filled with zeros.

Suspended Queue   As discussed in Chapter 9, BizTalk Server's Suspended Queue is like the Postal Service's Dead-Letter Office. This is where messages go when there is just no place else to send them. There are any number of reasons a message might wind up in the Suspended Queue, but the result is always the same. Someone has to intervene because BizTalk Server doesn't know what to do next. The most common reasons for messages going into the Suspended Queue are invalid documents being passed in to BizTalk Server and BizTalk Server being unable to deliver documents to their destination even after attempting multiple times.

class MicrosoftBizTalkServer_SuspendedQueue   This class represents the contents of the Suspended Queue. The messages in this queue have failed processing at some point. Messages on this queue require outside intervention before processing can continue. This class is derived from the base Queue class. All of the properties of the Queue class are available in instances of this class. Note that the instances returned from this class represent specific messages in a queue, not the queue itself (see Table 18-14 and Table 18-15).

The Suspended Queue class has several more methods than the other queue classes, because the only thing that can be done to a message that isn't in the Suspended Queue

Name	Type	Access	Description
DocName	String(256)	R	This is the name of the document definition associated with this document.
ErrorDescription	String(64)	R	Contains up to 64 characters of the Error message generated for this message. The method ViewErrorDescription can be used to retrieve the entire error message.
QGUID	String(256)	R	This is the GUID associated with the submission of this document. This property can be used to correlate a Suspended Queue entry with the original submission that caused the error.
State	Long	R	This code represents the point in the processing of this document where the error occurred.

Table 18-14.   *Suspended Queue Properties*

Name	Parameters	Description
Resubmit	None	This method is used to resubmit a message to the Work Queue for processing. Depending on the type of error that caused the message to reach the Suspended Queue, submission may or may not be possible.
ViewDocument	Output only: Document as Byte( ) CodePage as Long	This method returns the document that generated the error. In addition, an identifier is returned for the proper Unicode code page for the document.
ViewError Description	Output only: CompleteErrorDescription as String	This method returns the full text of the error message.
ViewInterchange	Output only: Document as Byte( ) CodePage as Long	This method returns the entire interchange that generated the error. In addition, an identifier is returned for the proper Unicode code page for the interchange. This is used for parsing errors where the interchange could not be separated into documents.

Table 18-15. *Suspended Queue Methods*

is to move it there. Most of these methods are used to retrieve diagnostic information about why the message landed in the Suspended Queue.

```
Dim BTS 'As SWbemServices
Dim osMessages 'As SWbemObjectSet
Dim objMessage 'As SWbemObject

Set BTS = GetObject( _
  "winmgmts:\\.\root\MicrosoftBizTalkServer")

Set osMessages = BTS.ExecQuery( _
  "Select * from MicrosoftBizTalkServer_SuspendedQueue" _
  & " where ErrorDescription='Transmission Failure'")

For Each objMessage In osMessages
  objMessage.Resubmit
Next
```

Suppose that your company lost its network connection for an hour. All of the messages that were supposed to be delivered to your trading partners via that network failed to transmit. These documents are now in the Suspended Queue. Instead of manually resubmitting each one, the preceding script can be used to resubmit all of the messages in the Suspended Queue that arrived there due to a transmission failure. Any other messages in the queue will be unaffected.

The cause of the error is offered in two forms. The short form of the error message is what you see in the BizTalk Server Administration when you examine the Suspended Queue. This can be retrieved from the ErrorDescription property, or it can be part of a query as it was in our example. The full text of the error message can be retrieved into a string variable using the ViewErrorDescription method. Anyone who has used BizTalk Server for any length of time has probably come to the conclusion that both of these error descriptions are too vague and generalized to be of much help in most cases. Fortunately, more detailed information is available in the Application Event Log. The QGUID property in this class can be used to search the event log for the relevant entries using the event log's own WMI provider.

The ViewInterchange and ViewDocument methods are used to retrieve the data that was not processed. Both methods are used to retrieve the full text of a document or interchange that is on the Suspended Queue. BizTalk Server stores all such data as Unicode strings. These methods return the code page for the document and the document as an array of BYTEs. If you need these converted to a string, you will have to do that yourself. A description of this processing is available in the BizTalk WMI Help File mentioned earlier.

The State property gives a great deal of information regarding the status of a document or interchange on the Suspended Queue. Different ranges of values have different meanings and restrictions.

Entries in the Suspended Queue States (Set 1) contain entire interchanges that could not be processed (see the following table). The ViewInterchange( ) method should be used to retrieve the data, and it is not valid to resubmit the interchange from the Suspended Queue.

Value	State
0	Initial
1	Custom component processing
2	Parsing

The states in the following table, Suspended Queue States (Set 2), represent document processing stages. Use the ViewDocument( ) method to retrieve this data. Except for state 3 (Document validation), it is valid to attempt resubmission of these documents.

Value	State
3	Document validation
4	Channel selection
5	Field tracking
6	Correlating
7	Mapping
8	Serializing

The final set of states, Suspended Queue States (Set 3), is once again for interchanges (see the following table). Therefore, using ViewInterchange( ) to view them is appropriate, as is attempting resubmission.

Value	State
9	Encoding
10	Signing
11	Encrypting
12	Transmitting

Receive Functions

BizTalk receive functions are a wonderfully convenient way to get data into your BizTalk Server. Essentially, a receive function is a small program that monitors a data source waiting for a document to appear. This data source is either a File or an MSMQ Messaging Queue. When data arrives, it is submitted to BizTalk Server using the same BizTalk Server Interchange component that we have used before. The only thing magical about receive functions is that we no longer have to write custom service programs to perform this rather straightforward function.

While receive functions are simple to understand, they are somewhat tricky to use, even through the BizTalk Server Administration. The reason is that there are so many different ways to use them. Receive from Files or Queues? Submit using an Open Source or not? Specify the channel name, document name, source, and destination information, some combination, or nothing at all? Regrettably, the designers of BizTalk Server's WMI provider didn't choose to create subclasses for different types of receive functions. They are all implemented in one class where the same properties take on different meanings depending on the type of receive function being defined.

class MicrosoftBizTalkServer_ReceiveFunction   This class represents either a File receive function or an MSMQ receive function. Some properties act differently depending on the type of receiver. Receive function objects have no methods, only properties. See Table 18-16.

Name	Type	Access	Description
Name(KEY)	String(256)	RW	Name of the receive function.
DateModified	Datetime	R	Date this instance was last modified. Format: CCYYMMDDHHNNSS…
GroupName	String(256)	R	Name of the BizTalk Server group in which this receive function resides.
Comment	String(256)	RW	User-supplied free-form text about the receive function.
DisableReceive Function	Boolean	RW	Indicates whether the receive function has been disabled or not. Defaults to 0 (not disabled).
FilenameMask	String(256)	RW	File Receivers Only: This is the filename, including wildcards, that the File Receiver will wait to receive. For example, "*.xml."
IsPassThrough	Boolean	RW	Indicates whether the Submit( ) call made by the receive function is made with the pass-through flag turned on or not. Defaults to 0 (not pass-through).
OpennessFlag	Long	RW	Indicates the "openness" of the submission when an interchange is received. Values: 1—Not open 2—Open source 4—Open destination
Password	String(63)	RW	For receive functions that require logon credentials, this property contains the Password.

Table 18-16.   *Receive Function Properties*

Name	Type	Access	Description
PollingLocation	String(260)	RW	For File Receivers: The directory that will be monitored by the File receive function. This does not include the filename. See the FilenameMask property. For MSMQ Receivers: Name of the queue to be monitored for incoming messages. For example, "Direct=OS:.\private$\TestQ" refers to the "TestQ" private queue on the local system.
PreProcessor	String(256)	RW	When a custom pre-processor component is used, this property contains the Class ID (GUID) of the component.
ProcessingServer	String(63)	RW	A receive function only runs on a single server within the group. This property represents the server on which this receive function runs.
ProtocolType	Long	RW	Indicates the type of receive function this instance implements. Values: 1—File receive function 2—MSMQ receive function
Username	String(256)	RW	For receive functions that require logon credentials, this property contains the User ID.
ChannelName	String(64)	RW	When submitting directly to a channel, this property contains the channel's name. Note that this contains the channel's name, not its ID in the Management database. Therefore, if the name of the channel is changed, the receive function must be updated.
DocumentName	String(256)	RW	Name of the Document Definition passed to the Submit( ) call.
DestinationID	String(256)	RW	ID of the receiving organization. This must be correct for the Destination Qualifier given.

Table 18-16.   *Receive Function Properties* (continued)

Name	Type	Access	Description
DestinationQualifier	String(64)	RW	Qualifier for the receiving organization. Examples: DUNS number (09), Mutually Defined (ZZ), etc. The two-character qualifier is stored, not the qualifier name.
EnvelopeName	String(256)	RW	This property represents the name of an envelope definition instance in the BizTalk Messaging Management database.
SourceID	String(256)	RW	ID of the sending organization. This must be correct for the Source Qualifier given.
SourceQualifier	String(64)	RW	Qualifier for the sending organization. Examples: DUNS number (09), Mutually Defined (ZZ), etc. The two-character qualifier is stored, not the qualifier name.

Table 18-16. *Receive Function Properties* (continued)

The procedure for adding or altering receive functions varies depending on the type of receiver being manipulated, but disabling or deleting a receive function is always done either as follows:

```
Dim objRecvFunc 'As SWbemObject

Set objRecvFunc = GetObject( _
    "winmgmts:\\.\root\MicrosoftBizTalkServer:" _
    & "MicrosoftBizTalkServer_ReceiveFunction" _
    & "='RCVFUNC Example Receive Function'")

' to disable a receive function
objRecvFunc.DisableReceiveFunction = -1
objRecvFunc.Put_ (1) ' Update
```

or:

```
' remove the receive function
objRecvFunc.Delete_
```

Managing File Receive Functions

To create File receive functions, we must specify where to look for the files and what filenames to look for. The directories we look in can be local or accessed through UNC names. The filenames are typically specified using a mask such as "*.txt". The following script shows how to create or alter a File receive function:

```
Dim BTS 'As SWbemServices
Dim objRecvFuncClass 'As SWbemObject
Dim objRecvFunc 'As SWbemObject
Dim strWQL 'As String

Set BTS = GetObject( _
    "winmgmts:\\.\root\MicrosoftBizTalkServer")

' Get a class object for the ReceiveFunction class
Set objRecvFuncClass = _
    BTS.Get("MicrosoftBizTalkServer_ReceiveFunction")

' Spawn a new instance object
Set objRecvFunc = objRecvFuncClass.SpawnInstance_

objRecvFunc.Name = "RCVFUNC Example Receive Function"
objRecvFunc.GroupName = "BizTalk Server Group"
objRecvFunc.FilenameMask = "*.txt"
objRecvFunc.ProcessingServer = "BTSDev"
objRecvFunc.ProtocolType = 1 'ADMIN_PROTOCOL_TYPE_FILE
objRecvFunc.PollingLocation = "C:\PICKUP"
objRecvFunc.DocumentName = "FlatFile Orders"
objRecvFunc.OpennessFlag = 1 'NOT_OPEN
objRecvFunc.SourceID = "Provider"
objRecvFunc.SourceQualifier = "Organization Name"
objRecvFunc.DestinationID = "Home Organization"
objRecvFunc.DestinationQualifier = "Organization Name"

' This query will determine whether this
' should be an Update or Create
strWQL = "select * " _
        & " from MicrosoftBizTalkServer_ReceiveFunction " _
        & "where Name='" & objRecvFunc.Name & "'"

If BTS.ExecQuery(strWQL).Count > 0 Then
    objRecvFunc.Put_ (1) ' Update
Else
    objRecvFunc.Put_ (2) ' Create
End If
```

This example demonstrates several important points. We start by creating an SWbemServices object. This object is used to create a class object for the ReceiveFunction class. The class object is then used to create a new, empty ReceiveFunction object by invoking the SpawnInstance_ method. The properties of this object are then set. Finally, before creating the receive function, we query the BizTalk Server service to determine whether there is already a receive function by this name. If so, we perform an update instead of a create by passing a "1" to the Put_ method instead of a "2".

In this case, we specified the document name, source, and destination. Alternatively, we could have specified the channel and envelope (required because this is a flat-file schema). We could also simply not specify any of these properties. In that case, the documents would have to be fully self-routing.

Managing MSMQ Receive Functions

Manipulating MSMQ-based receive functions is very similar to managing File receive functions. The difference is that the PollingLocation refers to a queue instead of a file directory.

```
Dim BTS 'As SWbemServices
Dim objRecvFuncClass 'As SWbemObject
Dim objRecvFunc 'As SWbemObject
Dim strWQL 'As String

Set BTS = GetObject( _
    "winmgmts:\\.\root\MicrosoftBizTalkServer")

' Get a class object for the ReceiveFunction class
Set objRecvFuncClass = _
    BTS.Get("MicrosoftBizTalkServer_ReceiveFunction")
' Spawn a new instance object
Set objRecvFunc = objRecvFuncClass.SpawnInstance_

objRecvFunc.Name = "MSMQ Example Receive Function"
objRecvFunc.GroupName = "BizTalk Server Group"
objRecvFunc.ProcessingServer = "BTSDev"
objRecvFunc.ProtocolType = 2 'ADMIN_PROTOCOL_TYPE_MSMQ
objRecvFunc.PollingLocation = "Direct=OS:.\private$\TestQ"
objRecvFunc.OpennessFlag = 1 'NOT_OPEN
objRecvFunc.DocumentName = "FlatFile Orders"
```

```
objRecvFunc.EnvelopeName = "FF Orders Env"
objRecvFunc.SourceID = "Provider"
objRecvFunc.SourceQualifier = "Organization Name"
objRecvFunc.DestinationID = "Home Organization"
objRecvFunc.DestinationQualifier = "Organization Name"

' This query will determine whether this
' should be an Update or Create
strWQL = "select * " _
        & " from MicrosoftBizTalkServer_ReceiveFunction " _
        & "where Name='" & objRecvFunc.Name & "'"

If BTS.ExecQuery(strWQL).Count > 0 Then
    objRecvFunc.Put_ (1) ' Update
Else
    objRecvFunc.Put_ (2) ' Create
End If
```

Notice the format of the PollingLocation. While an MSMQ queue has a moniker that begins with "queue:", that is not used in this case. Instead, BizTalk Server expects to receive a string like "Direct=OS:.\private$\TestQ".

Association Classes

BizTalk's WMI provider defines two classes known as *association classes*. An association class relates a set of managed objects in a parent/child relationship much like a Foreign Key in a relational database. Each association class has exactly two properties: Antecedent and Dependant. The Antecedent property contains the moniker path of the parent object. The Dependant property contains the moniker path of the child object. There are two such classes for BizTalk Server that map the Server group to either servers or receive functions within that group. The class names are MicrosofBizTalkServer_GroupServer and MicrosoftBizTalkServer_GroupReceiveFunction, respectively.

Event Classes

The final two classes defined by BizTalk's WMI provider are event classes. In WMI, event classes are used to notify management applications when certain conditions arise. WMI events can be raised by the CIMOM or by a WMI provider. When an event is thrown, all applications that have subscribed to the event are notified. The event classes in the following table are available for BizTalk Server.

Class	Description
DocSuspendedEvent	This event is triggered when a document is placed on the Suspended Queue. A management application can use this event to get immediate notification of suspended documents and interchanges instead of polling the queue periodically. The document GUID is provided for identification.
InterchangeProvError	If an error occurs during the creation of a class instance, this event is thrown. The name of the WMI provider that threw the error is given.

Chapter 19

BizTalk Server
Accelerators

Since the release of BizTalk Server 2000, various companies—including Microsoft—have created Application Integration Components (AICs) called *adapters* to allow BizTalk Server to communicate with existing systems and third-party products. Also, various companies have extended BizTalk Server through the creation of custom parsers and serializers to manipulate the document formats required by various *vertical markets*, such as the IT sector or the finance sector.

One of the key areas of interest for many organizations in the IT sector is the ability to integrate with existing business-to-business (B2B) standard processes, such as those provided by RosettaNet. Also, because of BizTalk Server's support for EDI data formats, organizations in healthcare-related industries have asked for that support to be extended to the EDI-based documents they deal with, so that they may bring their processes into line with new U.S. government regulations embodied in the Healthcare Insurance Portability and Accountability Act (HIPAA). Further, a more generic, extensible set of tools has been requested to allow supplier companies to quickly integrate into online marketplaces such as Ariba and Commerce One. In each case, Microsoft has responded with a complete collection of resources—as opposed to a single adapter or parser—designed to accelerate the deployment of such solutions.

Although many companies, such as J.D. Edwards, Navision, bSquare, and Compaq, have created adapters to ease integration with legacy systems, in this chapter we will concentrate on the three *accelerators* that Microsoft is making available for use with BizTalk Server. Because these accelerators are only of interest to particular companies or industries, this chapter will not go into complete detail on each one, providing instead an overview of the tools and services included.

BizTalk Server Accelerator for RosettaNet

Companies in the IT sector that wish to use BizTalk Server to integrate with the standard processes required by RosettaNet can take advantage of the BizTalk Server Accelerator for RosettaNet. This software provides a number of tools, components, and XLANG schedules to assist customers in the creation of *Partner Interface Processes (PIPs)*, and the deployment of the *RosettaNet Implementation Framework (RNIF)*.

Introduction to RosettaNet

RosettaNet is a not-for-profit consortium of IT companies, founded in June 1998, whose membership includes over 400 manufacturers of computers, components, and semiconductors. Its stated goal is to create and implement open electronic business standards for automated supply-chain solutions. One of these standards takes the form of a networked–application integration framework called the RosettaNet Implementation Framework (RNIF). The RNIF describes packaging, transport, and routing specifications and mandates the use of XML for information exchange. These specifications allow

RosettaNet partners to collaboratively execute automated business processes called Partner Interface Processes (PIPs), and they ensure interoperability between compliant partners. Dictionaries provide a common set of properties for PIPs. They include the *RosettaNet Business Dictionary*, which designates the properties used in business activities, and the *RosettaNet Technical Dictionary*, which provides properties for defining products.

 The RosettaNet web site at http://www.rosettanet.org/ has many downloadable white papers and resources on the RosettaNet Implementation Framework, Partner Interface Processes, and the Business and Technical dictionaries.

RosettaNet Implementation Framework

The BizTalk Server Accelerator for RosettaNet supports RNIF 1.1. This framework specification enables RosettaNet partners to implement system-to-system electronic business processes by communicating according to strictly defined protocols. These protocols specify message formats and message exchange sequences. The BizTalk Server Accelerator for RosettaNet also includes definitions for authorization, authentication, encryption, and nonrepudiation to provide for secure communications. The architecture of this framework is based on the Open Systems Interconnect (OSI) model for networked systems and specifies seven sublayers that correspond to the Application layer of the OSI model, and a Security layer as follows:

OSI Layer	RNIF Sublayer
Application Layer	Action Sublayer
	Transaction Sublayer
	Process Sublayer
	Service Sublayer
	Agent Sublayer
	Message Handling Sublayer
	Transfer Sublayer
Presentation Layer	
Session Layer	Security Layer
Transport Layer	
Network Layer	
Data Link Layer	
Physical Layer	

Partner Interface Processes

RosettaNet PIPs are specialized XML-based specifications that define the exchange of business data between trading partners in a supply chain. Each PIP specification is a message in three sections, each of which is a MIME-encoded XML document. These sections define the business and technical terms of the message. For each type of PIP, there is also a precisely defined list of rules governing the creation of a PIP, known as a *PIP Implementation Guideline*. These guidelines define the vocabulary, structure, data elements, and data values for each PIP. Because PIPs are XML based, Document Type Definitions (DTDs) are used to describe the implementation guidelines in a machine-readable way. However, as we saw in Chapter 2, DTDs are limited in the way they represent certain data structures, so PIP implementation guidelines are usually sent out to partners in an HTML format as well.

> **Note** *One vital thing to realize at this point is that PIPs are not business documents, such as purchase orders or invoices. Instead, they are processes that describe the exchange of business documents. The BizTalk Server Accelerator for RosettaNet implements these PIPs as XLANG schedules, as we will see later.*

RosettaNet describes related PIPs by means of logical groupings called *segments* and *clusters*. In RosettaNet, 17 segments in total are grouped into eight clusters. However, Microsoft BizTalk Server Accelerator for RosettaNet only provides built-in support for three of those clusters. These are listed in Table 19-1.

The RosettaNet Support cluster provides administrative functionality for other processes; specifically, it includes the failure notification implementation. The Product Introduction cluster provides processes for the distribution of new product information to buyer organizations so that online catalogs can be populated. The Order Management cluster includes PIP implementations to allow trading partners to request and deliver product price and availability information, issue and accept purchase orders, and issue and validate invoices. The full list of clusters is as follows:

> 0—RosettaNet Support
> 1—Partner, Product, and Service Review
> 2—Product Introduction
> 3—Order Management
> 4—Inventory Management
> 5—Marketing Information Management
> 6—Service and Support
> 7—Manufacturing

The Software Development Kit (SDK) included with the BizTalk Server Accelerator for RosettaNet includes information and samples to assist implementers in the creation

Cluster	Segment	PIP
0—RosettaNet Support	A—Administrative	1—Notification of Failure
2—Product Introduction	A—Preparation for Distribution	1—Distribute New Product Information
3—Order Management	A—Quote and Order Entry	2—Request Price and Availability
		4—Manage Purchase Order
		7—Notify of Purchase Order Acceptance
	B—Transportation andDistribution	2—Notify of Advance Shipment
	C—Returns and Finance	3—Notify of Invoice
		4—Notify of Invoice Reject

Table 19-1.   *Supported Clusters in BizTalk Server Accelerator for RosettaNet*

of further PIPs by extending generic patterns for requestors, responders, notifiers, and notification handlers.

RosettaNet Messages

The messages that flow between partners in a PIP take the form of XML documents. However, they are not stand-alone well-formed XML documents. A RosettaNet message actually takes the form of a multipart MIME-encoded interchange containing three XML documents and their associated DTDs packaged together into a single interchange. BizTalk Server cannot parse these interchanges using its existing components, so the BizTalk Server Accelerator for RosettaNet installs an additional parser to work with this data format. The parser converts the interchange into a well-formed XML document by removing the DTDs and MIME-encoding and by wrapping the three parts of the interchange in a single root element called *RosettaNetMessage*, as shown in Figure 19-1. There is also a corresponding serializer to package outgoing interchanges. The three parts of the message visible in Figure 19-1 are Preamble, Service Header, and Service Content.

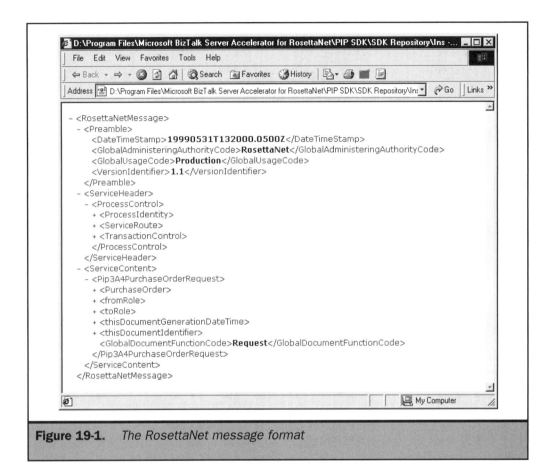

```
- <RosettaNetMessage>
  - <Preamble>
      <DateTimeStamp>19990531T132000.0500Z</DateTimeStamp>
      <GlobalAdministeringAuthorityCode>RosettaNet</GlobalAdministeringAuthorityCode>
      <GlobalUsageCode>Production</GlobalUsageCode>
      <VersionIdentifier>1.1</VersionIdentifier>
  </Preamble>
  - <ServiceHeader>
    - <ProcessControl>
      + <ProcessIdentity>
      + <ServiceRoute>
      + <TransactionControl>
      </ProcessControl>
    </ServiceHeader>
  - <ServiceContent>
    - <Pip3A4PurchaseOrderRequest>
      + <PurchaseOrder>
      + <fromRole>
      + <toRole>
      + <thisDocumentGenerationDateTime>
      + <thisDocumentIdentifier>
        <GlobalDocumentFunctionCode>Request</GlobalDocumentFunctionCode>
      </Pip3A4PurchaseOrderRequest>
    </ServiceContent>
  </RosettaNetMessage>
```

Figure 19-1. *The RosettaNet message format*

Using the RosettaNet Accelerator

The BizTalk Server Accelerator for RosettaNet allows organizations to implement the RosettaNet standards by creating a variety of applications, XLANG schedules, and adapters. After installing the accelerator, a number of PIPs are ready to use, and these can be selected using the PIP Administrator application. The PIP Schema Manager application then provides a way to configure the RosettaNet messages used by a process. To implement a process, the Messaging Configuration Wizard creates the necessary organizations, document definitions, envelopes, channels, and messaging ports. Finally, the PIP XLANG Schedule Tester allows you to simulate a given role in a PIP to try out your configuration.

Installing the Accelerator

Installing BizTalk Server Accelerator for RosettaNet is a straightforward affair. The hardware and software requirements are that you have BizTalk Server and all the prerequisite software that BizTalk Server needs. The only information required during setup is the name of the SQL Server database where the PIP configurations should be stored. Complete the following steps in the Microsoft BizTalk Server Accelerator for RosettaNet Wizard to install the software.

1. Click Next at the opening screen.

2. Accept the license agreement and click Next.

3. Enter your user and company information, type the product key in the boxes provided, and click Next.

4. Accept the default installation folder or click Browse to choose a different location, and click Next.

5. Select the features you wish to install as shown next. You will usually want to include all features, but you may not need the source files for the PIP Adapter Development Kit. Click Next when you have finished.

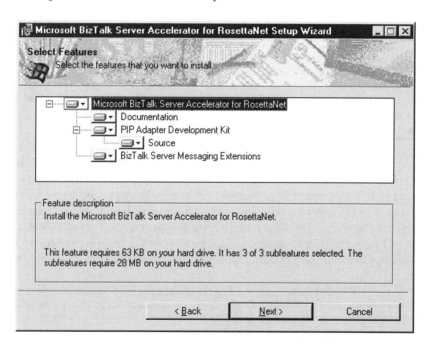

6. Ensure the option to create the accelerator databases is selected, and type the name of the SQL Server computer. Click Test Connection if necessary to confirm that the server is available. Type the name of the database, or leave the default name BTSKInstances, as shown. Click Next when you have finished.

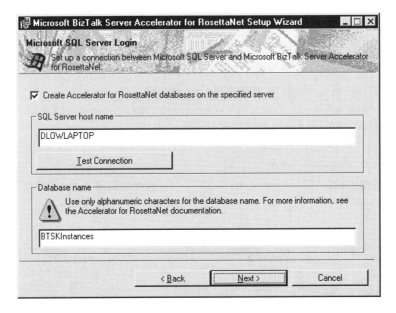

7. Click Install to copy the accelerator files, register the components, and create the database.

8. Click Finish to exit the wizard.

After you have installed the software, you will see a few changes apart from the new entries in the Start menu and the extra SQL Server database. First, there is a new parser called RNIF1_1Support.RNOParser.1. This should be moved to the top of the parser list using BizTalk Server Administration if you will be handling RosettaNet messages primarily. Also, there is a new private message queue called RNMsgOut; this is used for testing PIPs prior to deploying them in a production environment. Later, I will discuss how to modify a PIP XLANG schedule to send data to a trading partner.

Using BizTalk Server Administration to change the order of installed parsers was covered in Chapter 9.

In Chapter 13, we saw that the COM+ applications installed for BizTalk Server were configured to use the interactive user account—that is, the applications run in the security context of the user who is physically logged onto the machine. There are three new COM+ applications created when you install the RosettaNet Accelerator, and these applications are configured the same way. For production environments, you should therefore modify the properties of the BizTalk Server Accelerator for RosettaNet Core PIP Services, BizTalk Server Accelerator for RosettaNet XLANG Persistence Helpers, and BizTalk Server Accelerator for RosettaNet Messaging Extensions applications to run in the context of a service account. These changes can be made in the Component Services Microsoft Management Console (MMC), as outlined in Chapter 13.

Note *The BizTalk Server Accelerator for RosettaNet Messaging Extensions COM+ application is not created automatically during installation of the Accelerator. Instead, a script called create_COM_BTM_extensions.vbs is provided in the Setup Scripts directory under the install folder to add the application. Similarly, another script called remove_COM_BTM_extensions.vbs allows you to delete the application.*

If you need to uninstall the accelerator, this can be done through Add/Remove Programs in the Control Panel. This will only remove the program files, however—you will need to delete any messaging objects, document specifications, and databases manually.

RosettaNet Roles

Before exploring how each part of the Accelerator is used to describe a PIP, it's important to understand how an organization participates in the process. In the supported PIPs listed in Table 19-1, there are two main types of processes—transactions and notifications. In either case, each trading partner taking part will fulfill one of two roles—*requestor* (notifier) or *responder* (handler). In the case of a transaction process, the PIP outlines how each role behaves and the actions that must be carried out by each party to fulfill the obligations of that role, as shown:

Similarly, for notification PIPs, the role of each trading partner is defined as follows:

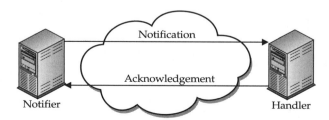

To configure an organization to play either role in a PIP, you will use the XLANG schedules and utilities included in the accelerator. For each PIP, there are two XLANG schedules supplied—one for the requestor or notifier (also called the initiator), and one for the responder or notification handler. The PIP executes by calling an adapter component created using the SDK. This adapter, which will implement either the IPIPInitiatorApplication or IPIPResponderApplication interface, depending on the role, will transport a RosettaNet message to a trading partner via BizTalk Messaging.

Implementing PIPs

To implement a RosettaNet PIP, follow these steps:

1. Select a PIP specification–compliant implementation.
2. Build an application or data source adapter component.
3. Bind the PIP XLANG schedule to the adapter component.
4. Bind the PIP XLANG schedule to BizTalk Messaging.
5. Compile the XLANG schedule.
6. Execute the XLANG schedule.

Select a PIP   First, you must decide which PIP to use. As stated, there are seven segments included with the accelerator, but you can create further PIP implementations by modifying existing PIPs or by extending the supplied PIP patterns in the SDK. This involves editing a suitable XLANG schedule with BizTalk Orchestration Designer to match the appropriate RosettaNet message.

Build an Adapter   Once you have decided on a PIP, you will then have to build an adapter component by creating a new ActiveX DLL that implements the IPIPInitiatorApplication or IPIPResponderApplication interfaces. The project should also reference the Microsoft BizTalk Server Accelerator for RosettaNet PIP Application Interfaces 1.0 Type library. You can either implement the interfaces in Visual Basic, or you can modify the StubInitiatorApplication and StubResponderApplication C++ implementations included in the SDK. The interfaces have the following methods:

IPIPInitiatorApplication	**IPIPResponderApplication**
HandleError	HandleError
HandleResponseMessage	
HandleRNException	
HandleRNReceiptAcknowledgementException	HandleRNReceiptAcknowledgementException
HandleRNReceiptAcknowledgement	HandleRNReceiptAcknowledgement

IPIPInitiatorApplication	IPIPResponderApplication
HandleUnexpectedResponse	
HandleUnexpectedSignal	HandleUnexpectedSignal
InitializeRequestMessage	StartRequestHandling
ValidateResponseMessage	ValidateRequestMessage

You should override these methods as required. For example, you could override the StartRequestHandling method of the IPIPResponderApplication interface to save an incoming request to a file or to a database. If you create the adapter in Visual Basic, you should also register it on the server using regsvr32.exe.

Bind the XLANG Schedule to the Adapter   The XLANG schedules supplied with the RosettaNet Accelerator already contain implementations of the StubInitiatorApplication or StubResponderApplication components, depending on the role. After you have created an adapter, you will need to bind the appropriate port in the XLANG schedule to your new component. To do this, locate the AppCalloutPort port in the XLANG schedule drawing (the .skv file), and double-click the attached stub component. If you implemented the appropriate interfaces, you will be able to replace the stub component with your own adapter without having to make any further configuration changes.

Bind the XLANG Schedule to BizTalk Messaging   The XLANG schedules for each PIP also contain a message queuing implementation that can be used for testing purposes. This allows you to execute the PIP without actually sending any data to a trading partner. Instead, the data is sent to a private message queue called RNMsgOut. To implement the PIP in a production environment, however, you will need to replace the message queuing implementation with a COM component that references the Microsoft BizTalk Server Accelerator for RosettaNet Submit Services library. This is a DLL containing an instance of the CPIPAdapterSubmit class, which has the following methods:

Method	Description
SendRNMessage	Sends an XML message through an unsigned channel
SendSignedRNMessage	Sends an XML message through a signed channel
SendSyncRNMessage	Sends an XML message synchronously through an unsigned channel
SendSyncSignedRNMessage	Sends an XML message synchronously through a signed channel

Luckily, the included PIPs already include such a COM component, and the changes you will have to make depend on the role. If you are editing an XLANG schedule for a requestor role, you will have to detach the Send Request Message and Send Ack actions from the SendRequestPort port. You will then connect them to the SendRNMessage_in and SendRNMessage_in_2 messages, respectively, on the RNSendPort port. If you are editing an XLANG schedule for a responder role, you will have to detach the Send Response and Send Ack actions from the RNMsgOutAck port. Similarly, you will then connect them to the SendRNMessage_in and SendRNMessage_in_2 messages, respectively, on the RNSendPort port. In each case, the Method Communication Wizard will appear. Select the option to initiate a synchronous method call, and add a reference to the appropriate existing synchronous message pair. You will also have to reconfigure the message flow on the Data page of the XLANG schedule drawing.

Compile the XLANG Schedule   After you have made the necessary changes to the XLANG schedule drawing, you can compile it by choosing File | Make <*filename*>.skx. This will create the executable schedule representing the PIP. The schedule can then be executed using the methods of the CPIPAdapterManager interface.

Execute the XLANG Schedule   You can create a new instance of a PIP XLANG schedule by calling the StartActivity and DeliverInitiationMessage methods of the CPIPAdapterManager interface. The initiator role should use the StartActivity method to return the flow ID for the appropriate XLANG schedule. This will be determined based on the submitted parameters to the method call, such as the Global Process Indicator Code (3A2, 3A4, and so on) and the DUNS (Data Universal Numbering System) numbers for the initiator and responder organizations. The DeliverInitiationMessage method then submits a RosettaNet message to the XLANG schedule determined by the flow ID.

Similarly, the responder role can call the DeliverResponseMessage method. This requires the flow ID of the XLANG schedule that received the original request. Executing this method will deliver the response message back to the requestor, where it will be picked up by the original XLANG schedule to complete the process.

Accelerator Tools

The BizTalk Server Accelerator for RosettaNet comes with a number of tools that can simplify the implementation of PIPs. The utilities are as follows:

Utility	Purpose
Messaging Configuration Wizard	Allows you to quickly create the messaging objects required to transport messages between trading partners
PIP Administrator	Lets you determine the location of the appropriate XLANG schedule for each PIP segment and role

Utility	Purpose
PIP Schema Manager	Provides a way for you to consolidate your RosettaNet messages into a single schema
PIP XLANG Schedule Tester	Tests PIP implementations by simulating a PIP role and submitting sample message data

Messaging Configuration Wizard   Running the wizard steps you through the process of creating the appropriate organizations, document definitions, envelopes, channels, and messaging ports required by a PIP implementation. The wizard also handles the configuration of each object, such as selecting the correct serializer component, encoding component, and digital certificates for the signing of messages. On the first page after the welcome screen, you create or select the source organization, its DUNS number, and an optional digital certificate for signing outbound messages. On the next page, you create or select the destination organization, its DUNS number, and an optional certificate for verifying digital signatures on inbound messages. You also specify the URLs on the destination organization's web site to which messages and failure notices should be posted. This page is shown in Figure 19-2.

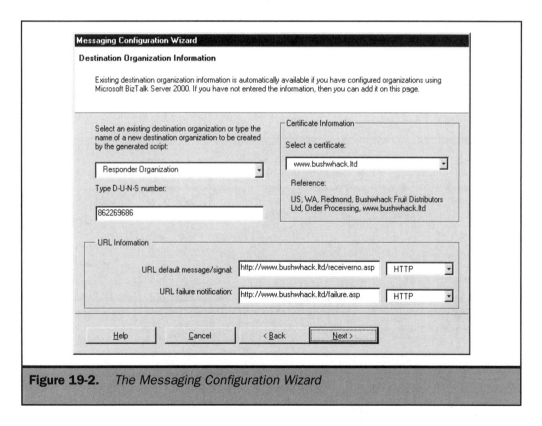

Figure 19-2.   *The Messaging Configuration Wizard*

The next page of the wizard shows you the channels and messaging ports to be created. There are three channels and three messaging ports for outbound messages, and two channels and one messaging port for inbound messages. For example, if the names of the organizations were Org1 and Org2, the following objects would be created:

Outbound Channels	**Outbound Messaging Ports**
Org1 to Org2 unsigned	Org2 unsigned out
Org1 to Org2 signed	Org2 signed out
Org1 to Org2 failure	Org2 failure out

Inbound Channels	**Inbound Messaging Ports**
Org2 PIPMgr	Org1 PIPMgr in
Org2 PIPMgr signed	

The final page of the wizard does not actually create the objects, however. Instead, it creates a script that uses the BizTalk Messaging Configuration Object Model to create the objects. The script is saved to your hard drive so that it can be run at any time, perhaps to move a development environment to a production environment. Figure 19-3 shows how these objects interact with the XLANG schedules that implement a PIP. The diagram only shows the first part of the PIP for compactness, but the other stages are implemented the same way.

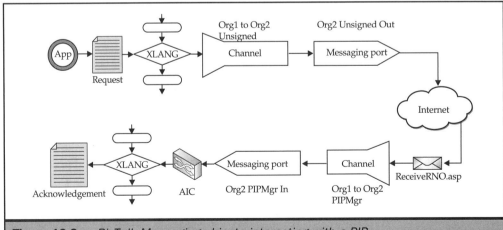

Figure 19-3.   *BizTalk Messaging objects interacting with a PIP*

Note *The BizTalk Messaging Configuration Object Model was covered in Chapter 16.*

First, an application that calls the StartActivity method of the CPIPAdapterManager interface submits a document to the appropriate initiator XLANG schedule, depending on the parameters passed to the DeliverInitiationMessage method. The XLANG schedule will then execute a COM component that implements the CPIPAdapterSubmit interface. This passes the document to BizTalk Messaging, where it will be picked up by a channel called "Org1 to Org2 unsigned" (where Org1 and Org2 are the names of the organizations specified in the Messaging Configuration Wizard). This, in turn, feeds into a messaging port called "Org2 unsigned out", which transports the document via HTTP to an Active Server Page (ASP) on the trading partner's web server. This ASP submits the document to BizTalk Messaging, where it is received by a channel called "Org2 PIPMgr in". (Note that this channel refers to Org2 rather than Org1 as listed in the preceding table because we are now looking at the trading partner.) This messaging port is configured to send the document to an Application Integration Component (AIC) that implements the CPIPAdapter interface and calls the ActivatePIP method to start the responder XLANG schedule and pass the message in. The acknowledgement generated is then passed back to the initiator through BizTalk Messaging as before.

Note *A sample ASP called ReceiveRNO.asp is included in the SDK. This file should be used in place of the generic ASP receive sample included with BizTalk Server, because it checks that the document uses the correct MIME type for the RosettaNet message standard.*

PIP Administrator This tool presents a grid of recognized PIP roles and their associated XLANG schedules, as shown in Figure 19-4. In this utility, you can select a role for a particular segment and choose the XLANG schedule that should be used to implement that role. The appropriate schedule will then be loaded to execute the corresponding PIP when the StartActivity method of the CPIPAdapterManager interface is called. To change the properties for any role, double-click the entry. To create a new segment role and associate an XLANG schedule with it, choose Action | Register New XLANG Schedule. You can then choose the Global Process Indicator Code (for example, 1B1), the Global Process Code (for example, Manage Product Information Subscriptions), the Global Business Action Code (for example, Subscription Request), the source and destination organizations for which this schedule should be valid, and whether this role is an initiator.

PIP Schema Manager This application allows you to merge new RNIF DTDs into the BizTalk Messaging RosettaNet Universal Message. The RosettaNet Universal Message is a document specification used by BizTalk Messaging for the RosettaNet Message document definition. This document definition is the only one used by BizTalk Messaging, regardless of the type of business document being exchanged. For this reason, an XML schema for each business message type that you wish to use should be merged into this file, which is saved as RosettaNetMessage.xml in the WebDAV Repository.

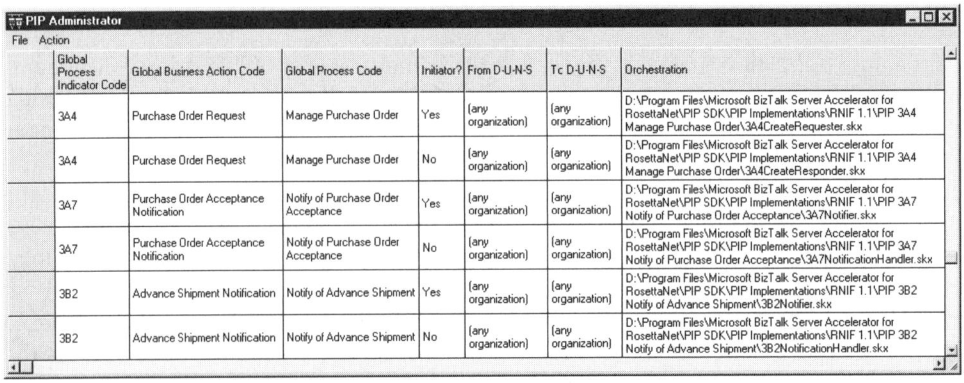

PIP Administrator

File Action

Global Process Indicator Code	Global Business Action Code	Global Process Code	Initiator?	From D-U-N-S	To D-U-N-S	Orchestration
3A4	Purchase Order Request	Manage Purchase Order	Yes	(any organization)	(any organization)	D:\Program Files\Microsoft BizTalk Server Accelerator for RosettaNet\PIP SDK\PIP Implementations\RNIF 1.1\PIP 3A4 Manage Purchase Order\3A4CreateRequester.skx
3A4	Purchase Order Request	Manage Purchase Order	No	(any organization)	(any organization)	D:\Program Files\Microsoft BizTalk Server Accelerator for RosettaNet\PIP SDK\PIP Implementations\RNIF 1.1\PIP 3A4 Manage Purchase Order\3A4CreateResponder.skx
3A7	Purchase Order Acceptance Notification	Notify of Purchase Order Acceptance	Yes	(any organization)	(any organization)	D:\Program Files\Microsoft BizTalk Server Accelerator for RosettaNet\PIP SDK\PIP Implementations\RNIF 1.1\PIP 3A7 Notify of Purchase Order Acceptance\3A7Notifier.skx
3A7	Purchase Order Acceptance Notification	Notify of Purchase Order Acceptance	No	(any organization)	(any organization)	D:\Program Files\Microsoft BizTalk Server Accelerator for RosettaNet\PIP SDK\PIP Implementations\RNIF 1.1\PIP 3A7 Notify of Purchase Order Acceptance\3A7NotificationHandler.skx
3B2	Advance Shipment Notification	Notify of Advance Shipment	Yes	(any organization)	(any organization)	D:\Program Files\Microsoft BizTalk Server Accelerator for RosettaNet\PIP SDK\PIP Implementations\RNIF 1.1\PIP 3B2 Notify of Advance Shipment\3B2Notifier.skx
3B2	Advance Shipment Notification	Notify of Advance Shipment	No	(any organization)	(any organization)	D:\Program Files\Microsoft BizTalk Server Accelerator for RosettaNet\PIP SDK\PIP Implementations\RNIF 1.1\PIP 3B2 Notify of Advance Shipment\3B2NotificationHandler.skx

Figure 19-4. *The PIP Administrator*

First of all, you must obtain the RNIF DTD for the business document you wish to use, such as a 2A2 Product Information Query. This DTD should be imported into BizTalk Editor and saved as an XML schema using UTF-8 encoding. The resulting schema can then be merged into the Consolidated Message specification that contains the schemata for the Preamble and Service Header portions of a RosettaNet message. Merging these two specifications gives you a complete specification for the RosettaNet business message that corresponds to this type of business document. This step is shown in Figure 19-5.

Note *The full set of RosettaNet DTDs is available at http://www.commercedesk.com/rosettanetrepository/.*

After you have created the consolidated business message schema that includes the schema for the business document, you must then merge that consolidated business message schema into the RosettaNet Universal Message schema, which contains all business document types. To do this, browse to the consolidated business message schema in the Document Specification To Merge From field, browse to the RosettaNet Message in the Document Specification To Merge To field, and enter the path and filename for the new RosettaNet Message in the Output File field. This new RosettaNet Message specification should be stored in the WebDAV Repository, and the RosettaNet Message document definition in BizTalk Messaging should be updated to point to it.

PIP XLANG Schedule Tester This utility provides a way for you to test your PIP implementations without having to actually send data to a business partner. This is done

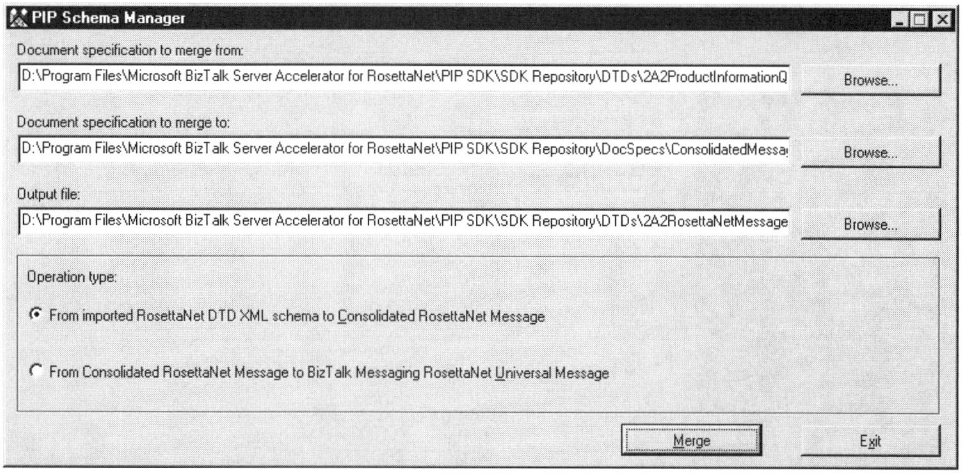

Figure 19-5.   *The PIP Schema Manager*

by saving the business messages to a private message queue called RNMsgOut that is created when the accelerator is installed. By default, the XLANG schedules shipped with the accelerator are configured to use this message queue. In a production environment, they should be modified to use a component that implements the CPIPAdapterSubmit interface instead. This will allow you to send business messages to trading partners via BizTalk Messaging.

When you execute the PIP XLANG Schedule Tester, the application acts as the other trading partner with which you exchange messages. For example, on the opening page of the application, you can choose between the four main roles. If you select Transaction Initiator, then the PIP XLANG Schedule Tester will act as the Transaction Responder. If you then click Next, you can browse to an instance of an appropriate RosettaNet business message. This message will be displayed in the web browser control, as shown in Figure 19-6. Clicking Next will then activate the appropriate XLANG schedule (as determined by the properties configured through the PIP Administrator tool). The window will show the events that have fired in the schedule. You can also use the BizTalk Server XLANG Monitor application to confirm the schedule is running and query the events.

After you click Next again, the utility allows you to select the signal message type, such as Acknowledgement. Browse to an appropriate acknowledgement instance, view the acknowledgement in the web browser control, and click Next. The PIP XLANG

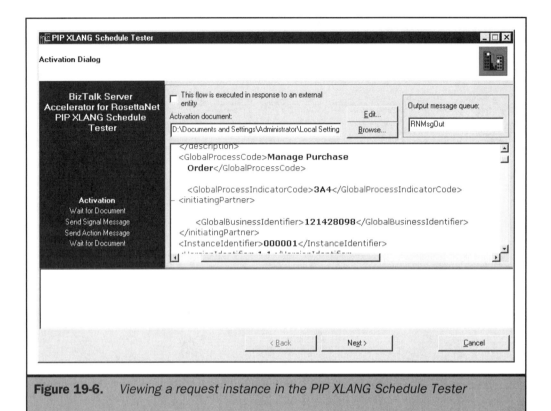

Figure 19-6. *Viewing a request instance in the PIP XLANG Schedule Tester*

Schedule Tester will pass this acknowledgement back into the XLANG schedule so that it may be retrieved by the initiator. At the next stage, you are asked to provide an instance of a response document. Browse to an appropriate file and click Next. The PIP XLANG Schedule Tester also passes this message into the XLANG schedule. Earlier in this chapter, during our discussion of roles, I described how the initiator sends a request, and the responder sends back an acknowledgement and a response. After the response has been received, the initiator must send an acknowledgement to the responder, which, in this case, is the RNMsgOut message queue. Click Next to move to the final stage. Here, we can again poll the message queue to see the response acknowledgement generated by the initiator and passed to the queue. This final step is shown in Figure 19-7. If you are also examining the XLANG Monitor application, this should now show the schedule as completed. Click Finish to exit the PIP XLANG Schedule Tester.

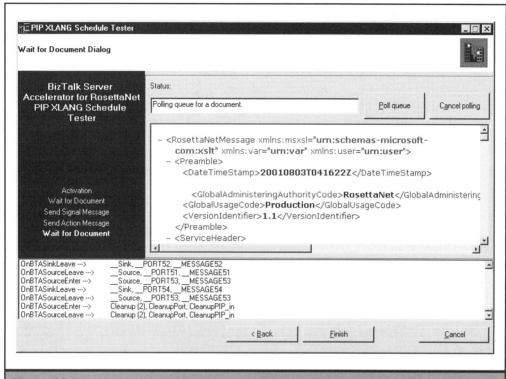

Figure 19-7.   *Viewing the response in the PIP XLANG Schedule Tester*

BizTalk Server Accelerator for HIPAA

Organizations in the United States who exchange healthcare-related information, such as health insurance claims or benefit inquiries, have to comply with new U.S. government regulations covering the electronic transmission of such data. These guidelines, embodied in the Health Insurance Portability and Accountability Act (HIPAA) of 1996, also mandate the use of a single content format for each type of document exchanged. This format is based on the ANSI X12 EDI standard, so Microsoft has released the BizTalk Server Accelerator for HIPAA to help organizations become compliant before the act is instituted in October 2002. The accelerator includes HIPAA-compliant templates and HIPAA- specific parser, serializer, and validation components to handle them. The accelerator also includes a claims processing sample using BizTalk Orchestration and relevant documentation.

Introduction to HIPAA

The Health Insurance Portability and Accountability Act (HIPAA) of 1996 defines important new protections for U.S. citizens with regard to health insurance coverage, such as increasing an individual's ability to secure healthcare when starting a new job, or maintaining an individual's insurance coverage if he or she changes jobs. These regulations also protect individuals or groups who suffer a change in conditions or health that previously may have led to discrimination. Apart from these benefits to consumers, however, the act also provides administrative simplifications that are designed to reduce the cost and overhead for organizations involved in the healthcare industry, by standardizing the electronic transmission of administrative and financial transactions. These simplifications also define privacy standards, security standards, and identifier standards that mandate how organizations may exchange healthcare-related data electronically.

HIPAA Transaction Sets

In particular, HIPAA defines a set of document standards, known as *transaction sets* and based on ANSI X12 EDI formats, which represent health insurance claims, benefit inquiries, benefit enrollment requests, and payment orders. The full list of HIPAA transaction sets is shown in Table 19-2.

Identifier	Document Description
270	Eligibility, coverage, or benefit inquiry
271	Eligibility, coverage, or benefit information
276	Healthcare claim status request
276	Healthcare claim status notification
278	Healthcare services review: request for review
278	Healthcare services review: response to request for review
820	Payment order/remittance advice
834	Benefit enrollment and maintenance
835	Healthcare claim payment/advice
837	Healthcare claim: professional
837	Healthcare claim: dental
837	Healthcare claim: institutional

Table 19-2.   *The HIPAA Transaction Sets*

The BizTalk document specifications included with the BizTalk Server Accelerator for HIPAA were created in association with the Washington Publication Company, who are the exclusive publishers of the corresponding HIPAA implementation guides. These guides explain in detail the structure of each transaction set, and they are freely downloadable from http://www.wpc-edi.com/hipaa/. Each implementation guide also includes sample documents that may be used to test a BizTalk specification. After installing the accelerator, you will also find an extra HTML Help file in the \Program Files\Microsoft BizTalk Accelerator or HIPAA\Documentation folder that describes the various data structures used by each transaction set, although this is only a subset of the information available in the corresponding implementation guide.

Using the HIPAA Accelerator

Many organizations involved in the healthcare industry currently use different document standards, perhaps tied to a format required by custom-built software. Replacing or reconfiguring these formats and systems to comply with HIPAA could be extremely time-consuming and expensive. However, as we've seen throughout this book, BizTalk Server can be used as an enterprise application integration server to transform documents and provide communication between internal systems. Similarly, BizTalk Server can allow an organization to use one data format internally while communicating different data formats with external partners. In this way, BizTalk Server can help reconcile the new HIPAA transaction sets with existing data formats to make it easier for organizations to comply with the regulations laid out under HIPAA.

The set of utilities provided by the BizTalk Accelerator for HIPAA is not as extensive as that included with either of the other accelerators discussed in this chapter. That's not to say, however, that the Accelerator for HIPAA is lacking in support—just that there is not much required to achieve the desired result. The accelerator consists of BizTalk-specific schemas representing the transaction sets listed in Table 19-2 and of corresponding HIPAA-specific parser, serializer, and validation components. There is also a sample claims-processing orchestration scenario consisting of an XLANG schedule, supporting COM components, BizTalk Messaging configuration scripts, and a procedure tracking database. Finally, an HIPAA Prescriptive Architecture Guide details how certain security and privacy aspects of the act should be implemented.

Installing the Accelerator

Installing the BizTalk Server Accelerator for HIPAA is so straightforward that it almost doesn't require any discussion, but this book is supposed to be a complete reference, so I'd better not leave it out. The hardware and software prerequisites are the same as those for BizTalk Server itself, but you must also have BizTalk Server Service Pack 1A installed beforehand—Service Pack 1 is not sufficient. In fact, the software will not install unless Service Pack 1A is present. To install the accelerator, you should double-click the installer program and perform the following steps:

1. Click Next at the welcome page of the installation wizard.

2. Accept the license agreement and click Next.

3. Enter your name and organization details, and choose whether the installation should be available for all users or just the currently logged-on user. Click Next.

4. Choose the installation location and click Next.

5. Choose either the Complete or Custom installation option and click Next.

6. If you chose the Custom installation option, select the components you want installed. The available choices are HIPAA Components, Schema, Documentation, and Sample. Click Next when you have finished.

7. Click Install to copy the files and register the components.

8. Click Finish.

See? Told you it was easy. In fact, the only thing to beware of regarding the installation is that a new parser component called BizTalk.ParserHipaaX12.1 is registered. This parser is automatically moved up in the parser call sequence so that it is above the generic BizTalk.ParserX12.1 component. This is important—if you need to rearrange the parser call sequence at any point, you should always ensure that the HIPAA parser is higher in the list than the generic X12 parser. This will not cause problems for X12 interchanges, however, because the HIPAA parser can handle both HIPAA X12 and generic X12 transaction sets.

Note *To uninstall the Accelerator, simply execute the installer file again, and choose Remove.*

Exchanging HIPAA Documents

To exchange HIPAA business documents with other compliant organizations, you will use the X12-based document formats listed in Table 19-2. However, your own internal applications may require that each document be in a different structure, such as XML or Flat-File. As discussed throughout this book, this is the kind of thing at which BizTalk Server excels. To exchange HIPAA documents with other systems, whether internal or external, you can make use of BizTalk Messaging and BizTalk Orchestration services.

To use the supplied specifications with BizTalk Messaging, you will need to create the appropriate organizations, applications, document definitions, envelopes, messaging ports, and channels. Specifically, to work with HIPAA-compliant documents, you should create a document definition for each transaction set required. Each document definition must then point to the appropriate HIPAA transaction set specification, which must be stored in the WebDAV Repository. You will also need to define the selection criteria for each document definition. In addition, to allow BizTalk Messaging to use the correct parser and serializer components, you must create an X12 envelope.

Note *Using BizTalk Messaging Manager to create and configure organizations, applications, document definitions, envelopes, messaging ports, and channels was discussed in Chapter 6.*

You can also use BizTalk Editor to validate HIPAA documents against their corresponding specifications. This can be done using a sample document instance such as those provided in the HIPAA implementation guides. For example, the following is a sample Healthcare Claim: Dental (837) document in its original format:

```
BHT*0019*00*0123*19990210*1023*CH~
xzsREF*87*004010X097~
NM1*41*2*PREMIER BILLING SERVICE*****46*TGJ23~
PER*IC*JERRY*TE*7176149999~
NM1*40*2*INSURANCE COMPANY XYZ*****46*66783JJT~
HL*1**20*1~
NM1*85*2*DENTAL ASSOCIATES*****34*587654321~
N3*234 SEAWAY ST~
N4*MIAMI*FL*33111~
HL*2*1*22*1~
SBR*P*****6***CI~
NM1*IL*1*SMITH*JANE****MI*111223333~
NM1*PR*2*INSURANCE COMPANY XYZ*****PI*66783JJT~
HL*3*2*23*0~
PAT*19~
NM1*QC*1*SMITH*TED~
N3*236 N MAIN ST~
N4*MIAMI*FL*33413~
DMG*D8*19730501*M~
CLM*26403774*150***11::1*Y**Y*Y~
DTP*472*D8*19990209~
REF*D9*17312345600006351~
NM1*82*1*KILDARE*BEN****34*999996666~
PRV*PE*ZZ*122300000N~
LX*1~
SV3*AD:D2150*100****1~
TOO*JP*12*M:O~
LX*2~
SV3*AD:D1110*50****1~
```

Pretty, isn't it? To see how BizTalk Messaging will convert this to XML (and from XML to any other format we choose), we can validate the instance in BizTalk Editor. As discussed in Chapter 4, load the appropriate specification into BizTalk Editor, and choose Tools | Validate Instance. If the document is valid, BizTalk Editor will show the corresponding XML in the Output pane, as shown in Figure 19-8.

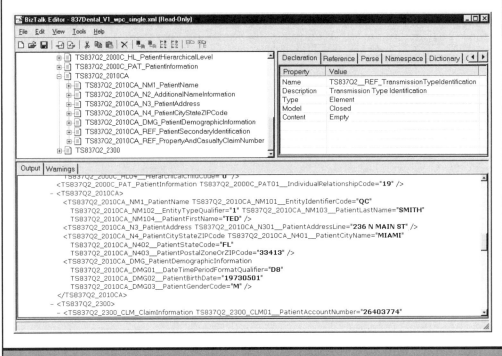

Figure 19-8. *Validating HIPAA instances in BizTalk Editor*

Running the Claims Processing Sample

The BizTalk Server Accelerator for HIPAA also includes a claims processing scenario that uses BizTalk Orchestration to handle insurance claims and to correlate processed payments with the appropriate claim. A SQL Server database called BTSHIPAA is created for the sample to hold the processed data. An SMTP server must also be available to send generated e-mail alerts that warn when claims are almost overdue or have become overdue. The scenario can be used to represent either a healthcare provider, such as a doctor or hospital, or a payer of claims, such as an insurance company or healthcare maintenance organization (HMO).

To install the sample, double-click install.exe in the \Program Files\Microsoft BizTalk Accelerator for HIPAA\Samples\Claims Processing\setup folder to run the installation program shown in Figure 19-9. In this application, you can choose the SQL Server computer on which to create the database, the user name and password required to register the components and create the receive functions, the details of the imaginary organization, such as name and type (payer or provider), and the configuration details for the scenario, such as the payment period and the number of days after which a warning should be sent by e-mail.

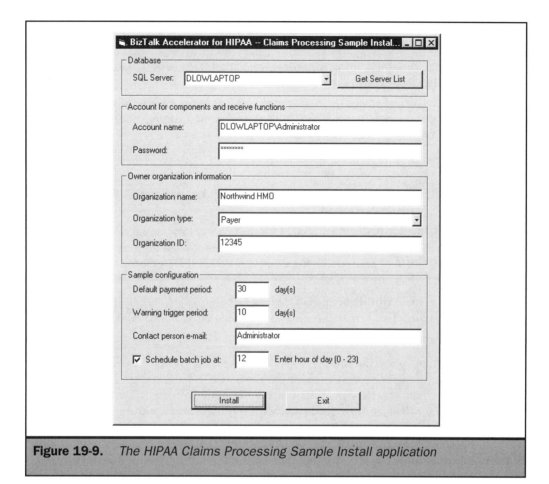

Figure 19-9. *The HIPAA Claims Processing Sample Install application*

After you click the Install button, the application performs the following tasks:

■ Creates a new COM+ application called "BizTalk Accelerator for HIPAA—Claims Processing Sample" and adds the components in BTHAIC.dll and BTSHipaaSamp.dll to it.

■ Creates Registry entries under HKLM\SOFTWARE\Microsoft\BTS HIPAA Sample\ for the new BTSHipaaSamp component containing the configuration data specified in the install application.

■ Creates a new SQL Server database called BTSHIPAA to hold claim and payment data.

■ Adds the organization information specified in the install application to the bth_organizations table in the database.

- Creates a virtual directory called btshipaa pointing to the \Claims Processing \ASP folder.

- Creates BizTalk Messaging organizations called BTSHIPAA_Samp_Payer_Org and BTSHIPAA_Samp_Provider_Org.

- Creates a BizTalk Messaging document definition for a claim payment called BTSHIPAA_Samp_835_Doc and another for an institutional claim called BTSHIPAA_Samp_837I_Doc.

- Creates BizTalk Messaging channels called BTSHIPAA_Samp_835_Chan and BTSHIPAA_Samp_837I_Chan.

- Creates BizTalk Messaging ports called BTSHIPAA_Samp_835_Port and BTSHIPAA_Samp_837I_Port.

- Creates folders called 835 and 837I under \Claims Processing\FilePickup as drop locations for the sample document instances and file receive functions called BTSHIPAA_Samp_835_RecvFunc and BTSHIPAA_Samp_837I_RecvFunc pointing to those directories.

- Registers \sked\RunProcessAlerts.vbs as a batch job to run at the designated time each day. This script executes the ProcessAlerts.skx XLANG schedule whose workflow is shown in Figure 19-10.

Making a Claim   To run the sample, copy the 837I.txt file from the \Claims Processing \TestData folder to the \Claims Processing\FilePickup\837I folder. It will be picked up by the appropriate receive function, which will pass it into the BTSHIPAA_ Samp_ 837I_Chan channel. This, in turn, feeds the XML representation of the claims document into the BTSHIPAA_Samp_837I_Port messaging port, where it is processed by the BTHAIC Proc837I Application Integration Component (AIC). The AIC adds the provider or payer information to the bth_organizations table in the database (if it is not already there), gets the payment period from that table, and creates a new record in the bth_ claims table, storing a record for each line item in the claim in the bth_lineitems table.

Registering a Payment   After you have registered a claim, you can address the claim by providing a payment. This is done by copying the 835.txt file from the \Claims Processing\TestData folder to the \Claims Processing\FilePickup\835 folder. As before, this will be picked up by a file receive function and fed into BizTalk Messaging, where it will be processed by the BTHAIC Proc835 AIC. This AIC checks whether the payment information already exists in the bth_payments table. If not, the AIC adds a record to that table for the payment and a record to the bth_paymentitems table for each line item in the payment.

Checking the Status of Claims and Payments   The sample also provides a web site where you can check submitted claims to see whether they have been addressed. The Claims Status page of this site is shown in Figure 19-11. If a payment (an 835 document)

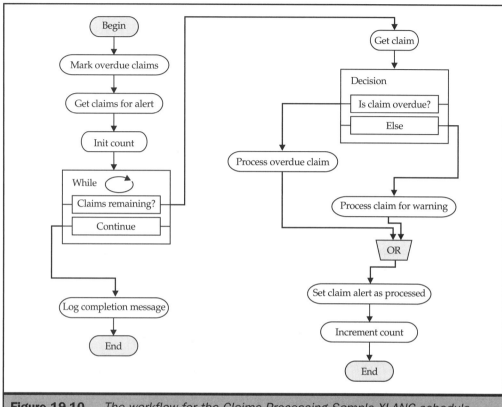

Figure 19-10.   *The workflow for the Claims Processing Sample XLANG schedule*

has not been received to address a particular claim, the web site allows you to manually address the claim by checking the appropriate box and clicking the Address Selected Claims button. The web site also allows you to configure the payer or provider organization chosen for the scenario, including setting the e-mail address of the person to whom overdue claim alerts should be sent and the default payment period.

HIPAA Documentation

Apart from the standard help files, the BizTalk Server Accelerator for HIPAA comes with two extra pieces of documentation. The HIPAA Transaction Set Reference contains information about each of the 12 transaction sets implemented in HIPAA, providing descriptions of each loop, segment, and element found therein. It also describes the structure of the Interchange and Functional Group headers and footers used in the X12 structures. Because these apply to all X12 formats, this in itself is a valuable learning tool.

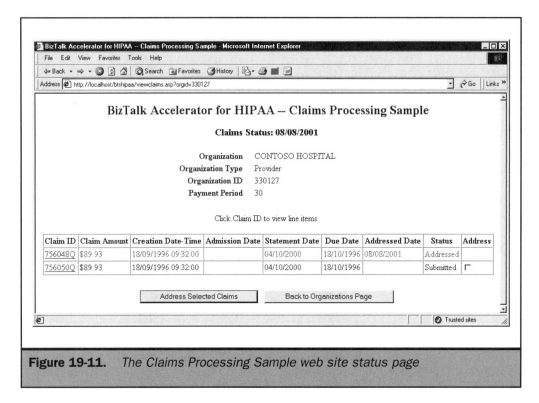

Figure 19-11. *The Claims Processing Sample web site status page*

Finally, there is also a Prescriptive Architecture Guide, which offers important background information and practical guidelines to assist in the implementation of HIPAA standards through all phases of working with the accelerator. It should not be thought of as a technical manual, however; it is intended for project management personnel in organizations that are facing up to HIPAA compliance. It also provides a concise summary of what's required for HIPAA compliance without having to read through several thousand pages of a government bill, including a high-level discussion of how the BizTalk Accelerator for HIPAA can be used to provide this compliance. The guide has the following main sections:

Planning: Readiness Assessment

                    Training

                    Infrastructure

Deployment: Gap Analysis

                    Accelerator Implementation

                    Testing

Operations: Administration

Optimization

Change Management

Accelerator for Suppliers

At the beginning of this book, I described how BizTalk Server began life as an extension of the business-to-business functionality in Microsoft Site Server 3.0 Commerce Edition. Site Server has since been superseded by Microsoft Commerce Server 2000, a full-featured server product for business-to-consumer and business-to-business e-commerce solutions. One of the early design goals for both BizTalk Server and Commerce Server was that they should integrate easily to form part of a larger supply-chain solution. A certain amount of integration is available out-of-the-box, as discussed in Chapter 14. From the perspective of supplier organizations, however, it is not possible without extensive configuration to allow Commerce Server to distribute product catalogs to trading partners and to have customers of those trading partners submit purchase orders directly to Commerce Server. The Microsoft BizTalk Accelerator for Suppliers (AFS) addresses these supplier-enablement issues by providing a low-cost solution to accelerate time-to-market. It also includes resources to allow Commerce Server to participate in online marketplaces such as those provided by Commerce One, Clarus, and Ariba.

Introduction to Supplier Enablement

Supplier enablement is a relatively new term in business-to-business e-commerce—so new that the spell-checker in my word processor didn't recognize it! However, it does exist and it can present a real challenge to organizations that are trying to automate and modernize their supply chains. Supplier enablement involves providing mechanisms for suppliers to engage in electronic trading with business partners through a variety of channels, such as *corporate procurement applications* and *marketplaces*. In this way, new avenues for conducting online business are established, and this can provide benefits not just for companies, but also for consumers. It can make it easier for suppliers to broaden their reach, forge new trading partner relationships, and, ultimately, improve their revenue while streamlining their processes. However, supplier enablement is not about the establishment of complete supply chains, although it is an important part of that process. Such solutions will typically require integration with internal enterprise resource planning (ERP) and customer relationship management (CRM) systems, but, as we have seen throughout this book, that is also possible with BizTalk Server.

Marketplaces

In recent years, many companies have begun providing services to consumers and suppliers to centralize and simplify the procurement process. These services often take the form of private or public web sites called *marketplaces*, where products and services from multiple suppliers are available to small and large buyers alike. Often, these marketplaces are specific to a vertical market, such as the automobile or IT industries, but lately, horizontal marketplaces that provide consumers with a greater range of products across multiple industries have become active. The sale of products from many different suppliers is possible through the aggregation of product catalogs from each of those suppliers.

Marketplaces can function in a variety of ways. Some only serve to connect consumers with suppliers by providing a portal where customers can browse available products. The actual purchasing, however, is done by directing the consumer to the supplier at purchase time. Other marketplaces strive to provide discounts to their customers by collecting orders from multiple buyers and then purchasing the products in bulk. Yet others attempt to make the purchasing process as seamless as possible, acting as a proxy for different suppliers, by displaying aggregated catalog details, as shown next.

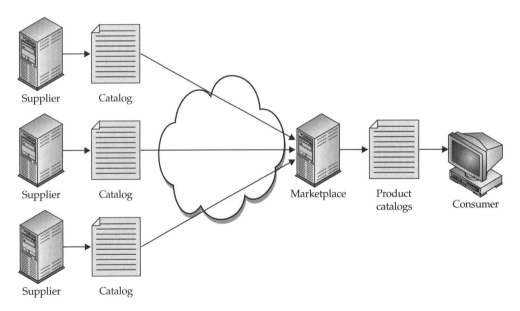

Also, accepting customer orders and passing them transparently through to the supplier results in a better shopping experience for the consumer. Obviously, this type of functionality can present a range of problems to all involved. Problems can arise not just due to the variety of transport mechanisms and data formats that will be required to support each party in the process, but also because it will be necessary to automate these business processes to make such a venture viable. If you're not thinking BizTalk Server at this point, go back to the beginning of the book and start reading again!

Before getting into the specifics of how the BizTalk Accelerator for Suppliers can provide this type of functionality, let me take a moment to introduce some important terminology and concepts relating to supplier enablement.

Buyer Application   A business-to-consumer e-commerce web site created with Microsoft Commerce Server is an excellent example of a buyer application, providing online business-to-consumer e-commerce functionality through a web site. Customers can view multiple product catalogs, select products for purchase by adding them to a virtual shopping basket, and complete the purchase of those products by providing the necessary payment details. Payment may be accepted in a variety of forms, such as by credit card or with electronic cash.

Corporate Procurement Application   If a buyer application is internal to an organization, there may be a need for extra functionality, whereby spending limits are imposed and purchase requests are forwarded as requisitions to an approving entity. The approval of purchases may then be performed automatically based on certain predefined criteria, or manually by an authorizing individual. When used within an organization in this way, a buyer application may be termed a corporate procurement application. The submission mechanism for approved purchases will then take the form of a purchase order generated automatically by the application and forwarded to the supplier.

Peer-to-Peer Trading   Suppose a company is engaged in supplying products directly to consumers through a buyer application or corporate procurement application, without going through an online marketplace. If the consumer then submits orders directly to the supplier, then the consumer and the supplier can be said to have a peer-to-peer trading partner relationship. This is also sometimes referred to as a "direct" trading partner relationship.

Remote Shopping   This is a service offered by many online marketplaces that provide aggregated catalogs from multiple suppliers, whereby a customer using a buyer application is redirected to the supplier's web site when they elect to view details about a product or add a product to their local shopping basket. In this way, the supplier retains a certain amount of control over how the product information is presented. After being directed to the supplier, the customer can continue browsing and selecting products. Each product selected is then added to the "remote" shopping basket held by that supplier. When the customer has finished choosing products for a particular supplier, their choices are reflected in the "local" shopping basket provided by the buyer application. Upon checkout, purchase orders are automatically generated and forwarded to each supplier as appropriate. Although "remote shopping" is the generic term used to describe this process, the name of the feature will vary depending on the implementation. For example, Ariba calls it "Punchout", Commerce One provides "RoundTrip", and Clarus refers to it as "Tap Out".

Vendors A number of different vendor companies provide online marketplace applications. As described, these vendors allow browsing of products from multiple suppliers collected through catalog publishing. Many also provide remote basket shopping functionality. However, each vendor may use a different data format for the catalogs they accept. As supplied, AFS supports the following vendors and their associated data formats:

Vendor	Protocol(s)
Ariba	Commerce Extensible Markup Language (cXML) 1.1 and 1.2
Clarus	Commerce Extensible Markup Language (cXML) 1.1
Commerce One	XML Common Business Language (xCBL) 3.0 SAP Open Catalog Interface (OCI) 2.0b
VerticalNet	Commerce Extensible Markup Language (cXML) 1.1

However, although a vendor may provide support for a particular data format, the implementation may differ from that provided by other vendors. For example, Ariba and VerticalNet both support cXML 1.1, but the specifics of how catalogs are constructed for each vendor differ in their implementation. Therefore, it is important to familiarize yourself with how messages should be formatted to comply with each vendor with which you communicate.

The documentation provided with AFS contains an extensive overview of supplier enablement, including the driving factors behind it, the types of organization involved, and the different ways in which it can be implemented. You can also find more information at http://www.cxml.org/ and http://www.xcbl.org/.

Using the Accelerator

AFS includes resources to enable suppliers to publish product catalogs to online marketplaces and receive purchase orders from customers of those marketplaces. To do this, AFS provides additional tools and configuration for both Commerce Server 2000 and BizTalk Server. After installation, product catalogs may be exported from Commerce Server, transformed by BizTalk Server, and published to an online marketplace. From there, purchase orders may be posted back to your web site, where they will be submitted to BizTalk Server. BizTalk Server will then transform them into the correct format to be handled by the Commerce Server Order Processing Pipeline (OPP). It is possible to install only the functionality required by either Commerce Server or BizTalk Server, and it is also possible to install only the Software Development Kit (SDK) so that all configuration can be done manually as needed.

Installing the Accelerator

Before installing AFS, it is important to decide how it will be used and where each component should go. In a development environment, it is possible that you will have both Commerce Server and BizTalk Server on the same machine, in which case you can perform a complete installation. If you are in a production environment, or if your development environment consists of separate Commerce Server and BizTalk Server installations, you can choose to only install the resources necessary for each server. As a prerequisite for installing AFS, you must ensure that the computer on which the BizTalk Server components will be installed has BizTalk Server (and all its required software) and Message Queuing Services (MSMQ). Also ensure that the computer on which the Commerce Server components will be installed has Commerce Server (and all its required software) with Commerce Server Service Pack 1. This service pack is required because it changes the default XML format used for product catalogs so that they may be mapped to cXML or xCBL formats more easily.

To install the software, double-click the executable and perform the following steps:

1. Click Next on the Welcome page.

2. Click Accept to accept the license agreement and click Next.

3. Enter your customer information, choose whether the application should be available for just the logged-on user or all users, and click Next.

4. Choose either the Complete or Custom installation option and click Next.

5. If you chose Custom, you can select the components you wish to install. The available choices are BizTalk Server Components, Commerce Server Components, SDK And Samples, and Online Documentation.

6. Accept the default installation location or click Change to select a new location, and click Next.

7. If your installation includes Commerce Server Components, enter appropriate user name, password, and domain information for an account with permissions to write to a file share on the BizTalk Server computer that will be used as a receive file location for catalog publishing. Click Next.

8. If your installation includes BizTalk Server Components, you will need to enter the URL to which purchase orders should be posted from trading partners. If you will be installing or have already installed the AFS solution site on another Commerce Server computer, or if you will be implementing the purchase order receive functionality of that solution site on an existing Commerce Server site, enter the URL for that site. If you are performing a complete installation on a computer with both BizTalk Server and Commerce Server, accept the defaults. Click Next when you have finished.

9. Click Install to begin copying files and configuring resources.

If you are installing AFS on a Commerce Server computer, the Commerce Site Packager utility will start so that you can install the AFS solution site. This site is only available with AFS and is an enhanced version of the Retail solution site available at http://www.microsoft.com/commerceserver/, with additional features such as remote basket shopping and purchase order reception. Perform the following tasks to install the solution site:

1. In the Commerce Site Packager Wizard, select the Quick Unpack option and click Next.

2. Type a name for the site, or accept SupplierAccelerator as the default. On this page, you may also select the IIS web site on which the site should be created, and you will need to provide the name of the SQL Server computer on which to store the site databases and the appropriate user credentials. Click Next when you have finished.

3. There is an extra site resource in the AFS site that allows Commerce Server to send catalogs to BizTalk Server. When prompted, enter the name of the BizTalk Server on which AFS is installed and click OK.

4. When prompted for the Data Warehouse information, enter appropriate values for the name of the Data Warehouse global resource. Enter the name of the corresponding database and SQL Server Analysis server on which it will reside. Click OK to continue.

5. You will then be asked to configure the Profiling System resources. Click Next and then OK to accept the defaults on the two pages that appear.

6. After the site has been unpacked, click Finish.

You will also need to install the Business Desk client application on a computer running Internet Explorer 5.5, and either SQL Server Client Tools or Office 2000. Business Desk is a DHTML application used by business managers, IT professionals, and developers to configure a Commerce Server site. This client-side application communicates with an ASP application created on Commerce Server during the unpacking of the AFS site. In a development or testing environment, you may choose to install the application on either the Commerce Server or BizTalk Server computer. AFS includes additional utilities known as *modules* that will appear in the Business Desk interface to configure catalog publishing and manage orders. Perform the following steps to install the Business Desk client:

1. In Internet Explorer 5.5 or later, browse to http:// *<computername>/<sitename>* bizdesk/, where *<computername>* is the name of the Commerce Server computer on which you installed the AFS solution site, and *<sitename>* is the name you gave the site in the Commerce Site Packager.

2. After the necessary components have been installed in the browser, the Browse For Folder dialog box will appear, as shown. Create a new folder to hold the application and click OK.

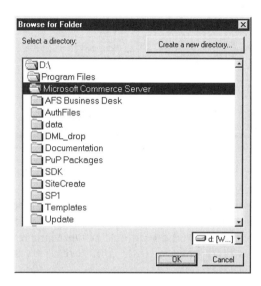

3. After installation, you can click the hyperlink in the browser window to start Business Desk, or you can double-click either of the icons created on the desktop and in the Start menu.

Publishing Catalogs

One of the most important features that AFS provides from a supplier-enablement perspective is the ability to share catalogs with trading partners. This is supported through additional modules supplied for the Commerce Server Business Desk application and through messaging objects, receive functions, and AICs supplied for BizTalk Server. The process by which catalogs are published is shown in Figure 19-12.

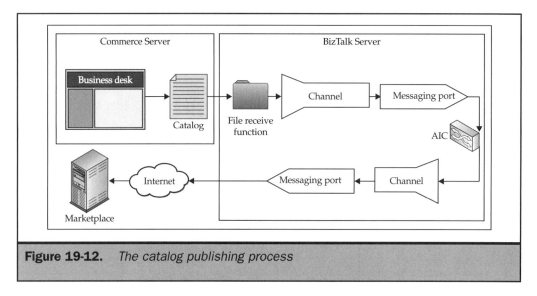

Figure 19-12. *The catalog publishing process*

First, you must use Commerce Server Business Desk to publish an existing catalog. After AFS has been installed on the Commerce Server computer, the AFS solution site contains three extra Business Desk modules, grouped under a new category called Accelerator for Suppliers. The three modules are Trading Partner Manager, Catalog Publisher, and Orders Manager. In the Trading Partner Manager module, click the New Trading Partner button on the toolbar to configure a new trading partner, as shown next.

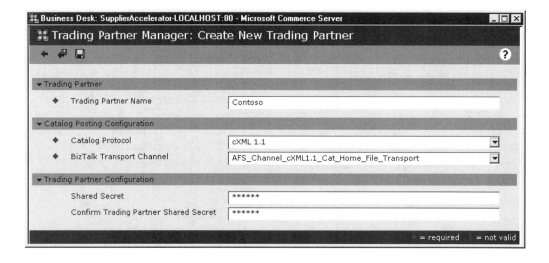

Enter the name of the trading partner, and choose the catalog format they expect. The available options are cXML 1.1, cXML 1.2, and xCBL 3.0. You should then choose the appropriate BizTalk Messaging channel to transport the Commerce Server catalog to that trading partner. AFS creates three channel-messaging port pairs for this purpose, so the available channels are

- AFS_Channel_cXML1.1_Cat_Home_File_Transport
- AFS_Channel_cXML1.2_Cat_Home_File_Transport
- AFS_Channel_xCBL3.0_Cat_Home_File_Transport

You can also specify a shared secret that will be used by your trading partner to verify the catalog. For obvious reasons, you should ensure that catalogs are always published using an encrypted transport such as HTTPS. Click the Save And Back To List button on the toolbar to submit your changes. You can then use the Catalog Publisher module to select the catalog you wish to publish. Click the New Catalog Publication button on the toolbar to configure the publish settings, as shown next.

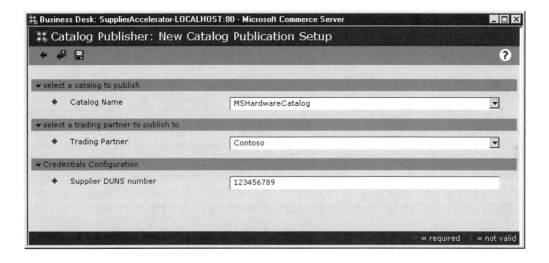

Enter the name of the catalog you wish to publish, and select a trading partner that you previously configured with the Trading Partner Manager module. You must also specify the Data Universal Numbering System (DUNS) number for your organization. Click the Save And Back To List toolbar button to accept the changes. When the list of publications appears, select the publication to submit and click the Publish Catalog toolbar button. This will cause the catalog to be wrapped in a BizTalk Framework 2.0 envelope and dropped into a shared network folder called \\<computername>\afscatalogpublish$, where <computername> is the name of the computer running BizTalk

Server. When AFS is installed on the BizTalk Server computer, it automatically creates a folder called AFSCatalogPub under \<UserProfile>\Application Data, where <UserProfile> represents the folder containing the Windows 2000 profile settings for the user who installed the software. If you specified during installation that the software should be available to anyone who uses the computer, then this is the All Users folder.

AFS also creates three file receive functions to pick up published catalogs and submit them to the appropriate BizTalk Server channel. The receive functions are

- AFS_RecFunc_CS2K_Cat_To_cXML1_1_Cat
- AFS_RecFunc_CS2K_Cat_To_cXML1_2_Cat
- AFS_RecFunc_CS2K_Cat_To_xCBL3_0_Cat

Each one polls the AFSCatalogPub folder on the BizTalk Server computer for documents with an appropriate name. When a catalog is published from Commerce Server, it is given a name in the form <CatalogName>_<GUID><format>.xml, where <CatalogName> is the name of the catalog, <GUID> is a unique identifier, and <format> is either cXML1_1, "cXML1_2, or xCBL3_0. Each receive function is also configured to point to a specific channel to convert the catalog into the format required by the trading partner. These channels are

- AFS_Channel_CS2K_Cat_To_cXML1.1_Cat
- AFS_Channel_CS2K_Cat_To_cXML1.2_Cat
- AFS_Channel_CS2K_Cat_To_xCBL3.0_Cat

Each channel is configured with the appropriate document definitions and map file to transform the catalog from the Commerce Server 1.5 format. This format is an updated version available when Commerce Server Service Pack 1 is installed, because BizTalk Mapper is not able to transform the original Commerce Server 1.0 catalog format. However, you should note that each map file provides a minimal transformation based on the sample hardware catalog included with the Accelerator. If your catalog schema is different, you will have to manually edit the map file to suit your needs.

Each channel also feeds into a messaging port that uses an AIC to perform some postprocessing tasks. Such tasks include extracting the name of the transport channel that will be used to send the catalog to the trading partner, removing the BizTalk Framework 2.0 envelope, inserting the DUNS number of the supplier into the catalog, and submitting the catalog to the corresponding transport channel. Each transport channel feeds into a messaging port that is configured by default to send the transformed catalog to a folder in the file system. These channels do not perform any other transformations. In a production environment, each messaging port would be reconfigured to post the catalog to a real trading partner.

Creating and configuring messaging ports was covered in Chapter 6.

Receiving Purchase Orders

AFS provides the capability for suppliers to receive purchase orders from a trading partner and to automatically process them using the Commerce Server Order Processing Pipeline (OPP). This functionality is provided by an Active Server Pages (ASP) script that accepts submitted orders and transports them via a message queue to BizTalk Server. When AFS is installed, additional messaging objects are created on the BizTalk Server computer to transform the purchase orders into the format that Commerce Server expects. Out of the box, AFS allows suppliers to accept purchase orders in cXML 1.1, cXML 1.2, and xCBL 3.0 formats. The process by which orders are received and transformed is shown in detail in Figure 19-13.

Purchase orders are posted using HTTP from a trading partner to a file called ReceivePO.asp on the Commerce Server computer. This ASP then drops the purchase order into a message queue. AFS creates three private message queues on the BizTalk Server computer when it is installed. These queues are

- cXML1.1_poreceive
- cXML1.2_poreceive
- xCBL3.0_poreceive

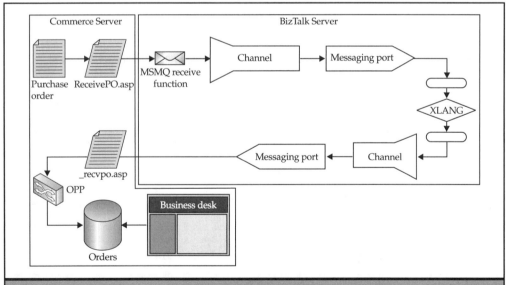

Figure 19-13.   *The purchase order reception process*

AFS also creates three corresponding message-queuing receive functions on BizTalk Server. These receive functions are

- AFS_RecFunc_cXML1_1_PO_To_CS2K_PO
- AFS_RecFunc_cXML1_2_PO_To_CS2K_PO
- AFS_RecFunc_xCBL3_0_PO_To_CS2K_PO

Each message-queuing receive function is configured to monitor the appropriate queue and to submit purchase orders to corresponding channels created by AFS on BizTalk Server. The channels created are

- AFS_Channel_cXML1.1_PO_To_CS2K_PO
- AFS_Channel_cXML1.2_PO_To_CS2K_PO
- AFS_Channel_xCBL3.0_PO_To_CS2K_PO

Each of these channels accepts a purchase order in one of the three supported formats and transforms the order into the format required by Commerce Server. This format is not changed by the addition of Service Pack 1, because BizTalk Mapper is able to deal with the original Commerce Server purchase order structure. Again, each channel is configured with the appropriate document definitions and map file to effect the transformation. These transform channels then feed into corresponding messaging ports, each of which wraps the purchase order in a BizTalk Framework 2.0 envelope and passes it on to an XLANG schedule called PO_Receive.skx that is supplied with AFS. The XLANG schedule drawing is shown in Figure 19-14.

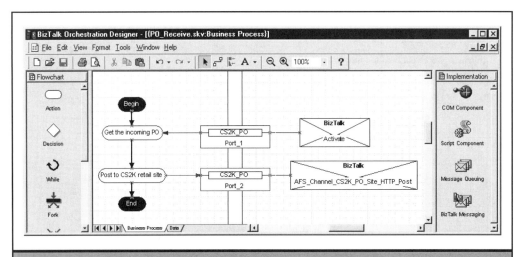

Figure 19-14.   *The AFS purchase order reception XLANG schedule*

As you can see, the XLANG schedule doesn't actually do an awful lot—it simply accepts the purchase order from BizTalk Messaging and then submits it back to BizTalk Messaging. However, if your business rules require that the purchase order should be validated in some way upon receipt, or if it needs to undergo further processing before being passed to Commerce Server, then the XLANG schedule can be extended to provide that functionality. A single channel called AFS_Channel_CS2K_PO_Site_HTTP_Post is created by AFS to accept purchase orders passed on from the XLANG schedule. This channel, in turn, feeds into a single messaging port that is used to submit the purchase order to a file called _recvpo.asp on the Commerce Server site.

This ASP extracts the trading partner information from the BizTalk Framework 2.0 envelope and then removes the envelope. The trading partner information is used to verify the organization details and to create a trading partner profile if none exists. For example, the shared secret in the purchase order must be the same one that was originally configured for the trading partner in Business Desk, or else the order will be rejected as shown. The ASP then converts the information in the purchase order into a Commerce Server dictionary object and submits the order dictionary to the OPP, where it is processed according to the logic of the site and stored in the orders table in the database. After processing, the order can then be queried using the Orders Manager module in the Commerce Server Business Desk application.

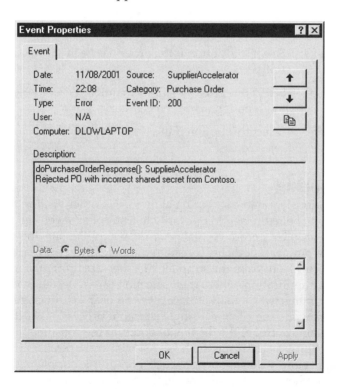

The Orders Manager module only shows orders submitted from trading partners. To view all orders, you should use the Order Status module in the Orders category.

Using the Orders Manager module, you can search for orders from trading partners using a variety of criteria, such as Order Number, Trading Partner, Order Date, and Order Status. When your search is complete, you can select an order and click the Open button on the toolbar to view the details. A sample order is shown in Figure 19-15. On this page, you can change the status of the order and also the fulfillment status. The available options for Order Status are Basket, New Order, and Saved Order. Orders that arrive from trading partners are automatically set to New Order, but that has nothing to do with the famous '80s pop group who released "Blue Monday". New status options can be added using the Data Codes module that appears under the Orders category in Business Desk. The available options for Fulfillment Status are shown in Figure 19-15. The following table describes each option:

Status	Description
Auto	Select this status to automatically process the order.
Auto 24hrs	Select this option to process the order within 24 hours.
Fulfilled	Select this option if the order has been fulfilled.
Manual	Select this option to allow manual intervention before processing.
Rejected	Select this option if the order has been rejected.

Remote Shopping

As discussed previously, remote shopping allows a customer visiting a marketplace buyer application to be redirected temporarily to a supplier's web site, where they can then browse that supplier's product catalogs. In that supplier site, they will then add products to a shopping basket that is considered remote from the marketplace. When they are ready to check out from the supplier site, they are brought back to the marketplace buyer application, where their selections are reflected in the local shopping basket. In this way, a marketplace allows a user to browse products from multiple suppliers while completing a single checkout process. Also, this feature allows the supplier to retain control of the display of goods to the consumer and implement important promotional mechanisms such as cross-sell and up-sell. Otherwise, the marketplace might simply display the products of multiple suppliers side by side, preventing the supplier from capitalizing on their identity and brand. Remote

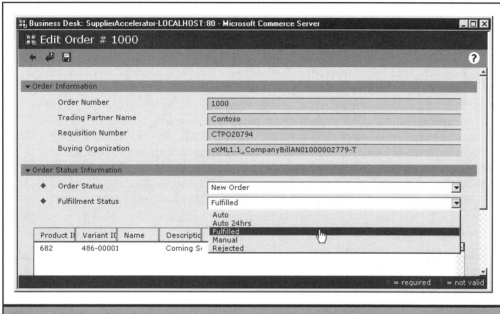

Figure 19-15.   *The Orders Manager module in Business Desk*

shopping also allows suppliers to customize product pricing for marketplace shoppers through personalization mechanisms and to provide custom configuration routines such as those used in the purchase of a composite product like a personal computer.

Although remote shopping functionality is included in AFS, it does not involve BizTalk Server in any way. Because this book is not called *Commerce Server: The Complete Reference*, I will only provide a brief overview of how AFS implements remote basket shopping for different marketplace vendors.

Commerce One RoundTrip   Commerce One provides remote shopping in its marketplace software through its *RoundTrip* feature. This uses the SAP Open Catalog Interface (OCI) 2.0b standard. When a customer using Commerce One elects to browse a catalog owned by a supplier using AFS, they are redirected to a page called OCIAccept .asp on the Commerce Server site. This page creates an anonymous session and redirects the user to RemoteBasketNav.asp. This page, in turn, redirects the user to RemoteBasket .asp, from where they can browse the product catalog and add products to the remote basket. An application-level variable called m_bIsRemoteBasketSession is set to true here, so that other pages in the site can detect that a remote basket session is in operation. When the customer decides to check out, they are brought to FormPostRemoteBasket .asp, which submits the details of the items in the basket back to Commerce One, where the items are displayed in that application's local shopping basket.

Ariba Punchout   Ariba provides remote shopping in its CSN application with a feature called *Punchout* that uses the cXML 1.2 standard. Punchout differs from Commerce One RoundTrip in that a remote basket session can be initiated at the product level rather than at the catalog level. As a result, when a customer of Ariba CSN chooses to add a product marked for Punchout to their local shopping basket, CSN makes a request to a page called punchout.asp on the supplier's AFS site. The marking of products in this way is done by using Business Desk to create a custom property called RemotelyConfigurable for each product. If the value of this property is "yes", then CSN will know that Punchout is available for this product.

When called, the punchout.asp file creates a remote shopping basket containing the selected product and sends an acknowledgement back to CSN, which then launches a remote shopping browser window. In this new browser, RemoteBasketNav.asp is requested, and it redirects the user to different pages, based on the operation being performed. The available operations are Inspect, Create, and Edit. These operations and the pages used to implement them are described in the following table:

Operation	Description
Inspect	When the user chooses to view the contents of the shopping basket, they are redirected to either InspectBasket.asp or InspectProduct.asp, depending on whether the Inspect request contained a specific product ID. In the page InspectBasket.asp, the user can view the contents of the shopping basket and click a link to view details about each product. The user can also check out at this point. In the page InspectProduct.asp, the user can view details about a specific product and click a link back to the page displaying the basket. Both of these pages are read only.
Create	When the user initiates a remote basket session without selecting a product, they are redirected to RemoteBasket.asp, from where they can check out regardless of whether the basket is empty. If they have selected a product, they are brought to product.asp, where they can choose to add the product to the remote shopping basket, at which point they are brought back to RemoteBasket.asp.
Edit	If a user decides to change the quantity of a product or remove a product from the basket, they will again be directed to either product.asp or RemoteBasket.asp, depending on whether a product ID is specified.

If the user clicks the Check Out button on either RemoteBasket.asp or InspectBasket .asp, they are again sent to FormPostRemoteBasket.asp, which builds a cXML 1.2 Punchout message containing the order details. The form on this page is then submitted to return the user to Ariba CSN.

Clarus Tap Out   Consumers using Clarus' marketplace application can avail themselves of remote shopping functionality using the *Tap Out* feature, which uses the cXML 1.1 standard. The only difference between Ariba Punchout and Clarus Tap Out is that Tap Out only allows remote shopping sessions to be initiated at the catalog level rather than the product level. Because it is based on cXML, the functionality provided by AFS for Clarus shoppers is almost identical to that provided for Ariba CSN users, in that the same Inspect, Create, and Edit operations are supported. However, the shopping basket always starts out empty after a Create request, because the session cannot be initiated for a specific product.

The Complete Reference

BizTalk Server

Part VII

BizTalk Server 2002 Enterprise Edition

The
Complete
Reference

BizTalk
Server

Chapter 20

What's Changed in BizTalk Server 2002

J ust months after the release of Microsoft BizTalk Server 2000, it is already in production in large enterprises such as Ford, DellWare, Coca-Cola, Siemens, Volvo, Marks and Spencer, and even the United Kingdom government. In July 2001, Service Pack 1 for BizTalk Server was released (and, subsequently, Service Pack 1A, which provides compatibility with Visio 2002) to address the inevitable issues that are present in version 1.0 of any product. The fixes and features in the service pack have been discussed throughout this book in the relevant chapters.

By the end of 2001, Microsoft will have released the next version of BizTalk Server—BizTalk Server 2002 Enterprise Edition. Code-named "Bizet" during its development, BizTalk Server 2002 has been designed more as a service release than as a major upgrade, with fixes and features aimed primarily at enterprise customers. In fact, the product only ships as BizTalk Server 2002 Enterprise Edition; there is no Standard Edition option for smaller companies. However, the changes that have been made permeate throughout the package with some completely new features also in evidence. For example, there is a SEED Wizard to simplify the configuration of BizTalk Messaging for new business partners, and full integration with Microsoft Application Center and Microsoft Operations Manager for the deployment and monitoring of enterprise installations is now provided. These new features will be discussed in detail in the next chapter. However, there are also enhancements to existing aspects of the product. For example, there is improved functionality for non-XML instances and XSD support in BizTalk Editor, true instance testing and grid pages in BizTalk Mapper, XLANG schedule throttling and instance identifiers in BizTalk Orchestration, and a new HTTP receive function in BizTalk Administration. In this chapter, I will discuss these changes and enhancements.

BizTalk Editor Changes

BizTalk Editor, the tool used to create document specifications, was discussed in depth in Chapter 4. In BizTalk Server 2002, there are some changes that address requests made by customers to simplify the creation and testing of these specifications. It is now possible to validate EDI interchanges without having to remove the interchange and functional group headers and footers. You can also specify default delimiters for this purpose. In addition, it is possible now to create native instances of different document formats for testing purposes. From an XML perspective, the *mixed* content model—that is, a mixture of child elements and text nodes beneath an element—is also supported. Finally, although full support for W3C XML Schema Definitions (XSD) will probably have to wait until the next version of BizTalk Server, with BizTalk Server 2002 it is possible to export an XSD schema from BizTalk Editor.

Working with Document Instances

In BizTalk Server 2000, it was possible to validate document instances against a specification and also create sample instances from a specification. However, when using BizTalk Editor to create EDI-based document specifications, some limitations made it difficult to test interchanges for compliance. For example, if the EDI formats you were working with used particular delimiters, you had to set those delimiters every time you validated an instance against a specification. Further, if you wished to validate a specification against an EDI interchange, it was not possible without first stripping the interchange down to a single transaction set with no headers or footers. Also, it was only possible to create instances of XML-based specifications. BizTalk Editor 2002 solves these problems.

Validating Instances

If you wish to test various EDI instances against specifications created in BizTalk Editor, you can now preconfigure the delimiters that your documents use. This functionality is available by selecting Tools | Options. The BizTalk Editor Options dialog box, shown in Figure 20-1, now has an extra tab—Document Delimiters—where you can specify the default delimiters to be used when testing EDI instances. You can set the default record, field, and subfield delimiters, as well as the escape character used to allow delimiter characters to appear as actual data in EDIFACT documents. You can also choose whether the Document Delimiters dialog box should be displayed during instance testing to allow overriding of these defaults.

Note   *The Repeating Field Delimiter option is disabled. In a future release, this will allow you to set the character used to delimit repeating fields found in later X12 versions such as 4030.*

If you choose Tools | Validate Instance and select a file that is a complete EDI interchange, BizTalk Editor will automatically select the appropriate delimiters as specified in the interchange header. For example, in ANSI X12 interchanges, the

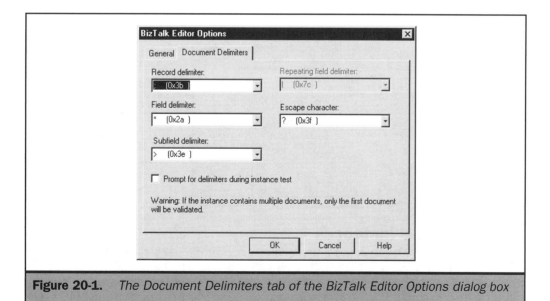

Figure 20-1.   *The Document Delimiters tab of the BizTalk Editor Options dialog box*

component element delimiter will always be found at position 105 in the interchange header; the element delimiter will always be found at position 4 in the interchange header; and the segment delimiter will always be found at position 106. As a result, BizTalk Editor is able to find the required delimiters automatically; discard the interchange, functional group, and transaction set envelopes; and then validate the document within against the specification.

If an interchange contains multiple transaction sets, or multiple functional groups, only the first document found will be validated.

Similarly, if you want to validate a document instance that is not contained within an EDI envelope, you can choose Tools | Validate Instance just as you did in BizTalk Editor 2000. However, if the delimiters found match those configured in the BizTalk Editor Options dialog box, the instance will be validated automatically. If the default delimiters are not found, BizTalk Editor will display the Document Delimiters dialog box, as shown next. In this dialog box, you can specify the delimiters for this particular instance only. However, if the Prompt For Delimiters During Instance Test check box is cleared as shown in Figure 20-1, then a mismatch between the delimiters found in the document and the defaults set in the BizTalk Editor Options dialog box will cause an error.

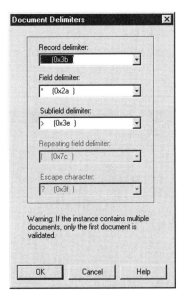

Creating Native Instances

In BizTalk Server 2000, you could only use BizTalk Editor to create sample instances based on XML specifications. In BizTalk Server 2002, that functionality has been extended to create instances for other document formats. To create a native instance, select Tools | Create Native Instance. If the specification format is X12 or EDIFACT, the Document

Delimiters dialog box will appear so that you can specify the delimiters to use for the instance. These will be used by the serializer to create the instance. You will then be asked to provide a filename and to specify where the file should be saved. The resulting document is also shown on the Output tab. For example, using a delimited flat-file specification, choosing Tools | Create Native Instance gives the output shown in Figure 20-2.

XML Enhancements

As discussed in Chapter 2, XML is core to the functionality of BizTalk Server. BizTalk Editor can be used to create XML-based document specifications for use in BizTalk Messaging. These specifications are saved in a format that is an extension of the XML Data Reduced schema structure created by Microsoft. Since BizTalk Server 2000 was released, the World Wide Web Consortium (W3C) has recommended a new XML Schema Definitions (XSD) format that supersedes XDR. BizTalk Editor in BizTalk Server 2002 now allows you to export specifications in this new schema format. There is also support included for the Mixed content model, where elements can have both child elements and text content.

Exporting XSD Schemas

To export an XSD schema, simply choose Tools | Export XSD Schema. You will be prompted to save the file.

Note   *XSD schemas are always saved in UTF-16 format.*

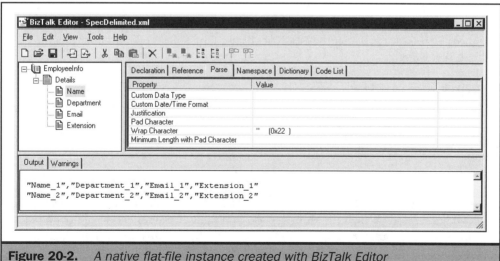

Figure 20-2. *A native flat-file instance created with BizTalk Editor*

BIZTALK SERVER 2002
ENTERPRISE EDITION

Using Mixed Content

To use mixed content in XML-based specifications, select the appropriate record in BizTalk Editor. On the Declaration tab, choose Mixed from the drop-down menu in the value field for the Content property, and click Yes if a dialog box appears warning you that certain properties may be cleared. You must then change the value of the Order property on the Declaration tab to Many.

If you import a well-formed XML document instance to create a specification, you will have to set the value of the Content property to Mixed manually if you wish to enable the mixed content model, unless the document being imported already contains mixed content.

BizTalk Mapper Changes

In Chapter 5, I discussed BizTalk Mapper, the tool in BizTalk Server 2000 that is used to create transformations that allow BizTalk Messaging to convert between different document structures. Some of the limitations that were mentioned in that chapter included the lack of support for JScript in Scripting functoids, the small mapping grid region that is either overcrowded or too awkward to navigate, and the unforgivable omission of complete instance testing. BizTalk Server 2002 includes an enhanced BizTalk Mapper that more than makes up for past transgressions.

Testing Maps

One complaint that was frequently directed at BizTalk Mapper in BizTalk Server 2000 was that it was not possible to test a document instance to see how it would be transformed by a map file. In BizTalk Server 2002, you can use BizTalk Mapper to test both XML and native instances, view the output, and validate both the input and output document instances against their respective specifications. This feature is available through Tools | Test Map.

Testing Instances

Under Tools | Test Map in BizTalk Mapper, there are six different ways to test a map. Table 20-1 summarizes the choices and the scenarios in which they are valid. The menu options available depend on the type of the source and destination specifications being mapped. First, it is always possible to test a map by having BizTalk Mapper generate sample XML based on the structure of the source specification. This sample XML is the same type of data that is created in BizTalk Editor by choosing Tools | Create Instance, and this functionality was present in BizTalk Mapper 2000. However, if you choose to use XML generated by BizTalk Mapper, you don't get a true reflection of how a real document will be transformed. You can still supply test values for every field in the specification just as you did in BizTalk Mapper 2000, but that can be extremely time-consuming for large specifications.

Source Specification Type	Destination Specification Type	Testing Options
XML	Non-XML	Generated XML to XML Generated XML to Native Instance XML to XML Instance XML to Native
Non-XML	XML	Generated XML to XML Instance XML to XML Native Instance to XML
XML	XML	Generated XML to XML Instance XML to XML
Non-XML	Non-XML	Generated XML to XML Generated XML to Native Instance XML to XML Instance XML to Native Native Instance to XML Native Instance to Native

Table 20-1.   *Testing Options Available in BizTalk Mapper*

In BizTalk Mapper 2002, you can now choose to have the generated XML transformed into a native instance. This option is only available if the destination specification is not XML based. BizTalk Mapper will generate sample XML, transform it using the map file, and then serialize the data into the format of the destination specification. However, you still don't get a true reflection of how real-world data will be transformed. Consequently, the most useful options for testing maps involve the use of real document instances. If the source specification is XML based, you can browse to an XML file that is an actual instance of the specification. If the destination specification is also XML, you can obviously only transform the instance into XML. However, if the destination specification is an EDI or flat-file specification, you also have the option to test the XML instance and see how the resulting document will look in its native format.

If the source specification is not XML based, you have the option to use either a native or XML instance for testing. Testing a native instance is closest to the actual operation of BizTalk Messaging, because the native instance first must be parsed by the appropriate parser into XML and then transformed using XSLT. Choosing to test an XML instance does not require the initial parsing phase. If your destination specification is not XML based, you have the most options available. You can choose to transform either an XML or native instance into either an XML or native instance. Again, the latter option is closest to how BizTalk Messaging actually works, because after the instance has been transformed by the XSLT, it must be serialized into the correct native format.

To test a map, choose an option from the Tools | Test Map submenu. If you choose an instance-based test, you will be prompted to browse for the instance file. If the instance is EDI based, you may also be asked to specify the delimiters. If the instance is an interchange, BizTalk Mapper will be able to determine the delimiters automatically. Otherwise, you will only be prompted if the delimiters found do not match the defaults set in the BizTalk Mapper Options dialog box, as discussed later in this section.

Note   *If an EDI instance contains multiple documents, only the first document will be transformed.*

For example, if you open a map that transforms an X12 850 purchase order to a Common PO format and choose Tools | Test Map | Native Instance To XML, you are prompted to provide an instance of an X12 850 document. If you then supply an appropriate EDI instance and specify the correct delimiters, the transformed document will be displayed on the Output tab, as shown in Figure 20-3.

Tip   *The EDI Introduction and EDI and Receipts samples in the BizTalk Server 2002 SDK provide maps and instances for testing document specifications and maps.*

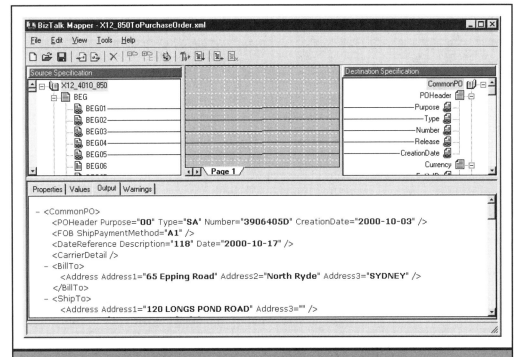

Figure 20-3.   *An X12 850 instance transformed in BizTalk Mapper*

Mapper Options

To accommodate some of the new functionality in BizTalk Mapper, the BizTalk Mapper Options dialog box contains some new settings. On the General tab, you can specify whether content should be validated before and/or after an instance test. On the Document Delimiters tab, you can set default delimiters for EDI instance testing; and on the XSLT Output tab, you can choose whether to omit the XML declaration from compiled XSLT files.

General Tab

The General tab of the BizTalk Mapper Options dialog box is shown in Figure 20-4. On this tab, there are two new settings—Validate Content Before Map Test and Validate Content After Map Test. As you can probably guess, these options allow you to specify whether an instance should be validated against the source specification during an instance test and whether the generated instance should be validated against the destination specification after an instance test has transformed the content.

During an instance test, if you have selected the first option and the instance being tested does not validate against the source specification, an error will be displayed on the Warnings tab, as shown in Figure 20-5. Similarly, if you have selected the second option and the transformed instance does not validate against the destination specification, the Warnings tab will again display information about the error.

BIZTALK SERVER 2002
ENTERPRISE EDITION

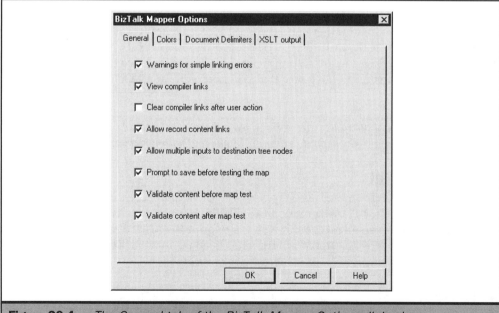

Figure 20-4.   *The General tab of the BizTalk Mapper Options dialog box*

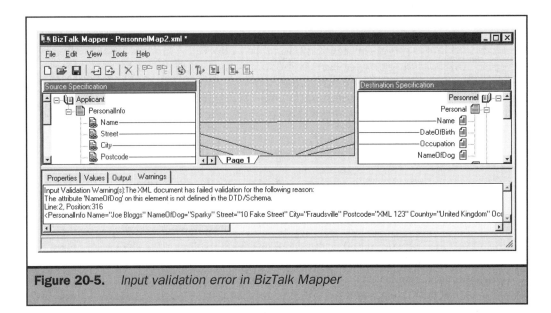

Figure 20-5. *Input validation error in BizTalk Mapper*

Document Delimiters Tab

On the Document Delimiters tab, you can specify default delimiters to be used during instance testing involving EDI specification formats. Just as in BizTalk Editor, if you set these delimiters and the instance being tested does not use those delimiters, you will be prompted to set them manually unless the Prompt For Delimiters During Instance Test check box is cleared. In the Delimiter Type drop-down menu at the top of the tab, you can also choose whether you are setting delimiters for the instance being tested (Source Delimiter) or the transformed instance that is generated (Target Delimiter), as shown in Figure 20-6.

Note *The settings configured here are maintained independent of those configured in BizTalk Editor, so changing the default delimiters in one tool will not update the other.*

XSLT Output Tab

When you create a map in BizTalk Mapper, you are actually creating an Extensible Stylesheet Language for Transformation (XSLT) file. XSLT was discussed in Chapter 2. One of the options available to you in XSLT is to omit the XML declaration from the resulting document after the transformation has been performed. The XML declaration looks like the following:

```
<?xml version="1.0" encoding="UTF-16" standalone="yes"?>
```

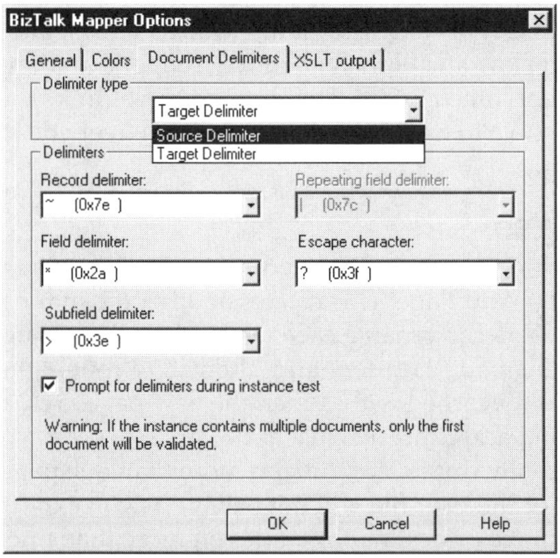

Figure 20-6. *The Document Delimiters tab of the BizTalk Mapper Options dialog box*

On most occasions, you will not want this declaration to be inserted into the destination document. The XML declaration is optional, and it will not cause an error if it is not included. However, there may be a situation in which you will want to ensure that it is present to help an XML parser decode a document. Because the first five characters of the XML declaration must be "<?xml", some processors use this fact to determine the encoding scheme for the document—in particular, whether the encoding is single byte (as in UTF-8) or double byte (as in UTF-16). If the processor can read the first five characters, then it will be able to read the rest of the declaration and thus determine the encoding scheme in use.

In XSLT, there is an xsl:output instruction element that is used to decide the format of a transformed document. For example, the following instruction:

```
<xsl:output method="xml" omit-xml-declaration="yes"/>
```

specifies that the transformed document will be XML (as opposed to text or HTML) but that the XML declaration should not be included. You can set this option for map files created by BizTalk Mapper on the XSLT Output tab of the BizTalk Mapper Options dialog box.

Grid Pages

Often you will find yourself creating maps to transform large document specifications. As a result, your map files will become increasingly complicated, particularly if numerous functoids must be employed to effect the transformation. Unfortunately, the grid region in BizTalk Mapper is quite small relative to how much is likely to be going on in there.

In BizTalk Mapper 2000, you were able to pan up, down, left, and right to move across the grid, and you were also able to quickly jump to an area using the Grid Preview feature. However, this made it slow and clumsy to move from one section to another, and the grid itself would still become cluttered as the number of links increased. In BizTalk Mapper 2002, it is possible to organize maps more effectively by dividing a large map into multiple grid pages.

Adding Grid Pages

If your map file is starting to get complicated, you can add a new page to the mapping grid by choosing Edit | Add Page. This creates another tab in the mapping grid area, as shown in Figure 20-7. You can rename each tab by double-clicking it—in this example, the tabs have been renamed "Header" and "Items" to reflect the portions of the specifications they are concerned with. When the new page is created, it is blank, but you can create links and add functoids just as before. However, you must make sure that you don't accidentally duplicate a link on more than one page. If you do, either you will get an error, or the map file will not behave as you expect. Similarly, don't inadvertently reuse source or destination nodes on more than one page. As you can see in Figure 20-7, sharing out links and functoids across pages makes the grid considerably less cluttered, particularly if compiler links are also visible.

Note *The total number of grid pages that can exist is 20.*

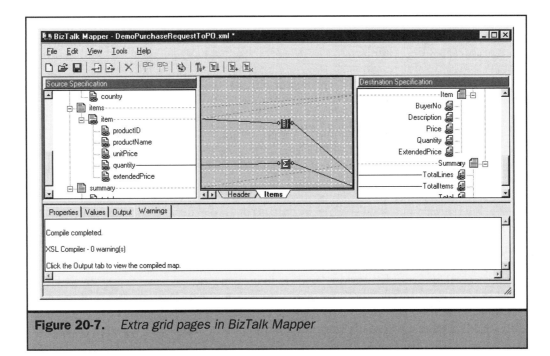

Figure 20-7. *Extra grid pages in BizTalk Mapper*

Move Links and Functoids Between Grid Pages

This is all well and good if you're creating a new map, but what if you have an existing map that could do with a bit of cleaning up? No problem—you can click a link or functoid on any grid page to select it, and then simply drag it down to the tab representing the grid page where you would like it to be moved. To move a functoid, you have to ensure that all of the inbound and outbound links are visible and not leading to collapsed nodes. This will move the functoid and attached links to the new page. You should notice that you are not actually modifying the XSLT or the behavior of the map file by doing this; you are simply arranging how it is displayed in BizTalk Mapper. To remove a grid page, you can choose Edit | Delete Page, but exercise caution—after you click OK in the BizTalk Mapper dialog box asking you to confirm the action, any links and functoids that were on that page are gone for good.

 If the grid page to which you want to drag a functoid or link is not visible, click the small left or right arrow beside the grid tabs until it comes into view.

Using JScript in Functoids

In BizTalk Server 2000, it was possible to create Scripting and custom BizTalk Mapper functoids using Visual Basic Scripting Edition (VBScript). In BizTalk Server 2002, you can now create Scripting and custom functoids using JScript, which is Microsoft's version of ECMAScript.

Creating a Scripting Functoid Using JScript

On the Advanced tab in the Functoid Palette, there is a Scripting functoid that can be used to implement custom functionality in a map. To create the functoid using JScript, simply select JScript on the Script tab of the functoid. The syntax of the default function template will change to use the JScript function syntax as shown.

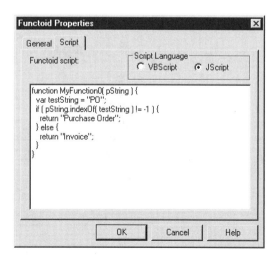

This example tests the value of the input parameter and returns the string "Purchase Order" if the input contains the string "PO". Otherwise, it returns the string "Invoice". A map file that uses this functoid to set the value of the DocumentType field in a destination document is shown in Figure 20-8. This example also uses logical functoids to check the value output by the Scripting functoid to decide which of the PurchaseOrder or Invoice records in the destination document should be created.

Creating a Compiled Functoid Using JScript

In Chapter 16, the creation of custom compiled functoids was discussed. Custom functoids are useful if there is particular functionality that you wish to have readily available without having to re-create scripting functoids again and again. In Visual Basic, these functoids implement the CannedFunctoid class; and in Visual C++, you can use the IFunctoid interface.

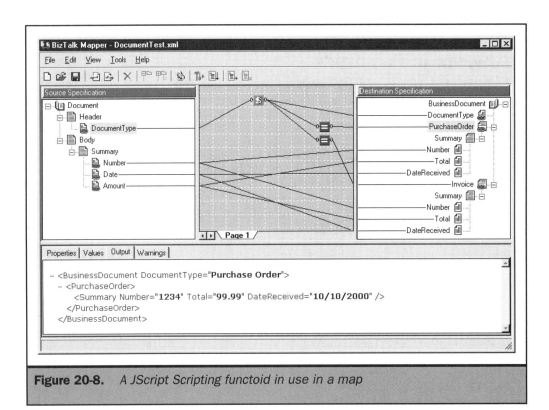

Figure 20-8.   *A JScript Scripting functoid in use in a map*

In either case, you will still implement the actual functionality of the functoid by providing script that can be inserted into XSLT. With BizTalk Server 2002, you can now create custom compiled functoids that make use of JScript.

When creating your custom functoid, you use the GetFunctionDescripter method to set specific information about the functoid that will be queried by BizTalk Mapper when displaying the functoid in the interface. One of the parameters of this method is an enumerated type called SCRIPT_CATEGORY that can have the values SCRIPT_CATEGORY_VBSCRIPT (0), SCRIPT_CATEGORY_JSCRIPT (1), or SCRIPT_CATEGORY_XSLSCRIPT (2). In BizTalk Server 2000, only the first value could be used; but in BizTalk Server 2002, you can specify that the functoid will be implemented using JScript by setting the SCRIPT_CATEGORY parameter to SCRIPT_CATEGORY_JSCRIPT. XSL Script is still not supported.

Copying Descendant Text Nodes

Earlier in this chapter, I covered how mixed content was now supported in BizTalk Editor. As a result, you can now have documents with records that contain both child elements and text. However, as discussed in Chapter 3, I would still recommend that you avoid using this structure in your documents, because it is an ineffective use of XML. This functionality is only really provided for organizations that require compatibility with existing document structures that may be already in use. Either way, this content would have caused problems with BizTalk Mapper in BizTalk Server 2000, because you could only copy a single node value from a source specification. However, there is another new feature in BizTalk Mapper that provides the ability to copy both text and subcontent values from a node in the source specification. This results in the concatenated values of all descendant text nodes being copied to the destination document. For example, consider a source document with the following content:

```
<Price>
    <Currency>IRP</Currency>
    19.99
</Price>
```

If you create a link from the Price node in a source specification to a node in a destination specification, by default, only the text content of the node will be copied, that is, "19.99". In BizTalk Mapper 2002, you can right-click the link and choose Properties. On the Compiler tab of the Link Properties dialog box, there is an extra option, Copy Text And Sub-Content Value, in the Source Specification Links region. Choosing this option instead of the default results in "IRP19.99" being copied to the destination document, as shown in Figure 20-9.

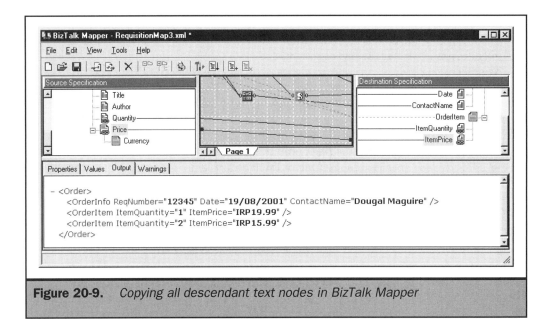

Figure 20-9. *Copying all descendant text nodes in BizTalk Mapper*

BizTalk Administration Changes

In BizTalk Server 2002, almost every aspect of the product has been updated to include new functionality, or to address issues raised by customers of BizTalk Server 2000. Along with changes that affect the development of solutions using BizTalk Editor, BizTalk Mapper, and BizTalk Orchestration, there are also differences that affect the installation and management of BizTalk servers or server groups. In the next chapter, we will see brand-new features that make it easier to disseminate configuration information to business partners, and to deploy and monitor enterprise solutions. Here, I will discuss some changes that have been made to existing features that are also of particular interest to administrators. These include the addition of a new HTTP receive function, considerations for the installation of BizTalk Server and prerequisite software, and issues related to security.

Installing BizTalk Server 2002

The installation of BizTalk Server 2000 was covered in depth in Chapter 3. All of the information in that chapter still holds for BizTalk Server 2002 with some minor exceptions. The list of prerequisite software has been updated, and the configuration of SQL Server has been changed in response to requests from customers.

Prerequisite Software

The supported platform for BizTalk Server 2002 is now Windows 2000 with Service Pack 2. As discussed previously in this book, it was always necessary to install certain pre–Service

Pack 2 hotfixes to ensure a stable installation. But since the release of Service Pack 1 for BizTalk Server 2000, Microsoft has recommended that Windows 2000 Service Pack 2 should be installed. That recommendation has now been formalized as a prerequisite.

Similarly, Microsoft now requires that SQL Server 2000 Service Pack 1 is installed on database servers used by BizTalk Server 2002. If you are using SQL Server 7.0 for this purpose, then SQL Server 7.0 Service Pack 3 is now required. Furthermore, SQL Server must be configured using Windows-only authentication. This differs from BizTalk Server 2000, where Mixed Mode authentication was required. Authentication and security considerations are discussed more fully later in this section.

Finally, the documentation for BizTalk Server 2002 informs us that the new version of BizTalk Orchestration Designer requires Visio 2002, and this product will be included in the BizTalk Server 2002 Enterprise Edition package.

HTTP Receive Functions

In BizTalk Server 2000, file and message-queuing receive functions were provided through the BizTalk Administration interface to allow applications to submit documents to BizTalk Messaging. As discussed in Chapter 9, both internal and external applications could post business documents to file folders or message queues, from where they would be submitted asynchronously to BizTalk Server for processing. In BizTalk Server 2002, that functionality has been extended to HTTP. Although it was always possible to configure a location on a web server to which trading partners could post documents, it was necessary to write the active server page (ASP) or Internet Server Application Programming Interface (ISAPI) extension manually to perform the submission. The new HTTP receive function makes this task much simpler for administrators, as well as providing previously unavailable synchronous receive function processing via the SubmitSync method of the IInterchange interface.

However, before you can create an HTTP receive function, you have to configure IIS by creating a virtual directory to hold the DLL and setting the appropriate virtual directory permissions. You must also ensure that the user account used by IIS has permission to access the BizTalk Messaging Management database.

Configuring IIS for HTTP Receive Functions

The HTTP receive function is implemented in BizTalk Server 2002 as a DLL called BizTalkHTTPReceive.dll. This DLL is available in the Program Files\Microsoft BizTalk Server\HTTP Receive directory by default. To use it, you must first create and configure an IIS virtual directory. To do this, perform the following steps:

1. Create a new folder and copy BizTalkHTTPReceive.dll into it.

2. In Internet Services Manager, use the New Virtual Directory to create a new virtual directory pointing to this folder. You should ensure that the virtual directory has Execute access permissions as shown next. If there will be no other files in this folder, such as static HTML files or ASP files, you can also remove Read and Run Scripts access permissions.

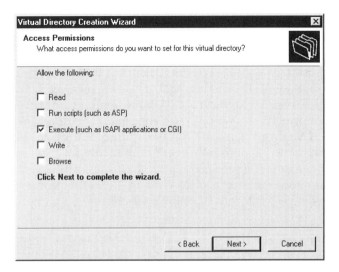

3. In Internet Services Manager, select the appropriate application protection level for the virtual directory. The choices are Low, Medium, and High.

■ If you choose Low (IIS Process), you must ensure that the service account used by the World Wide Web Publishing service has the appropriate network permissions to access the BizTalk Messaging Management database. Similarly, you must ensure that this account can use the BizTalk Server Interchange Application and BizTalk Server Internal Utilities COM+ applications.

■ If you choose Medium (Pooled), you must ensure that the service account configured as the identity for the IIS Out-Of-Process Pooled Applications COM+ application has the appropriate network permissions to access the BizTalk Messaging Management database. Similarly, you must ensure that this account can use the BizTalk Server Interchange Application and BizTalk Server Internal Utilities COM+ applications.

■ If you choose High (Isolated), you must ensure that the service account configured as the identity for the IIS-{Default Web Site//Root/ <virtual_directory_name>} COM+ application has the appropriate network permissions to access the BizTalk Messaging Management database. Similarly, you must ensure that this account can use the BizTalk Server Interchange Application and BizTalk Server Internal Utilities COM+ applications.

Creating HTTP Receive Functions

After configuring IIS appropriately, you can create HTTP receive functions in the BizTalk Server Administration Microsoft Management Console (MMC) to submit documents synchronously or asynchronously to BizTalk Messaging. Documents posted to the receive function can also be dropped off to a file location. To create an HTTP receive function, perform the following steps:

1. In BizTalk Server Administration, expand the Microsoft BizTalk Server 2002 and <GroupName> nodes.

2. Right-click the Receive Functions node, and choose New | HTTP Receive Function from the context menu. The Add An HTTP Receive Function dialog box appears, as shown in Figure 20-10.

3. In the Name field, type a unique name for the receive function. You can also type an optional comment in the Comment field.

4. From the Server On Which The Receive Function Will Run drop-down menu, select the computer on which the IIS virtual directory is located.

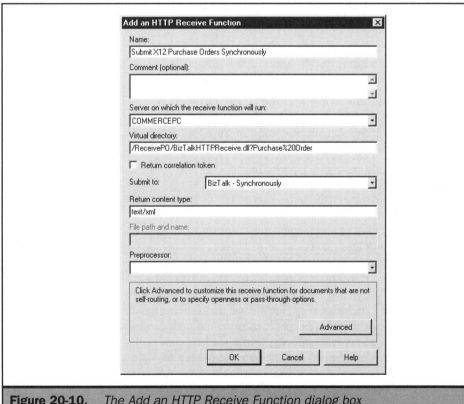

Figure 20-10.   The Add an HTTP Receive Function dialog box

5. In the Virtual Directory field, type the name of the virtual directory to which the DLL was copied. The path should include the name of the DLL, as shown in Figure 20-10, even if BizTalkHTTPReceive.dll has been configured as a default document for that virtual directory. You can also append an optional query string to uniquely identify this receive function if the same virtual directory will be used to retrieve different types of documents. In this case, you should ensure that your trading partners or applications use the appropriate query string when posting documents.

6. Select the Return Correlation Token check box if you want the receive function to automatically generate a token that can be used to check the processing status of the document. Correlation tokens will be discussed in detail shortly.

7. In the Submit To drop-down menu, choose whether the document should be submitted asynchronously or synchronously to BizTalk Messaging, or whether it should be dropped into a file location.

   ■ If you select BizTalk—Synchronously, you will also need to complete the Return Content Type field to specify the MIME type that BizTalk Messaging should use to construct the document that will be returned to the posting client.

   ■ If you select File, you will also need to complete the File Path And Name field to specify the name and location used by the HTTP receive function to deliver the submitted document to the file system.

8. As with file and message-queuing receive functions, you can choose a preprocessor component from the Preprocessor drop-down menu, and you can specify further routing information for non-self-routing documents by clicking the Advanced button.

9. Click OK to save the receive function.

One thing you might be wondering is when to choose each type of receive function. The decision will normally depend on the scenario in which the receive function is used. For example, you will choose an asynchronous submission if the channel that will receive the submitted document feeds into a messaging port that uses an asynchronous transport such as SMTP or Message Queuing. This will be necessary because these transport methods could not return a synchronous response. Similarly, if the channel feeds into a messaging port that uses a synchronous transport such as HTTP or AIC, then you might choose to submit the document synchronously. However, this will still depend on whether the endpoint of the transport mechanism is configured to return a meaningful response. If, for example, an Active Server Page (ASP) on a trading partner's web server were not designed to return anything more useful than a standard HTTP status code, you would probably choose an asynchronous submission. Still, sometimes we will want our HTTP receive functions to provide the impression of a synchronous submission, even if that is not actually possible. This is where correlation tokens come in handy.

Correlation Tokens

BizTalk Server 2002 HTTP receive functions can be used to submit documents synchronously to BizTalk Messaging. If a client application were posting a document directly to the receive function DLL, then a response generated by BizTalk Messaging via the Loopback transport option can be returned to the client. For example, this would enable a transformed business document to be instantly displayed in the posting client's browser. However, because the HTTP receive function must be created on a computer running BizTalk Server, that would require providing your trading partners with direct access to your BizTalk Server computers via the Internet. As discussed in Chapter 13, this is not good practice from a security perspective.

Instead, you could have an Internet-facing web server located in the demilitarized zone (DMZ) on your network to which trading partners could post documents. An ASP on this web server could then post the submitted document to the HTTP receive function located behind the internal firewall. However, this does not provide direct synchronous communication. For this reason, you should configure the HTTP receive function to submit documents to BizTalk Messaging asynchronously, and opt to have the receive function return a *correlation token*. This is a small XML-based message as shown.

Note   *Correlation tokens have nothing to do with the correlation process discussed in Chapter 8 that allows BizTalk Messaging to submit response documents to running XLANG schedules.*

This token contains a submission GUID for the document submitted to BizTalk Messaging. In our scenario, this token could be sent back as a response to the ASP on the web server in the DMZ to indicate that the document has been submitted to BizTalk Messaging. The ASP could then check the status of the document's progress through BizTalk Messaging using the GUID. When a response document is available, it can be picked up by the ASP and returned to the originating client as if it were a synchronous response.

Note   *If you use the HTTP receive function to submit the document to a file, the correlation token contains the file path and filename instead of the submission GUID.*

Optimizing HTTP Receive Functions

As with file and message queuing receive functions, a number of extra settings can be configured to improve the performance of HTTP receive functions. These settings are not present in the Registry by default, but they can be implemented by adding a new key called HTTPListener under the following key:

```
HKEY_LOCAL_MACHINE\System\CurrentControlSet\Services\BTSSvc
```

The values that can be configured for this key are listed in the following sections. Each value should be added as a DWORD.

WorkerThreads   Because the receive function manages a thread pool, you can use this setting to configure how many threads should be made available. The default value is 6, but you may need to increase this if you process a lot of documents using the receive function, or if the error log gives the message "The BizTalk HTTP receive function *<name>* could not retrieve a thread from the thread pool."

QueueFactor   This setting configures the number of requests that will be maintained for threads in the thread pool. Consequently, you should also increase this value from the default of 3 if you process a lot of documents using HTTP receive functions, or if the error log displays the message "The BizTalk HTTP receive function *<name>* could not post the work item to the thread pool. Try increasing the length of the thread pool queue under the registry key 'Queue Factor'."

AsyncBufferSize   This setting determines the size of the buffer that is used when blocks of data are read asynchronously from IIS. For example, the maximum amount of data that can be read synchronously from IIS is 48KB. For data larger than 48KB, the overrun must be read asynchronously in chunks of 4,096 bytes, which is the default setting for this Registry value.

MaxSyncFileDropSize   This value represents the maximum size of a file that can be read into memory and written to disk in one attempt. The default is 1,048,576 bytes (1MB), and anything larger than that will be written asynchronously in smaller chunks. If you have enough memory on your system, you can increase this setting to improve HTTP receive function performance. However, you should decrease this setting if resources are limited.

MaxLargeAsyncBuffers   As mentioned, when the data submitted to IIS is greater than 48KB, it will be read into asynchronous buffers in smaller chunks. This Registry value represents the maximum number of buffers that will be created if the size of the data is greater than 48KB but less than MaxSyncFileDropSize. These buffers are also used if the data is being submitted directly to BizTalk Messaging. The default value is 18, and this can be increased to improve the performance of the HTTP receive function if larger files are being submitted. But, again, it should be reduced if resources are limited.

ConfigRefreshInit   This value is the number of milliseconds between visits to the Messaging Management database for updated information. The default value is 60,000 (one minute), but you should increase this value if the database is not modified frequently.

Security Features

Securing BizTalk Server 2000 was discussed in depth in Chapter 13, and you'll be glad to hear that all the advice given in that chapter still holds for BizTalk Server 2002. To reflect the enterprise-centric nature of BizTalk Server 2002, some important security changes have been implemented in response to feedback from enterprise customers. Specifically, these changes are concerned with the authentication mode used to access SQL Server, simplifying the process of changing service account passwords, and providing authentication to proxy servers.

SQL Server Authentication

Although this section is entitled "SQL Server Authentication", I'm here to tell you that SQL Server authentication is no longer supported. BizTalk Server 2002 now uses Windows-only authentication to log onto SQL Server. This is much more secure and circumvents certain access problems for larger enterprise installations. As a result, either before or after the installation of BizTalk Server 2002, you should ensure that SQL Server is configured for Windows-only rather than SQL Server and Windows (Mixed Mode) authentication by examining the Security tab of the SQL Server Properties dialog box in SQL Server Enterprise Manager.

With the authentication mode set to Windows-only, you will have to ensure that the service account used by the BizTalk Messaging service can access the SQL Server computer. In particular, if BizTalk Server and SQL Server are installed on different machines, you will need to use a domain account for the BizTalk Messaging service, rather than a local computer account. This domain account should have administrative privileges on both the BizTalk Server and SQL Server computers. If the account was not chosen during the installation of BizTalk Server, it will also be necessary to manually assign the Log On Locally and Act As Part Of The Operating System rights to the service account through the Local Security Policy MMC.

Note *Creating and configuring service accounts was discussed in depth in Chapter 13.*

Furthermore, if BizTalk Server and SQL Server are installed on different computers, the BizTalk Messaging service account you create will have to be assigned to the appropriate roles and afforded the necessary privileges on SQL Server to access the Messaging Management, Document Tracking, and Shared Queue databases. To do this, perform the following steps:

1. Open SQL Server Enterprise Manager.

2. Expand the Microsoft SQL Server, SQL Server Group, *<ServerName>*, and Security nodes.

3. Right-click the Logins node, and select New Login from the context menu.

4. On the General tab, ensure that Windows Authentication is selected, and either type the name of the service account or click the Browse button to choose one. Also, type or select the appropriate domain in the Domain combo box.

5. On the Server Roles tab, select the System Administrators check box.

6. On the Database Access tab, select the check box for the InterchangeBTM database, and select the db_owner check box under Database roles for InterchangeBTM.

7. Repeat step 6 for the InterchangeDTA database, selecting the db_owner and dta_ui_role check boxes.

8. Repeat step 6 for the InterchangeSQ database, selecting the db_owner check box.

Similarly, you will also need to ensure that the service account used by the XLANG Scheduler COM+ application is also a domain account. Again, this account should be mapped to a new login on the SQL Server computer hosting the XLANG database, and that login should have the appropriate permissions to create tables and create procedures on the Orchestration persistence database.

Changing Service Account Credentials

As a general rule, it is good security practice to change the names of powerful accounts used in your domain from time to time. At the very least, you should change the passwords used by these accounts on a frequent basis. For example, the user account used by the BizTalk Messaging service typically has administrative access to multiple computers and databases, and also the rights to log on as a service and to act as part of the operating system. Therefore, you should consider changing it regularly to frustrate crackers. However, in an enterprise scenario, you could have multiple BizTalk Server computers in multiple BizTalk Server groups that will all need to use the same service account. Changing its credentials will involve changing the user name and/or password used on every BizTalk Server computer that shares the BizTalk Messaging Management database.

BizTalk Server 2002 provides a command-line utility called BTS_SvcPW to simplify this process. The utility can be used to change both the user account and password used on every BizTalk Server computer that is registered in the BizTalk Messaging Management database. The syntax of the command is as follows:

```
BTS_SvcPW /s:sqlserver /d:database /u:username /n:newusername /p:newpassword
```

where *sqlserver* is the name of the computer where the BizTalk Messaging Management database is stored, *database* is the name of the BizTalk Messaging Management database, *username* is the name of an existing account used by BizTalk Messaging service on one or more computers, *newusername* is the name of the new user account that should be used for the BizTalk Messaging service, and *newpassword* is the new password that should be used for the BizTalk Messaging service account.

First of all, the *sqlserver* and *database* arguments are required. The *username* argument is only required if you want to specify a particular account whose details should be changed. This would be if you only wanted to change the password of the existing account, or if there were multiple service accounts in use, and you only wanted one to be changed. The *newusername* argument is only required if you have not specified the name of an existing account, and you wish to change the name of the account used by all BizTalk Messaging services. Finally, the *newpassword* argument is required to specify the new password that should be used for the relevant services. If you do not include this argument, you will be prompted for it.

Note   *You can also receive help at the command prompt by typing* **bts_svcpw /?**.

After running the utility, a file called bts_svcpw.log is created in the root of the drive where BizTalk Server 2002 is installed. Subsequent uses of the utility cause new entries to be appended to the log file, as shown here.

Specifying Proxy Server Credentials

In the original BizTalk Server 2000 release, you could configure the uniform resource locator (URL) and port number for a proxy server existing between BizTalk Server and the outside world. You could also override this information on any messaging port that used HTTP. However, it was not possible to provide a user name and password to this proxy server, so many BizTalk Server computers sat in loneliness, unable to go out and play on the Internet. With the arrival of BizTalk Server 2000 Service Pack 1, salvation was at hand, because you could now provide a user name and password to a proxy server by accessing the advanced properties for each HTTP-based messaging port. However, it was still annoying to have to do that individually for every HTTP-based messaging port you were using.

Finally, in BizTalk Server 2002, you can specify a default user name and password in BizTalk Server Administration to provide authentication details to a proxy server on your network. To do this, open the BizTalk Server Administration MMC, expand the Microsoft BizTalk Server 2000 node, right-click the node representing the relevant server group, and click Properties in the context menu. On the General tab, select the Use A Proxy Server check box, and enter the appropriate information.

BizTalk Orchestration Changes

BizTalk Orchestration and the use of BizTalk Orchestration Designer to create XLANG schedules were discussed in detail in Chapters 7 and 8. In BizTalk Server 2002, there are numerous improvements to the design and operation of BizTalk Orchestration. First, the Orchestration Designer interface is now based on Visio 2002 rather than Visio 2000, so it looks a lot prettier, but there is also new functionality, such as per-instance queues and schedule throttling to optimize the execution of multiple XLANG schedule instances. One final addition that doesn't really require a section to itself is the ability to configure long-running and timed transactions to persist schedule state to the XLANG database. This is enabled through the properties dialog box for such transactions, although keeping this setting disabled can provide greater throughput if such persistence is not deemed crucial.

Schedule Throttling

In BizTalk Server 2002, a new COM+ application called XLANG Schedule Pool is created that consists of 25 components called SimpleSkedPool.SimplePool1.1, SimpleSkedPool. SimplePool2.1, and so on. These components allow you to pool XLANG schedule instances to take advantage of COM+ object pooling. In this way, you can set the maximum number of instances that can be active at any one time, the minimum number of instances that should be kept in memory to improve instantiation, and the timeout period for which schedule instances should wait on a slot to become available in the pool.

This feature is deceptively important. Not only does it provide you with a mechanism to optimize the creation of XLANG schedules, but it can also serve as a security precaution. Theoretically, an unscrupulous user (or even a scrupulous but socially maladjusted one) could execute a denial-of-service (DOS) attack on BizTalk Server by submitting an exceptionally large number of documents for processing by an XLANG schedule to use up available resources on the server. While schedule throttling does not prevent such an attack from being launched, it does remove the weakness that such an attack would be designed to exploit.

 Other types of denial-of-service attacks were discussed in Chapter 13 on securing BizTalk Server.

Enabling Throttling

To enable XLANG schedule throttling, you can right-click the Begin shape in the XLANG schedule drawing that should be throttled. In the properties dialog box, shown following, you can choose from 25 different object pools, as provided by the XLANG Scheduler Pool COM+ application. After you configure the schedule in this way, you can then modify the component that provides the pool in the Component Services MMC. First, you have to enable changes. To do this, right-click the XLANG Schedule Pool application, and choose Properties from the context menu. On the Advanced tab, deselect the Disable Changes check box and click OK. Then click Yes in the warning dialog box that appears.

XLANG schedules created with BizTalk Server 2000 will not be affected by schedule throttling in BizTalk Server 2002, because they will not be configured to take advantage of object pooling.

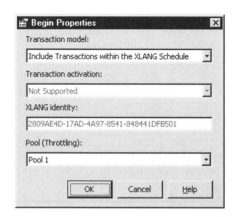

To modify the schedule pool, expand the XLANG Schedule Pool node in the Component Services MMC, right-click the Component representing the pool you chose in BizTalk Orchestration Designer, and select Properties from the context menu. The Activation tab of the SimpleSkedPool.SimplePool1.1 Properties dialog box is shown in Figure 20-11. On this tab, you can set the properties listed in the following sections.

Minimum Pool Size   Adjust this property to configure the minimum number of objects that should be kept in memory at all times. Keeping a certain number of instances in memory requires extra resources, but can greatly improve instantiation times. If your system processes high numbers of documents in short-lived schedules, increasing this value from its default setting of 1 can improve performance. If you are processing longer schedules on a less frequent basis, you should keep this value low.

Maximum Pool Size   Adjust this property to configure the maximum number of schedule instances that can be created at any one time. If your system processes high numbers of documents in short-lived schedules, you should increase this value from its default setting of 25 to achieve higher throughput. However, if you are processing long-running schedules, you might want to decrease this value to preserve resources. When the maximum is reached, no new schedule instances will be created until an existing schedule is dehydrated or completes.

 If an application creates a reference to an XLANG schedule instance, the instance will not be removed from memory unless either it is explicitly destroyed by the application that created it, or the reference to it goes out of scope.

Creation Timeout   Adjust this property to set the period in milliseconds that a pending schedule instance should wait before a slot in the object pool becomes available.

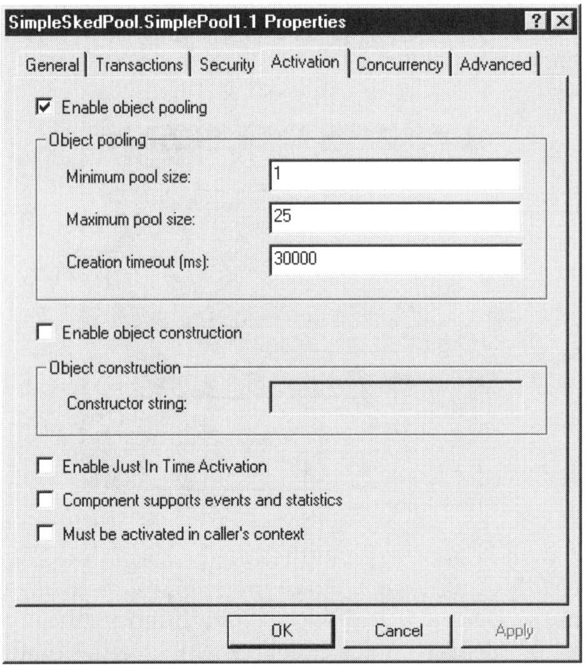

Figure 20-11. *The SimpleSkedPool.SimplePool1.1 Properties dialog box*

Instance IDs

In BizTalk Server 2000, every XLANG schedule instance created by the XLANG Scheduler COM+ application is given a unique instance ID. These instance IDs allow any given instance in memory to be directly addressable. Through this mechanism, it is possible to return messages to running instances and ensure that if an instance sends a message out through BizTalk Messaging, any response received will be returned to the same instance from which the original message was sent. This process, called *correlation*, was discussed in detail in Chapter 8. In this way, we can be sure that if there are multiple instances of the same XLANG schedule in memory waiting for responses, the correct instance will pick up each individual response.

In BizTalk Server 2002, you can use these instance IDs in two new ways. First, the unique ID for any given schedule instance is now available as a constant value at design time, so it can be inserted into a message field, or otherwise used in calculations and rules. Second, the ID can also be used as the label for messages stored in message queues. As a result, you can pick up a particular message from a message queue using its instance

ID instead of the generic message label or XML root element that would have been used before. This allows you to use a single message queue for multiple instances of short-lived or even long-running schedules and still be able to correlate messages with specific schedule instances. Obviously, this avoids the use of per-instance message queues that can quickly eat up resources on servers processing high volumes of documents.

Example: Using Instance IDs for Correlation

Because these two features are closely related and will often be used together, it is best to illustrate them using an example. In this scenario, a simple purchase order (PO) document with a unique PO number will be submitted to an XLANG schedule. The schedule will insert its instance ID into a special field in the message, and the PO will then be sent to BizTalk Messaging, where it will be transformed into an invoice. The invoice will then be dropped into a message queue and labeled with the unique instance ID. The XLANG schedule, in turn, will be configured to receive messages from a message queue based on the instance ID. In this way, even if multiple POs are submitted at once, each running XLANG schedule instance will only remove the correct invoice from the message queue. The logical flow of this scenario is shown in Figure 20-12.

First, you should create document specifications in BizTalk Editor representing a simple PO and a simple Invoice. You should also create a map in BizTalk Mapper to transform a PO into an invoice. Figure 20-13 shows this map, which also illustrates the structure of the PO and invoice specifications. You can then create a PO instance as follows:

```
<SimplePO ID="">
  <Document PONumber="201" Total="99.99" />
</SimplePO>
```

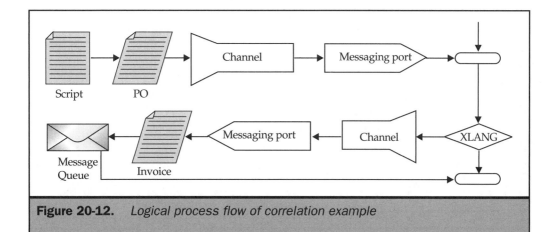

Figure 20-12. *Logical process flow of correlation example*

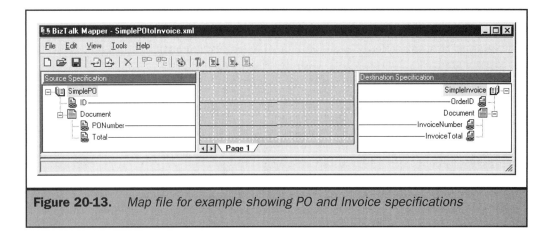

Figure 20-13. *Map file for example showing PO and Invoice specifications*

To receive the PO and transport it to the XLANG schedule, you will need to create a channel and messaging port with the following properties:

Channel	Name	Channel to Pick Up Simple PO
	Source	Source Organization
	Inbound Document	Simple PO
	Outbound Document	Simple PO
Messaging Port	Name	Port to Send Simple PO to XLANG
	Destination	XLANG Schedule
	Orchestration Port	ReceivePO

Then, to submit the PO to the channel, create a simple script as follows:

```
On Error Resume Next
Dim objInterchange, guidSub, docPO
Set objInterchange = CreateObject("BizTalk.Interchange")

set docPO = CreateObject("MSXML2.DOMDocument")
docPO.load "D:\SimplePO.xml"

for PONumber = 201 to 210
  docPO.documentElement.firstChild.setAttribute "PONumber", PONumber
  guidSub = objInterchange.Submit _
          (1,docPO.xml, , , , , ,"Channel to Pick Up Simple PO")
  if 0 <> err.number then
```

```
    WScript.Echo "Fail " + err.description
  Else
    WScript.Echo "Document with PO Number " & PONumber & " Submitted!"
  end if
next

Set objInterchange = nothing
```

This script will read the PO from the D: drive and modify the PONumber attribute
before submitting it to BizTalk Messaging. This is done ten times with unique PO numbers
to demonstrate correlation with multiple schedule instances in memory. Now we can look
at how to create the XLANG schedule that makes use of instance IDs for correlation.

Creating the Correlation XLANG Schedule

In BizTalk Orchestration Designer, create the XLANG schedule drawing shown in
Figure 20-14. As illustrated, the first BizTalk Messaging port should be configured to
activate the schedule. The second BizTalk Messaging port should be configured to feed
into a static channel called **Channel to Map PO to Invoice**. The Message Queuing port
should be configured to read from a single well-known private queue called **ReceiveInvoice**.
Finally, a Windows Script Component is used to correlate the received invoice with the
original PO. The code for this component is as follows:

```
<component>
<?component error="true" debug="true"?>
<registration
    description="CorrelationSample"
    progid="Sample.Correlate"
    version="1.00"
    classid="{34f72183-7c5a-4bb4-947f-09806ecd9e63}">
</registration>

<public>
    <method name="Correlate">
        <PARAMETER name="PONumber"/>
        <PARAMETER name="InvoiceNumber"/>
    </method>
</public>

<script language="VBScript">
<![CDATA[
function Correlate(num1, num2)
```

```
    strResponse = "Purchase Order: " & num1 & vbCrLf
    strResponse = strResponse & "Invoice Number: " & num2 & vbCrLf
    if num1 = num2 then
        strResult = "They match!"
    else
        strResult = "They don't match!"
    end if
    strResponse = strResponse + strResult
    MsgBox strResponse, , "Correlation Report"
end function
]]>
</script>
</component>
```

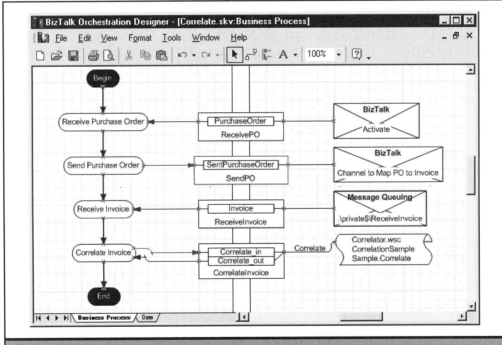

Figure 20-14. *The XLANG schedule used in the correlation example*

After adding the Action and Port shapes, you then need to connect them to create the message flow. For the ReceivePO port, create a new message called **PurchaseOrder** with message type SimplePO. Also browse to the Simple PO document specification and add references to the ID and PONumber fields. For the SendPO port, create a new message called **SentPurchaseOrder** that also has message type SimplePO. Browse to the Simple PO specification, and this time, only add a reference to the ID field. For the ReceiveInvoice port, you should create a new message called **Invoice** with message type SimpleInvoice. In BizTalk Server 2002, Orchestration Designer provides the ability to use the unique schedule instance ID as the message label. You will want to use this functionality to pick up the correct invoice from the queue, so select the Use Instance Id As Message Label check box as shown. Then browse to the Simple Invoice specification, and add a reference to the InvoiceNumber field.

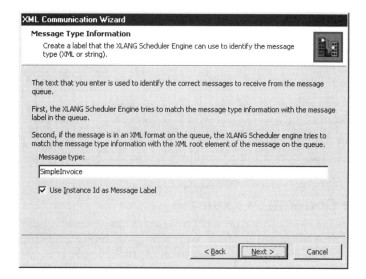

The XLANG schedule is almost finished. The last thing to do is configure the message flow through the schedule. The Data page for the schedule is shown in Figure 20-15. Note that there is a new constant value available in BizTalk Server 2002 called _Instance_Id_ that is inserted into the PO before it is sent off to be transformed by BizTalk Messaging. Also note that the PONumber field from the original PO and the InvoiceNumber field from the returned invoice are used as inputs to the Windows Script Component to test for correlation.

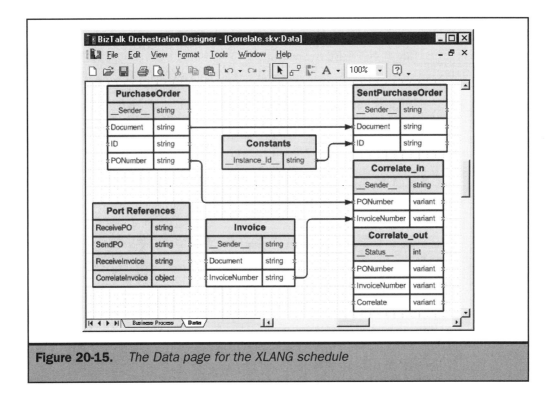

Figure 20-15. The Data page for the XLANG schedule

Testing the Correlation Example

Before we can test the example, we need to create a channel–messaging port pair to receive the PO from the XLANG schedule, transform it into an invoice, and transport it to a message queue. Use the following settings to create the channel and messaging port:

Channel	Name	Channel to Map PO to Invoice
	Source	XLANG
	Inbound Document	Simple PO
	Outbound Document	Simple Invoice
Messaging Port	Name	Port to Send Simple Invoice
	Destination	http://<server_name>/dropinvoice.asp

From this information, you can see that the messaging port delivers the transformed invoice to an Active Server Page (ASP). This is a crucial step, because we need to ensure that the invoice is dropped into a message queue using the instance ID of the schedule from which it came as the message label. This is not possible in BizTalk Messaging, so, instead, we use an ASP to transfer the invoice to the message queue. The code for dropinvoice.asp is as follows:

```
<%
' ---------- Receive Invoice and Retrieve Instance ID ----------
Dim docInvoice, instanceID
set docInvoice = server.createObject("MSXML2.DOMDocument")
docInvoice.load Request
instanceID = docInvoice.documentElement.getAttribute("OrderID")


' ---------- Drop Invoice into ReceiveInvoice Message Queue -----
Dim PRQueue, QueueMsg, MSMQTx, MSMQTxDisp, QueueInfo, objADO
Const MQ_SEND_ACCESS = 2
Const MQ_DENY_NONE = 0

'------------ Create Stream object and Save XML Document to It ---
Set objADO = CreateObject("ADODB.Stream")
objADO.open
objADO.CharSet = "us-ascii"
objADO.WriteText docInvoice.xml
objADO.Position = 0

'------------ Create required MSMQ objects ----------------------
Set QueueInfo = Server.CreateObject("MSMQ.MSMQQueueInfo")
Set PRQueue = Server.CreateObject("MSMQ.MSMQQueue")
QueueInfo.FormatName = "DIRECT=OS:.\private$\ReceiveInvoice"
Set PRQueue = QueueInfo.Open(MQ_SEND_ACCESS, MQ_DENY_NONE)
Set QueueMsg = Server.CreateObject("MSMQ.MSMQMessage")

'------------ Use Extracted Instance ID as Message Label ---------
QueueMsg.Label = instanceID
QueueMsg.Body = objADO.ReadText

'------------ Send Invoice to Queue -----------------------------
Set MSMQTxDisp = Server.CreateObject("MSMQ.MSMQTransactionDispenser")
Set MSMQTx = MSMQTxDisp.BeginTransaction
QueueMsg.Send PRQueue,MSMQTx
MSMQTx.commit

'------------ Clean Up ------------------------------------------
Set MSMQTx = nothing
Set MSMQTxDisp = nothing
Set QueueMsg = nothing
Set PRQueue = Nothing
Set QueueInfo = Nothing
Set objADO = Nothing
Set docInvoice = Nothing
%>
```

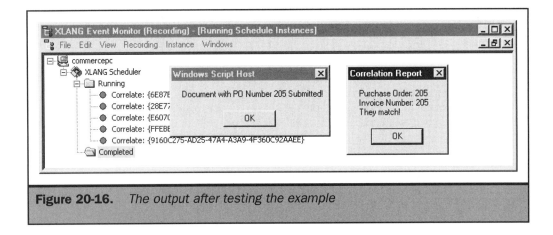

Figure 20-16. *The output after testing the example*

As you can see, the script uses XML Document Object Model (DOM) programming to extract the unique instance ID from the received invoice. When the message is being created on the queue, that ID is used as the label. As a result, when the schedule instances go to retrieve messages from the message queue, they will look for their own instance ID, as instructed during the configuration of the Invoice message. If you run the VBScript file given earlier to submit ten PO instances to BizTalk Messaging, you should see ten successive message boxes showing each PO instance number, followed by another sequence of ten message boxes displaying a message that the invoice successfully correlated with the PO. Usually, these message boxes will come up in a random order, proving that the invoices are not just being processed sequentially. You can also use XLANG Monitor to examine the running instances, as shown in Figure 20-16.

SDK Changes

The Software Development Kit (SDK) in BizTalk Server 2000 provided many useful tools and examples to help developers come to grips with the finer points of creating BizTalk Server solutions. In BizTalk Server 2002, the SDK has been extended to include more samples for both BizTalk Messaging and BizTalk Orchestration. It would not be worthwhile to provide a complete discussion of every new example because the documentation of those samples provides adequate information, but I will briefly discuss the additions and provide detail on an important work-around for existing limits to Microsoft Message Queuing Services (MSMQ).

New Messaging Samples

There are numerous new samples in the BizTalk Server 2002 SDK to assist implementers in the development of BizTalk Messaging solutions. These examples are summarized in Table 20-2.

Directory	Description
BTConfigAssistant	Although this is not a new sample in the SDK, the BT Configuration Assistant has been updated in BizTalk Server 2002. It now supports the deployment of receive functions along with messaging configuration objects.
Custom Counter	This example demonstrates how to count the number of documents in the Document Tracking database that match a particular set of criteria.
DateFunctoidNet	This sample demonstrates how to create a custom BizTalk Mapper functoid using the new C# programming language and the .NET Framework. The functionality of the new functoid is the same as that included as a Visual Basic sample with BizTalk Server 2000.
EDIIntroduction	This sample demonstrates configuring BizTalk Messaging to transform an XML-based purchase order acknowledgement into an X12 855.
EDIandReceipts	This sample demonstrates configuring BizTalk Messaging to accept an inbound X12 850 purchase order and to automatically generate an X12 997 functional acknowledgement (receipt). The purchase order is also mapped to an XML-based format for transport to an internal application.
Encryption	This sample demonstrates how to exchange documents securely between trading partners by configuring BizTalk Messaging to use digital certificates for signing and for encryption.
Flat-FileDelimited	This sample demonstrates how to create a delimited flat-file document specification in BizTalk Editor and how to use BizTalk Messaging to convert it into an XML document.
Flat-FilePositional	This sample demonstrates how to create a positional flat-file document specification in BizTalk Editor and how to use BizTalk Messaging to convert it into an XML document.
HTTP Receive Function	This sample demonstrates how to create an HTTP receive function to accept purchase orders transmitted using HTTP and how those documents are then submitted to BizTalk Messaging.
Mapping Twice	This sample demonstrates how to synchronously submit a document to BizTalk Messaging for transformation by a channel, and how to use the Loopback transport to return the resulting document to an application so that it may be submitted again to allow a second transformation to occur.

Table 20-2.   *Messaging Samples Included in the BizTalk Server 2002 SDK*

BIZTALK SERVER 2002
ENTERPRISE EDITION

Directory	Description
MSMQ 4MB Limit	This sample demonstrates how documents larger than 4MB (Unicode) or 2MB (ASCII) may be submitted via Message Queuing to BizTalk Server, as discussed later in this section.
Multi-Part MIME Attachment	This sample demonstrates how MIME-encoded documents containing attachments can be submitted to BizTalk Messaging.
Queue Sniffer	This tool allows you to access messages in local or remote message queues and view, delete, or forward those messages to other queues.
Refresh Messaging Manager	This tool allows you to refresh document definitions, envelopes, and channels used by BizTalk Messaging to ensure they are using the most up-to-date specifications and maps.
ReliableMessaging	This sample demonstrates how to submit a BizTalk Framework 2.0–compliant purchase order to BizTalk Server and how reliable receipts are generated.
Self-Routing	This sample demonstrates how documents can contain routing information to determine how they are processed by BizTalk Messaging. This also illustrates the use of the Dictionary tab in BizTalk Editor to identify fields that contain routing information and the use of envelopes to specify routing information for flat files.
Send To Remote Queue	This sample demonstrates how to use a COM object within an XLANG schedule to forward a document on to a remote message queue.
Suspended Queue Monitoring	This sample demonstrates how to generate an alert if a document is sent to the Suspended Queue. This makes use of the BizTalk Server Management Pack included with the product for use with Microsoft Operations Manager.
WMI	This sample demonstrates how to use the Windows Management Instrumentation object to create BizTalk Messaging organizations, document definitions, messaging ports, channels, and receive functions.

Table 20-2. *Messaging Samples Included in the BizTalk Server 2002 SDK* (continued)

MSMQ 4MB Limit

One particular shortcoming for many customers using BizTalk Server 2000 was the size limit on documents processed using Microsoft Message Queuing Services (MSMQ). It is not possible to submit documents larger than 2MB (ASCII) or 4MB (Unicode) to MSMQ. Unfortunately, this limit is not specific to BizTalk Server; it is built into the service. Further, this limit will still exist in Windows.NET Server when it is released. One of the SDK samples provides a work-around for this limitation using an Application Integration Component (AIC) and an XLANG schedule.

This limitation causes most problems for submitting documents to XLANG schedules via message queues. The work-around included in the SDK makes use of a SQL Server database to hold the document and instead passes a smaller document that contains a unique identifier to the XLANG schedule. This identifier can then be used by a COM component within the schedule to query the database and extract the full document. The workflow for the MSMQ 4MB Limit sample is illustrated in Figure 20-17. As shown, the sample makes use of a file receive function to accept a large purchase order (PO). The receive function then submits the PO to a channel, which feeds into a messaging port configured to use an AIC. This AIC performs two tasks. First, it extracts the unique identifier (in this case, a customer ID) from the PO and posts it to a message queue. Second, it inserts the PO into a SQL Server database using the BulkLoad component shipped with the XML for SQL Server Web Release 1 add-on.

Note *The XML for SQL Server Web Release 1 add-on can be downloaded from http://msdn.microsoft.com/xml/.*

A message-queuing receive function is also configured to retrieve the message containing the customer ID from the message queue and submit it to another channel. This channel is associated with a messaging port configured to instantiate an XLANG schedule. The XLANG schedule accepts the small document, extracts the unique customer identifier, and passes it to a COM component. This COM component looks up the SQL Server database using the identifier and retrieves the appropriate PO. The PO is then manipulated by the COM component to produce a summary, which is then dropped off to the file system.

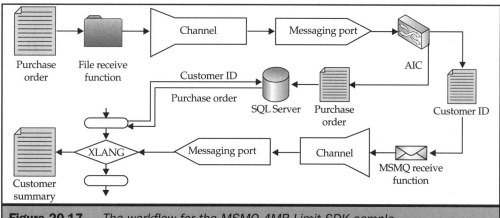

Figure 20-17.   *The workflow for the MSMQ 4MB Limit SDK sample*

Testing the Sample

To successfully install this sample, you must first ensure that the read-only attribute is removed from all files in the \Program Files\SDK\Messaging Samples\MSMQ 4MB Limit folder and its subfolders. Executing setup.cmd in the setup subfolder registers the DLLs for the AIC and the COM component, creates the necessary receive functions and messaging objects, and generates a new SQL Server database called LargeFileReceive. You will then have to manually copy the document specifications in the setup\docs subfolder to the Microsoft subfolder of the BizTalk Server WebDAV Repository. Because the AIC uses the BulkLoad component, you must also download and install the XML for SQL Server Web Release 1 add-on. You will then only need to modify one part of the sample—the XLANG schedule.

To modify the XLANG schedule, open MSMQ 4MB Limit.skv in BizTalk Orchestration Designer. Double-click the msg_CustomerID message in the port_CustomerID port, and proceed through the wizard until you reach the Message Specification Information page. Click the Browse button and navigate to the Microsoft subfolder of the BizTalk Server WebDAV Repository. Select the customerid.xml specification and click Finish. You should then double-click the GetSQLData COM component and proceed through the wizard, stopping at the Class Information page to select the appropriate ProgID, which is GetSQLData.getData. After completing the wizard, you will be prompted to modify the Data page of the schedule to reestablish the message flow. On the Data page, ensure that the CustomerID field in the msg_CustomerID message reference is feeding into the strCust_ID field of the getData_in message. Save and compile the XLANG schedule and you're ready to go.

There are two PO instances provided for testing. One is fairly compact, whereas the other is over 5MB. To test the sample with either of these instances, copy the file into the PODrop subfolder. After a while (about five minutes if you're using the large PO), the file will disappear. When the XLANG schedule has completed, a message box will appear showing the summary information. This data is also saved to the POSummary subfolder. During testing of the larger file, don't get worried if your system starts to thrash about. You can expect MSCIS.exe, which is the BizTalk Messaging Service, to operate at full strength to process the document, using much of the available processor resources and 80MB (or more) of memory.

New Orchestration Samples

Again, there are many new Orchestration samples provided with the SDK to accelerate the development of sophisticated BizTalk Orchestration solutions. These samples are summarized in Table 20-3.

Directory	Description
Export SKV to SKX	This sample demonstrates how to programmatically convert an XLANG schedule drawing into an executable XLANG schedule. To run the sample, copy the Export2SKX.vbs to the location of the drawing you want to convert. You can then use a command prompt to execute the script using the following syntax: Export2SKX.vbs *<sourcefilename.skv> <targetfilename.skx>*
Schedule Throttling	This sample demonstrates how to use the new throttling functionality of BizTalk Orchestration and the XLANG Scheduler Pool COM+ application to set the minimum and maximum number of XLANG schedule instances that should be created at any one time.
XLANG_async	This sample demonstrates how an Active Server Page (ASP) normally engages in synchronous operation with an XLANG schedule such that if the ASP initiates the XLANG schedule, it will not finish until the schedule completes. However, there is also an asynchronous example that demonstrates how an ASP can instantiate an XLANG schedule that may be long-running. In this scenario, the ASP decouples from the schedule by storing a work ID in a SQL Server database. The ASP can then query the database as needed to determine the status of the schedule.
XLANGTrace	This sample demonstrates how a COM object can be used to insert tracing operations into an XLANG schedule. This causes information about the state of the schedule and the data being processed to be written to a SQL Server database. The object has the following input parameters to record schedule data: message_label: String to hold name Action shape names message_ID: String to hold schedule instance IDs message_userkey: String to hold unique document identifiers message_body: String to hold actual document instances

Table 20-3.   *Orchestration Samples Included in the BizTalk Server 2002 SDK*

Chapter 21

What's New in BizTalk Server 2002?

869

izTalk Server 2002 Enterprise Edition will have been released by the end of 2001. In the previous chapter, I discussed changes and enhancements to existing features such as BizTalk Editor, BizTalk Mapper, BizTalk Administration, and BizTalk Orchestration. These changes have been implemented primarily to solve problems faced by small and large customers alike. However, brand-new features are also built into the product to address specific issues encountered by enterprise customers. In particular, there is the SEED Wizard for the efficient packaging and deployment of messaging configuration settings to trading partners, integration with Microsoft Application Center to simplify the deployment and management of clustered BizTalk Server solutions, and the Microsoft Operations Manager Pack for BizTalk Server to facilitate the monitoring and optimization of enterprisewide installations.

BizTalk SEED Wizard

In an enterprise environment, your organization will typically deal with many types of documents from many different trading partners. Often, as your enterprise grows, you will need to add new trading partners who will have to configure their own processes to ensure they are sending documents to you in the correct format and receiving responses from you in their own format. Similarly, changes to an existing trading-partner relationship may require new document formats to be incorporated. For obvious reasons, it can be difficult to correctly establish the document formats required on either end of the agreement.

The BizTalk SEED Wizard is a tool to accelerate business-to-business trading-partner integration, either within an enterprise or between disparate organizations. The wizard accomplishes this by allowing administrators to create a package containing document specifications and sample instances for both incoming and outgoing document formats. This package can then be made available for download to new and existing business partners, who can then install the package on their own systems and perform tests to validate the structures.

Creating SEED Packages

The SEED Wizard defines two types of organizations. First, there is the *initiator* organization, which creates a SEED package consisting of incoming and outgoing document specifications and instances. This package can then be made available to business partners, who are termed "recipients". Each *recipient* organization can download the package and use the SEED Wizard to install the specifications and instances. During the installation of the package, the recipient can perform local and remote tests on the specifications using automatically configured receive functions, channels, document definitions, and messaging ports. To run these tests, there are Active Server Page (ASP) files in the \Program Files\Microsoft BizTalk Server\SEED directory called slingback.asp, trigger.asp, and localsubmit.asp. Both the initiator organization and the recipient organization should create virtual directories on their respective web servers containing these files.

For example, let's say that Bushwhack Fruit Distributors is the initiator organization. They accept XML-based purchase orders from trading partners such as SuperSave MegaMarkets and return invoices to those partners. Bushwhack Fruit Distributors can use the SEED Wizard to package the purchase order specification representing the inbound documents they receive, and also to package the invoice specification representing the outbound documents they send to companies like SuperSave MegaMarkets.

On the Welcome page of the SEED Wizard, an organization accepts the role of initiator or recipient, by choosing to create or install a SEED package as shown. In the first part of this scenario, we will take the standpoint of Bushwhack Fruit Distributors, who are acting as an initiator and therefore creating a SEED package. Click Next to continue.

On the Package Creation Process – Organization Information page, enter the name of the initiator organization. This name will be used to create a BizTalk Messaging organization on the recipient's system when they download and install the package. Click Next to continue.

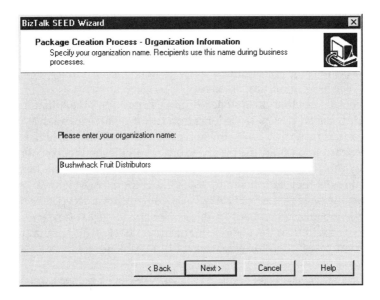

Configuring Inbound Documents for Packaging

On the Package Creation Process – Document Specifications page, click Add to configure a document specification. This will bring up the Configure Document dialog box, as shown next. In this dialog box, you should first choose whether you are configuring a document that will be arriving Inbound To Initiator or Outbound From Initiator, by selecting the appropriate option. We will first configure the inbound document, which is a purchase order. Click the first Browse button to select the appropriate document specification from the WebDAV Repository. Then click the second Browse button to choose a corresponding document instance from the local file system.

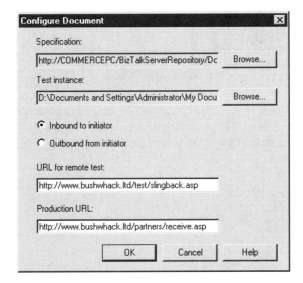

The BizTalk SEED Wizard only supports XML-based document specifications and instances. Attempting to choose an EDI or Flat-File instance will produce an error.

As mentioned, there are three ASP files included for use with the SEED Wizard. The first of these, called slingback.asp, reads a posted document and then returns that same document to provide simple synchronous testing. The initiator organization should configure a publicly accessible virtual directory containing this ASP, and you should enter this path in the URL For Remote Test field. Finally, in the Production URL field, you should enter the path to an ASP that is used by the initiator organization to accept real business documents from trading partners. After deployment to a recipient organization, this URL will be used at the end of the testing process to configure a messaging port. Click OK when you have finished configuring the inbound document.

Configuring Outbound Documents for Packaging

Because Bushwhack Fruit Distributors will also be sending invoice documents to its trading partners, it's important that we also provide an invoice specification and sample instance. To do this, click Add again to open up the Configure Document dialog box. This time select the Outbound From Initiator option, and browse for the appropriate invoice document specification and instance. The second ASP that is provided with the SEED Wizard is called trigger.asp, and again, this should be placed in a publicly accessible virtual directory on the initiator's web server for testing purposes. This page forwards an instance document on to another ASP that has been specially configured for local testing on the recipient's system. Enter the path to trigger.asp on the initiator system as shown, and then click OK. Click Next when you have finished configuring document specifications.

Configure Document	☒
Specification:	
http://COMMERCEPC/BizTalkServerRepository/Dc [Browse...]	
Test instance:	
D:\Documents and Settings\Administrator\My Docu [Browse...]	
○ Inbound to initiator	
⊙ Outbound from initiator	
URL for remote test:	
http://www.bushwhack.ltd/test/trigger.asp	
Production URL:	
[OK] [Cancel] [Help]	

On the final page of the BizTalk SEED Wizard, enter the path and filename for the SEED package, or click the Browse button to choose a location. The package that is created is an XML file, as shown in Figure 21-1. The Specification and Instance nodes

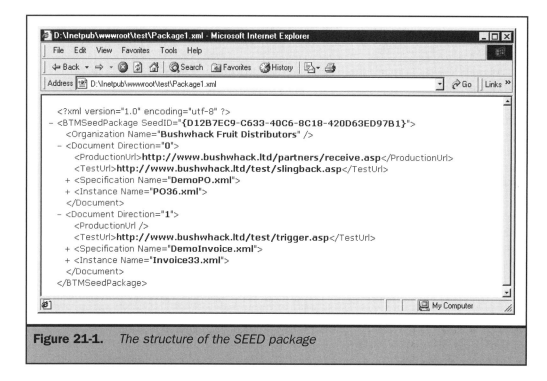

Figure 21-1. *The structure of the SEED package*

have been collapsed to save space, but they only contain the BizTalk Editor document specification and sample instance, respectively. Bushwhack Fruit Distributors could now place this package on their web site for downloading by trading partners using BizTalk Server 2002.

Installing SEED Packages

After a SEED package has been made available to trading partners of the initiator organization, they can use the BizTalk SEED Wizard to install the package on their system. To continue our scenario, SuperSave MegaMarkets is an organization that does business with Bushwhack Fruit Distributors. They have downloaded the SEED package from the Bushwhack web site so that they can quickly deploy the necessary configuration and begin electronic trading with the company.

On the Welcome page of the BizTalk SEED Wizard, choose the option to install a SEED package and click Next. On the Package Installation Process – Package Selection page, click Browse to select the newly downloaded package file. The wizard will then provide you with a summary of the information contained in the package, as shown here:

On the Package Installation Process–Test Information page, enter values for the time-out period after which a local or remote test will be deemed to have failed. Similarly, enter the interval between test instances as shown next. Both times are specified in seconds. If you will be testing large documents, or if the connection between your system and the initiator system is slow, you may need to increase these values. They should be suitable for most scenarios, however.

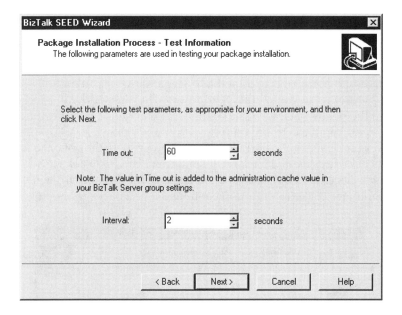

Configuring Inbound Documents for Deployment

The next page that appears is the Package Installation Process – Document Deployment page. On this page, you will be presented with the list of documents found in the SEED package, as shown next. Each of these needs to be tested before deployment.

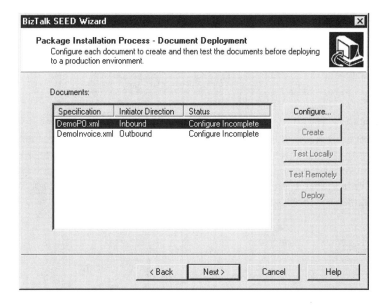

BIZTALK SERVER 2002
ENTERPRISE EDITION

We will first configure the document that will be inbound with respect to the initiator; this is the purchase order that will be sent from SuperSave MegaMarkets to Bushwhack Fruit Distributors. Select the document marked "Inbound" and click Configure. This displays the Inbound Document (To Initiator) Configuration dialog box, shown next. In this dialog box, you should specify the information that will be used to perform local testing using the inbound specification and document instance contained in the package. Under Receive Function, select a directory on the recipient system that will be used as the pick-up location for a file receive function. This can be specified using a local or Universal Naming Convention (UNC) file path. The File Types To Poll For field will already contain "*.xml" as a filter for instances arriving into this directory, and this should be suitable for most scenarios. In the Test Drop Location field, you should also type the location of or browse to a folder that will be used as a drop location for files that pass through the BizTalk Messaging configuration that will be created in the next step. This folder should be empty to avoid possible conflicts.

After the configuration of the inbound document specification (with respect to the initiator) is complete, you can click the Create button. This creates a sample BizTalk Messaging configuration consisting of a receive function to pick up document instances placed by the wizard in the specified location, a channel to accept the document instance submitted by the receive function, a document definition pointing to the inbound specification contained in the package, and a messaging port configured to transport the document instance to the file path specified in the last step. Upon creation, the Test Locally button is enabled in the wizard.

Testing Inbound Documents

When you click the Test Locally button, the wizard places a copy of the document instance in the receive function location. From there, it is picked up by the created receive function and submitted to the test channel. This channel performs no mapping, instead simply passing the document through to the test messaging port, which drops the document into the specified folder. The wizard checks to see that the file was delivered successfully and then deletes it. Note that this test only involves the recipient's local system. If the local test was successful, the Test Remotely button is enabled in the wizard.

 The receive function, channel, document definition, and messaging port are all called <packagename>_<specificationname>, for example, "Package1_TestPO".

When you click the Test Remotely button, the wizard reconfigures the messaging port to point to the remote test URL configured earlier, such as http://www.bushwhack.ltd/test/slingback.asp. Then it programmatically calls the SubmitSync method of the IInterchange object to pass the sample instance into the channel. Because slingback.asp is written to simply return the received document, the recipient knows that the initiator organization is able to receive the document at the test location. After completing the remote test successfully, the Deploy button is enabled in the wizard.

To complete the process of configuring the recipient system to send documents to the initiator organization, click the Deploy button. The wizard has already tested that instance documents dropped into a local folder will be successfully processed by BizTalk Messaging. Similarly, the remote test has proven that these instances will be accepted by a test page when sent to the initiator's web server. The only thing left to do is to replace the URL of the test page with the production URL for the initiator organization. Because this was also provided by the initiator during the creation of the SEED package, clicking Deploy reconfigures the messaging port to point to this URL. Now the recipient has a pick-up location into which they can drop business documents, and BizTalk Messaging will pick them up and transport them to the initiator.

Configuring Outbound Documents for Deployment

After deploying the inbound document specification, you can configure the outbound specification. Remember, this document will be outbound with respect to the initiator, so it represents documents that will be submitted by the initiator to the recipient. In our scenario, this is an invoice that will be sent from Bushwhack Fruit Distributors to SuperSave MegaMarkets. To begin the process, first click the Configure button. This will display the Outbound Document (To Initiator) Configuration dialog box, shown next. The name of this dialog box is confusing—again, we are talking about an outbound document coming from the initiator to the recipient.

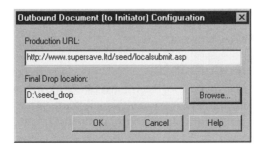

In the Production URL field, type the address of the third ASP file used by the SEED Wizard—localsubmit.asp. This file is located on the recipient's web server and is used during the remote test as a location to which the initiator can send documents. You should also type in a folder where the file should be dropped at the end of the process. Click OK to confirm the configuration, and then click the Create button, which is now enabled. When you click Create, the SEED Wizard configures BizTalk Messaging on the recipient's system by creating a channel, document definition, and messaging port, which are again named *<packagename>_<specificationname>*, for example, Package1_TestInvoice. Upon creation, the Test Locally button is enabled in the wizard.

Testing Outbound Documents

When you click the Test Locally button, the wizard programmatically submits the outbound document instance (in this case, an invoice) to the created channel. This channel, in turn, feeds into the created messaging port that drops the document into the specified local drop folder and then deletes it. As with the inbound document, this test is really only checking to make sure that the channel-messaging port pair is working correctly. After the local test, the Test Remotely button is enabled in the wizard.

Before discussing exactly what happens when the Test Remotely button is clicked, you should remember that when the outbound document specification was originally configured by the initiator organization, the URL for remote testing was set to point to a file called trigger.asp on the initiator's web server. Also, during the configuration of the outbound document for installation on the recipient, the production URL was set to point to a file called localsubmit.asp on the recipient's web server. This information is crucial to understanding what follows.

When you click the Test Remotely button, the Wizard posts the outbound document instance to trigger.asp on the initiator system. Actually, the document instance is wrapped in an XML envelope that includes both the name of the channel on the recipient's system that will be used to process the returned document, and the URL for localsubmit.asp on the recipient's system. Upon receipt of this interchange, trigger.asp removes part of the envelope and programmatically submits the rest to a hidden channel on the initiator called BTMSeedTestChannel. This channel is automatically created when BizTalk Server 2002 is installed on any system, along with a hidden document definition called BTMSeedTestDocument and a hidden messaging port called BTMSeedTestPort that is configured as open destination. This new interchange (which contains the document instance and the name of the recipient channel) is submitted to the hidden channel with the localsubmit.asp file on the recipient's system set as the destination.

> **Note**   *There is also an organization called SEED Test Organization that is configured as the source organization when the document is returned using the hidden channel.*

When the interchange is received by localsubmit.asp on the recipient system, it is submitted programmatically to BizTalk Messaging using the name of the channel extracted from the envelope. This is the channel created during the installation of the SEED package. After the removal of the outer envelope, the interchange now looks like this:

```
<SubmitData>
    <ChannelName>Package1_TestInvoice</ChannelName>
    <InstanceData><Invoice>…data…</Invoice></InstanceData>
</SubmitData>
```

with the original document instance embedded as a child of the *InstanceData* element. As with the local test, the channel feeds into a messaging port that drops the file into a folder on the recipient's system, from which it is then deleted. If all goes well, then the remote test is deemed to have passed, because it has been proven that the initiator can use BizTalk Messaging to send documents to the production URL specified for the recipient's system and they, in turn, will be processed by BizTalk Messaging.

Because the outbound documents from the initiator will not usually be wrapped in an envelope that contains the name of the channel on the recipient's system, the channel name should be hard-coded into localsubmit.asp for use in production.

Application Center Integration

Microsoft Application Center allows you to create clusters of applications for increased scalability, manageability, and availability. These applications can be web applications, shared COM components, or COM+ applications. In Chapter 12, we discussed how to create a cluster of servers to hold COM components so that XLANG schedules running on multiple BizTalk Server 2000 computers could use the dynamic Component Load Balancing feature provided by Application Center. BizTalk Server 2002 extends this integration by providing a specific set of BizTalk Server resources that can be added to server clusters. Further, using Application Center with BizTalk Server 2002 eases the process of moving BizTalk Server resources such as receive functions, messaging ports, distribution lists, and XLANG schedules from a development or staging environment to a live production environment. Applied in conjunction with the BTConfigAssistant discussed in Chapter 12, this can address many problems faced by administrators who need to redeploy existing BizTalk Server solutions.

Installing Application Center

To become fully proficient with Application Center, you should refer to the online documentation supplied with that product. However, I'll step through the basics to get you up and running. First, you will need to install Application Center. The installation process is very straightforward, so I'll only point out the most important information here. You can install Application Center either before or after the installation of BizTalk Server 2002, but if you will be installing it on a system that already has SQL Server 2000 with SQL Server 2000 Service Pack 1 (which is likely), you must address a serious issue.

 If you are new to Application Center 2000, or if you are looking for more in-depth information on the product, you can download the Application Center 2000 Resource Kit from http://www.microsoft.com/applicationcenter/.

Bypassing SQL Server 2000 Service Pack 1

Application Center uses the Microsoft SQL Server Desktop Engine (MSDE) to provide storage for performance counter and event logging data. Unfortunately, MSDE will not install properly on top of SQL Server 2000 Service Pack 1, because there are certain files that the installation program recognizes as being newer, so it will not replace them. This causes the installation to halt and roll back before completion. To circumvent this problem, you have to convince the setup utility that SQL Server 2000 Service Pack 1 is not present. Follow these steps to perform this work-around:

1. In the \Program Files\Microsoft SQL Server\80\Tools\Binn folder, rename semnt.dll, sqlsvc.dll, and sqlresld.dll to have a .dld file extension.

2. In the \Program Files\Microsoft SQL Server\80\Tools\Binn\Resources\1033 folder, rename semnt.rll and sqlsvc.rll to have an .rld file extension.

3. Install Application Center as normal. Do not reboot when the installation is finished.

4. Application Center installs its own version of the files listed in steps 1 and 2. Delete these replaced versions and rename the original files back to have a .dll or .rll file extension as necessary.

5. Reboot the server.

 Further information about this problem is available in the Microsoft Knowledge Base article Q296628.

Installing Application Center

To install Application Center, insert the product CD-ROM and double-click setup.hta in the root folder of the CD-ROM. This will start an HTML application, as shown next, with options to install Windows 2000 Service Pack 1 and certain pre-Service Pack 2 hotfixes on your system. If you have already installed Windows 2000 Service Pack 2 (required for BizTalk Server 2002), you can proceed directly to step 3. You can also proceed straight to the installation of the product by double-clicking setup.exe in the root folder of the CD-ROM, but this will not create a setup log. If you use setup.hta, a file called AC_Setup.log is created in the system root folder (\Winnt, by default).

 The available installation options are Typical and Custom. If you want to install the monitoring samples provided, you must select Custom.

To enable the addition of BizTalk Server resources to a clustered application, you must then install Application Center Service Pack 1 from the ACPatch directory on the BizTalk Server 2002 CD-ROM.

 The patch available with the beta version of BizTalk Server 2002 is a prerelease version of Application Center Service Pack 1. This version of the patch is specific to BizTalk Server 2000 machines and should not be installed on other Application Center servers.

Creating a Cluster

After Application Center has been installed, you can create a cluster for your applications. To do this, you must first connect to a server running Application Center to act as the cluster controller. In the Application Center Microsoft Management Console (MMC), right-click the Application Center node, and select Connect from the context menu. In the Connect To Server dialog box, enter the name of the server, as shown next, or click Browse to find a server on your network. You will then see the New Server dialog box, in which you can either create a new cluster or join an existing cluster. For the cluster controller, you should opt to create a new cluster. This will start the New Cluster Wizard.

In the New Cluster Wizard, enter a name and optional description for the cluster and click Next. You can choose from three different cluster types—General/Web Cluster, COM+ Application Cluster, or COM+ Routing Cluster. The first option will do in most scenarios. Click Next, and then choose the type of load balancing that will be used. In most enterprise deployment scenarios, you will have two network interface cards installed in each cluster member server, so the Network Load Balancing (NLB) option will be preferred. Click Next to continue. The remaining steps of the wizard allow you to confirm the network interface card (NIC) used for management traffic (the back plane), the e-mail address to which alerts should be sent, and the server through which they should be sent. Click Finish on the final page of the wizard to create the cluster.

Note *If you have only one NIC on your server, you can simulate NLB operations across a cluster by installing the Microsoft Loopback Adapter through the Add/Remove Hardware Control Panel. Consult the Application Center documentation for further information on creating and joining clusters.*

Creating an Application

Application Center clusters provide two types of load balancing—network load balancing, where requests for resources such as web pages are routed to members of the cluster via the Windows 2000 Network Load Balancing (NLB) service or another third-party load balancing solution, and Component Load Balancing (CLB), where requests for COM components or COM+ applications are shared among member servers configured to host those components. Configuring Application Center for Component Load Balancing was covered in Chapter 12, so I won't go through it again. However, what's new in BizTalk Server 2002 is the ability to add to these applications specific BizTalk Server resources, such as messaging ports, distribution lists, receive functions, and XLANG schedules.

To create an application that will host these resources, expand the cluster node in the Application Center MMC, and right-click the Applications node. The available applications will appear in the Applications pane on the right side of the window. Click the New button at the top of this pane to add a new application, and enter a name for the application. After the new application has appeared in the Applications pane on the right, you can add new resources to it. Select the new application in the Applications pane, and click the Resource Type drop-down menu in the lower pane. For custom counters, receive functions, messaging ports, and distribution lists, select BizTalk from the available resource types, as shown in Figure 21-2. To add XLANG schedules to the application, choose File System Paths from the list.

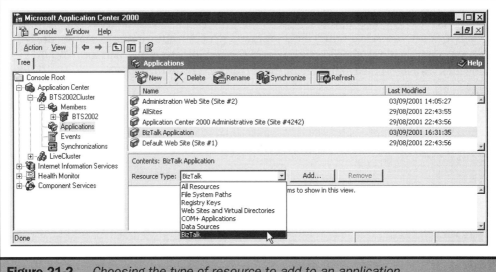

Figure 21-2.   *Choosing the type of resource to add to an application*

Adding BizTalk Resources

If you have chosen BizTalk resources from the Resource Type drop-down menu, click Add to see the individual resource types that can be configured. As shown following, the available types are BizTalkCustomCounters, BizTalkPortGroups, BizTalkPorts, and BizTalkReceiveFunctions.

Note	*The creation of custom counters using the sample provided in the SDK will be discussed in the section on Microsoft Operations Manager Integration later in this chapter.*

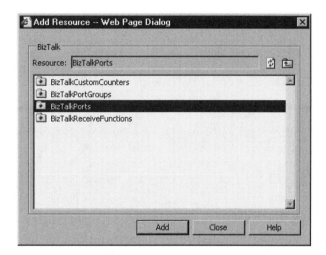

If you want to add all available resources of a particular type, select that type in the Add Resource–Web Page Dialog dialog box and click the Add button. If you only want to add a specific instance of a resource, double-click that resource type. For example, double-click BizTalkPorts to see the list of available messaging ports to add to the application, as shown next. Select each individual resource and click Add to add that resource to the application. Click Close when you have finished adding resources.

BIZTALK SERVER 2002
ENTERPRISE EDITION

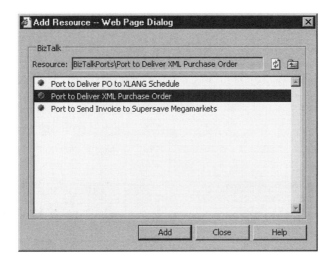

Adding XLANG Resources

If you have chosen File System Paths from the Resource Type drop-down menu, click Add to see the available drives from which to add resources. In the Add Resource–Web Page Dialog dialog box, double-click the drive containing the XLANG schedule, and browse to the SKX file. Click Close when you have finished adding resources.

Deploying an Application

When an application has been created on an Application Center cluster, the resources in that application are made available to all members of the cluster. However, Application Center is also designed to simplify the process of replicating content from staging to production servers. In this scenario, you may have a test cluster configured to stage your applications, and after suitable testing, you will want to deploy those applications to a production cluster.

 Unlike other resources handled by Application Center 2000, changes made to BizTalk Server resources are not synchronized automatically. If you make changes to any of the resources, you will need to redeploy the application.

To deploy an application, right-click the Applications node in the Application Center MMC, and select New Deployment from the context menu. In the New Deployment Wizard, click Next to advance past the opening page. On the Deployment Target Options page, choose a name for the deployment, and select the option to deploy content outside the current cluster, as shown next. Click Next to continue.

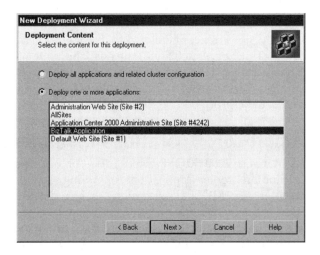

On the Deployment Target Authentication page, enter the appropriate credentials to create the content on the target cluster and click Next. On the Deployment Targets page, enter the name of the controller server of the cluster to which the content should be deployed, or click Browse to find the server on the network. Click Add and then click Next to continue. On the Deployment Content page, you can choose to deploy all applications from the staging cluster, or just deploy individual applications as shown here. To select multiple individual applications, use the CTRL key.

On the Deployment Options page, you can set or clear the option to deploy folder and file NTFS permissions as may be required for XLANG schedule files. Click Next to reach the final page of the wizard and then click Finish. The application will then be deployed to the production cluster.

To replicate and deploy applications, you must ensure that the directory structures on each member server and on each cluster controller are identical. For example, BizTalk Server must be installed on the same drive in the same folder on each server, and the physical folder containing the web server directories must be the same. Consult the Application Center documentation for more information.

Removing Application Resources

As mentioned, Application Center 2000 does not automatically replicate BizTalk Server resources between servers in a cluster. For this reason, if you make changes to any of the resources, you will need to redeploy the application. For a successful redeployment, you may need to delete existing resources from a target server. To remove messaging ports and distribution lists, use BizTalk Messaging Manager. To remove receive functions, use BizTalk Server Administration. To remove custom counters, modify the VBScript file that created the counters, as discussed in the next section. To remove XLANG schedules, simply delete the files in Windows Explorer.

Microsoft Operations Manager Integration

Another enterprise-level feature that many thought lacking from BizTalk Server 2000 was the ability to properly monitor events related to the operation of the product. This has been addressed in BizTalk Server 2002 with the availability of a Management Pack for Microsoft Operations Manager 2000. Through this management pack, you can monitor the performance of BizTalk Server groups, generate alerts based on server events, and apply management rules to be processed on these servers.

Introduction to Microsoft Operations Manager 2000

Microsoft Operations Manager 2000 (MOM) is a product for securing, monitoring, and managing desktop computers, server applications, operating system software, and web farms throughout an enterprise. MOM allows you to retrieve detailed information on application and system events, to generate reports based on the overall performance of server applications in various formats, and to send alerts in response to specific processing rules. MOM itself is not included with BizTalk Server 2002, but the management pack that establishes processing rules for BizTalk Server is bundled with BizTalk Server 2002 Enterprise Edition. These rules allow you to specify the action that should take place in response to an event, such as the execution of a script or the sending of e-mail to support personnel. The collection and monitoring of these events is enabled through data providers such as Windows Management Instrumentation (WMI), Windows event logs, performance counters, and Simple Network Management Protocol (SNMP) traps. You can also import further management packs for Windows NT and Windows 2000 event collection, Windows 2000 Active Directory, Internet Information Services (IIS), Message Queuing Services, and SQL Server, among others.

MOM Concepts

To properly appreciate how MOM can provide enterprise-level monitoring and management for BizTalk Server, it is important to understand some basic concepts used by MOM. MOM employs agents, consolidators, agent managers, data access servers, configuration groups, and rule groups to provide a centralized and remotely accessible platform for system support.

Agents   MOM installs services called *agents* on each computer that should be monitored as part of the enterprise. Specifically, the agent is installed on each managed computer by the agent manager assigned to that computer. These agents trap events and apply processing rules such as the generation of an alert, the execution of a batch file, or the forwarding of information to a consolidator. Agents also send a periodic *heartbeat* to a consolidator to keep the consolidator apprised of its status. The consolidator may reply to this heartbeat with an update to the agent's processing rules.

Consolidators   MOM also employs specific computers in a configuration group as consolidators. Each consolidator accepts event information from individual agents and applies further processing rules on those events, such as the execution of a script or the notification of support personnel. Consolidators also send information to a specified Data Access Server (DAS), which acts as a gateway to the central MOM database. In addition, consolidators act as agent managers for computers assigned to it, by installing agent services on those machines and updating the processing rules for those agents. The consolidator service also doubles as an agent service, trapping events specific to the consolidator computer.

Data Access Servers   Because there will be multiple agents and consolidators in a configuration group that all need to read data from and send data to the central MOM database, one or more machines will act as Data Access Server (DAS) computers, regulating the flow of information between agents, consolidators, and the database. The DAS also handles the retrieval of information for the administrative interfaces, such as the MOM Microsoft Management Console (MMC) and the MOM Web Console.

Configuration Groups   As with Windows domains, it makes sense to organize groups of computers that will be managed by MOM into logical groupings, perhaps determined by organizational boundaries or geographic location. Each of these configuration groups consists of one database, one or more DAS computers, one or more consolidators, and any number of agents. However, a single agent can be a member of multiple configuration groups, for example, to report information to different personnel.

Rule Groups MOM organizes everything according to rules. These rules are either processing rule groups that consist of filters, event traps, performance thresholds, and automated responses, or computer grouping rules that group computers together to collect related events or apply processing rules to each server in that group.

BizTalk Server Management Pack

The BizTalk Server Management Pack that comes with BizTalk Server 2002 can be used to implement important optimization and monitoring capabilities for enterprises that include BizTalk Server. These capabilities could include configuring the sending of e-mail in response to user-defined events, creating custom alerts based on the values or trends of certain performance counters, or executing specific scripts to handle the arrival of documents in the Retry or Suspended queues, which can be monitored in real time. Out of the box, the management pack includes a number of built-in event processing rules, performance processing rules, and samples that can help you manage BizTalk Server computers in your enterprise, and these can be extended or customized to meet your particular requirements.

To install the management pack, perform the following tasks:

1. Open the MOM Administrator Console, and expand the Microsoft Operations Manager and Rules nodes.

2. Right-click the Processing Rule Groups node, and select Import Management Pack from the context menu.

3. In the Import Management Pack dialog box, browse to
   <Install_CD>\MOM\BizTalk2002.akm and click Import, as shown here.

4. In the Import Processing Rule Groups dialog box, review the list of imported processing rule groups shown following and click OK.

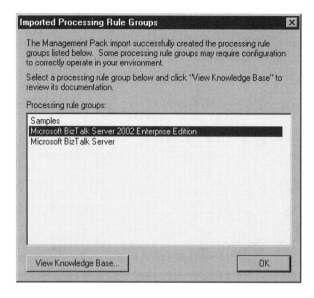

BizTalk Server Rules

When the management pack is imported, you will notice that certain preconfigured event processing rules already exist, as shown in Figure 21-3. These rules correspond to the complete set of events that can arise in the Windows 2000 application Event Log for BizTalk Server. Each of these events is configured to generate an alert and optionally to execute a response. You can also create custom rules to filter events, to detect missing events, to consolidate similar events, or to collect specific events.

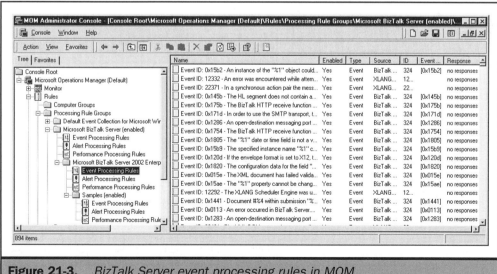

Figure 21-3. *BizTalk Server event processing rules in MOM*

A number of preconfigured performance processing rules also exist, as shown in Figure 21-4. These rules depend on BizTalk Server performance monitor counters and are either *measuring rules* that sample certain counters at predefined intervals or *threshold rules* that compare the value of counters to specified levels. By default, each of the measuring rules is enabled, and each of the threshold rules is disabled. To enable one of these rules, double-click on the rule and select the Enabled check box on the General tab as shown here.

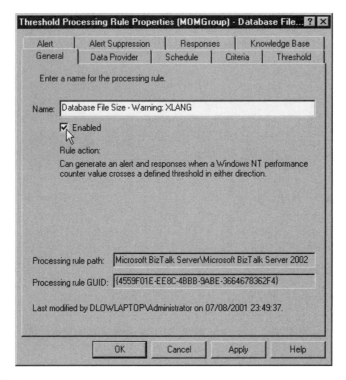

The BizTalk Server management pack also comes with sample rules that you can use as templates for your own purposes or to evaluate how certain features behave. The samples provided are as follows:

Category	Rule
Event rules	Sample–Suspended Queue Alert
Alert rules	Sample–Notification on Transport Failure with Event ID 0x0159
Performance processing rules	Sample–Suspended Queue Size Threshold
	Sample–Custom Counter
	Sample–Notify when too many failed schedules per unit time

For example, to use the Sample–Suspended Queue Size Threshold, you have to first enable the rule. To do this, double-click the rule in the right pane of the MOM Administration Console, and select the Enabled check box on the General tab. On the Threshold tab, enter a value in the Greater Than field, as shown here.

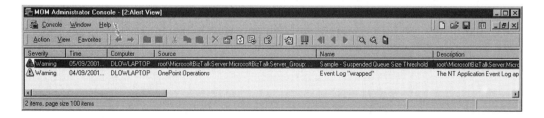

If you then submit more than five malformed documents to BizTalk Messaging, you will generate an alert. You can view unresolved alerts by clicking the All Open Alerts node under the Monitor node in the MOM Administration Console, as shown next. The next section will look at the Custom Counter sample in more detail.

 Note *There is also a Suspended Queue Monitoring sample in the SDK under Messaging Samples to quickly create suspended queue items.*

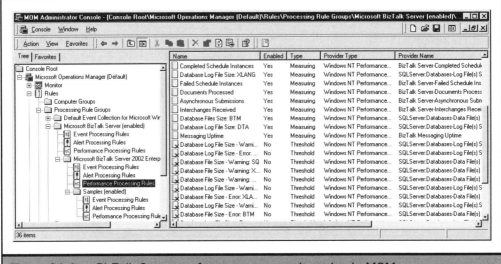

Figure 21-4. *BizTalk Server performance processing rules in MOM*

Custom Counter Sample

The BizTalk Server 2002 Software Development Kit (SDK) comes with a sample that makes use of the WMI interfaces to create custom counters. These counters can be used to keep track of documents entering the Document Tracking Activity (DTA) database that satisfy certain criteria. For example, you may be interested in checking how many purchase orders from SuperSave MegaMarkets have arrived in the last seven days, or you may wish to configure an alert to be sent if the number of invoices sent out to SuperSave MegaMarkets increases above ten per day. The sample uses MSBTS_CustomCounterSetting and MSBTS_CustomCounter WMI classes, which are created in the InterchangeProvSchema.mof file located in the \Program Files\Microsoft BizTalk Server\setup folder.

For information about how to use the other classes created in the InterchangeProvSchema.mof file, refer to Chapter 19.

Configuring the Custom Counter Sample

As with all samples in the SDK, a full set of instructions is included on how to set up the scenario required by the sample, so I will only summarize the important points here. To create the environment for the sample, perform the following tasks:

1. In the MOM Administrator console, expand the Microsoft Operations Manager, Rules, Processing Rule Groups, Microsoft BizTalk Server, Microsoft BizTalk Server 2002 Enterprise Edition, and Samples nodes. Click the Performance Processing Rules node, and double-click the Sample–Custom Counter icon in the right pane. Select the Enabled check box on the General tab, and click OK.

2. Create a folder called **CustomCounterSample** on the C: drive, and create folders called **SrcOrg** and **DestOrg** beneath it.

3. Copy the POReq.xml file from the \Program Files\Microsoft BizTalk Server\ SDK\Messaging Samples\Custom Counter folder to the \Program Files\ Microsoft BizTalk Server\BizTalkServerRepository\DocSpecs\Microsoft folder.

4. Run the CustomCounterConfig.vbs file. This script creates the following objects:

Object	Name
Organization	SrcOrg for Custom Counter
	DestOrg for Custom Counter
Document definition	POReq
Messaging port	Messaging Port for Custom Counter Sample
Channel	Channel for Custom Counter Sample
File receive function	CustomCounterSample

5. Open a Command Prompt, browse to the Custom Counter folder under \Program Files\Microsoft BizTalk Server\SDK\Messaging Samples, and run CreateCustomCounter_Organizations.vbs.

 You can also right-click the script in Windows Explorer and in the context menu, choose the Open command that is not the default action. This will cause the script to be run by wscript.exe rather than cscript.exe so that feedback is given in message boxes displayed on the screen.

Running the Custom Counter Sample

When you run the script, it creates a counter that monitors instances of the POReq document definition being passed from the source organization to the destination organization. It also validates the counter to ensure it has been properly configured.

To pass an appropriate document that the counter can measure through BizTalk Messaging, remove the read-only attribute from the PORequest.xml file in the Custom Counter sample folder, and paste a copy of it into the C:\CustomCounterSample\

SrcOrg folder. The file will be picked up by the receive function and dropped into the C:\CustomCounterSample\DestOrg folder as output.xml. No mapping is performed on the document, but each time it passes through BizTalk Messaging, a new record is created in the DTA database, and this will be logged by the custom counter. The counter is configured to generate an Alert of severity "Information", and this will be visible by clicking the All Open Alerts node in the MOM Administrator Console as before.

Management Pack Views

The BizTalk Server 2002 management pack also includes a number of performance data views that can be used to graphically monitor the performance of different aspects of BizTalk Server. The available views are

Activated Schedule Instances	Database Log File Size: XLANG
Asynchronous Submissions	Dehydrated Schedule Instances
Completed Schedule Instances	Documents Processed
Database File Size: BTM	Documents Received
Database File Size: DTA	Failed Schedule Instances
Database File Size: SQ	Interchanges Received
Database File Size: XLANG	Items Suspended
Database Log File Size: BTM	Messaging Uptime
Database Log File Size: DTA	Synchronous Submissions
Database Log File Size: SQ	Transactions Aborted

Note   *To view a description of these counters, search for "Performance Counters" in the BizTalk Server 2002 documentation.*

To display any of these views graphically, perform the following tasks:

1. In the MOM Administrator Console, expand the Microsoft Operations Manager, Monitor, Public Views, Microsoft BizTalk Server, and Microsoft BizTalk Server 2002 Enterprise Edition nodes.

2. Click any one of the view nodes, and double-click the node that appears in the right pane of the console.

3. In the Performance Data Properties (MOM Group) dialog box, select the Graph The Values check box, and select an appropriate scale, as shown next. Click OK.

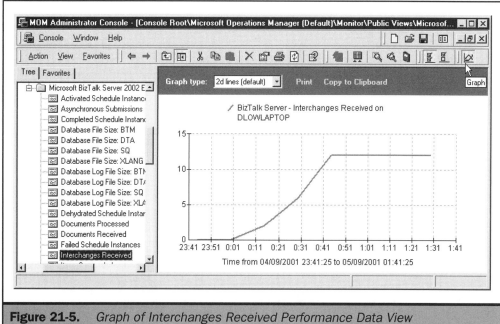

4. In the rebar of the MMC, click the Graph button, as shown in Figure 21-5, to view the graphic data.

Figure 21-5.   *Graph of Interchanges Received Performance Data View*

The
Complete
Reference

Part VIII

Appendix

Appendix

BizTalk Framework 2.0: Document and Message Specification

BizTalk Framework 2.0: Document and Message Specification

This specification provides a general overview of the BizTalk Framework 2.0 conceptual architecture, including the BizTalk Document and BizTalk Message. It provides detailed specifications for the construction of BizTalk Documents and Messages, and their secure transport over a number of Internet-standard transport and transfer protocols.

1. Introduction

The growing maturity of Internet-based secure transport protocols, combined with ubiquitous support for these protocols across networking, hardware, and software platforms, is enabling businesses to develop new ways to facilitate efficient and automated interactions. These interactions can occur between their own internal lines of business; productivity and knowledge management applications; the applications used by their customers and partners; and services provided by their commercial and corporate providers.

The challenges associated with enabling such efficient, automated interactions between applications across business boundaries, and in a cost effective manner, are similar to those associated with enabling them within an enterprise or departmental boundary. However, a new dimension of challenges in the areas of security and reliability must be addressed in order to communicate with other organizations.

These requirements for interaction across business boundaries include, but are not limited to, the following:

- A sufficiently-flexible and rich universal language to specify, package, publish, and exchange both structured and unstructured information across application or business boundaries.

- A flexible and rich universal language to specify and execute transformation rules to convert information from one format to the other as application and business boundaries are crossed.

- Platform-neutral, application-level communication protocols that enable automated interactions across application or business boundaries.

- Platform-neutral mechanisms for securing messages for integrity, privacy and non-repudiation.

Extensible Markup Language (XML) and XML-based schema languages provide a strong set of technologies with a low barrier to entry. These languages enable one to describe and exchange structured information between collaborating applications or business partners in a platform- and middleware-neutral manner.

As a result, domain-specific standards bodies and industry initiatives have started to adopt XML and XML-based schema languages to specify both their vocabularies and content models. These schemas are becoming widely published and implemented to facilitate communication between both applications and businesses. Wide support of XML has also resulted in independent solution providers developing solutions that enable the exchange of XML-based information with other third-party or custom-developed applications. Several solution- or middleware/platform-specific approaches have been taken to address the lack of middleware-neutral, application-level communication protocols. However, no single proprietary solution or middleware platform meets all the needs of a complex deployment environment.

These proprietary initiatives have generally resulted in customers facing broad interoperability issues on their own. The BizTalk™ Framework addresses these interoperability challenges in a platform- and technology-neutral manner. It provides specifications for the design and development of XML-based messaging solutions for communication between applications and organizations. This specification builds upon standard and emerging Internet technologies such as Hypertext Transfer Protocol (HTTP), Multipurpose Internet Mail Extensions (MIME), Extensible Markup Language (XML), and Simple Object Access Protocol (SOAP). Subsequent versions of the BizTalk Framework will be enhanced to leverage additional XML and Internet-related, messaging-standards work as appropriate.

It is important to note that the BizTalk™ Framework does not attempt to address all aspects of business-to-business electronic commerce. For instance, it does not deal directly with legal issues, agreements regarding arbitration, and recovery from catastrophic failures, nor does it specify specific business processes such as those for purchasing or securities trading. The BizTalk™ Framework provides a set of basic mechanisms required for most business-to-business electronic exchanges. It is expected that other specifications and standards, consistent with the BizTalk™ Framework, will be developed for the application- and domain-specific aspects.

2. Specification Scope and Evolution

This specification provides a general overview of the BizTalk Framework conceptual architecture, including the fundamental notions of BizTalk Document and BizTalk Message. It then provides detailed specifications for the construction of BizTalk Documents and Messages, and their secure transport over a number of Internet-standard transport and transfer protocols, as described below.

BizTalk Documents follow a number of rules for structure and content in order to provide rich functionality and predictable semantics. This specification describes the following aspects of BizTalk Documents and their semantics:

- Overall structure of BizTalk Documents.

- BizTalk headers for document routing, properties, catalog, and process management.
- Structure and handling of BizTalk Documents that require reliable delivery.

When implementing solutions using the BizTalk Framework, specific transport, encoding, and security mechanisms must be used to secure and deliver messages. This specification describes the following mechanisms and aspects of BizTalk Message encoding and transport:

- Transport bindings for Internet transfer protocols
- MIME-based transfer encoding and attachment packaging
- Signatures and encryption based on S/MIME

This specification is intended to define messaging interaction between BizTalk Framework 2.0 Compliant servers, referred to as *BFC servers* in this specification.

2.1 Relationship to BizTalk Framework 1.0

The BizTalk Framework 2.0 specification is a major revision of the BizTalk Framework 1.0 specification. BizTalk Framework 2.0 includes the following new features:

- Transport bindings
- Reliable message delivery
- MIME encoding for attachments
- Security based on S/MIME

In addition, BizTalk Framework 2.0 has been influenced by many recent standards efforts including, but not limited to, the following:

- SOAP Version 1.1 [SOAP]
- XML Schema Part 1: Structures [XSD1]
- XML Schema Part 2: Data types [XSD2]

The influence of SOAP 1.1 is most pervasive since BizTalk Framework 2.0 is an extension of SOAP 1.1, whereas BizTalk Framework 1.0 was "pre-SOAP." In addition, the opportunity for a major revision was used to rationalize the semantics, naming, and structure of many BizTags in the light of experience and the requirements of the new features in this specification. The use of SOAP 1.1 as the starting point aligns BizTalk Framework 2.0 with the direction set by the newly chartered XML Protocols activity of the W3C [XP].

One of the goals of BizTalk Framework 2.0 is to sufficiently explain wire-level behavior so that it's useful as the basis for interoperation among compliant servers.

The semantics of many BizTags has been defined much more specifically than in BizTalk Framework 1.0. The structure and content of BizTalk Documents described in BizTalk Framework 1.0 have been preserved wherever possible, but precise semantics and consistency with standards have been given higher priority in order to provide a solid foundation for the future.

2.2 Versioning Model

BizTalk Framework 2.0 follows SOAP 1.1 in not defining a traditional versioning model based on major and minor version numbers. The version is implied by the namespace URIs used to qualify the BizTalk-specific header entries defined in this specification. Normal SOAP 1.1 rules for the **SOAP-ENV:mustUnderstand** attribute imply that if the header entries that are required to be understood carry the wrong namespace or are deemed ill-formed in some other fashion, the BFC server should respond with a **SOAP-ENV:mustUnderstand** fault.

In the context of the HTTP binding specified in section 10, this fault indication may be returned in the HTTP response. However, if the message is processed asynchronously, the HTTP response will be **202 accepted** and the fault should be returned asynchronously, whenever possible. See section 10 for further discussion of SOAP protocol binding.

3. Use of XML Schema Data Types

This specification uses the type-qualification **xsi:type** attribute as well as a number of specific data types from the XML Schema specifications [XSD1, XSD2]. These are listed below with explanations. This specification, however, does not mandate the use of a specific method for defining XML schemas.

The **xsi:type** attribute allows an element to explicitly assert its type in a specific XML document instance. This can be used to validate the structure of the element.

The data type **timeInstant** represents a specific instant of time. The value space of **timeInstant** is the space of combinations of date and time of day values as defined in section 5.4 of the ISO 8601 [ISO8601] standard.

The **uriReference** data type represents a URI reference as defined in Section 4 of [URI]. A URI reference may be absolute or relative, and may have an optional fragment identifier.

A **complexType** is an element with content that is not a simple type, such as a string or a decimal number; the element contains sub-elements and/or attributes with their own content.

The XML schema data types are referenced in the text without the use of the xsd: prefix (signifying that they belong to the "http://www.w3.org/2000/08/XMLSchema" namespace) for brevity. The prefix and namespace are shown in the examples.

4. BizTalk Concepts

4.1 Terminology

This document uses a set of BizTalk-specific terms, as defined below:

- **BizTalk Framework Compliant (BFC) Server.** A BFC Server is represented by the set of services providing the message-processing functionality defined in the BizTalk Framework specifications.

Application   An Application is the line-of-business system where the business data or logic are stored and executed. An application also includes any additional adapters that may be required to emit or consume Business Documents (see below) and communicate with a BFC server.

Business Document   A Business Document is a well-formed XML document containing business data. This data may represent a purchase order, invoice, sales forecast, or any other business information. One or more Business Documents form the body of a BizTalk Document (see below).

   The BizTalk Framework does not prescribe the content or structure (schema) of individual Business Documents. The details of the Business Document content and structure, or Schema, are defined and agreed upon by the business entities involved.

Schema   A Schema is the metadata used to describe the structure of a class of XML documents, in particular for a class of Business Documents. This formal description is used by application developers to create systems that process corresponding Business Documents, or by parsers that validate a Business Document's conformance to the Schema at run time. Organizations may publish their Schemas in the BizTalk Schemas Library, or through other means.

> **Note**   *Schemas for Business Documents do not contain any BizTags, as described in this specification. A schema contains only those tags required to support the business transaction, as agreed to by the cooperating business entities. General requirements and guidelines for Schema implementations are defined in the BizTalk Schema Guidelines.*

BizTalk Document   A BizTalk Document is a SOAP 1.1 message in which the body of the message contains the Business Documents, and the header contains BizTalk-specific header entries for enhanced message-handling semantics. The following concepts apply to BizTalk Documents.

Lifetime   The time period during which a Document is meaningful. A Document must not be sent, accepted, processed or acknowledged beyond its lifetime.

- **Identity**: A universally unique token used to identify a Document.

Acceptance   The act of being accepted for delivery by a receiver. A received Document is accepted if it is recognized as being intended for an endpoint served by the receiver, including Documents that are copies or duplicates of previously received Documents (based on the identity). Acceptance does not mean that all header entries and the body have been inspected and their contents verified for any specific purpose.

- **Idempotence**: the ability of a Document to be transmitted and accepted more than once with the same effect as being transmitted and accepted once.

Receipts   Biztalk Framework includes end-to-end protocols that prescribe certain receipts to be sent by the receiver in order to ensure delivery semantics in some cases. These receipts are first-class BizTalk Documents with a prescribed syntax. There are two receipt kinds defined in this specification:

- **Delivery**: a receipt to acknowledge that the receiver accepted a given Document for delivery.

- **Commitment**: a receipt to acknowledge that, in addition to being accepted, a given Document has been inspected at the destination endpoint, all header entries marked mustUnderstand="1" have been understood, the correctness of their contents as well as the contents of the body has been verified, and there is a commitment to process the Document.

BizTag   BizTags are the set of XML tags (both mandatory and optional) that are used to specify Business Document handling. More precisely, BizTags are elements and attributes defined in this specification and used to construct BizTalk-specific SOAP header entries in the BizTalk Document. They are processed by the BFC Server, or by other applications facilitating the document interchange.

- **BizTalk Message:** A BizTalk Message is the unit of wire-level interchange between BFC Servers. BizTalk Messages are used to send BizTalk Documents, and any related files, between BFC Servers. A BizTalk Message must always contain a primary BizTalk Document that defines the semantics of the Message within the BizTalk Framework. It may in addition contain one or more attachments (see below), including well-formed XML documents, some of which may themselves be BizTalk Documents. BizTalk Documents carried as attachments are treated just like any other XML documents and have no special significance for the semantics of the BizTalk Message. The structure of a BizTalk Message is dependent on the transport being used to carry the message and often includes transport-specific headers.

- **Transport:** The actual interchange of BizTalk Messages between BFC servers presupposes a communication mechanism that is used to carry Messages physically from the source to the destination business entity. We use the term transport to refer to this mechanism. Transports used in this context will vary widely in their characteristics, ranging from simple datagram and file transfer protocols to transfer protocols such as HTTP and SMTP, and sophisticated, message-oriented middleware. This specification does not differentiate between transports based on their capabilities. Transport characteristics affect only the transport bindings specified in section 10.

- **Endpoint**: BizTalk Framework compliant source or destination of a BizTalk Message.

- **Address**: the location of an endpoint, resolvable in context for the purposes of message transport and delivery.

Attachment   Attachments are generally non-XML files or other related information that is not transmitted as a Business Document within the body of the BizTalk Document. These may be related images, large compressed files, or any other information format or content that is not an appropriate Business Document. Attachments may be carried within the BizTalk Message enclosing the BizTalk Document, or they may be external to the Message, and simply referenced within the Document.

4.2 Logical Layering

The logical implementation model for the BizTalk Framework is composed of three layers. The layering described here is for illustrative and explanatory purposes. As the BizTalk Framework specification definitively specifies only the wire format for BizTalk Messages and the protocol for reliable messaging, alternative logical layering may be used, provided it supports equivalent functionality, without affecting compliance with this specification. These logical layers include the application (and appropriate adapters), the BFC Server, and transport. The application is the ultimate source and destination of the content of BizTalk Messages, and communicates with other applications by sending Business Documents back and forth through BFC Servers. Multiple BFC Servers communicate with one another over a variety of protocols, such as HTTP, SMTP, and Microsoft Message Queue (MSMQ). The BizTalk Framework does not prescribe what these transport protocols are, and is independent of the implementation details of each.

The application is responsible for generating the Business Documents and any attachments to be transmitted to its peer(s) and submitting them to the BFC Server. The responsibility for wrapping the Business Documents in a BizTalk Document may rest with either the application or the BFC server, depending on the implementation of the BFC server. The server processes the document and any attachments and constructs a BizTalk Message as appropriate for the transport protocol. The BFC Server uses information contained in the BizTags to determine the correct transport-specific destination address. The server then hands the message to the transport layer for transmission to the destination BFC Server. The interfaces between the business application, the BFC Server, and the transport layer are implementation specific.

5. BizTalk Document Structure

The following is an example of a simple BizTalk Document.

```
<SOAP-ENV:Envelope
            xmlns:SOAP-ENV="http://schemas.xmlsoap.org/soap/envelope/"
            xmlns:xsi="http://www.w3.org/1999/XMLSchema-instance">
  <SOAP-ENV:Header>
    <eps:endpoints SOAP-ENV:mustUnderstand="1"
              xmlns:eps="http://schemas.biztalk.org/btf-2-0/endpoints"
              xmlns:agr="http://www.trading-agreements.org/types/">
      <eps:to>
        <eps:address xsi:type="agr:department">Book Orders</eps:address>
      </eps:to>
      <eps:from>
        <eps:address xsi:type="agr:organization">Book Lovers</eps:address>
      </eps:from>
    </eps:endpoints>
    <prop:properties SOAP-ENV:mustUnderstand="1"
              xmlns:prop="http://schemas.biztalk.org/btf-2-0/properties">
<prop:identity>uuid:74b9f5d0-33fb-4a81-b02b5b760641c1d6</prop:identity>
      <prop:sentAt>2000-05-14T03:00:00+08:00</prop:sentAt>
      <prop:expiresAt>2000-05-15T04:00:00+08:00</prop:expiresAt>
      <prop:topic>http://electrocommerce.org/purchase_order/</prop:topic>
    </prop:properties>
  </SOAP-ENV:Header>
  <SOAP-ENV:Body>
    <po:PurchaseOrder xmlns:po="http://electrocommerce.org/purchase_order/">
      <po:Title>Essential BizTalk</po:Title>
    </po:PurchaseOrder>
  </SOAP-ENV:Body>
</SOAP-ENV:Envelope>
```

This BizTalk Document consists of a standard SOAP 1.1 message that contains the
following:

- An application-specific Business Document (in this case a book purchase order),
  with its own application-defined XML namespace, carried in the body of the
  SOAP message.
- BizTalk-specific <endpoints> and <properties> SOAP header entries,
  constructed using BizTags defined in standard BizTag namespaces, with
  schema and semantics defined in this specification.

In general, the body of the SOAP message constituting a BizTalk Document contains several related Business Documents, and the header of the SOAP message contains several BizTalk-specific (and potentially other) header entries. The use of the **SOAP-ENV:mustUnderstand** attribute with a value of "1" implies (in accordance with the SOAP 1.1 specification) that the destination business entity receiving this Document must understand and correctly process the header entries so attributed, or if the header entry is not understood, the processing of the Document must be terminated with failure.

All BizTags are defined within standard BizTag namespaces with URIs derived by extension from the prefix http://schemas.biztalk.org/btf-2-0/. The scope of semantic significance for the BizTag namespaces is always confined to the header of the outermost BizTalk Document. If a BizTalk Document is carried whole in the body of another BizTalk Document, the BizTags in the inner document are "dormant" and ineffective—they are treated as business data for the purposes of processing the outer Document.

It is worth noting that the <to> and <from> routing tags, described in more detail below, often use business-entity names for source and destination addressing, rather than transport addresses such as HTTP URLs. The form and interpretation of the address content is indicated by the **xsi:type** attribute. The BizTalk Document structure and function are independent of the transports over which the Documents are carried.

6. BizTalk Document Body

The <Body> element of the SOAP message that constitutes a BizTalk Document contains the Business Documents being carried. In general, a BizTalk Document may carry a set of related Business Documents (for instance, a purchase order and a shipper's name and address for shipping that order).

Related Business Documents often have shared content. SOAP has a straightforward mechanism for encoding data targeted by multiple references; it uses XML ID attributes and relative URIs. Consider a simple elaboration of the purchase order example above in which both the purchase order and the shipping information reference information about the book. The <Body> element of the following BizTalk Document shows how this could be expressed using SOAP encoding rules.

```
<SOAP-ENV:Envelope
            xmlns:SOAP-ENV="http://schemas.xmlsoap.org/soap/envelope/"
            xmlns:SOAP-ENC="http://schemas.xmlsoap.org/soap/encoding/"
            xmlns:xsi="http://www.w3.org/1999/XMLSchema-instance">
<SOAP-ENV:Header>
    <!-- headers omitted for brevity -->
</SOAP-ENV:Header>
<SOAP-ENV:Body>
```

```
    <po:PurchaseOrder xmlns:po="http://electrocommerce.org/purchase_order/">
        <po:item href="#theBook"/>
        <!-- and other purchasing information -->
    </po:PurchaseOrder>

    <ship:shippingInfo xmlns:ship="http://electrocommerce.org/shippingInfo/">
        <ship:content href="#theBook"/>
        <!-- and other shipping information -->
    </ship:shippingInfo>

    <book xmlns="http://electrocommerce.org/bookInfo/"  id="theBook"
                                                        SOAP-ENC:root="0">

        <Title>Essential BizTalk</Title>
        <!-- and other book information -->
    </book>
    </SOAP-ENV:Body>
</SOAP-ENV:Envelope>
```

This example also illustrates a problem that occurs when this technique is used. We would like the destination business entity to view this BizTalk Document as containing two Business Documents: the purchase order and the shipping information. However, the <Body> of the SOAP message contains three child elements. We need a way to distinguish the Business Documents from the elements that appear as direct children of <Body> because they are shared via multiple references.

SOAP provides the **SOAP-ENC:root** attribute as a method for signaling that an element is not an independent entity. Every immediate child of the <Body> element in a BizTalk Document is a contained Business Document *unless* that child carries the **SOAP-ENC:root** attribute with a value of "0".

7. BizTalk Document Header Entries

This section describes the BizTalk-specific SOAP header entries that may occur in a BizTalk Document. They are concerned with Document routing, Document identification and other properties, Document delivery services requested, a catalog of Document contents and attachments, and tracking of the business process context of which the Document is a part. The following table lists the BizTags used to mark the header entries and their properties. Each header entry is described in more detail in the following sections.

Tag Name	Mandatory	Kind	Type	Occurs
endpoints	yes	element	complexType	once
properties	yes	element	complexType	once
services	no	element	complexType	once
manifest	no	element	complexType	once
process	no	element	complexType	once

7.1 Document Source and Destination

Document source and destination is specified by a SOAP header entry marked by the <endpoints> BizTag. The endpoints header entry from the initial BizTalk Document example is shown below:

```
<eps:endpoints SOAP-ENV:mustUnderstand="1"
          xmlns:SOAP-ENV="http://schemas.xmlsoap.org/soap/envelope/"
          xmlns:xsi="http://www.w3.org/1999/XMLSchema-instance"
          xmlns:eps="http://schemas.biztalk.org/btf-2-0/endpoints"
          xmlns:agr="http://www.trading-agreements.org/types/">
      <eps:to>
          <eps:address xsi:type="agr:department">Book Orders</eps:address>
      </eps:to>
      <eps:from>
          <eps:address xsi:type="agr:organization">Book Lovers</eps:address>
      </eps:from>
</eps:endpoints>
```

As noted in the context of the initial example, the source and destination are specified as names of business entities in the element marked by the <address> BizTag, and these names in general reflect business-related namespaces (such as DUNS numbers) rather than transport endpoints. The selection of transports and transport endpoints, over which the BizTalk Document is carried, often occurs separately between the business entities involved. It is entirely possible that multiple transports and transport endpoints are available for the communication and that they will change over time, without changing the names of the business entities (in <address>) and the structure of the BizTalk Documents exchanged between the entities. The exact routing logic used to deliver the BizTalk Document once it reaches the BFC server that is associated with the destination business entity is implementation dependent. Of course, the use of transport endpoints or resource locators (URLs) is by no means precluded as the content of the <address> elements.

Understanding and processing the <endpoints> header entry and all its contents at the recipient BFC server is always mandatory during successful processing of a BizTalk Document. The encoding of the <endpoints> element must always contain the **SOAP-ENV:mustUnderstand="1"** attribute to reflect this. The following table lists the BizTags used to construct the sub-elements of the <endpoints> header entry and their properties.

Tag Name	Mandatory	Kind	Type	Occurs
to	yes	element	complexType	once
from	yes	element	complexType	once

The <to> tag contains the specification of the destination business entity to which the BizTalk Document is to be delivered. This element contains exactly one occurrence of an <address> sub-element.

The <from> tag contains the specification of the source business entity from which the BizTalk Document originates. This element contains exactly one occurrence of an <address> sub-element.

The <address> element contains the identification of a business entity in string form. The <address> element has a required **xsi:type** attribute. The value of the **xsi:type** attribute signifies the category of the address as well as the permissible structure of the string form of the address. Several categories, including organization name and URI reference, are used in examples in this specification.

7.2 Document Identification and Properties

Document identity information and other properties are specified by a SOAP header entry marked by the <properties> BizTag. The properties header entry from the initial BizTalk Document example is shown below.

```
        <prop:properties SOAP-ENV:mustUnderstand="1"

xmlns:prop="http://schemas.biztalk.org/btf-2-0/properties">

<prop:identity>uuid:74b9f5d0-33fb-4a81-b02b5b760641c1d6</prop:identity>
        <prop:sentAt>2000-05-14T03:00:00+08:00</prop:sentAt>
        <prop:expiresAt>2000-05-15T04:00:00+08:00</prop:expiresAt>

<prop:topic>http://electrocommerce.org/purchase_order/</prop:topic>
        </prop:properties>
```

Understanding and processing the <properties> header entry and all its contents at the recipient BFC server is always mandatory during successful processing of a BizTalk Document. The encoding of the <properties> element must always contain the **SOAP-ENV:mustUnderstand="1"** attribute to reflect this. The following table lists the BizTags used to construct the sub-elements of the <properties> header entry.

Tag Name	Mandatory	Kind	Type	Occurs
identity	yes	element	uriReference	once
sentAt	yes	element	timeInstant	once
expiresAt	yes	element	timeInstant	once
topic	yes	element	uriReference	once

The <identity> tag is a URI reference that uniquely identifies the BizTalk Document for purposes of logging, tracking, error handling, or other Document processing and correlation requirements. The <identity> tag must be universally unique. This could be accomplished, for instance, with Universally Unique Identifiers (UUIDs), as illustrated in the example above, or with cryptographic hash algorithms such as MD5 applied to the Business Document(s). The choice of <identity> tag form and the process of generating <identity> tag is implementation specific.

The <sentAt> tag is the sending timestamp of the Document. In the context of the transmission-retry behavior discussed in Section 8, this timestamp must always reflect the time at which the properties element was created.

The <topic> tag contains a URI reference that uniquely identifies the overall purpose of the BizTalk Document. The <topic> tag may be used for interest-based routing (publish/subscribe via topic-based addressing) and to verify the consistency of the BizTalk Document content with its intent. The latter use occurs in the HTTP binding as described in section 10. Although the process for creation of this element is implementation specific, it is recommended that the topic is either specified by the sending application or is inferred in a standard way by the BFC server from the Business Documents carried in the BizTalk Document, e.g. by using the namespace URI of the (first) Business Document as the topic.

The <expiresAt> tag is the expiration timestamp of the Document. Beyond the point in time stamped in this element, the associated BizTalk Document is considered to have expired and must not be processed or acknowledged by the destination business entity. Care should be taken in specifying the expiration time, providing for a reasonable margin of error in time synchronization across distributed systems.

> **Note**
>
> *The business logic of the source business entity typically allocates a definite time interval for the performance of the business action represented by a BizTalk Document; it needs to be notified about failure to deliver the Document within the allocated time. There are two basic approaches to Document lifetime encoding: time to live (TTL) or maximum latency, and absolute expiration time. Both approaches have weaknesses. TTL is immune to time synchronization problems across machines, and is therefore best when low-latency messages are carried over fast transports. However, it effectively assumes instantaneous transport, which is an unreasonable assumption for some transports. Given the transport independence of the BizTalk Framework, use of TTL is problematic. The problem with using absolute expiration time (encoded as coordinated universal time) is the well-known clock-synchronization problem in distributed systems. However, the latency for messages that is expected in current usage of the BizTalk Framework tends to be high enough that synchronization is not expected to be a major issue. We therefore use absolute time encoding to specify lifetime. In future versions, the BizTalk Framework may support both kinds of lifetime encoding.*

7.3 Delivery Services

Reliable delivery services for a BizTalk Document are specified by an optional SOAP header entry marked by the <services> BizTag. A services header entry is shown below.

```
<services        xmlns="http://schemas.biztalk.org/btf-2-0/services"
                 xmlns:SOAP-ENV="http://schemas.xmlsoap.org/soap/envelope/"
                 xmlns:xsi="http://www.w3.org/1999/XMLSchema-instance"
                 xmlns:xsd="http://www.w3.org/2000/08/XMLSchema"
                 xmlns:agr="http://www.trading-agreements.org/types/"
                 SOAP-ENV:mustUnderstand="1">
    <deliveryReceiptRequest>
      <sendTo>
        <address xsi:type="agr:httpURL">
             http://www.we-love-books.org/receipts
        </address>
      </sendTo>
      <sendBy>2000-05-14T08:00:00+08:00</sendBy>
    </deliveryReceiptRequest>
    <commitmentReceiptRequest>
      <sendTo>
        <address xsi:type="agr:duns_number">11-111-1111</address>
      </sendTo>
```

```
      <sendBy>2000-05-14T10:00:00+08:00</sendBy>
    </commitmentReceiptRequest>
  </services>
```

When present, understanding and processing of the <services> header entry and all its contents at the recipient BFC server is always mandatory during successful processing of a BizTalk Document. The encoding of the <process> element must always contain the **SOAP-ENV:mustUnderstand="1"** attribute to reflect this.

The <deliveryReceiptRequest> is an optional element that requests reliable delivery of the enclosing BizTalk Document. If the <deliveryReceiptRequest> element is present, (the BFC server at) the destination business entity is required to send a delivery receipt back to the address given in the <sendTo> sub-element upon receiving and accepting the BizTalk Document. The Document-handling behavior related to this element and the structure and content of receipts is described in more detail in section 8.

The <commitmentReceiptRequest> is an optional element that requests an acknowledgement allowing the sender to determine the receiving business entity's decision regarding processing of the enclosing BizTalk Document. If the <commitmentReceiptRequest> element is present, (the BFC server at) the destination business entity is required to send a commitment receipt defining the (positive or negative) processing commitment back to the address given in the <sendTo> sub-element when it makes a decision regarding the processing of the BizTalk Document. The Document-handling behavior related to this element and the structure and content of receipts is described in more detail in section 8.

The <deliveryReceiptRequest> and <commitmentReceiptRequest> elements always contains the two sub-elements listed in the table below.

Tag Name	Mandatory	Kind	Type	Occurs
sendTo	Yes	element	uriReference	Once
sendBy	Yes	element	timeInstant	Once

The <sendTo> element contains an address sub-element that specifies the address (typically at the source business entity) to which the appropriate receipt for the BizTalk Document must be sent.

The <sendBy> element contains a time instant that specifies the absolute time by which the appropriate receipt for the BizTalk Document must be received by (the BFC server at) the source business entity. Failure to receive the receipt in time will typically initiate error-recovery behavior at the source.

See the Explanatory Note associated with the <expiresAt> tag for a discussion of the merits and pitfalls of the use of absolute time instants in this context. See section 8 for details of the reliability protocol, including the semantics of this deadline for each type of receipt.

7.4 Document Catalog

Document catalog information is specified by an optional SOAP header entry marked by the <manifest> BizTag; it may include (URI) references to both the Business Documents carried within the primary BizTalk Document in the BizTalk Message, as well as any additional attachments, such as images or binary data, that may be considered a part of the BizTalk Message, whether physically enclosed within the BizTalk Message or not. Details of the structure of references to the attachments that are carried within the BizTalk Message are dependent on MIME encoding rules and are discussed in section 9. An example of the manifest header entry taken from section 9.1 is shown below:

```
<fst:manifest xmlns:fst="http://schemas.biztalk.org/btf-2-0/manifest"
              SOAP-ENV:mustUnderstand="1">
     <fst:reference>
          <fst:document href="#insurance_claim_document_id">
          <fst:description>Insurance Claim</fst:description>
     </fst:reference>
     <fst:reference>
          <fst:attachment href="CID:claim.tiff@claiming-it.com">
          <fst:description>
               Facsimile of Signed Claim Document
          </fst:description>
     </fst:reference>
     <fst:reference>
          <fst:attachment href="CID:car.jpeg@claiming-it.com">
          <fst:description>Photo of Damaged Car</fst:description>
     </fst:reference>
</fst:manifest>
```

The manifest serves two primary purposes in the primary BizTalk Document in a BizTalk Message when the content of the Message consists of a multipart/related MIME package that includes one or more attachments as described in section 9.

The presence of the <manifest> header entry serves to mark the Document as part of a compound package. The presence of the <manifest> header entry is mandatory in this situation, and it must also be marked with a mustUnderstand attribute value of "1".

The contents of the <manifest> header entry allow the integrity of the compound package to be checked, for instance prior to acknowledgement with receipts: the header entry must catalog all attachments that are present in the enclosing BizTalk Message.

The <manifest> header entry, when present, may also optionally catalog the Business Documents carried in the enclosing BizTalk Document, and references to external resources, as described below.

The <manifest> element is a sequence of <reference> elements, as shown in the table below.

Tag Name	Mandatory	Kind	Type	Occurs
reference	yes	element	complexType	one or more times

Each <reference> element contains sub-elements containing a reference to an item in the BizTalk Message and optionally freeform text describing the item as shown in the following table:

Tag Name	Mandatory	Kind	Type	Occurs
document/ attachment	yes	element	SOAP reference	once
description	no	element	string	once

The actual reference to the item must be contained as the value of a SOAP **href** attribute in an element with one of two possible tags: <document> and <attachment>. The value of the href attribute must be a URI reference that resolves to the resource denoted by the enclosing <reference> element. More specifically,

- The <document> element must contain an href attribute whose value is a fragment identifier of the form #id that resolves to a Business Document within the enclosing BizTalk Document.
- The <attachment> element must contain an href attribute whose value is a URI reference that resolves to a resource outside the enclosing BizTalk Document. There are two cases for such resources:
  - An attachment within the enclosing BizTalk Message.
  - External resources, such as large files that are considered attachments, but whose content is not carried within the BizTalk Message itself.

The optional <description> element contains a text description of the Business Document or attachment. The content is mixed (text with and without XML markup). It may be used as a supporting comment, or as a keyword for additional implementation-specific processing or reporting requirements.

7.5 Process Management

Process-management information is specified by an optional SOAP header entry marked by the <process> BizTag that includes information about the business process that provides the processing context for the BizTalk Document. An example of the process header entry is shown next:

```
<prc:process SOAP-ENV:mustUnderstand="1"
                    xmlns:SOAP-ENV="http://schemas.xmlsoap.org/soap/envelope/"
                    xmlns:dtl="http://www.tradingagreements.org/process/detail/"
                    xmlns:eps="http://schemas.biztalk.org/btf-2-0/endpoints"
                    xmlns:prc="http://schemas.biztalk.org/btf-2-0/process">
    <prc:type>purchasing:Book_Purchase_Process</prc:type>
    <prc:instance>purchasing:Book_Purchase_Process#12345</prc:instance>
    <prc:detail>
        <dtl:targetPort>po_request</dtl:targetPort>
        <dtl:exceptionAddress>
            <eps:address
xsi:type="dtl:escrow">common_escrow_provider</eps:address>
        </dtl:exceptionAddress>
    </prc:detail>
</prc:process>
```

When present, understanding and processing of the <process> header entry and all its contents at the recipient BFC server is always mandatory during successful processing of a BizTalk Document. The encoding of the <process> element must always contain the **SOAP-ENV:mustUnderstand="1"** attribute to reflect this. The following table lists the BizTags used to construct the sub-elements of the <process> header entry and their properties:

Tag Name	Mandatory	Kind	Type	Occurs
type	yes	element	uriReference	once
instance	yes	element	uriReference	once
detail	no	element	anyType	once

The <type> element contains a URI reference that signifies the type of business process involved, for example, the process of purchasing a book. This is a pattern of interchange of (typically) multiple BizTalk Documents that is agreed upon among two or more business partners. The pattern defines the "rules of the game" and is usually repeated many times.

The <instance> element contains a URI reference that uniquely identifies a specific instance of the business process that this BizTalk Document is associated with (for example, an instance of the process of purchasing a book in which Booklovers Anonymous is in the process of purchasing a copy of Essential BizTalk). This is needed for correlation, as multiple instances of a given business process may be executing concurrently. A common way to construct this URI is to extend the URI for the process type with a fragment identifier signifying an instance—often a sequence number, as in the example above.

The <detail> element provides an extensibility point for further information that may be required to identify a step or an entry point within the business process instance, or other details such as response locations or exception handling directions. The contents of this element are implementation and application dependent.

8. Reliable Delivery of BizTalk Documents

BizTalk facilitates asynchronous document exchanges involved in e-commerce and Enterprise Application Integration, where specific delivery guarantees and error detection and reporting are necessary for integration of business functions across domain boundaries. High-performance-messaging middleware solutions for the Internet are emerging and should be used for this purpose when available. However, given the broad scope of deployment scenarios for BizTalk Framework-based application integration, and the continued use of transports with lower guarantees of service, it is important to provide a simple standard solution for reliable delivery of BizTalk Documents that can be easily implemented by BFC servers. Furthermore, standard business processes require confirmation not just of delivery and physical acceptance of a message, but also separately of verification of message content and intent to perform the business action requested.

The solution for both these requirements is described in the current section and is based on two simple notions:

- Document receipts.
- Idempotent delivery.

The overall purpose is to ensure a defined outcome for BizTalk Document delivery, acceptance and processing commitment. The following points summarize the ideas on which the functionality described here is based:

Delivery and commitment receipts provide a way for (the BFC server at) the source business entity to assure itself that the BizTalk Document was received and accepted (delivery receipt), or inspected for correctness of content and committed for processing (commitment receipt), using the identity for correlation.

- Given the possibility of multiple transmissions of the same BizTalk Document due to retry, (the BFC server at) the destination business entity may apply idempotent delivery rules to detect and eliminate duplicate Documents, again using the identity for correlation.

- If (the BFC server at) the source business entity does not receive a delivery receipt within the timeout period specified in the <sendBy> sub-element in the

<deliveryReceiptRequest> element, a delivery failure report will be generated and corrective action taken.

■ If (the BFC server at) the source business entity does not receive a commitment receipt within the timeout period specified in the <sendBy> sub-element in the <commitmentReceiptRequest> element, this is treated as being equivalent to receiving a negative commitment receipt with no additional detail.

Note that there is a small but finite possibility that the Document will be delivered to the destination business entity, verified and processed and a delivery and/or commitment failure report will nevertheless be generated at the source business entity, since any/all receipts may be lost due to transport failure.

The rest of this section describes the structure of a receipt document and the typical behavior of the source and destination business entities engaged in reliable delivery of BizTalk Documents. The details of actual behavior are implementation dependent and the description here is meant to serve as a guideline.

8.1 Structure and Content of Receipts

8.1.1 Delivery Receipts

A BizTalk Framework delivery receipt is a BizTalk Document that contains an additional <deliveryReceipt> header entry, and an empty body, as shown in the example below. Like all BizTalk Documents, the receipt has its own identity and expiration deadline. The expiration of the delivery receipt must coincide with the delivery deadline specified in the <sendBy> sub-element of the <deliveryReceiptRequest> element of the <services> header entry in the Document whose delivery is being acknowledged by this receipt.

The content of the receipt unambiguously identifies the BizTalk Document being acknowledged, by including the universally unique identity of the Document in the special <deliveryReceipt> header entry that distinguishes a receipt of this kind. A timestamp for the time at which the Document was received at the destination is also provided in the <deliveryReceipt> header entry.

The following receipt corresponds to the initial example in sections 7 and the <deliveryReceiptRequest> in section 7.3:

```
<SOAP-ENV:Envelope
    xmlns:SOAP-ENV="http://schemas.xmlsoap.org/soap/envelope"
    xmlns:xsd="http://www.w3.org/2000/08/XMLSchema"
    xmlns:xsi="http://www.w3.org/1999/XMLSchema-instance">
  <SOAP-ENV:Header>
    <endpoints SOAP-ENV:mustUnderstand="1"
               xmlns:ta="http://schemas.trading-agreements.com/"
               xmlns="http://schemas.biztalk.org/btf-2-0/endpoints">
```

```
    <to>
      <address xsi:type="ta:httpURL">
              http://www.we-love-books.org/receipts
      </address>
    </to>
    <from>
      <address xsi:type="ta:department">Book Orders</address>
    </from>
  </endpoints>
  <properties SOAP-ENV:mustUnderstand="1"
              xmlns="http://schemas.biztalk.org/btf-2-0/properties">
    <identity>uuid:24d304a0-b6e1-493a-b457-4b86c684d6f3</identity>
    <sentAt>2000-05-13T10:34:00-08:00</sentAt>
    <expiresAt>2000-05-14T08:00:00+08:00</expiresAt>
    <!-- expiration is at delivery deadline -->
    <topic>http://electrocommerce.org/delivery_receipt/</topic>
  </properties>
  <deliveryReceipt xmlns="http://schemas.biztalk.org/btf-2-0/receipts"
                   SOAP-ENV:mustUnderstand="1">
    <receivedAt>2000-05-13T10:04:00-08:00</receivedAt>
    <identity>uuid:74b9f5d0-33fb-4a81-b02b-5b760641c1d6</identity>
    <!—the above is the identity of the original message -->
  </deliveryReceipt>
 </SOAP-ENV:Header>
 <SOAP-ENV:Body/>
 <!-- the body is always empty in a delivery receipt -->
</SOAP-ENV:Envelope>
```

Understanding and processing of the <deliveryReceipt> header entry and all its contents at the recipient BFC server is always mandatory during successful processing of a receipt. The encoding of the <deliveryReceipt> element must always contain the **SOAP-ENV:mustUnderstand="1"** attribute to reflect this. The following table lists the BizTags used to construct the sub-elements of the <deliveryReceipt> header entry and their properties:

Tag Name	Mandatory	Kind	Type	Occurs
receivedAt	yes	element	timeInstant	Once

Tag Name	Mandatory	Kind	Type	Occurs
identity	yes	element	uriReference	Once

The <receivedAt> tag is the receiving timestamp for the Document acknowledged by this receipt. In the case of multiple copies of the BizTalk Document being received and accepted (see below for a discussion of the term "accepted"), the receiving timestamp may reflect either the time at which the first copy was received or the time at which the copy being acknowledged was received.

8.1.2 Commitment Receipts

A BizTalk Framework commitment receipt is a BizTalk Document that contains an additional <commitmentReceipt> header entry, as shown in the example below. Like all BizTalk Documents, the receipt has its own identity and expiration deadline. The expiration of the commitment receipt must coincide with the commitment deadline specified in the <sendBy> sub-element of the <commitmentReceiptRequest> element of the <services> header entry in the Document whose processing commitment is being acknowledged by this receipt.

The content of the receipt unambiguously identifies the BizTalk Document being acknowledged, by including the universally unique identity of the Document in the special <commitmentReceipt> header entry that distinguishes a receipt of this kind. A timestamp for the time at which the commitment to process the Document occurred is provided in the <commitmentReceipt> header entry.

The following receipt corresponds to the initial example in sections 7 and the <commitmentReceiptRequest> in section 7.3:

```
<SOAP-ENV:Envelope
    xmlns:SOAP-ENV="http://schemas.xmlsoap.org/soap/envelope"
    xmlns:xsd="http://www.w3.org/2000/08/XMLSchema"
    xmlns:xsi="http://www.w3.org/1999/XMLSchema-instance">
  <SOAP-ENV:Header>
    <endpoints SOAP-ENV:mustUnderstand="1"
            xmlns="http://schemas.biztalk.org/btf-2-0/endpoints"
            xmlns:ta="http://schemas.trading-agreements.com/">
      <to>
        <address xsi:type="ta:duns_number">11-111-1111</address>
      </to>
      <from>
        <address xsi:type="ta:department">Book Orders</address>
      </from>
    </endpoints>
    <properties SOAP-ENV:mustUnderstand="1"
```

```
                  xmlns="http://schemas.biztalk.org/btf-2-0/properties">
     <identity>uuid:1d394ac1-cadf-47cf-9a1e-aaa40531b97d</identity>
     <sentAt>2000-05-13T10:55:00-08:00</sentAt>
     <expiresAt>2000-05-14T10:00:00+08:00</expiresAt>
     <!-- expiration is at commitment deadline -->
     <topic>http://electrocommerce.org/commitment_receipt/</topic>
   </properties>
   <commitmentReceipt xmlns="http://schemas.biztalk.org/btf-2-0/receipts"
                      xmlns:cmt="http://schemas.electrocommerce.org/commitment/"
                      SOAP-ENV:mustUnderstand="1">
     <decidedAt>2000-05-13T10:44:00-08:00</decidedAt>
     <decision>negative</decision>
     <identity>uuid:74b9f5d0-33fb-4a81-b02b-5b760641c1d6</identity>
     <!-- the above is the identity of the original message -->
     <commitmentCode>cmt:outOfStock</commitmentCode>
     <commitmentDetail>
        <cmt:restockExpectedOn>2000-06-15</cmt:restockExpectedOn>
     </commitmentDetail>
   </commitmentReceipt>
 </SOAP-ENV:Header>
 <SOAP-ENV:Body/>
</SOAP-ENV:Envelope>
```

Understanding and processing of the <commitmentReceipt> header entry and all its contents at the recipient BFC server is always mandatory during successful processing of a receipt. The encoding of the <commitmentReceipt> element must always contain the SOAP-ENV:mustUnderstand="1" attribute to reflect this. The following table lists the BizTags used to construct the sub-elements of the <commitmentReceipt> header entry and their properties:

Tag Name	Mandatory	Kind	Type	Occurs
decidedAt	yes	element	timeInstant	once
decision	yes	element	positive/negative	once
identity	yes	element	uriReference	once
commitmentCode	no	element	QName	once
commitmentDetail	no	element	anyType	once

The <decidedAt> element contains the processing decision timestamp for the Document acknowledged by this receipt.

The <decision> element contains the actual decision, with possible values of positive or negative.

The <identity> element contains the identity of the Document to which the commitment decision applies.

The <commitmentCode> is an optional element that contains a qualified name (in the XSD sense [XSD1]) that specifies a more specific status regarding the processing decision—this is especially useful in the case of a negative decision and is then analogous to a fault code.

The <commitmentDetail> is an optional element that contains further details about the processing decision.

The content of the <commitmentCode> and <commitmentDetail> elements is application dependent. The <SOAP-ENV:Body> element of the commitment receipt may optionally contain one or more business documents referenced from the contents of the <commitmentDetail> element. The structure and interpretation of such documents is application dependent.

8.2 Endpoint Behavior for Reliable Delivery

This section describes guidelines for the behavior of (the BFC servers at) the source and destination business entities when engaged in reliable delivery of BizTalk Documents and Messages using the delivery receipt mechanism. However, this specification definitively specifies only wire-level behavior. Actual behavior at a business entity regarding transmission retry, duplicate removal, storage and archival of business documents and the management of durable storage resources is implementation dependent and does not affect compliance with this specification.

This section does not address the behavior of source and destination business entities regarding commitment receipts, since the semantics of commitment and the generation and handling of commitment receipts are strongly application dependent. The commitment receipt mechanism is meant to provide a standard framework within which such application-specific commitment semantics can be expressed at the wire level. Additional support for commitment receipts in BFC servers is entirely implementation specific.

8.2.1 Behavior of the Source Business Entity

In accordance with common practice, it is assumed that the BizTalk Document being transmitted has been persisted in durable storage at the source business entity. It is strongly recommended that persistence in durable storage occur before a BizTalk Document is transmitted in the case of Documents that require reliable delivery with a defined outcome.

The only special behavior required from a source business entity for reliable delivery of a BizTalk Document is to add an appropriate <deliveryReceiptRequest>

element to the <services> header entry, and to correlate and process the delivery receipt (as well as lack thereof within the deadline) appropriately. The following description is a guideline for heuristic retry behavior that is likely to increase the probability of successful delivery in the presence of unreliable transports. The only required behavior in the context of retries is that the content of the BizTalk Document including header entries must not be altered in any way for a retry. In particular, the content of the <sentAt> property must remain the same, that is, what it was set to for the first transmission attempt.

The retry behavior of the source business entity is typically based on a parameter: the retry interval. This parameter may be fixed or may be configurable for each business relationship or even each transport used in the context of a given relationship. There is typically also a maximum retry count. The basic behavior pattern is very simple. Keep transmitting the document to the destination business entity at a frequency determined by the retry interval until one of the following occurs:

- A receipt is received.
- The <sendBy> deadline in the <deliveryReceiptRequest> expires.
- The maximum retry count is exceeded.

At the end of this process, if a delivery receipt has not been received, and the <sendBy> deadline expires, the delivery of the BizTalk Document is said to have failed. Normal operating procedure if this occurs is to notify the source application in an appropriate way, for instance by placing a copy of the Document in a dead-letter queue, but this is clearly implementation dependent.

It is worth noting that retries need not occur over the same transport that was used for the first transmission attempt. If multiple transport endpoints are available for transmission to the destination business entity as specified in the <to> address in the <endpoints> header entry, new transport endpoints may be tried during retry attempts.

Actual implementations may use more elaborate algorithms for scalability and efficiency of resource use, as well as to account for peculiarities of the implementation context, such as intermittent connectivity.

8.2.2 Behavior of the Destination Business Entity

In accordance with common practice, it is assumed that, upon being accepted, each BizTalk Document will be persisted in durable storage at the destination business entity. It is strongly recommended that persistence in durable storage occur before a receipt is sent in the case of reliable delivery. In addition, idempotent delivery requires a minimum duration of archival for some information as noted below.

The only special behavior required from a destination business entity for reliable delivery of BizTalk Documents is to transmit a receipt for each accepted Document in which the <deliveryReceiptRequest> element of the <services> header entry is present. The receipt must be sent to the address specified in the <sendTo> sub-element. As defined in section 4.1, the term "accepted Document" in this case means the Document is recognized as being intended for an endpoint at the destination entity, including Documents that are copies or duplicates of previously received Documents (based on the identity). Documents that are received after the time instant specified in <expiresAt> is past are not accepted and must not be acknowledged with a receipt. Documents that are received after the time instant specified in the <sendBy> sub-element of the <deliveryReceiptRequest> is past but before the time instant specified in <expiresAt> is past *are* accepted and *must* be acknowledged with a receipt. The structure of receipts and the required correlation between a Document and its receipt has been described above.

A destination business entity may in addition perform idempotent delivery of BizTalk Documents to the target applications at its own end. This may be a part of the business process agreed upon between the parties involved, or an independent configuration parameter at the destination that is either constant or configurable for each business or service relationship. Idempotent delivery implies that a BizTalk Document received at a destination business entity is delivered exactly once to its intended recipient application, even when it is received multiple times due to transport behavior or transmission retries at the source.

The guideline for duplicate removal to achieve idempotent delivery, when required, is to archive in durable store all BizTalk Documents accepted, at least until they expire (that is until the time instant specified in <expiresAt> is past). It is actually sufficient to archive only the identity of the BizTalk Document, given the requirement that the identity must be universally unique. Note that the duplicate removal process needs to be applied only after a Document is accepted.

8.3 Delivery, Commitment, and Processing Deadlines

It is important to understand the distinct semantics of the three deadlines that may be associated with a BizTalk Document. The <sendBy> sub-element of <deliveryReceiptRequest> contains the *delivery deadline*, the <sendBy> sub-element of <commitmentReceiptRequest> contains the *commitment deadline*, and the content of the <expiresAt> property contains the *processing deadline*. Only the last one must be associated with every BizTalk Document, the others are optional. The reason for providing multiple deadlines is that business actions often require a nontrivial amount of time for commitment, and following commitment, for actual processing. If the action associated with a BizTalk Document is expected to take at most 4 hours to commit and process, and must be completed within 12 hours of transmission of the Document, then the delivery deadline for this Document must be 8 hours rather than 12 hours. This flexibility is required in designing realistic business processes. The semantics of the deadlines can be stated as follows:

- The delivery deadline concerns *acceptance* of the BizTalk Document by the destination business entity. The acceptance of a Document is described in section 8.2.2. Acknowledgement of acceptance must be received by the source business entity by the delivery deadline in the form of a delivery receipt.

■ The commitment deadline concerns *examination of content and verification of ability and willingness to process* the BizTalk Document by the destination business entity. The precise semantics of such commitment is application-specific. Acknowledgement of commitment must be received by the source business entity by the commitment deadline in the form of a commitment receipt.

■ The processing deadline is the point in time beyond which the BizTalk Document, if unprocessed, is null and void. The Document must not be delivered to an application for normal processing or acknowledged in any way by the destination business entity after this point in time.

The following points clarify what happens as each deadline expires:

When the delivery deadline expires:

■ The sending BFC server should notify the sending application if a delivery receipt has not been received. This alerts the sending application to the possibility that the receiving application may not have received the Document, or if it did, may not have enough time to process it.

■ There is no essential significance for the receiving BFC server. The receiving server continues to accept and acknowledge Documents past this deadline. This means that receipts may be generated and received past this deadline. In fact, the receiver has no absolute need to know the delivery deadline. However, if the receiving server does not know when the delivery receipt is expected, it may choose to delay sending the receipt for internal optimization reasons, causing unnecessary complications at the sender; or, being aware of these consequences, it may give the receipt transmission the highest possible priority reducing its possibilities for internal optimization. The delivery deadline serves as a useful priority hint to the receiver for sending the delivery receipt, which is especially useful in intermittent connection scenarios.

When the commitment deadline expires:

■ The sending BFC server must treat this as being equivalent to receiving a negative commitment receipt with no additional (<commitmentCode> and <commitmentDetail>) information. This alerts the sending application to the possibility that the receiving application may not have committed to processing the Document, or if it did, may not have enough time to process it.

■ The implication for the receiving BFC server is the same as in the case of expiration of the delivery deadline.

When the processing deadline expires:

- There is no special behavior recommended for the sending BFC server. The significance of expiration of this deadline at the source is entirely application-defined.

- The receiving BFC server should reject all Documents that arrive past the processing deadline. They should not be acknowledged with any kind of receipt and should not be delivered to any application for normal processing.

9. BizTalk Documents with Attachments

Business processes often require Business Documents to be transmitted together with attachments of various sorts, ranging from facsimile images of legal documents to engineering drawings. The attachments are often in some binary format. This section specifies the following:

A standard way to associate a primary BizTalk Document with one or more attachments in a multipart MIME structure for transport.

- The relationship between the MIME structure for attachments and the <manifest> header entry in the primary BizTalk Document.

Most Internet transports are capable of transporting MIME encoded content, although some special considerations are required for HTTP as described in the HTTP binding section.

9.1 Multipart MIME Structure

The compound content of a BizTalk Message, consisting of a primary BizTalk Document and one or more attachments, must be carried in a MIME structure that follows the rules for the multipart/related MIME media type as described in [MULTIPART].

The following example shows a BizTalk Document with two attachments that constitutes an automobile insurance claim. The primary BizTalk Document contains the claim data, and is transmitted along with a facsimile image of the signed claim form (Claim.tiff) and a digital photo of the damaged car (Car.jpeg).

```
MIME-Version: 1.0
Content-Type: Multipart/Related;
        boundary=biztalk_2_0_related_boundary_example;
        type=text/xml;
        start="<claim.xml@claiming-it.com>"
Content-Description: This is the optional message description.

--biztalk_2_0_related_boundary_example
```

```
Content-Type: text/xml; charset=UTF-8
Content-Transfer-Encoding: 8bit
Content-ID: <claim.xml@claiming-it.com>

<?xml version='1.0' ?>
<SOAP-ENV:Envelope
              xmlns:SOAP-ENV="http://schemas.xmlsoap.org/soap/envelope/">
    <SOAP-ENV:Header>
        <!-- endpoints and properties header entries omitted for brevity -->
         <manifest xmlns="http://schemas.biztalk.org/btf-2-0/manifest"
                  mustUnderstand="1">
            <reference>
                <document href="#insurance_claim_document_id"/>
                <description>Insurance Claim</description>
            </reference>
            <reference>
                <attachment href="CID:claim.tiff@claiming-it.com"/>
                <description>Facsimile of Signed Claim Document</description>
            </reference>
            <reference>
                <attachment href="CID:car.jpeg@claiming-it.com"/>
                <description>Photo of Damaged Car</description>
            </reference>
        </manifest>
    </SOAP-ENV:Header>
    <SOAP-ENV:Body>
        <claim:Insurance_Claim_Auto id="insurance_claim_document_id"
                       xmlns:claim="http://schemas.risky-stuff.com/Auto-Claim">
            <!-- ...claim details... -->
        </claim:Insurance_Claim_Auto>
    </SOAP-ENV:Body>
</SOAP-ENV:Envelope>

--biztalk_2_0_related_boundary_example
Content-Type: image/tiff
Content-Transfer-Encoding: base64
Content-ID: <claim.tiff@claiming-it.com>

   ...Base64 encoded TIFF image...

--biztalk_2_0_related_boundary_example
Content-Type: image/jpeg
```

```
Content-Transfer-Encoding: binary
Content-ID: <car.jpeg@claiming-it.com>

   ...Raw JPEG image...

--biztalk_2_0_related_boundary_example--
```

The rules for the structure of the <attachment> elements describing the attachments in the <manifest> header entry of the primary BizTalk Document are explained in the next section. The rules for the use of the multipart/related media type are given in [MULTIPART]. In addition, the primary BizTalk Document must be carried in the root part of the multipart/related structure. And furthermore, every part, including the root part, must be labeled with a Content-ID MIME header structured in accordance with [MIME1].

The use of a multipart/related container as described in this section is explicitly permitted even when the number of attachments to the root part is zero. This is a degenerate case with only a root part which can serve the purpose of insulating another more problematic content type from the transport layer, as discussed in section 10 which describes S/MIME security. It may also serve to precisely and unambiguously demarcate the content of the BizTalk Message for purposes such as non-repudiation receipts. The use of the <manifest> header entry in the primary BizTalk Document is not mandatory in this degenerate case.

9.2 Manifest Structure for Attachments

The relationship of the <reference> elements within the <manifest> header entry that denotes MIME part attachments is simple. Each such <reference> element contains an <attachment> sub-element, which contains a SOAP "href" attribute whose value is the location of the associated attachment in the form of the Content-ID URL based on the Content-ID of the MIME part that constitutes the attachment. The URL formed in accordance with the definition of Content-ID URLs in [CID].

10. Securing BizTalk Documents and Messages

Business processes very often require the ability to secure individual messages for authentication, integrity, non-repudiation or privacy. Transport-level mechanisms such as Secure Socket Layer (SSL) are sufficient for single-hop privacy and authentication but do not satisfy requirements for signing and encryption of individual messages and message parts for multi-hop transport and routing which is very common in business scenarios. The BizTalk Framework supports S/MIME version 3 described in [SMIME] for securing BizTalk Messages and their parts.

The entity being secured may be a BizTalk Document, an attachment, or an entire multipart/related MIME container structured according to section 9. Three securing modes are supported: enveloping (encryption) only, signing only, and both signing and encryption. These are applied according to the rules described in sections 3.3, 3.4 and 3.5 of [SMIME], respectively. More specifically, for signing, the BizTalk Framework only supports the detached signature (multipart/signed) mode, as described in section 3.4.3 of [SMIME].

It is worth noting that the combination of attachments, S/MIME support and the use of SOAP href attributes permits the header entries and Business Documents carried in a BizTalk message to be treated differently for encryption. This is often required when header entries must be in the clear for processing by intermediaries and infrastructure components, whereas Business Documents need to be encrypted with public keys whose private key counterparts cannot be made available to intermediaries and infrastructure components. The combination of features mentioned above makes it possible to place Business Documents in one or more attachments in encrypted form and place references to them in the body of the BizTalk Document, using the same URL form used in manifest header entries. The BizTalk Document can then be carried in the clear without compromising the privacy of the Business Documents. The following example shows how the insurance claim example in Section 9 might appear if the main XML claim document needed to be carried in encrypted form. The reference to the encrypted XML claim document in the Body of the BizTalk Document uses standard SOAP referencing, and is a simple mechanism to maintain a standard form for the BizTalk Document whether the claim document is embedded or referenced as an attachment. An empty Body element would be workable as well.

```
MIME-Version: 1.0
Content-Type: Multipart/Related;
        boundary=biztalk_2_0_related_boundary_example;
        type=text/xml;
        start="<claim.xml@claiming-it.com>"
Content-Description: This is the optional message description.

--biztalk_2_0_related_boundary_example
Content-Type: text/xml; charset=UTF-8
Content-Transfer-Encoding: 8bit
Content-ID: <claim.xml@claiming-it.com>

<?xml version='1.0' ?>
<SOAP-ENV:Envelope
              xmlns:SOAP-ENV="http://schemas.xmlsoap.org/soap/envelope/">
   <SOAP-ENV:Header>
      <!-- endpoints and properties header entries omitted for brevity -->
```

```
        <manifest xmlns="http://schemas.biztalk.org/btf-2-0/manifest"
                mustUnderstand="1">
            <reference>
                <attachment href="CID:insurance_claim@claiming-it.com">
                <description>Insurance Claim</description>
            </reference>
            <reference>
                <attachment href="CID:claim.tiff@claiming-it.com">
                <description>Facsimile of Signed Claim Document</description>
            </reference>
            <reference>
                <attachment href="CID:car.jpeg@claiming-it.com">
                <description>Photo of Damaged Car</description>
        </reference>
        </manifest>
    </SOAP-ENV:Header>
    <SOAP-ENV:Body>
        <claim:Insurance_Claim_Auto href="CID:insurance_claim@claiming-it.com"
                        xmlns:claim="http://schemas.risky-stuff.com/Auto-Claim">
    </SOAP-ENV:Body>
</SOAP-ENV:Envelope>

--biztalk_2_0_related_boundary_example
Content-Type: application/pkcs7-mime; smime-type=enveloped-data;
          name=smime.p7m
Content-Transfer-Encoding: base64
Content-Description: encrypted claim document
Content-Disposition: attachment; filename=smime.p7m
Content-ID:<insurance_claim@claiming-it.com>

rfvbnj756tbBghyHhHUujhJhjH77n8HHGT9HG4VQpfyF467GhIGfHfYT6
7n8HHGghyHhHUujhJh4VQpfyF467GhIGfHfYGTrfvbnjT6jH7756tbB9H
f8HHGTrfvhJhjH776tbB9HG4VQbnj7567GhIGfHfYT6ghyHhHUujpfyF4
0GhIGfHfQbnj756YT64V

--biztalk_2_0_related_boundary_example
Content-Type: image/tiff
Content-Transfer-Encoding: base64
Content-ID: <claim.tiff@claiming-it.com>
```

```
   ...Base64 encoded TIFF image

--biztalk_2_0_related_boundary_example
Content-Type: image/jpeg
Content-Transfer-Encoding: binary
Content-ID: <car.jpeg@claiming-it.com>

   ...Raw JPEG image

--biztalk_2_0_related_boundary_example--
```

10.1 S/MIME Packaging

There are two kinds of BizTalk Framework entities which can be secured with S/MIME:

- A BizTalk Document, which may have attachments, and in that case it is S/MIME secured separately from the attachments and carried in S/MIME encoded form in the root part of the multipart package.

- An entire multipart package consisting of a primary BizTalk Document and one or more attachments, where the primary BizTalk Document is in text/xml form and has not been secured with S/MIME.

Since an attachment to a BizTalk Document is a completely arbitrary entity, this specification does not mandate any restrictions on what encoding, including S/MIME encoding, may have been applied to it.

In both cases, the BizTalk Framework mandates that the outermost content type of the resulting secured entity must either be multipart/related or the entity must be suitably wrapped to make it so. The multipart/related content type results naturally in the case where a BizTalk Document is secured independently of one or more attachments. In the other two cases, where either an unattached BizTalk Document or a package consisting of a BizTalk Document with attachments is secured as a whole with S/MIME, the result is an S/MIME specific content type, which must be further wrapped in a degenerate multipart/related container with only a root part. This restriction is meant to permit only two top level content types for BizTalk Messages: text/xml and multipart/related, which have very simple semantics and are compatible with both HTTP and SMTP without difficulty. S/MIME content types carried directly over SMTP may sometimes be subject to premature S/MIME decoding by mail agents. The application/pkcs7-mime content-type used for S/MIME encrypted entities is almost always accompanied with headers such as content-disposition and content-transfer-encoding that are incompatible with HTTP.

The following example shows the (unattached) BizTalk Document from section 5 secured with a detached signature, and wrapped in a degenerate multipart/related container for transport.

```
MIME-Version: 1.0
Content-Type: Multipart/Related;
        boundary=biztalk_2_0_related_boundary_example;
        type=multipart/signed

--biztalk_2_0_related_boundary_example
Content-Type: Multipart/Signed;
                protocol="application/pkcs7-signature";
                micalg=sha1; boundary=smime-boundary-1234

--smime-boundary-1234
<SOAP-ENV:Envelope
                xmlns:SOAP-ENV="http://schemas.xmlsoap.org/soap/envelope/"
                xmlns:xsi="http://www.w3.org/1999/XMLSchema-instance">
    <SOAP-ENV:Header>
      <eps:endpoints SOAP-ENV:mustUnderstand="1"
                xmlns:eps="http://schemas.biztalk.org/btf-2-0/endpoints"
                xmlns:agr="http://www.trading-agreements.org/types/">
        <eps:to>
            <eps:address xsi:type="agr:department">Book Orders</eps:address>
        </eps:to>
        <eps:from>
            <eps:address xsi:type="agr:organization">Book Lovers</eps:address>
        </eps:from>
      </eps:endpoints>
      <prop:properties SOAP-ENV:mustUnderstand="1"
                xmlns:prop="http://schemas.biztalk.org/btf-2-0/properties">
        <prop:identity>uuid:74b9f5d0-33fb-4a81-b02b5b760641c1d6</prop:identity>
        <prop:sentAt>2000-05-14T03:00:00+08:00</prop:sentAt>
        <prop:expiresAt>2000-05-15T04:00:00+08:00</prop:expiresAt>
        <prop:topic>http://electrocommerce.org/purchase_order/</prop:topic>
      </prop:properties>
    </SOAP-ENV:Header>
    <SOAP-ENV:Body>
      <po:PurchaseOrder xmlns:po="http://electrocommerce.org/purchase_order/">
```

```
            <po:Title>Essential BizTalk</po:Title>
        </po:PurchaseOrder>
    </SOAP-ENV:Body>
</SOAP-ENV:Envelope>
--smime-boundary-1234
Content-Type: application/pkcs7-signature; name=smime.p7s
Content-Transfer-Encoding: base64
Content-Disposition: attachment; filename=smime.p7s

 .. base64 encoded detached signature

--smime-boundary-1234--
--biztalk_2_0_related_boundary_example--
```

11. Transport Bindings

11.1 HTTP Binding

This section describes the usage of the HTTP protocol for carrying BizTalk Documents, with or without attachments.

HTTP is a request/response protocol, whereas the BizTalk Framework architecture is based on asynchronous messaging. The HTTP resource being accessed as the target of a BizTalk Message is always assumed to be a message transfer agent, in the sense that the resource is not necessarily a SOAP processor as defined in the SOAP 1.1 specification, or a BFC Server as defined in this one. The meaning and contents of the HTTP response therefore only reflect the results of the attempted transfer of custody of the Message to the message transfer agent. Specifically, a successful response (2xx status code) does not necessarily imply the following:

The Message and its primary BizTalk Document have been accepted by the destination business entity in the sense of section 8.2.2.

or

The integrity and namespace validity of the SOAP envelope have been verified.

This is because the message transfer agent is in general distinct from the destination business entity—for instance it may be an HTTP server forwarding messages to that entity through a message queuing arrangement.

The HTTP binding described here is a special case of the SOAP 1.1 HTTP binding and extends the latter in describing the use of the multipart/related MIME media type for carrying attachments with SOAP messages. All rules of the SOAP 1.1 HTTP binding apply to the simple case of plain BizTalk Documents (which are SOAP messages) being carried over HTTP. The rules for message structure differ from SOAP 1.1 for BizTalk Documents with attachments, as described below. Note that the HTTP binding described here does not use the SOAP remote procedure call (RPC) or synchronous request/response pattern. In particular, receipt messages generated as a part of the reliable delivery mechanism described in section 8 are always independent messages sent as HTTP requests. They are never delivered in the HTTP response corresponding to the HTTP request in which the BizTalk Document being acknowledged was carried.

The rules regarding HTTP status codes in the HTTP response apply regardless of the presence of attachments. Specifically, in the common asynchronous case where the HTTP (success) response is returned before the document has been processed, status code 202 accepted must be used. It is possible and permissible to delay the response until the document has been processed; in those cases, the HTTP response status code will provide more definitive information regarding the outcome, in accordance with SOAP 1.1 rules. Specifically, status code 200 may only be used after the receiver, or downstream processors to which processing may be delegated in full or in part, have fully examined the document, determined that all mandatory headers are in fact understood, and performed the actions indicated by the message contents. In other words, after the BizTalk Message has been processed.

11.1.1 Example of a Simple BizTalk Message

The following example shows the BizTalk Document from the initial example being carried as part of an HTTP message using the POST verb.

```
POST /bookPurchase HTTP/1.1
Host: www.we-have-books.com
Content-Type: text/xml; charset="utf-8"
Content-Length: nnnn
SOAPAction: "http://electrocommerce.org/purchase_order/"

<?xml version='1.0' ?>
<SOAP-ENV:Envelope
            xmlns:SOAP-ENV="http://schemas.xmlsoap.org/soap/envelope/"
            xmlns:xsi="http://www.w3.org/1999/XMLSchema-instance">
    <SOAP-ENV:Header>
      <eps:endpoints SOAP-ENV:mustUnderstand="1"
                xmlns:eps="http://schemas.biztalk.org/btf-2-0/endpoints"
                xmlns:agr="http://www.trading-agreements.org/types/">
        <eps:to>
          <eps:address xsi:type="agr:department">
              Book Order Department
          </eps:address>
        </eps:to>
        <eps:from>
          <eps:address xsi:type="agr:organization">
```

```
                    Booklovers Anonymous
            </eps:address>
        </eps:from>
    </eps:endpoints>
    <prop:properties SOAP-ENV:mustUnderstand="1"
                xmlns:prop="http://schemas.biztalk.org/btf-2-0/properties">
        <prop:identity>uuid:74b9f5d0-33fb-4a81-b02b5b760641c1d6</prop:identity>
        <prop:sentAt>2000-05-14T03:00:00+08:00</prop:sentAt>
        <prop:expiresAt>2000-05-15T04:00:00+08:00</prop:expiresAt>
        <prop:topic>http://electrocommerce.org/purchase_order/</prop:topic>
    </prop:properties>
    </SOAP-ENV:Header>
    <SOAP-ENV:Body>
        <po:PurchaseOrder xmlns:po="http://electrocommerce.org/purchase_order/">
            <po:Title>Essential BizTalk</po:Title>
        </po:PurchaseOrder>
    </SOAP-ENV:Body>
</SOAP-ENV:Envelope>
```

This case falls squarely within the domain of the HTTP binding rules of SOAP 1.1 since the BizTalk Message payload consists of a single SOAP message.

The only rule in addition to SOAP 1.1 is the correlation for the SOAPAction HTTP header. The value of this header must be the URI reference contained in the mandatory <topic> element in the mandatory <properties> header entry.

11.1.2 Example of a BizTalk Message Including Attachments

```
POST /insuranceClaims HTTP/1.1
Host: www.risky-stuff.com
Content-Type: Multipart/Related;
        boundary=biztalk_2_0_related_boundary_example;
        type=text/xml;
        start="<claim.xml@claiming-it.com>"
Content-Length: nnnn
SOAPAction: "http://schemas.risky-stuff.com/Auto-Claim"
Content-Description: This is the optional message description.

--biztalk_2_0_related_boundary_example
Content-Type: text/xml; charset=UTF-8
Content-Transfer-Encoding: 8bit
Content-ID: <claim.xml@claiming-it.com>
```

```
<?xml version='1.0' ?>
<SOAP-ENV:Envelope
            xmlns:SOAP-ENV="http://schemas.xmlsoap.org/soap/envelope/"
            xmlns:xsi="http://www.w3.org/1999/XMLSchema-instance"
            xmlns:xsd="http://www.w3.org/2000/08/XMLSchema-datatypes">
    <SOAP-ENV:Header  xmlns:agr="http://www.trading-agreements.org/types/">
        <!-- manifest header entry omitted for brevity -->
        <endpoints SOAP-ENV:mustUnderstand="1"
                xmlns="http://schemas.biztalk.org/btf-2-0/endpoints">
          <to>
            <address xsi:type="agr:dept">insurance_claim_department</address>
          </to>
          <from>
            <address xsi:type="agr:agent">agent:/WA/Issaquah#id=12345</address>
          </from>
        </endpoints>
        <prop:properties SOAP-ENV:mustUnderstand="1"
                    xmlns:prop="http://schemas.biztalk.org/btf-2-0/properties">
          <!-- other elements omitted for brevity -->
          <topic>http://schemas.risky-stuff.com/Auto-Claim</topic>
        </prop:properties>
    </SOAP-ENV:Header>
    <SOAP-ENV:Body>
        <Insurance_Claim_Auto xmlns="http://schemas.risky-stuff.com/Auto-Claim"
                        id="insurance_claim_document_id">
            <!-- ...claim details... -->
        </Insurance_Claim_Auto>
    </SOAP-ENV:Body>
</SOAP-ENV:Envelope>

--biztalk_2_0_related_boundary_example
Content-Type: image/tiff
Content-Transfer-Encoding: base64
Content-ID: <claim.tiff@claiming-it.com>

   ...Base 64 encoded TIFF image

--biztalk_2_0_related_boundary_example
Content-Type: image/jpeg
Content-Transfer-Encoding: binary
Content-ID: <car.jpeg@claiming-it.com>
```

APPENDIX

```
...Raw JPEG image

--biztalk_2_0_related_boundary_example--
```

The basic approach to carrying multipart MIME structure in an HTTP message in this specification is to use the multipart media type header to the HTTP level, and treat it as a native HTTP header. The rules for forming a BizTalk Message in the case of a BizTalk Document with attachments, encoded in a multipart/related MIME structure according to section 9.1, are as follows.

- The Content-Type: multipart/related MIME header must appear as an HTTP header. The rules for parameters of this header specified in section 9.1 apply here as well.

- No other headers with semantics defined by MIME specifications (such as Content-Transfer-Encoding) are permitted to appear as HTTP headers. Specifically, the MIME-Version: 1.0 header must not appear as an HTTP header. Note that HTTP itself uses many MIME-like headers with semantics defined by HTTP 1.1. These may, of course, appear freely.

- The MIME parts containing the primary BizTalk Document and the attachments constitute the HTTP entity body and must appear exactly as described in section 9.1, including appropriate MIME headers.

11.2 SMTP Binding

In comparison with the HTTP binding there is far less that needs to be specified for the SMTP binding. SMTP is an asynchronous transfer protocol, in consonance with the asynchronous messaging model of the BizTalk Framework, so there are no response messages that need to be specified. There is no native SMTP binding yet defined for SOAP 1.1, and there are no SOAP-specific headers defined for SMTP, unlike HTTP. SMTP is completely compatible with MIME and fully supports MIME semantics, which are indeed intended for use primarily with SMTP. The content-type of text/xml is used for unsecured and unattached BizTalk Documents, and the content-type of multipart/related is used in all other cases, including BizTalk entities secured with S/MIME, as described in section 10.1. Since XML documents often use 7-bit incompatible charsets such as UTF-8 or UTF-16, a suitable content-transfer-encoding such as bin64 or quoted-printable may be applied when the message is likely to be carried over mail infrastructure that is only capable of carrying 7-bit textual content.

12. References

12.1 Normative References

Each BizTalk Framework document lists the existing or emerging Internet standards that it is built upon as normative references. Some of the content of the normative references may need to be reproduced for expository purposes in BizTalk Framework specifications. In all such cases, the normative references are authoritative. Every effort has been made to avoid discrepancies between the normative references and their usage in BizTalk Framework specifications. However, if a discrepancy is found, the normative reference provides the correct interpretation and the BizTalk Framework specification is in need of correction.

The following specifications are normative for this specification:

- [XML] Extensible Markup Language (XML) 1.0: http://www.w3.org/TR/1998/REC-xml-19980210.
- [SOAP] Simple Object Access Protocol (SOAP) Version 1.1: http://www.w3.org/TR/SOAP.
- [XMLNS] Namespaces in XML: http://www.w3.org/TR/1999/REC-xml-names-19990114.
- [URL] Uniform Resource Identifiers (URI): Generic Syntax: http://www.ietf.org/rfc/rfc2396.txt.
- [ISO8601] ISO 8601: Representations of dates and times: http://www.iso.ch/markete/8601.pdf.
- [HTTP] Hypertext Transfer Protocol—HTTP/1.1: http://www.ietf.org/rfc/rfc2616.txt.
- [XML-MIME] XML Media Types: http://www.ietf.org/rfc/rfc2376.txt.
- [MULTIPAR] The MIME Multipart/Related Content-type: http://www.ietf.org/rfc/rfc2387.txt.
- [MIME1] MIME Part One: Format of Internet Message Bodies: http://www.ietf.org/rfc/rfc2045.txt.
- [MIME2] MIME Part Two: Media Types: http://www.ietf.org/rfc/rfc2046.txt.
- [MIME3] MIME Part Three: Message Header Extensions for Non-ASCII Text: http://www.ietf.org/rfc/rfc2047.txt.
- [MIME4] MIME Part Four: Registration Procedures: http://www.ietf.org/rfc/rfc2048.txt.
- [SMIME] S/MIME Version 3 Message Specification: http://www.ietf.org/rfc/rfc2633.txt.

- [CID] Content-ID and Message-ID Uniform Resource Locators: http://www.ietf.org/rfc/rfc2111.txt.

12.2 Non-Normative References

The following specifications have had an influence on this specification, but the relationship is not foundational and their content is not normative for this specification:

- [XDR] XML-Data Reduced (XDR): http://www.ltg.ed.ac.uk/~ht/XMLData-Reduced.htm.
- [XSD1] XML Schema Part 1: Structures: http://www.w3.org/TR/xmlschema-1.
- [XSD2] XML Schema Part 2: Data types: http://www.w3.org/TR/xmlschema-2.
- [XP] XML Protocol: http://www.w3.org/2000/xp/.

Appendix A. BizTalk Document Schemas

A.1 XDR Schemas

A.1.1 Endpoints header entry

```xml
<?xml version="1.0" ?>
<!--
   BizTalk Framework 2.0
   BizTalk Document Schema: endpoints header entry
   Copyright 2000 Microsoft Corporation
-->
<Schema
   name="biztalk_2_0_endpoints.xml"
   xmlns="urn:schemas-microsoft-com:xml-data"
   xmlns:dt="urn:schemas-microsoft-com:datatypes"
   xmlns:SOAP-ENV="http://schemas.xmlsoap.org/soap/envelope/"
   xmlns:xsi="http://www.w3.org/1999/XMLSchema-instance">

   <!-- endpoints header entry element -->
   <ElementType name="endpoints" content="eltOnly">
      <attribute type="SOAP-ENV:mustUnderstand" default="1"
required="yes"/>
      <element type="to"            minOccurs="1" maxOccurs="1"/>
      <element type="from"          minOccurs="1" maxOccurs="1"/>
```

```
  </ElementType>

  <ElementType name="to" content="eltOnly" >
      <element type="address"          minOccurs="1" maxOccurs="1"/>
  </ElementType>

  <ElementType name="from" content="eltOnly">
      <element type="address"          minOccurs="1" maxOccurs="1"/>
  </ElementType>

  <ElementType name="address" content="textOnly" dt:type="string">
        <attribute type="xsi:type" required="yes"/>
  </ElementType>
</Schema>
```

A.1.2 Properties header entry

```
<?xml version="1.0" ?>

<!--
   BizTalk Framework 2.0
   BizTalk Document Schema: properties header entry
   Copyright 2000 Microsoft Corporation
-->

<Schema
   name="biztalk_2_0_properties.xml"
   xmlns="urn:schemas-microsoft-com:xml-data"
   xmlns:dt="urn:schemas-microsoft-com:datatypes"
   xmlns:xsi="http://www.w3.org/1999/XMLSchema-instance"
   xmlns:SOAP-ENV="http://schemas.xmlsoap.org/soap/envelope/">

   <ElementType name="properties" content="eltOnly">
        <attribute type ="SOAP-ENV:mustUnderstand" default="1"
required="yes"/>
        <element type="identity"         minOccurs="1" maxOccurs="1"/>
        <element type="sentAt"           minOccurs="1" maxOccurs="1"/>
        <element type="expiresAt"        minOccurs="1" maxOccurs="1"/>
        <element type="topic"            minOccurs="1" maxOccurs="1"/>
    </ElementType>
```

```
<ElementType name="identity" content="textOnly" dt:type="uri"/>
<ElementType name="sentAt" content="textOnly" dt:type="dateTime.tz"/>
<ElementType name="expiresAt" content="textOnly" dt:type="dateTime.tz"/>
<ElementType name="topic" content="textOnly" dt:type="uri"/>

</Schema>
```

A.1.3 Services header entry

```
<?xml version="1.0" ?>
<!--
    BizTalk Framework 2.0
    BizTalk Document Schema: services header entry
    Copyright 2000 Microsoft Corporation
-->
<Schema
    name="biztalk_2_0_services.xml"
    xmlns="urn:schemas-microsoft-com:xml-data"
    xmlns:dt="urn:schemas-microsoft-com:datatypes">

    <!-- services header entry element -->
    <ElementType name="services" content="eltOnly">
        <element type="deliveryReceiptRequest"     minOccurs="0" maxOccurs="1"/>
        <element type="commitmentReceiptRequest"   minOccurs="0" maxOccurs="1"/>
    </ElementType>

    <ElementType name="deliveryReceiptRequest" content="eltOnly" >
        <element type="sendTo"      minOccurs="1" maxOccurs="1"/>
        <element type="sendBy"      minOccurs="1" maxOccurs="1"/>
    </ElementType>

    <ElementType name="commitmentReceiptRequest" content="eltOnly" >
        <element type="sendTo"      minOccurs="1" maxOccurs="1"/>
        <element type="sendBy"      minOccurs="1" maxOccurs="1"/>
    </ElementType>

    <ElementType name="address" content="textOnly" dt:type="string">
        <attribute type="xsi:type" required="yes"/>
    </ElementType>

    <ElementType name="sendTo" content="eltOnly">
```

```
        <element type="address"           minOccurs="1" maxOccurs="1"/>
    </ElementType>
    <ElementType name="sendBy" content="textOnly" dt:type="dateTime.tz"/>
</Schema>
```

A.1.4 Manifest header entry

```
<?xml version="1.0" ?>
<!--
   BizTalk Framework 2.0
   BizTalk Document Schema: manifest header entry
   Copyright 2000 Microsoft Corporation
-->
<Schema
    name="biztalk_2_0_manifest.xml"
    xmlns="urn:schemas-microsoft-com:xml-data"
    xmlns:dt="urn:schemas-microsoft-com:datatypes">

   <ElementType name="manifest" content="eltOnly">
      <element type="reference" minOccurs="1" maxOccurs="*"/>
   </ElementType>

   <ElementType name="reference" content="eltOnly">
      <group minOccurs="1" maxOccurs="1" order="one">
         <element type="document">
         <element type="attachment">
      </group>
      <element type="description" minOccurs="0" maxOccurs="1"/>
   </ElementType>

   <ElementType name="document" content="eltOnly">
      <attribute type="href" required="yes"/>
   </ElementType>

   <ElementType name="attachment" content="eltOnly">
        <attribute type="href" required="yes"/>
   </ElementType>

   <AttributeType name="href" dt:type="uri"/>

   <ElementType name="description" content="mixed"/>
```

```
</Schema>
```

A.1.5 Process header entry

```
<?xml version="1.0" ?>

<!--
   BizTalk Framework 2.0
   BizTalk Document Schema: process header entry
   Copyright 2000 Microsoft Corporation
-->

<Schema
   name="biztalk_2_0_process.xml"
   xmlns="urn:schemas-microsoft-com:xml-data"
   xmlns:dt="urn:schemas-microsoft-com:datatypes"
   xmlns:SOAP-ENV="http://schemas.xmlsoap.org/soap/envelope/">

   <ElementType name="process" content="eltOnly">
      <attribute type="SOAP-ENV:mustUnderstand" default="1" required="yes"/>
      <element type="type"         minOccurs="1" maxOccurs="1"/>
      <element type="instance"     minOccurs="1" maxOccurs="1"/>
      <element type="detail"       minOccurs="0" maxOccurs="1"/>
   </ElementType>

   <ElementType name="type" content="textOnly" dt:type="uri"/>
   <ElementType name="instance" content="textOnly" dt:type="uri"/>
   <ElementType name="detail" content="eltOnly" model="open"/>

</Schema>
```

A.1.6 deliveryReceipt header entry

```
<?xml version="1.0" ?>

<!--
   BizTalk Framework 2.0
   BizTalk Document Schema: receipt header entry
```

```
    Copyright 2000 Microsoft Corporation
-->

<Schema
    name="biztalk_2_0_process_receipt_header.xml"
    xmlns="urn:schemas-microsoft-com:xml-data"
    xmlns:dt="urn:schemas-microsoft-com:datatypes"
    xmlns:SOAP-ENV="http://schemas.xmlsoap.org/soap/envelope/">

    ElementType name="deliveryReceipt" content="eltOnly">
        <attribute type="SOAP-ENV:mustUnderstand" default="1" required="yes"/>
        <element type="receivedAt" minOccurs="1" maxOccurs="1"/>
        <element type="identity" minOccurs="1" maxOccurs="1"/>
    </ElementType>

    <ElementType name="receivedAt" content="textOnly" dt:type="dateTime.tz"/>
    <ElementType name="identity" content="textOnly" dt:type="uri"/>

</Schema>
```

A.1.7 commitmentReceipt header entry

```
<?xml version="1.0" ?>

<!--
    BizTalk Framework 2.0
    BizTalk Document Schema: receipt header entry
    Copyright 2000 Microsoft Corporation
-->

<Schema
    name="biztalk_2_0_process_receipt_header.xml"
    xmlns="urn:schemas-microsoft-com:xml-data"
    xmlns:dt="urn:schemas-microsoft-com:datatypes"
    xmlns:SOAP-ENV="http://schemas.xmlsoap.org/soap/envelope/">

    <ElementType name="commitmentReceipt" content="eltOnly">
        <attribute type="SOAP-ENV:mustUnderstand" default="1" required="yes"/>
        <element type="identity" minOccurs="1" maxOccurs="1"/>
        <element type="decidedAt" minOccurs="1" maxOccurs="1"/>
        <element type="decision" minOccurs="1" maxOccurs="1"/>
```

```
      <element type="commitmentCode" minOccurs="0" maxOccurs="1"/>
      <element type="commitmentDetail" minOccurs="0" maxOccurs="1"/>
   </ElementType>

   <ElementType name="identity" content="textOnly" dt:type="uri"/>
   <ElementType name="decidedAt" content="textOnly" dt:type="dateTime.tz"/>
   <ElementType name="decision" content="textOnly" dt:type="string"/>
   <ElementType name="commitmentCode" content="textOnly" dt:type="string"/>
   <ElementType name="commitmentDetail" content="eltOnly" model="open"/>

</Schema>
```

A.1.8 SOAP 1.1 Envelope for BizTalk Document

```
<?xml version="1.0" ?>
<!--
   BizTalk Framework 2.0
   BizTalk Document Schema: envelope
   Copyright 2000 Microsoft Corporation

   This schema is based on the SOAP 1.1 schema
-->

<Schema
   name="biztalk_2_0_document_envelope.xml"
   xmlns="urn:schemas-microsoft-com:xml-data"
   xmlns:dt="urn:schemas-microsoft-com:datatypes">

  <!--
     SOAP envelope, header and body
  -->

  <ElementType name="Envelope" content="eltOnly">
     <element type="Header" minOccurs="1" maxOccurs="1"/>
     <element type="Body" minOccurs="1" maxOccurs="1"/>
  </ElementType>

  <ElementType name="Header" content="eltOnly" model="open"
               xmlns:eps="http://schemas.biztalk.org/btf-2-0/endpoints"
               xmlns:prop="http://schemas.biztalk.org/btf-2-0/properties"
               xmlns:fst="http://schemas.biztalk.org/btf-2-0/manifest"
```

```
                    xmlns:prc="http://schemas.biztalk.org/btf-2-0/process">
    <element type="eps:endpoints"        minOccurs="1" maxOccurs="1"/>
    <element type="prop:properties"      minOccurs="1" maxOccurs="1"/>
    <element type="fst:services"         minOccurs="0" maxOccurs="1"/>
    <element type="fst:manifest"         minOccurs="0" maxOccurs="1"/>
    <element type="prc:process"          minOccurs="0" maxOccurs="1"/>
</ElementType>

<ElementType name="Body" content="eltOnly" model="open"/>

 <!--
     Global Attributes.  The following attributes are intended
     to be usable via qualified attribute names on any Element type
     referencing them.
-->
 <AttributeType name="mustUnderstand" default="0" dt:type="Boolean"/>
 <AttributeType name="actor" dt:type="uri"/>

<!--
     'encodingStyle' indicates any canonicalization conventions followed
     in the contents of the containing element.  For example, the value
     'http://schemas.xmlsoap.org/soap/encoding/' indicates
     the pattern described in SOAP specification.
-->
 <AttributeType name="encodingStyle" dt:type="string"/>

<!--
   SOAP fault reporting structure
-->
<ElementType name="Fault" content="eltOnly">
    <element type="faultcode" minOccurs="1" maxOccurs="1"/>
    <element type="faultstring" minOccurs="1" maxOccurs="1"/>
    <element type="faultactor" minOccurs="0" maxOccurs="1"/>
    <element type="detail" minOccurs="0" maxOccurs="1"/>
</ElementType>

<ElementType name="faultcode" content="textOnly" dt:type="string"/>
<ElementType name="faultstring" content="textOnly" dt:type="string"/>
<ElementType name="faultactor" content="textOnly" dt:type="uri"/>

<ElementType name="detail" content="eltOnly" model="open"/>
```

```
</Schema>
```

A.2 XSD Schemas

A.2.1 Endpoints Header Entry

```xml
<?xml version="1.0" ?>
<schema xmlns="http://www.w3.org/2000/08/XMLSchema"
        xmlns:xsi="http://www.w3.org/1999/XMLSchema-instance"
        xmlns:tns="http://schemas.biztalk.org/btf-2-0/endpoints"
        targetNamespace="http://schemas.biztalk.org/btf-2-0/endpoints"
        xmlns:SOAP-ENV="http://schemas.xmlsoap.org/soap/envelope/"
        xmlns:SOAP-ENC="http://schemas.xmlsoap.org/soap/encoding/"
        elementFormDefault="qualified"
        attributeFormDefault="qualified">
    <annotation>
      <documentation>
        BizTalk Framework 2.0
        BizTalk Document Schema: endpoints header entry
        Copyright 2000 Microsoft Corporation
      </documentation>
    </annotation>
    <element name="endpoints" type="tns:endpoints"/>
    <complexType name="endpoints">
      <attribute ref="SOAP-ENV:mustUnderstand" use="required" value="1" />
      <sequence>
        <element name="to" type="tns:endpoint"/>
        <element name="from" type="tns:endpoint"/>
      </sequence>
    </complexType>

    <complexType name="endpoint">
      <element name="address" type="tns:address"/>
    </complexType>

    <complexType name="address">
      <simpleContent>
        <extension base="string">
          <attribute ref="xsi:type" use="required"/>
        </extension>
```

```
            </simpleContent>
        </complexType>
</schema>
```

A.2.2 Properties Header Entry

```xml
<?xml version="1.0" ?>
<schema xmlns="http://www.w3.org/2000/08/XMLSchema"
        xmlns:xsi="http://www.w3.org/1999/XMLSchema-instance"
        xmlns:tns="http://schemas.biztalk.org/btf-2-0/properties"
        targetNamespace="http://schemas.biztalk.org/btf-2-0/properties"
        xmlns:SOAP-ENV="http://schemas.xmlsoap.org/soap/envelope/"
        xmlns:SOAP-ENC="http://schemas.xmlsoap.org/soap/encoding/"
        elementFormDefault="qualified"
        attributeFormDefault="qualified">
    <annotation>
        <documentation>
        BizTalk Framework 2.0
        BizTalk Document Schema: properties header entry
        Copyright 2000 Microsoft Corporation
        </documentation>
    </annotation>
    <element name="properties" type="tns:properties"/>
    <complexType name="properties">
        <attribute ref="SOAP-ENV:mustUnderstand" use="required" value="1" />
        <sequence>
            <element name="identity" type="uriReference"/>
            <element name="sentAt" type="timeInstant"/>
            <element name="expiresAt" type="timeInstant"/>
            <element name="topic" type="uriReference"/>
        </sequence>
    </complexType>
</schema>
```

A.2.3 Services Header Entry

```xml
<?xml version="1.0" ?>
<schema xmlns="http://www.w3.org/2000/08/XMLSchema"
        xmlns:xsi="http://www.w3.org/1999/XMLSchema-instance"
        xmlns:tns="http://schemas.biztalk.org/btf-2-0/services"
```

```
            targetNamespace="http://schemas.biztalk.org/btf-2-0/services"
            xmlns:SOAP-ENV="http://schemas.xmlsoap.org/soap/envelope/"
            xmlns:SOAP-ENC="http://schemas.xmlsoap.org/soap/encoding/"
            elementFormDefault="qualified"
            attributeFormDefault="qualified">
    <annotation>
       <documentation>
         BizTalk Framework 2.0
         BizTalk Document Schema: services header entry
         Copyright 2000 Microsoft Corporation
       </documentation>
    </annotation>
    <element name="services" type="tns:services"/>
    <complexType name="services">
       <attribute ref="SOAP-ENV:mustUnderstand" use="required" value="1"/>
       <sequence>
           <element name="deliveryReceiptRequest" type="tns:receiptRequest"
                                                  minOccurs="0"/>
           <element name="commitmentReceiptRequest"
type="tns:receiptRequest"
                                                       minOccurs="0"/>
       </sequence>
    </complexType>
    <complexType name="receiptRequest">
       <element name="sendTo" type="eps:endpoint"/>
       <element name="sendBy" type="timeInstant"/>
    </complexType>
</schema>
```

A.2.4 Manifest Header Entry

```
<?xml version="1.0" ?>
<schema xmlns="http://www.w3.org/2000/08/XMLSchema"
        xmlns:xsi="http://www.w3.org/1999/XMLSchema-instance"
        xmlns:tns="http://schemas.biztalk.org/btf-2-0/manifest"
        targetNamespace="http://schemas.biztalk.org/btf-2-0/manifest"
        xmlns:SOAP-ENV="http://schemas.xmlsoap.org/soap/envelope/"
        xmlns:SOAP-ENC="http://schemas.xmlsoap.org/soap/encoding/"
        elementFormDefault="qualified"
        attributeFormDefault="qualified">
    <annotation>
```

```
        <documentation>
          BizTalk Framework 2.0
          BizTalk Document Schema: manifest header entry
          Copyright 2000 Microsoft Corporation
        </documentation>
      </annotation>
      <element name="manifest" type="tns:manifest"/>
      <complexType name="manifest">
        <attribute ref="SOAP-ENV:mustUnderstand" use="optional" default="0"/>
        <element name="reference" minOccurs="1" maxOccurs="unbounded">
            <complexType>
              <sequence>
                <choice>
                    <element name="document" type="tns:itemType">
                    <element name="attachment" type="tns:itemType">
                </choice>
                <element name="description" type="tns:markup" minOccurs="0"/>
              </sequence>
            </complexType>
        </element>
      </complexType>

      <complexType name="itemType">
        <attribute ref="SOAP-ENC:href" use="required"/>
      </complexType>

      <complexType name="markup" mixed="true">
        <simpleContent>
            <extension base="string"/>
        </simpleContent>
      </complexType>
</schema>
```

A.2.5 Process Header Entry

```
<?xml version="1.0" ?>
<schema xmlns="http://www.w3.org/2000/08/XMLSchema"
        xmlns:xsi="http://www.w3.org/1999/XMLSchema-instance"
        xmlns:tns="http://schemas.biztalk.org/btf-2-0/process"
```

```
        targetNamespace="http://schemas.biztalk.org/btf-2-0/process"
        xmlns:SOAP-ENV="http://schemas.xmlsoap.org/soap/envelope/"
        xmlns:SOAP-ENC="http://schemas.xmlsoap.org/soap/encoding/"
        elementFormDefault="qualified"
        attributeFormDefault="qualified">
    <annotation>
       <documentation>
         BizTalk Framework 2.0
         BizTalk Document Schema: process header entry
         Copyright 2000 Microsoft Corporation
       </documentation>
    </annotation>
    <element name="process" type="tns:process"/>
    <complexType name="process">
       <attribute ref="SOAP-ENV:mustUnderstand" use="required" value="1"/>
       <sequence>
          <element name="type" type="uriReference"/>
          <element name="instance" type="uriReference"/>
          <element name="detail" type="anyType" minOccurs="0">
       </sequence>
    </complexType>
</schema>
```

A.2.6 Receipt Header Entries

```
<?xml version="1.0" ?>
<schema xmlns="http://www.w3.org/2000/08/XMLSchema"
        xmlns:tns="http://schemas.biztalk.org/btf-2-0/receipts"
        xmlns:SOAP-ENV="http://schemas.xmlsoap.org/soap/envelope/"
        targetNamespace="http://schemas.biztalk.org/btf-2-0/receipts"
        elementFormDefault="qualified"
        attributeFormDefault="qualified">
    <annotation>
       <documentation>
         BizTalk Framework 2.0
         BizTalk Document Schema: receipt header entries
         Copyright 2000 Microsoft Corporation
       </documentation>
    </annotation>

    <element name="deliveryReceipt" type="tns:deliveryReceipt"/>
```

```
<element name="commitmentReceipt" type="tns:commitmentReceipt"/>

<complexType name="deliveryReceipt">
    <attribute ref="SOAP-ENV:mustUnderstand" value="1" use="required"/>
    <sequence>
        <element name="receivedAt" type="timeInstant"/>
        <element name="identity" type="uriReference"/>
    </sequence>
</complexType>

<complexType name="commitmentReceipt">
    <attribute ref="SOAP-ENV:mustUnderstand" value="1" use="required"/>
    <sequence>
        <element name="identity" type="uriReference"/>
        <element name="decidedAt" type="timeInstant"/>
        <element name="decision" type="tns:decision"/>
        <element name="commitmentCode" type="QName"/>
        <element name="commitmentDetail" type="anyType" minOccurs="0"/>
    </sequence>
</complexType>

<simpleType name="decision">
    <restriction base="string">
        <enumeration value="positive"/>
        <enumeration value="negative"/>
    </restriction>
</simpleType>
</schema>
```

A.2.7 BizTalk Document Envelope

```
<?xml version="1.0" ?>
<schema xmlns="http://www.w3.org/2000/08/XMLSchema"
        xmlns:SOAP-ENV="http://schemas.xmlsoap.org/soap/envelope/"
        targetNamespace="http://schemas.xmlsoap.org/soap/envelope/"
        elementFormDefault="qualified"
        attributeFormDefault="qualified">
    <annotation>
        <documentation>
            BizTalk Framework 2.0
            BizTalk Document Schema: BizTalk Document Envelope
```

APPENDIX

```
           Copyright 2000 Microsoft Corporation
         </documentation>
      </annotation>

 <!-- specify required and optional BTF2 headers -->
 <redefine schemaLocation="http://schemas.xmlsoap.org/soap/envelope/">
  <complexType name="Header"
         xmlns:eps="http://schemas.biztalk.org/btf-2-0/endpoints"
         xmlns:prop="http://schemas.biztalk.org/btf-2-0/properties"
         xmlns:svc="http://schemas.biztalk.org/btf-2-0/services"
         xmlns:fst="http://schemas.biztalk.org/btf-2-0/manifest"
         xmlns:prc="http://schemas.biztalk.org/btf-2-0/process"
         xmlns:rct="http://schemas.biztalk.org/btf-2-0/receipts">
      <all>
        <sequence>
           <element ref="eps:endpoints"/>
           <element ref="prop:properties"/>
           <element ref="svc:services" minOccurs="0"/>
           <element ref="fst:manifest" minOccurs="0"/>
           <element ref="prc:process" minOccurs="0"/>
           <choice>
              <element ref="rct:deliveryReceipt" minOccurs="0"/>
              <element ref="rct:commitmentReceipt" minOccurs="0"/>
           </choice>
        </sequence>
        <any minOccurs="0" maxOccurs="unbounded"/>
        <anyAttribute/>
      </all>
  </complexType>
 </redefine>
</schema>
```

APPENDIX

Index

INTERNATIONAL CONTACT INFORMATION

AUSTRALIA
McGraw-Hill Book Company Australia Pty. Ltd.
TEL +61-2-9417-9899
FAX +61-2-9417-5687
http://www.mcgraw-hill.com.au
books-it_sydney@mcgraw-hill.com

CANADA
McGraw-Hill Ryerson Ltd.
TEL +905-430-5000
FAX +905-430-5020
http://www.mcgrawhill.ca

GREECE, MIDDLE EAST,
NORTHERN AFRICA
McGraw-Hill Hellas
TEL +30-1-656-0990-3-4
FAX +30-1-654-5525

MEXICO (Also serving Latin America)
McGraw-Hill Interamericana Editores S.A. de C.V.
TEL +525-117-1583
FAX +525-117-1589
http://www.mcgraw-hill.com.mx
fernando_castellanos@mcgraw-hill.com

SINGAPORE (Serving Asia)
McGraw-Hill Book Company
TEL +65-863-1580
FAX +65-862-3354
http://www.mcgraw-hill.com.sg
mghasia@mcgraw-hill.com

SOUTH AFRICA
McGraw-Hill South Africa
TEL +27-11-622-7512
FAX +27-11-622-9045
robyn_swanepoel@mcgraw-hill.com

UNITED KINGDOM & EUROPE
(Excluding Southern Europe)
McGraw-Hill Education Europe
TEL +44-1-628-502500
FAX +44-1-628-770224
http://www.mcgraw-hill.co.uk
computing_neurope@mcgraw-hill.com

ALL OTHER INQUIRIES Contact:
Osborne/McGraw-Hill
TEL +1-510-549-6600
FAX +1-510-883-7600
http://www.osborne.com
omg_international@mcgraw-hill.com

About the CD-ROMs

- Microsoft® BizTalk™ Server 2000 Enterprise Edition 120-Day Evaluation CD-ROM

- Microsoft® SQL Server™ 2000 Enterprise Edition 120-Day Evaluation CD-ROM

- Microsoft® Visio™ 2000 SR1-A 120-Day Evaluation CD-ROM

System Requirements:

To install Microsoft BizTalk Server 2000 Enterprise Edition, Microsoft SQL Server 2000 Enterprise Edition, and Microsoft Visio 2000 SR1-A, you need:*

- PC with 300 MHz or higher Pentium II-compatible CPU running Microsoft Windows® 2000 Professional, Windows 2000 Server, or Windows 2000 Advanced Server with Service Pack 1 or later**

- 128 MB of RAM

- A 6-gigabyte (GB) hard disk

- One local hard-disk partition formatted with the NTFS file system

- CD-ROM or DVD-ROM drive

- VGA or Super VGA monitor

- Keyboard

- Microsoft Mouse, Microsoft IntelliMouse, or compatible pointing device (optional)

To download SP1 for Windows 2000 and for more information, please see the Windows 2000 web site http://www.microsoft.com/windows2000/default.asp.

* Actual system requirements will vary based on your deployment configuration, expected load, and the features you choose to install.
** Latest Service Pack recommended.

LICENSE AGREEMENT

THIS PRODUCT (THE "PRODUCT") CONTAINS PROPRIETARY SOFTWARE, DATA AND INFORMATION (INCLUDING DOCUMENTATION) OWNED BY THE McGRAW-HILL COMPANIES, INC. ("McGRAW-HILL") AND ITS LICENSORS. YOUR RIGHT TO USE THE PRODUCT IS GOVERNED BY THE TERMS AND CONDITIONS OF THIS AGREEMENT.

LICENSE: Throughout this License Agreement, "you" shall mean either the individual or the entity whose agent opens this package. You are granted a non-exclusive and non-transferable license to use the Product subject to the following terms:

(i) If you have licensed a single user version of the Product, the Product may only be used on a single computer (i.e., a single CPU). If you licensed and paid the fee applicable to a local area network or wide area network version of the Product, you are subject to the terms of the following subparagraph (ii).

(ii) If you have licensed a local area network version, you may use the Product on unlimited workstations located in one single building selected by you that is served by such local area network. If you have licensed a wide area network version, you may use the Product on unlimited workstations located in multiple buildings on the same site selected by you that is served by such wide area network; provided, however, that any building will not be considered located in the same site if it is more than five (5) miles away from any building included in such site. In addition, you may only use a local area or wide area network version of the Product on one single server. If you wish to use the Product on more than one server, you must obtain written authorization from McGraw-Hill and pay additional fees.

(iii) You may make one copy of the Product for back-up purposes only and you must maintain an accurate record as to the location of the back-up at all times.

COPYRIGHT; RESTRICTIONS ON USE AND TRANSFER: All rights (including copyright) in and to the Product are owned by McGraw-Hill and its licensors. You are the owner of the enclosed disc on which the Product is recorded. You may not use, copy, decompile, disassemble, reverse engineer, modify, reproduce, create derivative works, transmit, distribute, sublicense, store in a database or retrieval system of any kind, rent or transfer the Product, or any portion thereof, in any form or by any means (including electronically or otherwise) except as expressly provided for in this License Agreement. You must reproduce the copyright notices, trademark notices, legends and logos of McGraw-Hill and its licensors that appear on the Product on the back-up copy of the Product which you are permitted to make hereunder. All rights in the Product not expressly granted herein are reserved by McGraw-Hill and its licensors.

TERM: This License Agreement is effective until terminated. It will terminate if you fail to comply with any term or condition of this License Agreement. Upon termination, you are obligated to return to McGraw-Hill the Product together with all copies thereof and to purge all copies of the Product included in any and all servers and computer facilities.

DISCLAIMER OF WARRANTY: THE PRODUCT AND THE BACK-UP COPY ARE LICENSED "AS IS." McGRAW-HILL, ITS LICENSORS AND THE AUTHORS MAKE NO WARRANTIES, EXPRESS OR IMPLIED, AS TO THE RESULTS TO BE OBTAINED BY ANY PERSON OR ENTITY FROM USE OF THE PRODUCT, ANY INFORMATION OR DATA INCLUDED THEREIN AND/OR ANY TECHNICAL SUPPORT SERVICES PROVIDED HEREUNDER, IF ANY ("TECHNICAL SUPPORT SERVICES"). McGRAW-HILL, ITS LICENSORS AND THE AUTHORS MAKE NO EXPRESS OR IMPLIED WARRANTIES OF MERCHANTABILITY OR FITNESS FOR A PARTICULAR PURPOSE OR USE WITH RESPECT TO THE PRODUCT. McGRAW-HILL, ITS LICENSORS, AND THE AUTHORS MAKE NO GUARANTEE THAT YOU WILL PASS ANY CERTIFICATION EXAM WHATSOEVER BY USING THIS PRODUCT. NEITHER McGRAW-HILL, ANY OF ITS LICENSORS NOR THE AUTHORS WARRANT THAT THE FUNCTIONS CONTAINED IN THE PRODUCT WILL MEET YOUR REQUIREMENTS OR THAT THE OPERATION OF THE PRODUCT WILL BE UNINTERRUPTED OR ERROR FREE. YOU ASSUME THE ENTIRE RISK WITH RESPECT TO THE QUALITY AND PERFORMANCE OF THE PRODUCT.

LIMITED WARRANTY FOR DISC: To the original licensee only, McGraw-Hill warrants that the enclosed disc on which the Product is recorded is free from defects in materials and workmanship under normal use and service for a period of ninety (90) days from the date of purchase. In the event of a defect in the disc covered by the foregoing warranty, McGraw-Hill will replace the disc.

LIMITATION OF LIABILITY: NEITHER McGRAW-HILL, ITS LICENSORS NOR THE AUTHORS SHALL BE LIABLE FOR ANY INDIRECT, SPECIAL OR CONSEQUENTIAL DAMAGES, SUCH AS BUT NOT LIMITED TO, LOSS OF ANTICIPATED PROFITS OR BENEFITS, RESULTING FROM THE USE OR INABILITY TO USE THE PRODUCT EVEN IF ANY OF THEM HAS BEEN ADVISED OF THE POSSIBILITY OF SUCH DAMAGES. THIS LIMITATION OF LIABILITY SHALL APPLY TO ANY CLAIM OR CAUSE WHATSOEVER WHETHER SUCH CLAIM OR CAUSE ARISES IN CONTRACT, TORT, OR OTHERWISE. Some states do not allow the exclusion or limitation of indirect, special or consequential damages, so the above limitation may not apply to you.

U.S. GOVERNMENT RESTRICTED RIGHTS: Any software included in the Product is provided with restricted rights subject to subparagraphs (c), (1) and (2) of the Commercial Computer Software-Restricted Rights clause at 48 C.F.R. 52.227-19. The terms of this Agreement applicable to the use of the data in the Product are those under which the data are generally made available to the general public by McGraw-Hill. Except as provided herein, no reproduction, use, or disclosure rights are granted with respect to the data included in the Product and no right to modify or create derivative works from any such data is hereby granted.

GENERAL: This License Agreement constitutes the entire agreement between the parties relating to the Product. The terms of any Purchase Order shall have no effect on the terms of this License Agreement. Failure of McGraw-Hill to insist at any time on strict compliance with this License Agreement shall not constitute a waiver of any rights under this License Agreement. This License Agreement shall be construed and governed in accordance with the laws of the State of New York. If any provision of this License Agreement is held to be contrary to law, that provision will be enforced to the maximum extent permissible and the remaining provisions will remain in full force and effect.

This program was reproduced by Osborne McGraw-Hill under a special arrangement with Microsoft Corporation. For this reason, [PUBLISHER] is responsible for the product warranty and for support. If your diskette is defective, please return it to Osborne McGraw-Hill, which will arrange for its replacement. PLEASE DO NOT RETURN IT TO MICROSOFT CORPORATION. Any product support will be provided, if at all, by Osborne McGraw-Hill. PLEASE DO NOT CONTACT MICROSOFT CORPORATION FOR PRODUCT SUPPORT. End users of this Microsoft program shall not be considered "registered owners" of a Microsoft product and therefore shall not be eligible for upgrades, promotions or other benefits available to "registered owners" of Microsoft products.